About the Series Editor

André LaMothe, CEO, Xtreme Games LLC, has been involved in the computer industry for more than 25 years. He wrote his first game for the TRS-80 and has been hooked ever since! His experience includes 2D/3D graphics, AI research at NASA, compiler design, robotics, virtual reality, and telecommunications. His books are top sellers in the game programming genre, and his experience is echoed in the Premier Press *Game Development* books.

Letter from the Series Editor

Today there are many 3D graphics and game programming books to choose from. However, the development of a 3D game engine is usually left as an exercise for the reader because the majority of 3D engine work involves the implementation of the 3D rendering pipeline itself. Unfortunately, many readers still have problems putting theory into practice and creating a professional quality 3D game engine that can be used to develop actual production-ready games. Fortunately for us, Stefan Zerbst has stepped up to the plate and taken the opposite approach for *3D Game Engine Programming*. Instead of assuming you know nothing about math or 3D graphics, he assumes that you are familiar with these areas and comfortable with C++ and the DirectX/3D API. Given this assumption, for the first time really, an entire book is dedicated to creating the framework for and implementing an entire 3D game engine, aptly named the "ZFXEngine." (I will let you learn what it stands for.)

With that in mind, this book targets the intermediate or advanced 2D/3D game programmer who wants to see in detail the construction of an entire 3D engine ready to develop commercial games and not just demos. The ZFXEngine is a fully featured 3D engine supporting advanced 3D graphics, shading, model loading, spatial partitioning, networking, audio, scene management, and more. If you can read and understand everything in this book, not only will you be in a superior position to develop your own 3D game engine, but you will also have the background to take the lead position at a studio, defining and developing an engine for them.

And as if that wasn't enough, the book ends with the implementation of a deathmatch shooter to show you just a sample of what the ZFXEngine and the concepts herein can do. In conclusion, this book will round out even the most wicked 3D graphics programmer, or give the newbie 3D graphics programmer a roadmap to where he is going. I highly recommend it!

Sincerely,

André LaMothe
Series Editor, Premier *Game Development* series
ceo@nurve.net

THOMSON
COURSE TECHNOLOGY

Professional ■ Trade ■ Reference

3D
Game Engine Programming

Stefan Zerbst

with Oliver Düvel

Series Editor
André LaMothe, CEO, Xtreme Games LLC

THOMSON
COURSE TECHNOLOGY

Professional ■ Trade ■ Reference

3D
Game Engine Programming

Stefan Zerbst
with Oliver Düvel

Series Editor
André LaMothe, CEO, Xtreme Games LLC

Premier Press

© 2004 by Thomson Course Technology PTR. All rights reserved. No part of this book may be reproduced or transmitted in any form or by any means, electronic or mechanical, including photocopying, recording, or by any information storage or retrieval system without written permission from Thomson Course Technology PTR, except for the inclusion of brief quotations in a review.

The Premier Press and Thomson Course Technology PTR logo and related trade dress are trademarks of Thomson Course Technology PTR and may not be used without written permission.

Microsoft DirectX 9 SDK is Copyright Microsoft Corporation, 2002. All rights reserved. Images from *DOOM* and *QUAKE* © 1994, 1996 id Software, Inc. All rights reserved. Images from *Return to Castle Wolfenstein* © 2002 id Software, Inc. All rights reserved. Special thanks to id Software for their support and help with this project.

All other trademarks are the property of their respective owners.

Important: Thomson Course Technology PTR cannot provide software support. Please contact the appropriate software manufacturer's technical support line or Web site for assistance.

Thomson Course Technology PTR and the author have attempted throughout this book to distinguish proprietary trademarks from descriptive terms by following the capitalization style used by the manufacturer.

Information contained in this book has been obtained by Thomson Course Technology PTR from sources believed to be reliable. However, because of the possibility of human or mechanical error by our sources, Thomson Course Technology PTR, or others, the Publisher does not guarantee the accuracy, adequacy, or completeness of any information and is not responsible for any errors or omissions or the results obtained from use of such information. Readers should be particularly aware of the fact that the Internet is an ever-changing entity. Some facts may have changed since this book went to press.

Educational facilities, companies, and organizations interested in multiple copies or licensing of this book should contact the publisher for quantity discount information. Training manuals, CD-ROMs, and portions of this book are also available individually or can be tailored for specific needs.

ISBN: 1-59200-351-6
Library of Congress Catalog Card Number: 2004090737
Printed in the United States of America

04 05 06 07 08 BH 10 9 8 7 6 5 4 3 2 1

THOMSON
COURSE TECHNOLOGY
Professional ■ Trade ■ Reference

Thomson Course Technology PTR, a division of
Thomson Course Technology
25 Thomson Place
Boston, MA 02210
http://www.courseptr.com

SVP, Thomson Course Technology PTR:
Andy Shafran

Publisher:
Stacy L. Hiquet

Senior Marketing Manager:
Sarah O'Donnell

Marketing Manager:
Heather Hurley

Manager of Editorial Services:
Heather Talbot

Senior Acquisitions Editor:
Emi Smith

Senior Editor:
Mark Garvey

Associate Marketing Managers:
Kristin Eisenzopf and Sarah Dubois

Developmental Editor:
Ginny Bess

Project Editor:
Kevin Sullivan, Argosy Publishing

Technical Reviewer:
Richard Fine

Thomson Course Technology PTR Market Coordinator:
Amanda Weaver

Interior Layout Tech:
Sharon Burkhardt, Argosy Publishing

Cover Designer:
Steve Deschene

CD-ROM Producer:
Brandon Penticuff

Indexer:
Maureen Shepherd

Proofreader:
Sherri Dietrich

To my beloved wife Rike and our son Tim

Acknowledgments

In a world designed by the men in gray who decide how we live in brief, there's a master plan for the company men from the cradle to the company grave.

"Return of Alex," Die Toten Hosen

Writing about the things I like is pretty much one of my favorite hobbies. After all, it is a good way to pull even more people over to the dark side. This book is about the dark side of programming 3D engines for video game applications, and I hope to pull as many of you into the fun side of programming computer graphics stuff as I can.

It took some time to write the original version of this book as well as complete the English translation for it. A lot of things happened during that time, but the most important event was my little son Tim's arrival into this world. Even if doing 3D graphics is a lot of fun, Tim taught me that a baby's smile is way more beautiful than the most perfect 3D scene with per-pixel lighting, real-time shadows, and glow effects.

Besides my baby Tim, a lot of other people took their share in bringing this book about, and I would like to thank all of those people. I first want to mention Oli (Oliver Düvel), who wrote the chapter on character animation and a large portion of the network device chapter. For the original version of this book, Marcus Beck and Boris Karnikowski looked after me and helped me get the book done. Working with them was a pleasure, as they were friendly and motivated me. The same applies for Emi Smith, who organized the English version of the book and who tolerated my tardiness on due dates with a smile on her face and in her friendly e-mails. Thanks, Emi. And thanks to André LaMothe for establishing the contact.

Marco Kögler was kind enough to help me out with tips and tricks and listened carefully when I described scene management and lighting ideas to him. He pointed out weaknesses in the approaches and helped me with per-pixel lighting topics. Finally, I would like to thank the band Toten Hosen for the great music that kept me going and Jacobs for the instant coffee that kept me running.

Last, but not least, thanks to Rike, who makes all this possible.

Stefan Zerbst

Diligence is neither an ability nor a talent. It is a matter of habit.
Peter F. Drucker

These days, it is important to create video games that fascinate the player. To create this fascination, a video game needs very basic elements, such as network modes and character animation. The goal of these elements is to increase the level of interactivity the game is design for.

Personally, I am always astonished by the development of the character animation techniques employed in video games. Starting with plain, animated image files called sprites in the 80s and ending with the highly precise animations of characters with facial expressions moving through virtual game worlds, animations techniques are developing at amazing speeds.

I've had a lot of fun contributing to this book, and I hope you will have as much fun reading it.

Oliver Düvel

About the Authors

Stefan Zerbst started programming on the ancient C16 and now holds a German Diplom degree in Computer Science in Economics. During his studies he founded the German hobby game development community ZFX (www.zfx.info), which is the biggest and most active development community in Germany. He has already published two best-selling books about game programming and also shares his comprehensive experience in this field by holding lectures about game programming at a German university and the online academy Gameversity (ww.gameversity.com).

Oliver Düvel works as a project manager in the field of support for a medium-sized software company in Germany. He started programming in the early 1980s and did his first vector and matrix programs using assembler to visualize three-dimensional objects.

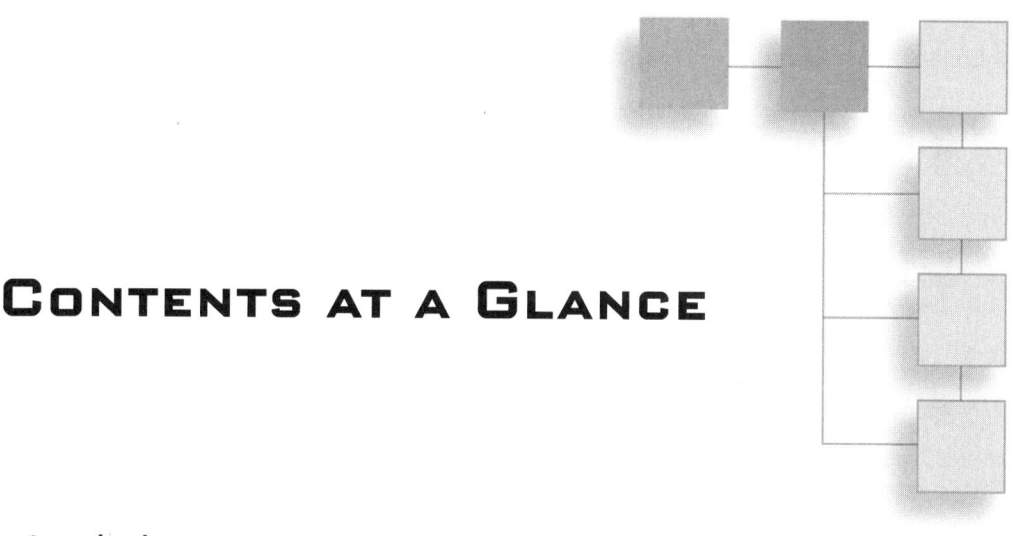

Contents at a Glance

Introduction xxiv

Part I Introduction to the Topics 1

Chapter 1
3D Engines and Game Programming 3

Chapter 2
Designing the Engine 31

Chapter 3
Engineering the Engine 41

Chapter 4
Fast 3D Calculus 91

Part II Rendering Graphics 187

Chapter 5
Materials, Textures, and Transparency 189

Chapter 6
The Render Device of the Engine 235

Chapter 7
3D Pipelines and Shaders 335

Chapter 8
Loading and Animating 3D Models 387

Part III   Support Modules for the Engine   445

Chapter 9
The Input Interface of the Engine 447

Chapter 10
The Audio Interface of the Engine 483

Chapter 11
The Network Interface of the Engine 503

Chapter 12
Timing and Movement in the Engine 569

Chapter 13
Scene Management 585

Part IV   Black Art of Game Programming   665

Chapter 14
Computer-Aided Design (CAD) Tools 667

Chapter 15
Deathmatch Shooter 787

Epilogue 843
Index 845

Contents

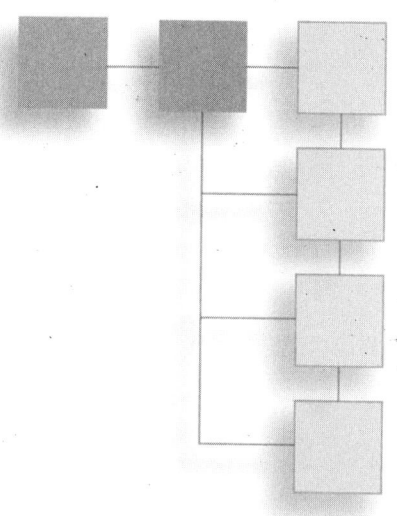

Introduction xxiv

PART I **INTRODUCTION TO THE TOPICS**   **1**

Chapter 1 **3D Engines and Game Programming** 3
Buzzword Engine 3
    Engines versus APIs 4
    What Exactly Is an Engine? 5
A Kind of Magic 6
    Nostalgia and Modern Times 7
    The Problems of Modern Times 8
    Wizardry and Art: Creating the Magic .9
The Development Process of a Video Game 10
    Professional Perspectives 12
    Game Programming 13
    Lead Programmer / Technical Director 14
    Game Design 14
    Game Proposal 17
    Publisher, Publishing, and Revenues .23
    Alternatives 26
Direct3D versus OpenGL Wars 26
    Flame Wars 27
    Drivers and Hardware 27

What Are We Going to Use? 27
Why Do It the Hard Way If There Is an Easy Way? 28
    D3DX Helper Library 28
    Knowing Instead of Copying 29
Get Ready to Rock 29

Chapter 2 Designing the Engine 31
Requirements for the Engine 31
    Naming the Engine 31
    Is the Game Code Autonomous? 32
    Other Video Game Engine Requirements 33
API Independence through Interface Definitions 34
The Structure of the Engine 35
    Interfaces and Dynamic Link Libraries 36
    Static Libraries 37
Components of the Engine 37
    ZFXRenderDevice Interface 37
    ZFXInputDevice Interface 37
    ZFXAudioDevice Interface 38
    ZFXNetworkDevice Interface 38
    ZFX3D Library 38
    ZFXGeneral Library 39
One Look Back, Two Steps Forward 39

Chapter 3 Engineering the Engine 41
What Is an Interface? 41
    Abstract Classes 42
    Virtual Member Functions 43
Defining the Interface 43
    About DLLs 44
    More About the Renderer 45
Workspace for the Implementations 45
    Loading DLLs 46
    Exporting Classes from DLLs 46
    ZFXRenderer: A Static Library As Manager 47
    ZFXD3D: A DLL As Render Device .48
    ZFXRenderDevice: An Abstract Class As Interface 50
Implementing the Static Library 52
    Loading DLLs 55

Sniffing for Exported Functions inside DLLs 56
Implementing the DLL 58
    Enumeration from the DirectX SDK .60
    What Is Coming Next? 60
    Exported Functions 61
    Comfort by Dialogs 63
    Initialization, Enumeration, and Shutdown 70
    Changing between Child Views 77
    Render Functions 79
Testing the Implementation 82
One Look Back, Two Steps Forward 89

Chapter 4   Fast 3D Calculus 91

Fast, Faster, the Fastest 92
    Assembler Programming Basics 94
    How Do I Tell My Compiler? 108
    Identifying the CPU 109
    Checking for SSE Support at Runtime 114
Working with Vectors 115
    Basic Arithmetic Operations 117
    Complex Vector Operations Using SSE 120
Working with Matrices 126
    Basic Operations 127
Working with Rays 131
    Basic Operations 132
    Intersections with Triangles 134
    Intersections with Planes 136
    Intersections with Bounding Boxes 138
Working with Planes 143
    Basic Operations 145
    Intersections with Triangles 146
    Intersections between Planes 147
    Intersections with Bounding Boxes 148
Working with AABBs and OBBs 150
    Basic Operations and Culling 153
    Intersections with Triangles 157
    Intersections Between Bounding Boxes 160
    Planes of an AABB 160
    Ray Contained in an AABB 161

Contents

- Working with Polygons 162
  - Basic Operations 163
  - Setting the Points for the Polygon 164
  - Clipping a Polygon 167
  - Culling with Bounding Boxes 173
  - Intersections with Rays 175
- Working with Quaternions 177
  - Introduction to 4D Space 177
  - Basic Operations 180
  - Multiplication of Two Quaternions 181
  - Building from Euler Angles 182
  - Building a Rotation Matrix 183
- One Look Back, Two Steps Forward 184

Part II   Rendering Graphics   187

Chapter 5   Materials, Textures, and Transparency 189

- Middle Management 190
  - About Management 191
  - Our Own Middle Management 191
  - Employing a Texture Manager 192
- A Class for Skins 193
  - Textures 193
  - Light and Material 194
  - Basic Structures 200
  - Interface Definition for a Skin Manager 204
  - The Skin Manager of the Render Device 207
  - Comparing Colors and Materials 211
  - Getting Skins 212
- Adding Skins and Textures 213
- Adding Textures 215
  - Adding Textures to Skins 216
  - Adding Textures As Normal Maps 219
  - Loading Graphic Files As Textures 221
- Adjusting the Transparency of Textures 226
  - Transparency in Computer Graphics 226
  - Again, Color Formats 228
  - Alpha Color Keys via Alpha Channels 229

Contents   xvii

        Overall Transparency via Alpha Channels 231
        One Look Back, Two Steps Forward 233

Chapter 6   **The Render Device of the Engine** **235**
        Project Settings 236
        View and Projection 237
            Multiple Viewing Stages 240
            Viewports, View Matrices, and the Frustum 242
            Orthogonal Projection 250
            Perspective Projection 252
            Combined Transformation Matrices 254
            Activating View and Projection 256
            Converting from 3D to 2D and Vice Versa 260
            Summing Up View and Projection 264
            Setting the World Transformation 265
        Vertex Structures 266
        Shader Support 267
            Prerequisites for Using Shaders 268
            Vertex Shader 272
            Pixel Shader 277
        Activating Render States 278
        Rendering Primitives Efficiently 282
            Hardware and Performance Foundation 283
            Caching During Rendering 286
            Static Versus Dynamic Vertex and Index Buffers 287
            Interface Definition of a Vertex Cache Manager 289
            Vertex Cache Object 290
            Vertex Cache Manager 303
        Rendering Text, Points, and Lines 319
            Creating Fonts and Rendering Text 320
        Rendering Point Lists 323
            Rendering Line Lists 325
        Presenting a Scene 327
        Demo Application Using the DLL 330
            Multiple Windows with Multiple Viewports 330
            Simple Geometry Loader 332
        One Look Back, Two Steps Forward 334

Chapter 7 3D Pipelines and Shaders 335
Shader Basics 336
- 3D Pipeline 336
- Applications, CPU Limited or GPU Limited 338
- Overusing Shaders 339
- Vertex Manipulation Using Vertex Shaders 340
- Pixel Manipulation Using Pixel Shaders 342

Shader Techniques and Samples 344
- Sample 1: Basic Transformations 344
- Sample 2: Single-Pass Multitexturing 351
- Sample 3: Directional Lighting per Vertex 354
- Sample 4: Per-Pixel Omni Lights 359
- Sample 5: Grayscale Filter 369
- Sample 6: Bump Mapping 370

One Look Back, Two Steps Forward 386

Chapter 8 Loading and Animating 3D Models 387
Triumphant Advance of Skeletal Animation 388
- Key Frame Animations 388
- Skeletal Animation and Skinned Meshes 390

The CBF File Format 394
- What Is a Chunk? 394
- Reading a Chunk 396
- The Main Function 397
- Reading the Header 398
- Reading the Vertices 400
- Reading Faces 403
- Reading the Mesh 404
- Reading the Material 405
- Reading the Joints 407
- Reading the Main Joint 410
- Reading the Key Frame Rotations 411
- Reading the Key Frame Positions 412
- Read the Animations 414
- Set the Scaling of the Model 416

Processing the Data in the Memory 418
- Preparing the Data 419
- Setting Up Bones for the Skeletal Animation 423
- Animating the Model 428

	Prepare the Animation	430
	Animating the Vertices	435
Using the Animated Model		438
	Updating the Model	438
	Rendering the Model	439
	Rendering the Bones	440
	Rendering the Normals	442
One Look Back, Two Steps Forward		444

Part III Support Modules for the Engine 445

Chapter 9 The Input Interface of the Engine 447

Good Old Interface Design	448
Interface Definition for an Input Class	449
Base Class for Input Devices	450
Creating and Destroying an Input Device	452
Making It Run	453
Querying the Input	454
Getting Down to the Keys	458
ZFXKeyboard Class	458
Initializing and Releasing	459
Updating	460
Querying the Input	460
The Pied Piper of Redmond	461
ZFXMouse Class	462
Initializing and Releasing	463
Updating	464
No Joy without a Joystick	467
ZFXJoystick Class	467
Initializing and Releasing	468
Updating	471
Implementing the Interface	472
Initializing and Releasing	473
Updating the Input	475
Querying the Input	476
Demo Application	477
One Look Back, Two Steps Forward	481

Contents

Chapter 10 The Audio Interface of the Engine 483
   Quick and Painlessly 483
      The Same Old Interface 484
      Interface Definition for an Audio Class 485
   Implementing the Interface 487
      ZFXDA Class 487
      Initializing and Releasing 490
      Loading and Playing Sounds 494
   Demo Application 501
   One Look Back, Two Steps Forward 501

Chapter 11 The Network Interface of the Engine 503
   Network Games 504
      Session-Based Video Games 504
      Persistent Worlds 506
      Lag 508
   Network Architecture 508
      Peer-to-Peer 509
      Client/Server Networks 509
   Network Technology 511
      The OSI Model 511
      Protocols 513
      Network APIs 514
   Implementing a Network Library 515
      The Same Old Interface Tea 516
      Server Versus Clients 517
      Packing Packages 517
      Waiting Queues 518
      Socket Objects 523
      Interface Definition for a Network Class 537
      WinSock API Encapsulation 539
   Demo Application 553
      Chat Application 553
      File Transfer Application 559
   One Look Back, Two Steps Forward 567

Chapter 12 Timing and Movement in the Engine 569
   Different Camera Modes 570
      Free Cameras 570

	The First-Person Camera 570
	The Third-Person Camera 571
	The Fixed Camera 572
	Movement by a ZFXMovementController 572
	What Is a Movement Controller? 572
	Implementing the Base Class 573
	Deriving a Free Camera 577
	Deriving a First-Person Camera 579
	Demo Application 584
	One Look Back, Two Steps Forward 584
Chapter 13	**Scene Management 585**
	The Concept of Scene Management 586
	Scene Management Techniques 587
	No Solution Is Also a Solution 588
	Continuous and Discrete Level of Detail 588
	Quadtrees 590
	Octrees 600
	Binary Space Partitioning Trees 602
	Portal Engines 614
	Potential Visibility Set 621
	Implementing a BSP Tree 622
	Class Declaration 624
	Creating and Releasing Instances 625
	Recursive Creation of the Tree 626
	Selecting the Best Splitter 629
	Traversing the Tree 631
	Collision Detection 633
	Implementing an Octree 636
	Class Declaration 637
	Creating and Releasing Instances 638
	Initializing a Child Node 639
	Recursive Creation of the Tree 641
	Clip the Polygon List to a Node 643
	Collision Detection in the Octree 645
	Player's Height in the Octree 647
	Traversing the Tree 650
	Demo Application: Octree and BSP Tree 653
	Rendering ZFXPolygon Instances 654

	Loading the Level Data	.656
	Calculating a Frame	.659
	Remarkable Things in the Demo	.662
One Look Back, Two Steps Forward		.663

Part IV   Black Art of Game Programming   665

Chapter 14   Computer-Aided Design (CAD) Tools 667

Using CAD Tools 667
   Engineer, Architect, and Game Developer 668
   Level-Editing Tools 668
Low-Polygon Editor: PanBox-Edit 670
   PanBox-Edit Capabilities 671
   WinAPI Framework 672
Class Design of the Tool 672
   Basic Structure of a Level 673
   The Foundation of All Existence: CLevelObject 675
   At the Lowest Level: CPolygon 678
   Complex Models: CPolymesh 698
   Into a New World: CPortal 716
   Let There Be Light: CLight 721
   Interactive Objects: CEntity 726
   Go Fish: CSpawn 732
   Local Management: CSector 733
   All Together Now: CLevel 761
   Your Call: CSelectionBuffer 764
Selected Aspects of the GUI 777
   Class Declaration 778
   Important Attributes 781
   Update Function 782
   Creating a Polygon 783
One Look Back, Two Steps Forward 785

Chapter 15   Deathmatch Shooter 787

Deathmatch Shooter: Pandora's Legacy 787
   Simple Game Design 788
   Old Classes Redone 788
In the Shadows of Ourselves 789

The Theory of Shadow Volumes	789
Implementing Shadow Volumes	795
Loading a Level	806
Supporting Data Structures	807
Loading Routine in CGameLevel	807
Loading Routine in CGameSector	809
Connecting Portals	818
Rendering a Level	821
Rendering the Geometry	821
Rendering Shadows in the Level	828
Integrating Characters	831
CGameCharacter, Base Class for Players and NPCs	831
Network Messages Concerning Characters	834
CGame, a Class of Its Own	836
Updating the Game	836
Networking Tasks	837
One Look Back, Two Steps Forward	841

Epilogue 843

Index 845

Introduction

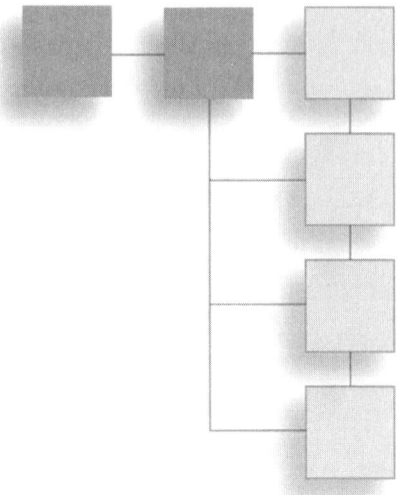

We don't market our developed products. We develop a market for the products we manufacture.

Akio Morita, Founder of Sony Corporation

There always comes the time when you have to write the introduction to your book. This is a difficult thing to do, as my experience tells me that people rarely read introductions because they want to get started immediately. I perfectly understand and welcome that desire to get to the guts of the book. However, please give me a chance and take a quick look at what I have to say about what will keep you awake for the next couple of nights. . . at least.

What Is Contained in this Book?

One of the most important questions you might have is, "What exactly is this book, with its hundreds of pages, about?" It's human nature to be curious, so I will tell you.

This book enables you to develop a video game engine on a comparably high level. To achieve this objective, you need to master some secondary goals first. Therefore, I first show you how to do the mysterious 3D graphics and 3D mathematics you have heard about, but didn't know could be so easy. You will also need to know about other areas of video game programming, such as getting input from the keyboard, mouse, and joystick, and sending data over network connections.

But I don't stop when the engine has reached a basic working level. I think it is imperative not only to show how to develop an engine, but also to show you how to use it in different projects. The first project in which I utilize the engine's renderer involves a complex tool used for low-polygon modeling and level building. Yes, your eyes are correct. You will see how to implement a tool similar to the ones big video game developers use to build their levels or similar to those you can find all over the Internet as freeware or shareware, such as the former *World Craft*.

The first half of the book reveals only half of the truth. To see the engine in real action requires a test scenario for which you can utilize all of the interfaces of the engine, not only the renderer. The second half of the book involves writing a multiplayer deathmatch shooter using the engine. This way, you can see how the pieces you worked so hard at in the first half of the book finally come together.

This book contains all of the source code needed for the modules and interfaces developed for the engine and for the tools and games. You can actually learn on-the-fly how to program Direct3D, DirectMusic, DirectInput, and WinSock if you don't know how to do this yet. You will also learn about interface definitions and how to keep API-specific things out of your applications.

The bottom line is that this book will demand a lot of you. However, it will show you comprehensive examples that reveal the steps that add up to a 3D video game.

What Is not Contained in this Book?

There are also some things that are not contained in this book. Actually there are a lot of things not contained in this book, but let's stick to things related to video game programming for now.

This is a book about programming video game engines. It is not a book about how to program with DirectX or OpenGL. I expect you to have a basic knowledge of the DirectX interfaces and the Direct3D interface in particular. I do not require you to know more about Direct3D than how to render a texture triangle to the screen. If you know how to do this, you will be able to follow along in this book. You do need experience with DirectX because it is a daunting program, especially the first time you use it. The other nice things Direct3D can do are not that difficult to learn; you will learn those tasks on-the-fly in this book.

However, if you have never worked with a DirectX interface, I strongly recommend you install the DirectX SDK and read the tutorials contained in the DirectX documentation. They are very well structured and will teach you the basics. There are also a lot of Internet sites and books that feature numerous tutorials and lessons on DirectX.

Another prerequisite you need is knowledge of C and C++. If you don't know how to program in C, you will get lost in this book. There is no way around this. Don't fool yourself and try to start without C programming knowledge or experience. I will not use fancy C++ techniques in this book, with the exception of discussions on classes. Do not panic if you are not a C or C++ expert. With some familiarity of C/C++, you should be able to follow the programs easily.

If you are already an expert in C++, know that you will not find a lot of C++ techniques used throughout this book. I use classes in this book to create a better structure for the engine design. However, there are a lot of fancy things that can be done with pure C++. These techniques are not emphasized in this book.

> **Tip**
>
> If you want to learn to use C++ in the way it is meant to be used, taking advantage of its features and capabilities, I recommend you read *C++ for Game Programmers,* by Noel Llopis; *Modern C++ Design,* by Andrei Alexander; and *Effective C++,* by Scott Meyers. These will give you a head start when it comes to applied design patterns and C++ gotchas, tips, and tricks.

Finally, I want to say that there are a lot of different genres and types of 3D environments a video game can take place in—not to mention 2D video games of course. There are adventures, sports games, simulations, and so on that are played in environments that utilize space, terrain, indoor settings, and so on. In this book, I do not talk about how to create these environments. Environments like these are special topics, so if you want to learn about them, pick up another book. I concentrate on first-person shooter games, and I show you some ways to create such a video game.

Of course you can use the engine you will develop throughout this book in other types of games. However, there is no such thing as an integrated support for terrain in the form of heightmaps, quad trees, the so-called ROAM (real-time optimally adapting meshes) algorithm, or anything like that. You are welcome to implement this engine for your own needs or enrich the engine's interfaces to create a new engine.

Roadmap

The concept of this book is easy to explain. The book is divided into four parts, which you should read in order of their appearance. The following sections provide a brief overview of what to expect from each part.

Act One

Part I describes the basic concepts that are prerequisites for the other chapters in the book. It will start in Chapter 1, "3D Engines and Game Programming," with a rather general introduction to the topic of programming and developing video games. You will learn about the relationships between video game development and business administration and organizational tasks. Believe me, it's interesting to know what type of money a developer earns or what they don't earn for that matter. Chapter 2, "Designing the Engine," provides a roadmap of how the engine of this book is designed. Chapter 3, "Engineering the

Engine," is the first that allows you to start coding. This is the kick-off for the engine you will develop in the remaining pages of the book. You will learn how to implement API-independent interfaces that add up to a working game engine. Chapter 4, "Fast 3D Calculus," which is the last one of the first part, is equivalent to what you learned in math class. It's all about vectors, matrices, quaternions, and so on. To keep the focus on more advanced topics, I also discuss optimization techniques.

> **Tip**
>
> The term API stands for Application Programming Interface and normally refers to a library that implements a certain functionality while providing an interface for the user to access this functionality. The WinAPI, for example, offers the possibility to access some functionalities of the Windows operating system. The Direct3D and the OpenGL API let you use your graphics adapter's functionality.

Act Two

Part II is about the guts of the engine. You will learn how to deal with the most complex part of the engine. As you might have guessed, this complex part is the render device. I show you how to load graphic files as textures, render triangles to the screen, develop your own vertex shaders and pixel shaders, and so on. Another topic in Part II is the animation of 3D models. Animation is not about rendering graphics, it is about producing graphical output to the screen, so I moved this topic into Part II where it fits best.

You might ask yourself why rendering graphics takes a whole section of its own whereas the input device, the sound device, and even the network device do not take up this much space. You will learn in the first half of the book that there are many issues related to the rendering issue. If you want to automate several tasks without the user of your engine performing numerous low-level switches, you have to keep track of render state settings to maintain integrity while your engine runs. This complex issue demands much space in a book on programming video games.

Act Three

I previously mentioned the input device, the sound device, and the network device. Part III provides a chapter on each of these devices to show you how to use DirectInput, DirectAudio, and the WinSock API. In addition, Chapter 12, "Timing and Movement in the Engine," covers camera movement and perfect timing for your 3D applications.

Part III also includes a lengthy chapter on scene management issues. Although graphics hardware gets better and better virtually each day, there is still a need to control scenes (or the level data) as much as possible so that you can select only the parts of the scene that are visible and need to be processed. You might have heard buzz words, such as binary space partitioning (BSP) trees and octrees. At the end of Part III, you will learn what these terms are used for and how to implement them. You will also learn to praise the math I teach you in Part I. Utilizing your 3D math library by implementing BSP trees and similar scene management algorithms is a walk in the park.

Act Four

When you have completed Part III of this book, I can honestly say that there isn't much left to show you about engine development. At the end of Part III, you will have a comprehensive game engine at your disposal. However, to give you the complete picture, there are two things you still need to know. Both of these deal with the use of the engine in a software project.

First, I want to show you how to develop tools you need to write for your video game projects. The term that comes to mind is *level editor*. I show you how to implement a level editor that lets you build your own 3D levels from scratch with a graphical user interface. This means that you do not have to hack weird numbers into your text pad or parse a text file to build polygons. It involves just a point and a click of the mouse. You can even misuse the level editor as a low-poly model editor.

The other thing I want to show you is how to apply the game engine to implement a network deathmatch first-person shooter. You will load the levels you created with the level-editing tool from Part I of this book and implement a program that allows you to easily walk through the levels in first-person shooter style. You can connect several clients to the game session and then hunt and freeze each other using ice guns.

Tools of the Trade

The most important thing you need to program video games and engines is your brain! That said, there are a number of other tools that are helpful. The first one is the integrated development environment (IDE). Most of you already use an IDE, even if you have not heard of the term. We are just talking about programs, such as Microsoft Visual Studio. An IDE is nothing more than an environment that teams up a smart text editor for source code, a compiler for a certain programming language, a linker if it is necessary for that language, and other helpful tools, such as a debugger.

To use the examples provided in this book you will need to use an IDE that supports DirectX, such as Visual Studio. I use the Standard edition of Visual Studio, version 6.0. There are other IDEs that can deal with DirectX, so check the manual of your preferred tool to find out if it can, too. Figure I.1 shows a screen shot of Visual C++ 6.0.

As previously mentioned, the engine I develop in this book is API-independent. That is, if you watch its interfaces and use the engine, you will notice under the hood that you still have to implement the engine using a specific API. In this book, I use DirectX 9, so you need to use the DirectX SDK if you want to rebuild the examples from this book.

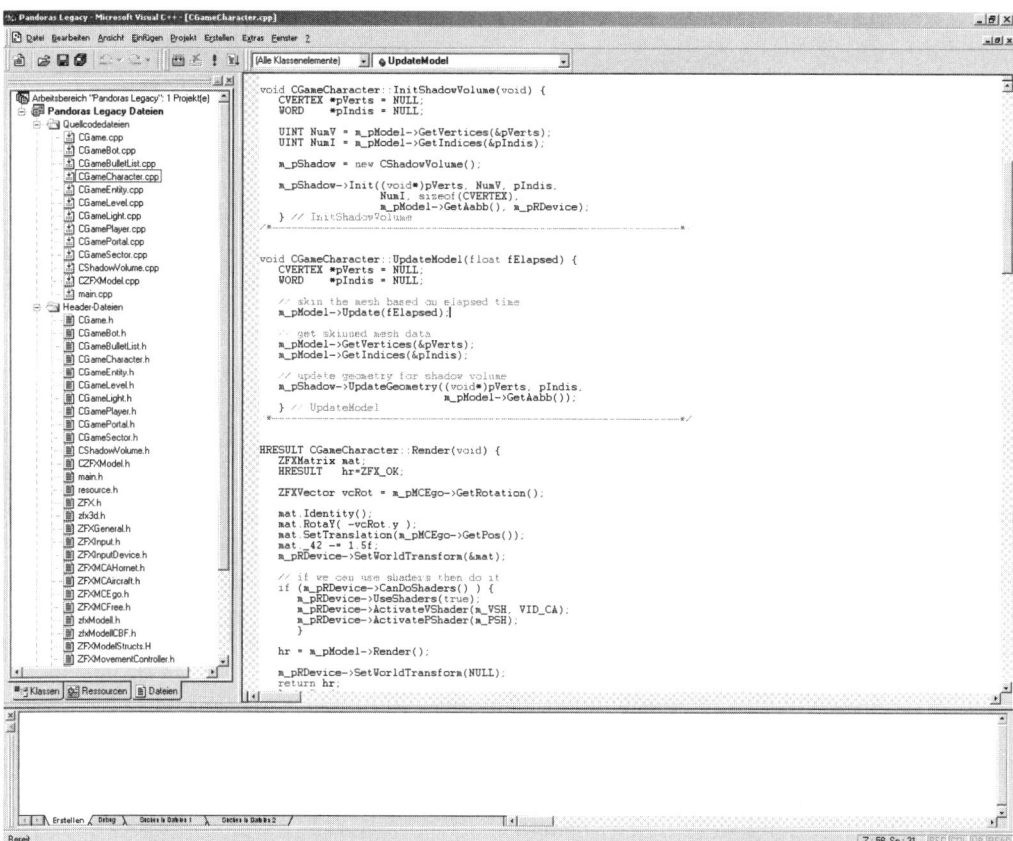

Figure I.1 Microsoft Visual C++ 6.0 in action.

However, if you do this, you will need to utilize other computer system prerequisites. DirectX, from version 9.0 and up, demands the Windows operating system versions 98SE, 200, ME, or XP, whereas Windows 95 is no longer supported.

The final tool you need to work with is a level-editing tool. Fortunately, there is no need to download or buy a certain tool because you can program your own tool for this job. Figure I.2 shows a screen shot of this tool.

Hardware Requirements

When most real world developers work on a professional video game, they still (or again) have to write several code paths depending on the hardware. (Actually, hardware-abstracting APIs, such as DirectX or OpenGL, should be making such paths obsolete.) Compared to these developers, I am in a lucky position. I do not want to develop examples that are good

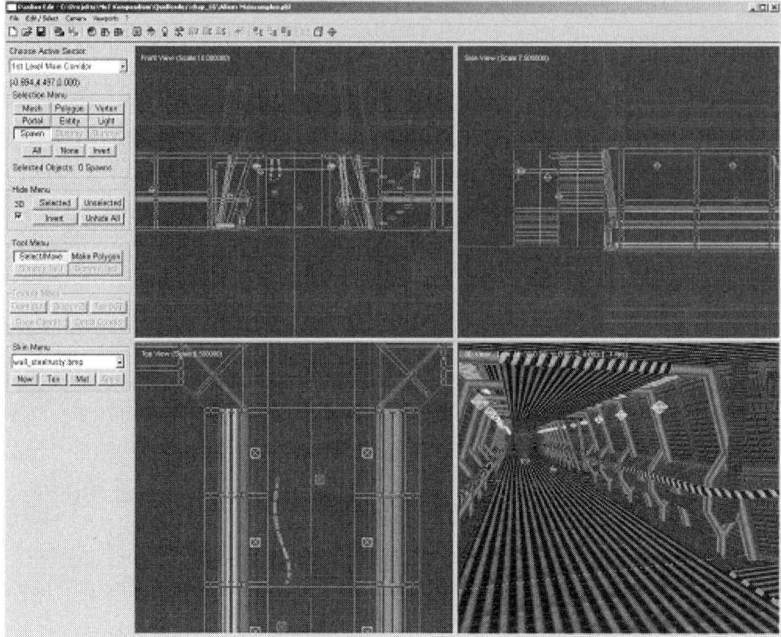

Figure I.2 A screenshot of the *PanBox* level-editing tool.

enough for oldies such as TNT chips or similar hardware that is considered ancient trash. You probably already have a graphics adapter that is modern and that can handle vertex shaders and pixel shaders in version 1.1. If your graphics adapter cannot do this, you will have to live with the more advanced example in this book. The reason for this is that I use vertex and pixel shaders to bring light to the samples.

A Word about ZFX

You will read a lot about the three innocent letters ZFX in this book. So I want to take the chance here and explain to you what this is all about. Lots of people assume those letters to be an acronym for something. But actually they aren't. They developed more or less historically because I used them for whatever reason from my beginning in programming computer graphics as a prefix for my own function names.

Nowadays ZFX stands for a team of guys including myself who are running the German hobby game developer website http://www.zfx.info. Currently those persons are Oliver Düvel, Steffen Engel, Carl Eilers, Eike Anderson, and myself. The core of this website is a huge discussion bulletin board / forum as well as a bunch of tutorials, votes, images of the day, and the like. The Figure I.3 shows a snapshot of the website.

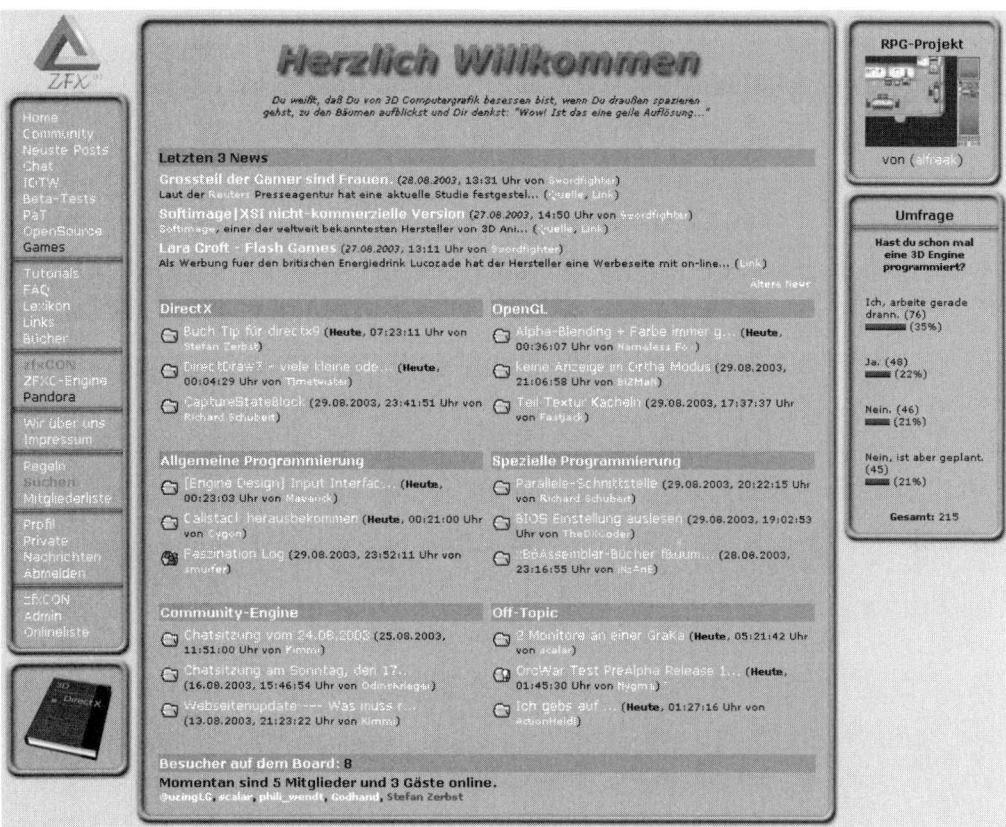

Figure I.3 The ZFX website (written in the German language only).

If you happen to use the German tongue or speak German as a second language, visit our website and take part in the huge exchange of hobby developers who help each other or show off what they achieved to date.

Our team organized an event called zfxCON, which took place for the first time in 2003. It was a huge success at which professional developers and famous authors (Wolfgang Engel, for example) participated. I want to thank Emi and Premier Press, who sent us a bunch of books as part of their sponsorship for this event.

Unfortunately, we run the website in the German language only. English-speaking programmers can check out some other good sites, such as flipcode.com, gamedev.net, and others.

You are now done with the introduction. I've had a lot to say about the book, its historical birth, its development, and so on. I'm happy you are still with me. Let's move on to the more substantive stuff.

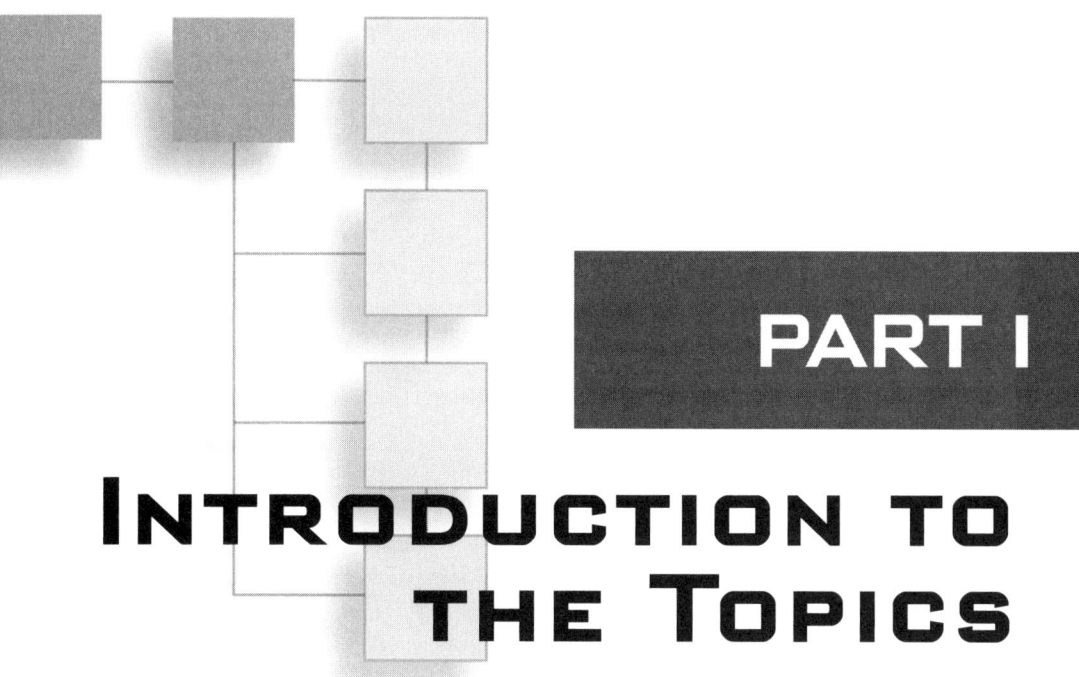

PART I

INTRODUCTION TO THE TOPICS

CHAPTER 1
3D Engines and Game Programming 3

CHAPTER 2
Designing the Engine 31

CHAPTER 3
Engineering the Engine 41

CHAPTER 4
Fast 3D Calculus 91

CHAPTER 1

3D Engines and Game Programming

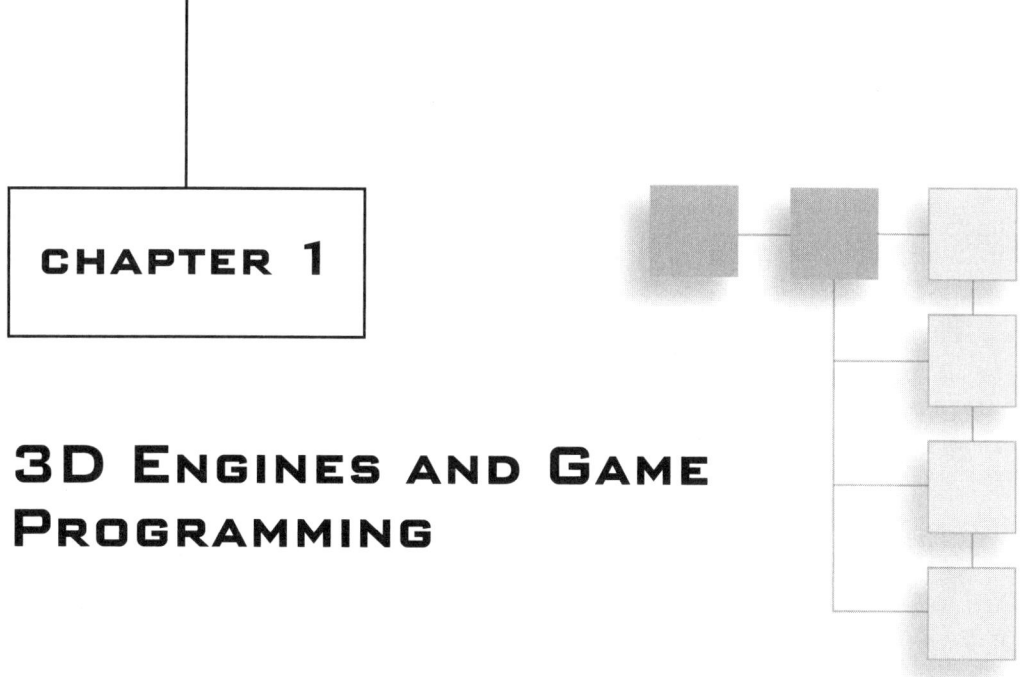

We would like to be treated as objects of human lust today and not as musicians.
Campino, lead singer of the band Toten Hosen, shortly before women-only concert

This chapter covers the basics of programming game engines and video games. In particular it covers the following objectives:

- Defining an engine
- Learning about graphic-rendering APIs (application programming interfaces)
- Setting up a video game as a business project

Buzzword *Engine*

The terms *engine* and *3D engine* are very popular and used by hobby game programmers all over the world. However, the guys who use these buzzwords to name their code projects do not always fully understand the meaning of them. It is important to clarify what we mean by engine or 3D engine; therefore, before jumping into the code, I clarify the meaning for you.

You might define an engine as a machine that is used to propel a vehicle. With regard to game programming, an engine is a part of your project that propels certain functionalities of your program. It is quite clear that if you put a key into a car's ignition lock and turn it, the car's engine should crank up and the car should start. You then put your foot on the accelerator to get the car to move. Inside, your car's engine transfers kinetic energy to the axle-drive shaft to make things move. The driver does not need to know exactly what is going on inside the engine, nor does he care if he just wants to drive the car.

The very same concept applies to 3D engines. You call the `Turn_Key_in_Ignition_Lock()` function to crank things up. The 3D engine then gets your graphics adapter ready to run. When you floor the virtual accelerator (in this case, you send 3D models to the graphics adapter), the 3D engine makes the 3D models show up on your screen. The engine's job is to do all the nasty low-level stuff, such as communicating with the graphics adapter, setting its render states, transforming the models, and dealing with the abstruse math (such as rotation matrices). This sort of dirty work is necessary, but it is work you don't want to do to program a video game, or do you?

You should want to do the dirty work because this book is about programming an engine and not a video game. Hence, you should be interested in how the engine actually works and how you can implement all those things a programmer of a video game would not have to care about because he is just using a certain engine. I will show you how to program an engine that can do all of those low-level things a game programmer doesn't need to bother with—and probably doesn't want to.

Engines versus APIs

Today, several libraries are used to provide the most basic functions of a 3D engine. In addition, some libraries even deserve the name *3D engine*. Examples of these libraries include DirectGraphics, OpenGL, Java3D, and OpenInventor. We focus on the two big APIs, DirectGraphics and OpenGL, and ignore the more comprehensive 3D-engine approaches, such as Java3D or OpenInventor. These two big APIs are less integrated parts of graphics programming, because they use graphics-adapter drivers that interface between your software application and the hardware graphics adapter. However, such APIs are not 3D engines even if they are dealing heavily with 3D graphics as such.

DirectGraphics and OpenGL do not only project 3D data to 2D space and put color onto the output pixel data. However, you should understand why it is still better to call such libraries 3D pipelines rather than 3D engines. The pipeline takes in 3D data and outputs 2D data. But if you fire up my Web browser and search for 3D engines, you will find virtually thousands of websites that show off programs by people who develop their own 3D engine that might feature impressive "can-do" lists such as the following:

- Triangle hardware rasterizing
- Hardware transformation and lighting
- Texture filtering and anti-aliasing
- Blending up to four textures in single pass

You might ask how these features are implemented and why such an impressive engine can render only a single triangle. Unfortunately, most new people mistake the 3D pipeline for a 3D engine. If you initialize Direct3D or OpenGL, you automatically access features like those in the previous list. However, you don't get access to a free 3D engine. Nowadays

I can bring Direct3D online in about ten lines of code if I want to do it smoothly. But if doing that could provide me with a 3D engine there would have been no need for me to write this book. In conclusion, if you come across a homemade engine that can render a hardware-transformed, lit, and rasterized triangle, understand that it is a simple test program that shows you how to crank up a graphics API and feed the 3D pipeline that already exists in the hardware.

What Exactly Is an Engine?

In the previous section, I explained to you what a 3D engine is not. Maybe it would be helpful if I explained what I think a 3D engine actually is. Actually, there is no such thing as a single definition of what an engine is. If you ask ten graphic programmers what their definition of a 3D engine is, you will get about twenty different definitions. In the most general sense, the multiple definitions are similar. However, if you ask for specifics, you will see that no two programmers have the same opinion. Instead, let's not simply try to define what an engine is but focus on some general principles of what an engine should do for us.

An engine has to:

- Manage all data in its responsibility area
- Compute all data according to its task area
- Pass on all data to its following instance, if necessary
- Accept data to manage and to compute from preceding instances

Personally, I hate such definitions, especially when I was studying and just every single author thought he needed to come up with his very own definition because all the other already existing 23,342,735 definitions of the same thing lack this or that in his humble opinion. So do me a favor and don't take my definition of what an engine needs to do as a God-given law. It is not. You will have an implicit understanding of what an engine should do for you, just as I and lots of other guys out there do.

I use different terms such as *3D engine*, *game engine*, and *engine*. The general term *engine* is used for all kinds of engines. I think of an engine that is designed to be used in a video game project as one that contains several sub-engines. Examples of sub-engines include 3D engines, sound engines, input engines, network engines, physics engines, artificial intelligence (AI) engines, and so on.

I want to show you a simple example of an engine and how my loose definition applies to it. Imagine that you write a program as a library that contains functions to load, manipulate, and play sound files. You call this a *sound engine*. Think about what users of your engine want it to do for them. They want it to be simple. For example, users want one function call to initialize the library or to instantiate an object from the sound engine class. They want one function call to load a sound file and one function call for each time a sound is to be played. Finally, they want one function to shut the engine down or delete the engine object.

Those who would use your sound engine don't care how your engine parses sound files to get the data or how it communicates with the sound card. Your engine needs to take care of storing the sound data and providing an ID or an object so the user can access it, accepting instructions from preceding instances (like those generated by the user, for example) to play a sound, and how to pass it on to following instances to let them play the sound.

The previous example is a simple one of how engines work. However, you can think of this example in a more complex way. For example, think about a custom memory manager that manages the memory blocks where the sound files are stored.

The most complex engine is a 3D engine. The days of pumping 3D data into a graphics adapter's 3D pipeline are long gone because the graphic accelerator cards do more jobs on their own inside the 3D pipeline. Nowadays a 3D engine needs to organize things in a way suitable to speed things up. The so-called *object and scene management* is one of the most important parts. In a perfect situation, the user would name scene data to the engine and the engine itself would take care of organizing and structuring the data. After initialization time, the user would then need to make only some render calls and not care about state switches and similar things. The engine should catch those render calls and apply them in the most performant way.

To conclude, there is not a strict definition of what an engine needs to do *exactly* or doesn't need to do. It is clear, however, that there is a difference between the 3D pipeline and a 3D engine. Later, we will talk about the 3D pipeline in detail because it is imperative that you understand how your hardware works to avoid certain bottlenecks. The concept of a 3D engine is discussed in several chapters because it is important that you understand how to implement the engine I call the ZFXEngine. This engine is a game engine, which means it consists of several sub-engines. You will see the structure of the ZFXEngine in Chapter 2, "Designing the Engine," but for now I will tell you one final criterion that I think each engine must comply with: An engine should be independent of the project and capable of working with other video game projects and non-game multimedia software projects without the need to modify the engine's code. In other words: The engine's code must not include any game-related code, and it has to be reusable.

A Kind of Magic

Ignoring the technical point of view, you can clearly see the magic of video games. Today, you can buy a graphics adapter for about a hundred U.S. dollars that is the size of a small, thin book and that lets you do awesome things no one would have dared to dream a decade ago. Thinks like creating the illusion of a real world inside your computer with a graphical representation that within the next few years will be comparable to a photo-realistic rendering.

Just think about it. Some decades ago, hardware to calculate mathematical equations and put pixels out to a pretty small black-and-white screen would have cost you a pretty penny and it would have filled a whole room. Clearly, nowadays we are better off because we can afford to do these things as a hobby or even as professional with a bit of luck at our disposal, because the necessary hardware is widely available and affordable.

Nostalgia and Modern Times

Moving away from the technical aspects and definitions toward the fascination of video, I like to dream about the good old days. Those of you who can still remember *Wing Commander I* can understand the kind of nostalgic feeling. *Wing Command I* had small, cute sprites that wandered around on the screen at a resolution of 320x200 and the display of 256 sensational colors in a poorly depicted, fake 3D world. The buzzword describing such a video game from today's computer graphics point of view would be *pixel-pulp*. Even on a small-sized monitor the displayed image would suffer serious staircase effects, and, due to the low number of pixels available to set to different colors, it was not possible to have a lot of details in the displayed objects.

Although it wasn't the standard of game we see today, it hit the mark. If you played these games when they first came out, you might remember the astonished, happy faces of the people who played them. Personally, I still remember the night a friend of mine got this amazing new game called *Doom* as a birthday gift. A whole bunch of people skipped a party and gathered in front of the computer. It was not until dawn that the roaring of the chain saw ceased and the last monster was cut down.

Note

> The video game *Doom*, from id Software, played a very special role in the development of video games in general. It introduced concepts and algorithms that are still used in today's video games. Naturally, those algorithms were adapted to a real 3D world and modern graphics adapters, but this still holds true. We will revisit *Doom* and its successors.

The hardware manufacturers were as happy as the gamers. People updated their hardware by buying a new graphics adapter, memory, CPU, or even a whole new computer just to play the next-generation games. As a matter of fact, people were willing to invest several hundred dollars to upgrade their systems. This boom in the hardware market made it possible for the manufacturers to increase their sales and lower their prices. New hardware hit the shelves in increasingly shorter periods of time.

Just take a look at your computer now. It most certainly has a graphics adapter that can render five million polygons per second. And you most certainly bought it for a couple hundred dollars, correct?

The Problems of Modern Times

Unfortunately, programmers new to 3D computer graphics tend to render a million polygons without any kind of scene management and optimizations because the hardware is so incredibly fast these days. Reality hits when you try to switch on effects, such as multi-texturing, bump mapping, and per-pixel lighting on all these polygons. Before you can say "Rats," your graphics adapter will say its good-bye.

The faster the hardware is, the more effects gamers want to see in the video games they buy. This leads to a situation where you have to watch the polygon count just like you would have had to do several years ago. There are a lot ways to do this and to achieve a smart polygon count for the available hardware. A few graphics adapter generations ago, programmers needed to take care of algorithms at a very low level to speed up rotation calculations and prevent pixel overdraw at all costs. Each cycle of the CPU was considered extremely valuable, and you had to think twice before you were willing to invest it. Today, you need to optimize on a much higher level. Do you just render a few hundred pixels twice each frame? Do you just transform and render several hundred polygons without culling on a per-polygon basis? So what? This is no problem today.

The modern technique in the field of computer graphics introduced the concept of division of labor and specializing. Do you remember Taylor from your last course on economics? He was the guy who came up with the idea of specialization in industrial manufacturing of goods. On the one hand, you now have the CPU calculation algorithms the programmer designed. Since the advent of computers there have been no changes about that except for the lightning speed today's processors run at. On the other hand, you have an additional full-blown processor that sites on the graphics adapter. This machine is doing the graphics-related stuff and it is solely optimized for that purpose. So finally the idea of specialization made its way into the hardware architecture of computers and their graphics adapters.

The challenge today is not to optimize every single detail at the lowest level you can reach. The challenge starts with distributing the workload evenly between the two processors at your disposal. The advent of shaders introduced even more changes in the way you write graphic applications, as there is now the possibility of writing your very own programs for the processor that sits on the graphics adapter, instead of using the hardwired functionalities the graphics adapter's driver exposes to you and to your programs running on the main processor.

Tip
The processor sitting on the graphics adapter is called the graphics processing unit (GPU), as opposed to the main board's processor, which is called the central processing unit (CPU).

The trick is that you need to look at the traffic between the two processors because the AGP (*accelerated graphics port*) bus connecting the two is about ten times slower in moving the data than the memory feeding the CPU and the GPU. Over the course of this book, I show you how to prevent that kind of traffic or at least how to minimize it. The point I'm getting at is that it is imperative for you to understand that new technology demands new concepts and ways of approaching old-fashioned problems to deal with them in a more optimized way.

> **Tip**
>
> I still remember the day I posted on my website the first screen shots of the simple first-person shooter game that I developed while writing this book. I gave away the fact that the game does not use a binary space partitioning (BSP) tree with a potential visibility set (PVS). This made people angry, and I had to defend my decision to create the game this way. As you will see in Chapter 13, "Scene Management," this kind of technique is outdated and simply cannot use modern graphics adapters in a way they are meant to be used. The point is, don't just use what you know was good yesterday. Utilize what the future will bring.

To put it simply, you must know your enemy to defeat him. Actually, I don't like that kind of aggressive thinking, so I'd better put it this way: If you can't defeat your enemy, just ally with him. Your enemy is the hardware sitting smugly inside your computer that refuses to render as many polygons with as many effects per pixel as you would like. Now, if you think of that little beast as your friend and team up with it, you will get closer to your goal. You have to understand how the hardware works to take advantage of the knowledge instead of using Rambo-like strategies.

Wizardry and Art: Creating the Magic

If you approach the graphics adapter and video game programming with an open mind, you will feel the magic this field offers. This is a magic you, the programmer, can create and control. There are programmers who are just that: programmers. However, there are also programmers who are artists or wizards, if you will. Using their wizard force, they can create the magic of a real video game that features smart light and shadow effects and a realistic atmosphere.

You should never make fun of this fact or think that creating magic is less important than creating the video game itself. On the contrary, this aspect is the most important one in creating a video game that people will like. It's at the core of the work. The final product is a lot more than just bits and bytes created from a couple of lines of code; at least this is not the case for developers and players. Publishers with their marketing and business people definitely take another point of view on this topic, even if they do not officially agree to it. And rightly so. Their job is just to sell the product. The developers and players will also see the entertainment issue, that a video game is after all a toy.

For you the developer, the final product should be a piece of valuable, unique artwork. Your team's graphic artists will create textures for your objects, just like a painter will do his painting. Your team's modelers will create 3D models just like a sculptor would do his statues. You need real musicians to create a sound atmosphere fitting the game's scheme perfectly. So who still wants to say that the final video game is not an artwork of its very own kind?

There is one major difference between video games and most other kinds of art. As Richard Rouse III described it in *Game Design: Theory and Practice* (Wordware Publishing; 2nd ed., 2004), a video game is an interactive form of art.

However, a video game is more than "just" artwork of its own kind. If you do your job right, the final game will emit a magical attraction that puts the players under the spell of the game. As opposed to games, normal plain application software is developed as a solution to a given problem. Video games, on the other hand, have no real problem to solve for the user. I don't want to dive into the sociological aspects of why people play games, but it all boils down to the same fact. People play games for fun; the program itself is the reason people use it.

A video game is very similar to a virtual theme park. People come to these parks to enjoy themselves, be it during a Magic Mountain ride or while having a snack in a theme restaurant in Las Vegas. Human beings never had much time to spend on leisure activities over the course of history. People want to go to fantastic places, switch their brains to relax mode, and be enchanted by the atmosphere. The same thing applies to video games. The task of a video game is to take people out of their normal lives and make them a special agent, a jet fighter pilot, or a Formula One driver. They should survive dangerous missions while risking their virtual lives trying to save the world or the virginity of a bunch of babes.

Inside the world that you as a programmer or developer create, you are God. Period. "Why is that?" you might ask. It's the case if you define a God as an entity with the power to formulate laws of nature and put them to work in the (virtual) universe. Should a character in the virtual world also be able to control a bit of this magic, or should gravity have an effect upward, not downward, with respect to mass centers? You have the power to let things happen or not.

Whether you believe in a real existing God or not, the concept still applies in your virtual world and this is your place of being a (virtual) God.

The Development Process of a Video Game

Now that you've heard about the motives that drive developers to develop video games (or at least what should drive them), I want to tell you something about the project management and business administration that accompanies a video game project. The creation and development of a video game is a lengthy process, not a single, linear task. Newcomers

> **The Responsibility of Gods**
>
> Even if the creation processes and the wonders a video game developer executes as half-god are taking place in a virtual world, those things still have an effect on the real world. I know this might be a bit unusual, but in my humble opinion there is no way around discussing some of these effects or at least mentioning them here.
>
> Recent incidents illustrate how video games are held responsible for very cruel crimes committed by teenagers in the United States as well as in Germany. The video games were held responsible, especially those in which the player is interactive and acts out cruel and brutal activities. Some video games even educate players on how to kill or how to fire weapons.
>
> Indeed, a lot of games take place in a setting in which the player can play at ancient, current, or future wars with any kind of weapon. Most games are about killing other beings that are typically evil and must be wiped out for the sake of Earth's well-being.
>
> I don't want to delve too much into such topics here, but there is one thing I you should know about my opinion. As a matter of fact, developers and designers of a video game can have an influence on the player. You must be aware of the fact that you have a responsibility to minimize negative effects your game could possibly have on others. We don't need to discuss that you simply cannot take into account every weird mind out there and what that mind might make of playing the game. However, you should ask yourself if realistic human-destruction physics, such as blood drops influenced by gravity or realistic wounds after weapon fire, are really needed to increase the game's quality and atmosphere. Another question you might ask is: Is the United States Army a suitable publisher for a totally free video war game? The question here is whether or not the amusement of the people is the primary interest of the publisher in this case. In my opinion the publisher should always entertain through video games. If you want to be a top-notch video game developer after reading this book, please also bear in mind that you have at least two responsibilities:
>
> - You have to offer the player the best you can achieve on current hardware.
> - You have the responsibility to try your best to ensure that the game is always seen as just that: a game.

to this genre most likely stem from a video-game-playing generation and do not know what happens in the business world. Most do not care about the business world.

Those who do not care might be very lucky and survive in the business world, but they would be better off understanding something about that world. In the following sections, I give you some insight from a bird's eye perspective. This perspective will help you understand issues, such as the money a developer actually earns from developing an average video game and whether or not one can make a living developing video games.

Professional Perspectives

If you really intend to get into the business of developing video games as a professional and make a living out of it, then read the following pages carefully. These sections will give you an understanding of the cross-connections a video game project depends on and how the development process actually works, starting with that particular idea you have that eventually leads to a product the customer can buy. And that is the first perspective you should be take as a professional. A video game is a product that will be sold on a rough market. The second perspective is whether or not you want to make a living of producing such products.

Games Are Products

Do not fool yourself—games are products. Even if we talk about games—meaning things people just play—we are still talking about a business, and this business is just as difficult as other kinds of businesses in the world. It doesn't matter if it's soap, cars, or rubbish bags. Business is business.

> **Note**
>
> About a decade ago China restricted the growth in population by forcing people to have only one child. This led to a phenomenon called "little emperors" or "little princesses." All the money the relatives spent for a bunch of children before could be used to buy more leisure goods and toys for fewer children. The toy industry was the most booming business in the Chinese market at that time, making tons of money. Do not mistake games for "just toys" from a business point of view. Even if children play with toys like video games there is still a serious business effort involved and the market is as rough as any other out there.

Successful video games are sold in numbers of a few hundred thousand worldwide per system, meaning PC and different consoles. Very successful titles break the one million mark, and only the premium, AAA titles manage to sell several million copies. You might think of John Carmack now, whose hobby is collecting Ferraris financed by video games he developed with his team, including *Doom* and *Quake*.

This is why I think it is imperative and even interesting to learn about the process of developing a video game from a commercial point of view. The following pages deal with that development process in a reverse order from when they actually happen.

Job or Profession?

The first question to ask yourself is, "What kind of vision do you have regarding what you want to achieve programming engines and video games?" There are two answers when doing this as a profession. The first answer would be to work as a programmer, artist, modeler, or whatever in a team for somebody else. The second answer is to start your own development studio as an independent company. The alternative is to program engines or video games as a hobby or for fun.

Both professional options have advantages and disadvantages. If you want a job in another person's development studio, you will have to fight your way in a tough job market to find an open position. If you get a job, you are always in danger of losing it.

Do you think you are better off starting your own company? Not really. Starting your own company makes you responsible for pushing the project forward to a successful end, and you have to find people who know the business and will do what you want from them. Those people also need to share your vision. Finally, you also have to find a publisher and/or financer. If you are only a programmer without knowledge of business topics, you will be lost before you even get started.

These points apply even more in the United States where you need as many lawyers protecting you from being sued as you have employees.

Tip
> For the last few years there is some kind of new profession around in the video game business that is called a *game agent*. Like an agent managing a Hollywood movie star, a game agent works for a video game development studio. His task is to make contacts between "his" development studios and publishers, to bargain contracts, and the like. Time will tell whether or not this way of using an agent is promising.

Game Programming

First of all I would like to talk a bit about what most people mistake for being the core of creating a video game. That is the process of game programming.

One of the biggest misunderstandings about video game programming is that most people, especially programmers, like to think that the programming is the most important part of developing a video game. Naturally, the image of a long-haired freak comes to mind. He has a glowing cigarette in the corner of his mouth, and a cup of jet-black coffee is handy during his 3 o'clock in the morning hacking ritual as he punches algorithms into the keyboard.

Agreed, the freak is not the misunderstanding. The misunderstanding is the importance that people associate with programming itself. Naturally, programming is a time-consuming process; that is true. In the end, the product consists of several thousand lines of code. Consider this: What are those freaks hacking into their keyboards? What do they come up with spontaneously? What do they think will end with a cool result? Programming is not a creative process at all. The freaks just have to hack into the keyboard exactly what is written in the design document—in more or less detail.

Actually, the programming of a video game is the most uncreative and most boring part of developing a video game. It's diligent work, but in the end, it is nothing more than just programming what is given in very specific task lists.

Okay, calm down. It is indeed not as bad as I just described it here. But I wanted to bring it to you the hard way so nobody around here gets the idea that you can develop a video game by just switching on your computer and writing some code that comes to mind. The implementation of the design document will raise several unexpected problems during the planning phase of the project. Even in this very late phase of the project, creativity and feedback loops are important.

This book, like most of its brothers and sisters related to game development, focuses on the programming aspect. So you can still see that there is indeed at least some importance connected with that part of video game development. Or to put it as mathematicians would: It is a necessary, but not a sufficient condition. Or to speak in a language more of us can understand: You should know programming by heart to have your brain cells freed for all those other things that differentiate a video game from a plain, boring software application.

Lead Programmer / Technical Director

For each sub-complex in a development team, which will consist of about ten to thirty people, there needs to be a leader. Such sub-complexes are graphic arts, programming, sound and music, and so on. The job of the lead programmer, which is sometimes also called technical director, is the coordination and organization of the team's programmers.

The lead programmer has the last word if there are differences that cannot be solved in discussions inside the team. He has also a lot of responsibility. He has to come up with a list of tasks, which he delegates to his team. And he is also held responsible for the things that go wrong.

Game Design

Well, now we have talked about game programming as representative for all tasks inside a video game development project that are concerned with implementing things like graphics artwork, models, sound, and so on.

The natural progression is to discuss game design. Game design is everything that is concerned with planning what the programmers should implement. It involves a general plan of how the game should look when it is done, what kind of atmosphere and game play it will provide, and so on. The most important part when it comes to game design is the design document.

The Design Document

The first step when you start planning the game is to write a design document. It is the heart and soul of the project. To say it in a simple way, you can think of the design document as the actual game in written form. It documents all aspects of the game, such as drawings and graphics of the locations, settings, and characters. Additionally, you will find the storyline, a description of the cut scenes, the user interface, and the possible actions a player can do while playing the game.

To make the point even more obvious, you can say that if you hand out the design document to a game development team that has nothing to do with the project at all, they must be able to create the same game as the original team would have done. Now, that's more or less impossible to do because a project lives and dies with the commitment of the original project members and their visions. Another team might be able to implement it the same way, but will not provide the same atmosphere unless they are as passionate about the project as the original design team.

The creation and completion of such a design document is a long process and involves a huge amount of work. It forces you to think through every aspect of the game in advance, thus forcing you to describe every single detail of the game. The bottom line is: What is not contained in the design document will not be implemented in the final game. So it is easy to accept that you will need to work for as long as one year to complete this document. During this time, there are also other tasks to be fulfilled, such as finding a publisher, doing market research, forming the team, and so on.

Creating a thorough design document is a task that must be completed before you start implementing anything. At least this would be the optimal way to go in theory. Naturally, there will be changes to the design document. You cannot think about every single detail upfront, so the design document needs to be revisited and corrected throughout the development process. (In practice, about 80% of the design document would be ready before work on the implementation starts.)

Lead Designer

It might be clear by now what a so-called lead designer has to do. In cooperation with the team, he has to write the design document. This task demands that he have the game already inside his head. He must feel the atmosphere that the game should put the player into, and he is responsible for seeing that the team implements the game in exactly the way he designed it. (Note that, normally, the team does not have a say in the design document but is only consulted by the lead designer if he wants additional opinions. But there are also companies like Valve out there that pass on the idea of an all-mighty, "god-like" game designer. Instead their "cabal" design process involves a whole team group [see http://www.gamasutra.com/features/19991210/birdwell_01.htm].)

It is not necessary for the lead designer to be a programmer or have knowledge about programming, artwork, or anything at all. However, he must be able to communicate with programmers, artists, sound designers, and the other team members in a way they understand. There is an interesting story on www.gamasutra.com where Warren Spector describes the development process of the game *Deus Ex* (see http://www.gamasutra.com/features/20001206/spector_01.htm).

Because *Deus Ex* was to break all boundaries of conventional genres and because there were two guys suited for the position of lead designer, an unusual decision was made. As Spector discusses, they used two design teams, each one with its own lead designer. To anticipate the outcome of this decision, I'll tell you that this was described in the "what went wrong" part of the post mortem. The different points of views and philosophies of the two lead designers led to tensions inside the team(s) and did not create the synergies everybody hoped for. Reflective of this tension were the names of the teams; one was called Team 1 and the other called Team A because neither of the teams wanted to be number 2 or B.

After some months they switched strategies and melded the two teams into one, using only a single lead designer. Now I think you can imagine that this decision was accompanied by technical problems as well as social ones. But still, it proved to be the right decision to let the project survive successfully.

From this interesting story you can learn a lot. There is no such thing as a working anarchy in project management. I would describe the most suitable structure for project management as a kind of democratic dictatorship. All team members should raise their voices and argue for their points of view on important decisions. As long as the majority of the team favors the same points of view, it is most likely the best way to do it. Still, there is the need for one single leader to have the right to say that a certain way is the way it will be done. Obviously, this needs to be the same person for the duration of the project.

Caution

Every video game project has its lead designer even if you cannot identify him because there is not one with the title of lead designer. You can simply define the lead designer as the one person who has the final word in all decisions concerning the project. . . except for the financer, of course.

Implementing the Design

I want to raise a point again. The design document is not a fixed constant in the project. It should remain consistent from the kickoff until the project is done, but the need to apply changes to it will arise. You must therefore ensure that the vision of the game and its whole atmosphere is not changed after you start to implement the project. To say the least, the design document is part of the contract you have agreed on and signed with your publisher. There is a lot more to say about game design, but there are several books that do a good job of this. I recommend Richard Rouse III's book, which is called *Game Design: Theory and Practice* (Wordware Publishing; 2nd ed., 2004).

Game Proposal

People will mistake the game proposal for the game design document or vice versa. The game proposal is a meta-document that contains several sub-documents. Although the game design document deals only with game-specific aspects important for implementation, the game proposal deals with each aspect of the project as a whole. The design document concentrates on the game whereas the game proposal also takes the environment into account. While the design document should communicate the implementation issues to the implementers the game proposal should communicate the whole project to the business people of the development company and the publisher.

A publisher will want you to do some work that you might not think is part of your job as a game developer. The game proposal is the document you as a development studio take to a publisher to convince him to accept this project and give you financial backing. You should therefore put a lot of effort into the proposal.

The million-dollar question is what are you supposed to write into this game proposal and why is the design document not enough? Well, we will arrive at an answer for the second part of the question while discussing the answer to the first part of the question. There is no single right game-proposal template you can use or copy. Nor can you say exactly what should be contained in it or how many pages it should have, and you cannot provide a sample table of contents. This can be very annoying; however, the reason for this is that each and every project in the video game development world is different. Very huge projects generally need long game proposals. Smaller projects generally require shorter game proposals. It's that simple. I can show you what *should* be contained in every game proposal at the least. If you want to learn more about this, I strongly recommend Luke Ahearn's book *Designing 3D Games That Sell!* (Charles River Media, 2001). You will find a thorough introduction to the topics related to game proposal as well as a lot on business administration and marketing, which provide you with a basic knowledge of business issues.

In this book, Ahearn names the following parts of a game proposal, which are:

- Game treatment
- Competitive analysis
- Design document
- Team introduction
- Budget
- Schedule

Whoa, wait. Are you surprised to see the game design document in this list? Why? It is only natural that the design document be part of the game proposal package. Except for the game treatment, all other parts of the game proposal deal with the environment in which the development process will take place.

In the following sections, I explain the game proposal part, except for the design document.

Game Treatment

You might know the term *executive summary*. In general, if you take a look at business operations, you will see a lot of documents written about various issues. Normally, those documents contain hundreds of pages. The people responsible for writing these documents obviously put a lot of effort in writing them.

On the other hand, a single person is generally responsible for making the final decisions regarding whether to back up a particular project, revisit it, or just skip it based on that document. Unfortunately, the higher a manager sits in the company's hierarchy, the less time he has to spend on each task. No need to say that he simply cannot read hundreds of pages of a dozen documents he has on his desk each day. Senior executives do not want to read this many documents. This is why all of those documents are accompanied with an executive summary that outlines the major points described extensively in the document. The executive summary also draws the conclusions from the documents. The manager can then read the executive summary and make a decision based on the summary. If necessary, he might look at other parts of the document only after he has looked at the executive summary.

Back to the video game business world: You can think of the game treatment as the executive summary of the game project you want to sell to a publisher. A manager sits in the publisher's office at his desk and receives a lot of game proposals from dozens of new game development teams asking the publisher for a contract. This manager has to make a decision about these proposals in a limited amount of time, and the manager must sort them by priority and interest. Interesting things come first, less interesting things come next, and uninteresting things are tossed in the trash can.

To get to the point, the game treatment should describe the main aspects of your game in about two or three pages. It needs to be written so that the manager sees that you are top-notch at what you do, and that your game is the next AAA title that will sell like crazy.

Competitive Analysis

The next part the game proposal must have is the competitive analysis. I will never forget the course in strategic planning for international marketing I took while studying in Finland. Our instructor, who was a very good one by the way, sharpened his students' minds to focus on only one thing when designing products. This one thing he called *competitive advantage*.

> **Note**
>
> In Finland I also learned from the same instructor that there is no such thing as a plain product. All products are services that should serve to satisfy certain needs of the consumers. If you think this way, you will automatically end up with better products because you are not thinking in terms of products, but in terms of what your potential customers want.

The competitive advantage is the one and only reason why people will buy your product (video game) and not your competitor's. There are several aspects that can give you the competitive advantage. It is the famously low price, the ultra-high quality, a special gimmick no other game can offer, or a special technology. It doesn't matter what it is, but it does matter that you can name at least one competitive advantage in your game proposal.

From a publisher's point of view the market is always narrow. It is difficult to place a new product in that market and compete against all the other video games out there. In the competitive analysis you have to do two things. First, you have to analyze the market and list all currently existing or soon-to-come video games that are somehow similar to your project (placed in the same genre). The second thing you are required to do is to compare your project against the ones in your list. You need to explain and prove here that your game will get its market share against the competition and why it will get and hold it.

As you can see, the competitive analysis is not much more than justifying your video game against all the others out there and making the publisher believe that he will achieve major sales with it. If you manage to sell this idea to him, you will get the business deal.

Team Introduction

Another point to consider is that the project is always about the people. You have people to work with, you have people to sell your work to, and, unfortunately, you most often have people to work against because of business politics.

The publisher wants to know who you are and what you have managed to achieve in your life. If he gives you a contract, you will most likely be working together along with your team for at least one year. You will want to know the people on the publisher's side you will work with for the next couple of months. The publisher will want to know your team. Therefore, you should include a description of your team in the proposal.

You have a problem if you are a newcomer and just started a video game development studio. If this is the case, refer to your education and other software projects you have worked with and completed. You should also include your experience *playing* games.

I received an application from a graphic artist who wanted to work in the field of video games and create models and graphics for a game. It was quite obvious after a few email exchanges that he knew nothing about video games. He knew some names of famous games, but that was it. You do not need someone who is not interested in playing games on a team that wants to develop a game.

Budget

Now that the easy stuff is behind us, let's discuss some of the "real" business stuff. I happened to take part in an event designed by the consulting company Accenture (formerly known as Anderson Consulting) at my university. We students had to develop a business plan for a fictitious customer and consult for him with regard to certain aspects of his company. After one group of students presented their findings to the fictitious customer (who was one of the Accenture guys), he asked one question that broke all our necks because we didn't expect it: "How much will it cost?"

The consultant got us on icy ground. We thought he would ask us details or for an action plan for his company, but he didn't. And rightly so. He told us that from his experience, most responsible managers of his real customers are only interested in what it will cost them. All the other details are discussed later on.

In the budget part of the game proposal, the publisher wants to know what you and your team will cost him if he lets you develop the game for him. After all, he is the one who has to give you the money. A budget is nothing more than a list of costs that will occur over the time you need to finish the project successfully. This is what you should know about a budget if you happen to review or write a general business plan.

Note
By now, you should realize that developing a video game takes a lot more than hacking codes into your computer. You also have to deal with market analysis, budget plans, and project management. And you'd better deal well with these topics or your project will die faster than you can say *hasta la vista*.

In case you have never written a budget, I will provide you with a very simple example here to get you started. The most obvious entries in a budget plan are the costs that stem from salaries for your teammates and yourself, of course. Then you will have one-time costs, such as licenses for engines or software tools.

Keep in mind that it is easy to forget costs, such as rent for office space, office equipment costs, traveling expenses, and so on. Even if you use lower estimates, the costs can easily add up to several tens of thousands of dollars. Refer to Table 1.1 to see an example budget.

I want to discuss the sample budget entries you see in Table 1.1. First of all, this is a team for a very small project. Hence, the budget is also very low, coming in around $650,000. The project duration is only twenty-four months, and there are only eight people working on the project. I assume in this budget that the team is not aiming for a AAA title and

Table 1.1 Simplified Sample Budget of 24-Month Project

Item	Cost x Number	Total Cost
Project		
Project Manager	U.S. $6,000 x 24	U.S. $144,000
Programming		
Lead Programmer	U.S. $4,000 x 24	U.S. $96,000
Game Programmer	U.S. $3,000 x 24	U.S. $72,000
Tool Programmer	U.S. $3,000 x 24	U.S. $72,000
Graphics and Artwork		
Level-Designer (Lead)	U.S. $2,500 x 24	U.S. $60,000
Level-Designer	U.S. $2,000 x 24	U.S. $48,000
Graphics Artist	U.S. $2,500 x 24	U.S. $60,000
Modeler	U.S. $2,000 x 24	U.S. $48,000
Licenses and Software		
Discreet "3D Studio Max 5"	U.S. $5,000 x 3	U.S. $15,000
id Software "Quake II Engine"	U.S. $10,000 x 1	U.S. $10,000
Adobe "Photoshop 7"	U.S. $1,200 x 1	U.S. $1,200
Rent and Equipment		
Office rent	U.S. $1.000 x 1	U.S. $24,000
Computer	U.S. $1.000 x 7	U.S. $7,000
Total		U.S. **$657,200**

therefore they use only older technology, such as the Quake II engine, which is cheap compared with its successors. However, you will always find other modern engines at roughly the same cost. They are just less famous.

Also, real-world modelers would ask you as project manager for other, more expensive software than 3D Studio. Tools such as Maya or XSI are what modelers like to work with and if you want to buy them, including all the fancy add-on tools and plugins, you would at least double the cost for a license.

Finally, the sample budget does not include costs for you and your lead designer to travel to the publisher, which would need to be done multiple times. A lot of other costs are missing, such as costs for a lawyer to check the contracts, the outsourced creation of sound effects and music, and so on. But this sample should serve as a simple one.

Schedule

As you have seen in the sample budget, you need to know how long it will take you to bring the project to a successful end. The biggest part of the budget is the salaries for your employees and they add up month by month. To know how much time you will need, you have to set up a schedule that describes the project in as much detail as possible.

The schedule, as part of the game proposal, does not only say how long it will take you, but also which milestones and miniature milestones should be achieved at which point in the project process. First of all, this schedule lets the publisher make his own estimations about when the product is ready to hit the retailers' shelves. This is an important scheduling point because the retail delivery time is when the product can drive home revenues for the publisher. The schedule also provides the publisher with the opportunity to control the project at any phase of its lifetime. The publisher can just look at the schedule and ask you if you reached the milestones stated.

The bad news is that it is quite complicated for a relatively new programmer who might not have worked on a commercial project to estimate the time he would need to implement a certain algorithm or functionality. The same applies for artists and other team members. The only way to make such estimations is from experience. I recommend that you act as a professional in your next hobby projects. You need to set up a document along with your project in which you write down the dates when you achieve what you think is at least a medium-sized goal of your project. Also write down how many working hours you spent from the last major point to get to the current one.

Tracking your hobby projects will increase your knowledge of what you can do in a given amount of time. Or, to put it the other way around, you can track how much time you would need to implement a given list of features or milestones. There is no better way of doing project estimations and nobody other than you can do this for your part of the cake. The only thing you need to do is to stay honest. Don't cheat yourself to show off in front of others. That's not the reason why you tracked your work in the first place. By cheating you will eventually get to the point where you run out of time and can't meet a specific deadline at all, causing unnecessary stress on yourself and the whole project. If you stay as honest as possible from the start you will get better and better at estimating time schedules for your workload.

Other Elements of a Game Proposal

Now you know the minimum requirements of a game proposal. However, there are a few more things to consider. These are:

- Everything that you think is of importance with regard to the project or the environment, such as the target audience or your business partners, should be included in the game proposal.

- The minimum system specifications (of the customers' computers) you are targeting for and the like.

Publisher, Publishing, and Revenues

You think now you know all the business stuff you need to know to start developing a video game? Well, this is still not true. You actually know only about the development process of the game and you have learned that there is a lot more to it than just hacking some code into the keyboard and putting nice textures on your polygons. But everything we discussed so far is mostly concerned with the developer's point of view on developing a video game.

Do you know how the video game finds its way onto the retailers' shelves and how much money you will earn? The process is similar to the path that is taken by books. An author will write a book, just like a development team will develop a game. Prior to writing a book the author is required to write a proposal about what the book should include and the author will go to a publisher and convince him that he needs this book in his line of products.

If the author and a publisher agree on the project, your contact person within the publisher typically needs to "sell" this project internally to his superiors, which is normally just a formality. I happened to stumble into a situation where a project of mine was canceled by a superior of my contact person because of business politics. However, if you get your contract signed, you start writing the book or developing the game. When you are done, you hand the final product over to the publisher and then you go through a feedback stage, which involves correcting cycles. Then it is the task of the publisher to manufacture and produce and distribute the book or game to wholesalers and/or retailers. The publisher therefore needs salesmen who travel around and present the product, pushing the traders to accept the product for their range of products.

There are a few other catches in publishing, such as buying a good place on the shelf. The publisher is also responsible for selling licenses and doing marketing and commercials for the product. Ultimately, exactly what needs to be done is a matter of detailed contract bargaining.

Note
Publishers normally like to accept video game projects that are in a very early stage of development. This way, the publisher can push the developers to change details to make the product fit better into the publisher's line of products and what he thinks the market wants. Still, it is helpful to present a load of concept art, screenshots, and a working demo to impress the people you want to convince.

Earning Revenues

Also a matter of contract is the amount of money the development team will get when the product is done. Typically, you receive your revenues as a percentage of the profit from each sold unit. Roughly speaking, the wholesalers and retailers take as much as 50 percent of the final price of the product a gamer has to pay at the retailer's store. The remainder goes to the publisher.

> **Note**
>
> Percentages and calculations in this section are based mainly on the German market. U.S. and other markets may differ in terms of exact figures.

The publisher uses the money to finance his marketing, the manufacturing process, the physical distribution, and so on. So what do you see from all this money? Well, depending on the contract you bargained, you can expect to get something in the range of 10–25 percent of the revenues the publisher receives. This is what you call royalties, and as you can see it is not that much. Just take a title, for example, that costs about $50.00 in the retail store. For each sold unit, the publisher gets $25.00 and hands over about $3.75 to the development team. That is you.

Well, how does this sound to you? You get less than $4.00 from each unit sold. In addition, you have to share this money with your whole team. You might argue that you sell hundreds of thousands of units and the money adds up to a good amount. This is true. However, you are forgetting one thing. Let's revisit the sample budget shown in Table 1.1. You need about two years' time to get the project done, and you burn about $700,000 while doing the project.

No development team can afford to spend that much money because they simply don't have that much money. Try to go to a bank and get the money. The only way to achieve this is through a bank robbery. So how can a team develop a game without money? The answer is quite simple: they don't have to. The publishers are not nasty, greedy monsters. They want you to do video games and so they give you the money you need. That is also part of the contract, and typically a development team gets certain sums of money connected to milestones of the schedule they achieve.

The catch is that the publisher has no money to give away as a gift. Instead, the money you receive is an advance on the royalties. If the money finally starts to roll into the publisher's house from sales of the finished video game, he won't give you any money until the amount of royalties you should have received compensate the amount of money the publisher gave you as an advance. Only after that will you get royalties, if the game sells even more units than it cost you to make the game.

This does not sound so good anymore because it does not sound like huge amounts of money are coming into your pockets. Let's stay with that simple example and do some calculations with it. Let's suppose your game is a successful one and you manage to sell about

150,000 units. For a small project of a small team, this is a great success and more than you should hope for in the first place.

The retailers will make a turnover of about $7.5 million, accumulated over the whole period in which these units were sold. This could easily be a year or more. The publisher will get 3.75 million from this turnover and has to pay the bills from this money. Still, he has a remarkable amount of money as profit.

So finally, all the royalties the development team would get amount to about $570,000. Wow, there is more than half a million dollars for the development team. This would be nice indeed, but as you will notice, the publisher won't give you any money before he is compensated for the $650,000 he paid you as an advance. And the end result of the story is that you will get no more money from this project. You already burned more money for the development process than you will get from the publisher in total.

So no Ferraris, no champagne, no caviar. You did, however, manage to get a salary for two years. You will have to look out for the next project and work even harder to make it a better one and hope for bigger sales next time. The good news is that you normally don't have to give money back to the publisher because he takes the risk of not selling enough units to compensate for the advance he gave you. This is a matter of contract, however, so be sure to settle on that issue before you begin work.

A Very Normal Professional

From this point of view, the profession of a video game developer is a job like any other out there. You don't get a huge bag full of money after you have done your work. You will get monthly payments to make your living like most other people do, and, like most other people would say, you are underpaid for sure. If the programming team would work in normal application software development you would find they get paid better. However, their jobs might be boring if they took the typical programming job.

You can argue that you will produce more quality and sell a lot more units for sure. This might be true, but selling more often means you need a bigger team and a longer duration of time for the development process, and this can lead to much higher development costs. AAA titles nowadays need budgets like Hollywood movie productions.

It is more realistic to think of starting as a small newcomer and grow from project to project. After you manage a successful title, you will be able to ask for higher revenues, force the publisher to pay for some of the tools you need, and so on. This will earn you more money but also more responsibility. The bigger your team gets, the more responsibility you have to pay your employees and to keep money available for unexpected expenses.

This also leads to the fact that you as the boss of such a development team get more and more away from actually developing video games. You will find yourself trying to acquire new projects while old ones are not totally finished to prevent your team from being without work. You will also have to ask for payment after one project is completed, and you will find yourself in meetings with publishers and making dates with the press to promote your video games.

Alternatives

As you can see, the current way in the video game business seems strange. The ones doing most of the work are the ones who gain the least profit from it. And there are no guarantees of anything. The publishers will always have the right to quit the project any time they want, even without granting you the rights to the work you already did.

So the best bet would be to find another way of publishing your game and of financing it. Unfortunately, bank loans are no way to go as banks will not give you the money unless you are an experienced developer who can also get a good contract from a publisher. There is no difference between who takes his share from the cake, the bank or the publisher.

You can consider the Internet. In these days when broadband connections are available at comparably low cost nearly everywhere in your target markets, this might be a viable option. You will never reach the same number of customers that a retailer could, but maybe you would be satisfied with fewer sales and bigger profits for you because there is no retailer, no wholesaler, and no publisher asking for its share. You don't lose about 86 percent of the revenue to them. Note that you could also try to convince a publisher to accept your game for retail distribution, while also allowing you to distribute it online on your own.

Another alternative would be to skip all this business stuff for the sake of free software and just remain a hobby game developer as you might currently be doing. You would most likely not have the time to create something that could compete against million-dollar-budget productions, but you would have your fun without worrying about money or making a living. And believe me, you would be worrying.

Now, we finally leave that business stuff for the remainder of the book and will concentrate on programming issues only. I promise.

Direct3D versus OpenGL Wars

As you might already know, the two main APIs existing today for communicating with graphics hardware are OpenGL and Direct3D (which is nowadays called DirectGraphics). The two APIs use different concepts to fulfill their job. OpenGL is a plain functional library, whereas Direct3D is purely object-oriented using the component object model (COM). I don't want to go into history issues here, but you can say that since version 8.0, Direct3D is much easier and more logical to use than it was previously.

Direct3D, and the whole DirectX package (which provides much more functionality than just 3D graphics) for that matter, is updated more frequently than OpenGL. People like to say that is because OpenGL was designed in a much better way, hence there is no need for frequent updates. The thing is, if you are using DirectX you need a new version to support new features the hardware offers. But if you use OpenGL you need new drivers providing new so-called extensions to support the new features such as shaders (a.k.a. vertex programs and fragment programs).

After all it's pretty much the same. DirectX comes in new versions officially and OpenGL uses this kind of plug-in system. And that leads us to another topic I find important to talk about here.

Flame Wars

Unfortunately, you will always find lots of flame war discussions going on in online bulletin boards or messaging systems. Those flame wars about Direct3D and OpenGL are spinning around the one and only question that comes in several different variations. Which one is better, which one is faster, which one is more comfortable, which one is higher, smells better and tastes ace? The base those discussions are built upon is always the same: ignorance or lack of knowledge and competence. Most "arguments" used in such discussions sound more like the one you would get from the brother of the cousin of the sister of the guy whose friend driving his grandpa's car ran over the cat of your neighbor lately.

OpenGL and Direct3D are said to be getting closer to each other with every new release of DirectX. There are still major differences in how you should use certain features from those APIs. Anyone trying to port a program from one API to the other without making certain changes will find the ported version to be much slower than the original one. You could now conclude that the API you ported the program to is a lot slower than the API you came from. This is how rumors start. Whoever is educated enough to know both APIs pretty well or to know his own limitations is smart enough not to take part is such pointless flame wars. So do me a favor. If you stumble across such a discussion, ignore it. There is no point trying to cure some misguided minds from their wrong opinions.

Drivers and Hardware

Another thing most people who discuss OpenGL versus Direct3D forget about is the system you run a program on. Certain hardware might be better suited to be used with OpenGL, whereas others might be better off using Direct3D. The drivers you use on a machine also matter.

What Are We Going to Use?

I see the goal of this book as developing an engine that is totally independent of a particular graphics API. Well, that is not true 100 percent of the time, but more or less. You will find the structure of the ZFXEngine to be oriented according to the Direct3D way of doing things. If you want to implement the interfaces of the engine using OpenGL, then you may struggle and find things to be complicated. The reason is simple: I'm just used to Direct3D.

The next question you might ask is why you would want to develop an engine that is totally independent of a certain graphics API. Actually, at the moment it is not all that common in commercial game engines to implement more than one graphics API. That would be a waste of time because one working renderer is enough to power a video game. You are here to learn something, and after all it is still a good idea to abstract your game code away from everything that depends on a certain API—other than your very own API, of course.

Going this way you always have the ability to switch away from a certain API any time you want. This would mean implementing your interfaces with another API you want to use instead, but you don't need to change your game code.

I already mentioned that I use DirectX for the remainder of this book, with one exception. For the network part of the engine I do not use DirectPlay, but the Windows Socket API. Also, the more boring components of the engine are not very detailed but are well-suited to do their jobs. I'm talking about the sound sub-engine and the input sub-engine featuring DirectMusic and DirectInput, respectively.

Why Do It the Hard Way If There Is an Easy Way?

One of my favorite topics you can start lots of flame wars about is whether to use already existing helper libraries or to reinvent lots of wheels with your own implementations. I will walk the hardest way I can see in this book, following my motto: Only those who have been in Hell can see Heaven. You are going to learn in this book how to use your hands at a very low level to write as many functions as you can for yourself. There are a lot of tools out there that would provide an easy way and that would make your life much easier, like STL, Windows API functions, FMOD, or the D3DX helper functions from the DirectX SDK (*Software Development Kit*). But as I already mentioned, you are here to learn something and I refuse to teach you just how to call library functions other people wrote for you. If this is what you want then you are better off using a reference to a certain library or tool than reading a book about programming.

D3DX Helper Library

Since version 7 of the DirectX SDK, Microsoft kindly provided us programmers with a really big and cool helper library. That one is called Direct3D Extensions, which boils down to Direct3DX or just D3DX. Besides other helpful stuff you will find especially its math functions and objects pretty good, fast, and comprehensive.

Unfortunately, this leads to a situation where even absolute beginners can throw fascinating 3D graphics onto the screen pretty fast, transforming geometry or even picking single pixels out of whole meshes. But then move on and ask them why they did this and that and why it works. The answer you will get sounds like this: "Er ... well, I just copied the code from this example here...."

As a matter of fact, the D3DX library lets you do a lot of things. That is pretty good as long as you know what you are doing and why those functions work the way they do. In developing a video game or just an engine, there will come a situation for sure where you will not find a D3DX function that fits your needs. You are instead forced to write your own implementation for this purpose, only to notice that you have not the slightest idea of 3D mathematics at all.

I don't want to let you run into this situation, so for the most part of the book I will show you how to actually do those calculations. It's true that the D3DX library was written by lots of people who know their jobs very well. The library is using SIMD (*single instruction stream, multiple data stream*) technology such as AMD's 3DNow! or Intel's SSE. I will introduce you to what that means in Chapter 4, "Fast 3D Calculus," so just hang on a bit. For now it's only important that those technologies are pretty fast compared with plain C++ code.

Knowing Instead of Copying

To be able to complete on your own the 3D math calculations that are not provided by the library of your choice, you simply must understand some very basic 3D math stuff. Trust me, there will be situations when there is no fitting D3DX function, and then you are pretty lucky if you know how to grab and color a pixel from a bitmap, how to calculate a rotation matrix, and how to adjust a billboard to the screen.

Be aware that D3DX is still a very fast beast for what it does. My intention in this book is not to show you how you should program your engines and video games from scratch. I want you to see and learn how to do this basic stuff. If you decide to go for D3DX afterward, you are welcome to do so. The big difference then is that when you use the D3DX functions, you also know how and why they work.

Get Ready to Rock

This chapter talked about what I think an engine actually is or should be. You also learned about the big business around video games, which might be especially interesting for those among you who hope to work commercially in this field some time soon. The third topic involved graphic APIs including Direct3D. The following hundreds of pages will be a bit of hard work for you, but they will also be fun.

It's clear that everybody has some favorite topics related to video game programming. I can already hear the curses of the hard-core math-haters fighting their way through the

3D mathematics chapter. Also, there are those who regard nasty initialization work and framework programs to set off a new project as the eighth plague of mankind.

I will do my best to explain all those topics to you in a way that is easy to follow and to finally understand. There are some topics out there you hate, but you need to understand them in order to become a good graphics or video game engine programmer. So just fight your way through. After the long road of suffering, you will be rewarded with the knowledge you worked so hard for.

What most humans fear and therefore hate and fight against is uncertainty. Uncertainty about the things that are lurking behind the next corner and will inevitably come. I still remember back some years ago when I was a soldier, sitting at the very low end of the command chain as an ordinary private in an armored personnel carrier speeding through the bumpy terrain. Inside the APC it's total jet-black darkness and you can't see your hand in front of your eyes. Suddenly, the driver hits the brakes. The tailgate is opening and you have to jump out of the vehicle and head for the next cover. The squad leader, typically a noncommissioned officer, points his arm in the direction you should aim your gun at. At least this guy knows what you came for and what mission the squad has to fulfill. But it's already in question whether they told him which country he is actually operating in. If this guy is hit during the mission the squad has no idea about anything. At the least, the APC commander will know where the rest of the platoon is located, and the platoon leader ought to know where the other platoons of the company should be. The company commander, finally, should know how the battalion is distributed around and which country you are actually in right now—we hope.

Okay, I'm exaggerating a bit here. But there is no doubt about the hierarchy of knowledge inside an army. And indeed, such a hierarchy does make sense in certain situations. But not in a software development project, for sure. So, I don't want you to be the machine gunner I was, riding the APC in virtual and real darkness. I want you to know what lies ahead of you in this book. Therefore, the next chapter is also just some discussion about software design and not any coding yet. But if you stay with me, then you will have quite a good idea of what is to come in the next hundreds of pages in this book, leaving little or no uncertainty for you. Let's go.

Chapter 2

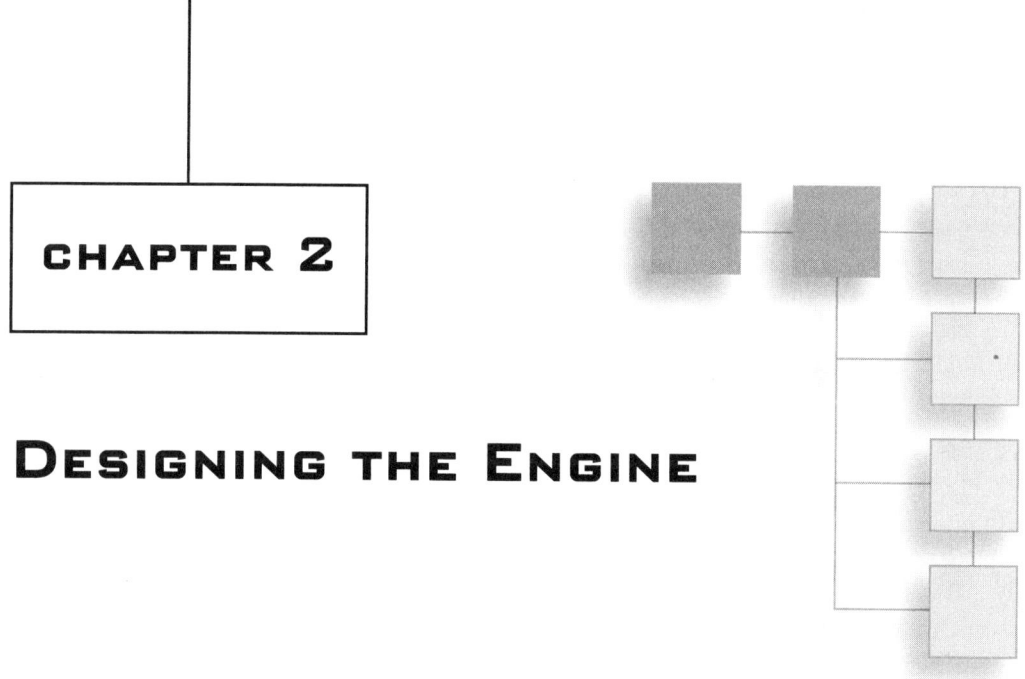

Designing the Engine

The one I love, who craves for the impossible.

Johann Wolfgang von Goethe

The good old Goethe knew to value the pursuit of impossible things. The task at hand does look overwhelming. Our master told us we must develop a video game engine that astonishes his people. There is no excuse or retreat for us. We must oppose and defeat our foe.

The following objectives are covered in this chapter:

- Designing a basic game engine
- Creating engines that are independent from the game application using them
- Building an engine from single parts

Requirements for the Engine

One of the most important things to do when you bring a child into this world is naming that child. Don't laugh. The same is true of software projects. Names or titles of software projects, or any other project for that matter, are very important.

Naming the Engine

I will stick to an old fashioned tradition here and name the engine we will discuss throughout this book—ZFXEngine 2.0. This stems from the actual ZFXEngine, which was something of a local legend among German hobby game developers a few years ago. I used this very pure code framework, which I happened to call an engine, to power my very first online tutorial about programming a Wing Commander-style game, such as the 3D space shooter.

> **Note**
>
> There is a new job in many of today's industries. The job is called a name inventor. Names are that important. Car manufacturers, for example, will not release a new car to market without having a name inventor invent a new name for it. The name must be suitable to not just local people, but people from all over the world.

Is the Game Code Autonomous?

In Chapter 1, "3D Engines and Game Programming," you learned that game engine code must follow this rule: It must be autonomous. That is, the code must not be tied to a specific project, but it must be capable of standing on its own and working with other projects.

This minimum requirement actually says that there must not be any part, function call, parameter, structure, or data type in the engine's source code that belongs to a specific video game project. If this is the case, the code cannot be used for another engine or project without rewriting parts of it.

Many object-oriented programmers believe this is the main goal of using object-oriented programming, and if it is used, the code would be autonomous or usable in other engines. But that is not really true—object-orientation as such does not create code independent from other related projects automatically. That is still subject to some design issues you have to resolve.

Think about the design issues involved with 3D space shooters. Assume that a game code class named `CIhtarlikFighter` implements a really cool alien space pilot. There are two ways to bring an instance of this class onto your screen. First, you can send the render device a list of vertices, indices, textures, and stage settings and let it render the primitives you sent it. However, you can also give the instance of the `CIhtarlikFighter` class to the render device and let it extract all the information it needs to render this itself. The following code shows how these two strategies work:

```
CIhtarlikFighter *pFighter = new CIhtarlikFighter();

// Strategy 1:
g_pRenderer->Render( pFighter->GetVertices(),
                     pFighter->GetNumVertices(),
                     pFighter->GetIndices(),
                     pFighter->GetNumIndices(),
                     pFighter->GetTexture() );

// Strategy 2:
g_pRenderer->Render( pFighter );
```

As you can see, the second strategy is a bare-bones object-oriented example. You don't have to write a lot of accessor functions to get the data out of the object. Just let the render device do the dirty work for you. However, to render this object to get the needed information from it, the render device must know the class definition of `CIhtarlikFighter`. The engine containing the render device is bound to be dependent on the game code containing this class. There is no way to compile your engine's source code without providing it with the game code class `CIhtarlikFighter`.

Hold on! Don't turn in your object-oriented wings by voting for the second strategy. The second strategy is a good choice. If the renderer knows all particular objects that can be rendered, he can do a lot of internal optimizations. You can also use a higher level approach and more comprehensive objects. A higher level approach normally results in more optimized rendering methods. However, there is a price, in that only a fixed number of specific objects can be rendered because arbitrary objects cannot be processed by the renderer. The renderer and hence its programmer need to know the architecture of the objects in advance.

Regarding the first strategy, you can see that to get the information out of the object, you have to go to a lower level, down to the objects the render device knows, such as vertices and indices that add up to triangles. Your game code can create as many objects as you want without the render device needing to know all of the objects in advance. This is the case as long as all of those objects can provide you with access to the vertices, indices, and so on. You can also compile and use your game engine without having to provide the `CIhtarlikFighter` class.

As you might have guessed, I use the second strategy for the engine developed in this book. I want to keep it as independent and as generalized as possible.

Other Video Game Engine Requirements

There are a few other requirements for a video game engine in general and the one we discuss throughout this book in particular. I don't want to go into much detail here, so I will just show you want I think is needed for a video game engine in order to be of any use for us. A video game engine should be flexible and easy to use. In addition, it should be able to do the following:

- Render primitives efficiently
- Query input from the keyboard, the mouse, and the joystick
- Play sound effects
- Provide network connections

API Independence through Interface Definitions

If you encounter a hobby game programmer working on his own rendering engine, you might ask the million dollar question, which is, "What API will you use?" At some point, when you have learned much more about programming a video game, you will realize that this question is not relevant.

Tip

> The API matters only if you need to meet certain constraints, such as the intended operating system or the target platform. This might be the case with the Linux operating system, where DirectX is missing, or with video game consoles that have a certain built-in operating system, for example.

The trick is to avoid the dependency that results from using certain APIs such as DirectX, for example; to do this, use API-independent interface classes that interface your game code with a hidden implementation of the interface. Actually, this hidden implementation does use a particular API (DirectX, for example), but the real trick is that you can also exchange this implementation with another implementation that uses a different API (OpenGL, for example) and the very same interface. The good news is that this is not as difficult as it seems. In fact, in Chapter 3, "Engineering the Engine," I show you how to do this. In the meantime, don't take part in silly discussions about Direct3D versus OpenGL and who has the bigger... er, implementation of a certain API.

For now, you should also understand that an interface can be defined in C++ just like a class declaration because an interface is just an abstract base class in C++ that contains only public member functions, which are purely virtual in nature. This means those functions are declared only; they are not implemented. An interface is, after all, nothing more than a template for an object with a list of functions a real object must implement. Don't mistake the word template here as the templates you can use in C++ programming.

Caution

> You would also call a base class an interface or an adapter if it implements its functions only by delegating them to another class's instance, which it holds as a member variable. This kind of scheme is used to hide implementation details from the user because this second class is known only to the base class.

Now this abstract base class idea might sound strange to those of you who have not worked with interface programming. Look at Figure 2.1 in which you can see an interface called IObject. IObject's definition is declared in the file IObject.h. This interface is backed up by three different implementations. All three of them, called CObjectA, CObjectB, and CObjectC, provide exactly the same functionalities with exactly the same functions calls. Naturally, the function calls are the ones defined in the interface, but the implementations of these functions in the three objects are different, although they lead to the same result.

On the left side in the figure, you see the application that uses the interface. This application does not know about CObjectA, CObjectB, or CobjectC, and it doesn't care about them. It talks only to the interface that has to complete the job that the application wants it to complete, such as rendering a bunch of primitives, for example.

But now the dog seems to be chasing its own tail. As a programmer you will ask yourself how to actually implement this base class and an appropriate hidden derived class without getting stuck in a situation like this:

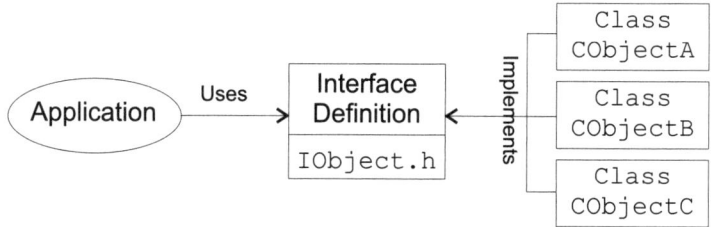

Figure 2.1 An interface declares a number of functions that can be used by an application that uses the interface. However, the real implementation of the functions takes place in real classes that implement the interface.

```
CApplication *pMyApp = new CApplication();

// assume CApplication::m_pObject is of type IObject* and initialized

pMyApp->m_pObj = new CObjectA();
```

You cannot build an instance from IObject because there is no implementation of that interface class, so instead you just build an instance from any one of the three implementing classes. Still, you want to reference to the object with a pointer using the interface class type, as shown above. Hence, the three implementing classes must be derived from the interface class. The problem is that now the application must know about the three implementing classes—or at least about one of them—because it has to call the class's constructor.

To avoid this problem, prevent the application from directly creating objects derived from an interface. In Chapter 3, you learn how to implement a manager that creates such derived objects without the application seeing them and then returns them to the application as pointers of the interface type that the applications knows.

The Structure of the Engine

It's time to talk about the actual design of the ZFXEngine 2.0. Figure 2.2 shows the structure of the engine. At first glance, it might seem a bit confusing so take a second look at it. There are a lot of dependencies, DLLs, and static libraries (lib) located around the application that uses the engine. Do not panic; I explain the meaning of each of the libraries in the following sections. As for the dependencies, these just show you how the libraries of the engine are related with each other and with the application using the engine as such.

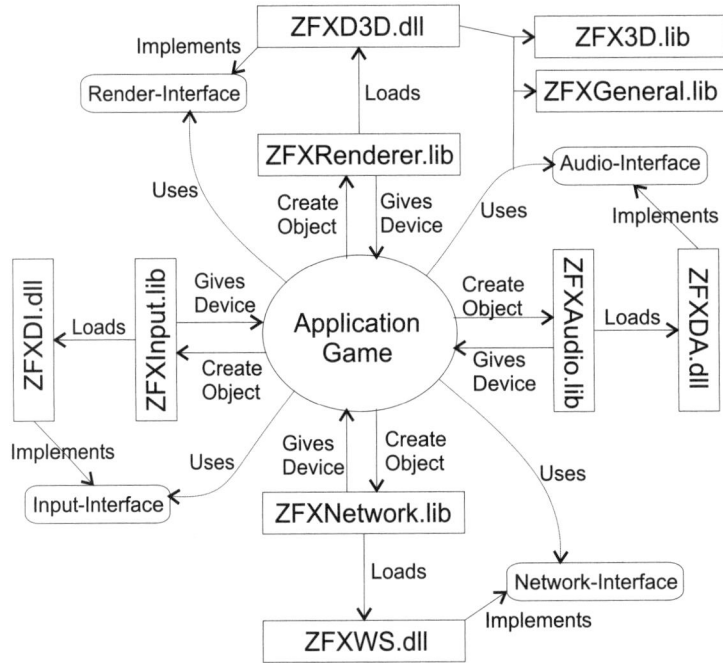

Figure 2.2 The ZFXEngine 2.0 uses four interfaces and two static libraries. The interfaces are implemented inside at least one DLL that is loaded using a static linked library.

Interfaces and Dynamic Link Libraries

The engine is not just one single compiled file that is used by an application. It consists of four interfaces and two static libraries. An application that uses the engine can decide whether to use all of the modules together as a comprehensive team, or just to use parts of the engine while ignoring the other parts.

There are four main modules of the engine. Each one is defined using an interface and each is implemented in a single DLL of its own. The main modules are the render device, the network device, the audio device, and the input device. There are also additional static libraries for each of the four main modules. Those libraries are needed for one purpose. They have to take care of loading the DLL. You will see how this works in Chapter 3.

Note also that the same scheme is used for each of the modules. The application uses a pointer of the interface class type. Hence, it can use only the functions defined in the interface. A single DLL implements the interfaces and the DLL is loaded by a static library. As previously stated, each interface can have several different implementations. Each is a DLL of its own, but each is also loaded by the very same static library. The static library hands over the address of an object created from the implementing class inside the DLL to the application, which uses this object via the interface definition.

If this sounds strange, you are probably the type of person who needs to see the source code of a project to grasp what is going on. The next chapter skips this theory and works at the level of the source code.

Static Libraries

In addition to the four main modules and their interfaces, DLLs, and static libraries, there are two other static libraries. You can see them in the upper right corner of Figure 2.2. Those are named ZFX3D.lib and ZFXGeneral.lib. They implement helper classes and helper functions that are not directly part of the engine.

Components of the Engine

The following sections explain each of the main modules and the ZFX3D.lib and ZFXGeneral.lib static libraries.

ZFXRenderDevice Interface

The most complex and comprehensive module of the ZFXEngine 2.0 is its render device, which implements the ZFXRenderDevice interface. In Chapter 3, I define this interface and show its implementation in Direct3D. I focus more on this interface, DLL, and static library in Chapter 3. You will see how to apply these programming techniques to a real-world example, though the example is reduced to a minimum so that you can concentrate on the interfacing issues to understand how they work.

In Chapter 6, "The Render Device of the Engine," I revisit this interface in more detail and show you how to render graphical primitives with it. Although I discuss Direct3D in the next chapter, you could also use OpenGL or whatever API you find suitable and like to work with the most. No problem using interfaces.

ZFXInputDevice Interface

The input module of the ZFXEngine 2.0 is used to make access to the keyboard, the mouse, and the joystick available to the user. You will learn how to abstract the low level work so that you can check the state of a button on any of the three input devices using a single function call without having to get data from the devices, analyze the data, or transform it into output values. You can even query the values of the mouse or joystick movements a player has made in a similarly easy way.

For the implementation of this interface, I use DirectInput. But as we will work with an interface here as well, you are free to use whatever API you like, such as SDL.

ZFXAudioDevice Interface

The third module of the ZFXEngine 2.0 is the audio module. In Chapter 1, "3D Engines and Game Programming," I discussed the definition of a video game, or what it should be. Without audio media, it would fail to be a true multimedia experience. If you happened to play a video game without your speakers (if your mate did not have additional speakers on his second computer on your last network deathmatch session), you know what a video game is without the sound—it's like a coffee cup without coffee. Even the most ancient video games featured sound effects. They were bound to stick to the good old "beep" sound from the built-in computer speakers, but even the Comodore C16 offered that kind of feature to players. There is no question that we need a module to play sound effects and music files for our video games. I use DirectMusic and DirectSound to implement the *ZFXAudioDevice* interface, but again you can use whatever API you like the most and replace my implementation.

ZFXNetworkDevice Interface

A few years ago, playing games over a network against or with other human players was a special feature of a video game. Today, it is considered a standard feature; not having this feature is considered a big minus for a video game. You are not required to program a massively multiplayer, online role playing game, or MMORPG. A plain, simple network mode, such as a Deathmatch, can be found in all serious commercial 3D titles.

Most startup game programmers have a lot of respect for network programming. They think it is quite a complicated task and they are afraid to discuss IP addresses, protocols, and LAN connections. I don't want to get too detailed on this subject. However, the *ZFXNetworkDevice* will enable you to open network connections, to connect clients to a server, and to send data over a network. This gets you started in network programming and it is more than enough to program a Deathmatch mode for a first-person shooter.

When I show the implementation details to you, there is no question that you will say, "Oh I never thought that this would be so easy." I use the Windows Sockets API, or WinSock as most people call it. I could have used DirectPlay, but I wanted you to understand networking. DirectPlay is a component of DirectX that does this network stuff on a higher level. There are no problems with switching to DirectPlay after you understood the guts of network programming.

ZFX3D Library

The name of this static library might be a bit misleading. The ZFX3D library does not contain things that are directly connected to 3D graphics. It contains the calculus you need to develop 3D video games or applications. Most of those classes and functions operate in the third dimension of course, such as vectors, rays, and planes. I decided to make this library a static one because there is no need for an interface. Most of the implementation is done in C/C++, hence there is no need to use different APIs with different implementations for the same interface.

If you read carefully, you might wonder why I just said that most of this calculus stuff is written in C/C++. What about the other parts? To boost things up a bit, I implemented certain functionalities in a special form of assembly language. Don't be scared if you are a bit rusty on assembly language because we are not exactly using assembler here. Assembler is even worse, as you will see in Chapter 4, "Fast 3D Calculus."

In that math chapter, I teach you a bit about Streaming SIMD Extensions (SSE), which are a special kind of assembler that runs on supporting CPUs only. But if your CPU does not support SSE features, do not worry. I will provide a fallback path to plain C/C++ implementations. In Chapter 4 you get the whole story.

ZFXGeneral Library

The final part in the big engine puzzle is the *ZFXGeneral* library that contains, as you might have guessed, a few general items. This library is not necessarily a part of a game engine, but it makes life easier for applications that use the game engine for 3D video games or 3D programs. Most of the classes in this general library deal with camera movement that prevents the application from messing around with rotation matrixes and suffering gimbal lock, which is a problem common to camera movements. In Chapter 4, we discuss gimbal lock in the context of avoiding it by using quaternions. Thus, you can also think about integrating the classes into the math library. However, they are more about applying math versus the math itself.

One Look Back, Two Steps Forward

This chapter covered the most important things you need to know about the design of the ZFXEngine 2.0. I made this a short one because I think you are already eager to start coding. But the more you know about the design, the easier it will be to follow what you have to do later on when we are discussing the implementation of the engine.

Now take a look in the mirror and tell me if there is a flashing "information overload" warning blinking on your forehead. The next chapter is about real-life source code, so warm up your fingers and start your developing environment. When you hack the code into the keyboard, you will see the pieces fall into place and you will understand the matrix. Trust me, and turn the pages now.

CHAPTER 3

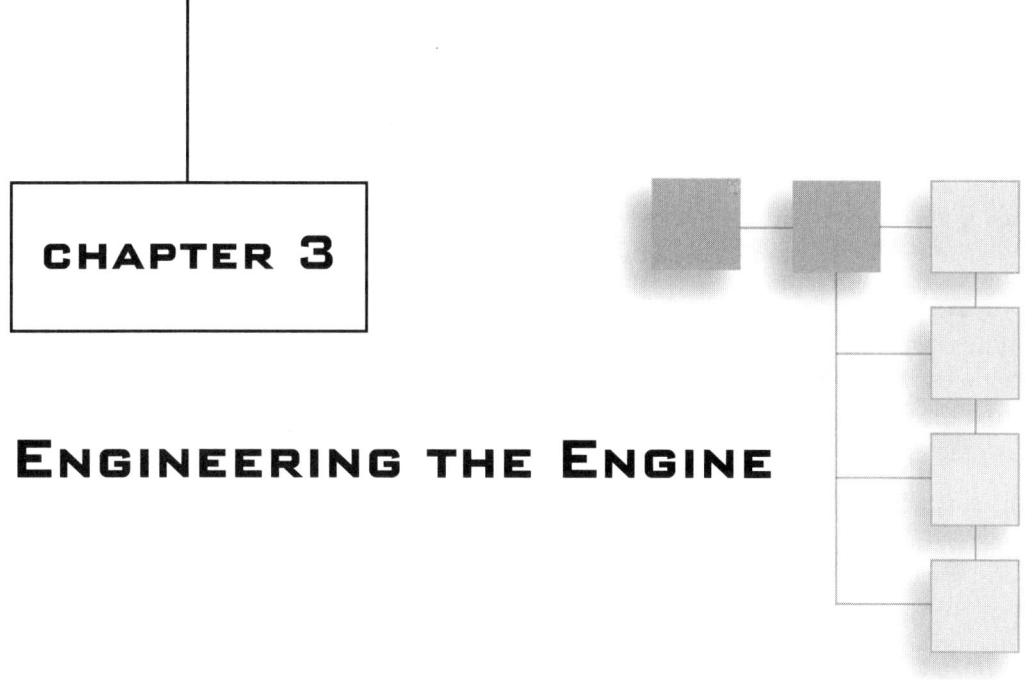

Engineering the Engine

What you get if you don't get what you want is experience.

Desire Nick

You are probably tired of listening to design issues and general game programming and engine programming topics. If you think like me then you want to finally get down to work on some code. If so, this is the chapter for you. From now on, you will develop the ZFXEngine step-by-step, chapter-by-chapter. Don't worry. I will guide you.

This chapter covers the following objectives:

- Creating static and dynamic linked libraries (DLLs)
- Using Windows dialogs to interact with programs
- Developing a renderer for the ZFXEngine as a static library
- Initializing and cranking up Direct3D using a custom DLL
- Writing a framework program using the ZFXEngine

What Is an Interface?

An interface is a pretty smart concept related to the design of code. Note that we are talking about interfaces in object-oriented design here as opposed to user interfaces, for example. Just think about it: the bigger a software project becomes, the more problems arise from multiple different people screwing around with the code and sometimes screwing it up badly. Interfaces are just a way of insulating yourself from a particular implementation. In an object-oriented software engineering world, big projects should be made up of separate code objects that are reusable whenever possible and that are independent from your colleagues' work. However, how would you prevent a hard-core coder from changing the object's implementation, forcing you to rewrite the code that is related to this object?

An interface protects your work from this type of hard-core programmer. Interfaces are a concept independent of any particular language. Generally speaking, an interface sits between two objects or persons, and its task is to provide a means of communication between them. Using C++ you can define a class as an interface that uses a bunch of abstract methods. You might ask how this helps you to organize software projects.

It's actually fairly easy. Let's suppose your super-coder colleague has to implement an object A, and it's your job to implement object B that uses some of object A's public methods. You can define an interface for object A, and the implementation your colleague plays with has to inherit from the interface class you both agree on or that was given to you by the project's lead programmer. No matter how much the super-coder colleague messes around in his code, he has to provide only the methods declared in the interface—or risk being fired, as there is always more than one option.

Finally, you are in a quite secure position. Even if the implementation of object A stalls, you can do your implementation of object B based on the interface definition; the program will work with any and all objects that implement the interface. This is the basic interchangeability of interfaces. For different platforms you can have different implementations of the same interface.

Note

Basically you can define the layout of a class by just writing a specification document. But using interfaces is a means of enforcing the specification.

Abstract Classes

There are several ways to create interfaces. The most common way in object-oriented programming is to create an interface as a class that has no implementations. In C++, you create a class that declares only public member functions but provides no implementation for them. For those of you who have not yet dealt with C++, this might sound new. However, hang on, it gets even more difficult. The point is that you cannot instance an object from such a class because the compiler would complain that there is at least one implementation missing that such an object would need. However, it is not our intention to get objects from this interface class. Its only purpose is to act as the base class from which other classes inherit. Then those derived classes provide the implementations prescribed by the interface.

Now for the freaky stuff. Such functions you don't provide an implementation for are called *pure virtual functions*. A C++ class containing at least one pure virtual function is called an *abstract class* because you can't create instances of this class. Finally, such an abstract class is what we call an *interface*. So there is one more new thing to learn for you C coders who have avoided C++ until now. How do I declare a pure virtual function, and what is *virtual* supposed to mean?

Virtual Member Functions

Actually, from a coder's point of view it's pretty easy. You just have to use the C++ keyword `virtual` while declaring the function. I don't want to dive too deeply into C++ right now, but at least you should know the meaning of this keyword. To keep it simple, let me put it this way: If a class inherits from another class, it can declare and implement member functions featuring the same name as functions in the class they are derived from. Normally, an object would call the function from the base class if the derived class does not declare a function with the same name even if the object is of the derived class's type. However, if it does declare the same function, you can quickly mess up the code. Because with normal, non-virtual functions, the type of the pointer to your object, rather than the type of the object, is used to decide which function to call.

This means you can cast the pointer to your object of the derived class and use a pointer of the base class type instead. This way, your code would call the base class's function, which is normally not what you want. By declaring the function as virtual, it is now the type of the object that determines which implementation to call and not the type of the pointer you use to access the object. Take a look at the following line of code, which shows a sample of an abstract class:

```
class CMyClass
   {
   public:
      virtual void MyPureVirtualFunction( void ) = 0;
   };
```

This is as simple as it looks. The =0 in the function declaration is the part responsible for making the function pure virtual: it tells the compiler that there must not be an implementation for this function in this class. Furthermore it forces each non-abstract class deriving from this base class to provide an implementation for this function. Otherwise the code could not be compiled. Guess what? You have now mastered what you need to know about declaring pure virtual functions and creating abstract classes.

Defining the Interface

You should have a quite good understanding of why a big software project needs interfaces and what their benefits are. And as you already might suppose, I designed the ZFXEngine to use interfaces. This engine is not a very big project, but it is larger than what you would call a small one. My goal in designing the engine is simply to prevent

API-dependency, as discussed previously. I will define an interface that exposes all functionalities that output graphics to the screen using the engine. After that, I will derive a class from this interface and implement the functions using Direct3D. Note that you can also derive a class of your own and implement the functions using OpenGL. Finally, I will put the implementation into a dynamic link library (DLL).

> **Note**
>
> Normally your compiler compiles your code into object files, which are then linked together to a program executable file by the linker. However, you can also link those object files together to a static library, which is in turn linked by any program that uses this library. If you link your object files as DLLs, each program using the library is not linked to it, but needs to load it at runtime.

About DLLs

The big advantage of DLLs should be clear. You can write a bunch of programs using the engine's interface, and you only need to load my implementation of the interface featuring Direct3D. Okay, okay. You can also load your own implementation featuring OpenGL or a software renderer. The point is that you can load the DLL at runtime. There is no need to recompile your code each time you make changes in the implementation of the engine because your code that uses the engine does not use the derived class in the DLL. The implementation is used via the interface. As long as the interface does not change, you can change whatever you want inside the DLL and provide the newly compiled version of it to your software project. You could even unload the old version during runtime and load the new one. If a new DirectX or OpenGL version comes along, you won't have a problem. You just need to rewrite your interface implementation inside the library and distribute the new library to your engine users. They don't need to rebuild their programs to use the new version. It is just used. This process is opposed to that with static libraries, which are effectively copied right into the executable file during the compilation and linking of your project.

> **Tip**
>
> On Linux systems, there are also libraries loaded at runtime just like DLLs on Windows systems. However, Linux folks call these *shared objects* (.so).

You can also use this technique for every component in your engine. You can have a DLL for the audio component featuring sound effects and music, you can encapsulate your input system in a DLL, and so on. Can you see where this path leads us? We will rebuild a system similar to DirectX itself, but in a high-level manner. Actually, this is ultimately what we do in the course of this book. You can also use other strategies, such as putting everything into one very big DLL.

Another advantage of using such DLLs is that you can build prototype implementations. The game programmers or application programmers can have a full working version of the engine ready to go in a short amount of time. This is not to speak of performance, however. This version is definitely not very good. However, it will work, so the other coders can do their job without waiting for you to get the engine on track. When the optimized version of the engine is done, you can hand over the new DLL and it will power the game or application code immediately without rebuilding the project or making changes to the code.

More About the Renderer

For the purpose of this book, I implement a DLL for the renderer using only Direct3D. In Chapters 9–11 I add libraries for audio, input, and network capabilities to the engine. If you feel more comfortable with OpenGL, you can provide your own implementation in your own DLL and run the engine using OpenGL for rendering. If you happen to use Linux, you can create a shared object using OpenGL and also implement the interfaces.

> **Caution**
>
> Actually, I'm not providing platform-independent code here. I want to keep the code as straightforward and simple as possible, so some interface functions use plain Windows structures. With a careful design, you can come up with an interface that will do the job on both systems.

Also of importance is the fact that the class that inherits from the interface and implements it cannot provide additional public member functions. Well, it can, but you must remember that the user of your engine does not see this derived class. The user sees only the functions declared in the interface because he or she only has a pointer of the interface type, even if that points to an object built from the derived class. There is no way for the user to access other functions of the object except those from the interface.

Workspace for the Implementations

Fire up the development environment of your choice, preferably Microsoft Visual C++, and get ready to hack some lines of code. Oh, but wait. A few other issues come to mind that you might find interesting. We spoke only about loading the DLL at runtime. There are two ways to do that. If you create a DLL using Visual C++, you will end up with the .dll file itself and an additional .lib file (a static library). The first way of loading a DLL is to link to this static library, while the second way is to load the DLL with a specific function call. The next section shows you how both ways work.

Loading DLLs

Huh? What is that static library doing there? Again, it is one way to load the DLL. However, it comes with the disadvantage that all applications that use your engine need to link to that static library. Thus, any time you make changes to the DLL code that also affect this .lib file, you also need to recompile the application's code using the DLL to relink the new static library. Such a change is, for example, changing the public interface of the DLL or any other exported function. That is not good, so we will use the second way to load a DLL without the accompanying static library. Windows provides a function you will see in action shortly that can be used to load DLLs. Here is its prototype:

```
HINSTANCE LoadLibrary( LPCTSTR plLibFileName );
```

This seems too easy, doesn't it? If you agree, you are right. It's never this easy. By linking to the static library, you tell Windows that you want that DLL automatically loaded at program startup, and you tell the linker about all the functions contained in the DLL—so that when you use them like regular functions in your program, it doesn't complain that it can't find them. Without this kind of list, you just don't know what is inside the DLL. If you use the Windows function to load the DLL at runtime without the static library, your application is not able to find the functions or classes inside the DLL.

This way of dynamically loading a DLL would be stupid if there weren't a way to get around the obstacles. Indeed there is a workaround. You have to declare the functions you want the application to access as __declspec(dllexport). The application can then get a pointer to these functions and can them. There is another way. You can write a def file that lists the functions inside the DLL that should be exported. Then you have the list of exported functions in a single place to check, rather than distributed over several header files, for example. This is the way we will go, so more on this is coming soon.

> **Note**
> If you use the Windows function to load a DLL at runtime, you will not be able to use the functions inside the DLL. You first have to use another function called GetProcAddress() to get a pointer to a function you know the name of.

Exporting Classes from DLLs

There is one final catch. Who said it would be easy? The problem is that there is no easy way to export a class from a DLL if you load the DLL yourself and don't use the static library it came with. I can provide you with an easy solution. First, we will define a class derived from the interface and implement this class inside the DLL. Then we will write a function inside the DLL that creates an object of this class, casts this object to the interface type, and returns it to the caller. You might have already guessed that this function is exported from the DLL. In addition, there is no need to export anything other than this function from the DLL. The user knows about the interface and he can do everything with the returned object the interface allows him to do.

ZFXRenderer: A Static Library As Manager

Are you still with me? Now we will implement a static library called ZFXRenderer. The only purpose of this static library is to do the loading of our DLL. Please note that this is *not* the static library that the compiler will auto-generate for our DLL project. I implement this static library only to take the workload of loading the DLL from the user. You can still make changes inside the DLL without recompiling.

There is another job the static library needs to do. I will show you how to implement the renderer using Direct3D. However, to do an OpenGL implementation, you need to decide somewhere in the program which DLL to load. This task is also done by the ZFXRenderer, which you will see in action later in this chapter.

You will need to deal with that ZFXRenderer library only two times. First, you need it during initialization to create and obtain a render device. You see that I'm trying to adhere to DirectX naming conventions, so the thing actually sitting in my DLL and doing all that rendering of things is the ZFXRenderDevice. To finally make the puzzle pieces come together I will show that the ZFXRenderDevice is actually the abstract class we will use as the interface for our rendering implementation. The second time you need to deal with the ZFXRenderer is during the shutdown of the engine. You are required to delete that object in order to free its allocated resources.

Next, you need to learn how to set up a project in Visual C++. You also need to know which files to add and what kind of code to hack into those files to make this kind of system run. Don't panic if you feel a bit overwhelmed with the perhaps unfamiliar terms flying around in your head like slow motion bullets on weird paths. Well, I should not play Max Payne that often I guess, but I'm somehow connected to Finland, having lived and studied there for half a year.

Note
> The description of how to set up the projects in this book is meant to explain how it's done using Visual C++ 6.0. If you use a newer version, check your software's manual. Also note that DirectX 9 no longer supports versions of Visual C++ or Visual Studio older than version 6.0.

Open Visual C++. In the File menu, select the New option. A dialog comes up; select the Project tab and select Win 32 Library (static) from the list of options. In the field on the right, enter the name for the project, which is ZFXRenderer. This confirms for Visual C++ that you are done with your settings. (For Visual C++ .NET 2003, select Project from the New option in the File menu. Chose Visual C++ Projects as Win32 Project, then click OK.

Now click on Application Settings, select Static Library, uncheck Precompiled Header, and finally click on Finish.)

You should now have an empty project space to work in. You can add files to that project in Visual C++ 6.0 by navigating to the Project menu and selecting the Add to Project option and the New suboption. In the dialog box that appears, select the File tab. In the list, you can select either C/C++ Header File or C/C++ Source Code File, depending on which kind of file you want to add. After that you can name the file that Visual Studio should create and add for you to the project space. (In Visual C++ 2003, select the Add New Item option from the File menu, select Visual C++, and select C++ File (.cpp) or Header File (.h). Then type the name of the file and click on Open.) Now, please add the following files:

- ZFXRenderer.cpp
- ZFXRenderer.h
- ZFXRenderDevice.h

The first two files will contain the implementation of the class ZFXRenderer. The third file is used to take the definition of the interface, that is, the abstract class that the implementation in our DLL will be derived from. Now I will show you how to integrate the abstract class into the workspace that is open on your screen.

Tip

You can find all the source code on the CD-ROM that comes with this book, so you don't necessarily have to write all the files from scratch and you don't even have to set up the workspace and projects. I think it's always better to know what is going on and how you can set up a workspace of your own.

ZFXD3D: A DLL As Render Device

Currently, you have a Visual C++ workspace that contains one project named ZFXRenderer. Most of you have worked with only one project in one workspace. It is time to change that. A workspace in Visual C++ can hold more than just one single project. Otherwise, there is no need to separate the project from the workspace. Add a second project to your workspace.

Tip

Since the advent of Visual Studio .NET (7.0 and higher), the workspaces were renamed with a fancier name. They are called *solutions* (*.sln) now.

Whenever you have two or more projects that are somehow related, it is a good idea to keep them all in the same workspace. Chances are that you will work on several of them in parallel. In one workspace, you can easily change between projects. Ask yourself how your projects will be related. It is pretty easy. You have one static library acting as a manager that is responsible for loading a DLL that implements the ZFXRenderDevice interface. In addition to the static library project, you have to add a project into the workspace for each implementation you will provide for the interface. There needs to be at least one such implementation, which I will show you in this chapter using Direct3D. If you want to implement the interface using OpenGL or a software renderer, you need to add another project to the workspace similar to the ZFXD3D project.

ZFXD3D is the name of the DLL project and also of the class inside this DLL project that implements the render interface ZFXRenderDevice. To add this project to the workspace, the steps necessary are quite similar to the ones for adding new components, such as files, to the workspace. However, for Visual C++ 6.0, instead of choosing files, select the Projects tab. From the list, select Win 32 Dynamic-Link Library. In the Name field, add a subdirectory called ZFXD3D and also use the same name for the project itself, such as ZFXD3D/ZFXD3D. Click the OK button and select that you want a plain, empty project. In Visual C++ 2003, select the Add Project / New Project option from the File menu, select Visual C++ Projects / Win32, type in the name (ZFXD3D in this case), and click OK. Then click on Application Settings, select DLL, check the Empty Project option, and click Finish.

Tip

Using the Active Project option in the Project menu, or from the Context menu, you can decide which of the projects inside the workspace is to be the active one. This is the one to be compiled when you hit the Build button and the one where all project-related settings and options are being used. If you want to add new files, for example, they can be added to the active project in Visual C++ 6.0. The active project is displayed in bold letters in the workspace treeview, so make sure that when you compile, add new files, and so on, you have the correct project set as active.

You should now have a second project sitting inside the workspace. This new project ZFXD3D is still missing files, but you will change that. You know how to add new files to a project, so take advantage of this knowledge and add the following files to the project:

- ZFXD3D_init.cpp
- ZFXD3D_enum.cpp
- ZFXD3D_main.cpp
- ZFXD3D.h
- ZFXD3D.def

I use the first four of these files to implement the class ZFXD3D. As discussed previously, this class implements the interface ZFXRenderDevice. We have not defined this interface, but we will come to that soon. The name ZFXD3D gives away the fact that we use Direct3D as the means of communication with the hardware. This class creates quite a bit of work so we just get started in this chapter. We will revisit the class in Chapter 5, "Materials, Textures, and Transparency." I personally don't like my files to get too long so I put the implementation of this class into several files to maintain structure in the project. All functions that are needed to initialize (and shut down for that matter) are defined in the file with the suffix `_init`. The enumeration of Direct3D needs a chapter of its own; I put everything related to that enumeration of available video and buffer modes into a separate file with the suffix `_enum`. This leaves only the file with the suffix `_main` for all the other things needed at runtime.

Finally, there is the mysterious file `ZFXD3D.def`. If you use a DLL, you need to tell the application which functions sit inside the DLL and which are meant to be called by an application. You can either export those functions directly by using `declspec(dllexport)` or you can use a def file containing the names of the exported functions. There is nothing magical about doing this.

Now that you have set up workspaces and added files to the project you can load a DLL that implements the render interface. We will discus this in the next section. After that, we will implement the ZFXD3D dynamic library project that implements the render device interface.

ZFXRenderDevice: An Abstract Class As Interface

Before you can start to implement anything, you first need to think about the interface. The interfaces of an engine need to be defined and fixed before anything else can take place. This is because everything in the engine is connected to these interfaces in some way. The programmers ordered to implement the interfaces naturally need to know the complete interface definition before they can get started. Those who write the programs that will use the interface to render something to the screen will also need the complete specification of the interfaces to see what they can or cannot perform—and more importantly, how to perform things with the interface.

All functions using functions from a particular API, such as Direct3D or OpenGL, must be hidden by interfaces. This way you end up with an engine that is not strictly dependent on a certain graphics library, and so not dependent on a certain operating system such as Windows or Linux. I already said that platform-independence is not that easy to achieve. There are always some things pestering you, starting with opening up a simple window of an operating system's specified data types. Therefore, as discussed previously, you must strive for platform-independence. The code in this book is graphics-API–independent, although it is still slightly bound to the operating system Windows.

The code in this chapter is fairly simple. I use this chapter only to demonstrate the idea of interfaces and API-independence, not to show off fancy rendering effects. We will get to the fancier code later.

You will not see a lot on the front end, but on the back end, the engine will do a lot more, such as detect underlying hardware and initialize Direct3D, providing a comfortable dialog where the user can select the settings he chooses. But now I have talked enough. Following is the definition of the interface:

```cpp
// File: ZFXRenderDevice.h
#define MAX_3DHWND 8

class ZFXRenderDevice
   {
   protected:
      HWND       m_hWndMain;            // main window
      HWND       m_hWnd[MAX_3DHWND];    // render window(s)
      UINT       m_nNumhWnd;            // number of render-windows
      UINT       m_nActivehWnd;         // active window
      HINSTANCE  m_hDLL;                // DLL module
      DWORD      m_dwWidth;             // screen width
      DWORD      m_dwHeight;            // screen height
      bool       m_bWindowed;           // windowed mode?
      char       m_chAdapter[256];      // graphics adapter name
      FILE       *m_pLog;               // logfile
      bool       m_bRunning;

   public:
      ZFXRenderDevice(void) {};
      virtual ~ZFXRenderDevice(void) {};

      // INIT/RELEASE STUFF:
      // ==================
      virtual HRESULT Init(HWND, const HWND*, int,
                           int, int, bool)=0;
      virtual void    Release(void)     =0;
      virtual bool    IsRunning(void)   =0;


      // RENDERING STUFF:
      // ================
      virtual HRESULT UseWindow(UINT nHwnd)=0;
      virtual HRESULT BeginRendering(bool bClearPixel,
                                     bool bClearDepth,
                                     bool bClearStencil)
                                     =0;
```

```
    virtual void     EndRendering(void)=0;
    virtual HRESULT  Clear(bool bClearPixel,
                           bool bClearDepth,
                           bool bClearStencil) =0;

    virtual void     SetClearColor(float fRed,
                                   float fGreen,
                                   float fBlue)=0;
}; // class
typedef struct ZFXRenderDevice *LPZFXRENDERDEVICE;
```

> **Caution**
>
> Be warned: Do not show this code to hard-core C++ object-oriented programming gurus. These programmers would criticize this code because when you define an interface, you should not define attributes in the abstract class. This is a code design issue. In this book, I am less strict about design matters, saving the derived classes from having something close to a billion attributes.

If you are new to C++, you will notice the *virtual destructor* of the interface. The same reasoning that leads to virtual functions also leads to virtual destructors. No matter what pointer you use to point to an object, make sure that the correct destructor of the object is called by making the destructor virtual. Normally, every constructor is virtual unless you can guarantee that no one will ever cast a pointer to an object into something else. Believe me, you can't do that.

In addition to the constructor and destructor, there are several other functions that are defined as purely virtual. You will see the meaning of each function when we implement the functions, but I think the names are already hint at what the functions are meant to do later on. From a graphical point of view there is not much to do yet. You can use the method `ZFXRenderDevice::SetClearColor` to change the screen color and clear the screen explicitly using the appropriate function. Clearing the color is already implicitly contained in the `ZFXRenderDevice::BeginRendering` call. But don't worry if you think there is not much we can use this interface for. For now you are right, but later you will be able to use most of Direct3D's functionality through this interface. In addition, you will have learned how to add other things not explicitly covered in this book.

Implementing the Static Library

The anchor for our work with a DLL is the static library `ZFXRenderer`. Its task is to decide which DLL to load. The DLL in turn represents a render device that can be used to output graphics on the screen. The implementation of this static library is quite short and will not change over the course of this book. You need to recompile it only in one of two cases. The first case is if you get into a situation where you indeed need to change something in the implementation. This will happen, for example, in a situation where you add another DLL to the workspace and want the static library to load this new DLL. The second case where you need to recompile the static library is when you are making changes to the `ZFXRenderDevice` interface definition, because the static library uses its header and handles pointers of the interface type.

That made clear, I show you now the header file for the static library's only class. It is, not surprisingly, called `ZFXRenderer`.

```
// file: ZFXRenderer.h
#include "ZFXRenderDevice.h"

class ZFXRenderer
   {
   public:
      ZFXRenderer(HINSTANCE hInst);
      ~ZFXRenderer(void);

      HRESULT            CreateDevice(char *chAPI);
      void               Release(void);
      LPZFXRENDERDEVICE  GetDevice(void)
                             { return m_pDevice; }
      HINSTANCE          GetModule(void)
                             { return m_hDLL;    }

   private:
      ZFXRenderDevice   *m_pDevice;
      HINSTANCE          m_hInst;
      HMODULE            m_hDLL;
   }; // class
typedef struct ZFXRenderer *LPZFXRENDERER;
```

This is the whole class that will not change anymore, correct? Well, yes, as I told you, this class is short and easy to implement. The constructor simply takes the Windows instance handle from the application using the ZFXEngine and stores it in one of its attributes. The class will use it later on. Even more important is the attribute m_hDLL, which will receive the handle from Windows for the loaded DLL. The third attribute m_pDevice is the most important one around. It is a pointer to an object that implements the `ZFXRenderDevice` interface. That object will be created using the `ZFXRenderer::CreateDevice` method. This method takes a string as the input parameter specifying the DLL to be loaded.

You will be even more disappointed when you look at the constructor and destructor of this class. They are quite short, as there is not really much to do:

```
ZFXRenderer::ZFXRenderer(HINSTANCE hInst)
   {
   m_hInst   = hInst;
   m_hDLL    = NULL;
   m_pDevice = NULL;
   }

ZFXRenderer::~ZFXRenderer(void)
   {
   Release();
   }
```

Okay, before we move on to the more interesting stuff of this class, namely, the creation of the interface-implementing object, we need to take a look at some other functions that are also contained in the header file ZFXRenderDevice.h but that are not part of the class itself:

```
// file: ZFXRenderDevice.h
extern "C"
   {
   HRESULT CreateRenderDevice(HINSTANCE hDLL, ZFXRenderDevice **pInterface);

   typedef HRESULT (*CREATERENDERDEVICE)
                    (HINSTANCE hDLL, ZFXRenderDevice **pInterface);

   HRESULT ReleaseRenderDevice(ZFXRenderDevice **pInterface);

   typedef HRESULT(*RELEASERENDERDEVICE)
                    (ZFXRenderDevice **pInterface);
   }
```

Here, I define the symbols CREATERENDERDEVICE and RELEASERENDERDEVICE for pointers to the given functions CreateRenderDevice() and ReleaseRenderDevice(). Those functions are declared as extern to indicate that we do not implement them here. This must be done in another part of the source code, but it is stated here that we need to work with those functions in our static library. As discussed previously, there is no direct way to export a class straight from a DLL without knowing its declaration. However, you can use the functions you see in the previous code to get a pointer of the interface type to an object implementing the interface. These functions will be implemented in the DLL in a moment. This static library knows only that those functions are somewhere around to be used and it uses them.

Oh, and the "C" means that the functions should be exported in plain C style without C++ name mangling. The overhead of object orientation forces C++ to twist around the function names and parameter lists a bit, but we don't want to worry about that and so we enforce plain C usage of those functions here.

Loading DLLs

The following function is responsible for creating an object that implements the interface. It takes a string as a parameter that specifies the name identifying the DLL to be used. To keep things simple here, I included one possible option for this string, namely "Direct3D". This will identify that the caller wants to load the implementation of the interface that features Direct3D. Any other string will result in an error message thrown out by the function, as you can see for yourself in the following code:

```
HRESULT ZFXRenderer::CreateDevice(char *chAPI)
   {
   char buffer[300];

   if (strcmp(chAPI, "Direct3D") == 0)
      {
      m_hDLL = LoadLibrary ("ZFXD3D.dll");
      if (!m_hDLL)
         {
         MessageBox(NULL,
            "Loading ZFXD3D.dll failed.",
            "ZFXEngine - error", MB_OK | MB_ICONERROR);
         return E_FAIL;
         }
      }
   else
      {
      _snprintf(buffer, 300, "API '%s' not supported.", chAPI);
      MessageBox(NULL, buffer, "ZFXEngine - error",
               MB_OK | MB_ICONERROR);
      return E_FAIL;
      }

   CREATERENDERDEVICE _CreateRenderDevice = 0;
   HRESULT hr;

   // pointer to DLL function 'CreateRenderDevice'
   _CreateRenderDevice = (CREATERENDERDEVICE)
                     GetProcAddress(m_hDLL,
                           "CreateRenderDevice");
```

```
   if ( !_CreateRenderDevice ) return E_FAIL;

   // call DLL function to create the device
   hr = _CreateRenderDevice(m_hDLL, &m_pDevice);
   if (FAILED(hr))
      {
      MessageBox(NULL,
         "CreateRenderDevice() from lib failed.",
         "ZFXEngine - error", MB_OK | MB_ICONERROR);
      m_pDevice = NULL;
      return E_FAIL;
      }

   return S_OK;
   } // CreateDevice
```

If the function gets a string that specifies a DLL that it recognizes, then the function will do all the things necessary to load the DLL and create an object of the interface implementation. If the caller uses the Direct3D API, the function will load the `ZFXD3D.dll`. You will see this library's implementation shortly. The function uses the following Windows API function to load a DLL at runtime:

```
HINSTANCE LoadLibrary( LPCTSTR lpLibFileName );
```

For the single parameter of this thing, pass in the name of the DLL you want to load. Now for the guts of this function. It will ensure that the DLL is loaded into memory only once. If another application is already using the DLL, the function ensures that the memory is mapped in a way that this application will also have access to the DLL. This is another advantage of using DLLs. They are loaded only one time when they are needed.

Now the return value gets interesting. If the call succeeds, you will get an instance handle from Windows. Whenever you need to call Windows API functions inside the dynamic link library that are requesting an instance handle as parameter, you must not use the application's instance handle but the handle of the library itself—that is, the return value of this function.

Sniffing for Exported Functions inside DLLs

Let's suppose now that the call was successful and we loaded the DLL. Now we want an object from the class `ZFXD3D` inside the DLL, but you can't see this class inside the DLL. For this reason, I define the external function `CreateRenderDevice()`, which must be implemented in the DLL. The problem now is to catch up with this function implementation. Unlike static libraries, you don't know the address of a function inside a DLL at compile time so you cannot just call the function. The linker would not be able to find it because it does not have the compiled version of the DLL at hand.

There is a way around this potential disaster. You can just sniff inside a DLL and seek the address of any exported function at runtime. This is done using the following Windows API function:

FARPROC GetProcAddress(HMODULE hModule, LPCTSTR lpProcName);

You have to pass in the handle of the loaded DLL as the first parameter to this function. Don't get freaked by Microsoft messing around with different handle names, as they are all more or less the same type. The HMODULE handle you need to use here is the same handle returned by the LoadLibrary() function, even if it was called HINSTANCE when it was returned.

You can see how this all is connected. You can use this function to get the address of the CreateRenderDevice() inside the DLL and store this address in the pointer called _CreateRenderDevice. Then you can call the function, and if everything goes well, you have a valid object of the class ZFXD3D from the DLL stored in the attribute m_pDevice. Please note that this attribute is the interface type ZFXRenderDevice. The static library does not need to know anything about the class ZFXD3D at all.

That's how interfaces work. Neat, isn't it? To make this clearer, I will now show you the ZFXRenderer::Release method. It does the very same thing, except that it sniffs for and calls the ReleaseRenderDevice() function from the DLL.

```
void ZFXRenderer::Release(void)
   {
   RELEASERENDERDEVICE _ReleaseRenderDevice = 0;
   HRESULT hr;

   if (m_hDLL)
      {
      // pointer to dll function 'ReleaseRenderDevice'
      _ReleaseRenderDevice = (RELEASERENDERDEVICE)
                             GetProcAddress(m_hDLL,
                                "ReleaseRenderDevice");
      }
   // call dll's release function
   if (m_pDevice)
      {
      hr = _ReleaseRenderDevice(&m_pDevice);
      if (FAILED(hr))
         {
         m_pDevice = NULL;
         }
```

```
    }
} // Release
```

As you will see in a moment, the object that implements the interface is created inside the DLL. Therefore, I let the DLL do the release job of this object as well because the object's memory has been allocated on the DLL's heap. To do this, you have to get the pointer to the release function that is exported. If you have that pointer, call the function and hand to it the object that should be deleted. Again, there's no magic behind this.

Maybe the definitions `CREATERENDERDEVICE` and `RELEASERENDERDEVICE` are a bit confusing for you, but they actually tell the compiler which parameter list belongs to that function pointer. Without that, the compiler would not be able to verify if you called the function in a way that doesn't blow up the call stack.

Now for the good news. I'm glad you made it so far. As far as I can see, we just suffered slight losses in taking that hill here. Good job, Soldier. You're done with the static library loading a DLL now. The bad news? Well, there is another hill to be taken tonight. Now, move it!

Implementing the DLL

Change the active project to the ZFXD3D project. I'll show you now how to encapsulate Direct3D inside this project. The benefit of the encapsulation is that anyone using our engine does not need to know a single piece of information about Direct3D. He does not need to have the DirectX SDK (*Software Development Kit*) installed and there is no need to mess around with Direct3D data types or classes.

Note the attribute `m_pChain[MAX_3DHWND]` in the following class definition. Even if the engine we implement in this book is a small demo project, I want to make it as complete as possible. One of the frequently asked questions in bulletin boards about game programming goes like this: "I want to render graphics into multiple child views for my editor. How do I do that?"

There are a number of ways to achieve this goal using DirectX, but the way it's meant to be done is to use the so-called Direct3D swap chains, which are basically used to take one rendered image each. I will go into more detail about that later. For now, note that our engine supports up to `MAX_3DHWND` different child windows that you can render your graphics into. The handles to those different windows are stored in the attribute `m_pChain`.

```
// file: ZFXD3D.h

#define MAX_3DHWND 8

class ZFXD3D : public ZFXRenderDevice
    {
```

```cpp
public:
   ZFXD3D(HINSTANCE hDLL);
   ~ZFXD3D(void);

   // initialization
   HRESULT Init(HWND, const HWND*, int, int, int,
                bool);

   BOOL CALLBACK DlgProc(HWND, UINT, WPARAM, LPARAM);

   // interface functions
   void    Release(void);
   bool    IsRunning(void) { return m_bRunning; }
   HRESULT BeginRendering(bool,bool,bool);
   HRESULT Clear(bool,bool,bool);
   void    EndRendering(void);
   void    SetClearColor(float, float, float);
   HRESULT UseWindow(UINT nHwnd);

private:
   ZFXD3DEnum            *m_pEnum;
   LPDIRECT3D9            m_pD3D;
   LPDIRECT3DDEVICE9      m_pDevice;
   LPDIRECT3DSWAPCHAIN9   m_pChain[MAX_3DHWND];
   D3DPRESENT_PARAMETERS  m_d3dpp;
   D3DCOLOR               m_ClearColor;
   bool                   m_bIsSceneRunning;
   bool                   m_bStencil;

   // start the API
   HRESULT Go(void);

   void Log(char *, ...);
}; // class
```

As you can see, there are eight public functions in this class in addition to the constructor and destructor. Seven of these functions need to be there as they stem from the interface that this class inherits from. The other function is called ZFXD3D::DlgProc. Although this function is public, don't forget that the class ZFXD3D itself cannot be seen from outside the DLL so the public attribute resolves effectively to "can be seen by all objects inside the DLL." This function is needed to process the messages connected to the dialog box that the engine uses to let the user select some settings for the display modes and stuff.

> **Note**
>
> Member functions in derived classes that override virtual member functions from the parent class(es) are automatically tagged as virtual by the compiler. There is no way around being virtual for those functions even if you don't use the keyword `virtual` explicitly. Naturally, it is advisable to use the keyword anyway so one can see at first glance that those functions are virtual.

Enumeration from the DirectX SDK

Several attributes in the `ZFXD3D` class store the most important Direct3D objects and information about the graphics adapter capabilities or active settings. You need some functions to get the graphics adapter to reveal its deepest secrets, namely, its capabilities. This is all part of the enumeration of available graphics adapters and their modes. In this implementation, I use a class `ZFXD3DEnum` to do this job, and its methods are quite similar to the stuff provided by the DirectX SDK common files. I don't want to bore you by explaining the DirectX framework to you.

If you are unsure about those enumeration things and want to learn them first, feel free to dig through the common files and see how enumeration is done there. My implementation is nothing more than a boiled-down version of it. So you can take a look at my class instead, because I think it is easier to grasp. You can find the class implementation on the CD-ROM accompanying this book.

What Is Coming Next?

Before we get started implementing the DLL's `ZFXD3D` class, I want to make sure that you know what is coming next. The interface demands that we provide an `Init()` function to crank up the graphics API our DLL wants to use. It is advisable to make this powering-up process as flexible as possible and use as little hard coding as possible. One thing people like to do to achieve that flexibility is write an init file containing all the values for screen width and height and things and so on. During powering up, the engine parses the init file. But I want to do it another way. I will show you how to implement a Windows dialog box that pops up during initialization and lets the user select some settings to influence these values in the most flexible way.

Still, our engine is very easy to work with. You only need to call one initialization function and that will kick off an internal process that includes enumeration and the dialog box to let the user decide which settings should be used (such as fullscreen or windowed, and so on). If you take a look at the DirectX SDK samples, you see that you can switch all those settings at runtime. This comes along with some overhead of resetting the Direct3D device, so I'm not going to include this feature in the ZFXEngine. I want to keep the code as simple to follow as possible. You can always refer to the DirectX SDK common files to see how to switch at runtime.

Okay, but before we can start implementing our class I want to show you the implementation of the exported functions. These are the functions the static library sniffs for via `GetProAddress()`.

Exported Functions

You still remember the empty files we created for the ZFXD3D project, don't you? If you do, then you also remember that mysterious `ZFXD3D.def` file, which is somehow related to exporting functions from a DLL. I already talked about exporting functions from a DLL and how you can do it. The following "code" is what you need to write into the def file to export the functions the static library `ZFXRenderer` will sniff for:

```
; file: ZFXD3D.def
; DLL exports the following functions
LIBRARY "ZFXD3D.dll"
EXPORTS
    CreateRenderDevice
    ReleaseRenderDevice
; end of file :-)
```

As you might have already guessed, the semicolon defines a comment in a def file. Then you need to write the name of the library after the keyword `LIBRARY` so that the file can be identified as belonging to the named DLL and to define exports for that library. After that you use the keyword `EXPORTS` to name your wishes, that is, to name the symbols that should be exported from the DLL and that are therefore visible and accessible to other applications using this DLL. Here you only have to define the two functions we already talked about by their names. The parameter lists for the functions are not needed when you export them.

Caution

If you are using Visual C++ or Visual Studio .NET (version 7.0 or newer), you will sometimes get into trouble with the def files. The trouble is that they don't work and as a result of this, the functions are not exported. The `GetProcAddress()` function then returns a `NULL` pointer because it cannot find what you want it to look for.

When this happens, you need to remove the function declarations `CreateRenderDevice()` and `ReleaseRenderDevice()` from the file `ZFXRenderDevice.h`, but the two `typedef` instructions must remain in place there. Now move the two declarations into a header file inside the DLL project ZFXD3D and add the following prefix to the declarations and function definitions: `extern "C" __declspec(dllexport)`

Now these two functions are marked as exports inside the DLL and will be found by the `GetProcAddress()` call.

Now get ready to see how cute these two exported functions really are. There is not much behind them other than creating an object or deleting it. But please note that though the object created is from the class ZFXD3D, it is returned as a reference with a pointer of the interface type ZFXRenderDevice:

```
// file: ZFXD3D_init.cpp
#include "ZFX.h"

HRESULT CreateRenderDevice( HINSTANCE hDLL, ZFXRenderDevice **pDevice )
   {
   if ( !*pDevice )
      {
      *pDevice = new ZFXD3D( hDLL );
      return ZFX_OK;
      }
   return ZFX_FAIL;
   }


HRESULT ReleaseRenderDevice( ZFXRenderDevice **pDevice )
   {
   if ( !*pDevice )
      {
      return ZFX_FAIL;
      }
   delete *pDevice;
   *pDevice = NULL;
   return ZFX_OK;
   }
```

If you want to create such an object, you need to know the handle to the loaded DLL, as this is used by the constructor of the ZFXD3D class. You need this handle to open up a dialog from inside the DLL, for example, or to access any other kind of resource stored in the DLL, such as icons. The release of the object is just a plain delete call to the object, which forces its destructor to go to work and then free all memory used for the object itself. The interesting thing here is that you don't need to cast the interface type pointer to a ZFXD3D pointer. Because of the virtual destructor, the delete call correctly calls the ZFXD3D class's constructor, as this is the class the object originally stems from. There are times when object-oriented programming makes life easier, as you might know.

To recap, you made the class ZFXD3D available from outside the DLL without the need for the user to know this class at all. If you just know the interface definition, you can use the render device object.

Comfort By Dialogs

To keep the engine as flexible as possible to demonstrate what you can do to satisfy your customers, I'll now show you how to use a dialog to make settings during the startup phase of the engine. Then I'll talk about that nasty enumeration stuff Direct3D comes along with, but hey, OpenGL has its extensions, which you need to verify before using them.

Assume you are done with an enumeration, so you have a whole list of modes and capabilities the current hardware provides. So what do you do with it? Should you as engine programmer select what you think is the best possible option for the user? Definitely do not do this. Instead, use a container that displays the most important findings of the enumeration process. This container is a simple dialog in which the user can choose the settings he prefers.

Creating the Dialog

You need to activate the ZFXD3D project now. Go to the Insert menu and select Resource. From the upcoming dialog, select Dialog, and then select the New button. You just created a new resource object and Visual C++ changes to its resource editor automatically.

By double-clicking on a control element (button, drop down list, and so on) or on the dialog box itself, you make the Attributes dialog box for this item show up. The most important field here is the one named ID. Here you need to provide a unique identifier. Try it out and identify the dialog box as "dlgChangeDevice". It is very important here to include the quotation marks in the ID field as well. Otherwise, you have to resolve the ID to the actual name of the dialog if you want to show it.

You are probably familiar with creating custom dialogs in the resource editor. If not, play around with it for a few minutes. It's not complicated. Then insert the controls from the list below into the dialog. Give them the IDs shown in the list. This time, don't use quotation marks because for the controls of a dialog it is much easier to use a macro to resolve a plain ID that the resource editor can connect to. This is a plain number as opposed to a real string.

- Combo box named IDC_ADAPTER
- Combo box named IDC_MODE
- Combo box named IDC_ADAPTERFMT
- Combo box named IDC_BACKFMT
- Combo box named IDC_DEVICE
- Radio button named IDC_FULL
- Radio button named IDC_WND
- Buttons named IDOK and IDCANCEL

The combo box controls are used to offer the available graphics adapters and their video modes for selection to the user. Most adapters are capable of using several video modes or screen resolutions (800x600 or 1024x768, for example). Then there are two combo boxes for the color format because, since Direct3D 9, it is possible to use different formats for the front buffer and the back buffer if the program is running in windowed mode. You are not bound to the current desktop format the user is running.

The last combo box is used for the type of the Direct3D device. There are only two types available. First is the HAL device, the Hardware Abstraction Layer. This is the graphics adapter. The other one is the REF, the Reference Rasterizer. I hope you already know that Direct3D can emulate almost everything in software if the hardware is not able to do it. The REF enables you to run most of the Direct3D features on ancient hardware that does not even provide hardware transformation and lighting.

> **Caution**
>
> Using the REF is not recommended, except for testing scenarios in which you don't have the hardware available to do the features you want to test. It is incredibly slow and not meant for real-time applications. Even the poorest hardware can beat a software implementation on features it actually provides. Furthermore, the REF device isn't even guaranteed to be available in a non-debug install of DirectX.

The two radio buttons in the dialog can be used to select whether to start the engine in windowed or fullscreen mode. Figure 3.1 shows how the dialog box will look in the running engine program later on.

If you are still with me and have followed all these steps, select the Save button in Visual C++ to save the project. Note that a dialog box asks you to save your resource first. Save the list, and then select the `ZFXD3D` directory; name the file `dlgChangeDevice.rc`. This auto-generates a file called `resource.h`, which contains some ID stuff and definitions in a script form. Visual C++ needs this to build the dialog when you compile the project.

Add the two files I just mentioned to the project into a resource directory. This enables you to use the dialog you just created. The resource header must be included in every file where you want to use something from the dialog. Mostly this is when you want to access the control elements in the dialogs and need their IDs for Windows function calls.

But first, let's review dialog boxes and how to call them from a program. A dialog box in Windows is basically the same kind of object as a window. The same is true for the control elements that sit inside the dialog. So if you want to get messages from these controls or send messages to them, you need to have a callback procedure for the dialog like you would have for a simple window.

The following Windows API function lets you show a dialog box and name the callback procedure that should handle the messages coming from the open dialog:

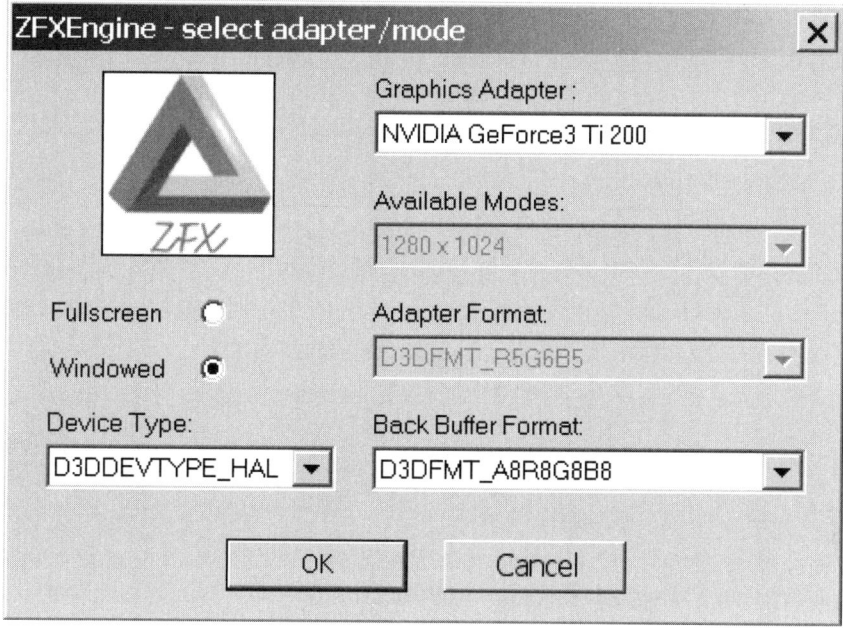

Figure 3.1 The selection dialog as it will appear in the final program version

```
int DialogBox( HINSTANCE hInstance, LPCTSTR lpTemplate, HWND hWndParent,
               DLGPROC lpDialogFunc );
```

The first parameter has to be the instance handle of the module containing the resource. As you work inside a DLL, it needs to be the DLL's handle. You remember the value we retrieved as return value from the `LoadLibraryEx()` call? And the dialog here is the only reason we need to know this handle in this project. This is why the constructor of the `ZFXD3D` class asks for it. Next, you need to understand the meaning of the parameters.

The second parameter must be the ID of a template used for the dialog. This is the dialog box you designed using the resource editor. If you had given it a plain ID you would need to resolve this now by using the `MAKEINTRESOURCE()` macro. However, you were smart enough to use a real string as the ID so you can enter that string here to load the dialog. The next parameter is the handle of the parent window. You see, the dialog is just a window, a child to its dad.

The last parameter is the name of the callback procedure that should handle the window's messages. This is a problem because object-oriented programmers want a member function as a callback routine. That is not possible because the existence of the callback function must be ensured at compile time, but a normal member function's existence is bound to the existence of an object of the according class. Now you could use a static member function. This would be okay, but it comes at the price of not having access to member variables of the class.

Chapter 3 ■ Engineering the Engine

Message Procedure for the Dialog

The thing is, you want this kind of access. In this instance, you want to read the user's selections right into some member variables of the class. I will return to this problem in a moment, but first I want to show you what the callback function should look like:

```
ZFXDEVICEINFO   g_xDevice;
D3DDISPLAYMODE  g_Dspmd;
D3DFORMAT       g_fmtA;
D3DFORMAT       g_fmtB;

BOOL CALLBACK ZFXD3D::DlgProc( HWND hDlg, UINT message,
                               WPARAM wParam, LPARAM lParam )
   {
   DIBSECTION dibSection;
   BOOL       bWnd=FALSE;

   // get handles
   HWND hFULL       = GetDlgItem(hDlg, IDC_FULL);
   HWND hWND        = GetDlgItem(hDlg, IDC_WND);
   HWND hADAPTER    = GetDlgItem(hDlg, IDC_ADAPTER);
   HWND hMODE       = GetDlgItem(hDlg, IDC_MODE);
   HWND hADAPTERFMT = GetDlgItem(hDlg, IDC_ADAPTERFMT);
   HWND hBACKFMT    = GetDlgItem(hDlg, IDC_BACKFMT);
   HWND hDEVICE     = GetDlgItem(hDlg, IDC_DEVICE);

   switch (message)
     {
     // preselect windowed mode
     case WM_INITDIALOG:
        {
        SendMessage(hWND, BM_SETCHECK, BST_CHECKED, 0);
        m_pEnum->Enum(hADAPTER, hMODE, hDEVICE,
                      hADAPTERFMT, hBACKFMT,
                      hWND, hFULL, m_pLog);

        return TRUE;
        }

     // render logo ( g_hBMP is initialized in Init() )
     case WM_PAINT:
        {
        if (g_hBMP)
```

Implementing the DLL 67

```
            {
        GetObject(g_hBMP, sizeof(DIBSECTION),
                  &dibSection);
        HDC      hdc = GetDC(hDlg);
        HDRAWDIB hdd = DrawDibOpen();
        DrawDibDraw(hdd, hdc, 50, 10, 95, 99,
                    &dibSection.dsBmih,
                    dibSection.dsBm.bmBits, 0, 0,
                    dibSection.dsBmih.biWidth,
                    dibSection.dsBmih.biHeight, 0);
        DrawDibClose(hdd);
        ReleaseDC(hDlg, hdc);
            }
    } break;

// a control reports a message
case WM_COMMAND:
    {
    switch (LOWORD(wParam))
        {
        // OK button
        case IDOK:
            {
            m_bWindowed = SendMessage(hFULL,
                          BM_GETCHECK, 0, 0) != BST_CHECKED;
            m_pEnum->GetSelections(&g_xDevice,
                                   &g_Dspmd,
                                   &g_fmtA,
                                   &g_fmtB);
            GetWindowText(hADAPTER,m_chAdapter,256);
            EndDialog(hDlg, 1);
            return TRUE;
            } break;

         // cancel button
        case IDCANCEL:
            {
            EndDialog(hDlg, 0);
            return TRUE;
            } break;

        case IDC_ADAPTER:
```

```
                    {
                    if(HIWORD(wParam)==CBN_SELCHANGE)
                        m_pEnum->ChangedAdapter();
                    } break;
                case IDC_DEVICE:
                    {
                    if(HIWORD(wParam)==CBN_SELCHANGE)
                        m_pEnum->ChangedDevice();
                    } break;
                case IDC_ADAPTERFMT:
                    {
                    if(HIWORD(wParam)==CBN_SELCHANGE)
                        m_pEnum->ChangedAdapterFmt();
                    } break;
                case IDC_FULL: case IDC_WND:
                    {
                    m_pEnum->ChangedWindowMode();
                    } break;

                } // switch [CMD]
            } break; // case [CMD]
        } // switch [MSG]
    return FALSE;
    }
```

On initialization of the dialog, there are already some actions that need to take place. The most important is that you have to call the `ZFXD3DEnum::Enum` function. This kicks off all those enumeration things I talked about earlier, which you should know from the DirectX SDK common files. As parameters, the function wants to get the handles to all the controls of the dialog to fill them with the findings of the enumerations. This way an instance of the `ZFXD3DEnum` class always has access to the control element of the dialog and can read or write the dialog's contents. When this call is done, the control elements of the dialog, especially the combo box lists, are filled with entries about the hardware capabilities.

The next part of the procedure renders a logo image into the dialog box. This is just to show off. You need only basic functionalities from the Windows API. If this is not the case, please refer to the MSDN Library (*Microsoft Developer Network*) for the functions used in this case. To make this work, you need to link the library `vfw32.lib` (video for Windows) and include its header `vfw.h`. Note that the bitmap file with the logo is already loaded in the function `ZFXD3D::Init`.

Finally, the callback procedure handles the message `WM_COMMAND`. This message is sent by Windows to the dialog when an event occurs from one of the control elements. You can now check the lower part of the `WPARAM` parameter, which contains the plain ID of the control that is involved. Windows provides the macro `LOWORD` to evaluate only the lower parts of a given parameter.

You can see that the procedure calls one of the following functions according to the event that happened. If the user changes the selection in the Device combo box, for example, then the function `ChangedDevice()` from the class `ZFXD3DEnum` is called.

- `ZFXD3DEnum::ChangedAdapter`
- `ZFXD3DEnum::ChangedDevice`
- `ZFXD3DEnum::ChangedAdapterFmt`
- `ZFXD3DEnum::ChangedWindowMode`

All these functions have the same purpose. If the user changes one selection, it might influence the possible options for the other settings. The HAL might not have as many possible formats as the REF, for example. The `ZFXD3DEnum` class then walks through its enumerated lists and fills the dialog combo boxes with the possible choices available for the setting the user just selected. This is fairly simple.

Shutting Down the Dialog

The only two controls that are handled a bit differently are the OK button and the Cancel button. The following Windows API function makes the dialog disappear from the screen and your mind by destroying it.

`BOOL EndDialog( HWND hWnd, int nResult );`

Again you see that the dialog is just a window because for the first parameter you have to hand over the handle of the dialog you want to make quit. The second parameter is more interesting because it allows you to control a crucial return value we have not yet talked about. This return value is given to you by the `DialogBox()` function. Does this sound strange? It is not. You call `DialogBox()` somewhere inside your application. This brings up the dialog box and makes its callback procedure active, as long as you call `EndDialog()` from somewhere. As this dialog is modal, which means that the application is stalled as long as the dialog and its callback procedure are active, this call normally takes place in the callback procedure. From here, you can define what value should be returned to the point where the "normal" application waits for the dialog to end. This is the place where it all began: the `DialogBox()` call itself.

Now you can see that the dialog returns 0 in the case that the user canceled the dialog and 1 in the case that the user hit the OK button. It is also important to know that `DialogBox()` returns a value of -1 if the call itself fails because of a missing dialog resource or something similar. So you'd better not interfere with negative return values via the `EndDialog()` call.

But back to the OK Button case. You have to call the `ZFXD3DEnum::GetSelections` function there to make the class save the current settings from the dialog to global variables or `ZFXD3D` class variables. The structure `ZFXDEVICEINFO` contains a value from the enumeration that describes the device capabilities that should be used to initialize the Direct3D device, such as its modes and with which adapter it belongs. Again this structure is very similar to the one used in the DirectX SDK common files.

End the dialog and return 1 to signal a successful termination of the dialog. You can now look at how the initialization of the engine is done and how it uses the dialog. You still remember the problem of using callback functions in a class, don't you?

Initialization, Enumeration, and Shutdown

Everything starts with the constructor of the class `ZFXD3D` that is called from the exported function `CreateRenderDevice()`, which in turn is called by the static library class `ZFXRenderer` if the user wants to initialize the render device. So here is the constructor:

```
ZFXD3D *g_ZFXD3D=NULL;

ZFXD3D::ZFXD3D(HINSTANCE hDLL)
   {
   m_hDLL              = hDLL;
   m_pEnum             = NULL;
   m_pD3D              = NULL;
   m_pDevice           = NULL;
   m_pLog              = NULL;
   m_ClearColor        = D3DCOLOR_COLORVALUE(
                            0.0f, 0.0f, 0.0f, 1.0f);
   m_bRunning          = false;
   m_bIsSceneRunning   = false;

   m_nActivehWnd       = 0;

   g_ZFXD3D = this;
   }
```

The only interesting thing in this constructor is the global variable g_ZFXD3D. As you can see, we set it to the `this` pointer. Given that the user creates only one object of this class we now have a global pointer to that object. I agree that is not a smart way to build something like a singleton, but then it does its job. If you look at the DirectX SDK common files, you will find a big software company from Redmond does the very same thing, so I guess you and I can live with that quick 'n dirty solution in this book.

Have a quick look at the destructor and then follow me to further explanations about global variables and callback procedures.

Implementing the DLL

```
ZFXD3D::~ZFXD3D()
   {
   Release();
   }

void ZFXD3D::Release()
   {
   if (m_pEnum)
      {
      delete m_pEnum;
      m_pEnum = NULL;
      }
   if(m_pDevice)
      {
      m_pDevice->Release();
      m_pDevice = NULL;
      }
   if(m_pD3D)
      {
      m_pD3D->Release();
      m_pD3D = NULL;
      }
   fclose(m_pLog);
   }
```

Initializations Process Chain

Using the render device interface, you can call the following function to initialize the render device. (This function is short, which means you will need more functions to write and call.) But first dig your way through it.

```
HBITMAP g_hBMP;

HRESULT ZFXD3D::Init(HWND hWnd, const HWND *hWnd3D,
                     int nNumhWnd, int nMinDepth,
                     int nMinStencil, bool bSaveLog)
   {
   int nResult;

   m_pLog = fopen("log_renderdevice.txt", "w");
   if (!m_pLog) return ZFX_FAIL;

   // should I use child windows??
```

```cpp
   if (nNumhWnd > 0)
     {
     if (nNumhWnd > MAX_3DHWND) nNumhWnd = MAX_3DHWND;
     memcpy(&m_hWnd[0], hWnd3D, sizeof(HWND)*nNumhWnd);
     m_nNumhWnd = nNumhWnd;
     }
// else use main window handle
   else
     {
     m_hWnd[0] = hWnd;
     m_nNumhWnd = 0;
     }
   m_hWndMain = hWnd;;

   if (nMinStencil > 0) m_bStencil = true;

   // generate enum object
   m_pEnum = new ZFXD3DEnum(nMinDepth, nMinStencil);

   // load ZFX logo
   g_hBMP = (HBITMAP)LoadImage(NULL, "zfx.bmp",
                               IMAGE_BITMAP,0,0,
                               LR_LOADFROMFILE |
                               LR_CREATEDIBSECTION);

   // open up dialog
   nResult = DialogBox(m_hDLL, "dlgChangeDevice", hWnd,
                       DlgProcWrap);

   // free resources
   if (g_hBMP) DeleteObject(g_hBMP);

   // error in dialog
   if (nResult == -1)
      return ZFX_FAIL;
   // dialog canceled by user
   else if (nResult == 0)
      return ZFX_CANCELED;
   // dialog ok
   else
      return Go();
   }
```

There are several parameters to this function, so let's take them one by one. The first parameter is the handle of the application's main window. Easy. The second parameter is an array of handles with the number of entries following in the third parameter. You only need those if you don't want to render into the main application window and use one or more child windows instead. The function does nothing more than copy the data it needs from the parameters to the member variables.

The next two parameters specify the minimum bit depth you want to use for the depth buffer and the stencil buffer. The last parameter specifies whether the caller wants a secure log file that streams each entry at once, thereby making this secure even if the application crashes.

Okay, now back to the callback problem. The function quickly loads the bitmap file used for the logo and creates a ZFXD3DEnum object. Then it calls the dialog box. But instead of providing our ZFXD3D::DlgProc defined previously, which wouldn't work for reasons stated, it uses a callback procedure named DlgProcWrap(). This is a plain C function and looks like this:

```
BOOL CALLBACK DlgProcWrap(HWND hDlg,
                          UINT message,
                          WPARAM wParam,
                          LPARAM lParam)
   {
   return g_ZFXD3D->DlgProc(hDlg,
                            message,
                            wParam,
                            lParam);
   }
```

Again, this is not pretty, but it is a quick (and dirty) workaround to use the callback function from the ZFXD3D class. This callback procedure delegates the call and that is why the global object points to the last (and only) created instance of the ZFXD3D class.

Now if everything goes right, you will have filled some global and member variables with the settings based on the user's selections from the dialog. The only thing remaining is to crank up the Direct3D device (finally!). As this is a quite lengthy process, I provided its own function for it. It is called ZFXD3D::Go and it looks like this:

```
HRESULT ZFXD3D::Go(void)
   {
   ZFXCOMBOINFO   xCombo;
   HRESULT        hr;
   HWND           hwnd;
```

```cpp
// create Direct3D main object
if (m_pD3D)
   {
   m_pD3D->Release();
   m_pD3D = NULL;
   }
m_pD3D = Direct3DCreate9( D3D_SDK_VERSION );

if (!m_pD3D) return ZFX_CREATEAPI;

// get fitting combo
for (UINT i=0; i<g_xDevice.nNumCombo; i++)
   {
   if ( (g_xDevice.d3dCombo[i].bWindowed ==
         m_bWindowed)
      && (g_xDevice.d3dCombo[i].d3dDevType ==
          g_xDevice.d3dDevType)
      && (g_xDevice.d3dCombo[i].fmtAdapter ==
          g_fmtA)
      && (g_xDevice.d3dCombo[i].fmtBackBuffer ==
          g_fmtB) )
      {
      xCombo = g_xDevice.d3dCombo[i];
      break;
      }
   }

// fill in present parameters structure
ZeroMemory(&m_d3dpp, sizeof(m_d3dpp));
m_d3dpp.Windowed              = m_bWindowed;
m_d3dpp.BackBufferCount       = 1;
m_d3dpp.BackBufferFormat      = g_Dspmd.Format;
m_d3dpp.EnableAutoDepthStencil = TRUE;
m_d3dpp.MultiSampleType       = xCombo.msType;
m_d3dpp.AutoDepthStencilFormat = xCombo.fmtDepthStencil;
m_d3dpp.SwapEffect            = D3DSWAPEFFECT_DISCARD;

// stencil buffer active?
if ( (xCombo.fmtDepthStencil == D3DFMT_D24S8)
    || (xCombo.fmtDepthStencil == D3DFMT_D24X4S4)
    || (xCombo.fmtDepthStencil == D3DFMT_D15S1) )
   m_bStencil = true;
```

```cpp
else
   m_bStencil = false;

// fullscreen mode
if (!m_bWindowed)
   {
   m_d3dpp.hDeviceWindow    = hwnd = m_hWndMain;
   m_d3dpp.BackBufferWidth  = g_Dspmd.Width;
   m_d3dpp.BackBufferHeight = g_Dspmd.Height;
   ShowCursor(FALSE);
   }
// windowed mode
else
   {
   m_d3dpp.hDeviceWindow    = hwnd = m_hWnd[0];
   m_d3dpp.BackBufferWidth =
                     GetSystemMetrics(SM_CXSCREEN);
   m_d3dpp.BackBufferHeight =
                     GetSystemMetrics(SM_CYSCREEN);
   }

// create direct3d device
hr = m_pD3D->CreateDevice(g_xDevice.nAdapter,
                          g_xDevice.d3dDevType,
                          m_hWnd, xCombo.dwBehavior,
                          &m_d3dpp, &m_pDevice);

// create swap chains if needed
if ( (m_nNumhWnd > 0) && m_bWindowed)
   {
   for (UINT i=0; i<m_nNumhWnd; i++)
      {
      m_d3dpp.hDeviceWindow = m_hWnd[i];
      m_pDevice->CreateAdditionalSwapChain(
                 &m_d3dpp, &m_pChain[i]);
      }
   }

delete m_pEnum;
m_pEnum = NULL;

if (FAILED(hr)) return ZFX_CREATEDEVICE;
```

```
m_bRunning        = true;
m_bIsSceneRunning = false;
return ZFX_OK;
} // Go
```

In this function, you don't need to do anything other than run through the objects of the `ZFXCOMBOINFO` structures and find the one that fits the user's wishes. From this object, you can then retrieve the values you need to fill in the present parameters structure from Direct3D, and you can initialize the Direct3D device—finally!

There are some minor issues involved in running in either windowed or fullscreen mode. After that, the device is ready to go and ready to pump polygons to the graphics adapter. Please note that the name `combo` has nothing to do with a combo box control. This name was introduced in the DirectX 9 common files, and it describes a combination of front buffer and back buffer format, an adapter, a device type, a vertex processing type, and the depth-stencil format. I want to show you what is happening with the common files.

Caution

In this current design, you force the users of the engine to accept the dialog that pops up each time an end user runs his application. This might be useful for applications such as games that can run either windowed or fullscreen. But it is nonsense for applications meant to run in windowed mode only, such as tools and editors. Therefore, I added a method `ZFXRenderDevice::InitWindowed` as an alternative. This method cranks up the engine in windowed mode without querying the user for his wishes.

About Swap Chains

Let's reveal the magic of how you can render to multiple child windows using Direct3D. It's not that difficult. The Direct3D device uses so-called *swap chains* for this purpose. You say you've never heard of these? If you ever used Direct3D before, then you have actually used a swap chain.

Basically, a swap chain is nothing more than one or more back buffers. The standard Direct3D device has at least one built-in render target—the front buffer. If you use a back buffer, then you suddenly end up with two buffers you can render to that are swapped automatically if you call the `IDirect3DDevice::Present` function. There it is, the implicitly existing swap chain of the Direct3D device. The device simply cannot exist without a swap chain.

Now you can add as many swap chains as you like if you have enough memory. In the previous listing, you saw the function that can do exactly this, creating a swap chain and adding it to the device: `IDirect3DDevice::CreateAdditionalSwapChain`. As parameters you need to provide only the Direct3D present parameters structure and a pointer of the interface type `IDirect3DSwapChain9`.

I don't want to go into detailed descriptions here of how to use Direct3D interfaces, as it is not the topic of this book. However, I will point out all the functions you need to deal with those swap chains and let you explore in the DirectX SDK reference whatever you cannot grasp from my explanations. What I show you here is more than enough to get a grip on those swap chains.

After creating a new swap chain, which is connected to another window over the window handle you put into the present parameters structure, you can later change the active swap chain if you want to use another child window to render into. Next, I show you how to do this.

Changing between Child Views

Let's suppose the user provided an array of window handles to the `ZFXRenderDevice::Init` call because he wants to use multiple child views to render into. You have to make your engine capable of switching to any of those child windows whenever the user wants you to. To do this is actually quite easy, but there are some nasty details connected to it. Each time you render something to Direct3D, the pixel output is rendered onto what is called a render target. The back buffer is such a render target, but a texture could be a render target as well. I told you that a swap chain is basically nothing more than a separate back buffer, so the only thing you need to do is change the render target to a swap chain's back buffer if you want to render to another child window.

And that sounds even more complicated than it is. You have to pick the swap chain object and retrieve its back buffer object as a Direct3D surface object. The following function lets you do this: `IDirect3DSwapChain9::GetBackBuffer`. It awaits three parameters. First, it waits for the index of the back buffer, as there could be more than one. Second, it waits for the flag `D3DBACKBUFFER_TYPE_MONO`. In a later version of DirectX, there might be a support for stereo rendering, but for now there is only the flag I mentioned. The third parameter is a pointer to a Direct3D surface to be filled with the back buffer you requested.

After you get what you came for, you can set this surface as a render target for the Direct3D device. *Voilà*, you successfully changed the active swap chain of the device to another one. This means that until the next switch, Direct3D will render into the window connected with the swap chain that is now active.

It is that simple. The following function takes care of doing this job:

```
HRESULT ZFXD3D::UseWindow(UINT nHwnd)
   {
   LPDIRECT3DSURFACE9 pBack=NULL;

   if (!m_d3dpp.Windowed)
      return ZFX_OK;
   else if (nHwnd >= m_nNumhWnd)
```

```
        return ZFX_FAIL;

    // try to get the appropriate back buffer
    if (FAILED(m_pChain[nHwnd]->GetBackBuffer(0,
                                              D3DBACKBUFFER_TYPE_MONO,
                                              &pBack)))
        return ZFX_FAIL;

    // and activate it for the device
    m_pDevice->SetRenderTarget(0, pBack);
    pBack->Release();
    m_nActivehWnd = nHwnd;
    return ZFX_OK;
    }
```

> **Caution**
>
> Things are never easy. There is a slight catch concerning the change of a render target. The depth-stencil surface attached to the Direct3D device must not be smaller than the dimensions of the render target. Otherwise the whole screen will look pretty messed up. To keep things simple, I use the desktop size for the implicit Direct3D swap chain, and it will also be taken for the depth-stencil surface. You can also create a depth-stencil surface for each render target and change the depth-stencil surface if you change the render target.

We have completed the initialization stuff. Our engine is now able to initialize Direct3D in a comfortable way. You can also fire up a lot of child windows you might want to render into, and you can switch the active window in the blink of an eye.

Figure 3.2 shows you what the final demo in this chapter looks like. This is nothing spectacular at all. There is, however, a lot going on behind the scenes, as you learned in this chapter. The figure shows the engine running in windowed mode with four child windows. We are not yet able to render anything but we can already clear the client area of all the child windows, as you will see in a moment.

If you select fullscreen mode in the dialog during the startup phase of the engine, the engine is smart enough to ignore the list of child windows and use the main application window handle instead. It will also block the calls to ZFXD3D::UseWindow without an error. This way you cannot mess up the engine by making a wrong call. This intelligent logic sits inside the ZFXD3D::Init and ZFXD3D::UseWindow functions, as you might have noticed.

There are still some pieces missing from the puzzle. We have not yet implemented the last few functions the ZFXRenderDevice interface wants us to implement. These are the topic of the next section.

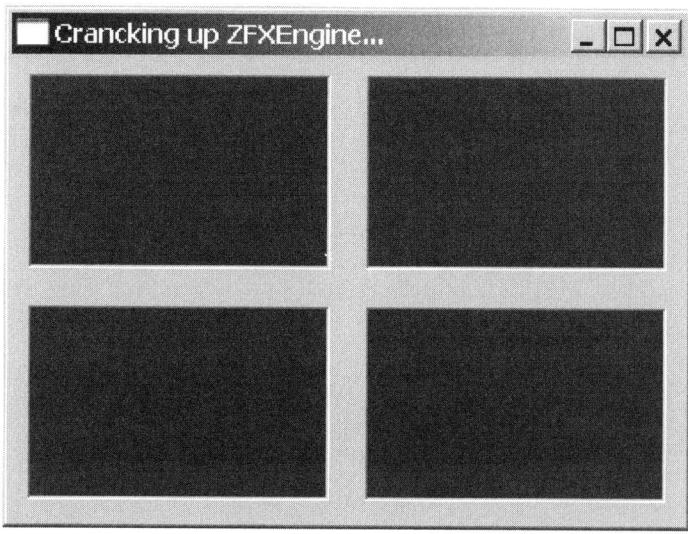

Figure 3.2 The engine running in windowed mode featuring four child windows

Render Functions

We did it. We initialized the render device that sits inside the DLL, and we used Direct3D. We can also release it and just clean up after our party. This does not take us anywhere if we cannot do anything at all between its initialization and its release. However, the main purpose of a render device should be to render something.

I guess you already have a lot to consider from this chapter and I don't want to throw a lot more on you. You will soon see that rendering is not very easy if you want to do it right and encapsulate it comfortably in an engine.

However, I can't just let you initialize and destroy render devices without seeing anything on your screen. Therefore, I will include the basic functionality to clear the screen using the render device. Take a look at the following interface functions or, better, at how they are now implemented in the ZFXD3D class using Direct3D.

```
HRESULT ZFXD3D::BeginRendering(bool bClearPixel,
                               bool bClearDepth,
                               bool bClearStencil)
   {
   DWORD dw=0;

   // anything to be cleared?
   if (bClearPixel || bClearDepth || bClearStencil)
      {
```

```
         if (bClearPixel)   dw |= D3DCLEAR_TARGET;
         if (bClearDepth)   dw |= D3DCLEAR_ZBUFFER;

         if (bClearStencil && m_bStencil)
            dw |= D3DCLEAR_STENCIL;

         if (FAILED(m_pDevice->Clear(0, NULL, dw,
                                     m_ClearColor,
                                     1.0f, 0)))
            return ZFX_FAIL;
         }

      if (FAILED(m_pDevice->BeginScene()))
         return ZFX_FAIL;

   m_bIsSceneRunning = true;
   return ZFX_OK;
   } // BeginRendering
/*----------------------------------*/


HRESULT ZFXD3D::Clear(bool bClearPixel,
                      bool bClearDepth,
                      bool bClearStencil)
   {
   DWORD dw=0;

   if (bClearPixel)   dw |= D3DCLEAR_TARGET;
   if (bClearDepth)   dw |= D3DCLEAR_ZBUFFER;

   if (bClearStencil && m_bStencil)
      dw |= D3DCLEAR_STENCIL;

   if (m_bIsSceneRunning)
      m_pDevice->EndScene();

   if (FAILED(m_pDevice->Clear(0, NULL, dw,
                               m_ClearColor,
                               1.0f, 0)))
      return ZFX_FAIL;

   if (m_bIsSceneRunning)
```

```
        m_pDevice->BeginScene();
   } // Clear
/*----------------------------*/


void ZFXD3D::EndRendering(void)
   {
   m_pDevice->EndScene();
   m_pDevice->Present(NULL, NULL, NULL, NULL);
   m_bIsSceneRunning = false;
   } // EndRendering
/*----------------------------*/


void ZFXD3D::SetClearColor(float fRed,
                           float fGreen,
                           float fBlue)
   {
   m_ClearColor = D3DCOLOR_COLORVALUE(fRed,
                                      fGreen,
                                      fBlue,
                                      1.0f);
   } // SetClearColor
/*----------------------------*/
```

Before you can render, you have to begin the *scene*, as Direct3D calls it. Each API uses naming conventions as it likes and so I called this one `BeginRendering()`, which looks more native to me and more or less explains itself. (Try to explain to someone what exactly a scene is and why you have to begin a scene.) This step itself is necessary to instruct the video adapter to prepare for rendering.

You have to provide three parameters of type `bool` to control which buffers will be cleared before you begin rendering. You will almost always want to wipe out the depth buffer—but only if you use one. The same applies for the stencil buffer. Ever tried to do a clear on a nonexistent depth or stencil buffer? Direct3D shows you some nice blinking colors if you do this.

Things get looser with the pixel buffer. It makes sense to clear the pixel buffer each frame; however, if you know you will render each pixel of the pixel buffer in the new frame, there is no need to clear the pixel buffer because its contents will be overwritten anyway. Therefore, it can save you time and an expensive fill rate if you can save yourself from clearing that buffer.

> **Note**
>
> In computer graphics, you encounter a lot of terms that mean the same thing. Or to put it the other way around, you find a lot of different terms describing the same object or concept. Roughly speaking, a pixel buffer is the same thing as back buffer–front buffer, frame buffer, or just render target.

The remaining functions are self-explanatory. A separate function does a clear without beginning a scene. You need that for some effects, such as when you have to clear buffers during a scene. If the engine sees that the scene is currently running, it will stop the scene, clear, and then start the scene again but without calling the IDirect3DDevice9::Present function from Direct3D.

This is done only when you explicitly end the rendering for the engine. Please note that you must not call IDirect3DDevice9::Present more than once for a swap chain per frame. Otherwise, Direct3D will thank you with its nice blinking colors or a messed up screen.

You are now truly, truly done with the implementation issues of this chapter. This I promise you. Both projects are complete and you have only to see the code that is needed to make a test run of your brand new, small but fine engine.

Testing the Implementation

Most of us have already worked with a 3D API, at least enough to know that it is a whole lot of work to crank up such an API, to keep an eye on errors that could occur, select screen modes, and so on. Those are the nasty things we locked away deep inside the DLL that implements the render device interface. As you will see, the more code we can abstract away from an application because of low-standard encapsulation work, the better it is and the shorter the source code of an application using the engine naturally gets.

If you would be so kind now, open a new project in Visual C++ as a Win32 Application and call it Demo or whatever you want it to be called. Please don't use animal names.

You already know how to create a new project and add new empty files to it; therefore, insert main.cpp and main.h into the project. To eliminate some batch file work and even more Visual C++ settings, copy the files the demo project needs to use from the ZFXRenderer directory and the subdirectories that contain the static library implementation and the compiled library itself.

It would be easier to use batch files called in the post-build step to copy these files and to give path names to the IDE (*Integrated Development Environment*) so that it can find the directories for itself. However, you then need to know your way around in Visual C++, so just copy the following files into the directory of your Demo project space:

- ZFXRenderer.h
- ZFXRenderDevice.h

- ZFXRenderer.lib
- ZFXD3D.dll

With this completed, you can start coding. You will need only four short functions. One of them naturally needs to be the WinMain() function, which is accompanied by a message procedure callback. The other two functions necessary for internal organization in the code are the function for initialization of the engine and the function to shut it down.

Here I list for you the program as I implemented it. Object-oriented programmers might call this a mess, but then it is only a demo and it is meant to be simple and to the point without creating a smart class encapsulation with the Windows API and without the cool design stuff. Following is the code:

```cpp
/////////////////////////////////////////////////////////
// FILE: main.h
LRESULT WINAPI MsgProc(HWND, UINT, WPARAM, LPARAM);
HRESULT ProgramStartup(char *chAPI);
HRESULT ProgramCleanup(void);
/////////////////////////////////////////////////////////
```

```cpp
/////////////////////////////////////////////////////////
// FILE: main.cpp

#define WIN32_MEAN_AND_LEAN

#include "ZFXRenderer.h"   // the interface
#include "ZFX.h"           // return values
#include "main.h"          // prototypes

// link the static library
#pragma comment(lib, "ZFXRenderer.lib")

// Windows stuff
HWND      g_hWnd  = NULL;
HINSTANCE g_hInst = NULL;
TCHAR     g_szAppClass[] = TEXT("FrameWorktest");

// application stuff
BOOL  g_bIsActive = FALSE;
bool  g_bDone     = false;
FILE  *pLog       = NULL;
```

```
// zfx objects
LPZFXRENDERER      g_pRenderer = NULL;
LPZFXRENDERDEVICE  g_pDevice   = NULL;


/**
 * WinMain entry point
 */
int WINAPI WinMain(HINSTANCE hInst,
                   HINSTANCE hPrevInstance,
                   LPSTR lpCmdLine, int nCmdShow)
   {
   WNDCLASSEX     wndclass;
   HRESULT        hr;
   HWND           hWnd;
   MSG            msg;

   // initialize the window
   wndclass.hIconSm       = LoadIcon(NULL,IDI_APPLICATION);
   wndclass.hIcon         = LoadIcon(NULL,IDI_APPLICATION);
   wndclass.cbSize        = sizeof(wndclass);
   wndclass.lpfnWndProc   = MsgProc;
   wndclass.cbClsExtra    = 0;
   wndclass.cbWndExtra    = 0;
   wndclass.hInstance     = hInst;
   wndclass.hCursor       = LoadCursor(NULL, IDC_ARROW);
   wndclass.hbrBackground = (HBRUSH)(COLOR_WINDOW);
   wndclass.lpszMenuName  = NULL;
   wndclass.lpszClassName = g_szAppClass;
   wndclass.style         = CS_HREDRAW | CS_VREDRAW |
                            CS_OWNDC | CS_DBLCLKS;

   if (RegisterClassEx(&wndclass) == 0)
      return 0;

   if (!(hWnd = CreateWindowEx(NULL, g_szAppClass,
              "Crancking up ZFXEngine...",
              WS_OVERLAPPEDWINDOW | WS_VISIBLE,
              GetSystemMetrics(SM_CXSCREEN)/2 -190,
              GetSystemMetrics(SM_CYSCREEN)/2 -140,
              380, 280, NULL, NULL, hInst, NULL)))
```

Testing the Implementation 85

```
      return 0;

g_hWnd  = hWnd;
g_hInst = hInst;

pLog = fopen("log_main.txt", "w");

// start the engine
if (FAILED( hr = ProgramStartup("Direct3D")))
   {
   fprintf(pLog, "error: ProgramStartup() failed\n");
   g_bDone = true;
   }
else if (hr == ZFX_CANCELED)
   {
   fprintf(pLog, "ProgramStartup() canceled\n");
   g_bDone = true;
   }
else
   g_pDevice->SetClearColor(0.1f, 0.3f, 0.1f);

while (!g_bDone)
   {
   while(PeekMessage(&msg, NULL, 0, 0, PM_REMOVE))
       {
       TranslateMessage(&msg);
       DispatchMessage(&msg);
       }

   if (g_bIsActive)
       {
       if (g_pDevice->IsRunning())
           {
           g_pDevice->BeginRendering(true,true,true);
           g_pDevice->EndRendering();
           }
       }
   }

// cleanup
ProgramCleanup();
```

```
      UnregisterClass(g_szAppClass, hInst);
      return (int)msg.wParam;
    } // WinMain
/*-------------------------*/



/**
 * MsgProc to proceed Windows messages.
 */
LRESULT WINAPI MsgProc(HWND hWnd, UINT msg,
                       WPARAM wParam,
                       LPARAM lParam)
   {
   switch(msg)
      {
      // application focus
      case WM_ACTIVATE:
         {
         g_bIsActive = (BOOL)wParam;
         } break;

      // key events
      case WM_KEYDOWN:
         {
         switch (wParam)
            {
            case VK_ESCAPE:
               {
               g_bDone = true;
               PostMessage(hWnd, WM_CLOSE, 0, 0);
               return 0;
               } break;
            }
         } break;

      // destroy window
      case WM_DESTROY:
         {
         g_bDone = true;
         PostQuitMessage(0);
         return 1;
         } break;
```

```
         default: break;
      }
   return DefWindowProc(hWnd, msg, wParam, lParam);
   }
/*--------------------------*/


/**
 * Create the render device object.
 */
HRESULT ProgramStartup(char *chAPI)
   {
   HWND hWnd3D[4];
   RECT rcWnd;
   int  x=0,y=0;

   // we don't have OpenGl at all :)
   if (strcmp(chAPI, "OpenGL")==0) return S_OK;

   // create the renderer object
   g_pRenderer = new ZFXRenderer(g_hInst);

   // create the render device
   if (FAILED( g_pRenderer->CreateDevice(chAPI) ))
      return E_FAIL;

   // save pointer to the render device
   g_pDevice = g_pRenderer->GetDevice();
   if(g_pDevice == NULL) return E_FAIL;

   // query client area size
   GetClientRect(g_hWnd, &rcWnd);

   for (int i=0; i<4; i++) {
      if ( (i==0) || (i==2) ) x = 10;
      else x = rcWnd.right/2 + 10;

      if ( (i==0) || (i==1) ) y = 10;
      else y = rcWnd.bottom/2 + 10;

      hWnd3D[i] = CreateWindowEx(WS_EX_CLIENTEDGE,
```

```
                        TEXT("static"), NULL, WS_CHILD |
                        SS_BLACKRECT | WS_VISIBLE, x, y,
                        rcWnd.right/2-20, rcWnd.bottom/2-20,
                        g_hWnd, NULL, g_hInst, NULL);
      }

   // initialize render device (show dialog box))
   return g_pDevice->Init(g_hWnd,   // main window
                        hWnd3D,     // child windows
                        4,          // 4 children
                        16,         // 16 bit Z-Buffer
                        0,          // 0 bit Stencil
                        false);
   } // ProgramStartup
/*------------------------*/


/**
 * Free allocated resources.
 */
HRESULT ProgramCleanup(void)
   {
   if (g_pRenderer)
      {
      delete g_pRenderer;
      g_pRenderer = NULL;
      }
   if (pLog) {
      fclose(pLog);
      pLog = NULL;
      }

   return S_OK;
   } // ProgramCleanup
/*------------------------*/
```

What you see here is nothing more than a typical Windows application that opens up one window to start and provides a message pump to process the messages the operation system throws in your direction. There is a little more going on here. This is what sits inside the `ProgramStartup()` function and involves initializing the basic engine.

First, I get an instance from the `ZFXRenderer` class, which is the static library used to load a DLL that implements the render device interface `ZFXRenderDevice`. Then I call the

`ZFXRenderer::CreateDevice` function, which initializes the render device and brings up a dialog in which you can select the settings to run the application in.

In the `ProgramStartup()` function you can also see some weird code that creates four child windows, which are distributed evenly inside the main window's client area. The handles of these windows are given to the initialization function, and if the user selects that he wants to run the engine in windowed mode, you will see the four child windows you can render into just as you saw in Figure 3.2. If the user selects fullscreen mode then it doesn't matter that you hand over the child window handles to the engine. They will get ignored.

To end the program you can either hit the Escape key or use the window termination symbol from the window's caption bar in windowed mode.

One Look Back, Two Steps Forward

This chapter served as a refresher on several topics. You revisited some of the basic programming skills, but you should have learned a lot of new things, namely interfaces and DLLs. Using these two concepts or techniques, you are now able to encapsulate an API and hide its usage deep inside a library. I showed you how you can apply these methods and build a generic engine as an intermediary between a low-level API and the high-level game code.

If you end up writing all API-related stuff right into the game code or use API-dependent calls inside the game code, you will find yourself in a dead end one day. Even a simple switch to the next version of an API you use inside your game code would mess things up, as you would have to write the whole game code from scratch. Don't even try to just rewrite this and that over here and over there. It would just make things worse.

If you cleanly separate your game code from all API-dependent code using a mid-level engine, encapsulating an API, and hiding it totally to outsiders, everything will be okay. You just need to rewrite the engine, leaving the calling methods untouched. Then you do not need to change the game code. It will work with the new API version as soon as the engine is wrapped around this new version.

Another point that might be new to you is the flexible handling of multiple child windows. This enables you to build tools using typical level-editor-style front, side, top and perspective views, as well as a separate view for a material editor and stuff like that. We will revisit this flexibility again when we add the option for multiple viewports inside these child windows in Chapter 6, "The Render Device of the Engine." A viewport is basically a window inside a window; however, the difference is that it is not a real Windows window.

You should now have a fully functionally workspace with two projects that are the kickoff for a simple engine. Nothing will stop us from expanding that basic framework into a comprehensive engine.

The next chapter deals with some other basics you will hate at first, but you will learn to love later on. Trust me. Put on your helmet, soldier, and take point. If you encounter math problems, then fire for effect.

CHAPTER 4

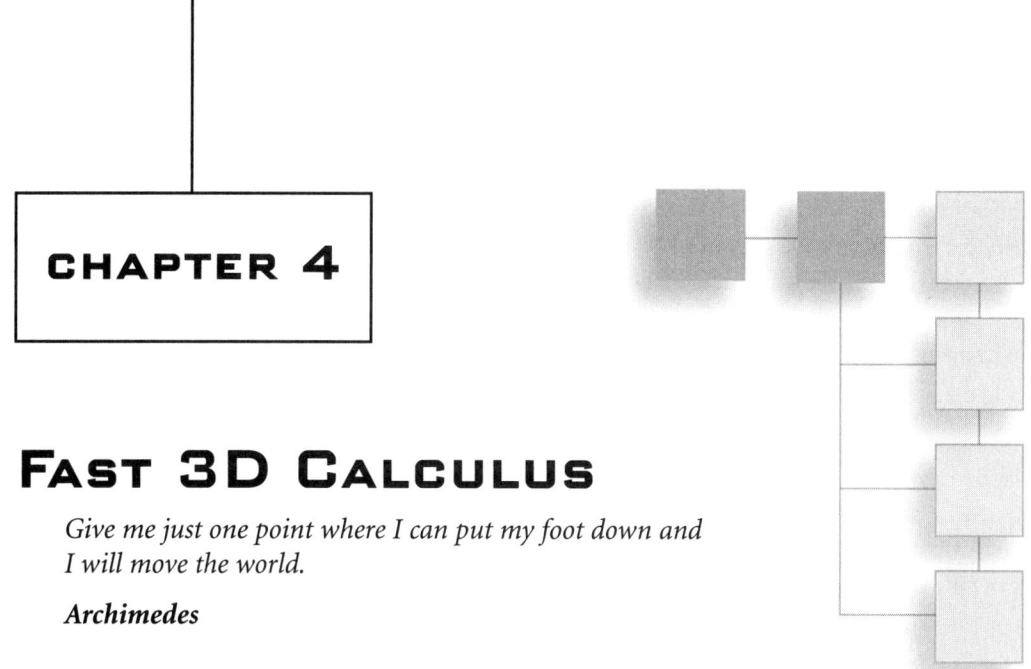

Fast 3D Calculus

*Give me just one point where I can put my foot down and
I will move the world.*

Archimedes

Thanks to modern 3D graphics application programming interfaces (APIs), programming a 3D engine nowadays is really easy. The fast hardware automates several processes, and this may make your engine look as if it is quite fast, too, on its first tests. However, when you attempt to run a real-life application on your engine, such as a full-blown commercial title, you may see its frame rate going down faster than you can say "son of a bitmap." In the ancient times of nonhardware transformation and lighting, you were directly bound to the speed of the CPU and the fill rate of the graphics adapter. Under these conditions, you had to let your graphics adapter idle while the CPU calculated this and that; then the CPU idled while the graphics adapter rendered one frame.

Compared to this approach, today's hardware is significantly more efficiently organized. Still, you can easily bring a high-end card to its knees pretty fast. The bottom line is that it still makes sense to optimize on several levels, high as well as low in certain places. This chapter repeats the basic calculus you need for 3D graphics, but focuses on optimization techniques to speed up such calculations.

This chapter covers the following objectives:

- Assembler programming basics
- Extended instruction sets for various CPUs (MMX, 3DNow!, and SSE)
- How to identify CPUs
- How to program processor-optimized vectors, matrices, and the like
- How to perform collision detection with rays, planes, polygons, and a lot more
- Quaternion basics

Fast, Faster, the Fastest

Repeated throughout this book is a philosophy you should make your own: Know your enemy, which is the graphics hardware. Another, perhaps friendlier way to put this is that you *must* team up with this enemy and make it your friend; after all, you simply cannot win against it.

A modern graphics adapter serves as a hardware transformation and lighting pipeline and facilitates several other advanced graphics hardware tasks. Unfortunately, many people lazily rely on the graphics adapter to actually do all those things. Those who use hardware features and shaders for just about everything may overload their graphics adapters, requiring a huge amount of work from them for each frame. They may consider this is how it's supposed to be. After all, the features are built in to the hardware and the adapter card is built to facilitate these features, right?

Simple answer: No. Such an approach leads to the central processing unit (CPU) being idle most of the time while the graphics processing unit (GPU) works itself virtually to death. In a better scenario, the programmer distributes the work more or less evenly between the CPU and the GPU. Don't forget that graphics are not the only calculations taking place in a 3D application or game; in addition, much collision detection and artificial intelligence (AI) math must be performed, tasks only the CPU can do. Before optimizing your code, first always profile your applications and see which parts of the program are executed most often; these should serve as your starting points for optimization. Second, don't attempt to optimize with programming tricks, twisting around data types and using weird assembler coding. Instead, always start the optimization process by reviewing your chosen algorithms to determine whether you can enhance performance by altering the algorithm.

If after following this logical optimization process you still need a boost, then you should look at low-level optimization possibilities. Low-level optimization refers to optimization you don't accomplish with high-level languages such as C/C++; that is, with low-level optimization, you trust yourself more than your compiler to better translate your code to an assembly language. Some people still consider that using assembler code leads to the best optimization. If you do have a good compiler, however, you should not start writing assembler code in your programs. Good compilers are written by people who *really* know their jobs. If you attempt to bypass the compiler and write your own assembler code, chances are you will slow down your code, because a good compiler's translation to assembler code or another machine language will be a better one.

Sometimes, however, you will understand what needs to occur (the job) better than the compiler. Therefore, this chapter identifies some ways to use special forms of assembly languages to speed up 3D math calculations.

A processor needs specific instructions regarding how to process the data flowing through its power lines. Those instructions must be strictly defined bit patterns containing binary numbers only. That is, the instructions must be comprised of combinations of power on and power off signals, the only language your computer hardware can really understand (hence the term *machine language*).

Because we humans often err when writing programs as bit strings, assembler languages were invented. In fact, an assembler program is very much the same thing as a bit string program. The main difference is that an assembler language provides names or macros for each and every bit string instruction a processor would understand. These names or macros are called mnemonic codes.

Note

The ancient Greek word *mneme* refers to human memory. *Mnemonics* or *mnemotechnology* is the discipline that deals with enhancing human memory with technical aids, to give a rather futuristic application example. But this science also deals with artificial memory issues such as shape-memory polymers, which can memorize a second permanent shape independent of their current shape. The transformation between the two shapes is initialized by an external stimulus such as change in temperature.

With high-level languages, programmers attempt to write computer programs in a language similar to a real, everyday human language. In contrast, assembler languages "speak" the language the hardware speaks and understands directly. Quite simply, computer languages move power (current/signal) into the processor register to make it respond to that power in the way it was built to respond.

As previously mentioned, high-level language compilers don't always result in optimal code. Perhaps this is because assembler languages were developed simultaneously with processors, whereas high-level languages took a longer time to be developed. For a long time (decades even), high-level languages were not as efficient as the human brain at optimizing assembler code. Therefore, programmers tend to use assembler languages quite a lot. However, high-level languages such as C/C++ do enable programmers to embed assembler code right into a function implementation. This is called *inline* assembler.

The inline assembler capability makes the programmer's job that much easier, enabling the programmer to write the main parts of the program in a high-level language. After all, learning such a language is easier than learning to think and talk like a machine. In addition, maintaining a high-level language program is much easier than trying to implement hardcore optimization tricks a real assembler guru may have hacked into a program. Inline assemblers enable programmers to take advantage of high-level language capabilities while still being able to write time-critical parts of a function in straight assembler code.

As previously mentioned, current high-level language compilers are very good. Unless you're an assembly language guru, you should definitely rely on a compiler for all your translation and compilation.

As good as compilers are at translating your instructions into meaningful assembly code, the efficient processing of that code is directly linked to CPU capabilities. New CPUs continue to be introduced into the market, promising to be faster and faster and even faster than all the others. You may be asking yourself why CPUs are always getting faster. Does their gain in speed depend only on their increased cycle frequency?

Well, yes. But not on that alone. If that were so, CPU developers would be frustrated by their inability to speed up processors beyond a certain limit. It's impossible to make that current flow faster than physical laws allow (at least so far).

Ask yourself why Intel and AMD salesmen always talk about processors optimized for multimedia applications in general and 3D graphics in particular. Also ask yourself how you can optimize a processor for processing graphics-related data and just what do MMX and 3DNow! stand for.

This chapter begins by answering those questions. After that, you will learn how to apply certain technologies in your own applications to speed up your 3D data processing.

Assembler Programming Basics

An exhaustive tutorial on programming assembler languages is beyond the scope of this book. You can find many good books on the market that provide such. However, to understand 3D data processing optimization techniques, you need to learn at least the very basics of assembler programming. This section covers the material you need to gain such an understanding.

For the purposes of this book, you do not need to know how to write complicated loops and functions in assembler languages. Instead, you need to understand the most common instructions assembler programs typically use. This section covers them. This material provides a foundation of information you will rely on throughout the rest of this chapter as you deal with one assembler language dialect. If you find yourself interested in learning more about assembler programming, you will find much more information in an assembler-only book.

Processor Architecture

A simple explanation of a processor is that it is just a bunch of memory slots (registers) that can hold data of a specific size. Programmers are able to manipulate the data in these memory slots; that is, they can move the data from one slot to another or change the values in the slots. Assembler languages provide a significant advantage in this regard. If you know how to move the data around optimally in a specific CPU (in a way the CPU understands and "likes"), you can write programs that run faster than those a compiler would output from a high-level language. Even today the resources a CPU offers to the programmer are quite limited. For general tasks, a CPU can provide only eight *registers* (the correct name for a memory slot inside a CPU). Each register can take a 32-bit value, which is a bit string of bit 0 to bit 31; each of these bits can be set to either 0 or 1. This boils down to the possibility of 2^{32} different values. The following list identifies all eight registers. You can see that each register is named with three letters that stand for its usage:

- EAX (extended accumulator)
- EBX (extended base)
- ECX (extended counter)
- EDX (extended data)
- ESI (extended source index)
- EDI (extended destination index)
- EBP (extended base pointer)
- ESP (extended stack pointer)

These register names derive from various important historical developments, and they used to be more important than they are now. The prefix *E*, for example, which is common to all registers, shows that those registers are *extended* to take 32 bits in 32-bit processors. The former generation of 16-bit processors just used the same register names but without that prefix. Nowadays it really doesn't matter what kind of data you put into which register. You can just use all the registers as equally well-suited memory slots to hold data. However, one exception does apply to this loose rule: You should leave the registers EBP and ESP alone because they are operating directly on the memory stack of the target platform. That means that they are changing values directly affecting the runtime behavior.

Therefore, unless you are absolutely, 100 percent certain about what you are doing with those registers, stay away from them. Otherwise you risk screwing up local variables or function parameters inside your program, perhaps making it do calculations on wrong memory addresses and producing bad results in the best case. In the worst case, you crash your operating system by tweaking imperative values.

Note

Oversimplifying, you can think of a computer dividing its memory resources into two big chunks of random access memory: the *heap* and the *stack*. The heap is a part of the memory from which the programmer can take packages. Each global function and global variable is saved behind an address in the heap. This is why the size of the element needs to be known in advance and why you cannot have arrays with dynamic size. The stack, on the other hand, is the storage for memory packages requested during runtime for things such as local variables or function parameters. Every time your program jumps from a function to a subfunction, a jump-back address is saved onto the stack. After calculating the subfunction, the program jumps back to this address and cleans up all the stack memory used by the subfunction.

It's important for you to understand one more thing before delving into assembler functions: Even today, it is quite possible to access the lower 16-bit index, 0 to 15, in a processor's register by just using the old name (AX, for example). And to split the memory up even more to have more storage than just eight registers, you can access the lower 8 bits of this 16-bit index, 0 to 7, as well as the upper 8-bit index, 8 to 15. You can do this by using the name AL and AH, respectively (where L stands for the lower 8 bits and H for the higher 8 bits). However, don't let this cause your head to swim. We will stick to using 32-bit registers because we are dealing with just single float values, which are 32-bit values.

Central Processing Unit (CPU)

Registers are just one part of the CPU. The processor would not be the brain of the computer if it were able only to store data. A brain's job is to process data (hence the name central *processing* unit). So besides the registers, the CPU enables you to perform mathematical and logical operations on the data contained in those registers. And if you are now thinking about those instructions mentioned above for registers, then you are on the right track. The most famous CPU instruction, which you will find in virtually every assembler program, is the MOV instruction. It is used to copy data from one register into another register. The following code snippet shows you how to write that in an assembler program:

```
MOV EDI, ESI    ;copy 32 bits of data from ESI to EDI
```

Each line of an assembler program has a similar syntax. First you name the instruction you want the CPU to perform. Then you identify the destination register where the result of the operation named in the instruction will be stored. The third part of this line is the source register from where the input data for the operation will be taken. A semicolon is not used to mark the end of a line; it is not necessary in assembler language. Instead, a semicolon starts a comment to the end of the line, as you can see in the preceding line of code.

The following line shows you how to add the value stored in the register ESI to the value stored in the register EDI. The result is stored in register EDI, and the content of register ESI is left unchanged:

```
ADD EDI, ESI    ;add value from ESI to value stored in EDI
```

After you get used to this syntax, it's pretty easy (that is, if you know what you are doing and what data resides in which register).

Floating-Point Unit (FPU)

The floating-point unit (FPU) is another part of the CPU and dates back to the good old 486 processor. Earlier processor architectures contained no room for an FPU; however, it was possible to buy an additional coprocessor as a standalone FPU (an expensive hardware investment).

For the purposes of this chapter, an exhaustive coverage of the FPU is unnecessary. However, its eight registers are of some interest because you will encounter them later in this chapter. Those eight registers are named R0 to R7 and are meant to take only one data type: an 80-bit type called *Extended Real*. Compared to the former 16-bit registers, they calculate floating-point numbers significantly better. Today's generation of 32-bit operating systems still use the 32-bit size `float` data type.

By now you should grasp the theoretical background of assembler languages and have the requisite understanding to start programming assembler code. Later in this chapter, you will actually write small assembler programs; don't worry, though, it is not as bad as it might sound right now. Before that, however, take the time to read the following sections that cover some additional instruction sets introduced with each new processor generation; these are the "magic" behind the increase in CPU performance with regard to processing 3D data and performing 3D calculations.

Introduction to SIMD

The acronym SIMD stands for *Single Instruction Multiple Data*. This name really gives away the whole secret behind SIMD technology and why this technology is able to boost processor performance. In fact, SIMD answers the question of what leads to the nonproportional decrease in processing time as compared to clock speed increases. It's really just that simple, and this section explains how this miracle works.

Normally, if you have an assembler program, the processing unit processes data and performs instructions on the data in a linear sequence. One by one. Each cycle of the CPU can be used to perform an operation or a part of a complex operation. Therefore, one way to increase the processing speed is to increase the tact rate or clock speed of the processor, and thus speed the processing of the sequential workload. Another totally different way to improve the speed is not to process the data in a one-by-one scheme. You just perform the same operation in parallel on different data packages. As you may infer from its name, the SIMD technology is basically doing exactly this. It performs a single instruction and, while paying the price for this one instruction, it performs the operation on multiple data packages at the same time.

SIMD assembler programs basically perform the same instruction on not just one register, but on several simultaneously. In contrast, plain old assembler programs call the very same instruction for every register on which they need to perform the data manipulation. From a technical point of view, this is not really correct; however, this explanation is enough for our purposes here. Actually, the SIMD instruction will also work on just a single register for one instruction, but the trick is that the register does not contain only one data package, but several. Registers used for SIMD instruction are bigger than the now old-fashioned 32-bit registers. The SIMD registers are more or less just like an array of variables you can work on, in parallel, at the same time in the same CPU cycle.

An example may help here. Think of a vector in three dimensions. You need three floating-point values with 32 bits each to describe this vector. Suppose you have a SIMD register that can take at least three times 32 bits, so it needs to be 96 bits in size (at least). Whereas a normal assembler would require three registers for one vector, a SIMD register needs only one register. Now suppose you have two vectors and you want to add them. With a normal assembler, you would need six registers to store those vectors and three instructions to add them component by component. With SIMD registers and instructions, you need only two registers and one instruction call. All three vector components in one register are processed at the very same time, in parallel.

Quite good, isn't it? And it gets even better. SIMD knows enough instructions to support just about everything a 3D graphics programmer needs for 3D calculus. You can perform vector additions, subtractions, multiplications, square root operations, and much more, as you will see soon.

Before that, however, you need to know a little about the historical development of SIMD assembler types. Don't mistake SIMD for a specific implementation or application of this parallel processing scheme. It is not. It is only a name for the concept of parallel data processing in such processing units that support a specific type of SIMD. The previous brief example referred to a SIMD technology that can take three floating-point values for a three-dimensional vector into one register. However, not all types of SIMD can do this, and not all types of SIMD are limited to only three values in one register.

In the following sections, you'll learn about various extensions with mysterious names such as MMX, 3DNow!, SSE, and SSE2. You may have already stumbled across one or more of those names at some point; the names are similar to specific SIMD implementation brands from various processor manufacturers. SSE might not be that well known, but MMX and 3DNow! were once extensively marketed (with those names appearing on stickers and labels on just every computer sold during that time). So read on and see what those different technologies are all about.

Multimedia Extensions (MMX)

The very first extension meant for multimedia applications with regard to SIMD technology in assembler programming was MMX (which stands for *Multimedia Extensions*). As mentioned previously, SIMD instructions are performed on only one register, but this register holds multiple data packages, not just a single variable. For this purpose, MMX defines several new data types. Each one of them is 64 bits in size. The reasoning behind this is that you should not put just a single 64-bit number into an MMX register, but an array of multiple numbers in a smaller bit size.

For example, the 64-bit size is big enough to accept an array of two 32-bit floating-point values. Although that is not really spectacular in itself, the amazing thing is that MMX knows that there is not a single 64-bit value there, but two distinct 32-bit values. If you call an instruction on that register, MMX is smart enough to process the instruction in parallel for both distinct numbers and not to mix up and mess around with the bits. Well, if you are still unimpressed then please stop now, remain a moment in silence, and then read on: The 64-bit size is large enough to store half a vector. (3D calculations often require programmers to work with 4D vectors, as discussed later.) So, whereas you once needed four instructions for most operations on 4D vectors, MMX cuts down the processing time by a factor of two. Applause please. (As you will learn in just a moment, however, that's not the whole story. MMX precision with regard to 3D graphics is quite poor because it can handle only integer values.)

MMX Registers

Although what you've read so far about MMX sounds good, there was a slight problem when MMX was first introduced. Processors didn't have 64-bit registers. And at that time, manufacturers didn't build processors with special registers for SIMD only. Intel took the easy way out and used the floating-point registers for that purpose. In fact, MMX is just using the lower 8 bytes of the 10-byte-sized floating-point registers. This comes at the cost of not being able to use the floating-point registers at the same time you are using MMX instructions, because both would want to operate on the very same physical registers in the processing unit.

The formerly floating-point registers known as R0 to R7 are used in MMX under the alias MM0 to MM7, but physically they are all the same.

MMX Data Types

The 64-bit data types introduced by MMX enabled programmers to accomplish many different operations that required a lot of data types. However, all of those new MMX data types had one thing in common: They were all integer data types and not floating-point values. For instance, you could use the *Short Packed Double Word* data type, which is an array of two 32-bit double word (like `DWORD`) values, or you could use the *Short Packed Word* data type, which is just an array of four 16-bit words. When the Short Packed Word data type is used, MMX knows that inside one register there are four values, and it can apply the same operation in parallel to those four values.

It is also interesting to note that if you use MMX the floating-point unit does not have control over its registers itself. The CPU takes them over, and thus MMX has total control over the registers. It's not necessary to say a lot more about MMX because it is really outdated technology.

MMX Instructions

All this theory may be boring you. Perhaps you're ready to see some code that illustrates all of these points. Okay, but first just a few brief words about instructions; then we'll get to some code for writing MMX assembler programs. Do not forget, however, that MMX is hopelessly outdated now. A number of other (newer) SIMD technologies are much better than MMX. The only reason for you to learn MMX would be if you need to maintain old source codes using MMX assembler or if you really want your 3D applications to support older CPUs.

One of those newer SIMD technologies is 3DNow! from AMD, which has been supported since the K6-2 processor. Intel, on the other hand, offers the SSE technology, which has been supported since the Pentium III processor series.

It's important for you to understand some MMX basics so that you can get a grip on all this stuff. The same concepts discussed here still apply to all SIMD technologies (even the most modern). Suppose, for instance, that we want to use an addition operation on two registers, and that both registers that will be subject to the addition operation contain a Packed Double Word. To add those registers component by component, you use the PADDD instruction. The prefix P indicates that you are working with packed data, that the data is packed into a single array for each register. The suffix D gives away the data type, which is a Double Word in this case:

```
PADDD MM1, MM0
```

This line of MMX assembler code tells the processing unit to add the contents of the MM0 register to the contents of the MM1 register, suspecting the data to be arrays of DWORD values. Although this does not look that spectacular, take a look at what you would have to do in C/C++ code to accomplish the same:

```
DWORD dwMM0[2] = { some_value, some_value };
DWORD dwMM1[2] = { some_value, some_value };

Add_PackedDoubleWords()
   {
   dwMM1[0] = dwMM0[0] + dwMM1[0];
   dwMM1[1] = dwMM0[1] + dwMM1[1];
   }
```

The component-by-component addition of arrays with the length of two can be done in a single instruction in MMX, whereas C/C++ requires two addition operations. From this, you should be able to understand why SIMD technologies facilitate faster code than C/C++ code, even if that code is translated to an optimized assembler language. Even normal assembler language does enable programmers to work with a single instruction on a whole array of data in parallel.

Another frequently required instruction is copying data between registers using the MOV instruction. Because MMX knows only those unusual 64-bit registers, however, you must use a specific copy instruction depending on the data type you want to move. The MMX instruction MOVQ is used to move 64 bits from an MMX register to another MMX register.

In some cases, however, you may want to move just half of the register, 32 bits. For that, you use the MMX instruction MOVD to move a DWORD value. You can use this, for example, to copy constants between MMX registers or to copy data from normal 32-bit CPU registers to an MMX register.

Intel invented the MMX technology, and it was first used in the Pentium processors. Now it's time to change focus and take a look at AMD and how they approached the topic of SIMD in their processor lines.

AMD Three-Dimensional (3DNow!)

After Intel took the lead in integrating SIMD technology in mainstream processing units, AMD needed to provide the same or even better technology in their processor lines. Basically, AMD used a quite similar approach regarding the use of the floating-point registers for their SIMD technology, and they also used the 64 bits of R0 to R7 and labeled them MM0 to MM7. However, the main difference as compared to MMX was the fact that AMD already used real floating-point values in the registers, whereas Intel's MMX had to work with integer values.

In 2D computer graphics, integer values had been fine to use to manipulate pixel data and the like. For 3D graphics and calculations using vectors and matrices, however, integer values are just not good enough. So you can think of AMD's 3DNow! technology as nearly the same as Intel's MMX but with much better precision. Whereas MMX was touted for its capability to boost the performance of multimedia applications, AMD's 3DNow! is touted for 3D graphics applications and games.

3DNow! enables programmers to use structures of two float values, as opposed to two DWORD integer values in MMX. So, finally, speeding up 3D graphics applications by roughly a factor of two became a reality. Another analogy with MMX is the naming conventions for the 3DNow! instruction set, which uses the same prefix P to mark the data as packed data, meaning multiple data packages in a single register. However, now there is also a second prefix, F, marking the data as floating-point values. Therefore, the instruction PFADD adds two floating-point arrays stored in two MM registers.

After a while, AMD realized that 3DNow! lacked some features. It had been introduced in the K6 processor series, but later on the instruction set was broadened and more functionality was added. That is especially true for the support of integer data types. Whereas MMX supported integer data types only and 3DNow! supported floating-point data types only, the second generation of 3DNow! supported integer data types as well. The Athlon processor series was the first one to support the second generation of 3DNow!, which was officially called Enhanced 3DNow!

3DNow! is now as obsolete as MMX. The information regarding 3DNow! is included here just to provide some historical background. In this book, I use Intel's Streaming SIMD

Extensions (SSE) for two reasons: It is modern enough to be a good choice, but not so modern that most readers' computers wouldn't have a processor that supports it.

Intel's Streaming SIMD Extensions (SSE)

By now, you already know a lot about SIMD technology. How it works, what it should achieve, and what kind of implementations started the SIMD story in the first place. So we can skip this introduction stuff and get down to the real applications of SIMD technology in a modern, virtual world.

The main drawback of MMX was its limitation to integer numbers. 3DNow! dealt with that drawback, but a bottleneck still existed: the parallel processing of only two 32-bit floating-point values. In the 3D computer graphics world, you need to work with four-dimensional vectors. This may sound weird at first, but just think of transformation matrices in the 3D world. As discussed later in this chapter, you need a 4x4 matrix to express several things in 3D graphics (starting from translation values and ending up with projection transformations). To multiply such matrices with vectors from 3D objects, those vectors also need to have four dimensions. And if you want to store the rows of a 4x4 matrix, you need an array of four floating-point values for each row anyway.

From a 3D graphics programmer's point of view, it would be the best if you would have a floating-point array with four entries as a basic unit that can be processed in parallel by the processor. And now for the good news: SSE offers exactly this kind of capability.

New Registers, the Cavalry Finally Arrived

Finally, the processor manufacturers (Intel in this instance) nixed the concept of reusing the floating-point unit registers R0 to R7 any longer for their SIMD implementations. Instead, Intel provided the Pentium III processor with a set of eight totally new built-in registers. Those new registers are big enough to take 128 bits of data. Even if you skipped too many math classes, you still don't need a single second to calculate that 128 bits are enough to store four 32-bit values in a single register. And it is obvious that floating-point numbers of normal precision, such as the float data type, are supported by SSE in those new registers. Intel calls this data type Packed Single Real, by the way.

It almost goes without saying that SSE is now a perfect match if you have arrays of four floating-point values (such as 4D vectors and 4x4 matrices, for example). Finally, we 3D programmers got what we came for. SSE enables programmers to perform instructions and operations on four floating-point numbers simultaneously, which means that you can do lots of 3D graphics-related tasks in just one instruction call using SSE rather than two calls using 3DNow! and rather than four calls using C/C++ or an assembler language.

Those new registers are named XMM0 to XMM7. However, you can still perform operations on scalar values. You don't have to process operations on all four values stored in such a register (as discussed shortly).

SSE Instructions

It's time for another example. Here is what the addition of values would look like in Intel's SSE (in this case, the two instructions ADDPS and ADDSS). The first instruction adds packed single-precision floating-point values. Again, packed means that you have an array of values and the operation is performed on all values at the same time. The second instruction adds scalar single-precision floating-point values. This means that only the first float value in the bits 0 to 31 from the source and destination registers are added. Take a look at some code so that you can see what all this means:

```
ADDPS XMM1, XMM0    ; adds two 4d vectors
ADDSS XMM1, XMM0    ; adds only the x-component of both vectors
```

And here is how the very same operations can be expressed in C-like pseudo code:

```
Add_PackedFloats()
   {
   fXMM1[0] = fXMM0[0] + fXMM1[0];
   fXMM1[1] = fXMM0[1] + fXMM1[1];
   fXMM1[2] = fXMM0[2] + fXMM1[2];
   fXMM1[3] = fXMM0[3] + fXMM1[3];
   }

Add_ScalarFloats()
   {
   fXMM1[0] = fXMM0[0] + fXMM1[0];
   }
```

Aligned or Not Aligned?

So far so good. Now we move on to copying data between two 128-bit SSE registers and between a normal 32-bit processor register and a 128-bit SSE register. You have to use a specific move instruction. Actually, there are several such instructions. If you want to move your data very fast from a 32-bit register to a 128-bit register or vice versa, use the instruction MOVAPS, which means **mov**e **a**ligned **p**acked **s**ingle-precision floating-point values. The term *aligned* refers to the fact that the data must be aligned in the memory in a specific pattern with specific boundaries. The address of the data's location must be dividable by 16, so that the data is 16-byte-aligned.

Now just think for a moment and you realize that 16 bytes are equal to 128 bits. Does that ring some bells? The XMM registers are 128 bits in size. So the copying of 16-byte-aligned data into 16-byte-sized registers is quite fast because the data does not need to be realigned in the XMM memory. You can make your data aligned to 16-byte boundaries by specifying __declspec(aligned(16)) for that data. If your compiler does not apply this macro in a correct manner, however, your program will crash if you execute the move instruction for aligned data (or any other SSE instruction using the APS suffix for that matter).

If you don't want to use the aligned data for whatever reason, you can still use SSE instructions of course. Instead of APS, you just have to use the suffix UPS (as in MOVUPS, for example), which means **u**naligned **p**acked **s**ingle-precision floating-point values. This is always the safe way to go if you cannot guarantee that the data is aligned to 16-byte memory boundaries. However, this is also the slower operation as compared to the aligned data operation because the data has to be aligned first before the processor can execute the operation on it.

Tip

Even if you work with nonaligned data, it is always true that the data is indeed aligned when it is sitting inside an XMM register. So if you perform operations on data where the source and the destination registers are both XMM registers, it is always safer and faster to use the instructions for aligned data.

Moving Data

The following samples in C-like syntax featuring inline assembler show the usage of the different MOV instructions in SSE. Note that only one of the vectors is aligned to 16-byte boundaries:

```
// given are two float-[4]-arrays, representing
// two vectors with valid data:
// __declspec(align(16)) float fVektor_A[4];
//                       float fVektor_U[4];
// Call: SSE_Add( &fVektor_A[0], &fVektor_U[0] );

void SSE_Add(float *fA, float *fU)
   {
   __asm {
      MOV     esi,    fA
      MOV     edi,    fU
      MOVAPS  XMM0,   [esi]
      MOVUPS  XMM1,   [edi]
      ADDPS   XMM0,   XMM1
      MOVAPS  XMM1,   XMM0
      MOVAPS  [esi],  XMM0
      MOVUPS  [edi],  XMM1
      }
   }
```

First of all, the addresses of the call by reference parameters are moved into normal assembler registers. Then the contents of the memory areas located at those addresses are moved into the SSE registers XMM0 and XMM1. Note the use of the move instructions for aligned and unaligned data.

Then the two SSE register are added using the ADDPS instruction, and the result is stored in the register XMM0. Then you copy the result into the register XMM1 as well, and finally the data is moved back to the normal registers ESI and EDI. Actually you are not copying the data itself into the ESI and EDI registers, but the addresses where the data is located (hence the need for the brackets).

After the function call, you have successfully calculated the result of the vector addition and stored the result in both vectors. This isn't necessarily a good idea, but the example does show you how to work with aligned and unaligned data in SSE.

Besides those two types of SSE move instructions discussed already, there are some more:

- MOVSS (copies a single 32-bit value from the lower bits of the register)
- MOVLPS (copies the lower 64 bits of an XMM register to another one)
- MOVHPS (copies the upper 64 bits of an XMM register to another one)
- MOVLHPS (copies the lower 64 bits into the upper 64 bits of the same register)
- MOVHLPS (copies the upper 64 bits into the lower 64 bits of the same register)

Shuffling Data

And now for the final SSE instruction discussed here, one that you'll need later on: an instruction to shuffle around the data packages sitting in one register. After you understand this, you will be able to implement the most common vector and matrix operations using SSE assembler.

While implementing certain operations in vector calculus, we may need to change the numbers in one register. SSE enables you to do so by using the SHUFPS instruction, which means **shuf**fle **p**acked **s**ingle-precision floating-point values. With this instruction, you can access each single element of a register and put some data into the specific field of the 128-bit register. All this shuffling may seem somewhat strange, so perhaps an example is in order:

```
SHUFPS XMM0, XMM1, 9Ch
```

Okay, maybe this example doesn't tell you everything you need to know. You know this call will shuffle some values, but what about that 9Ch in the last part of the instruction call? To shuffle not arbitrarily but with some sense, you need to control which values are taken from which element of the register and are put into which destination element. The hexadecimal value at the end of the instruction line tells the processor exactly that. The h in the value indicates that we are dealing with a hexadecimal number. Take a look at Table 4.1, which shows the conversion of some hexadecimal numbers to binary numbers.

So back to the sample call of the instruction. If you convert the hexadecimal number 9C into a binary 1, you get the following bit string:

10011100

And from this bit string, you can finally see which part of the register is shuffled into which other part. Two bits from that string are indicating one of the four elements in an XMM register. The first 2 bits represent the first element of the register in bits 0 through 31, the second 2 bits represent the second element in bits 32 through 63 in the register and so on.

Now the shuffling depends on how the bits are set. You have four elements you want to shuffle around. Each 2 bits from this bit string represent a position in the 128-bit register. So you just need to set the bits according to the shuffling you want to perform. You can identify the source for the shuffling from 2 bits as well. Element[0] is identified by the binary number 00, element[1] is identified by the binary number 01, element[2] is identified by the binary number 10, and element[3] is identified by the binary number 11.

You need to know one last thing to fully understand how shuffling works. The computer works with the least significant bit order, which means it interprets the bit string above not from the left to the right, but from the right to the left. Therefore, if you shuffle the register XMM0 and XMM1 using the hexadecimal number 9C you get the following result:

- XMM0 [0] contains the value from XMM0 [0] (identified by 00).
- XMM0 [1] contains the value from XMM0 [3] (identified by 11).
- XMM0 [2] contains the value from XMM1 [1] (identified by 01).
- XMM0 [3] contains the value from XMM1 [2] (identified by 10).

Table 4.1 Converting Hexadecimal Numbers to Binary Numbers

Hexadecimal	Binary	Hexadecimal	Binary
0	0000	8	1000
1	0001	9	1001
2	0010	A	1010
3	0011	B	1011
4	0100	C	1100
5	0101	D	1101
6	0110	E	1110
7	0111	F	1111

Because:

SHUFPS XMM0, XMM1, 9Ch

Equals:

SHUFPS XMM0, XMM1, 10 01 11 00

Where the bit string is read from the right to the left.

But wait. No, there is no error in the preceding bulleted list. The last two elements of the destination register can be filled only using the same register as the source. You can fill the upper two elements of the destination register only with values from a different source register. So keep this in mind when you start the shuffle game.

Broadcasting Data

Broadcasting data into an SSE register is something very similar to shuffling. Actually, it also uses the shuffling instruction. It is used to set the whole register (that is, all four elements of it) to the very same value as one of the four elements. Take a look at the following instruction line, which is broadcasting one value for the whole register:

SHUFPS XMM0, XMM0, 00h

This instruction shuffles with a bit string of 00000000, which means that all elements of the destination register XMM0 get the value from the source register's first element. If you were to broadcast using the hexadecimal number, however, you would broadcast the third element of the register into all the other elements.

Strange, eh? For now, let's let the shuffle be a shuffle and proceed to the final two stops on our trip through SIMD history before we get back to the keyboard and start coding.

Intel's Streaming SIMD Extensions, the Second (SSE2)

With the introduction of the new Pentium IV processor line, Intel boosted the SIMD capabilities of their flagship again. Whereas MMX was meant to work with 64-bit integer registers, the SSE SIMD was created to work with 128-bit floating-point data structures. Intel's new SIMD, called SSE2, also supports 128-bit integer data structure processing in the XMM registers. The whole palette of integer operations and data types available in MMX is also now available in the XMM registers via SSE2, but with twice the size as was available in MMX.

SSE2 is not used here because we need to work with floating-point values only in the 3D graphics calculus. SSE alone will do the job and, besides that, many readers probably don't have an SSE2-capable processor. If you own an AMD, you would be out in the cold with SSE2, but not with SSE. However, read on to see why Intel's SSE is okay with AMD's newer processor models.

AMD Three, Even More Dimensional (3DNow! Professional)

The latest versions of the AMD Athlon and the Athlon XP processor still use 3DNow! As mentioned previously, however, the 3DNow! SIMD technology has been extended and enhanced (drastically even). Before its enhancements, 3DNow! had been somewhat similar to MMX, but it did have additional support for floating-point numbers. However, AMD added 128-bit registers that could be used as four-element floating-point value memory slots, just like Intel's SSE. Even better, AMD decided not to create a competitive SIMD technology. They implemented the whole range of SSE instructions and just called this technology *3DNow! Professional*. In actuality, this is a hundred percent compatible with Intel's SSE instruction set.

Before 3dNow! Professional, programmers had only three application options for using SIMD, as follows:

1. Optimize the critical code only for 3DNow! or Enhanced 3DNow! if the target platform is an AMD processor; otherwise, use non-SIMD optimized code paths.
2. Optimize the critical code only for SSE or SSE2 if the target platform is an Intel processor; otherwise, use non-SIMD optimized code paths.
3. Provide a specific separate code path for each available SIMD technology (3DNow!, SSE, and SSE2, for example) and decide at runtime which one to use.

The good thing now is that you can use an SSE implementation and, unless you are targeting pretty old platforms, it is very likely that SSE will be supported by the hardware. Whether you use Intel's SSE or AMD's 3DNow! Professional doesn't matter, because the latter one can use the very same implementation and supports it one hundred percent.

How Do I Tell My Compiler?

From a technical point of view, you are now all set to go. As always, however, there is this damn catch 22 if you want to get started. Even if you know how to program SIMD assembler already, you can't start just yet, depending on the Integrated Development Environment (IDE) you are using. Actually a compiler needs to know the instruction set for all processors you want your code to work with. That is why there are several so-called processor packs out there to patch up older versions of the Microsoft Visual Studio IDE. Each time a manufacturer adds a new set of instructions, your compiler needs to learn these new assembler additions.

The problem with using Visual Studio 6.0 Standard edition is that it is impossible to program that SIMD stuff. If you are lucky and own the Professional or Enterprise edition, you have to get the service pack (at least version 4) and the processor pack from the Microsoft website. Then your IDE will be able to compile programs containing inline SIMD assembler programs.

The other alternative is to use a newer IDE (Microsoft Visual Studio .NET, for example). Even the "cute" Microsoft Visual C++ .NET supports SIMD assembler, making it the cheapest choice. In .NET, you also don't have to install service packs or processor packs to use the current kinds of SIMD.

> **Caution**
>
> Microsoft Visual Studio 6.0 Pro and Enterprise need the latest service pack and the processor pack to be able to deal with SIMD assembler. The Standard version does not support SIMD at all. However, all .NET versions can understand SIMD assembler without additional packs.

One final catch is the operating system. Not only the IDE and the processor need to be able to provide SIMD support, the operation system does too. If you use Windows 98SE or later, you are on the safe side.

Identifying the CPU

Many different SIMD approaches now exist, and all of them differ significantly. You have MMX, which is not really well-suited for 3D graphics applications. Then there is 3DNow! (three different versions), and don't forget SSE and SSE2. Depending on the processor the target machine can provide, you have to decide which kind of SIMD you want to use (and whether it is even available to you). This may remind some programmers of the time when it was necessary to program a separate code path for each available graphics adapter.

The bottom line is that you must write a function for your program to check which kind of SIMD is available when the program is running. Even though the examples in this book use SSE only, this section explains how to determine whether the various different SIMD technologies are available. Later on, we write our math functions with two code paths (one using SSE, if available; the other to use plain C/C++ in case SSE isn't available). If you want to support older SIMD technologies, you should also add a code path for the original 3DNow!

First you need to know which processor is available at the program runtime. Luckily, AMD and Intel are kind enough to provide detailed information about how to check for specific types of processors. You can download this information from their websites along with tons of other material about optimizing for certain processor models and the like. To start with, I use the following code to determine the available processor's features:

```
// file: ZFX3D.h
typedef struct CPUINFO_TYP {
   bool bSSE;       // Streaming SIMD Extensions
   bool bSSE2;      // Streaming SIMD Extensions 2
   bool b3DNOW;     // 3DNow! (vendor independent)
   bool bMMX;       // MMX support
```

```
    char name[48];      // cpu name
    bool bEXT;          // extended features available
    bool bMMXEX;        // MMX (AMD specific extensions)
    bool b3DNOWEX;      // 3DNow! (AMD specific extensions)
    char vendor[13];    // vendor name
} CPUINFO;
```

CPUID Instruction

Now you can write a function that will examine the CPU with regard to the features it supports. Since the release of the ancient 386 processor, CPUs have supported the so-called `CPUID` instruction, which is easy to use and reveals most of the interesting information. You just have to put a certain value into the `EAX` register and then call this instruction. It returns a result regarding a specific feature depending on the value you put into `EAX`. If you use the value 0, for example, the `CPUID` instruction will return the name of the processor's vendor. This name string must not be longer than 12 characters, and four at a time are returned into the registers EBX, EDX, and ECX, respectively.

If you put a value of 1 into EAX and call `CPUID`, the instruction will return a bit string into register EDX. This bit string is a feature list identifying what the processor can or cannot do. In addition, a so-called brand ID is written into register EBX for Intel processors and into register EAX for AMD processors.

Processor Feature List

You can check this feature list for specific bits to be set or not set. Each bit has a certain meaning, and all processor vendors have to interpret the bit string in the same way. The following features you can check for are the most interesting ones for our purposes:

- SSE support
- SSE2 support
- MMX support

Besides those standard features, there are extended features. However, not every processor can provide an extended features list. To get this list, if it exists, you put the value 0x80 into EAX and call the `CPUID` instruction. The processor then writes a value back into EAX, which you need to check to determine whether it's greater than 0x80. If it is greater, the processor does indeed have a list of extended features and is willing to hand it over to you. To get this list, put the value 0x80000001 into the EAX register and, again, just call `CPUID`. This returns the list of extended features into register EDX.

But what exactly are those extended features? Well, first of all, each processor could support 3DNow!, because this is an open standard every vendor can use. In the case of an Intel processor, you don't need to check for more extended features than that one. In case of an AMD processor, you can look for two more things. First, AMD offers an

Fast, Faster, the Fastest   111

extended MMX instruction set. Second, AMD has the extended (enhanced) 3DNow! instruction set.

Now you know all you need to know about identifying processors. The specific bits you need to check in the feature list or the extended feature list are contained in the technical documents AMD and Intel provide on their websites. It's unnecessary to list all of them here; the following function shows enough. It creates an object from our structure and fills the values into this object depending on what the processor can and cannot do:

```
CPUINFO GetCPUInfo() {
   CPUINFO info;
   char *pStr = info.vendor;
   int n=1;
   int *pn = &n;

   memset(&info, 0, sizeof(CPUINFO));

   // 1: Vendor name, SSE2, SSE, MMX support
   __try {
     _asm {
        mov   eax, 0           // get vendor name
        CPUID

        mov   esi,     pStr
        mov   [esi],   ebx     // first 4 Chars
        mov   [esi+4], edx     // next 4 Chars
        mov   [esi+8], ecx     // final 4 Chars

        mov   eax, 1           // Feature-List
        CPUID

        test edx, 04000000h    // test SSE2
        jz   _NOSSE2           // jump if negative
        mov  [info.bSSE2], 1   // true

__NOSSE2: test edx, 02000000h  // test SSE
        jz   _NOSSE            // jump if negative
        mov  [info.bSSE], 1    // true

__NOSSE:  test edx, 00800000h  // test MMX
        jz   _EXIT1            // jump if negative
        mov  [info.bMMX], 1    // true
__EXIT1:  // done
```

```
            }
        }
    _except(EXCEPTION_EXECUTE_HANDLER) {
        if ( _exception_code() ==
            STATUS_ILLEGAL_INSTRUCTION )
            return info;          // CPU inactive
        return info;              // unexpected error
        }

    // 2: Test Extended Features
    _asm {
        mov   eax, 80000000h      // Extended Features?
        CPUID
        cmp   eax, 80000000h      // > 0x80?
        jbe   _EXIT2              // jump if negative
        mov   [info.bEXT], 1      // true

        mov   eax, 80000001h      // Feat-Bits to EDX
        CPUID
        test edx, 80000000h       // test 3DNow!
        jz    _EXIT2              // jump if negative
        mov   [info.b3DNOW], 1    // true
__EXIT2: // fertig
        }

    // 3: vendor dependent things
    //    INTEL: CPU id
    //    AMD:   CPU id, 3dnow_ex, mmx_ex
    if ( (strncmp(info.vendor, "GenuineIntel", 12)==0)
         && info.bEXT) {          // INTEL
        _asm {
            mov   eax, 1          // Feature-List
            CPUID
            mov   esi,   pn       // Brand-ID
            mov   [esi], ebx
            }
        int m=0;
        memcpy(&m, pn, sizeof(char)); // only lower 8 bit
        n = m;
        }
    else if ( (strncmp(info.vendor, "AuthenticAMD",
            12)==0) && info.bEXT) {  // AMD
```

```
    _asm {
        mov  eax, 1              // Feature-List
        CPUID
        mov  esi,  pn            // CPU-Type
        mov  [esi], eax

        mov  eax, 0x80000001     // Ext.Feat. Bits
        CPUID

        test edx, 0x40000000     // AMD extended 3DNow!
        jz   _AMD1               // jump on error
        mov  [info.b3DNOWEX], 1  // true
_AMD1:  test edx, 0x00400000     // AMD extended MMX
        jz   _AMD2               // jump if negative
        mov  [info.bMMXEX], 1    // true
_AMD2:
    }
  }

  else {
     if (info.bEXT)
        ; /* UNKNOWN VENDOR */
     else
        ; /* NO Extended-Feature-List */
  }

  info.vendor[13] = '\0'
  GetCPUName(info.name, n, info.vendor );
  return info;
}
```

This function is divided into three major parts. You start warming up by extracting the vendor's name and saving it into our structure. For an Intel processor, this string is GenuineIntel; for AMD, it is AuthenticAMD. After that, you can just query the standard feature list and evaluate the support of SSE2, SSE, and MMX. If such a test is negative, the function just skips the next line, where the according field in the structure would be set to true.

The second part of this function checks whether the processor has a list of extended features. If it does, this list is queried. The only test you have to perform on the extended feature list is the support of 3DNow!. Then you can move on to the third part of the function.

Now you need to distinguish the different vendors. For Intel, you want to extract only the brand ID. For AMD, however, you can check for extended 3DNow! and extended MMX support. At the end of the function, you need to set the terminating string symbol \0 into the string with the vendor name. If you want to have the actual name of the processor model and not only its vendor number, you have to call the function GetCPUName. I don't want to show this function here because it is just a huge switch that sorts names such as Pentium IV to certain brand IDs and vendor names. You can take a look at this function on the CD-ROM.

> **Caution**
>
> For Intel, the identification of specific processors is not that easy. It is quite possible that the function will not recognize a processor name properly, so don't rely on that. However, all the important information about the vendor name and the processor's features will be right.

Checking for SSE Support at Runtime

As mentioned previously, it is unfortunately not the only requirement that the processor supports an SIMD technology. The operating system has to be able to support this, too. Although this might seem somewhat strange, the operating system must fulfill the task of saving the states of the 128-bit floating-point number SIMD registers to be able to restore them.

Luckily, however, there is a quite simple way to evaluate the operating system's support for SIMD assembler on the processor. You just need to call an SIMD instruction after ensuring that the processor can really support SIMD technology. If this call ends up in an exception, the operating system is not able to process this call. Hence it does not support this kind of SIMD. And here is what this looks like:

```
bool OSSupportsSSE() {
   __try
     {
     _asm xorps xmm0, xmm0
     }
   __except(EXCEPTION_EXECUTE_HANDLER) {
     if ( _exception_code() ==
          STATUS_ILLEGAL_INSTRUCTION )
        return false;   // sse not supported
     return false;      // unexpected error
     }
   return true;
   }
```

Finally, you just need to sum up the two functions just shown (the first one to check the processor features, and the second one to check whether the operating system supports SSE). The following little function evaluates the results of the two calls and sets the global variable g_bSSE to true if the current system supports SSE and to false otherwise:

```
bool g_bSSE = false;

bool ZFX3DInitCPU() {
   CPUINFO info = GetCPUInfo();
   bool    bOS  = OSSupportsSSE();

   if (info.bSSE && bOS) g_bSSE= true;
   else g_bSSE = false;

   return g_bSSE;
   }
```

Okay, if you call the function ZFX3DInitCPU() at runtime, you will know afterward whether the current system can handle SSE by just checking the state of the global variable g_bSSE. That being the good news, here's the bad: That was only the foundational work you need to do to build a comprehensive and fast math function library. Now it's time to do some serious coding.

Open your IDE and start a new project as a static library and call it zfx3d.lib. Alternatively, just use the project files from the accompanying CD-ROM. This library will contain all the math, the CPU identification issues, and even more by the time you finish this chapter.

Working with Vectors

The most basic thing you deal with in 3D computer graphics is the vector. A 3D vector is nothing more than a structure containing three floating-point values. A vector in 3D space has one extend on each of the three axes (which can also be 0, of course). Imagine, for a moment, a plain one-dimensional world. In such a world, you need only one value to describe a position, because such a one-dimensional world is comprised of just a row of single points attached together. You could think of a timeline as a one-dimensional world. You only need one coordinate to navigate in this world. With a specific date and a reference point (such as the birth of the universe), you can locate a specific point in time.

Actually, this is true only if there is indeed only one time and if there are no other universes existing in parallel using the same timeline in other dimensions. But I'm going off topic right now. Back to vectors. In a two-dimensional world, you need two coordinates to describe a certain position in this world. You can think of the earth's surface as a two-dimensional world. The height doesn't really matter; you would need values only for longitude and latitude.

Finally, welcome to the real three-dimensional world! Here you need three coordinates to specify an exact location in space (assuming you have an origin point of reference of the three axes in the world). I won't bother you anymore with vectoring stuff because I suppose you already know your business. However, let me just list here the two attributes that make a vector what it is. A vector has the following:

- A specific length (magnitude)
- A specific direction

Because a vector is so important for most of our work in the 3D graphics world, I will create a C++ class for vectors. The nice thing is that you can overload the operators in C++ and implement vector additions and the like pretty easily without the need to make an obvious function call in your code. Here is the vector class:

```
// file: zfx3d.h
class __declspec(dllexport) ZFXVector
   {
   public:
      float x, y, z, w;

      ZFXVector(void) { x=0, y=0, z=0, w=1.0f; }
      ZFXVector(float _x, float _y, float _z)
         { x = _x; y = _y; z = _z; w = 1.0f; }

      inline void  Set(float _x, float _y, float _z,
                       float _w=1.0f);
      inline float GetLength(void);
      inline float GetSqrLength(void) const;
      inline void  Negate(void);
      inline void  Normalize(void);
      inline float AngleWith(ZFXVector &v);
      inline void  Difference(const ZFXVector &u,
                              const ZFXVector &v);
      void operator += (const ZFXVector &v);
      void operator -= (const ZFXVector &v);
      void operator *= (float f);
      void operator /= (float f);
      float     operator * (ZFXVector &v) const;
      ZFXVector operator * (float f) const;
      ZFXVector operator * (ZFXMatrix &m) const;
      ZFXVector operator + (ZFXVector &v) const;
      ZFXVector operator - (ZFXVector &v) const;
```

```
        inline void Cross(const ZFXVector &u,
                          const ZFXVector &v);
};  // class
```

The `ZFXVector` class provides the most basic operations you want to perform on a vector. The first thing you will notice is that this class uses a four-dimensional vector rather than a three-dimensional one. This is the case because you need a four-dimensional vector to be able to multiply it with 4x4 matrices. However, normally the w component of this vector is not of any importance to us.

> **Tip**
>
> The C++ keyword operator enables you to overload certain operators. So you can really define functions that are called if someone uses an object of the given class together not only with a symbol (such as +, i, *, and /) but also with the = and == operators. It is also perfectly possible to use the – operator to perform an addition. But that would be stupid, to say the least.

Now I want to show you the implementations of this class. I won't go into much detail here about the math. If you do not already know about vector math, you can see how each of these operations work in the code.

> **Note**
>
> If you provide parameters to a function call, you should prefer a call by reference to a call by value. Otherwise, the computer has to create a copy of the parameter object on the stack, which is pretty time-consuming. This could also lead to errors if, for instance, you have an instance of a class that cannot be copied correctly if it is using dynamically allocated memory.

Basic Arithmetic Operations

If you overload a vector operator, such as the + sign, there are two different versions of this operator (in this case, + and +=). The difference is not just cosmetic; performance differs. With the + sign, you need to create a new object of the class and add the given two objects together. The creation of an object is the implicit call of the standard constructor. Then you need to return this new object, which results in copying the object over the stack. The += operator can use the instance's own attributes for the operation and store the result in those members. That is much faster than calling constructors and copying objects. Here is how those calls would look in the final code:

```
ZFXVector u, v, w; // filled with some values
w = u + v;
u += v;
```

The first case implicitly creates a new object and adds the components of u and v and stores the result in the new object, which is then copied into object w. The second case adds only v's components to those of u. Okay, that was the primer in operator overloading. Now you can start implementing the vector class. Watch out for our good friend SSE. I'm quite sure you will encounter SSE again pretty soon:

```
float _fabs(float f) {if (f<0.0f) return -f; return f;}

inline void ZFXVector::Set(float _x, float _y, float _z,
                           float _w) {
   x=_x; y=_y; z=_z; w=_w;
   }
/*------------------------------*/

void ZFXVector::operator += (const ZFXVector &v) {
   x += v.x;   y += v.y;   z += v.z;
   }
/*------------------------------*/

ZFXVector ZFXVector::operator + (const ZFXVector &v)
const {
    return ZFXVector(x+v.x, y+v.y, z+v.z);
    }
/*------------------------------*/

void ZFXVector::operator -= (const ZFXVector &v) {
   x -= v.x;   y -= v.y;   z -= v.z;
   }
/*------------------------------*/

ZFXVector ZFXVector::operator - (const ZFXVector &v)
const {
    return ZFXVector(x-v.x, y-v.y, z-v.z);
    }
/*------------------------------*/

void ZFXVector::operator *= (float f) {
   x *= f;   y *= f;   z *= f;
   }
/*------------------------------*/

void ZFXVector::operator /= (float f) {
   x /= f;   y /= f;   z /= f;
```

```
    }
/*------------------------------*/

ZFXVector ZFXVector::operator * (float f) const {
    return ZFXVector(x*f, y*f, z*f);
    }
/*------------------------------*/

float ZFXVector::operator * (const ZFXVector &v) const {
    return (v.x*x + v.y*y + v.z*z);
    }
/*------------------------------*/

inline float ZFXVector::GetSqrLength(void) const {
    return (x*x + y*y + z*z);
    }
/*------------------------------*/

inline void ZFXVector::Negate(void) {
    x = -x;   y = -y;   z = -z;
    }
/*------------------------------*/

inline void ZFXVector::Difference(const ZFXVector &u,
                                  const ZFXVector &v) {
    x = v2.x - v1.x;
    y = v2.y - v1.y;
    z = v2.z - v1.z;
    w = 1.0f;
    }
/*------------------------------*/

inline float ZFXVector::AngleWith(ZFXVector &v) {
    return (float)acos( ((*this) * v) /
            (this->GetLength()*v.GetLength()) );
    }
/*------------------------------*/
```

So you didn't discover good old SSE yet? And you ask yourself why. Why you fought all your way through the strange SIMD thing if you just don't use it here to add vectors or subtract them from each other. The answers are quite simple. SIMD is indeed fast. However, for every speed-up technique you can come up with one thing is true: If you use it in the wrong place, you will screw things up pretty bad. As you have seen earlier in this chapter, you must copy the data from the stack memory into the fast SSE registers. Then you can perform fast operations in the registers, and afterward you need to copy the results back from the XMM registers.

SIMD operations are fast, but not fast enough to copy the data around at least two times. If you have two copy operations and only one calculation operation (as in vector addition, for example), you can take it for granted that copying the data into SSE registers alone takes longer than applying the same operations three times for the single components in plain C++. You simply don't need a laser gun to fry doves.

The following section covers more complex operations on vectors that are pretty well suited as candidates for an additional code path using SSE.

Complex Vector Operations Using SSE

The function ZFXVector::GetSqrtLength, which you saw earlier, calculates only the squared length of a vector. If you are asking yourself why you need the squared length in vector math, then don't waste any more thoughts on it. In actuality, you don't really need the squared length of a vector for very many calculations. However, the problem is that calculating the real length of a vector involves a square root operation. Along with the trigonometric functions, the square root is the programmer's worst enemy when it comes down to math. Calculating the root of a number is a comparably slow operation, one you should avoid whenever possible.

Magnitude of a Vector

Now that you have read the word *slow*, just remember that slowness is fought best by speeding-up techniques. Again, SSE comes to mind. You can, in fact, come up with a function calculating the real length of a vector where the SSE version of the function is really faster than the C++ version:

```
inline float ZFXVector::GetLength(void) {
   float f;

   if (!g_bSSE) {
      f = (float)sqrt(x*x + y*y + z*z);
      }
   else {
      float *pf=&f;
      w = 0.0f;
      __asm {
            mov      ecx,    pf           ; point to result register
            mov      esi,    this         ; vector U
            movups   xmm0,   [esi]        ; vector U in XMM0
```

```
        mulps   xmm0,   xmm0           ; multiply
        movaps  xmm1,   xmm0           ; copy result
        shufps  xmm1,   xmm1, 4Eh      ; shuffle: f1,f0,f3,f2
        addps   xmm0,   xmm1
        movaps  xmm1,   xmm0           ; copy result
        shufps  xmm1,   xmm1, 11h
        addps   xmm0,   xmm1
        sqrtss  xmm0,   xmm0           ; square root
        movss   [ecx],  xmm0           ; move result to ECX which is f
        }
        w = 1.0f;
    }

    return f;
}
```

First of all, this function decides which code path to use. You still remember the global variable that knows whether the operating system and the processor support SSE at all, right? The if decision is the most simple one to implement, but using function pointers to different implementations would be faster, actually.

Note

Microsoft's D3DX math functions use different code paths as well. There are optimized versions of the math functions using 3DNow!, SSE, SSE2, and the like. The first call to a math function in D3DX starts the processor-evaluation process and then sets function pointers to the best-suited implementation. That is why the very first call to the D3DX library is always pretty slow.

In the SSE part of the function, you just put two pointers into normal registers. That is needed because you simply cannot use the result of an SSE calculation if it is still sitting inside an XMM register. Then you copy the data from this pointer, which is located in the ESI register, into an XMM register.

Note

To access the data behind an address located in an assembler register, you need to put the register's name into brackets [ ].

Now you multiply the contents of the register XMM0 with itself, as in this calculation:

[x*x   y*y   z*z   w*w]

The result of this operation is then copied into register XMM1 to be shuffled with 4Eh, which equals 01 00 11 10 according to Table 4.1. This will swap two components of the register that already contain the multiplied values. If you add this register to the register XMM0, you end up for now with the following values stored in XMM0:

```
[ x*x + z*z    y*y + w*w    z*z + x*x    w*w + y*y ]
```

And now you can already see what this kind of shuffling game aims at. Again, we copy this result into register XMM1 and play the shuffle game again (this time using 11h as shuffle value). We add the result back to register XMM0. Now each element of register XMM0 contains exactly the same value, which is the squared length of the vector, as follows:

```
x*x + y*y + z*z + w*w
```

It's kind of a waste that we have this value four times, because we need it only one time. Because of the parallel processing of SSE, however, the three additional calculations are free, and it would indeed be slower to copy single values only and do operations on them. The instruction SQRTSS is then used to calculate the square root of a single scalar value. That means that the instruction is performed on only the first element in the register. Equally, the instruction MOVSS copies only the first element of the register, which now contains the length of the vector, into the local variable that is returned at the end of the function. Congratulations, you just finished your very first SSE implementation successfully.

Note that the component w needs to be set to 0 before you can start the operation; otherwise, it will add to the length of the vector.

Normalizing a Vector

Normalizing a vector means that you want to make it have a length of one but maintain exactly the same direction as before. So you just need to scale the vector to unit length. You want this operation to be lightning fast; after all, it's one you will use frequently. Another candidate for SSE wizardry.

To bring a vector to unit length, calculate its length and then divide each component of the vector by the vector's length. This is pretty much the same as scaling down scalar numbers, which are more or less just one-dimensional vectors.

Because you are pretty clever, you can see that we have already calculated the length of a vector. So, you can use the same function just developed and apply a few changes to it. You don't actually have to calculate the square root; you can use another trick to make it faster. But first have a look at the code:

```
inline void ZFXVector::Normalize(void) {
   if (!g_bSSE) {
      float f = (float)sqrt(x*x + y*y + z*z);

      if (f != 0.0f) {
```

```
        x/=f; y/=f; z/=f;
        }
    }
    else {
        w = 0.0f;
        __asm {
            mov    esi,    this
            movups xmm0,   [esi]
            movaps xmm2,   xmm0
            mulps  xmm0,   xmm0
            movaps xmm1,   xmm0
            shufps xmm1,   xmm1, 4Eh
            addps  xmm0,   xmm1
            movaps xmm1,   xmm0
            shufps xmm1,   xmm1, 11h
            addps  xmm0,   xmm1

            rsqrtps xmm0,  xmm0      ; reciprocal square root
            mulps   xmm2,  xmm0      ; multiply
            movups  [esi], xmm2
        }
        w = 1.0f;
    }
}
```

Now think a bit about what you need to do. First you need to calculate the square root to get the length of the vector. Then you divide the vector by the result of the square root of some value a, as follows:

`vector / sqrt(a)`   <equals to>   `vector * 1 / sqrt(a)`

The last term, `1/sqrt`, is also called the reciprocal square root. The nice thing about it is that the processors have a lookup table with a list of results for this operation, accessible via the `rsqrtps` instruction. The lookup table doesn't always provide totally precise results, but normally it provides is a pretty good approximation that will serve your needs. So you just call this instruction and then multiply its result with the vector, which is then normalized. And that's it.

Tip

You could also normalize the vector by calculating the reciprocal square root using the instruction RSQRTSS for only the first component of the register and then broadcast the result into the whole register. However, doing so is slower than working with the lookup table. If you need to use the real square root, however, try this method.

Cross Product

Another operation you will perform frequently on vectors is the calculation of the cross product. If you have two arbitrarily oriented vectors in 3D space, you can build a third vector out of them by performing the cross-product operation. The interesting thing is that this third vector will be orthogonal to the other two, under the condition that the two vectors are not parallel.

An example of when you might need this operation is when you want to calculate the normal vector standing on a plane or on a polygon to calculate the lighting on this object. Again, the SSE version of this function is faster than the plain C++ version:

```
inline void ZFXVector::Cross(const ZFXVector &u, const ZFXVector &v)
   {
   if (!g_bSSE)
      {
      x = v1.y * v2.z - v1.z * v2.y;
      y = v1.z * v2.x - v1.x * v2.z;
      z = v1.x * v2.y - v1.y * v2.x;
      w = 1.0f;
      }
   else {
      __asm {
         mov esi, v1
         mov edi, v2

         movups xmm0, [esi]
         movups xmm1, [edi]
         movaps xmm2, xmm0
         movaps xmm3, xmm1

         shufps xmm0, xmm0, 0xc9
         shufps xmm1, xmm1, 0xd2
         mulps  xmm0, xmm1

         shufps xmm2, xmm2, 0xd2
         shufps xmm3, xmm3, 0xc9
         mulps  xmm2, xmm3

         subps  xmm0, xmm2

         mov    esi, this
         movups [esi], xmm0
         }
```

```
        w = 1.0f;
        }
    }
```

First you must copy the two vectors you want to cross into two XMM registers each. You must use one register to shuffle the data a bit and the other register to multiply the shuffled data with the original one. After that you have the correctly multiplied values sitting in registers XMM0 and XMM2. If you are a bit rusty on the cross-product operation, remind yourself by reviewing the C++ version of the code for this operation. As the final step, subtract the two vectors from each other by using the SUBPS instruction; this leads to the final result of the operation. This result is then copied to the address where this pointer is stored, thus making this object the result of the operation.

Note that the shuffle values use the prefix 0x rather than the suffix h, because otherwise the compiler would have trouble recognizing them as hexadecimal values. If shuffling is still somewhat confusing to you, take a pencil and a piece of paper and write down the contents of each register step by step. In the end, you will have the correct calculation, like the one in the C++ implementation path.

Vector Matrix Multiplication

Now that you are probably starting to get used to SIMD, here is one final operation. You'll often need to multiply a vector with a 4x4 matrix (hence the need for a fast operation to do so). You will implement the 4x4 matrix in the class called ZFXMatrix shortly, but for now just take it as an existing type in the math library.

Again, I suppose that you know how to multiply a vector with a matrix. If you're drawing a blank here, take a look at the C++ code path of the function to remind you:

```
ZFXVector ZFXVector::operator * (const ZFXMatrix &m)
const {
    ZFXVector vcResult;

    if (!g_bSSE) {
        vcResult.x = x*m._11 + y*m._21 + z*m._31 + m._41;
        vcResult.y = x*m._12 + y*m._22 + z*m._32 + m._42;
        vcResult.z = x*m._13 + y*m._23 + z*m._33 + m._43;
        vcResult.w = x*m._14 + y*m._24 + z*m._34 + m._44;

        vcResult.x = vcResult.x/vcResult.w;
        vcResult.y = vcResult.y/vcResult.w;
        vcResult.z = vcResult.z/vcResult.w;
        vcResult.w = 1.0f;
        }
```

```
    else {
        float *ptrRet = (float*)&vcResult;
        __asm {
            mov     ecx,    this        ; vector
            mov     edx,    m           ; matrix
            movss   xmm0,   [ecx]
            mov     eax,    ptrRet      ; result vector
            shufps  xmm0,   xmm0, 0
            movss   xmm1,   [ecx+4]
            mulps   xmm0,   [edx]
            shufps  xmm1,   xmm1, 0
            movss   xmm2,   [ecx+8]
            mulps   xmm1,   [edx+16]
            shufps  xmm2,   xmm2, 0
            movss   xmm3,   [ecx+12]
            mulps   xmm2,   [edx+32]
            shufps  xmm3,   xmm3, 0
            addps   xmm0,   xmm1
            mulps   xmm3,   [edx+48]
            addps   xmm2,   xmm3
            addps   xmm0,   xmm2
            movups  [eax],  xmm0        ; store as result
            mov     [eax+3], 1          ; w = 1
        }
    }
    return vcResult;
}
```

What you have learned about SSE should be enough to catch up with that implementation of a vector matrix multiplication. A lot of shuffling is occurring, but actually those are just broadcasts.

At this point, you have now worked your way through the vector class function by function and have mastered a lot of SSE implementations along the way. Always keep in mind that it is worth it to optimize all the things you use very often. *Very often*, in this case, means a hundred times per frame. Therefore, you should not be surprised that the vector class uses SSE optimizations for all of its functions that are the least bit complex. Now let's leave the vectors alone for a while and have a look at the matrix class, shall we?

Working with Matrices

Stories about matrices abound. What they are and what they are not. Who lives inside of them and who created them. In fact, most people new to linear algebra or 3D graphics math have some problems in understanding matrices. However, there is nothing spectacular about them. Just take matrices for what they really are: A 2D array of numbers. Nothing more and nothing less. Mathematicians can do a lot of strange things with matrices, but as far as I am concerned there is no better use for them than 3D graphics.

Matrices might not be as easy to visualize as vectors, but you will get used to them if you don't know them yet. As a reminder, you can perform several operations on vectors (for instance, translate them, rotate them, and scale them). Interestingly, you can combine all these operations into one transformation matrix and then just multiply the vector with that matrix. In actuality, this would save you a significant number of operations that would otherwise have to be done one by one on each vector.

That made clear here, it's time to take a look at the ZFXMatrix class:

```
// file: zfx3d.h
class __declspec(dllexport) ZFXMatrix
   {
   public:
      float _11, _12, _13, _14;
      float _21, _22, _23, _24;
      float _31, _32, _33, _34;
      float _41, _42, _43, _44;

      ZFXMatrix(void) { /* nothing to do */ ; }

      inline void Identity(void);       // make identity matrix
      inline void RotaX(float a);       // X-Axis
      inline void RotaY(float a);       // Y-Axis
      inline void RotaZ(float a);       // Z-Axis
      inline void RotaArbi(ZFXVector vcAxis, float a);
      inline void Translate(float dx, float dy, float dz);

      inline void TransposeOf(const ZFXMatrix &m);
      inline void InverseOf(const ZFXMatrix &m);

      ZFXMatrix operator * (const ZFXMatrix &m)  const;
      ZFXVector operator * (const ZFXVector &vc) const;
   }; // class
```

Basic Operations

As you can see, a matrix is nothing more than a collection of floating-point values. A matrix has a number of rows and columns. With regard to 3D computer graphics, you must always work with 4x4 matrices. (This book doesn't go into detail about this. For more information, take a look at some 3D graphics books or search the Internet.) The attributes in the matrix class are labeled _32, for example, which means that this element is in the third row and the second column of the matrix.

I list only the less-interesting functions here and don't insult you by explaining the obvious matrix things:

```
// build identity matrix
inline void ZFXMatrix::Identity(void) {
   float *f = (float*)&this->_11;
   memset(f, 0, sizeof(ZFXMatrix));
   _11 = _22 = _33 = _44 = 1.0f;
   }
/*---------------------------*/


// build rotation matrix around world X axis
inline void ZFXMatrix::RotaX(float a) {
   float fCos = cosf(a);
   float fSin = sinf(a);
   _22 =  fCos;
   _23 =  fSin;
   _32 = -fSin;
   _33 =  fCos;
   _11 = _44 = 1.0f;
   _12=_13=_14=_21=_24=_31=_34=_41=_42=_43=0.0f;
   }
/*---------------------------*/


// build rotation matrix around world Y axis
inline void ZFXMatrix::RotaY(float a) {
   float fCos = cosf(a);
   float fSin = sinf(a);

   _11 =  fCos;
   _13 = -fSin;
   _31 =  fSin;
   _33 =  fCos;

   _22 = _44 = 1.0f;
   _12 = _23 = _14 = _21 = _24 = _32 = _34 = _41 = _42 = _43 = 0.0f;
   }
/*---------------------------*/
```

```cpp
// build rotation matrix around world Z axis
inline void ZFXMatrix::RotaZ(float a) {
   float fCos = cosf(a);
   float fSin = sinf(a);
   _11 =  fCos;
   _12 =  fSin;
   _21 = -fSin;
   _22 =  fCos;
   _33 = _44 = 1.0f;
   _13=_14=_23=_24=_31=_32=_34=_41=_42=_43=0.0f;
   }
/*----------------------------*/

// build rotation matrix around arbitrary axis
inline void ZFXMatrix::RotaArbi(ZFXVector vcAxis, float a) {
   float fCos = cosf(a);
   float fSin = sinf(a);
   float fSum = 1.0f - fCos;

   vcAxis.Normalize();

   _11 = (vcAxis.x*vcAxis.x) * fSum + fCos;
   _12 = (vcAxis.x*vcAxis.y) * fSum - (vcAxis.z*fSin);
   _13 = (vcAxis.x*vcAxis.z) * fSum + (vcAxis.y*fSin);

   _21 = (vcAxis.y*vcAxis.x) * fSum + (vcAxis.z*fSin);
   _22 = (vcAxis.y*vcAxis.y) * fSum + fCos ;
   _23 = (vcAxis.y*vcAxis.z) * fSum - (vcAxis.x*fSin);

   _31 = (vcAxis.z*vcAxis.x) * fSum - (vcAxis.y*fSin);
   _32 = (vcAxis.z*vcAxis.y) * fSum + (vcAxis.x*fSin);
   _33 = (vcAxis.z*vcAxis.z) * fSum + fCos;

   _14 = _24 = _34 = _41 = _42 = _43 = 0.0f;
   _44 = 1.0f;
   }
/*----------------------------*/

// add translation values to the matrix
inline void ZFXMatrix::Translate(float dx, float dy, float dz) {
   _41 = dx;
   _42 = dy;
```

```
        _43 = dz;
        }
/*--------------------------*/

// build transposed matrix which is mirrored on the main axis
inline void ZFXMatrix::TransposeOf(const ZFXMatrix &m) {
    _11 = m._11;
    _21 = m._12;
    _31 = m._13;
    _41 = m._14;

    _12 = m._21;
    _22 = m._22;
    _32 = m._23;
    _42 = m._24;

    _13 = m._31;
    _23 = m._32;
    _33 = m._33;
    _43 = m._34;

    _14 = m._41;
    _24 = m._42;
    _34 = m._43;
    _44 = m._44;
    }
/*--------------------------*/
```

More functions are defined in the class ZFXMatrix, but it's not important for our purposes to go into more of them here. You have already seen how to multiply a vector with a matrix. The multiplication of two matrices is a bit more complex (and so I used an SSE implementation there). The same applies for the matrix inversion, which is a very lengthy function in SSE as well as in plain C++. Check your favorite math book and have a look at the code on the accompanying CD-ROM to see how this is done. This chapter just focuses on things you would not learn in most other books about graphics programming.

Now we proceed to rays, collision detection, and more advanced things like that. Give yourself a short break, however, and take a look at the whole implementation of the matrix class on the accompanying CD-ROM.

Working with Rays

Besides vectors and matrices, programmers often use a lot of other mathematical or geometrical objects, including rays, in 3D computer graphics and applications. Rays may not be that obvious while you are working on a 3D application; if you start working on a video game and encounter collision detection and things like that, however, you will be very pleased that you have them at your disposal.

Rays are a perfect match if you need to do collision detection for pretty small and pretty fast objects. And what kind of object would be smaller and faster than a bullet? However, rays are also needed to do picking of 3D objects, which actually means to be able to select objects by firing rays at them. In a 3D editor, for example, you want to click on the screen and select the object the cursor is pointing at. To do this, you need picking.

In case you have never heard of a ray, here are some basics. From a mathematical point of view, a ray is nothing more than a certain part of a line. A line is a rather one-dimensional object running from +infinity to −infinity at some angle and some location in space. A ray is similar to a line, except that it has a specific starting point, called the origin. From this origin, it runs in a specific direction, but it has infinite length as well. Another brother of those two objects is a line segment. A line segment is pretty similar to a ray, but it runs only for a specific distance. So, actually, you have two specific points in space, and the connection between them is the line segment.

Don't worry; this implementation sticks to rays. Line segments are sometimes required in collision detection, but you can always check a reference value against the length such a segment would have. You'll learn how to do that soon. For now, just take a look at the ZFXRay class implementing this object in the math library:

```
class __declspec(dllexport) ZFXRay {
   public:
      ZFXVector m_vcOrig,   // origin
                m_vcDir;    // direction

      ZFXRay(void) { /* nothing to do */ ; }

      inline void Set(ZFXVector vcOrig, ZFXVector vcDir);
      inline void DeTransform(const ZFXMatrix &m);

      // intersecting triangles
      bool Intersects(const ZFXVector &vc0,
                      const ZFXVector &vc1,
                      const ZFXVector &vc2, bool bCull,
                      float *t);
      bool Intersects(const ZFXVector &vc0,
```

```
                        const ZFXVector &vc1,
                        const ZFXVector &vc2, bool bCull,
                        float fL, float *t);

   // intersecting planes
   bool Intersects(const ZFXPlane &plane, bool bCull,
                   float *t, ZFXVector *vcHit);
   bool Intersects(const ZFXPlane &plane, bool bCull,
                   float fL, float *t,
                   ZFXVector *vcHit);

   // intersecting aabb
   bool Intersects(const ZFXAabb &aabb, ZFXVector *vcHit);

   // intersecting obb
   bool Intersects(const ZFXObb &obb, float *t);
   bool Intersects(const ZFXObb &obb, float fL, float *t);
   }; // class
```

In this class you can see two important things. The first one is that it is already using other objects from the math library, such as ZFXPlane and bounding boxes like ZFXAabb and ZFXObb. The other thing is that some of the functions are overloaded, featuring one additional parameter float fL. This one is used to give the ray a certain length for the call, which will effectively make the ray a line segment for this operation. For now, though, let's work through the functions one by one.

Basic Operations

A ray has just two attributes: an origin in space, and the direction it is running. This direction has to be normalized, but I want the user of a ray to ensure the normalization. Normalizing a vector is an expensive operation; in most instances, the user will already have a normalized vector he wants to build a ray from. That is why the following code to set the attributes of a ray will not check for normalization or renormalize the direction:

```
inline void ZFXRay::Set(ZFXVector vcOrig, ZFXVector vcDir)
   {
   m_vcOrig = vcOrig;
   m_vcDir  = vcDir;
   }
```

One of the most common operations for which you need to employ rays is collision detection. Normally, however, each separate 3D model is defined in its own local coordinate space relative to its own local origin. You call that model coordinates, local coordinates, or object coordinates. Then you use a transformation matrix while rendering the model so that it is transformed according to its current position and rotation to be in what is called world coordinates. This transformation is done on the graphics hardware, so normally you would not have the vertices of a model stored in world coordinates.

This creates a problem for collision detection. Each model uses a different coordinate space, and if you want to perform collision detection you have to use the same frame of reference (meaning the same coordinate system). The colliding objects (such as the ray) will mostly be given in world coordinates. One way to do collision detection is to transform all vertices of the model with its current transformation matrix on the CPU to have the model in world space. A pretty good working method, but pretty slow.

Instead of transforming hundreds of vertices by multiplying them with a matrix, you could reach the same result by multiplying just two vectors. How? Actually, it's pretty easy. You don't have to use the world space, you just need to use the same coordinate space. So why not leave the model in its local coordinates and transform the ray into the coordinate system of the model? It's quite easy, by the way, as you can see here:

```
inline void ZFXRay::DeTransform(const ZFXMatrix &_m)
   {
   ZFXMatrix mInv;
   ZFXMatrix m=_m;

   // inverse translation
   m_vcOrig.x -= m._41;
   m_vcOrig.y -= m._42;
   m_vcOrig.z -= m._43;

   // delete translation in the matrix
   m._41=0.0f;   m._42=0.0f;   m._43=0.0f;

   // invert matrix
   mInv.Inverse(&m);

   // apply inverse matrix
   m_vcOrig = m_vcOrig * mInv;
   m_vcDir  = m_vcDir  * mInv;
   }
```

This function takes a transformation matrix containing rotation and translation values. This could be a transformation matrix for a model. The ray is supposed to be in the world coordinate system. To transform the ray to the local coordinates of the model where the matrix comes from, you need to do the following things. First, you take the translation from the matrix and invert it by negating the values. Keep in mind the first three entries of the fourth row of a matrix store the translation values. Second, you apply this inverse translation to the origin of the ray. Then invert the transformation matrix, but make sure not to have any translation values in the matrix any more. Keep in mind that the direction vector *must not be* translated, because it only says something about the direction of the ray and not about a position in space. Finally, you apply the inverse transformation matrix, which now contains rotations only.

Now the ray is effectively transformed into the local coordinate system of an object that uses the given matrix as the transformation matrix to world space. With the ray being in the same frame of reference as this object, you could now perform collision detection between the two of them.

Tip

To perform collision detection or a similar comparison operation on two objects, both of them must be located in the very same coordinate system. To transform object A from world space into the coordinate space of object B, you need to apply the inverse world transformation matrix from object B to object A.

Intersections with Triangles

Now that you know how to transform a ray to the local coordinate system of an object, suppose you have a model and want to check for an intersection with a ray. To be very exact, you would need to loop through all triangles of the model and check each one of them for an intersection with the ray. The following function utilizes a quite fast algorithm from Möller and Trumbore. The algorithm works basically by translating the triangle to the origin of the coordinate system and makes it a unit triangle in the y and the z plane. The ray will be aligned on the x plane, thus making it easy to check for an intersection, as follows:

```
bool ZFXRay::Intersects(const ZFXVector vc0, const ZFXVector vc1,
                        const ZFXVector vc2, bool bCull, float *t)
   {
   ZFXVector pvec, tvec, qvec;

   ZFXVector edge1 = vc1 - vc0;
   ZFXVector edge2 = vc2 - vc0;

   pvec.Cross(m_vcDir, edge2);

   // if close to 0 ray is parallel
   float det = edge1 * pvec;

   // to account for poor float precision use
```

```cpp
   // so called epsilon value of 0.0001 instead
   // of comparing to exactly 0
   if ( (bCull) && (det < 0.0001f) )
      return false;
   else if ( (det < 0.0001f) && (det > -0.0001f) )
      return false;

   // distance to plane, < 0 means ray behind the plane
   tvec = m_vcOrig - vc0;
   float u = tvec * pvec;
   if (u < 0.0f || u > det)
      return false;

   qvec.Cross(tvec, edge1);
   float v = m_vcDir * qvec;
   if (v < 0.0f || u+v > det)
      return false;

   if (t) {
      *t = edge2 * qvec;
      float fInvDet = 1.0f / det;
      *t *= fInvDet;
      }
   return true;
   } // Intersects(Tri)
```

As you can see, not much math is involved, at least nothing that would be slow. Hence this is a very fast operation using only two cross products, some comparisons, and some multiplication and division in the worst case. A very nice outcome of the algorithm is the value this function stores in the floating-point parameter t if this pointer is given to the function. This value is the exact distance from the ray origin to the point of intersection. With this value at hand, you can calculate the point of intersection by multiplying this distance with the ray's direction and add this vector to the origin of the ray. It's really nice to place an explosion or bullet hole at this point in space.

Sometimes you will just want to check for an intersection with a line segment. The intersection with a ray would calculate any intersection no matter how far away from the ray's origin it is. This is nice for picking, for example, but if you want to know whether a laser beam hit a target, you need to take the laser's maximum firing distance into account. Therefore, you need to check for a collision of a line segment (from the laser gun's barrel to its maximum firing range). Using the parameter t, you can calculate this afterward. I like my functions to be very handy, however, so I added this function:

```
bool ZFXRay::Intersects(const ZFXVector vc0, const ZFXVector vc1,
                        const ZFXVector vc2, bool bCull,
                        float fL, float *t);
```

It is more or less the same as the one above. The only difference is that there is a new parameter, fL, which is the length of the ray on which you want to check for an intersection. If there happens to be an intersection between the ray and the triangle, the distance to the point of intersection is compared to the given length of the line segment you want to check. If it is greater than this length, there is no intersection on this segment with the given triangle.

Intersections with Planes

Even if the intersection of a ray with a triangle can be calculated very fast, this method suffers from one drawback. Every 3D model normally has thousands of triangles, and a 3D game usually has about a hundred models that would need to be checked for an intersection. So, even a very fast method is very slow if you perform it thousands of times each frame. Normally you would check only for an intersection of a ray with the triangles of a model if you know for sure that an intersection is likely.

But how do you know that? It's quite simple. You have some easier bounding volumes containing one (or even more) model(s) each. Such a bounding volume would be a simple cube or sphere. You can check this simple geometry for an intersection with a ray. Only if there is an intersection do you check the real triangles of the model for an intersection.

Okay, that said, we need to have intersection methods for a bunch of other objects as well. Here is the full story about the intersection between a ray and a plane:

```
bool ZFXRay::Intersects(const ZFXPlane &plane, bool bCull,
                        float *t, ZFXVector *vcHit)
   {
   float Vd = plane.m_vcN * m_vcDir;

   // ray parallel to the plane
   if (_fabs(Vd) < 0.00001f)
      return false;

   // plane normal point away from ray direction
   // => intersection with back face if any
   if (bCull && (Vd > 0.0f))
      return false;

   float Vo = -( (plane.m_vcN * m_vcOrig) + plane.m_fD);
```

```
    float _t = Vo / Vd;

    // intersection before ray origin
    if (_t < 0.0f)
       return false;

    if (vcHit) {
       (*vcHit) = m_vcOrig + (m_vcDir * _t);
       }

    if (t)
       (*t) = _t;

    return true;
    } // Intersects(Plane)
```

This function is also pretty short, and you can skip certain calculations if you don't want to know about the collision distance and the actual point of intersection. Just set the according parameters to NULL. Such a collision function is really helpful if you are working with binary space partitioning trees or similar data structures working a lot with rays. This is covered later in Chapter 13, "Scene Management."

Again, I want to have the same functionality for a line segment. On the CD-ROM, you will find the following function including the length of the line segment you want to check for an intersection:

```
bool ZFXRay::Intersects(const ZFXPlane &plane, bool bCull, float fL,
                       float *t, ZFXVector *vcHit);
```

It is basically the very same implementation as earlier, but now you just add a logical or comparison to the check for _t being smaller than 0. The check for the value of _t should look like this:

```
if ( (_t < 0.0f)  ||  (_t > fL) ) return false;
```

In this case, false is returned if the intersection at distance _t occurs either before the ray starts or beyond the specified length we want to check.

Now it's time to leave the playgrounds and head to the most important function related to collision detection between rays and models: the intersection function for rays against bounding boxes. As mentioned previously, each 3D model has a bounding box that enables you to check for an intersection much more quickly than checking the thousands of triangles of the model itself. If there is no intersection between the bounding box and the ray, none of the model's triangles could be intersected by the ray.

Intersections with Bounding Boxes

To fully understand bounding boxes, you need to know that there are two kinds of them. The easier one to calculate is the axis-aligned bounding box (AABB). This kind of box is aligned to the world coordinate axis, which makes it very easy to calculate. You just loop through all vertices of the model you want to have the box for and store the maximum and the minimum extend value for all three axes. As compared to the second kind of boxes, the oriented bounding boxes (OBBs), an AABB is not as precise because it will not fit optimally to a model that is somehow straddling the world axes.

An OBB is aligned to the local axis of the model and its object space, thus making it fit tighter around the model. However, don't mistake AABBs as useless. Actually, they are even more important than OBBs because their advantage is that they are much more easy to calculate than OOBs. Another advantage is that some data structures, such as the octree, are virtually built around using AABB. When we implement an octree later on, you will be quite happy to have a comprehensive class for AABB.

The following function is a version of Andrew Woo's algorithm to check for an intersection with a ray and an AABB. It appears to be rather lengthy, but take a closer look at it. I just unrolled the loop and treated every coordinate separately, so the same code repeats three times, using just another one of the x, y, and z coordinates:

```
bool ZFXRay::Intersects(const ZFXAabb &aabb, ZFXVector *vcHit)
   {
   bool bInside = true;
   ZFXVector MaxT;

   MaxT.Set(-1.0f, -1.0f, -1.0f);

   // find the x component
   if (m_vcOrig.x < aabb.vcMin.x) {
      (*vcHit).x = aabb.vcMin.x;
      bInside = false;
      if (m_vcDir.x != 0.0f)
         MaxT.x = (aabb.vcMin.x - m_vcOrig.x) / m_vcDir.x;
      }
   else if (m_vcOrig.x > aabb.vcMax.x) {
      (*vcHit).x = aabb.vcMax.x;
      bInside = false;
      if (m_vcDir.x != 0.0f)
         MaxT.x = (aabb.vcMax.x - m_vcOrig.x) / m_vcDir.x;
      }

   // find the y component
```

```
      if (m_vcOrig.y < aabb.vcMin.y) {
         (*vcHit).y = aabb.vcMin.y;
         bInside = false;
         if (m_vcDir.y != 0.0f)
            MaxT.y = (aabb.vcMin.y - m_vcOrig.y) / m_vcDir.y;
         }
      else if (m_vcOrig.y > aabb.vcMax.y) {
         (*vcHit).y = aabb.vcMax.y;
         bInside = false;
         if (m_vcDir.y != 0.0f)
            MaxT.y = (aabb.vcMax.y - m_vcOrig.y) / m_vcDir.y;
         }

      // find the z component
      if (m_vcOrig.z < aabb.vcMin.z) {
         (*vcHit).z = aabb.vcMin.z;
         bInside = false;
         if (m_vcDir.z != 0.0f)
            MaxT.z = (aabb.vcMin.z - m_vcOrig.z) / m_vcDir.z;
         }
      else if (m_vcOrig.z > aabb.vcMax.z) {
         (*vcHit).z = aabb.vcMax.z;
         bInside = false;
         if (m_vcDir.z != 0.0f)
            MaxT.z = (aabb.vcMax.z - m_vcOrig.z) / m_vcDir.z;
         }

      // ray origin inside the box
      if (bInside) {
         (*vcHit) = m_vcOrig;
         return true;
         }

      // find maximum value for maxT
      int nPlane = 0;

      if (MaxT.y > ((float*)&MaxT)[nPlane]) nPlane = 1;
      if (MaxT.z > ((float*)&MaxT)[nPlane]) nPlane = 2;

      if ( ((float*)&MaxT)[nPlane] < 0.0f) return false;

      if (nPlane != 0) {
```

```
         (*vcHit).x = m_vcOrig.x + MaxT.x * m_vcDir.x;
         if ( ((*vcHit).x < aabb.vcMin.x-0.00001f) ||
              ((*vcHit).x < aabb.vcMax.x+0.00001f) )
            return false;
         }
      if (nPlane != 1) {
         (*vcHit).y = m_vcOrig.y + MaxT.y * m_vcDir.y;
         if ( ((*vcHit).y < aabb.vcMin.y-0.00001f) ||
              ((*vcHit).y < aabb.vcMax.y+0.00001f) )
            return false;
         }
      if (nPlane != 0) {
         (*vcHit).z = m_vcOrig.z + MaxT.z * m_vcDir.z;
         if ( ((*vcHit).z < aabb.vcMin.z-0.00001f) ||
              ((*vcHit).z < aabb.vcMax.z+0.00001f) )
            return false;
         }
      return true;
      } // Intersects(Aabb)
```

As you can see, this method is very fast due to the lack of complicated calculations used. Everything just boils down to comparisons, additions, and subtractions. Note that this algorithm also deals with cases where the ray origin is sitting inside the bounding box. This is important to know because the point of intersection will then be returned as the origin of the vector.

Now for the second kind of bounding box. You are going to see the ZFXObb class in a moment, but for now just believe me that it does exist. If you want to check for an intersection between a ray and an OBB, a quite fast algorithm is available. Well, actually, more than just one is available, but this one best serves our needs. The following algorithm, called the *slabs method*, was developed by Möller and Haines. A loop could certainly be used to shorten this function; unrolling small loops is a minor optimization, however, so this is just three times the same code for different coordinates:

```
bool ZFXRay::Intersects(const ZFXObb *pObb, float *t)
   {
   float e, f, t1, t2, temp;
   float tmin = -99999.9f,
         tmax = +99999.9f;

   ZFXVector vcP = pObb->vcCenter - m_vcOrig;

   // 1. Slap
   e = pObb->vcA0 * vcP;
```

```
   f = pObb->vcA0 * m_vcDir;

// otherwise ray parallel to plane normal
if (_fabs(f) > 0.00001f) {

   t1 = (e + pObb->fA0) / f;
   t2 = (e - pObb->fA0) / f;

   if (t1 > t2) { temp=t1; t1=t2; t2=temp; }
   if (t1 > tmin) tmin = t1;
   if (t2 < tmax) tmax = t2;
   if (tmin > tmax) return false;
   if (tmax < 0.0f) return false;
   }
else if ( ((-e - pObb->fA0) > 0.0f) ||
          ((-e + pObb->fA0) < 0.0f) )
   return false;

// 2. Slap
e = pObb->vcA1 * vcP;
f = pObb->vcA1 * m_vcDir;
if (_fabs(f) > 0.00001f) {

   t1 = (e + pObb->fA1) / f;
   t2 = (e - pObb->fA1) / f;

   if (t1 > t2) { temp=t1; t1=t2; t2=temp; }
   if (t1 > tmin) tmin = t1;
   if (t2 < tmax) tmax = t2;
   if (tmin > tmax) return false;
   if (tmax < 0.0f) return false;
   }
else if ( ((-e - pObb->fA1) > 0.0f) ||
          ((-e + pObb->fA1) < 0.0f) )
   return false;

// 3. Slap
e = pObb->vcA2 * vcP;
f = pObb->vcA2 * m_vcDir;
if (_fabs(f) > 0.00001f) {

   t1 = (e + pObb->fA2) / f;
```

```
            t2 = (e - pObb->fA2) / f;

            if (t1 > t2) { temp=t1; t1=t2; t2=temp; }
            if (t1 > tmin) tmin = t1;
            if (t2 < tmax) tmax = t2;
            if (tmin > tmax) return false;
            if (tmax < 0.0f) return false;
            }
      else if ( ((-e - pObb->fA2) > 0.0f) ||
                ((-e + pObb->fA2) < 0.0f) )
         return false;

      if (tmin > 0.0f) {
         if (t) *t = tmin;
         return true;
         }
      if (t) *t = tmax;
      return true;
      }
```

Just like Woo's method for AABB, this is pretty fast because it uses only basic math operations and comparisons. No slow math functions are involved here. Basically, the algorithm calculates intersections between the ray and two planes defined by the box's sides closest to the ray. Both planes are hit for sure, but the ray hits the plane closer to its origin before it hits the other plane it intersects on this side of the bounding box. This slap test could also be used for the intersection between a ray and an AABB.

You can use the same function to test for an intersection between an OBB and a line segment. You just need to provide the length of the line segment to the intersection method and, before you return the value of t as the distance to the point of intersection, you just compare its value against this length. The accompanying CD-ROM includes this function. It's not printed out here because except for one addition comparison, it is the same as the one used for a ray to infinity. Its function declaration looks like this:

```
bool ZFXRay::Intersects(const ZFXObb *pObb, float fL, float *t);
```

Now we will let the rays be rays and move on to the next topic. Our math library is getting bigger and bigger with each page of this chapter. Although it's now starting to become a real tool we can work with, we still have some way to go before we are really done with it. Next stop, the planes in 3D space.

Working with Planes

Planes are also a quite abstract concept because they are areas with an infinite extend. Just think of a wall made of glass. But this wall has no border at all. It extends to the sides and up and down to infinity. And that's all there is to say about planes.

Well, not really. You can say a lot more about planes, and this is why we are here. You can define a plane with two vectors and say that those vectors are building the plane. The two vectors can be arbitrary, but they must not be parallel. Otherwise the plane would collapse into a line.

That said, a plane is like a disc in the space with an infinite radius and with an infinitely small thickness. To describe such a plane from a mathematical point of view, you need only three things, as the following formula shows:

```
V * N + d = 0
```

The symbol d is a variable that contains the shortest distance from the plane to the world coordinate system's origin. The symbol N stands for the normal vector of the plane. Just like a polygon, a plane has a front face and a back face. That becomes important if you define a volume bounded by planes and if you want to check whether an object is inside or outside of this volume. The same applies if you have a binary space partitioning tree (hang on until the scene management chapter) and want to check whether you are on the front side of a wall or on its back side. The side of the plane on which the normal vector resides and is pointing out of it is said to be the front side. By switching the normal's direction, you can flip the front face and back face attribute of a plane.

> **Note**
>
> A normal vector is a vector standing orthogonal on a plane. This is not to be mistaken with a normalized vector, which would mean that the vector just has a unit length of one. Although it is true that a normal vector should be normalized to simplify calculations involving the normal, a *normalized* vector does not necessarily mean that it is a *normal* vector.

The variable V in the formula is a vector of a point sitting on this plane. It really doesn't matter where it is located as long as it lies somewhere on the plane. If you want to know whether a given point lies on the plane, you only have to insert it into the formula and calculate its dot product with the plane's normal and add the distance d to the result. If the result equals 0, the point lies on the plane.

Another topic related to this plane equation is quite important. Now that you know that a plane has both a front side and a back side, you can move on and classify points with regard to a plane and on which side of the plane (if any) they are residing. A point could also be sitting on the plane, as you just learned. If the result of the formula is greater than

0, the point is on the plane's front side. If the result is less than 0, the point is on the plane's back side. You will need such a classification when you start dealing with binary space partitioning trees.

Enough of this theory, let's get back to code. Here is what the plane class looks like:

```
class __declspec(dllexport) ZFXPlane
   {
   public:
      ZFXVector m_vcN,        // normal vector
                m_vcPoint;    // point on plane
      float     m_fD;         // distance


      ZFXPlane(void) { /* nothing to do */ ; }

      inline void  Set(const ZFXVector &vcN,
                       const ZFXVector &vcPoint);
      inline void  Set(const ZFXVector &vcN,
                       const ZFXVector &vcPoint,
                       float fD);
      inline void Set(const ZFXVector &v0,
                      const ZFXVector &v1,
                      const ZFXVector &v2);

      // distance of a point to the plane
      inline float Distance(const ZFXVector &vcPoint);

      // classifying a point with respect to plane
      inline int   Classify(const ZFXVector &vcPoint);

      // intersection with a triangle
      bool Intersects(const ZFXVector &vc0,
                      const ZFXVector &vc1,
                      const ZFXVector &vc2);

      // intersection line of two planes
      bool Intersects(ZFXPlane &plane,
                      ZFXRay *pIntersection);

      // intersection with aabb / obb
      bool Intersects(const ZFXAabb &aabb);
      bool Intersects(const ZFXObb &obb);
   }; // class
```

We don't actually need that much functionality in our plane class right now. However, besides just classifying points with respect to the plane, in many cases you'll want to calculate the distance of a point to this plane (hence the according function). The remaining functions are all meant to deal with intersection detection between the plane and several other geometrical objects. Here you can see the importance of collision detection in 3D computer graphics applications. You have already seen the plane being used as collision partner in the ZFXRay class, too. You could also mirror that functionality in this class, but I want to keep it as small as possible so that you are not overwhelmed by bunches of overloaded versions of the Intersection() function.

Basic Operations

Most of the plane's basic operations can be done using the plane equation shown earlier. Therefore, the implementations shown here are comprised of just a few lines of code each. It's enough for you to see what's going on:

```
#define ZFXFRONT    0
#define ZFXBACK     1
#define ZFXPLANAR   2

// set plane's values but calculate distance to origin
inline void ZFXPlane::Set(const ZFXVector &vcN, const ZFXVector &vcPoint)
   {
   m_fD      = - ( vcN * vcPoint);
   m_vcN     = vcN;
   m_vcPoint = vcPoint;
   }
/*---------------------------*/

// set all plane's values directly
inline void ZFXPlane::Set(const ZFXVector &vcN, const ZFXVector &vcPoint,
                          float fD)
   {
   m_vcN     = vcN;
   m_fD      = fD;
   m_vcPoint = vcPoint;
   }
/*---------------------------*/

// calculate plane from three points forming two vectors
inline void ZFXPlane::Set(const ZFXVector &v0, const ZFXVector &v1,
                          const 7FXVector &v2)
   {
```

```
    ZFXVector vcEdge1 = v1 - v0;
    ZFXVector vcEdge2 = v2 - v0;

    m_vcN.Cross(vcEdge1, vcEdge2);
    m_fD = m_vcN * v0;
    }
/*------------------------------*/

// Calculate distance point to plane
// normal vector needs to be normalized
inline float ZFXPlane::Distance(const ZFXVector &vcP)
    {
    return ( _fabs((m_vcN*vcP) - m_fD) );
    }
/*------------------------------*/

// classify a point with respect to the plane
inline int ZFXPlane::Classify(const ZFXVector &vcP)
    {
    float f = (vcP * m_vcN) + m_fD;

    if (f >  0.00001) return ZFXFRONT;
    if (f < -0.00001) return ZFXBACK;
    return ZFXPLANAR;
    }
/*------------------------------*/
```

This should clear up any questions you might have about the plane equation and how to apply it. Now let's move on to the intersection functions of the plane class. You will need those while implementing scene management algorithms and things like that.

Intersections with Triangles

The calculation you need to do to decide whether a triangle has collided with a plane is actually pretty easy. A triangle consists of three points, and the plane class has a function to decide on which side of the plane a given point lies. If the triangle collides with the plane, all three points of the triangle will not be on the same side of the plane. Or to put it the other way round: A triangle does not intersect a plane if all three points of the triangle lie on the same side of the plane:

```
bool ZFXPlane::Intersects(const ZFXVector &vc0, const ZFXVector &vc1,
                          const ZFXVector &vc2)
    {
```

```
   int n = this->Classify(vc0);

   if ( (n == this->Classify(vc1)) && (n == this->Classify(vc2)) )
      return false;

   return true;
   } // Intersects(Tri)
```

Caution

The method `ZFXPlane::Intersects`, which checks for the intersection of a triangle with a plane, will also report an intersection if the triangle merely touches the plane. That means that at least one vertex lies on the plane and not yet on a different side than the other two points. Some applications might not want to interpret this as an intersection.

Intersections Between Planes

Interestingly, you can also calculate whether two planes are colliding. As you know, planes are extending themselves to infinity, so there is only one case in which two planes do not intersect each other: if both planes are parallel. If the planes intersect, however, the intersection has the form of a line, not a single point. But that should be obvious.

The following code is based on an implementation by David Eberly. The test for an intersection is actually pretty simple. To check for the parallel case, you only need to build the cross product of the planes' normal vectors. If the resulting vector of this cross product operation is the zero vector, you know the planes are parallel.

Tip

Check out David Eberly's website at www.magic-software.com. It contains lots of source code and mathematical papers about 3D graphics in general and intersection detection in particular.

```
bool ZFXPlane::Intersects(const ZFXPlane &plane, ZFXRay *pIntersection)
   {
   ZFXVector vcCross;
   float     fSqrLength;

   // if cross product equals 0 planes are parallel
   vcCross.Cross(this->m_vcN, plane.m_vcN);
   fSqrLength = vcCross.GetSqrLength();

   if (fSqrLength < 1e-08f)
      return false;
```

```
// intersection line if needed
if (pIntersection) {
   float fN00 = this->m_vcN.GetSqrLength();
   float fN01 = this->m_vcN * plane.m_vcN;
   float fN11 = plane.m_vcN.GetSqrLength();
   float fDet = fN00*fN11 - fN01*fN01;

   if (_fabs(fDet) < 1e-08f)
      return false;

   float fInvDet = 1.0f/fDet;
   float fC0 = (fN11*this->m_fD - fN01*plane.m_fD) *
               fInvDet;
   float fC1 = (fN00*plane.m_fD - fN01*this->m_fD) *
               fInvDet;

   (*pIntersection).m_vcDir  = vcCross;
   (*pIntersection).m_vcOrig = this->m_vcN * fC0
                             + plane.m_vcN * fC1;
   }
return true;
} // Intersects(Plane)
```

Most of this function is needed only if you want to know the intersection line (because calculating it requires more than just a few steps). Therefore, you should only ask for the intersection lines if you really need that data. The rest of the function is as easy as it gets.

Intersections with Bounding Boxes

To end this discussion about planes, I just want to show you how to calculate intersections between planes and bounding boxes. Because we are working with two types of bounding boxes, we need two different implementations here. Although you can still convert the AABB into an OBB or vice versa and use only one function, you need to know that each of the box types has its own advantage. In general, AABBs are always much easier to build and to calculate with than OBBs. On the other hand, OBBs deliver better results because they are approximating rough objects generally better than AABBs.

Let's start with the code for detecting an intersection between an AABB and a plane, shall we? The first thing you will notice is that the code is quite long. Actually, it is much longer than the code needed for an OBB. However, don't let the length of the code fool you. The function for the AABB is a very fast one because it is using only comparisons and only two dot products and additions in the worst case scenario. Here it comes:

```cpp
bool ZFXPlane::Intersects(const ZFXAabb &aabb) {
   ZFXVector Vmin, Vmax;

   // x-coordinate
   if (m_vcN.x >= 0.0f) {
      Vmin.x = aabb.vcMin.x;
      Vmax.x = aabb.vcMax.x;
      }
   else {
      Vmin.x = aabb.vcMax.x;
      Vmax.x = aabb.vcMin.x;
      }

   // y- coordinate
   if (m_vcN.y >= 0.0f) {
      Vmin.y = aabb.vcMin.y;
      Vmax.y = aabb.vcMax.y;
      }
   else {
      Vmin.y = aabb.vcMax.y;
      Vmax.y = aabb.vcMin.y;
      }

   // z- coordinate
   if (m_vcN.z >= 0.0f) {
      Vmin.z = aabb.vcMin.z;
      Vmax.z = aabb.vcMax.z;
      }
   else {
      Vmin.z = aabb.vcMax.z;
      Vmax.z = aabb.vcMin.z;
      }

   if ( ((m_vcN * Vmin) + m_fD) > 0.0f)
      return false;

   if ( ((m_vcN * Vmax) + m_fD) >= 0.0f)
      return true;

   return false;
   } // Intersects(AABB)
```

This algorithm can be found in Möller and Haines's book *Realtime Rendering*, and it's actually pretty smart. You decide for each coordinate which point of the AABB is closer to the plane by checking the orientation of the normal on the same coordinate. Then you build a minimum and a maximum vector of the AABB with respect to the plane. That means you have the point from the box that is closest to the plane and the one that is the most far away. By just inserting these points into the plane equation and checking the result, you can decide on which side of the plane the points lie. If the closest point is already on the front side, there is no intersection. Otherwise, an intersection occurs if the other point is not on the back side of the plane. And that's it.

Now take a look at the following function. It is evaluating whether an intersection between a plane and an OBB occurred. As you can see, it is quite short. Note that whereas an AABB is stored with only two points (the minimum and the maximum points in the box), an OBB needs more information. You need at least three normalized vectors representing the axis of the box along with three floating-point values representing the extends on each axis:

```
bool ZFXPlane::Intersects(const ZFXObb &obb)
   {
   float fRadius = _fabs( obb.fA0 * (m_vcN*obb.vcA0) )
                 + _fabs( obb.fA1 * (m_vcN*obb.vcA1) )
                 + _fabs( obb.fA2 * (m_vcN*obb.vcA2) );

   float fDistance = this->Distance(obb.vcCenter);
   return (fDistance <= fRadius);
   } // Intersects(OBB)
```

What the function is doing here is, geometrically speaking, just like projecting the box and the plane onto a line. To do this, you calculate the radius the projected box would have on the line. Then you calculate the distance from the center of the box to the plane. If this distance is greater than the radius, there is no intersection.

You'll encounter this test and the one used for AABB again very soon. The next part of this chapter covers the classes for the bounding boxes in detail. In these sections, you will again need to perform intersection tests between planes and boxes (while checking view frustums, because a view frustum is nothing more than just six planes).

Working with AABBs and OBBs

In this book, I work with two types of bounding boxes. The first one is the one aligned to the world axis and is called the axis-aligned bounding box (AABB, as mentioned earlier). The second type, the oriented bounding box (OBB), is the one aligned in a way to approximate a rough object as well as possible without enclosing too much free space (as an AABB most likely would). Now it's time for you to see the two classes that will do the job of bounding boxing 3D models in this book.

To describe an AABB, you only need to save its two extreme points. One extreme point is holding the maximum values for x, y, and z occurring in all the vertices of the enclosed object. The other extreme point is holding the minimum values for all three coordinates from the enclosed object. Here is the class definition:

```
class __declspec(dllexport) ZFXAabb {
   public:
      ZFXVector vcMin, vcMax; // extreme points
      ZFXVector vcCenter;     // center point

      //---------------------

      ZFXAabb(void) { /* nothing to do */ ; }

      void Construct(const ZFXObb *pObb);
      int  Cull(const ZFXPlane *pPlanes,
               int nNumPlanes);

      void GetPlanes(ZFXPlane *pPlanes);
      bool Contains(const ZFXRay &Ray, float fL);
   }; // class
```

Surprisingly, there are not many member functions for an AABB. However, you have seen the AABB as a visitor in other classes (ZFXRay and ZFXPlane) where it was needed. If you like, you can mirror the same functions here again (which is recommended for a full implementation). For the purposes of this book, however, the classes are presented as simply as possible (to let you get used to them). The last thing to notice is the comparably low memory consumed by this class. Note that there is no real need to save the center point. However, you should keep it handy.

Now for the other type of bounding box, the OBB. For an OBB, you have to store its local vectors to know about its orientation. Those vectors should be normalized direction vectors. Then you need to store the half extend of the box on each axis. This information is enough to describe an OBB and to work with it. Again, however, it's good to have its center precalculated. Here is the class definition:

```
class __declspec(dllexport) ZFXObb {
   public:
      float     fA0,  fA1,  fA2; // half extend on each axis
      ZFXVector vcA0, vcA1, vcA2; // axis vectors
      ZFXVector vcCenter;         // center point
```

```
      //----------------------

      ZFXObb(void) { /* nothing to do */ ; }

      inline void DeTransform(const ZFXObb &obb,
                              const ZFXMatrix &m);

      bool Intersects(const ZFXRay &Ray, float *t);
      bool Intersects(const ZFXRay Ray, float fL, float *t);

      bool Intersects(const ZFXObb &Obb);
      bool Intersects(const ZFXVector v0, const ZFXVector v1,
                      const ZFXVector v2);

      int  Cull(const ZFXPlane *pPlanes, int nNumPlanes);

   private:
      void ObbProj(const ZFXObb &Obb, const ZFXVector &vcV,
                   float *pfMin, float *pfMax);

      void TriProj(const ZFXVector &v0, const ZFXVector &v1,
                   const ZFXVector &v2, const ZFXVector &vcV,
                   float *pfMin, float *pfMax);
   }; // class
```

This class does actually define some intersection methods with a ray you have seen before in the ZFXRay class. But there are also some new ones in this class. (Otherwise it would be boring, now wouldn't it?) You will learn a function to check for the intersection of a triangle with an OBB and between two OBBs. In addition, you'll learn two private functions you need if you are going to implement the intersection with a triangle.

New to both classes of bounding boxes is the Cull() member function, which accepts an array of plane objects that make up a frustum. As may be obvious, these functions are needed to check for the visibility of the bounding boxes with a given view frustum.

> **Tip**
>
> Removing objects from the pipeline of further calculations for a frame because they are known not to be visible in this frame is called *object culling*. The most common type of early culling in 3D world-space is the view frustum culling, but there is also occlusion culling as well as some other culling techniques.

Basic Operations and Culling

Sometime it might be helpful to create an AABB out of an OBB, so I just wrote a function that does so. It works by multiplying the half extend of one axis with the axis direction vector. After doing this for all three axes, you have the three maximum points of the OBB on its own local axis. Then you need to seek only the maximum and minimum x, y, and z values out of those three vectors. With these values, you have just found the two extreme points of the AABB enclosing the OBB:

```
void ZFXAabb::Construct(const ZFXObb &Obb)
   {
   ZFXVector vcA0, vcA1, vcA2;
   ZFXVector _vcMax, _vcMin;

   vcA0 = Obb.vcA0 * Obb.fA0;
   vcA1 = Obb.vcA1 * Obb.fA1;
   vcA2 = Obb.vcA2 * Obb.fA2;

   if (vcA0.x > vcA1.x) {
      if (vcA0.x > vcA2.x)
           { vcMax.x = vcA0.x;  vcMin.x = -vcA0.x; }
      else { vcMax.x = vcA2.x;  vcMin.x = -vcA2.x; }
      }
   else {
      if (vcA1.x > vcA2.x)
           { vcMax.x = vcA1.x;  vcMin.x = -vcA1.x; }
      else { vcMax.x = vcA2.x;  vcMin.x = -vcA2.x; }
      }
   if (vcA0.y > vcA1.y) {
      if (vcA0.y > vcA2.y) {
           { vcMax.y = vcA0.y;  vcMin.y = -vcA0.y; }
      else { vcMax.y = vcA2.y;  vcMin.y = -vcA2.y; }
      }
   else {
      if (vcA1.y > vcA2.y)
           { vcMax.y = vcA1.y;  vcMin.y = -vcA1.y; }
      else { vcMax.y = vcA2.y;  vcMin.y = -vcA2.y; }
      }
   if (vcA0.z > vcA1.z) {
      if (vcA0.z > vcA2.z)
           { vcMax.z = vcA0.z;  vcMin.z = -vcA0.z; }
      else { vcMax.z = vcA2.z;  vcMin.z = -vcA2.z; }
      }
```

```
    else {
       if (vcA1.z > vcA2.z)
            { vcMax.z = vcA1.z;  vcMin.z = -vcA1.z; }
       else { vcMax.z = vcA2.z;  vcMin.z = -vcA2.z; }
       }
    vcMax += Obb.vcCenter;
    vcMin += Obb.vcCenter;
    } // construct
```

The second basic function of a bounding box is the culling test. Actually, that is not a basic function of bounding boxes, but it is the main reason why bounding volumes exist at all. The viewing volume of the camera can be thought of as a frustum bounded by six planes: a near plane, a far plane, two side planes, one top plane, and finally one bottom plane. Now all you need to do is to check whether the bounding box is on the outer side of only one of those planes. If it is totally on the outer side, it simply cannot be inside the viewing volume. Hence you can ignore the object inside the bounding box for the given frame.

Caution

I assume here that the normal vectors of the viewing volume planes are pointing outward. The space enclosed by those planes can then be thought of as the insides of the viewing volume.

You can cull an AABB if it is totally on the front side of one of the frustum planes. The following function calculates the temporary extreme points, similar to the AABB plane intersection test; if the AABB is not already on the front side of the plane, however, the final result is withheld until all six planes have been tested. If the AABB is on the front side of only one plane, the function can return immediately because the box can be culled. If the box is intersecting a plane, the function proceeds testing the other planes and returns its results accordingly. The extreme points depend on the coordinates of the normal vectors. If a certain coordinate of the normal vector is positive, then you take the coordinate from the box's maximum point as the coordinate for the temporary maximum extreme point, for example. If the normal's coordinate is negative, you take the minimum point's coordinate as the coordinate value for the temporary maximum extreme point. This sounds complicated, but as you can see from the code, it's actually pretty simple.

```
#define ZFXCLIPPED   3
#define ZFXCULLED    4
#define ZFXVISIBLE   5

int ZFXAabb::Cull(const ZFXPlane *pPlanes, int nNumPlanes)
    {
    ZFXVector  vcMin, vcMax;
    bool       bIntersects = false;
```

```
    // build and test extreme points
    for (int i=0; i<nNumPlanes; i++) {
        if (pPlanes[i].m_vcN.x >= 0.0f) {
            vcMin.x = this->vcMin.x;
            vcMax.x = this->vcMax.x;
            }
        else {
            vcMin.x = this->vcMax.x;
            vcMax.x = this->vcMin.x;
            }
        if (pPlanes[i].m_vcN.y >= 0.0f) {
            vcMin.y = this->vcMin.y;
            vcMax.y = this->vcMax.y;
            }
        else {
            vcMin.y = this->vcMax.y;
            vcMax.y = this->vcMin.y;
            }
        if (pPlanes[i].m_vcN.z >= 0.0f) {
            vcMin.z = this->vcMin.z;
            vcMax.z = this->vcMax.z;
            }
        else {
            vcMin.z = this->vcMax.z;
            vcMax.z = this->vcMin.z;
            }

        if ( ((pPlanes[i].m_vcN*vcMin) + pPlanes[i].m_fD) > 0.0f)
            return ZFXCULLED;

        if ( ((pPlanes[i].m_vcN*vcMax) + pPlanes[i].m_fD) >= 0.0f)
            bIntersects = true;
        } // for
    if (bIntersects) return ZFXCLIPPED;
    return ZFXVISIBLE;
    } // cull
```

I hope you still remember how we transformed a ray into the coordinate system of another object using the inverse transformation matrix. It is also useful to have a function at hand to transform an OBB using a matrix. Normally an OBB would be stored in local coordinates. If you want to test for an intersection in the world coordinate system, you just need to apply the world matrix of the object to its OBB. Again, please do not translate direction vectors. The translation should be applied only to position vectors such as the center of the box:

```
inline void ZFXObb::DeTransform(const ZFXObb &obb, const ZFXMatrix &m)
   {
   ZFXMatrix mat = m;
   ZFXVector vcT;

   // delete translation from matrix
   vcT.Set(mat._41, mat._42, mat._43);
   mat._41 = mat._42 = mat._43 = 0.0f;

   // rotate vectors
   this->vcCenter = mat * obb.vcCenter;
   this->vcA0     = mat * obb.vcA0;
   this->vcA1     = mat * obb.vcA1;
   this->vcA2     = mat * obb.vcA2;

   // translate center point
   this->vcCenter += vcT;

   fA0 = obb.fA0;
   fA1 = obb.fA1;
   fA2 = obb.fA2;
   } // Transform
```

Naturally, you also need the ability to cull OBBs with respect to a viewing frustum (made up of six planes). This function is very similar to the intersection test of a plane and an OBB. The function to cull an OBB looks like this:

```
int ZFXObb::Cull(const ZFXPlane *pPlanes, int nNumPlanes)
   {
   ZFXVector vN;
   int       nResult = ZFXVISIBLE;
   float     fRadius, fTest;

   // for all planes
   for (int i=0; i<nNumPlanes; i++)
      {
      // bend normals inwards
      vN = pPlanes[i].m_vcN * -1.0f;

      // calcuate box radius
      fRadius = _fabs(fA0 * (vN * vcA0))
```

```
              + _fabs(fA1 * (vN * vcA1))
              + _fabs(fA2 * (vN * vcA2));

      // reference value: (N*C - d) (#)
      fTest = vN * this->vcCenter - pPlanes[i].m_fD;

      // obb on far side of plane: (#) < -r
      if (fTest < -fRadius) return ZFXCULLED;

      // or intersecting plane
      else if (!(fTest > fRadius)) nResult = ZFXCLIPPED;
      } // for

   return nResult;
   }
```

The only difference here (besides the use of six planes rather than just one) is that you cannot use the function ZFXPlane::Distance. It would return the distance between the plane and the center of the OBB as an absolute value. For the intersection function, that was totally okay because you were only interested in a possible intersection. Now, however, it is important on which side of the plane the box resides. Only if the OBB is located totally on the front side of one of the frustum planes can you cull it.

Intersections with Triangles

Now for some hardcore math stuff. As you have seen, collision detection is not normally much of an issue. However, detecting the intersection of a triangle with an OBB is quite an adventure. The easiest way to do so is to use the separation axis method as described in the technical papers on David Eberly's website (http://www.magic-software.com/Documentation/MethodOfSeparatingAxes.pdf) and in his books.

Note

The separation axis method alone could fill an entire chapter. Instead of going into detail here about it, I strongly recommend that you at least take a look at the papers on David Eberly's website.

The calculation of a possible intersection between an OBB and a triangle basically works by projecting the OBB and the triangle onto a line and checking a bunch of separating axes. If one of the separating axes is separating the two objects, no intersection is possible any more:

```
// helper function
void ZFXObb::ObbProj(const ZFXObb &Obb, const ZFXVector &vcV,
                    float *pfMin, float *pfMax)
```

```
   {
   float fDP = vcV * Obb.vcCenter;
   float fR  = Obb.fA0 * _fabs(vcV * Obb.vcA0) +
               Obb.fA0 * _fabs(vcV * Obb.vcA1) +
               Obb.fA1 * _fabs(vcV * Obb.vcA2);
   *pfMin = fDP - fR;
   *pfMax = fDP + fR;
   } // ObbProj
/*--------------------------*/


// helper function
void ZFXObb::TriProj(const ZFXVector &v0, const ZFXVector &v1,
                     const ZFXVector &v2, const ZFXVector &vV,
                     float *pfMin, float *pfMax)
   {
   *pfMin = vcV * v0;
   *pfMax = *pfMin;

   float fDP = vcV * v1;
   if (fDP < *pfMin)      *pfMin = fDP;
   else if (fDP > *pfMax) *pfMax = fDP;

   fDP = vcV * v2;
   if (fDP < *pfMin)      *pfMin = fDP;
   else if (fDP > *pfMax) *pfMax = fDP;
   } // TriProj
/*--------------------------*/


// intersection function
bool ZFXObb::Intersects(const ZFXVector &v0, const ZFXVector &v1,
                        const ZFXVector &v2)
   {
   float    fMin0, fMax0, fMin1, fMax1;
   float    fD_C;
   ZFXVector vcV, vcTriEdge[3], vcA[3];

   // to enable loopings
   vcA[0] = this->vcA0;
   vcA[1] = this->vcA1;
   vcA[2] = this->vcA2;

   // direction of tri normals
```

```
vcTriEdge[0] = v1 - v0;
vcTriEdge[1] = v2 - v0;

vcV.Cross(vcTriEdge[0], vcTriEdge[1]);

fMin0 = vcV * v0;
fMax0 = fMin0;

this->ObbProj((*this), vcV, &fMin1, &fMax1);
if ( fMax1 < fMin0 || fMax0 < fMin1 )
    return false;

// direction of obb planes
// =====================
// axis 1:
vcV = this->vcA0;
this->TriProj(v0, v1, v2, vcV, &fMin0, &fMax0);
fD_C = vcV * this->vcCenter;
fMin1 = fD_C - this->fA0;
fMax1 = fD_C + this->fA0;
if ( fMax1 < fMin0 || fMax0 < fMin1 )
    return false;

// axis 2:
vcV = this->vcA1;
this->TriProj(v0, v1, v2, vcV, &fMin0, &fMax0);
fD_C = vcV * this->vcCenter;
fMin1 = fD_C - this->fA1;
fMax1 = fD_C + this->fA1;
if ( fMax1 < fMin0 || fMax0 < fMin1 )
    return false;

// axis 3:
vcV = this->vcA2;
this->TriProj(v0, v1, v2, vcV, &fMin0, &fMax0);
fD_C = vcV * this->vcCenter;
fMin1 = fD_C - this->fA2;
fMax1 = fD_C + this->fA2;
if ( fMax1 < fMin0 || fMax0 < fMin1 )
    return false;

// direction of tri-obb-edge cross products
```

```
         vcTriEdge[2] = vcTriEdge[1] - vcTriEdge[0];
         for (int j=0; j<3; j++) {
            for (int k=0; k<3; k++) {
               vcV.Cross(vcTriEdge[j], vcA[k]);

               this->TriProj(v0, v1, v2, vcV,
                             &fMin0, &fMax0);
               this->ObbProj((*this), vcV, &fMin1, &fMax1);

               if ( (fMax1 < fMin0) || (fMax0 < fMin1) )
                  return false;
               }
            }
         return true;
         } // Intersects(Tri)
/*----------------------------*/
```

Intersections Between Bounding Boxes

The very same method of using separation axis tests is also used to check whether two OBBs intersect each other. This method is described in the original paper about OBB trees by Gottschalk et al. in the SIGGRAPH proceedings in 1996. Another description is provided by David Eberly (again, check out his website). You can find this method on the accompanying CD-ROM, of course.

Planes of an AABB

Another little helper function is the next one. It is used to extract the planes that enclose an AABB. This is important later on when I show you the polygon class of the ZFXEngine 2.0. If you want to clip a polygon to be totally inside an AABB, you just need to know the AABB's planes and then you clip the polygon against each of the planes. I won't give away a big secret if I tell you that you will need that kind of functionality to implement an octree, will I?

Building the planes for an AABB is actually not a big trick. To build a plane, you just need to provide a point on that plane and a normal vector. Regarding the AABB, you have the minimum extreme point and the maximum extreme point, so you can say that the top side plane will contain the maximum point, for example, and you know that its normal vector is pointing straight upward because we build the planes with the normals pointing outward with respect to the AABB:

```
void ZFXAabb::GetPlanes(ZFXPlane *pPlanes)
   {
   ZFXVector vcN;
```

```
   if (!pPlanes) return;

// right
vcN.Set(1.0f, 0.0f, 0.0f);
pPlanes[0].Set(vcN, vcMax);

// left
vcN.Set(-1.0f, 0.0f, 0.0f);
pPlanes[1].Set(vcN, vcMin);

// front
vcN.Set(0.0f, 0.0f, -1.0f);
pPlanes[2].Set(vcN, vcMin);

// back
vcN.Set(0.0f, 0.0f, 1.0f);
pPlanes[3].Set(vcN, vcMax);

// top
vcN.Set(0.0f, 1.0f, 0.0f);
pPlanes[4].Set(vcN, vcMax);

// bottom
vcN.Set(0.0f, -1.0f, 0.0f);
pPlanes[5].Set(vcN, vcMin);
} // Intersects(point)
```

Ray Contained in an AABB

Did I say "octree" lately? Okay, that reminds me of another helper function you will come to love if you want to do collision detection inside an octree. *Inside* is the keyword here. The following functions will simply check whether a given line segment is totally inside an AABB. This helper can be used, for example, to check whether part of a ray is totally inside the node of an octree or whether you need to check the node's neighbors for further collisions as well:

```
bool ZFXAabb::Contains(const ZFXRay &Ray, float fL)
   {
   ZFXVector vcEnd = Ray.m_vcOrig + (Ray.m_vcDir*fL);

   return ( Intersects(Ray.m_vcOrig) && Intersects(vcEnd) );
   } // Contains
```

Again, no magic applied here. You just calculate the endpoint of the line segment and test that point as well as the ray's origin if they are contained in the AABB. If both are inside the bounding box, the whole line segment is totally inside the box. If at least one of the points is outside the box, you can say that the line segment is at least partially outside of the box. Maybe even totally outside. But that is not of our concern. Not this time.

Working with Polygons

Well, well. When I was designing this book, I was saying to myself, "No, you don't need to have a class for polygons in this book. You won't be dealing with polygons enough to justify a class of their own for them." At this very moment of writing, however, I just beamed myself through a temporary slit in the space-time continuum to a parallel dimension some weeks ahead of the time you think of as being the now and took a look at Chapter 13, "Scene Management." So now I'm back here and supply this class in advance (or hand it in after, depending on the temporary normality your point of view resides in).

You will undoubtedly hear about octrees, binary space partitioning trees, and portal systems and about implementing them. You can have a huge amount of code for those scene management algorithms or you can keep it to a minimum. I prefer the latter, so I decided to create a class for a polygon that will do all the basic tasks of such algorithms (such as clipping, splitting, culling, and other dirty things like that).

To put it simply, you will love this class after it is finished. Until then, however, here is your work list:

```
class __declspec(dllexport) ZFXPolygon
   {
   friend class ZFXPlane;

   private:
      ZFXPlane      m_Plane;    // plane of polygon
      int           m_NumP;     // number of points
      int           m_NumI;     // number of indices
      ZFXAabb       m_Aabb;     // bounding box
      unsigned int  m_Flag;     // for free use
      ZFXVector     *m_pPoints; // points
      unsigned int  *m_pIndis;  // indices

      void CalcBoundingBox(void);

   public:
      ZFXPolygon(void);
      ~ZFXPolygon(void);
```

```
    void         Set(const ZFXVector*, int, const unsigned int*, int);
    void         Clip(const ZFXPlane &Plane, ZFXPolygon *pFront,
                      ZFXPolygon *pBack);
    void         Clip(const ZFXAabb &aabb);
    int          Cull(const ZFXAabb &aabb);
    void         CopyOf(const ZFXPolygon &Poly);

    void         SwapFaces(void);
    bool         Intersects(const ZFXRay&, bool, float*);
    bool         Intersects(const ZFXRay&, bool float fL, float *t);

    int             GetNumPoints(void){return m_NumP;}
    int             GetNumIndis(void) {return m_NumI;}
    ZFXVector*      GetPoints(void)    {return m_pPoints;}
    unsigned int*   GetIndices(void)   {return m_pIndis;}
    ZFXPlane        GetPlane(void)     {return m_Plane;}
    ZFXAabb         GetAabb(void)      {return m_Aabb;}
    unsigned int    GetFlag(void)      {return m_Flag;}
    void            SetFlag(unsigned int n) {m_Flag = n;}
}; // class
```

The only thing worth mentioning is the flag of type `unsigned int`. There is no specific purpose for that flag, and a user of this class can use it for whatever he wants. Actually, the flag does have a specific purpose, but I won't tell you what it is just now. If you are working with a lot of polygons, however, it is really nice to be able to flag them to a range of values. Trust me.

Basic Operations

The first thing I will show you from this class is its constructor and its destructor (just to give you a little more information about this class, because there really is not much going on; the real show takes place in other locations):

```
ZFXPolygon::ZFXPolygon(void)
    {
    m_pPoints = NULL;
    m_pIndis  = NULL;
    m_NumP    = 0;
    m_NumI    = 0;
    m_Flag    = 0;
    memset(&m_Aabb, 0, sizeof(ZFXAabb));
    } // constructor
```

```
ZFXPolygon::~ZFXPolygon(void)
   {
   if (m_pPoints) {
      delete [] m_pPoints;
      m_pPoints = NULL;
      }
   if (m_pIndis) {
      delete [] m_pIndis;
      m_pIndis = NULL;
      }
   } // destructor
```

But now there are no more basic operations. Most of the functions in this class are pretty interesting and somewhat lengthy. As I just mentioned, however, fight your way through because you will love this puppy once it's done.

Setting the Points for the Polygon

If you create an instance from this class, it will contain nothing. It will be only an empty container that could hold a polygon's data. To actually fuel it with data, you must call the ZFXPolygon::Set function. That sounds easy, too easy. The problem is that a polygon can also have a back face and a front face, so it is important to always maintain its orientation in space.

You also already know that there is this thing called a normal vector pointing from the front face of the polygon or its plane outward. And you know how to calculate a normal vector for the incoming data. So far so good. Therefore, you just take the first three points of a polygon, build two vectors from them, and calculate the normal vector by performing the cross-product operation on them.

That's perfectly true, but watch out for the catch 22. For an arbitrary polygon, it is legal to have a bunch of neighboring points sitting on the very same edge of the polygon. Therefore, the two vectors you would build from the first three vertices can be parallel in a lot of cases. Crossing parallel vectors is senseless, however, because this operation will result in the zero vector. So before crossing those two vectors, you have to seek two vectors on the polygon's edge that are not parallel. Keeping this in mind, it is quite easy to write a function to set the data for a polygon and avoid this catch:

```
void ZFXPolygon::Set(const ZFXVector *pPoints, int nNumP,
                     const unsigned int *pIndis, int nNumI)
   {
   ZFXVector vcEdge0, vcEdge1;
   bool bGotEm = false;
```

```
   if (m_pPoints) delete [] m_pPoints;
   if (m_pIndis)  delete [] m_pIndis;

   m_pPoints = new ZFXVector[nNumP];
   m_pIndis  = new unsigned int[nNumI];

   m_NumP = nNumP;   m_NumI = nNumI;

   memcpy(m_pPoints,pPoints,sizeof(ZFXVector)*nNumP);
   memcpy(m_pIndis,pIndis,sizeof(unsigned int)*nNumI);

   vcEdge0 = m_pPoints[m_pIndis[1]] -
             m_pPoints[m_pIndis[0]];

   // calculate the plane
   for (int i=2; bGotEm==false; i++) {
      if ((i+1) > m_NumI) break;

      vcEdge1 = m_pPoints[m_pIndis[i]] -
                m_pPoints[m_pIndis[0]];

      vcEdge0.Normalize();
      vcEdge1.Normalize();

      // edges must not be parallel
      if (vcEdge0.AngleWith(vcEdge1) != 0.0)
         bGotEm = true;
      } // for

   m_Plane.m_vcN.Cross(vcEdge0, vcEdge1);
   m_Plane.m_vcN.Normalize();
   m_Plane.m_fD = -(m_Plane.m_vcN * m_pPoints[0]);
   m_Plane.m_vcPoint = m_pPoints[0];

   CalcBoundingBox();
   } // Set
```

Let me add one more thing about this polygon class. Normally, a polygon would consist of points only. In this class, I use indices as well to represent the triangulation of the polygon. In certain situations, it is just better to have the triangulation of the polygon to perform a per-triangle intersection, for example. Another reason is that I'm building polygons from geometrical model data, which is normally using indices as well.

The next function calculates the AABB for the polygon. It just loops through all points of the polygon and saves the minimum and maximum values:

```
void ZFXPolygon::CalcBoundingBox(void) {
   ZFXVector vcMax, vcMin;
   vcMax = vcMin = m_pPoints[0];

   for (int i=0; i<m_NumP; i++) {
      if ( m_pPoints[i].x > vcMax.x )
         vcMax.x = m_pPoints[i].x;
      else if ( m_pPoints[i].x < vcMin.x )
         vcMin.x = m_pPoints[i].x;

      if ( m_pPoints[i].y > vcMax.y )
         vcMax.y = m_pPoints[i].y;
      else if ( m_pPoints[i].y < vcMin.y )
         vcMin.y = m_pPoints[i].y;

      if ( m_pPoints[i].z > vcMax.z )
         vcMax.z = m_pPoints[i].z;
      else if ( m_pPoints[i].z < vcMin.z )
         vcMin.z = m_pPoints[i].z;
      } // for
   m_Aabb.vcMax    = vcMax;
   m_Aabb.vcMin    = vcMin;
   m_Aabb.vcCenter = (vcMax + vcMin) / 2.0f;
   } // CalcBoundingBox
```

Even if we are not if China or celebrating carnival in Rio, we need to take care of the two faces of the polygon. Here is a function that enables you to swap the orientation of a polygon. That means you change the front side and the back side. Actually, it would be enough to just invert the normal vector. Because the polygon class uses indices, however, you also need to reverse the list of indices. Otherwise the orientation of each single triangle would be exactly the opposite orientation of the polygon, meaning front-face-only collision detection on the polygon and on the polygon's triangles and producing different results. You wouldn't really like that:

```
void ZFXPolygon::SwapFaces(void) {
   unsigned int *pIndis = new unsigned int[m_NumI];

   // change sorting of indices to reverse order
   for (int i=0; i<m_NumI; i++)
      pIndis[m_NumI-i-1] = m_pIndis[i];
```

```
// invert normal direction
m_Plane.m_vcN *= -1.0f;
m_Plane.m_fD  *= -1.0f;

delete [] m_pIndis;
m_pIndis = pIndis;
} // SwapFaces
```

Caution

The class `ZFXPolygon` is explicitly not meant to be used during rendering. It is a class meant to perform collision detection; therefore it doesn't save vertex data, just mainly position data.

As you can see in this method, you must not forget about the plane equation. It is imperative that you negate this value. Otherwise the plane equation would describe another parallel plane in the same position but with a different orientation. So always make it your habit to look out for such details that could become your personal debugging hell later on.

Clipping a Polygon

Oh, and speaking of personal hells, here is the next small nightmare to overcome you. I will introduce you to the black art of clipping polygons. Actually, implementing this is not as bad as it sounds. However, it is a quite lengthy operation. I will show you two kinds of clipping. The first one is to clip a polygon to an AABB. After that clipping process, the polygon will be totally inside the box with no overlapping edges and corners because all those have been simply cut off.

The second case of clipping is the real guts of polygon clipping. It is about clipping a polygon at a plane and cutting off all parts of the polygon on a specific side of the plane. It is a bit tricky to maintain the integrity of the polygon, but I will guide you through the process. Let's start with the simple clipping to boost our motivation.

Clipping to an AABB

Well, well. Now I've probably really scared you. Don't worry, though; clipping a polygon against an AABB is really easy after all (that is, if you are already able to clip a polygon against a plane). It goes like this: Extract the planes from the AABB, and then clip the polygon against each of these planes. By doing so, you effectively clip the polygon against the AABB. Watch it:

```
void ZFXPolygon::Clip(const ZFXAabb &aabb)
   {
   ZFXPolygon BackPoly, ClippedPoly;
   ZFXPlane   Planes[6];
```

```
   bool       bClipped=false;

// cast away const
ZFXAabb *pAabb = ((ZFXAabb*)&aabb);

// get planes from aabb, normals pointing outwards
pAabb->GetPlanes(Planes);

// copy the polygon
ClippedPoly.CopyOf( *this );

// do the clipping
for (int i=0; i<6; i++) {
   if (Planes[i].Classify(ClippedPoly) == ZFXCLIPPED)
      {
      ClippedPoly.Clip(Planes[i], NULL, &BackPoly);
      ClippedPoly.CopyOf(BackPoly);
      bClipped = true;
      }
   }

if (bClipped) CopyOf(ClippedPoly);
} // Clip
```

The function ZFXAabb::GetPlanes will return the AABB's planes with its normals pointing outward. That means that you clip the polygon on one of the planes and keep the part of the polygon that is on the back side of the plane. You can already see the call to the function ZFXPolygon::Clip where you provide a plane and two pointers as parameters. The first pointer, which is set to NULL in this case, would return the front side part of the polygon after the clipping.

Oh, and there is also the new function ZFXPlane::Classify, which classifies not only a point but also a whole polygon. As you can imagine, you only need to loop through the points of the polygon and classify each one of them. If all of them are on the same side, you return the appropriate value. If there is at least one point on the other side than the others, the function will return the value ZFXCLIPPED, meaning that the plane intersects the polygon and that it should be clipped.

Clipping with a Plane

Now here you are. You fought all your way through the whole level just to encounter him: the level boss. The ultimate evil plane-polygon clipper. But you are still a marine and you've got a job to do. It is not all that complicated to create a function to clip a polygon.

You just have to think about what you want and need to do. You have a list of points from the polygon and a plane that should divide the group of points into two groups according to the side of the plane the points sit on. So why not just classify each point of the polygon at the plane and build a list of front-face points and back-face points?

That's a pretty good start. From this front list and back list, you could then build two new polygons (each one a result of the clipping process; one in front of the plane and one on its back side).

Actually, that is what we are going to do. As always, though, there is one catch. Seldom will a polygon be intersected by a plane in a way that the plane only intersects the polygon's edge in places where a point of the polygon is located. So we have to insert new points into the polygon where such a situation occurs. That makes clipping of polygons a bit different. Luckily, however, we already have a quite good math library at our disposal. So here's the outline of the clipping algorithm I will show you in a moment:

1. Create two empty lists for the points of the two new polygons.
2. Classify the first point of the polygon and sort it into the appropriate list (front-side list or back-side list). If it lies on the plane, sort it into both lists.
3. Take the next point of the polygon and classify it. Sort it into both lists if and only if the point lies on the plane. Otherwise take the preceding point from the list and look at the edge between the two points. If this edge intersects the plane, create a new point where the intersection occurs and insert the new point into both lists. Then insert the first point of this edge into the appropriate list.
4. If there are more points in the polygon, go back to Step 3. Otherwise go to Step 5.
5. If the front-side list and the back-side list contain at least three points (one or two points should be impossible), build a new index list for each of them. Take the first point of the polygon and use the following two points for a triangle. Then skip the second one and use the following point or the next triangle like so: ([0, 1, 2], [0, 2, 3], [0, 3, 4], . . .).
6. Create the real polygon objects from the point lists and the index lists. The new index list may have swapped the normal by accident. Compare it to the original polygon's normal and twist it around if needed.

Although I hope these listed steps make the whole task sound pretty, there is still a lot of work to do. It is not really complicated, however; it is only a lot of source code in one single function. But there is not much one could possibly and logically delegate to other functions without losing the overview of what is going on. So stay tuned and work your way through the code. To help you out a bit, I inserted comments in the code that are similar to the preceding listed steps:

```
void ZFXPolygon::Clip(const ZFXPlane &Plane, ZFXPolygon *pFront,
                      ZFXPolygon *pBack)
```

```
{
if (!pFront && !pBack) return;

ZFXVector vcHit, vcA, vcB;
ZFXRay    Ray;

// cast away const
ZFXPlane  *pPlane = ((ZFXPlane*)&Plane);

unsigned int nNumFront=0, // number of points front side
             nNumBack=0,  // number of points back side
             nLoop=0, nCurrent=0;

ZFXVector *pvcFront = new ZFXVector[m_NumP*3];
ZFXVector *pvcBack  = new ZFXVector[m_NumP*3];

// classify the first point
switch (pPlane->Classify(m_pPoints[0])) {
   case ZFXFRONT:
      pvcFront[nNumFront++] = m_pPoints[0];
      break;
   case ZFXBACK:
      pvcBack[nNumBack++] = m_pPoints[0];
      break;
   case ZFXPLANAR:
      pvcBack[nNumBack++]   = m_pPoints[0];
      pvcFront[nNumFront++] = m_pPoints[0];
      break;
   default: return;
   }

// loop through all points of the polygon
for (nLoop=1; nLoop < (m_NumP+1); nLoop++) {

   if (nLoop == m_NumP) nCurrent = 0;
   else nCurrent = nLoop;

   // take two neighbor points from the polygon
   vcA = m_pPoints[nLoop-1];
   vcB = m_pPoints[nCurrent];

   // classify them with respect to the plane
```

```cpp
      int nClass  = pPlane->Classify(vcB);
      int nClassA = pPlane->Classify(vcA);

      // if planar add to both sides
      if (nClass == ZFXPLANAR) {
         pvcBack[nNumBack++]   = m_pPoints[nCurrent];
         pvcFront[nNumFront++] = m_pPoints[nCurrent];
         }
      // test if an edge intersects the plane
      else {
         Ray.m_vcOrig = vcA;
         Ray.m_vcDir  = vcB - vcA;

         float fLength = Ray.m_vcDir.GetLength();

         if (fLength != 0.0f) Ray.m_vcDir /= fLength;

         if ( Ray.Intersects(Plane, false, fLength, 0,
                             &vcHit)
             && (nClassA != ZFXPLANAR)) {

            // then insert intersection point as
            // new point in both lists
            pvcBack[nNumBack++]   = vcHit;
            pvcFront[nNumFront++] = vcHit;
            }
         // sort the current point
         if (nCurrent == 0) continue;

         if (nClass == ZFXFRONT) {
            pvcFront[nNumFront++] =
                              m_pPoints[nCurrent];
            }
         else if (nClass == ZFXBACK) {
            pvcBack[nNumBack++] =
                              m_pPoints[nCurrent];
            }
         }
      } // for [NumP]

// now we have the vertices of the two polygons
// let's take care of the indices
```

```cpp
    unsigned int I0, I1, I2;
    unsigned int *pnFront = NULL;
    unsigned int *pnBack  = NULL;

    if (nNumFront > 2) {
       pnFront = new unsigned int[(nNumFront-2)*3];

       for (nLoop=0; nLoop < (nNumFront-2); nLoop++) {
          if (nLoop==0) { I0=0; I1=1; I2=2; }
          else { I1=I2; I2++; }

          pnFront[(nLoop*3)   ] = I0;
          pnFront[(nLoop*3) +1] = I1;
          pnFront[(nLoop*3) +2] = I2;
          }
       }

    if (nNumBack > 2) {
       pnBack  = new unsigned int[(nNumBack-2)*3];

       for (nLoop=0; nLoop < (nNumBack-2); nLoop++) {
          if (nLoop==0) { I0=0; I1=1; I2=2; }
          else { I1=I2; I2++; }

          pnBack[(nLoop*3)   ] = I0;
          pnBack[(nLoop*3) +1] = I1;
          pnBack[(nLoop*3) +2] = I2;
          }
       }

    // generate new polys
    if (pFront && pnFront) {
       pFront->Set(pvcFront, nNumFront, pnFront,
                   (nNumFront-2)*3);

       // maintain same orientation as original polygon
       if (pFront->GetPlane().m_vcN * m_Plane.m_vcN
          < 0.0f)
          pFront->SwapFaces();
       }
```

```
        if (pBack && pnBack) {
           pBack->Set(pvcBack, nNumBack, pnBack,
                      (nNumBack-2)*3);

           if (pBack->GetPlane().m_vcN * m_Plane.m_vcN
               < 0.0f)
              pBack->SwapFaces();
        }

        if (pvcFront) { delete [] pvcFront; }
        if (pvcBack)  { delete [] pvcBack;  }
        if (pnFront)  { delete [] pnFront;  }
        if (pnBack)   { delete [] pnBack;   }
        } // Clip
```

You made it! Good. As you can see, the actual polygon object that was used to call the function is left untouched. Instead, the function generates two new polygon objects and returns them to the caller via call-by-reference parameters. Another thing worth mentioning is that this function does not test whether the plane is intersecting the polygon at all. It supposes that the plane indeed does. However, the user should ensure this beforehand. My reasoning behind this is that I wanted to avoid a double call. It is most likely that the user will indeed call this function beforehand for his own purposes and then call the clipping function. Thus we avoid overhead by leaving the task to the user. Now you can use the function, as follows:

```
ZFXPolygon FrontPoly, BackPoly;
if ( g_Plane.Classify( g_Poly ) ) == ZFXCLIPPED )
   {
   g_Poly.Clip( g_Plane, &FrontPoly, &BackPoly );
   }
```

Now it's time to relax. This was the most complex part you will encounter in this chapter, so you can sit back a bit and take it easy for a while. Next up are just some intersection and culling functions for polygons with bounding boxes and with rays.

Culling with Bounding Boxes

In some situations, it is important to be able to calculate whether an object is totally inside an AABB or not. No, I won't mention the octree again here. In other situations, you have hierarchies of bounding boxes and need to sort polygons into them. As with a view frustum, we can think of the inside of an AABB as a visible area. In this case, there are three possibilities: A polygon could be totally visible, totally invisible (culled), or partially visible (intersecting).

Chapter 4 ■ Fast 3D Calculus

The first possibility is easy to evaluate. If all points of the polygon are inside the bounding box, the whole polygon is. The second possibility is not as easy as it seems. Even if all points are outside the box, the polygon can be way bigger than the box but intersecting it. That said, there is an easy solution to get around actually calculating this possibility. After all, if the polygon is not totally inside the box and if it is not intersecting the box, it must be totally outside, right?

The last possibility is not so trivial. We will just take each edge of the polygon and test whether it intersects one of the planes of the box. If it does, the function simply reports that there is an intersection. This is not really true, however, because the edge could also intersect the plane but not the rectangle of the box lying in this plane.

For the purposes of this book, we can live with that little approximation as long as we know about it. To be really accurate, you should then calculate the point of intersection and determine whether it lies inside the rectangle of the bounding box. For an AABB, this is quite easy because you can evaluate this in only two dimensions (because one dimension of the rectangle is always 0 due to its orientation along the according world axis). So now you have your homework for today. Take a look at the implementation of the approximating version of this function:

```
int ZFXPolygon::Cull(const ZFXAabb &aabb)
   {
   ZFXPlane Planes[6];
   int      nClass=0;
   int      nInside=0, nCurrent=0;
   bool     bFirst=true;
   ZFXRay   Ray;

   ZFXAabb *pAabb = ((ZFXAabb*)&aabb);

   // planes of aabb, normals pointing outwards
   pAabb->GetPlanes(Planes);

   // do aabb intersect at all
   if ( !m_Aabb.Intersects(aabb) )
      return ZFXCULLED; // no way

   // all planes of the box
   for (int p=0; p<6; p++) {

      // one time test if all points inside aabb
      if (bFirst) {
         for (int i=0; i<m_NumP; i++) {
```

```
            if ( pAabb->Intersects(m_pPoints[i]) )
                nInside++;
            }
         bFirst = false;

         // yes => polygon totally inside aabb
         if (nInside  == m_NumP) return ZFXVISIBLE;
         }

      // test intersection of plane with polygon edges
      for (int nLoop=1; nLoop < (m_NumP+1); nLoop++) {
         if (nLoop == m_NumP) nCurrent = 0;
         else nCurrent = nLoop;

         // edge from two neighbor points
         Ray.m_vcOrig = m_pPoints[nLoop-1];
         Ray.m_vcDir  = m_pPoints[nCurrent]
                      - m_pPoints[nLoop-1];

         float fLength = Ray.m_vcDir.GetLength();
         if (fLength != 0.0f) Ray.m_vcDir /= fLength;

         // if intersection aabb intersects polygon
         if (Ray.Intersects(Planes[p], false, fLength,
             0, NULL))
             return ZFXCLIPPED;
         }
      }

   // polygon not inside aabb and not intersection
   return ZFXCULLED;
   } // Cull
```

Intersections with Rays

Rays, rays, rays. Wherever you look in 3D graphics, it is most likely that you see hundreds of rays in each direction fired across the space to pick something, or to evaluate a collision, or to calculate lighting (if you happen to be in a raytracer).

Not surprisingly, you also need to have a collision detection for a polygon object that evaluates an intersection of the polygon with a ray and a line segment. Again, the line segment is just a ray and, in addition, a certain length we want the ray to be checked on. As you can see in this function, it was a right decision to store the index list for the triangulation along with the polygon's other data.

Now I gave you all three keywords. But I will repeat them again to make your brain rotate and click: *triangulation, ray, intersection*. Why invent the wheel twice? In this case, you already have the "wheel" inside the math library. We have a polygon built out of triangles, we have a ray to test for an intersection, and we have a function, ZFXRay::Intersection, to do exactly this. And here it comes:

```
bool ZFXPolygon::Intersects(const ZFXRay &Ray, bool bCull, float *t)
   {
   ZFXRay *pRay = (ZFXRay*)&Ray;

   for (int i=0; i<m_NumI; i+=3)
      {
      if (pRay->Intersects(m_pPoints[m_pIndis[i]],
                           m_pPoints[m_pIndis[i+1]],
                           m_pPoints[m_pIndis[i+2]],
                           false, t))
         {
         return true;
         }
      if (!bCull)
         {
         if (pRay->Intersects(m_pPoints[m_pIndis[i+2]],
                              m_pPoints[m_pIndis[i+1]],
                              m_pPoints[m_pIndis[i]],
                              false, t))
            {
            return true;
            }
         }
      }
   return false;
   } // Intersects
```

This functions works by taking three points of the polygon that are indicated by the index list to form a triangle. Then it checks this triangle for an intersection with the ray. If the user does not want the back face to be culled, the function reverses the order of the indices and repeats the test for the back-face triangle.

The very same function is also used for the intersection test with the line segment. In this case, however, the function will then use the line segment version of the triangle intersection test. You can find the complete code on the CD-ROM.

Working with Quaternions

Although you've come a long way through this chapter, there is still a lot of weird stuff out there. For instance, as of now, we haven't even touched one of the strangest concepts 3D mathematics offers to an interested freak. Well, I should have said 4D mathematics because I'm actually talking about the so-called quaternions.

Even if you were a top math student all the way through college, you most likely never even heard about quaternions. You probably did hear about vectors and matrices, for sure, even if teachers hid from you all the cool things you can do with them in computer graphics. Quaternions, on the other hand, are not something teachers generally cover.

If you are interested in computer graphics, however, you have probably at least heard about quaternions (a quite fashionable topic lately, among some circles). To provide you with an idea about what a quaternion is I will try to express it in a very simple way. If you want to describe an object's rotation in space, you can do in one of three ways. First, you can use a simple transformation matrix like the rotation matrices discussed previously in this chapter. Second, you can use the so-called Euler angles. You would only save the three angles by which the object is rotated on the three-world axis. Third, you can use quaternions. In a quaternion, you can store all the information about the orientation of an object, even reducing your need for memory storage in the process.

Introduction to 4D Space

Before implementing quaternions, you should know a bit about the background of quaternion mathematics. A quaternion is really nothing more than a four-dimensional number. Don't mistake this with a four-dimensional vector containing four one-dimensional numbers. A vector is just a collection of simple numbers bunched together for some reason (for instance, because of their position on a certain axis).

> **Note**
>
> It all started with one-dimensional, plain numbers, called scalars. Complex numbers, or two-dimensional numbers, followed. This understanding spurred the futile attempts to "invent" or "discover" three-dimensional numbers. (If you want to win a Nobel Prize, just find a three-dimensional number.) Although these attempts were technically failures, the search process led to the discovery of four-dimensional numbers, hypercomplex numbers called quaternions, which followed mathematical rules.

You may vaguely remember from school something about complex numbers. Perhaps you remember a teacher saying something about the impossibility of calculating the square root of a negative number. Well, that's an "old-school" impossibility. With complex numbers, you can do exactly that. But in the year 1843 Sir William Rowan Hamilton defined the first rules for quaternions as extensions to complex numbers.

Complex Numbers

Now it really starts to get strange. Complex numbers are described using a normal scalar number. In addition, however, a so-called imaginary part is added to the scalar number. This part is expressed in the formula using the letter *i*, as in *insane*.

```
k = (a + bi)
```

The two variables a and b in this formula are normal scalar values, and i is some kind of unit (such as kilogram, for instance). But the strange thing is that i also has a value, and now it really gets insane if you look at how this value is defined:

```
(i * i) = -1
```

That seems to be okay with our normal human brain. However, don't mistake this for a trivial formula, because it also implies the following:

```
(i * i) = -1    <=>    i = squareroot(-1)
```

All of a sudden you can now start calculating square roots for negative numbers (the result of such an operation being undefined in one-dimensional numbers). With complex numbers, the result of such an operation is just a complex number. You could also end up with a real one-dimensional result if you can kick the imaginary parts out of the equation. If you are really interested in this weird stuff, I recommend a doctor and a good book about analysis.

Quaternions

Quaternions are not *as strange* as complex numbers, they are even *more strange*. Whereas complex numbers have only one imaginary part, a quaternion has three of them. Normally you call them as i, j, and k:

```
(j * j) = -1     <=>     j = squareroot( -1 )
(k * k) = -1     <=>     k = squareroot( -1 )
```

Therefore, you can write down a quaternion using one real part and three additional imaginary parts. This would look like the following equation for quaternion q:

```
q = ( a + bi + cj + dk )
```

That does not ring any 3D bells in our ears, so I will provide another common way of writing down a quaternion by bunching up the imaginary values in an additional variable called v. In this form of the equation, however, the real scalar part of a quaternion is commonly called w rather than a:

```
q = [w, v]    where v = ( x, y, z )
```

A quaternion can be represented by a scalar value w and a 3D vector called v. From a 3D graphics point of view, you can think of this value w as the angle of a rotation applied to an object. The vector v is then representing the axis around which the rotation took part. The nice thing is that you don't need to store three rotation angles for the three-world axis. You can just add rotation after rotation to the quaternion, which would be changing its rotation vector and the angle value accordingly.

This is really a great thing because the quaternion math is, after all, much simpler than calculating rotation matrices and multiplying matrixes together to sum up different transformations. So read on, please.

Gimbal Lock, or Why Do We Need Quaternions?

The old-fashioned inertial navigation systems used fixed platforms that always maintained the same orientation in space with the aid of gyroscopes no matter how their carrier system (a rocket or plane) moved and was oriented in space. To make this possible, the platform needed to have a flexible connection to its carrier vessel that was able to rotate freely on all three axes.

Such a flexible connection between the platform and its carrier vessel was built using multiple gimbals of different sizes that were connected by two couplers opposing each other. The position of the two couplers of one gimbal was effectively setting the rotation axis for the next smaller gimbal ring. To allow a movement on three axes in space, you have to use three gimbals.

But then you have a problem. Performing some different flight maneuvers, you could accidentally align the inner gimbal to have exactly the same rotation axis as the outer gimbal. In such a case, you have lost the possibility to rotate on three axes and are bound to only two rotational degrees of freedom. Congratulations, you just suffered what is called a gimbal lock.

This problem can be solved using a fourth gimbal to prevent the lost of one rotation axis even if two gimbals are aligned to the same axis. By the way, the famous Apollo 13 mission suffered from the same problem after the steering unit was damaged by an explosion in the fuel tanks. In those days, the vessel was equipped with only a three-gimbal system, and the pilots were trained to perform only "safe" flight maneuvers not leading to a gimbal lock.

Back to the topic of 3D computer graphics, in which gimbal lock is also a potential problem. Normally, you work with the three-world axis as the reference platform. If you rotate the camera about 90 degrees on the z axis to the left, the vector of the camera's local x axis is now equal to the world's y axis.

In fact, if you look at famous first-person shooter games, you will notice that you can normally use only a very restricted camera. You can rotate on the y axis as much as you like, but the rotation on the x axis is always restricted to be smaller than ±90 degrees. The rotation around the z axis is even more restricted.

As you will see later on, quaternions are a way to have a camera with three degrees of freedom without the danger of getting your gimbals locked.

Basic Operations

Here is the class definition of a quaternion. It is surprisingly simple, but so is the quaternion equation itself:

```
class __declspec(dllexport) ZFXQuat
   {
   public:
      float x, y, z, w;

      ZFXQuat(void) { x=0.0f, y=0.0f, z=0.0f, w=1.0f; }

      ZFXQuat(float _x, float _y, float _z, float _w)
                  { x=_x; y=_y; z=_z; w=_w; }

      void GetMatrix(ZFXMatrix *m);

      void MakeFromEuler(float fPitch,
                         float fYaw,
                         float fRoll);

      ZFXQuat operator *  (const ZFXQuat &q)const;
      void    operator *= (const ZFXQuat &q);
   }; // class
```

As you can see, we don't need much functionality for our quaternion class. Note that the constructor initializes the quaternion as a so-called identity quaternion. Then you can also build the quaternion from three given Euler angles and you can calculate a real transformation matrix from a quaternion.

Tip

A quaternion built from the zero vector and the scalar value 1 is called the *identity quaternion*. It looks like this: q = [1, (0, 0, 0)]

As for the operators, you will find that I only implement the multiplication of two quaternions. Naturally, however, the quaternions also define their own rules for addition, subtraction, and some other operations. For the simple purposes of this book, though, we need only the multiplication. If you are interested in quaternion math, crank up your favorite web browser and search the web for the keyword *quaternion*. You will find tons of information.

Multiplication of Two Quaternions

Unlike the multiplication of scalar values, the multiplication of two quaternions is not commutative. (By the way, the same applies to matrices.) That means that quaternion C is not equal to quaternion D if C = A*B and D = B*A, where A and B are also quaternions. As you can already see from this equation, however, the result of a multiplication of two quaternions is again a quaternion. And this multiplication of two quaternions is defined as follows:

given: $q = [\ q_w,\ (q_v)\ ],\quad r = [\ r_w,\ (r_v)\ ]$

wanted: $q * r = [\ q_w r_w - q_v r_v,\ (\ q_v \times r_v + r_w q_v + q_w r_v)\ ]$

The real part of the new quaternion is built from the difference of the product of the two original real parts and the dot product of the two original vectors. The vector of the new quaternion is created from the sum of the cross product of the two original vectors and the scaling of those vectors with the scalar part of the other one.

Although this sounds complicated, at a source code level you see that it is not as bad as it sounds and boils down to some multiplication and subtraction:

```
void ZFXQuat::operator *= (const ZFXQuat &q)
   {
   float _x, _y, _z, _w;

   _w = w*q.w - x*q.x - y*q.y - z*q.z;
   _x = w*q.x + x*q.w + y*q.z - z*q.y;
   _y = w*q.y + y*q.w + z*q.x - x*q.z;
   _z = w*q.z + z*q.w + x*q.y - y*q.x;

   x = _x;
   y = _y;
   z = _z;
   w = _w;
   }
/*----------------------------*/

ZFXQuat ZFXQuat::operator * (const ZFXQuat &q) const
   {
```

```
    ZFXQuat qResult;

    qResult.w = w*q.w - x*q.x - y*q.y - z*q.z;
    qResult.x = w*q.x + x*q.w + y*q.z - z*q.y;
    qResult.y = w*q.y + y*q.w + z*q.x - x*q.z;
    qResult.z = w*q.z + z*q.w + x*q.y - y*q.x;

    return qResult;
    }
/*--------------------------*/
```

Building from Euler Angles

In today's world, quaternions are not yet part of the main 3D APIs. DirectX's D3DX helper library contains several functions to work with quaternions. However, you still need to be able to build quaternions from Euler angles and to build transformation matrices from quaternions. Euler angles are named after the Swiss mathematician Leonard Euler (1707–1783), and they describe an object's orientation in space by saving its rotation angles on three local axes in a cubic coordinate system.

If you know the three angles for an object, you can build a quaternion representing the very same rotation of the object. For a quaternion to be able to represent rotation information, however, it must be a unit quaternion with a magnitude of 1. For an arbitrary three-dimensional vector, a unit quaternion is defined as follows:

q = [cos(a), sin(a) v]

Again, the source code version might look simpler to you than the math equation (at least it certainly does to me):

```
void ZFXQuat::MakeFromEuler(float fPitch, float fYaw, float fRoll)
   {
   float cX, cY, cZ, sX, sY, sZ, cYcZ, sYsZ, cYsZ, sYcZ;

   fPitch *= 0.5f;
   fYaw   *= 0.5f;
   fRoll  *= 0.5f;

   cX = cosf(fPitch);
   cY = cosf(fYaw);
   cZ = cosf(fRoll);

   sX = sinf(fPitch);
   sY = sinf(fYaw);
```

```
sZ = sinf(fRoll);

cYcZ = cY * cZ;
sYsZ = sY * sZ;
cYsZ = cY * sZ;
sYcZ = sY * cZ;

w = cX * cYcZ + sX * sYsZ;
x = sX * cYcZ - cX * sYsZ;
y = cX * sYcZ + sX * cYsZ;
z = cX * cYsZ - sX * sYcZ;
} // MakeFromEuler
```

Building a Rotation Matrix

I just mentioned the modern 3D graphics APIs, and the same applies for graphics adapters. All of them are using transformation matrices rather than quaternions and Euler angles. However, it is perfectly possible to calculate your rotations using a quaternion and then build a rotation matrix from this quaternion to hand it over to the 3D API (or, for that matter, the graphics adapter). This transformation matrix would then represent exactly the same rotation as the quaternion did. Taking for granted that the quaternion is a unit quaternion, you can build a transformation matrix from it using the following scheme:

$$\begin{vmatrix} 1-2y^2-2z^2 & 2xy+2wz & 2xz-2wy & 0 \\ 2xy-2wz & 1-2x^2-2z^2 & 2yz+2wz & 0 \\ 2xz-2wy & 2yz+2wz & 1-2x^2-2y^2 & 0 \\ 0 & 0 & 0 & 1 \end{vmatrix}$$

Not too bad. And you don't even have to understand why it is true. (Let's leave the proofs to the mathematicians out there.)

```
void ZFXQuat::GetMatrix(ZFXMatrix *pMat)
   {
   float wx, wy, wz, xx, yy, yz, xy, xz, zz, x2, y2, z2;

   // identity matrix
   memset(pMat, 0, sizeof(ZFXMatrix));
   pMat->_44 = 1.0f;

   x2 = x + x;
   y2 = y + y;
   z2 = z + z;
```

```
    xx = x * x2;
    xy = x * y2;
    xz = x * z2;

    yy = y * y2;
    yz = y * z2;
    zz = z * z2;

    wx = w * x2;
    wy = w * y2;
    wz = w * z2;

    pMat->_11 = 1.0f - (yy + zz);
    pMat->_12 = xy - wz;
    pMat->_13 = xz + wy;

    pMat->_21 = xy + wz;
    pMat->_22 = 1.0f - (xx + zz);
    pMat->_23 = yz - wx;

    pMat->_31 = xz - wy;
    pMat->_32 = yz + wx;
    pMat->_33 = 1.0f - (xx + yy);
} // GetMatrix
```

That's all there is about quaternions as such in this book. Later in this book, I show you how to build a camera using quaternions and avoiding gimbal lock while allowing the user three degrees of rotational freedom without restrictions. If you're interested, search the Internet for more information about quaternions and more operations you can perform on them. It never hurts to have classes as comprehensive as possible.

One Look Back, Two Steps Forward

Wow. Let's slow down for a minute or two. The obligatory look back on this chapter reveals a whole bunch of little things concerning math, math, and more math. The good thing is that we managed to wrap up all those things into one single comprehensive math library specialized for use in 3D computer graphics applications. In addition, the chapter showed you how to use certain processor optimizations such as SSE as one kind of SIMD to speed up your performance (when possible, and when it makes sense to). Although you may have found some things in this chapter challenging, wouldn't life be boring without a few challenges?

To develop a useful engine, you really do need a sound knowledge of mathematics (at least of the match needed for 3D graphics). I can just show you the door; you are the one who has to walk through it. If you still feel a bit unsure about the math I showed you or if you already think you need more of this, buy a good book focusing on this topic. Although many books on the market promise all you need to know about mathematics for video games, one book really does give you your money's worth: David Eberly and Philip J. Schneider's book *Geometric Tools for Computer Graphics*. Their book covers all you need to know about math. What is not contained in their book is of no importance to computer graphics; I assure you of that.

That said, with the zfx3d.lib library you are well equipped to master all mathematical and geometrical obstacles waiting for you in this book. Even the object-oriented design of the library enhances its usability (even though it is not strictly, purely perfect C++ object orientation). The code is good enough to be easily maintained and used, and that is the single most important thing.

The next chapter leaves the area of 3D math to focus on the renderer. You will then learn a bit about materials and texture and 2D graphics. This is a warming up exercise for Chapter 6, "The Render Device of the Engine," where the real version of the renderer is implemented.

Review the code and the project files on the accompanying CD-ROM, and don't forget that you must meet the IDE requirements to compile the SSE codes in these sources. I built this project using Visual C++ .NET (7.0), so don't wonder why you cannot open this project using Visual Studio or Visual C++ 6.0. If you want to compile the library using these old tools without the processor pack and service packs mentioned earlier, you must remove the SSE instruction and stick to the pure C/C++ code paths.

If you can actually compile the library, don't forget about the operating system and the processor; these must also support the SSE assembler.

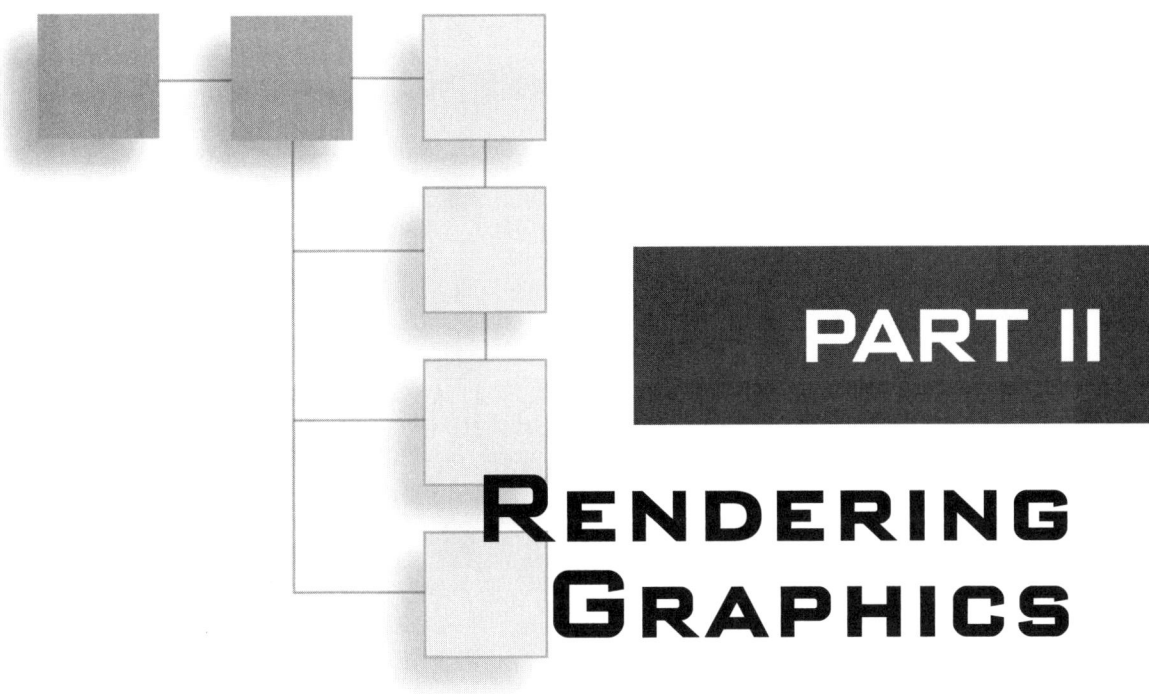

PART II
RENDERING GRAPHICS

CHAPTER 5
Materials, Textures, and Transparency .189

CHAPTER 6
The Render Device of the Engine 235

CHAPTER 7
3D Pipelines and Shaders 335

CHAPTER 8
Loading and Animating 3D Models 387

CHAPTER 5

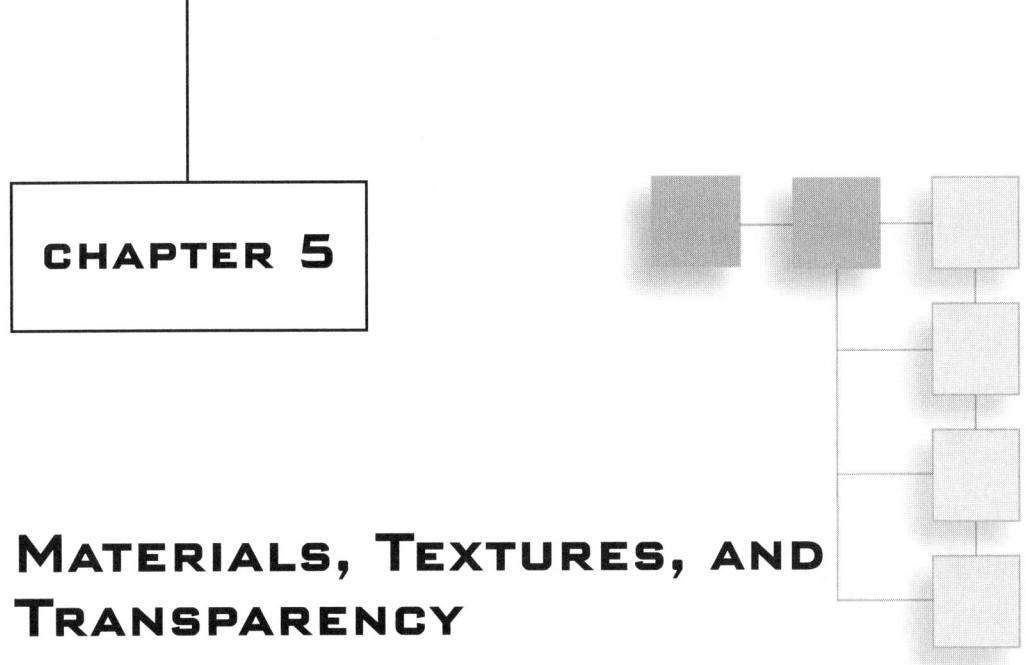

Materials, Textures, and Transparency

If two people are always thinking the same, one of them is superfluous.
Winston Churchill

The introductory quote from this chapter reveals a truth in a very unromantic way. Actually, this quote is about redundancy, which is relevant to what we are doing here—developing software for use in 3D computer graphics. One of the most fundamental things is that during this development you should avoid redundancy as much as possible. The speed of our code is directly connected to the overall performance of the running program. On the uppermost level, this means the code you never execute at all is as fast as it can get.

Now such code would be quite ridiculous, wouldn't it? Don't judge too quickly. Just think of scene management and culling away invisible or hidden objects. You would then not execute the code for those objects. I will show you scene management techniques in Chapter 13, "Scene Management."

For now, this chapter covers the following objectives:

- Manage resources without wasting memory
- Define and use light and materials
- Use texture to extend the realism of your models
- Load graphic files and use them as textures
- Create transparency effects on textures

Middle Management

If you need to skip unnecessary calculations in your code, you can do so in several ways, and reduce redundant usage of memory as well. Redundant code appears in situations in which you use constants throughout your code; however, always recalculate them. Do I need to say more than (Pi/2) or (2*Pi)?

Obviously, situations such as this can easily be found in the code and then wiped out quickly. However, there is a similar situation in which such a redundancy is not that obvious because even the uncontrolled use of memory leads to a penalty in speed. Just imagine the following situation: You load a 3D model from your disc and want to show it on the screen. This model has about 2,000 faces and uses a single graphics file as texture. However, the model format saves the texture by its filename for each face of the model that uses this texture.

> **Caution**
>
> The X file format from Microsoft is capable of doing such a silly thing—creating redundant textures and materials. Even the D3DXMesh helper class in the DirectX SDK is not smart enough to recognize multiple uses of the same texture and material. The X file format lets you alternatively save a unique texture/material definition once somewhere in the model file and then provide only references to those for each face. Unfortunately, most X file exporters for Maya, 3D Studio, or Softimage XSI do not use these references and define identical textures multiple times in the exported model file.

If you had a plain and simple model loader, you would just walk through the file and load the face vertex and index data. Each time you encountered a texture definition you would then load the texture along with the face data. The worst-case scenario takes place, in which you load the same graphics file as texture about 2,000 times. Even a small resolution texture consumes about a quarter of a megabyte of memory ($256 \times 256 = 24$ bits). Thus, the same texture in this example ends up using 500MB of memory.

Having to individually render 2,000 faces slows down your graphics adapter to the point where it's faster to draw the scene by hand. In addition, the 500MB of texture data makes using real-time rendering impossible. No graphics adapter exists yet that is able to spend 500MB of video memory for textures alone. So, you have to send a huge amount of that data during runtime from your system memory or the AGP memory over the bus system to the graphics adapter. This equals trying to push an elephant through a telephone line. We will talk about bus traffic issues later in Chapter 7, "3D Pipelines and Shaders," about shader programming.

The bottom line is that the circle to the introductory quote is now closing. In this example, we were dealing with texture data that was redundant about 2,000 times. But, as you can see, there is no sense in loading the same data multiple times. It would do the job to load the graphics file one time and reuse it for every face that needs to have this file as texture. Optically, you get the same result but internally you can render all 2,000 faces with a single call without having to switch the texture object during the rendering operations. But the gain in performance is like switching over from a one HP engine to the Enterprise's warp drive.

> **Tip**
>
> The gain in performance does not stem only from saving bus traffic for huge amounts of data. It also comes from the fact that modern graphics adapters like to render hundreds of faces in a single call much more than rendering single faces in a lot of calls. They are then able to use a load of optimizations, avoiding redundant transformations.

About Management

You might still be wondering why I'm talking about management all the time. Referring to the science of management as part of business administration, you can regard management from an institutional and from a functional point of view. This means there is always an institution (a person) who is managing something and there are functions (tasks) to be fulfilled by managing something.

In the early 1990s, you could see a trend in which big companies tried to thin out the middle management level to cut costs. This was also meant to keep the chain of communication as short as possible between the upper and the lower management levels. From a business point of view, a flat hierarchy makes sense.

But this is not necessarily true for other areas in which managing something is involved. Now transfer this managing idea to what we are dealing with here. In the area of software development, the upper management is the actual program running on a machine and demanding things from the hardware to be done. The lower level is the hardware itself, which has to fulfill several tasks to comply. In this scheme, the top management sends a bunch of polygons to the low-level guys, who are required to render them. Now you have a flat hierarchy without lengthy communication chains. However, you also have the 2,000 polygons problem as well.

Our Own Middle Management

Over the course of this book, you will encounter the same problem again and again: data, data, and data. I continually repeat this topic by implementing several manager classes or just managing functions in the code to handle upcoming data in a smart way to avoid redundancy.

In fact, it is not a good idea to bother top managers like a video game application with additional work. A top manager is just not interested in how many polygons a certain video game level has and which polygon uses which texture. If the manager had to handle this, he would be trapped in analyzing bunches of data, leaving little time for him to make important decisions, which is what he is actually supposed to do.

Enough of this manager talk for now. The bottom line is that you need to have some kind of middle management between the application and the hardware. And naturally the video game engine is exactly this kind of manager, or—to say the least—you need a different managing functionality inside the engine.

The tasks a manager has to fulfill can be as diverse as the definitions of different managing styles you can find in the science of business administration. We'll concentrate on managers made from silicon and electrical current. As opposed to big companies, you as a programmer still need to occupy lots of positions in middle management. In later chapters, you will see some other manager classes or functions implemented as well. Every time you have to deal with huge amounts of (possibly even redundant) data, it makes sense to employ a manager to do this. But who decides how to process the data and which data needs to be processed at a given point of time?

The top management (video game application) as well as the low-level management (hardware) sees only the data they need to see. The top level works with this data, whereas the low level must deal with only a bunch of polygons that are most likely visible. Now I'm sure you are beginning to see certain parallels to the loose definition of an engine I made in Chapter 1, "3D Engines and Game Programming." And indeed, an engine is mostly about managing data in the most efficient way, with regard to its subordinates as well as its superiors.

Employing a Texture Manager

In this chapter, you will get acquainted with the first manager sitting in the ZFXEngine 2.0. This manager must deal with materials and textures. A surface's light reflection behavior or even its light emitting behavior can be adjusted by tweaking its *material values*. *Textures*, on the other hand, are simple 2D graphics displayed on the surfaces. Therefore, they are similar to the image of an object in diffuse light and you can make a 3D rectangle look very detailed without actually building the 3D geometry for all the details.

When talking about managing resources to save memory and bus bandwidth, think about the example of a 3D model using the same texture 2,000 times. It is not difficult to load the texture only once for a 3D model. However, if you are dealing with hundreds of models and some of them share several textures, you still can load each file only one time into the memory.

You need only a list of textures; each time a model requests to get a certain texture, you can loop up in this list. If the texture is already loaded, you can return a pointer to the texture data to the model for further references to the texture. If the texture is not yet loaded and therefore does not appear in the list, you can load the data, add it to the list, and then return a pointer to its data.

Now you have successfully separated the additional data needed by a model from the place where the model data is stored. Thus, the textures are separated from the geometry data and a manager is responsible not only for loading, but also for providing access to the textures. The same scheme could apply to the models themselves. Think of a structure holding a platoon of tanks. Each one of the tanks of the platoon uses a 3D model of a tank. If the platoon uses only a single tank model, a model manager should sit between the platoon class and the model class that takes care of loading and storing each model only one time.

To illustrate this scheme, let's implement a manager for textures and materials.

A Class for Skins

We'll start by discussing the terms *texture*, *light*, and *material*. Then we'll get down to work and try to melt those terms into a single structure so we can manage the data more easily as opposed to separating textures and materials. We'll name this structure skin, but don't mistake it for a relation to animated model files using a technique called *skin and bones*. You will be introduced to that technique in Chapter 13.

At the end of this chapter, you will learn how to implement a manager that takes care of a combined structure holding a material and multiple textures each. A simple polygon typically comes with not just one texture applied to its surface, but with multiple ones—for example, a diffuse texture plus a detail map texture and a bump map. The focus of this chapter is on managing data and resources in a smart way.

Textures

Back to the 3D models you want to show on the screen. The fewer polygons you have to display, the faster the calculations that need to be done for each model and the faster it is displayed on the screen. For example, you shouldn't build a mosaic using a single polygon for each part of the mosaic. Instead, you should build a single rectangle for the whole mosaic. "It will look bad and nothing like a mosaic," you might say. You can fake the impression you get while looking at it if you use a texture displaying a mosaic and put that onto the rectangle.

A texture is just a plain 2D image. If a textured polygon is rendered, the graphics adapter calculates a position on the texture map based on the polygon's texture coordinates for each projected pixel making up the polygon. It then takes the corresponding color from the texture map and uses this color, which is modified with lighting to display on the screen. Using this little trick lets you fake a lot of details on otherwise plain surfaces.

Take a look at Figure 5.1, which displays the model of a tank. On the right side, this model uses no textures and does not really look like a tank anymore. On the left side, you see the same model with a simple texture applied to it. That model has wheels, tracks, and a lot of detail. However it has no more geometry than the naked textured model without a texture map.

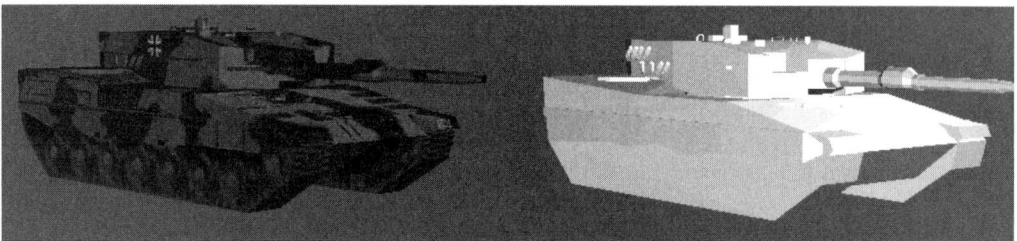

Figure 5.1 The model of a tank, shown with texture on the left side and without texture on the right side.

But nothing comes for free in this virtual 3D world. The same holds true for textured models. You have to pay a price if you fake details, and this price comes in terms of lighting the model. Normally, a 3D engine or 3D video game application does the lighting calculations on a per-vertex base. Thus, the lighting equations are evaluated for each vertex based on the vertex normal and the light direction or, better said, based on the angle between those two vectors. If you have a lot of details but they are faked without real vertices underneath them, all the lighting calculations will look wrong. If a texture displays sharp edges in the model, both faked surfaces sharing those sharp edges will have the same amount of light on them, which would not be the case in reality.

You can use several techniques to fake the lighting—lightmaps, dark maps, or bump maps, for example. Bump mapping is used later in this book and is illustrated with vertex shaders and pixel shaders in Chapter 7.

Light and Material

In a 3D scene, you want to have as much realism as possible. One of the main components that makes a computer image look realistic is lighting, along with the shadows the light creates. In 3D computer graphics, if you don't have sufficient lighting, your applications will look like an ancient video game where the hardware used to be too slow to make it look better.

In computer graphics, you deal with two kinds of light: ambient light and direct light. *Ambient* light is the light that is present at each point in a 3D scene with the same intensity and apparently coming from all directions with the same intensity. In nature, that kind of light stems from the direct light that is reflected all over the space on every object it hits, thus making each object an emitter of light for itself. This level of light existing all around is the ambient light level.

Direct light always comes from a light source whose position could be found by looking at where its light falls. In computer graphics, you can define a level of ambient light even without direct light because it makes things simpler. You don't calculate all the reflections; instead, you can define a level of ambient light that is used without additional calculations. For direct light, the computer graphics have the following three kinds of light sources:

- Directional light
- Point light
- Spot light

You can see the effects of those light sources in Figure 5.2, later in this chapter.

Directional Light

The light coming from very distant light sources is called *directional* light. The type of light source from which it comes doesn't matter because the observer is too far away from it. The light rays have already traveled such a long distance that you can think of those you see as being parallel to each other. This is a great simplification of the lighting calculations because you can think of each object in your scene as being lit by the same light vector. There is no change in angle and no change in intensity or color.

This might sound strange, but there is one kind of directional light we all know: the normal sunlight we see everyday. Think of the area of the city where you live—the sun itself is still so far away that its rays hit the whole area with a range of different angles. Yet you can think of the angle from each point in this area to the sun as being exactly the same because the range of angles is very small. That means that all the surfaces facing the light are lit all over with the same intensity.

Point Light

A *point* light source is a single point in space that emits light evenly in all directions. If you want to calculate your lighting with respect to a point light source, you need to know only the position of the light source as well as the light's color and intensity. A point light lights each point on a flat surface with a different intensity because each of those points has another angle to the point light that is taken into consideration.

The more directly a point is aligned to the incoming light vector, the more light that falls on this point. The less aligned the normal vector is with the light vector, the darker it is. Again, take a look at Figure 5.2 to see an area of different lighting intensity on the lit rectangle as opposed to the constant light intensity in the case of directional light.

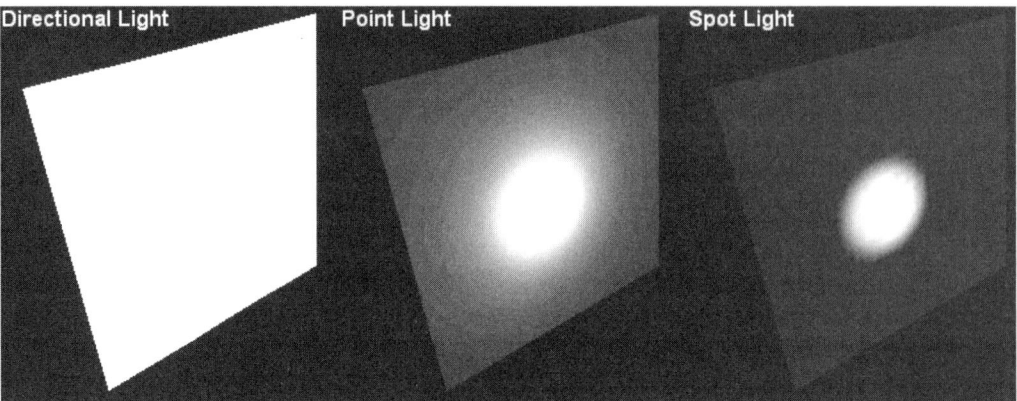

Figure 5.2 Lighting a gray rectangle by three types of light sources.

Calculating a point light is easy because you just have to put light onto each object inside the sphere of light surrounding the point light source.

Tip
There are many bad jokes out there about mathematicians. Lots of them go like this: Says one mathematician to the other: "I've come up with a solution for how to calculate the amount of milk given by a cow. Let's suppose the cow is spherical . . ." This joke is about the habit of mathematicians to approximate every object they need to calculate with a sphere first. That is because of the easiness of the math related to spheres.

Spot Light

The most complex light source is the *spot* light, and it is the light source that is most common in our technical world. Unfortunately, it is not easy to calculate lighting from it. Actually, a spot light is similar to a point light, but with the important restriction that it emits light into only a certain angle. Just think of a bulb whose socket prevents the light from going evenly in all directions. The same applies for lampshades and similar objects blocking light in a certain angle around its emitter.

To define a spot light, you need to set a lot of values. First, you need its position, color, and light intensity. Then you also need to know the direction in which the spot light is emitting its rays. This is opposed to the point light and the directional light where you need only the position or the direction of the light, respectively. Finally, you need to set an angle defining a cone through which the light is emitted. Actually, you need two of those cones. Figure 5.3 shows how those cones and angles relate to each other. The inner cone is where the light intensity is evenly distributed, and the outer cone is used to fade out the light intensity. The space between the inner and the outer cone is known as the penumbra.

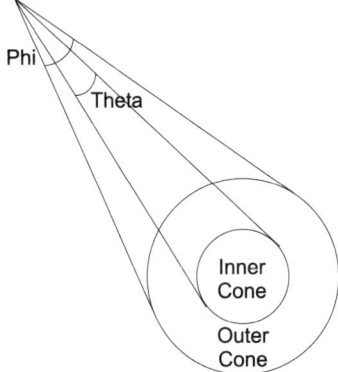

Figure 5.3 The two angles and their cones of a spot light.

About Hardware Lights

To light 3D scenes, Direct3D and OpenGL provide a structure for light sources you can fill with values and activate for the graphics adapter. This comes at a price and with certain restrictions. I will show you the structure for lights in Direct3D, but I'm not going to use hardware lighting. Later I'll show you how to implement lighting using vertex shaders and pixel shaders in Chapter 7. But I want you to know about hardware lights.

The restrictions connected to them are that you can activate only eight hardware lights at a time and the calculations they perform are not very fast because they cannot be optimized like vertex shaders can and have to be as general as possible. However, even if eight lights isn't enough for a 3D scene, you can always render your scene in small batches—for example, room by room. Just activate the room's eight light sources and render the room. Then activate the next room's light sources and render the next room, and so on.

Another restriction is that the hardware lights are evaluated per vertex and not per pixel. The rectangle displayed in Figure 5.2 could never be lit in such a way using hardware lights because only its four vertices can have different light intensity values between which the rectangle's color is interpolated. This is called Gouraud Shading. However, you cannot have a cone of light shining on the middle of the rectangle. If none of the vertices is inside the cone, the rectangle would have no light on it. You can get around this problem by subdividing the rectangle into dozens of small rectangles, thus making it have many vertices that can take different light values from hardware lights.

The more vertices you have for this rectangle, the better the lighting result will be, up to the point where you have a vertex for each pixel and the vertex lighting is equal to per-pixel lighting. As you already saw, this is not a good way of doing things because each additional vertex adds overhead and eats calculation time for transformations, and possibly bus transfer as well.

I still want to take a look at the structure that defines a hardware light in Direct3D. We talked about lights previously so can see what its fields mean.

```
typedef struct _D3DLIGHT9
    {
    D3DLIGHTTYPE Type;
    D3DCOLORVALUE Diffuse;
    D3DCOLORVALUE Specular;
    D3DCOLORVALUE Ambient;
    D3DVECTOR Position;
    D3DVECTOR Direction;
    float Range;
    float Falloff;
    float Attenuation0;
    float Attenuation1;
    float Attenuation2;
    float Theta;
    float Phi;
    } D3DLIGHT9;
```

The attenuation values are three constants in a formula that are used to calculate the actual attenuation value; that is, to calculate the way the light fades out as you get further from its position. Please refer to the DirectX documentation for further details. The different types of light are defined as this:

```
typedef enum _D3DLIGHTTYPE
    {
    D3DLIGHT_POINT = 1,
    D3DLIGHT_SPOT = 2,
    D3DLIGHT_DIRECTIONAL = 3,
    } D3DLIGHTTYPE;
```

To activate a hardware light, you need to do two things. First, you have to call the function IDirect3D9::SetLight to put the light into a slot indexed 0–7. But that will not yet activate the light. You need to call the function IDirect3D9::LightEnable, give the index of the slot, and provide a bool value that tells whether to activate or deactivate the light.

A directional light calculated by Direct3D can sometimes be useful if no fancy lighting effects are needed.

Material's Influence on Lighting

Just placing one or more light sources in a 3D scene has no effect on the objects being brighter or darker in the first place. Not yet. You could calculate the light intensity on certain points in the scene, but the objects in the scene are not visible yet. Crank up your flashback processor please and follow me up to your biology and physics classes in school: Without light, there is darkness. That is the easy part.

If you switch on a light source that then pumps photons into the scene, it gets more complicated. According to particle wave dualism, you can treat the light similarly to a bouncing billiard ball. You can actually see something in front of you, but what exactly do you see? Don't mistake what you see for really seeing the objects standing around you. That is not the case. Your eyes are just sensors that can detect photons hitting them, and your brain transforms the impacts into an image and interprets it.

That's the whole story: The light source emits photons into the space. The photons are then reflected by solid objects in the space, so they change their directions, bouncing off other objects and so on. During their journey, they lose energy due to collisions, and sometimes they happen to hit a human's eye. If this happens, the eye detects an impacting photon with a certain energy and color that was influenced by the object from which it was reflected. This is what you see, if you think you see an object. In reality, you see only the photons the object reflects roughly in your direction.

Why do different photons stemming from the same light source look different to the eye? Just think about a mirror: It can be as bright as the light source itself, but the wall on which the mirror is located looks different from that. You actually approach the sense of materials.

The material of an object determines how incoming photons are dealt with. If you talk about real material in nature, you talk about the chemical and physical attributes of a surface. A matt or rough surface, for example, is not really a matt but is very bumpy, as you can see under a microscope. The incoming photons therefore are reflected like billiard balls. However, they're not reflected in a single direction, but are reflected in different directions. So, there is no bright spot of light on them like there is on shiny materials.

If the surface of an object is really more or less flat, even through a microscope, most of the photons are reflected into roughly the same direction. Thus, the viewer can see a bright spot on such a surface if it hits the reflection angle to the light source.

However, we are not in nature; we're in a virtual environment. Nonetheless, you have a structure called material that can take several attributes to describe a surface's behavior under the influence of light. To make things easier, you would differentiate certain types of light in a scene. You have a separate ambient light, a separate diffuse light used for normal reflections like on matte surfaces, and a separate specular light. This is used for additional reflections on shiny surfaces. Just look at the `D3DLIGHT9` structure, and you can see that a hardware light source can emit those three types of light.

A material structure can be used during rendering. This material structure defines what percentage of the light in the scene of a certain type is reflected by the object. Only if there is at least a small percentage of any of the light reflected does the object get a color other than jet black. If you define a material to reflect no ambient and no diffuse lighting but all specular lighting, you would have a shiny surface. You will see the material in action soon.

Basic Structures

For the ZFXEngine 2.0, we also need some basic structures, as defined in the file ZFX.h, because the engine uses them as well as the user using the engine. The smallest unit you have to deal with when we are talking about material definitions is a color. So, I defined the following type to handle colors:

```
typedef struct ZFXCOLOR_TYPE
   {
   union {
      struct {
         float fR;
         float fG;
         float fB;
         float fA;
         };
      float c[4];
      };
   } ZFXCOLOR;
```

A color is built from four floating-point values specifying the red, green, blue, and alpha component of it. Those values must be given in the range from 0.0f to 1.0f, where 1.0f equals 100 percent. The alpha value defines the opacity of the color. If the alpha value is 1.0f, the color is totally opaque. If it is 0.0f, the color is totally transparent. In between, it would be transparent to some degree, making more distant objects behind the one using this color shine through.

With this structure, you can define a structure for a material. First, look at Figure 5.4, which summarizes what we've discussed about lighting, the types of light, and the types of light sources in the last paragraph. As you can see, the ambient light is separated from the direct light and is just added to the other light in the scene. The direct light splits into the three possible kinds of light sources with their light meeting at the material of a 3D object in the scene.

Depending on the material of an object, the calculations needed for the diffuse lighting model or for the specular lighting model are done. It is also possible to use both types of reflection on a single object and add those together. Finally, you have the output, which is a certain light intensity and light color used to modify a certain pixel or vertex. It's based on which type of lighting level you modify the texture or vertex color with.

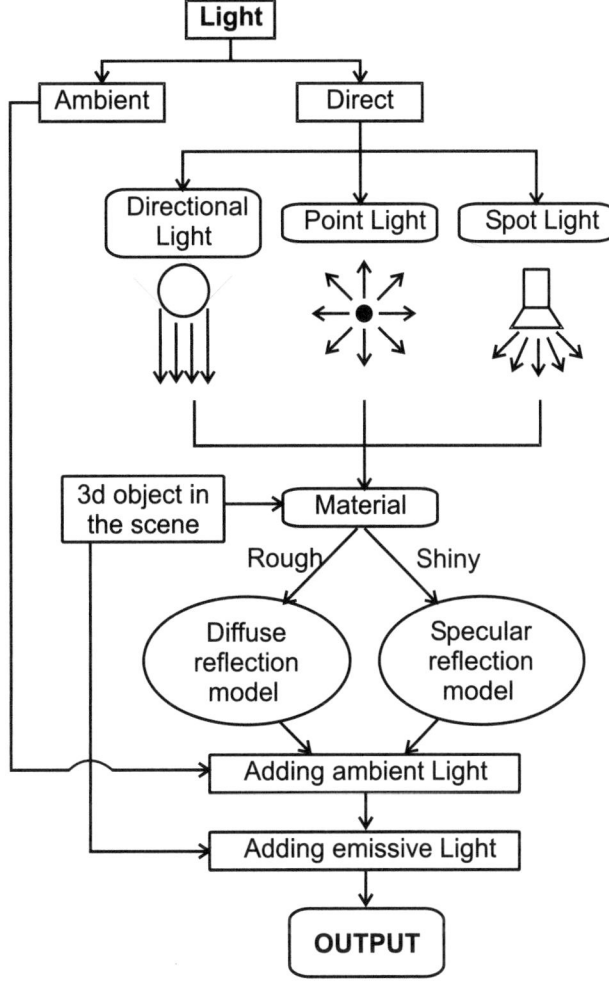

Figure 5.4 A simplified overview of the types of light and light sources in computer graphics.

The next structure I defined is the one used for materials. This is just a copy of the material structure used by Direct3D, but we want to stay API-independent. The structure uses four color values and the exponent used in the specular lighting formula. You might wonder why light sources can emit only three types of light (ambient, diffuse, and specular) when the material has information about four light types. You also might wonder why there is information about colors in the material at all. The colors stored in the material just say how much of the incoming light will be reflected by simply multiplying the color in the material with the color coming from the light source. Let's suppose you have a light source emitting diffuse light of the color RGB (1.0f, 0.5, 0.5f), which is a red-colored light. You also have an object with a material defining the diffuse light color of the material by

RGB (0.5f, 1.0f, 1.0f). The object will appear to be gray because the color of the light is multiplied by the color in the material, making the final diffuse color value for this object RGB (0.5f, 0.5f, 0.5f).

Before I tell you what the fourth color component is used for, take a look at the structure:

```
typedef struct ZFXMATERIAL_TYPE
   {
   ZFXCOLOR cDiffuse;    // RGBA diffuse light
   ZFXCOLOR cAmbient;    // RGBA ambient light
   ZFXCOLOR cSpecular;   // RGBA specular light
   ZFXCOLOR cEmissive;   // RGBA emissive light
   float    fPower;      // Specular power

   } ZFXMATERIAL;
```

The color value for the emissive term is interesting. Normally, you would add together the final color values from diffuse, ambient, and specular lighting to get the final color for the object including all types of light falling on it. However, in some situations you may want to have a bright object independent from the color in the scene. Think of a dark room that should be lit by a point light below its ceiling. You would set a pretty low light level to keep a dark atmosphere in this room. However, if you have an object such as a bulb hanging from the ceiling, the bulb would also be shaded very darkly like all the other polygons. That looks quite unrealistic, though. It should be brighter than the rest of the room, but you cannot achieve this in a simple way by normal lighting calculations.

To solve this situation, a material defines an additional color value that enables the object to add a fourth color to the final light calculated from the ambient, diffuse, and specular values. That is the *emissive* light. It is called *emissive* because this value makes an object look like it is a light source itself. The main difference between a material's emissive color and a real light source is that the material's emissive color affects only the object that uses the material. This color is not taken into consideration for other objects in the scene.

You can start your favorite first-person shooter now and fight your way to a dark room with a bulb hanging from the ceiling. That should not take too long because first-person shooters always have dark rooms. You will notice that the whole room's polygons are dark or poorly lit while the bulb is still shining yellow or white.

Note

> Please note that even if the lighting calculations done for each light source approximate the real light's behavior, three things will not be done by hardware lighting implementation. First, a light source you define and activate is just that—an invisible photon emitter. If you want to see the light source itself, you have to build a 3D model for it and place it at the same position in space.
>
> Second, if the player looks straight into the light source, there is no blend effect as would occur in reality. You have to implement this yourself.

Third, the lighting calculations are done only on a per-object or per-triangle basis. This leads to the effect that other triangles that might occlude light are not taken into consideration. Thus, no shadows are calculated. You are required to do this for yourself, as you will see later.

Okay, let's see what we've got. We have a structure for a color and a material. We lack only the structure for a texture file. Using Direct3D, we would simply utilize the IDirect3DTexture9 interface, but I want to keep this engine free from all API-related stuff. I also want the engine to manage its resources, so we need some additional information in this structure besides the texture data. Here is the structure used by the ZFXEngine 2.0:

```
typedef struct ZFXTEXTURE_TYPE {
   float    fAlpha;      // overall transparency value
   char     *chName;     // texture filename
   void     *pData;      // texture data
   ZFXCOLOR *pClrKeys;   // color key array
   DWORD    dwNum;       // number of color keys
   } ZFXTEXTURE;
```

This structure contains a pointer that holds the name of the graphics file used as texture. This name is also used as an ID for the texture, which means it is unique and you cannot load the same graphics file twice if the skin manager is in place. The void pointer is used to hold a pointer to the actual texture object, which is of type IDirect3DTexture9 in the case of Direct3D. The overall transparency value is the alpha value used for each pixel of the texture map. However, apart from that, you can also have an arbitrary number of colors that have different alpha values that are bigger than the overall transparency. I did call those *color keys*, but that does not mean they are transparent colors.

This structure and the transparency system enable a texture to be 50 percent transparent on all pixels but also have all black pixels with 75 percent transparency and all red pixels in the texture with 100 percent transparency. Shortly, you will see how to implement this transparency effect.

Before I let you implement something, I will show you another structure you will need during the implementation process. Now we have a structure for colors, materials, and textures. Any polygon you want to render must have at least one material but can have up to an infinite number of textures. However, it does not make sense to use more than eight textures on a single polygon. This would be already pretty slow. Most graphics adapters can render only four textures in a single pass, so using eight different textures on the same surface would require at least two render passes.

Tip

In single-pass rendering, a graphics adapter renders a triangle in one rendering pass This is opposed to multi-pass rendering, where you render the triangles more than once, blending the results of each rendering pass together for a final image. With multi-pass rendering you can put more textures onto a triangle than your graphics adapter can do at one time with a single pass. More frequently, multi-pass rendering is used for special effects, where, for example, the output of a first pass is used as input texture for the second pass.

Here is the structure called ZFXSKIN, which combines one material and up to eight textures. There is also a field in the structure that indicates whether the skin uses alpha values other than 1.0f.

```
typedef struct ZFXSKIN_TYPE
   {
   bool   bAlpha;
   UINT   nMaterial;
   UINT   nTexture[8];
   } ZFXSKIN;
```

As you can see, only the textures and material in the manager with an ID of the type unsigned int are saved. The manager keeps the real objects in storage and gives only those ID values to the user. In fact, those IDs are only indices to an array inside the manager where the data can be found.

Interface Definition for a Skin Manager

Now you can warm up your fingers and get the keyboard ready to start coding. For the remainder of this chapter, I will show you how to implement a manager that creates materials and loads textures while being sure not to load the same texture data twice. However, considering the materials, you could also decide not to check whether the same material is already defined. A material is made up from only four color values and one additional float value. Thus, storing these materials redundantly does not waste too much memory, while attempts to avoid redundancy are too expensive because of the search times necessary to loop through already created materials and compare 17 floating-point values for each existing material to identify a total match. Furthermore, the bad floating-point value accuracy could also let a total match slip through unrecognized or find a mismatch to be a perfect match. I also integrated checking for redundancy of materials to let you see how this anti-redundancy scheme actually works.

Here is the interface definition of the skin manager. It does not offer too many functions, but it is more than enough to be flexible and functional. First, take a look at it and then we'll discuss it and implement it into a class.

```
class ZFXSkinManager
   {
   protected:
      UINT         m_nNumSkins;        // num. skins
```

```cpp
      UINT         m_nNumMaterials; // num. materials
      UINT         m_nNumTextures;  // num. textures
      ZFXSKIN      *m_pSkins;
      ZFXMATERIAL  *m_pMaterials;
      ZFXTEXTURE   *m_pTextures;

   public:
      ZFXSkinManager(void) {};
      virtual ~ZFXSkinManager(void) {};

      virtual HRESULT AddSkin(const ZFXCOLOR *pcAmbient,
                              const ZFXCOLOR *pcDiffuse,
                              const ZFXCOLOR *pcEmissive,
                              const ZFXCOLOR *pcSpecular,
                              float fSpecPower,
                              UINT *nSkinID)=0;

      virtual HRESULT AddTexture(UINT nSkinID,
                                 const char *chName,
                                 bool bAlpha,
                                 float fAlpha,
                                 ZFXCOLOR *cColorKeys,
                                 DWORD dwNumColorKeys)
                                 =0;

      HRESULT AddTextureHeightmapAsBump(UINT nSkinID,
                                        const char *chName)=0;

      virtual bool      MaterialEqual( const ZFXMATERIAL *pMat0,
                                       const ZFXMATERIAL *pMat1)=0;

      virtual ZFXSKIN   GetSkin(UINT nSkinID)=0;

      virtual ZFXMATERIAL GetMaterial(UINT nMatID)=0;

      virtual const char* GetTextureName(UINT nTexID,
                                         float *pfAlpha,
                                         ZFXCOLOR *pAK,
                                         UCHAR *pNum)=0;

      virtual void      LogCurrentStatus(char *chLog,
                                         bool bDetail)=0;
   };
```

As you would demand from an interface, it is as simple as possible. There are only three pointers to become arrays and hold the data after it is loaded, along with three integers for the number of elements in each array. In addition to the constructor and the destructor, the two most important functions of this interface are `ZFXSkinManager::AddSkin` and `ZFXSkinManager::AddTexture`. The first one is used to create a new skin object. Therefore you have to provide all the parameters needed to create a new material object for this skin. You are also required to hand in a reference pointer to an `unsigned int` value where you want the ID of the new skin to be saved. An application creating a skin must save this value to access it later.

The second function adds a new texture to the skin. Its parameter list is a bit lengthy because you can already set some attributes for the texture. First, you need to name the skin for which the texture should be used along with the name of the graphics file used for the texture. The function then checks whether the skin can take one more texture and tries to load the specified graphics file. Then you can specify whether the texture has an alpha value and supply an alpha value used for each pixel as well as a list of color keys. In those lists, you specify a color that should become transparent to an arbitrary degree. For example, the color key RGBA(1.0f, 0.0f, 0.0f, 0.3f) makes all the pixels in the texture colored with RGB(1.0f, 0.0f, 0.0f) only 30 percent solid and 70 percent transparent.

This transparency is easy to set for the user. He needs to know only the color he wants to influence. Most games predefine a certain color to become 100 percent transparent later. This is mostly the color RGB(1.0f, 0.0f, 1.0f) or RGB(0.0f, 1.0f, 1.0f) because these colors would not be used in this pure form on textures that should have no color keys.

The function `ZFXSkinManager::LogCurrentStatus` is a useful debugging tool because it prints a log file and writes out all the materials and textures currently loaded with the manager. You can use this to make a dump of the manager during runtime to check whether all the textures were loaded correctly. The bool parameter controls whether you get a brief log or a lengthy one, writing out all the material and texture data.

I put this interface definition into the `ZFXRenderDevice.h` class because the skin manager should become an attribute of the render device in the next chapter. This attribute is declared as `ZFXSkinManager* m_pSkinMan`. This forces the user who wants to implement his own version of a render device with the ZFXEngine 2.0 render device definition to implement a skin manager as well. In a completely C++ object-oriented design, you would not define any attributes for interfaces. Luckily we are not in such a situation.

> **Note**
>
> Now we have an interface definition for a skin manager, and will implement it in the next paragraph by writing its implementation to the files `ZFXD3D_skinman.h` and `ZFXD3D_skinman.cpp`. These will be added to the ZFXEngine's DLL project for the render device in the next chapter. At the end of this chapter, you will have the final implementation of this manager but no testing application because the skin

manager is meant to work only with the render device. It will take some work to wire those two together, which will be done in the next chapter.

The Skin Manager of the Render Device

Finally, we've made it to the point where we start implementing the interface definition of the skin manager. The class implementing the interface is called `ZFXD3DSkinManager`. I will now show you the class declaration, and I will ask you to ignore the `ZFXD3DVCache` class for a while. This is a class you will not see until the next chapter, but keep in mind this class would really like to have access to the skin manager to make handling skins internally easier. Here is the class for the skin manager:

```
class ZFXD3DSkinManager : public ZFXSkinManager
   {
   friend class ZFXD3DVCache;

   public:
      ZFXD3DSkinManager(LPDIRECT3DDEVICE9 pDevice,
                        FILE *pLog);
      ~ZFXD3DSkinManager(void);

      HRESULT AddSkin(const ZFXCOLOR *pcAmbient,
                      const ZFXCOLOR *pcDiffuse,
                      const ZFXCOLOR *pcEmissive,
                      const ZFXCOLOR *pcSpecular,
                      float fSpecPower, UINT *nSkinID);

      HRESULT AddTexture(UINT nSkinID, const char *chName,
                         bool bAlpha, float fAlpha,
                         ZFXCOLOR *cColorKeys,
                         DWORD dwNumColorKeys);

      HRESULT AddTextureHeightmapAsBump(UINT nSkinID,
                                        const char *chName);

      bool MaterialEqual(const ZFXMATERIAL *pMat0,
                         const ZFXMATERIAL *pMat1);

      ZFXSKIN     GetSkin(UINT nSkinID);
      ZFXMATERIAL GetMaterial(UINT nMatID);
      const char* GetTextureName(UINT nTexID);
```

```
        void LogCurrentStatus(char *chLog, bool bDetailed);

protected:
    LPDIRECT3DDEVICE9  m_pDevice;
    FILE               *m_pLog;

    inline bool ColorEqual(const ZFXCOLOR *pCol0,
                           const ZFXCOLOR *pCol1);

    HRESULT CreateTexture(ZFXTEXTURE *pTexture,
                          bool bAlpha);

    HRESULT SetAlphaKey(LPDIRECT3DTEXTURE9 *ppTexture, UCHAR R,
                        UCHAR G, UCHAR B, UCHAR A);

    HRESULT SetTransparency(LPDIRECT3DTEXTURE9 *ppTexture,
                            UCHAR Alpha);

    DWORD   MakeD3DColor(UCHAR R, UCHAR G, UCHAR B, UCHAR A);

    void    Log(char *, ...);
};
```

You will notice that the constructor of this class has a parameter list and that it wants to have a pointer to a Direct3D device. You can also give this class a pointer to a FILE object, which would then be used as a log file.

About Log Files

Nothing is more helpful for debugging a complex project than a good, organized log file explaining the whole history of a test run of an application. There are at least two good ways to do this kind of manual debugging. The first method is to create a log file class that is then linked to every project where you want to debug. The disadvantage is that this class needs to be accessible everywhere, so you have to keep it with you all the time.

Another way is to just log some things into a text file. This task is not complicated, so I put a log function in every class that should be able to write to a debug log. Each important class in the ZFXEngine 2.0 has the same function used for the output into this log file.

To accomplish this task, each of the classes—such as ZFXRenderDevice or ZFXSkinManager, for example—has to provide not only the function to write to the log, but also a pointer called FILE *m_pLog. This could be a log file of its own, or it can be a pointer to an existing log file handed to the class in its constructor.

I also employed a global variable, `bool g_bLF`, which means log-flush. If this variable is set to `true`, the log file is flushed after each log call to retain the information even if the program crashes and prevents the logged data from being written from the buffer to the actual file. The function doing the logging process looks like this:

```
void ZFXSomeClassOfTheEngine::Log(char *chString, ...)
   {
   char ch[256];
   char *pArgs;

   pArgs = (char*) &chString + sizeof(chString);
   vsprintf(ch, chString, pArgs);
   fprintf(m_pLog, "[ ZFXSomeClassOfTheEngine]: ");
   fprintf(m_pLog, ch);
   fprintf(m_pLog, "\n");

   if (g_bLF)
      fflush(m_pLog);
   } // Log
```

This log function can be used just like the standard C function `fprintf()`, which means you can hand in an arbitrary number of parameters after the formatting string. The `pArgs` pointer is set to the start of the optional parameter list. The standard C function `vsprintf()` is then used to convert the data from such a parameter list to a real string based on the formatting string. This complete string is then saved as a string named `ch`.

For more comfort while reading, the output is prefixed by the name of the class it stems from. This is followed by the actual log file entry and a carriage return sign. If the user wants the log file to be crash-safe it is then flushed immediately.

Constructors and Destructors

Besides the log function, some more nonpublic functions are in the class definition of the skin manager. In the following paragraphs, we will discuss each of the functions in detail, but for now let's start with the following constructor:

```
ZFXD3DSkinManager::ZFXD3DSkinManager(LPDIRECT3DDEVICE9 pDevice, FILE *pLog)
   {
   m_nNumMaterials = 0;
   m_nNumTextures  = 0;
   m_nNumSkins     = 0;
   m_pMaterials    = NULL;
   m_pTextures     = NULL;
   m_pSkins        = NULL;
```

```
m_pLog        = pLog;
m_pDevice     = pDevice;
Log("online");
}
```

This is a typical constructor, as you have seen from hundreds of classes. You just have to initialize each pointer and each member variable of the class to some start value. That's all there is to it. However, the destructor is a bit more complex because it has to clean up all the things that happen between the construction and destruction:

```
ZFXD3DSkinManager::~ZFXD3DSkinManager(void)
   {
   // release Direct3D texture objects
   if ( m_pTextures ) {
      for (UINT i=0; i<m_nNumTextures; i++) {
         if (m_pTextures[i].pData) {
            ((LPDIRECT3DTEXTURE9)(m_pTextures[i].pData))
                                 ->Release();
            m_pTextures[i].pData = NULL;
            }
         if (m_pTextures[i].pClrKeys) {
            delete [] m_pTextures[i].pClrKeys;
            m_pTextures[i].pClrKeys = NULL;
            }
         if (m_pTextures[i].chName) {
            delete [] m_pTextures[i].chName;
            m_pTextures[i].chName = NULL;
            }
         }
      free( m_pTextures );
      m_pTextures = NULL;
      }

   // free memory
   if (m_pMaterials) {
      free(m_pMaterials);
      m_pMaterials = NULL;
      }

   if (m_pSkins) {
      free(m_pSkins);
      m_pSkins = NULL;
      }
```

```
        Log("offline (ok)");
     }
```

Dealing with memory issues is easy most of the time if you stick to some basic rules. Rule one is that you always must free the memory you allocated in your class. In this case, you have to destroy the IDirect3DTexture9 objects you created by releasing them. For each texture, you have to free the memory allocated for the color keys and the graphics filename as well. Finally, you also must allocate memory for the three arrays themselves, so they must also be granted freedom again.

Now that you know how to initialize and clean up the skin manager, I will introduce you to the implementations of its functions.

Comparing Colors and Materials

One of the most important tasks of the skin manager is to keep track of the loaded data and prevent unique data from being loaded into the memory more than one time. Remember what we talked about concerning redundancy in RAM and VRAM a few pages ago. The skin manager has two helper functions that enable it to compare two colors or two materials to see whether they use equal values.

```
inline bool ZFXD3DSkinManager::ColorEqual( const ZFXCOLOR *pCol0,
                                           const ZFXCOLOR *pCol1)
     {
    if ( (pCol0->fA != pCol1->fA) ||
         (pCol0->fR != pCol1->fR) ||
         (pCol0->fG != pCol1->fG) ||
         (pCol0->fB != pCol1->fB) )
       return false;

    return true;
    } // ColorEqual
/*----------------------------------*/

bool ZFXD3DSkinManager::MaterialEqual( const ZFXMATERIAL *pMat0,
                                       const ZFXMATERIAL *pMat1)
    {
    if (!ColorEqual(&pMat0->cAmbient,  &pMat1->cAmbient)
     || !ColorEqual(&pMat0->cDiffuse,  &pMat1->cDiffuse)
     || !ColorEqual(&pMat0->cEmissive, &pMat1->cEmissive)
     || !ColorEqual(&pMat0->cSpecular, &pMat1->cSpecular)
     || (pMat0->fPower != pMat1->fPower) )
       return false;
```

212   Chapter 5 ■ Materials, Textures, and Transparency

```
      return true;
   } // MaterialEqual
/*------------------------*/
```

That's not too complicated. Just compare each field in the structures and test them for being equal.

Getting Skins

If the engine is later used to render something with a skin that is a material and possibly has textures, such an object goes to the skin manager and requests that its material and texture be set for Direct3D. The following helper functions enable the skin manager to hand out the requested objects from its stock:

```
ZFXSKIN ZFXD3DSkinManager::GetSkin(UINT nSkinID)
   {


   if (nSkinID < m_nNumSkins)
      return m_pSkins[nSkinID];

   else {
      ZFXSKIN EmptySkin;
      return EmptySkin;
      }
   } // GetSkin
```

It is enough for an object to get a copy of the skin object for which it was created. But in some situations, the user wants to know about the material colors and the texture filename associated with a certain ID.

An example is the level editing tool you will see at the end of this book. There, you need to access material colors to display such settings in information dialog boxes and the like. Fortunately, accessing a given index in an array is not that complicated:

```
ZFXMATERIAL ZFXD3DSkinManager::GetMaterial(UINT nMatID)
   {

   if (nMatID < m_nNumMaterials)
      return m_pMaterials[nMatID];

   else {
      ZFXMATERIAL EmptyMaterial;
      return EmptyMaterial;
      }
```

            } // GetMaterial
/*----------------------------*/

const char* ZFXD3DSkinManager::GetTextureName(UINT nID, float *pfAlpha,
                                              ZFXCOLOR *pAK, UCHAR *pNum)
   {
   if (nID >= m_nNumTextures) return NULL;
   if (pfAlpha) *pfAlpha = m_pTextures[nID].fAlpha;
   if (pNum) *pNum = m_pTextures[nID].dwNum;

   if (m_pTextures[nID].pClrKeys && pAK) {
      memcpy(pAK, m_pTextures[nID].pClrKeys,
             sizeof(ZFXCOLOR) * m_pTextures[nID].dwNum);
      }

   return m_pTextures[nID].chName;
   } // GetTextureName

Adding Skins and Textures

If you want to create a new skin, you have to provide the information for the material used for the skin at the very least. A skin does not need to have a texture, but it must not exist without a material. When creating a new skin object in the manager, you must do two things. First, you need to find a free place in the m_pSkins array that is saving all the skins that were created with the manager. From the start, this pointer is empty, so you have to allocate memory dynamically. To prevent ongoing memory allocations during initialization, I make it a habit to initialize slots for 50 new objects each time more space is required. So, if the counter to the array can be divided by 50 without leaving a rest, I just reallocate the memory with 50 more units.

The second thing you must do is to loop through the m_pMaterials array of created materials and see whether an equal material was already created before. If this is the case, you don't need to create another one with the same values.

If you find an identical material in the array, you save only its ID in the new skin object. If you don't find one, you have to create a new material object; you also might need to allocate new memory for the material array, copy the settings of the requested material into the new one, and save the new ID with the new skin. Then you are done.

```
#define MAX_ID 65535

HRESULT ZFXD3DSkinManager::AddSkin( const ZFXCOLOR *pcAmbient,
                                    const ZFXCOLOR *pcDiffuse,
```

Chapter 5 ■ Materials, Textures, and Transparency

```
                                    const ZFXCOLOR *pcEmissive,
                                    const ZFXCOLOR *pcSpecular,
                                    float fSpecPower,
                                    UINT    *nSkinID)
   {
   UINT    nMat, n;
   bool    bMat=false;

   // allocate memory for 50 objects if needed
   if ( (m_nNumSkins%50) == 0 ) {
      n = (m_nNumSkins+50)*sizeof(ZFXSKIN);
      m_pSkins = (ZFXSKIN*)realloc(m_pSkins, n);
      if (!m_pSkins) return ZFX_OUTOFMEMORY;
      }

   ZFXMATERIAL mat;
   mat.cAmbient  = *pcAmbient;
   mat.cDiffuse  = *pcDiffuse;
   mat.cEmissive = *pcEmissive;
   mat.cSpecular = *pcSpecular;
   mat.fPower    = fSpecPower;

   // do we already have such a material?
   for (nMat=0; nMat<m_nNumMaterials; nMat++) {
      if ( MaterialEqual(&mat, &m_pMaterials[nMat]) ) {
         bMat = true;
         break;
         }
      } // for [MATERIALS]

   // if yes save its id if not create a new one
   if (bMat) m_pSkins[m_nNumSkins].nMaterial = nMat;
   else {
      m_pSkins[m_nNumSkins].nMaterial = m_nNumMaterials;

      // allocate memory for 50 objects if needed
      if ( (m_nNumMaterials%50) == 0 ) {
         n = (m_nNumMaterials+50)*sizeof(ZFXMATERIAL);
         m_pMaterials = (ZFXMATERIAL*)realloc(
                              m_pMaterials, n);
         if (!m_pMaterials) return ZFX_OUTOFMEMORY;
         }
```

```
        memcpy(&m_pMaterials[m_nNumMaterials], &mat,
               sizeof(ZFXMATERIAL));
        m_nNumMaterials++;
        }

    m_pSkins[m_nNumSkins].bAlpha = false;
    for (int i=0; i<8; i++)
        m_pSkins[m_nNumSkins].nTexture[i] = MAX_ID;

    // save id and increment counter
    (*nSkinID) = m_nNumSkins;
    m_nNumSkins++;

    return ZFX_OK;
    } // AddSkin
```

The ID is nothing more than just the index position of the objects in the array where they are saved. The first object in the array has an ID of 0, the second has an ID of 1, and so on. Now you can also see why I'm not saving the material data in the skin object itself. This way, we can have many skins while using only a single material for all of them. Most of the time the material for the geometrical objects looks similar, and in most cases, it is identical. So, we just saved a lot of redundant data from crowding our memory.

Please note that the `bool` value for the new skin is set to `false`, indicating that no alpha blending is needed for this skin object. Furthermore, the ID of all eight possible textures for this skin is set to MAX_ID, which is the maximum value a 16-bit variable can take. In the context of texture IDs, I interpret this value as being invalid. No texture is connected with this new skin object yet.

Adding Textures

After completing the first part of the skin manager, it is now able to create and manage skin objects as well as material objects. However, a skin could have up to eight textures connected with it, or it could have up to eight texture IDs connected with it. For example, most modern first-person shooters use a set of different textures for a single model of a slimy alien. First, they use the standard diffuse texture map and then use a bump map for per-pixel lighting, and maybe even a specular or light map. The whole sense of a skin batching together textures is that you don't need to hold several texture objects for a single model. You need only to hold one single skin object. There is no need to take care of texture anymore.

However, before I let you enjoy this luxury, you have to see how to add textures to a skin object.

Adding Textures to Skins

The function that lets you add a texture to a certain skin is similar to the one that lets you add a material. The function `ZFXSinManager::AddTexture` has a long parameter list, but I already discussed the meaning of the parameters while we were talking about the interface definition.

First, you need to know the ID of the skin to which you want to add a texture. Up to eight textures can be connected to a skin object. You can call the function up to eight times, and the order of the calls determines which texture is used for stage 0, stage 1, and so on. The texture added to a skin first becomes the texture used in stage 0, the next one is set to stage 1, and so on.

However, before you can allow a texture to become part of a skin, or at least be referenced by it, you need to apply two security checks. First, you have to check whether the given skin ID is valid. Otherwise, you could end up accessing memory over the bounds of the array where the skin objects are stored, leading to nonsense results in the best case. The second check you should perform is a check of how many textures are already connected to this skin. There must not be more than seven; otherwise, you cannot add another texture. Remember that I use the value `MAX_ID` to mark a free slot.

If the function call survives those two security checks, the manager can get down to its real work. Now it needs to look into its storage and check whether the requested texture is already created because another object is already using it. You can find that out by simply looping through the array of textures, called `m_pTextures`, and compare the name of each one with the name of the graphics file that should now be added as a texture. Again, the functions branch in two directions. If the texture is already created, the function can just take its ID and that's it.

However, if the function does not find the texture in its array, you need to create the new texture object for it. Again, you have to check the size of the array to see whether it can take at least one more object. In this object, you then save the values, such as the name of the texture. The actual graphics file that should be used as texture is loaded into a Direct3D texture object using the function `ZFXSkinManager::CreateTexture`.

You are now done, unless the user wants to have alpha bending on this texture map. Then you must take some additional steps. The two member functions, `ZFXSkinManager::SetAlphaKey` and `ZFXSkinManager::SetTransparency`, are called to take care of that. Note that the first one is called in a loop because there can be as many color keys as the user wants to have.

I hope you have a good idea of what the function to add a texture to an existing skin object should look like. Now you can compare that image to my implementation of the function:

```
HRESULT ZFXD3DSkinManager::AddTexture( UINT      nSkinID,
                                 const char *chName,
```

Adding Textures 217

```
                                    bool      bAlpha,
                                    float     fAlpha,
                                    ZFXCOLOR *cColorKeys,
                                    DWORD     dwNumColorKeys)
{
ZFXTEXTURE *pZFXTex=NULL;   // helper pointer
HRESULT hr;
UINT    nTex, n;
bool    bTex=false;

// is skin id valid at all?
if (nSkinID >= m_nNumSkins) return ZFX_INVALIDID;

// any of the eight texture slots free?
if (m_pSkins[nSkinID].nTexture[7] != MAX_ID)
   return ZFX_BUFFERSIZE;

// is this texture already loaded?
for (nTex=0; nTex<m_nNumTextures; nTex++) {
   if (strcmp(chName, m_pTextures[nTex].chName)==0) {
      bTex = true;
      break;
      }
   } // for [TEXTURES]

// load new texture if needed
if (!bTex) {
   // allocate memory for 50 objects if needed
   if ( (m_nNumTextures%50) == 0 ) {
      n = (m_nNumTextures+50)*sizeof(ZFXTEXTURE);
      m_pTextures = (ZFXTEXTURE*)realloc(
                                 m_pTextures, n);
      if (!m_pTextures) return ZFX_OUTOFMEMORY;
      }

   // alphablending needed?
   if (bAlpha) m_pSkins[nSkinID].bAlpha = true;
   else m_pTextures[m_nNumTextures].fAlpha = 1.0f;

   m_pTextures[m_nNumTextures].pClrKeys = NULL;

   // save texture name
```

```cpp
                m_pTextures[m_nNumTextures].chName =
                                new char[strlen(chName)+1];
   memcpy(m_pTextures[m_nNumTextures].chName, chName,
          strlen(chName)+1);

   // create new Direct3D texture object
   hr = CreateTexture(&m_pTextures[m_nNumTextures],
                      bAlpha);
   if (FAILED(hr)) return hr;

   // add alpha channel if needed
   if (bAlpha) {
      pZFXTex = &m_pTextures[m_nNumTextures];

      pZFXTex->dwNum = dwNumColorKeys;
      pZFXTex->pClrKeys = new
                         ZFXCOLOR[dwNumColorKeys];
      memcpy(pZFXTex->pClrKeys, cColorKeys,
             sizeof(ZFXCOLOR)*pZFXTex->dwNum);

      LPDIRECT3DTEXTURE9 pTex = (LPDIRECT3DTEXTURE9)
                                 pZFXTex->pData;

      // alpha keys are first
      for (DWORD dw=0; dw<dwNumColorKeys; dw++) {
         hr = SetAlphaKey(&pTex,
                    UCHAR(cColorKeys[dw].fR*255),
                    UCHAR(cColorKeys[dw].fG*255),
                    UCHAR(cColorKeys[dw].fB*255),
                    UCHAR(cColorKeys[dw].fA*255));
         if (FAILED(hr)) return hr;
         }

      if (fAlpha < 1.0f) {
         // now general transparency
         m_pTextures[m_nNumTextures].fAlpha=fAlpha;
         hr = SetTransparency(&pTex,
                         UCHAR(fAlpha*255));
         if (FAILED(hr)) return hr;
         }
      }
```

```
    // save id and increment counter
    nTex = m_nNumTextures;
    m_nNumTextures++;
    }

// save id to first free texture slot of the skin
for (int i=0; i<8; i++) {
    if (m_pSkins[nSkinID].nTexture[i] == MAX_ID) {
        m_pSkins[nSkinID].nTexture[i] = nTex;
        break;
        }
    }
return ZFX_OK;
} // AddTexture
```

It is imperative that you first set the alpha key values for the texture before you apply the general transparency. You will soon see why, but I can already tell you that the alpha key function is looking for colors using no alpha value other than 1.0f. If you apply some other general alpha value to it, this function is bound to fail.

Adding Textures As Normal Maps

`ZFXD3DSkinManager::AddTextureHeightmapAsBump` is similar to the previous function. If you are not acquainted with 3D graphics, you will wonder what this function is used for. I'm sure you've heard about bump mapping already, even if you don't know what it is yet. I will go into detail about bump mapping and how to implement it in Chapter 7.

However, I can already give away the open secret that you need some special kind of texture to perform bump mapping. You start by having a texture map not showing an image of the surface you want to texture in diffuse light but as a heightmap. That means lower areas in such heightmaps have darker colors and higher areas in the heightmap have brighter colors. From such a heightmap, you can build a special map used for bump mapping, which is what this function is the starting point for.

Most of the function is identical to the previous one, so we'll take a brief look at it. It's not very complicated because the tricky part is done in another function:

```
HRESULT ZFXD3DSkinManager::AddTextureHeightmapAsBump( UINT    nSkinID,
                                                     const char *chName)
    {
    ZFXTEXTURE  *pZFXTex=NULL;
    HRESULT     hr;
    UINT        nTex, n;
    bool        bTex=false;
```

Chapter 5 ■ Materials, Textures, and Transparency

```cpp
   // is skin ID valid at all
   if (nSkinID >= m_nNumSkins) return ZFX_INVALIDID;

   // all 8 stages for this skin already set?
   if (m_pSkins[nSkinID].nTexture[7] != MAX_ID) {
      Log("error: AddTexture() failed, all 8 stages set");
      return ZFX_BUFFERSIZE;
      }

   // do we already have this texture
   for (nTex=0; nTex<m_nNumTextures; nTex++) {
      if ( strcmp(chName, m_pTextures[nTex].chName) == 0 ) {
         bTex = true;
         break;
         }
      } // for [TEXTURES]

   // load new texture if not yet done
   if (!bTex) {
      // allocate 50 new memory slots for textures if necessary
      if ( (m_nNumTextures%50) == 0 ) {
         n = (m_nNumTextures+50)*sizeof(ZFXTEXTURE);
         m_pTextures = (ZFXTEXTURE*)realloc(m_pTextures, n);
         if (!m_pTextures) {
            Log("error: AddTexture() failed, realloc()");
            return ZFX_OUTOFMEMORY;
            }
         }

      // no alpha blending needed
      m_pTextures[m_nNumTextures].fAlpha = 1.0f;
      m_pTextures[m_nNumTextures].pClrKeys = NULL;

      // save texture name
      m_pTextures[m_nNumTextures].chName = new char[strlen(chName)+1];
      memcpy(m_pTextures[m_nNumTextures].chName, chName, strlen(chName)+1);

      // create d3d texture from that pointer
      hr = CreateTexture(&m_pTextures[m_nNumTextures], true);
      if (FAILED(hr)) {
```

Adding Textures

```
         Log("error: CreateTexture() failed");
         return hr;
         }

      // build normals from heightvalues
      hr = ConvertToNormalmap( &m_pTextures[m_nNumTextures] );
      if (FAILED(hr)) {
         Log("error: ConvertToNormalmap() failed");
         return hr;
         }

      // save ID and add to count
      nTex = m_nNumTextures;
      m_nNumTextures++;
      } // load texture

   // put texture ID to skin ID
   for (int i=0; i<8; i++) {
      if (m_pSkins[nSkinID].nTexture[i] == MAX_ID) {
         m_pSkins[nSkinID].nTexture[i] = nTex;
         break;
         }
      }
   return ZFX_OK;
   } // AddTextureHeightmapAsBump
```

After creating a texture object, if the requested map is not loaded yet, this function simply calls `ZFXD3DSkinManager::ConvertToNormalmap`. I'm not going to show you this function now because I need to explain how bump mapping with normal maps works first. So, we'll come back to this one in Chapter 7 when we talk about bump mapping.

Loading Graphic Files As Textures

When using the Windows operating system, there are dozens of methods you can use to load bitmap files into the memory and to get access to the pixel data. I used to write my own loader functions, but not all people like to reinvent the wheel again and again. So, in this book I will use the `LoadImage()` function from the WinAPI. By calling this function, we get a handle to the opened file to access its contents. The `GetObject()` function from the WinAPI then lends a helping hand because it can create a device-independent bitmap (DIB) section from this file. *DIB* is used to describe a bitmap data format that is independent from the graphics adapter and the operating system.

You are probably familiar with the WinAPI and know how to load a bitmap file. If you do not, I recommend you look up the functions I just named in the MSDN. Take a look at the functions, their parameters, and the structures involved.

In the DIB section, you have all the relevant data from the image at hand. This includes the bitmap header file, which is a structure holding information about the image such as its width, height, and bit depth. Then you can use the Direct3D function `IDirect3DDevice9::CreateTexture`, which creates an object of the type `IDirect3DTexture9`. Please note that this is an empty texture object from the start. This object is really nothing more than a linear array in memory that is meant to hold the pixel data, but you have to use this object type if you want to use the texture in Direct3D. Most important is the bit depth and color format used.

Converting Color Formats

The ZFXEngine 2.0 allows for only two different color formats in textures. This restriction applies to all the color formats supported by Direct3D, but it makes sense. I use only the `D3DFMT_R5G6B5` and `D3DFMT_A8R8G8B8` formats. The `D3DFMT_R5G6B5` format is a 16-bit format in which the red and blue components use 5 bits each, which equals 32 different values ($2^5 = 32$). The green component uses 6 bits and therefore equals 64 different values ($2^6 = 64$). That means you can have 32 different red values from a very dark red to a very bright one. There are no bits in this format for use with an alpha value, so I use this format only for textures not having any kind of transparency.

The second format I use has 32 bits, with 8 bits for the red, green, blue, and alpha components. That equals 256 different values for each component ($2^{32} = 256$). People tend to use 32-bit textures wherever possible, but you should always think about the target system you develop for. The latest graphics adapters like to have 32-bit textures and have enough memory to deal with them. However, considering older hardware, keep in mind that 32-bit textures consume twice as much memory as 16-bit textures. And in a 32-bit texture where you don't use transparency, you will waste 8 bits times the dimension of the texture.

If you are not satisfied with the visual quality of the 16-bit textures and your graphics artist is good enough, I recommend you use 32-bit textures for all the texture maps. I would like to show you how to deal with 16-bit textures as well.

After all, using a 16-bit texture is not that easy if you load its pixel data from a 24-bit texture. If you save a bitmap image, it will use 24 bits only—8 bits for red, green, and blue, respectively (I'm ignoring the ancient 8-bit palette mode). Actually, that is more or less the same format as Direct3D's `D3DFMT_A8R8G8B8` but without the alpha value, of course. You can already see that it is no problem to store the 24-bit data in a 32-bit texture, leaving 8 bits of space between each pixel.

Luckily, converting a 24-bit color into a 16-bit color is relatively simple. The following shifting macro can be used to build a 16-bit color value from three integer values ranging from 0 to 255, which equals an 8-bit variable:

```
#define RGB16BIT(r,g,b) ((b%32) + ((g%64) << 5) + ((r%32) << 11))
```

By calculating the modulo with the percent sign, you put the values into the valid boundaries between 0 and $x-1$, where x is the value for the modulo. Then you need to shift the values according to the position they should have in the final data structure. Shifting blue is unnecessary because it remains as the rightmost part of the color. The green value is shifted 5 bits to the left because it has an offset of 5 bits with regard to the blue component, and the red value is shifted the 5 bits offset for the blue component plus 6 bits, the size of the green component. Now you have a valid 16-bit value representing a color analog to the three 8-bit values. The accuracy of the smaller color value of 16 bits is below the 24-bit value, so some visible artifacts might result from converting.

Creating the Texture

With this macro, you can now write the function that creates the texture object and loads the graphic file data into the texture. If the user requests the texture to contain alpha values, the 32-bit format is used. Otherwise, the incoming 24-bit data needs to be converted to 16-bit data. This function takes care of the whole mess:

```
HRESULT ZFXD3DSkinManager::CreateTexture( ZFXTEXTURE *pTexture,
                                          bool bAlpha)
   {
   D3DLOCKED_RECT    d3dRect;
   D3DFORMAT         fmt;
   DIBSECTION        dibS;
   HRESULT           hr;
   int               LineWidth;
   void              *pMemory=NULL;

   HBITMAP hBMP = (HBITMAP)LoadImage(NULL,
                                     pTexture->chName,
                                     IMAGE_BITMAP,0,0,
                                     LR_LOADFROMFILE |
                                     LR_CREATEDIBSECTION);
   if (!hBMP) return ZFX_FILENOTFOUND;

   GetObject(hBMP, sizeof(DIBSECTION), &dibS);

   // we support only 24-bit bitmaps
   if (dibS.dsBmih.biBitCount != 24) {
```

224   Chapter 5 ■ Materials, Textures, and Transparency

```
      DeleteObject(hBMP);
      return ZFX_INVALIDFILE;
      }

   if (bAlpha) fmt = D3DFMT_A8R8G8B8;
   else fmt = D3DFMT_R5G6B5;

   long  lWidth   = dibS.dsBmih.biWidth;
   long  lHeight  = dibS.dsBmih.biHeight;
   BYTE *pBMPBits = (BYTE*)dibS.dsBm.bmBits;

   hr = m_pDevice->CreateTexture(lWidth, lHeight, 1, 0,
                                 fmt, D3DPOOL_MANAGED,
                                 (LPDIRECT3DTEXTURE9*)
                                 (&(pTexture->pData)),
                                 NULL);
   if (FAILED(hr)) return ZFX_FAIL;

   // set dummy pointer
   LPDIRECT3DTEXTURE9 pTex = ((LPDIRECT3DTEXTURE9)
                              pTexture->pData);

   if (FAILED(pTex->LockRect(0, &d3dRect, NULL, 0)))
      return ZFX_BUFFERLOCK;

   if (bAlpha) {
      LineWidth = d3dRect.Pitch >> 2; // 32 Bit = 4 Byte
      pMemory = (DWORD*)d3dRect.pBits;
      }
   else {
      LineWidth = d3dRect.Pitch >> 1; // 16 Bit = 2 Byte
      pMemory = (USHORT*)d3dRect.pBits;
      }

   // copy each pixel
   for (int cy = 0; cy < lHeight; cy++) {
      for (int cx = 0; cx < lWidth; cx++) {

         if (bAlpha)
            {
            DWORD Color = 0xff000000;
            int   i = (cy*lWidth + cx)*3;
```

```
                memcpy(&Color, &pBMPBits[i], sizeof(BYTE)*3);

                ((DWORD*)pMemory)[cx+(cy*LineWidth)]=Color;
                } // 32 Bit
            else
                {
                // convert 24 bit into 16 bit
                UCHAR B=(pBMPBits[(cy*lWidth+cx)*3 +0])>>3,
                      G=(pBMPBits[(cy*lWidth+cx)*3 +1])>>3,
                      R=(pBMPBits[(cy*lWidth+cx)*3 +2])>>3;


                // map values to 5, 6, and 5 bits respectively and call macro
                USHORT Color = RGB16BIT( (int)(((float) R / 255.0f) * 32.0f),
                                         (int)(((float) G / 255.0f) * 64.0f),
                                         (int)(((float) B / 255.0f) * 32.0f) );


                // write pixel as 16-bit color
                ((USHORT*)pMemory)[cx+(cy*LineWidth)]=Color;
                } // 16 Bit

            } // for
        } // for

    pTex->UnlockRect(0);
    DeleteObject(hBMP);
    return ZFX_OK;
    } // CreateTexture
```

So, are you a bit rusty working with Direct3D textures? No problem. I will point out the major details so you can look up the functions in the DirectX documentation in the DirectX SDK. To get access to the memory area where the texture stores its data, you simply call `IDirect3DTexture9::LockRect` to lock the texture for other resources to get access at the same time. In the Direct3D `D3DLOCKED_RECT` structure, you then find a pointer to this area called pBits, as well as a value called Pitch that is the width of a single row of the data area.

The data from a bitmap is stored in the memory as a linear array of pixels, but you can access the data by using the image's width and height values to calculate the position of a certain (x,y) pixel in the array, like so:

```
index = ( row_number * row_width ) + column_number * bytes_per_pixel
```

The x position of the pixel in question equals the column number, whereas the y position is the row number. The value from `Pitch` is the width of a row in bytes. A row generally should have the length of the number of pixels in a row times the bit depth. However, this must not be the case because some fill bits can appear at the end of each row. Thus, you should use the actual pitch value instead of the row width calculated by the width of the image. The previous code shifts the pitch value by two, which equals dividing it by four because one pixel is 4 bytes long. In the case of the 16-bit texture, the code divides by two because one 16-bit pixel is 2 bytes long. Inside the 24-bit pixel data array, we multiply by a value of three instead because a 24-bit pixel is 3 bytes long.

When all the data is then copied into the texture, you just have to unlock the texture and let it go back to work. The loaded bitmap image is now unnecessary, and the allocated memory can be freed as well by calling `DeleteObject()` from the WinAPI. Now we have successfully loaded a 24-bit image as a 16-bit or 32-bit texture.

Adjusting the Transparency of Textures

The virtual world would be boring or even displayed wrongly if there were no transparency effects. Just think of materials you can look through to a certain degree, such as force fields, windows, or even water. Achieving this effect is pretty simple, but most people use Direct3D D3DX helper files to create transparency effects in their textures or depend on a graphic artist to integrate the alpha value into the graphic files they load as textures.

I like to have as much flexibility as possible, so I wrote two functions that enable me to set the alpha values and adjust the transparency effects on the texture after I load a simple bitmap file not containing alpha values.

Figure 5.5 shows the image of two rectangles. A bigger one in the background has a texture with a lake scene. The smaller rectangle contains the image of a sphere on its texture, which is naturally surrounded by an ugly frame. Later in the chapter, I will revisit this scene two more times, but it will look much better than this.

Transparency in Computer Graphics

In my forum, I sometimes get questions concerning transparency where you can see that the people don't understand how transparency effects actually work and therefore get unexpected results.

The most famous example for transparency is a window made of glass. Even if you render a polygon for the window, you should still be able to see the objects on the far side of the window because its transparency lets most of the photons coming from the objects

Figure 5.5 Two rectangles overlapping using no transparency.

behind it pass right through. Please note that I assume your windows are at least a bit cleaned and have the transparency feature.

Does the graphics adapter look at which objects are behind a transparent texture and still show them on the screen? No, it doesn't. Remember that the graphics adapter has no understanding of a scene; it cannot even think in terms of polygons or triangles. After all, the graphics adapter just knows about pixels on the screen—or in its back buffer.

First, you must render all objects without transparency, making their projected pixels sit in the back buffer and the related depth values sit in the depth buffer. Next, you render the transparent objects, such as the glass window. After transforming and projecting the polygons of the window, the graphics adapter wants to start setting its pixels to the back buffer if the depth buffer agrees. If you enabled alpha blending, something else is going on as well. If the transparent pixel is more distant than the depth buffer allows for a certain position on the screen, the new pixel is rejected.

However, if the pixel is closer than the one sitting in the back buffer at the same position, the graphics adapter needs to blend them together. It then takes the color from the back buffer and adds it to the color of the partially transparent pixel. Each color is multiplied by a certain factor first, which is usually the alpha value for the new pixel and 1 minus the alpha value for the pixel from the back buffer. Thus, changing the alpha value controls how strongly the back buffer pixel will look through.

The most important thing to remember about this process is that what you see is normally never the object already sitting in the back buffer nor its pixels. You take a bit of the same color, yes, but you always make a totally new pixel for the transparency effect. Why is this important? It is important if you deal with an object that has one or more colors that are totally transparent. Its seems as if you still see the distant objects as they were before, but there is a big difference now. You still set a new pixel to the back buffer and the depth buffer even if the new pixel has a transparency of 100 percent and is therefore identical to the more distant pixel already that sits in the depth buffer.

This implies two problems. First, you still have to spend fill rate even if you are not changing the image. Second, the depth buffer is filled with a new, closer depth value even if there actually is nothing at this close distance due to 100 percent transparency.

Luckily, today's graphic adapters support a feature called *alpha testing*. If you activate that, the graphics adapter can recognize pixels with a certain threshold alpha value, which you can adjust, and it does not take any setting action, whether to the back buffer or to the depth buffer, if the threshold is crossed. This prevents a lot of depth buffer problems. But you should still stick to the following rules while using transparency:

- Render all polygons without transparency first.
- Render all objects using transparency and sort them by distance from back to front.

Again, Color Formats

And here it is again, our favorite friend—the color format and conversions between different types of it. Direct3D does not work with separated color components but uses a 32-bit value to combine the four components into a single structure like a DWORD. We need a function that lets us build such a 32-bit value from four 8-bit values, where each one is a red, green, blue, or alpha component of the color. The functions look like this:

```
DWORD ZFXD3DSkinManager::MakeD3DColor(UCHAR R, UCHAR G,
                                      UCHAR B, UCHAR A)
   {
   return (A << 24) | (R << 16) | (G << 8) | B;
   } // MakeD3DColor
```

As you can see, you simply need to shift the given 8-bit color values for the red, green, blue, and alpha components to their corresponding places to get the final 32-bit output value.

Alpha Color Keys via Alpha Channels

We will use this function to play around with different color values, as you will see shortly. We start by applying the color keys to a texture. Remember, you can hand over an array of colors you want to be transparent to a certain degree while adding a texture to a skin using the skin manager. For example, you could demand that all blue pixels in the texture be 50 percent transparent or that all jet black pixels in the texture be 100 percent transparent. Take a look at Figure 5.6 to see how a single color key with 100 percent transparency applied to the texture of the small rectangle in front helped us get rid of the ugly border surrounding the sphere in Figure 5.5.

This not only sounds easy to do, but it actually is. The only thing you have to do is loop through all the pixels and replace them all using the RGB color that is to be replaced with a newly built color value using exactly the same RGB values but with an adjusted alpha value:

```
HRESULT ZFXD3DSkinManager::SetAlphaKey( LPDIRECT3DTEXTURE9
                                        *ppTexture,
                                        UCHAR R, UCHAR G,
```

Figure 5.6 The topmost rectangle's texture featuring a color key.

```
                                         UCHAR B, UCHAR A) {
   D3DSURFACE_DESC   d3dDesc;
   D3DLOCKED_RECT    d3dRect;
   DWORD             dwKey, Color;

   // must be 32 bit ARGB format
   (*ppTexture)->GetLevelDesc(0, &d3dDesc);
   if (d3dDesc.Format != D3DFMT_A8R8G8B8)
      return ZFX_INVALIDPARAM;

   // color to be replaced
   dwKey = MakeD3DColor(R, G, B, 255);

   // color to replace old one with
   if (A > 0) Color = MakeD3DColor(R, G, B, A);
   else Color = MakeD3DColor(0, 0, 0, A);

   if (FAILED((*ppTexture)->LockRect(0, &d3dRect, NULL, 0)))
      return ZFX_BUFFERLOCK;

   // overwrite all pixels to be replaced
   for (DWORD y=0; y<d3dDesc.Height; y++) {
      for (DWORD x=0; x<d3dDesc.Width; x++)
         {
         if ( ((DWORD*)d3dRect.pBits)[d3dDesc.Width*y+x] == dwKey )
            {
            ((DWORD*)d3dRect.pBits)[d3dDesc.Width*y+x] = Color;
            }
         }
      }
   (*ppTexture)->UnlockRect(0);

   return ZFX_OK;
   } // SetAlphaKey
```

I want to mention one thing here: This function awaits the pixel of the RGB value in question to have an alpha value of 1.0. You could also easily write a function that compares only the RGB values, but I leave that to you as homework. This implementation must not have any alpha value set to one of the color key colors before this function call. Otherwise, it would fail to recognize the colors to be replaced.

Overall Transparency via Alpha Channels

As you have seen, the color keys are applied only to certain colors in the image—for example, to remove ugly frames from the texture. However, you can also demand a certain degree of transparency for the whole texture, as you would need for a window in which each pixel should be transparent regardless of the color it has.

Take a look at Figure 5.7. It is the same image as in Figure 5.6, but now the small rectangle in front has a certain degree of overall transparency on each pixel in addition to the color key, thus preventing the ugly frame from being seen.

This is even easier than searching for specific colors in the texture on which to place an alpha value. Take a look for yourself:

```
HRESULT ZFXD3DSkinManager::SetTransparency(LPDIRECT3DTEXTURE9 *ppTexture,
                                           UCHAR Alpha)
   {
   D3DSURFACE_DESC  d3dDesc;
   D3DLOCKED_RECT   d3dRect;
```

Figure 5.7 The topmost rectangle with a color key and overall transparency.

```
DWORD          Color;
UCHAR          A, R, G, B;

// must be 32 bit format
(*ppTexture)->GetLevelDesc(0, &d3dDesc);
if (d3dDesc.Format != D3DFMT_A8R8G8B8)
   return ZFX_INVALIDPARAM;

if (FAILED((*ppTexture)->LockRect(0, &d3dRect, NULL,
                                  0)))
   return ZFX_BUFFERLOCK;

// loop through all pixels
for (DWORD y=0; y<d3dDesc.Height; y++) {
   for (DWORD x=0; x<d3dDesc.Width; x++) {

      // get color from the pixel
      Color = ((DWORD*)d3dRect.pBits)[d3dDesc.Width*y+x];

      // calculate new ARGB value
      A = (UCHAR)( (Color & 0xff000000) >> 24);
      R = (UCHAR)( (Color & 0x00ff0000) >> 16);
      G = (UCHAR)( (Color & 0x0000ff00) >>  8);
      B = (UCHAR)( (Color & 0x000000ff) >>  0);

      // set only if new alpha value is lower
      if (A >= Alpha)
         A = Alpha;

      ((DWORD*)d3dRect.pBits)[d3dDesc.Width*y+x] =
                  MakeD3DColor(R, G, B, A);
      }
   }
(*ppTexture)->UnlockRect(0);

return ZFX_OK;
} // SetTransparency
```

There is one interesting thing to note. The new requested alpha value is set for a pixel only if its current alpha value is greater than the new one, meaning that its transparency is currently less. This restriction maintains the integrity of the color keys possibly set to the texture beforehand. If you want all blue pixels to be 100 percent transparent, they should also be 100 percent transparent even if you apply a 50 percent overall transparency for each pixel of the texture, right?

One Look Back, Two Steps Forward

You've survived another chapter. Maybe you think this chapter is boring because I cannot provide a running example to show off what you have learned. However, you have just mastered a huge amount of important low-level work on materials and textures. Please take your time and dig through the alpha setting topic again until you fully understand how to deal with different color formats.

You have learned how to manage resources in a suitable way to prevent yourself from mindlessly cramming your memory with redundant data all over the place. This basic field work enables the users of the engine to be as mindless as they want about calling a loading routine for the same graphics file repeatedly. And that is a really good thing because that is what makes the engine easy to use and what frees the user from organizing and managing those things for herself. After all, she wants to implement a graphics application and not resource managers.

From a theoretical point of view, you have learned a lot about lighting in 3D applications and you should now have a better understanding of lighting issues and why this remains one of the most interesting topics in developing video games. Only recently have video games begun to employ realtime lighting without too much preprocessing. However, there is still the need for smart ways to implement this to make it run in realtime.

So, what's missing in this chapter? I can show you the door, but only you can proceed from this point. The is focused on 3D graphics so there is no easy support for 2D sprites and things like that. You could, for example, add an encapsulation for the `IDirect3DSurface9` object that deals with 2D images only and apply the same management scheme for ease of use.

The next chapter will see a quantum jump in the capabilities of the engine. I've shown you enough material to get started displaying graphics to the screen. You will have to revisit the render device of the ZFXEngine 2.0, and I will show you how to boost is by 500 percent. Again, we will run into managing issues with enabling efficient rendering of single pieces of geometrical data, which would be impossible with pure Direct3D.

So, relax for a second or two and then get ready to start working again.

Chapter 6

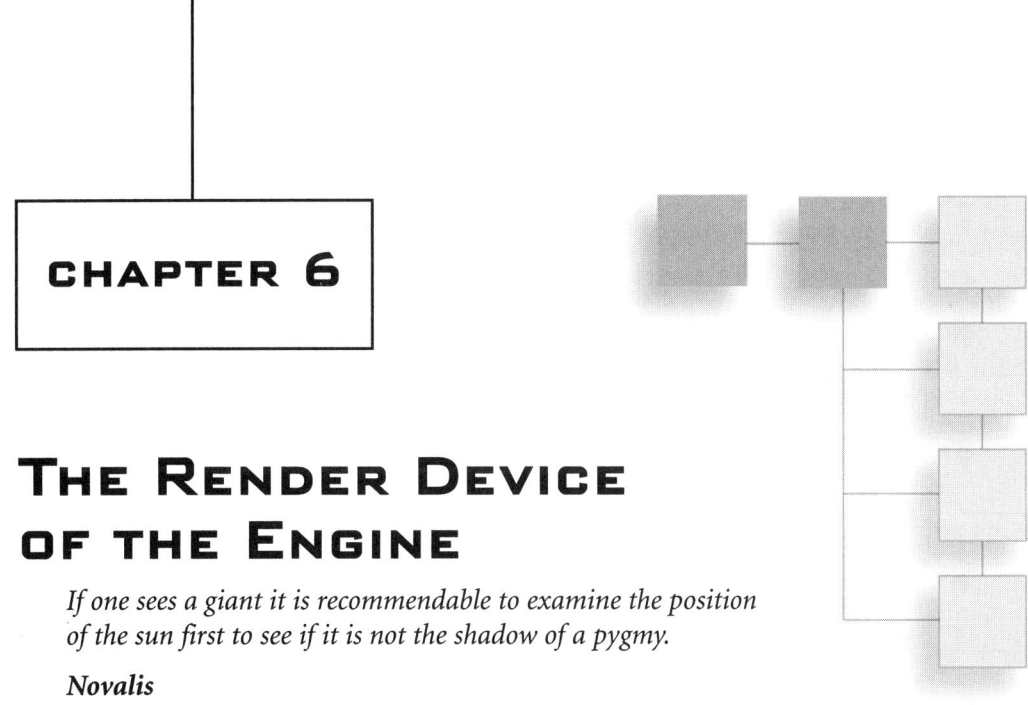

The Render Device of the Engine

If one sees a giant it is recommendable to examine the position of the sun first to see if it is not the shadow of a pygmy.

Novalis

Each computer program is a somewhat complex thing, analogous to an onion. The outer layers of a program are made out of the application or game code and the front end is the user interface. Whether this is the input mask of a database or the heads-up display of a first person shooter does not matter. The inner layers of the software deal with managing data on different levels as well as encapsulating certain APIs (Application Programming Interfaces), such as the WinAPI, Direct3D, or WinSock. The core of the onion is the communication with the hardware—for instance, sending the triangles to be rendered to the graphics adapter.

There are two competing design goals: simplicity and flexibility. An abstracted ideal 3D engine is one that is 100 percent flexible and as easy to use as possible. A rather ridiculous example is a 3D engine that can be cranked up, render a model, and shut itself down in only one function call. Pretty easy to use, isn't it? This is as inflexible as it gets. The more flexibility you add, the more function calls you have to execute and the more data you have to supply as parameters.

The designer of a 3D engine has to find an appropriate balance between simplicity and flexibility. Over the course of this chapter, we will work on enlarging and enriching the ZFXRenderDevice interface and its implementation into something we can actually work with. My goal is to hide as much of the internal processes as possible from the user of the engine, thus making it very easy to use.

This chapter covers the following objectives:

- Performing perspective and orthogonal projection
- Transforming coordinates from 3D to 2D and vice versa

- Dealing with static and dynamic vertex and index buffers
- Rendering small amounts of data efficiently by batching

You might think that you just encountered the proverbial giant. However, take Novalis's advice and change your position to see the source code from a more abstract point of view. There are some tricky details here, but from a distance you can hopefully see the shadow of the pygmy.

Project Settings

In this chapter, your workload gets heavier, but I will help carry it. First, you need to add files to the current project. You can copy the project from Chapter 3, "Engineering the Engine," but you need to add new files, which will carry some of the workload. Otherwise, you'll end up with source files that are much too long. You also need to add new empty header and source files to the project named ZFXD3D from Chapter 3. Add the following files (or just take the source code and project files provided on the CD-ROM):

- ZFXD3D_misc.cpp
- ZFXD3D_vcache.cpp
- ZFXD3D_vcache.h

The first of these three files should take several functions belonging to the class ZFXD3D. Keep the source files handy, because you don't want the whole class implementation sitting in a single file—plus, the render device implementation will get big as you proceed through this chapter. You also need to integrate the work you did in the last two chapters, so copy the zfx3d.h and zfx3d.lib files with the math functions to the new project folder as well as the skin manager files: ZFXD3D_skinman.cpp and its header ZFXD3D_skinman.h.

On the following pages, you will add a lot of things to the interface definition such as rendering primitives. This always means you have to change or add the code in two places. First, the interface definition in the ZFXRenderDevice class needs to be changed. Next, the actual implementation of the interface should also get the new function declarations and the implementations for them as well. You must change the ZFXD3D class, which contains the implementation of the interface. As usual, put all public functions and the most important attributes into the interface definition, thus the remaining private functions and implementation-specific attributes are members of the ZFXD3D class.

As long as you ignore strict object-oriented design, you can also add a public attribute to the interface class. You can always change the design of the engine, but at this point, keep it as simple and straightforward as possible. This attribute is a pointer to the skin manager the render device is using, as shown in the following:

```
// class ZFXRenderDevice:
   private:
```

```
    ZFXSkinManager *m_pSkinMan;
public:
    virtual ZFXSkinManager* GetSkinManager(void)=0;
```

Note that the public attribute is of the interface type ZFXSkinManager and not of its implementation ZFXD3DSkinManager. So, the user gets to the object only through the interface. You can give the user better-designed access to the skin manager in many ways, including inserting the attribute to the ZFXD3D class and providing an interface function for accessing it. This would be the way to do it for a real commercial project, but you want to keep it simple and easy to grasp at one glance.

Using my shortcut, the user of the ZFXEngine 2.0 can access the skin manager and create a new skin object, as shown in the following:

```
UINT nMySkin;
ZFXCOLOR cWhite = { 1.0f, 1.0f, 1.0f, 1.0f };
ZFXCOLOR cBlack = { 0.0f, 0.0f, 0.0f, 1.0f };
pDevice->GetSkinManager()->AddSkin( &cWhite, &cWhite, &cBlack,
                                    &cBack, 0.0f, &nMySkin);
```

You don't want to print the whole new interface ZFXRenderDevice and its sample implementation ZFXD3D. There are several new functions and attributes to add. Don't focus on the organization of the files and members; focus on the implementations. You can see the parts coming together on the CD-ROM.

As a rule of thumb, virtually all public functions are declared in the interface while all private functions are located in the class ZFXD3D. I will add some comments when I introduce new sections into the code.

View and Projection

Two fundamental aspects of the 2D presentation of a 3D scene are the view and projection. It is quite obvious that you have to project the data from the 3D space to the 2D space to incorporate the third coordinate into the other two. However, the type of projection you use is up to you. In this chapter, I show you the two most common types of projection: perspective projection and orthogonal projection.

Perspective projection is used to factor the distance of an object from the viewer into the two other coordinates. You might know this type of projection from most 3D games that have a first-person view. Even the third-person view uses perspective projection. The *orthogonal* projection is the projection used in editing tools, where you have 2D views of a 3D scene, or with 2D graphic objects such as HUD.

The other related aspect of a 3D engine is the view. This includes several things, but the most important one is the view matrix. In this matrix, the position and orientation of the viewer are set. Besides this matrix, there is also a rectangle that displays the projected scene, which is called a *viewport*.

Caution

A viewport is similar to a child window in the Windows operating system or any other window-based OS. However, don't mistake viewports for real child windows or as connections to different Windows child windows.

Basically, Direct3D renders to the whole client area of a window. You can define a viewport for Direct3D and then render to the viewport area only. The viewport must not be greater in size than the client area of the connected window, but it can be smaller. By rendering multiple times or different scenes into different viewports, you can have a virtual child window in Direct3D, which is used mostly for things like split screens.

You want to be as flexible as possible with regard to view and projection to achieve nice visual effects, like a sniper's scope, for example. Also, you should change between orthogonal and perspective projection as quickly as possible. If you want to program an editing tool that uses both, you have to switch between the projections at least once each frame. Calculating these matrices on occasion doesn't take too much time, but it is still faster to store precalculated values as often as possible. Many implementations therefore introduce multiple stages of viewing or projection settings. This means you can initialize different settings and switch between them afterward without needing to recalculate things. You can also change each stage setting, which involves recalculating the matrices. As long as you deal with only three or four different settings, there is no need to do so anymore. After all, calculating transformation matrices in computer graphics always involves trigonometric functions, which are comparably slow.

In the following, I show you several miscellaneous functions for the class ZFXD3D that will sit in the ZFXD3D_misc.cpp file. The following functions and attributes are defined as public members of the render device interface ZFXRenderDevice to enable it to deal with the view and projection issues:

```
// private:
     float           m_fNear,          // near plane
                     m_fFar;           // far plane
     ZFXENGINEMODE   m_Mode;           // 2D, 3D,...
     int             m_nStage;         // stage (0-3)
     ZFXVIEWPORT     m_VP[4];          // viewports

// public:
     // viewmatrix from vRight, vUp, vDir, vPos
     virtual HRESULT SetView3D(const ZFXVector&,
                               const ZFXVector&,
```

View and Projection

```
                           const ZFXVector&,
                           const ZFXVector&)=0;

// viewmatrix from position, fix point, WorldUp
virtual HRESULT SetViewLookAt(const ZFXVector&,
                              const ZFXVector&,
                              const ZFXVector&)=0;

// near and far clipping plane
virtual void SetClippingPlanes(float, float)=0;

// stage modus, 0:=perspective, 1:=ortho
virtual HRESULT SetMode(int, int n)=0;

// field of view and viewport for stage n
virtual HRESULT InitStage(float, RECT*, int n)=0;

// plane of the viewing frustum
virtual HRESULT GetFrustum(ZFXPlane*)=0;

// screen coordinates to world ray
virtual void Transform2Dto3D(const POINT &pt,
                             ZFXVector    *vc0,
                             ZFXVector    *vcD)=0;
// world coordinates to screen coordinates
virtual POINT Transform3Dto2D(const ZFXVector &vcP)=0;
```

In addition to the values for the near clipping plane and the far clipping plane, you see two new data types used for the attributes. They are defined in the ZFX.h file so the whole engine will have access to them, as will the user. The type ZFXVIEWPORT defines a simple viewport structure, which is an area on the back buffer that receives the rendered image. The remaining parts of the back buffer are not used by the render device as long as the viewport is not changed to include them:

```
// simple viewport type
typedef struct ZFXVIEWPORT_TYPE
   {
   DWORD X;   // position of upper ...
   DWORD Y;   // ... left corner
   DWORD Width;
   DWORD Height;
   } ZFXVIEWPORT;
```

The enumerated type `ZFXENGINEMODE` features three entries. It is used to switch the engine between three modes. What these modes are used for and how the switching takes places is covered later in this chapter. First, take a look at the enumeration:

```
typedef enum ZFXENGINEMODE_TYPE
   {
   EMD_PERSPECTIVE,   // perspective projection
   EMD_TWOD,          // world equals screen coordinates
   EMD_ORTHOGONAL     // orthogonal projection
   } ZFXENGINEMODE;
```

The perspective mode is used for perspective projection. Who would have guessed? The orthogonal mode is used for the orthogonal projection type. What about the mysterious 2D mode? This is a neat projection in which the world coordinates are treated by the projection as if they were already given in screen coordinates. This makes switching the vertex type from untransformed to transformed unnecessary. This is useful for rendering heads-up displays in game menus and the like.

From the names of the functions, you should be able to guess what they are actually meant for. The next paragraphs deal with each of them in detail, so hang on a bit if you're unclear about one of the other functions yet. Or like good old Leonardo da Vinci would say, impatience is the mother of stupidity.

Caution

If you're unclear about buzzwords, such as *view matrix, viewport, field of view (fov), view frustum,* and *near* and *far clipping plane,* you need to check a good book or tutorial about 3D graphics first to be able to follow the development of the engine in this book. Even if I implement these basic things here, the focus of explanation is on how they are tied together for the course of the engine.

Multiple Viewing Stages

By *multiple viewing stages*, I mean only that the ZFXEngine has four triples of perspective projection matrices, orthogonal projection matrices, and viewports that are saved in the engine together. Normally, you activate a projection matrix and a viewport and don't save the attributes, thus requiring recalculation of the projection matrix if you change it in between.

You need only one orthogonal projection matrix, and in reality only one perspective projection matrix is active at one time. However, for some special effects, you might need to change the perspective projection, such as for the aforementioned sniper scope effect where you want to zoom into the scene. But I like the engine to offer the possibility to save some settings for the user if he wants to.

View and Projection

The first stage should contain the normal projection mode. The second stage could then hold a perspective projection matrix for an 8x sharpshooter scope, while the third stage holds a 12x binocular. Because a certain viewport is always connected to a stage, you can also save the area where the image for the given projection should be rendered. You would need that if you wanted to render the zoomed view into a part of the screen only as an image in image—for example, when the scope view is shown above the normal scene.

To keep all the precalculated things in memory, you have to use attributes to hold these values; in this case, we use the new attributes of the class ZFXD3D. The user who applies the engine should not have to deal with matrices and so on. He should simply not care because that is what the engine is meant for. He should be required to only set the field of view angle and the viewport for a certain stage. The engine should then take care of the rest. This means the engine has to do some internal calculations and settings the user will not notice.

This seems to be a fair compromise between flexibility and simplicity. The new private attributes of the class ZFXD3D are shown here:

```
D3DMATRIX m_mView2D,       // viewmatrix 2D
          m_mView3D,       // viewmatrix 3D
          m_mProj2D,       // projection orthog.
          m_mProjP[4],     // projection persp.
          m_mProjO[4],     // projection orthog.
          m_mWorld,        // world transformation
          m_mViewProj;     // combo-matrix for 3D
          m_mWorldViewProj; // combo-matrix for 3D
```

Two matrices are used for the view matrix in 2D mode, which treats vertices as if they were already in screen coordinates. The 3D matrix is used for the perspective and orthogonal viewing mode. A matrix is used for the projection in 2D mode, and two arrays with four entries each holding matrices for perspective and orthogonal projection, respectively, are included. These arrays have four entries because each entry corresponds to a stage of the engine.

Finally, a world matrix holds the current world transform, and two combination matrices hold a multiplication of the current view matrix with the current projection matrix and a concatenation of the world, the view, and the projection matrix, respectively. Such combination matrices are used in several situations to do other calculations, such as extracting the view frustum from Direct3D or while transforming data from a 2D space to a 3D space, or vice versa.

Viewports, View Matrices, and the Frustum

Now we'll start the groundwork by setting up the view matrix. If you want to present a 3D scene to the screen, you must take the viewer's position in the 3D scene into account—that is, her position and her orientation. In the language of a computer graphics artist, this is called the *camera* or the *position and orientation of the camera.*

This makes sense because you can have several cameras in a video game or any graphics application but with only one viewer viewing through different cameras. Just imagine yourself commanding a platoon of soldiers and being able to switch to view the action from each soldier's perspective.

The following public function of the ZFXD3D class lets you set the position and orientation of a camera in a 3D space. The new bool attribute m_bUseShaders in the class is used to determine whether the present hardware has support for vertex and pixel shaders. If this is not the case, you only need to apply the changes to the transformation, projection, and view matrices by using the IDirect3DDevice9::SetTransform function call.

But if the engine is running using shaders, you don't need to set the new matrices for the Direct3D device because all the transformation is done by you in a vertex shader. Setting the matrices to the graphics adapter results in slowing things down:

```
HRESULT ZFXD3D::SetView3D(const ZFXVector &vcRight, const ZFXVector &vcUp,
                          const ZFXVector &vcDir,   const ZFXVector &vcPos)
   {
   if (!m_bRunning) return E_FAIL;

   m_mView3D._14 = m_mView3D._21 = m_mView3D._34 = 0.0f;
   m_mView3D._44 = 1.0f;

   m_mView3D._11 = vcRight.x;
   m_mView3D._21 = vcRight.y;
   m_mView3D._31 = vcRight.z;
   m_mView3D._41 = - (vcRight*vcPos);

   m_mView3D._12 = vcUp.x;
   m_mView3D._22 = vcUp.y;
   m_mView3D._32 = vcUp.z;
   m_mView3D._42 = - (vcUp*vcPos);

   m_mView3D._13 = vcDir.x;
   m_mView3D._23 = vcDir.y;
   m_mView3D._33 = vcDir.z;
   m_mView3D._43 = - (vcDir*vcPos);
```

```
if (!m_bUseShaders)
   {
   if (FAILED(m_pDevice->SetTransform(D3DTS_VIEW, &m_mView3D)))
      return ZFX_FAIL;
   }

CalcViewProjMatrix();
CalcWorldViewProjMatrix();
return ZFX_OK;
}
```

As you can see, the view matrix is not complicated to build. The first three entries of the first three columns contain the right, up, and direction vector of the camera (see Figure 6.1). These three orthogonal vectors span the camera's coordinate system. The first three fields of the last row in the matrix are calculated by building the dot product of the appropriate vector from the column above with the position vector of the camera. Finally, the last column stays because it used in an identity matrix.

To ensure the integrity of all the values inside the engine, you also have to recalculate the two combination matrices because the view matrix has changed now. The two functions

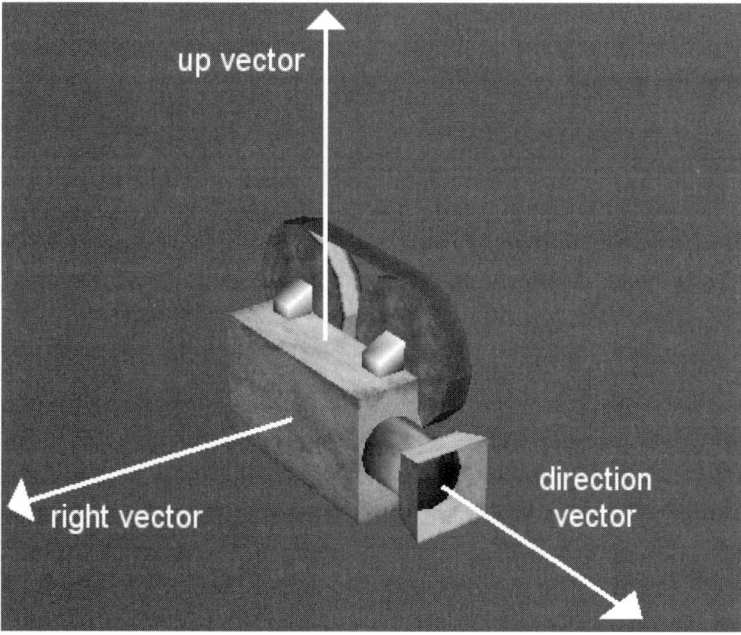

Figure 6.1 The three axes of a camera. The right vector is the unit vector of the x axis; the up vector is the one for the y axis; and the direction vector is the one for the z axis.

`ZFXD3D::CalcViewProjMatrix` and `ZFXD3D::CalcWorldViewProjMatrix` take care of the recalculations for you.

The function I just showed you is very useful if you have the position and orientation calculated and want to view the scene from this camera. Each time the camera moves or rotates you have to recalculate the values. Another common case is when you have the position of the camera and the position of an object the camera should look at. But you don't have the orientation for the camera. The camera is not able to move because it depends on the object it looks at to move and follows the object with its lens. This way, you can build a camera for a third-person view that is fixed on a certain character and is located a bit behind and above her.

We are now talking about the famous *look-at* matrix. It got its name because it is used as a view matrix that is doing exactly what I just described. You also need to know the position and orientation of the camera, but you only get the position of the camera and the position of the object the user wants the camera to look at. The rest is up to you to calculate. As with most things in computer graphics, that is not hard to do. You can calculate the direction vector by subtracting the starting point (the camera's location) from the end point (where the object is located) and normalizing the result. Then you have already done a third of the necessary work.

The up vector is a bit more demanding. You start by asking the user to provide the world coordinate system's up vector, which is normally [0,1,0]. By calculating the dot product between the world's up vector and the normalized direction vector, you get the cosine of the angle between them. Then you make a copy of the direction vector, scale that one with the dot product's value, and subtract this new vector from the world's up vector to get the camera's up vector. Basically, you are doing this to scale the direction vector with the difference in the angle to the orthogonal case and calculate this correction vector into the world's up vector. This should lead to a vector that is rotated once based on the world's up vector but orthogonal to the direction vector. I said this *should* lead to such a vector because in some cases it simply doesn't.

Such a case is when the final up vector you found is too short to contain any useful information. This happens if the object is located in a way that the direction vector from the camera to the object is more or less aligned to the world's up vector. The idea behind this approach is to have a vector that is already close to be the camera's up vector, but if the camera is looking nearly along the world's up vector, this no longer holds true. But don't worry. There are still two other vectors that can do the job. Just take the standard world's right or direction vector and try the same procedure again. It is very likely that at least one of the three tries will produce the correct result.

After you've found the up vector for the camera, simply build the cross product between it and the camera's direction vector to calculate a vector orthogonal to the two of them.

This is the right vector for the camera. And you now have all three vectors of the camera to build the final view matrix, as shown previously:

```
HRESULT ZFXD3D::SetViewLookAt(const ZFXVector &vcPos, const ZFXVector &vcPoint,
                              const ZFXVector &vcWorldUp)
   {
   ZFXVector vcDir, vcTemp, vcUp;

   vcDir = vcPoint - vcPos;
   vcDir.Normalize();

   // calculate up vector
   float fDot = vcWorldUp * vcDir;
   vcTemp = vcDir * fDot;
   vcUp = vcWorldUp - vcTemp;
   float fL = vcUp.GetLength();

   // if too short take y axis
   if (fL < 1e-6f) {
      ZFXVector vcY;
      vcY.Set(0.0f, 1.0f, 0.0f);

      vcTemp = vcDir * vcDir.y;
      vcUp = vcY - vcTemp;

      fL = vcUp.GetLength();

      // take z axis if still too short
      if (fL < 1e-6f) {
         vcY.Set(0.0f, 0.0f, 1.0f);

         vcTemp = vcDir * vcDir.z;
         vcUp = vcY - vcTemp;

         fL = vcUp.GetLength();

         // we tried our best
         if (fL < 1e-6f) return ZFX_FAIL;
         }
      }
   vcUp /= fL;

   // build right vector
```

```
    ZFXVector vcRight;
    vcRight.Cross(vcUp, vcDir);

    // create and activate final view matrix
    return SetView3D(vcRight, vcUp, vcDir, vcPos);
    }
```

If you are done with the calculations, the function calls `ZFXD3D::SetView3D` to activate the view matrix for the engine and for Direct3D. Now you have the functionality to reposition the viewer in the 3D scene.

Getting the Frustum

While talking about the view in 3D computer graphics, there is no way around the view frustum, which is one of the most important concepts because it can be used for quick, cheap, but very effective optimizations in the 3D scene to calculate only objects that are visible to a camera. Just like a human looking out a window, the monitor forms the boundary of what the viewer can see from the 3D world. Its frame provides a window not to the world outside your room, but to the virtual world inside your computer.

The frustum describes the volume that sits behind the window and contains everything you can see in the world, ignoring occlusions between objects. This viewing volume has the shape of the foot of a quadratic pyramid lying on its side. By checking whether an object is sitting inside the view frustum, you can tell if it is visible from a certain position and orientation in the 3D scene.

The view frustum is made of six planes. A near plane sits close to the projection plane, which is the screen of your monitor. No object closer than this near plane can be seen because it is behind the projection plane. On the opposite side is the far plane, which is simply to the largest distance at which you allow objects to be visible. In nature there is no such thing as a far plane, and theoretically, you can see to the end of the universe. You simply cannot see it because the incoming photons are too weak in their energy levels for you to detect them. Another reason is fog or particles in the atmosphere that block a lot of incoming signals from your view.

The location and the exact shape of the view frustum in world coordinates depend on the view matrix and the projection matrix. The projection defines the angles in the horizontal and vertical plane that are used for the view. The view matrix defines the position and orientation of the current camera. The engine saves a concatenation of the view and projection matrix in the attribute `m_mViewProj`; you can then extract the view frustum from this matrix. But you don't need to store it as a real 3D model. It is sufficient to save the six planes (the near and the far plane as well as the four planes for the two sides and the top and bottom) that restrict the space of the view frustum.

The following function shows you how to extract the planes from the matrix:
```
HRESULT ZFXD3D::GetFrustum(ZFXPlane *p)
   {
   // left plane
   p[0].m_vcN.x = -(m_mViewProj._14 + m_mViewProj._11);
   p[0].m_vcN.y = -(m_mViewProj._24 + m_mViewProj._21);
   p[0].m_vcN.z = -(m_mViewProj._34 + m_mViewProj._31);
   p[0].m_fD   = -(m_mViewProj._44 + m_mViewProj._41);

   // right plane
   p[1].m_vcN.x = -(m_mViewProj._14 - m_mViewProj._11);
   p[1].m_vcN.y = -(m_mViewProj._24 - m_mViewProj._21);
   p[1].m_vcN.z = -(m_mViewProj._34 - m_mViewProj._31);
   p[1].m_fD   = -(m_mViewProj._44 - m_mViewProj._41);

   // top plane
   p[2].m_vcN.x = -(m_mViewProj._14 - m_mViewProj._12);
   p[2].m_vcN.y = -(m_mViewProj._24 - m_mViewProj._22);
   p[2].m_vcN.z = -(m_mViewProj._34 - m_mViewProj._32);
   p[2].m_fD   = -(m_mViewProj._44 - m_mViewProj._42);

   // bottom plane
   p[3].m_vcN.x = -(m_mViewProj._14 + m_mViewProj._12);
   p[3].m_vcN.y = -(m_mViewProj._24 + m_mViewProj._22);
   p[3].m_vcN.z = -(m_mViewProj._34 + m_mViewProj._32);
   p[3].m_fD   = -(m_mViewProj._44 + m_mViewProj._42);

   // near plane
   p[4].m_vcN.x = -m_mViewProj._13;
   p[4].m_vcN.y = -m_mViewProj._23;
   p[4].m_vcN.z = -m_mViewProj._33;
   p[4].m_fD   = -m_mViewProj._43;

   // far plane
   p[5].m_vcN.x = -(m_mViewProj._14 - m_mViewProj._13);
   p[5].m_vcN.y = -(m_mViewProj._24 - m_mViewProj._23);
   p[5].m_vcN.z = -(m_mViewProj._34 - m_mViewProj._33);
   p[5].m_fD   = -(m_mViewProj._44 - m_mViewProj._43);

   // normalize normals
   for (int i=0;i<6;i++)
      {
```

```
        float fL = p[i].m_vcN.GetLength();
        p[i].m_vcN /= fL;
        p[i].m_fD  /= fL;
        }
    return ZFX_OK;
    }
```

Caution

The view frustum depends on the matrices used as the view and projection matrix. Each one of these two matrices changes the view frustum and must be recalculated if you want to work with it. The view matrix is likely to change each frame, so you have to extract the view frustum during each frame. But it is also up to the user to know that he needs to reextract the frustum if he changes the view matrix or the projection matrix.

Setting Clipping Planes

Two very important values for the view calculations are the value for the near clipping plane and the value for the far clipping plane. These two values determine the size of the view frustum along your direction vector, and the planes are parallel to the projection plane that receives the projected image.

To define the near plane and far plane, you therefore only need to give the distance values as floating-point numbers to set the distance at which the planes should be situated. The near plane value is the minimum distance an object or a projected pixel needs to have for the camera to be visible. If a pixel is closer to the camera or has a negative distance because it is behind the camera, it is not shown. The depth buffer calculations would get in trouble if you set the near plane's distance to a value of 0. A viewer would see artifacts if you did this. Always set the near plane's value to some value greater than 0.

The value for the far clipping plane is just that—the distance beyond which no object or pixel is rendered because it is too far away. Again, visual artifacts can appear if the range between the near plane and far plane is too big, such as 100,000,00 units. The reason is easy to understand. The values in the depth buffer are expressed in the range of 0.0f–1.0f. If you express distance values from near value 0.1f to far value 100.f, this has a much greater accuracy in the range [0.0f, 1.0f] than a near value of 0.01f and a far value of 100000.0f. The less accuracy the depth buffer has, the more often you will see visible artifacts such as distant objects shining through closer ones. If this happens, check your values for the near plane and the far plane first.

The far plane should be more distant than the near plane. The following function lets the user of our engine set the values for the near plane and far plane. By adjusting the far plane, you can effectively change the viewing distance of the camera. But these two values are used in other calculations in the 3D pipeline so they are also part of the projection matrix. So, if the user changes the values, you also have to recalculate the fields of the projection matrices that are using the near plane and far plane values:

```
void ZFXD3D::SetClippingPlanes(float fNear, float fFar)
   {
   m_fNear = fNear;
   m_fFar  = fFar;

   if (m_fNear <= 0.0f) m_fNear = 0.01f;
   if (m_fFar  <= 1.0f) m_fFar  = 1.00f;

   if (m_fNear >= m_fFar) {
      m_fNear = m_fFar;
      m_fFar  = m_fNear + 1.0f;
      }

   // adjust 2d matrices
   Prepare2D();

   // adjust orthogonal projection
   float Q = 1.0f / (m_fFar - m_fNear);
   float X = -Q * m_fNear;
   m_mProjO[0]._33 = m_mProjO[1]._33 = Q;
   m_mProjO[2]._33 = m_mProjO[3]._33 = Q;
   m_mProjO[0]._43 = m_mProjO[1]._43 = X;
   m_mProjO[2]._43 = m_mProjO[3]._43 = X;

   // adjust perspective projection
   Q *= m_fFar;
   X = -Q * m_fNear;
   m_mProjP[0]._33 = m_mProjP[1]._33 = Q;
   m_mProjP[2]._33 = m_mProjP[3]._33 = Q;
   m_mProjP[0]._43 = m_mProjP[1]._43 = X;
   m_mProjP[2]._43 = m_mProjP[3]._43 = X;
   }
```

This function also performs some security checks to prevent the near plane from being less than or equal to 0 to avoid screwing up the depth buffer calculations. It also prevents the far plane from being closer than the near plane.

Then the projection matrices in the arrays are recalculated. The third entries in the third and fourth rows depend on the near plane and the far plane's values. So, we just recalculate these and not the whole matrices because the other values stay as they are.

Next, I will explain the projection calculations to refresh your knowledge about computer graphics.

Orthogonal Projection

From your art class at school, you will certainly know some techniques of how to draw or paint 3D pictures on paper. You do this by drawing all the lines so they meet at a single point or by drawing all the lines going into the image at a 45-degree angle and at half length.

By projecting 3D information, you integrate the third dimension's information into the two other ones, thus making the third dimension's information unneeded and enabling the drawing of the image in two dimensions as on a flat paper. In computer graphics, you normally need only two types of projections: orthogonal projection and perspective one projection.

Orthogonal projection is sometimes also called *parallel projection*. Orthogonal projection is one type of a parallel projection, but there are other types of parallel projections as well.

In a parallel projection, you simply draw lines from each point that should be projected to the plane on which the image should be projected. The angle of the lines doesn't matter as long as all the lines are parallel to each other. This is where the name of this type of projection comes from. Parallel projection rejects the differences in distance that objects have to the projection plane. Think of a cube standing 2 meters in front of the camera and a second cube standing 100 meters away from it; both of them would look the same. This happens because they project their images to the projection plane without taking care of the distance.

If the angle of the projection lines is perpendicular to the projection plane, this is called an orthogonal projection. Figure 6.2 shows a 3D model of a brick wall and how it is projected to the projection plane, or the monitor. On the projected image, you can see only the front side of the wall even if the wall is not right in front of the viewer. In a perspective projection, you could also see the side of the wall. Compare this to Figure 6.3, which shows the same scene in a perspective projection.

If the distance of the projected objects does not matter, in the final image the objects will not look smaller. But they will also not look 3D if you are using an orthogonal projection. A parallel projection should be used if you are using it for an isometric game in which perspective correctness is neither needed nor wanted. But an orthogonal projection will look pretty boring. In fact, any objects built by a 3D artist will look like technical blueprints, so what do you need that kind of projection for?

Actually, I just mentioned what you will use this type of projection for: blueprints, or for designing and building 3D objects. A 3D indoor level editor has one perspective view and three views showing the level from the front, the side, and above, like some technical

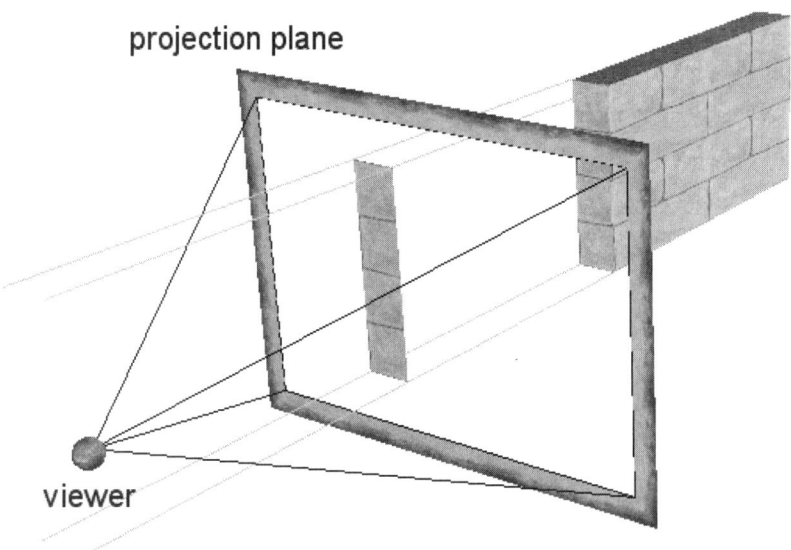

Figure 6.2 Orthogonal projection of a 3D scene onto a 2D projection plane.

drawings do. People tend to start drawing 2D images and lines when they begin to program a level editor. However, the apparent 2D views are in fact orthogonal views of the 3D level.

Do you still remember the three modes our engine can be run in? These are perspective mode, orthogonal mode, and 2D mode. This 2D mode works by using an orthogonal projection matrix and a special view matrix. This view matrix treats the vertices as if they were given with screen coordinates in their x and y components. You can build the orthogonal projection matrix and this special view matrix using the following function:

```
void ZFXD3D::Prepare2D(void)
   {
   // make identity matrix
   memset(&m_mProj2D, 0, sizeof(float)*16);
   memset(&m_mView2D, 0, sizeof(float)*16);
   m_mView2D._11 = m_mView2D._33 = m_mView2D._44 = 1.0f;

   // orthogonal projection matrix
   m_mProj2D._11 =  2.0f/(float)m_dwWidth;
   m_mProj2D._22 =  2.0f/(float)m_dwHeight;
   m_mProj2D._33 =  1.0f/(m_fFar-m_fNear);
   m_mProj2D._43 = -m_fNear*(1.0f/(m_fFar-m_fNear));
   m_mProj2D._44 =  1.0f;
```

```
    // 2d view matrix
    float tx, ty, tz;
    tx = -((int)m_dwWidth) + m_dwWidth * 0.5f;
    ty =   m_dwHeight - m_dwHeight  * 0.5f;
    tz =   m_fNear + 0.1f;

    m_mView2D._22 = -1.0f;
    m_mView2D._41 = tx;
    m_mView2D._42 = ty;
    m_mView2D._43 = tz;
    }
```

If you activate the 2D mode, this sets the matrices m_mProj2D and m_mView2D as the projection and view matrix for the Direct3D device. Then you can define triangles with vertices whose coordinates are given in screen space as opposed to world space or local space along with a world matrix. This way, you can render polygons for heads-up displays, menus, or maps onto the screen without the need to switch to a transformed vertex type, thereby avoiding the overhead of such a switch.

The projection matrix uses the width and height of the whole screen, independent from the active viewport. In the function ZFXD3D::InitStage, we use the same formula to create the orthogonal projection matrices for the four view stages but use the width and height of the stage's viewport.

Note

If you are a bit unsure of how the formulas for projection matrices work, make sure you read the related parts of the DirectX SDK documentation that contains several good paragraphs explaining the math behind the formulas and showing some examples of projection types and matrices.

Perspective Projection

The most important kind of projection in computer graphics is the one that makes the 3D scene look like the real world on the projection plane. This is, of course, the perspective projection, which now incorporates the depth information into the x and y component of the projected points. Perspective projection is used in all first-person and third-person video games.

This projection works explicitly by not using parallel projecting lines; instead it draws lines from the viewer to each point inside the viewing frustum. The point is rendered onto the image plane at the point at which this line hits the projection plane. As you can see in Figure 6.3, the points that are more distant from the viewer require projecting lines with a smaller angle than points that are closer to the viewer. Thus, the depth information is taken into account and distant polygons are projected to a smaller area on the projection plane as polygons closer to the plane.

Now you can also see the side and the top face of the wall, and the projected image looks like the perspective image it is supposed to.

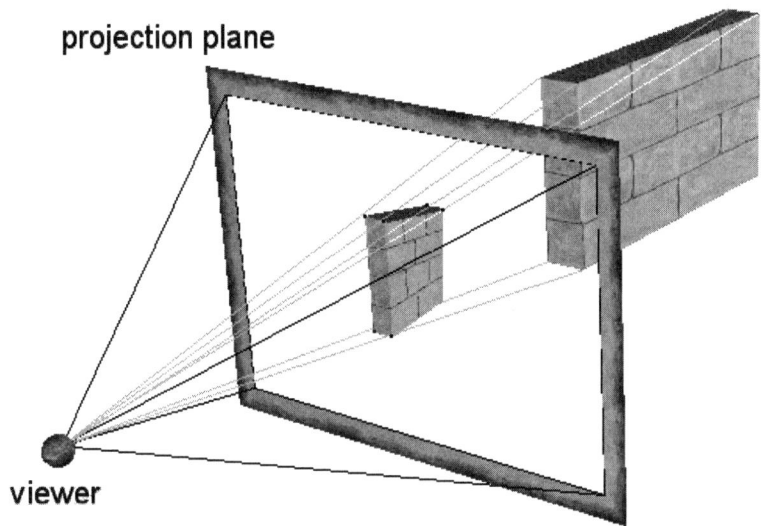

Figure 6.3 Perspective projection of a 3D scene onto a 2D projection plane.

Again, you should check the DirectX SDK documentation or a basic book about computer graphics or linear algebra to see how the formula behind this works. Here is the implementation that uses the formula for perspective projection to set up a projection matrix based on the horizontal field of view and the aspect ratio from the width to the height of the viewport:

```
HRESULT ZFXD3D::CalcPerspProjMatrix(float fFOV,
                                    float fAspect,
                                    D3DMATRIX *m)
   {
   if(fabs(m_fFar - m_fNear) < 0.01f)
      return ZFX_FAIL;

   float sinFOV2 = sinf(fFOV/2);

   if(fabs(sinFOV2) < 0.01f) return ZFX_FAIL;
```

```
    float cosFOV2 = cosf(fFOV/2);

    float w = fAspect * (cosFOV2 / sinFOV2);
    float h =   1.0f  * (cosFOV2 / sinFOV2);
    float Q = m_fFar / (m_fFar - m_fNear);

    memset(m, 0, sizeof(D3DMATRIX));
    (*m)._11 = w;
    (*m)._22 = h;
    (*m)._33 = Q;
    (*m)._34 = 1.0f;
    (*m)._43 = -Q*m_fNear;
    return ZFX_OK;
    } // CalcPerspProjMatrix
```

Please note the dependency of the perspective matrix on the values used for the near clipping plane and far clipping plane. You can see that it is always a good idea to calculate the sine and cosine values only once and store the result in a new temporary variable even if you will use the values only twice. This saves you some calculation time due to the slow nature of trigonometric functions.

Combined Transformation Matrices

Combining the transformation matrices is also a trivial task to accomplish. The function needs only to check which mode of the engine is currently active to be sure to pick the right matrices and the right stages. To use the engine's own matrix class, the function casts the attributes of the type D3DMATRIX into ZFXMatrix types. Then the two matrices for projection and view are combined by multiplication. Matrix multiplication is not commutative, so the order of matrices is important:

```
void ZFXD3D::CalcViewProjMatrix(void)
    {
    ZFXMatrix *pA;
    ZFXMatrix *pB;

    // 2D, perspective, or orthogonal
    if (m_Mode == EMD_TWOD)
       {
       pA = (ZFXMatrix*)&m_mProj2D;
       pB = (ZFXMatrix*)&m_mView2D;
       }
    else {
       pB = (ZFXMatrix*)&m_mView3D;
```

```
       if (m_Mode == EMD_PERSPECTIVE)
           pA = (ZFXMatrix*)&(m_mProjP[m_nStage]);
       else
           pA = (ZFXMatrix*)&(m_mProjO[m_nStage]);
       }
   ZFXMatrix *pM = (ZFXMatrix*)&m_mViewProj;
   (*pM) = (*pA) * (*pB);
   } // CalcViewProjMatrix
```

The same applies for the combination of the world, view, and projection matrix. But before multiplying the view matrix by the projection matrix, you multiply the world matrix by the view matrix and then multiply the resulting matrix by the projection matrix. By using this combo matrix, you can now transform vertices from world space to camera space and project them. Normally, you would not need to do this, but if you use shaders, as in the next chapter, you need this matrix. If you set a custom vertex shader for Direct3D, you need to do this transformation to the projected space in the shader, which is one reason such a combo matrix is necessary:

```
void ZFXD3D::CalcWorldViewProjMatrix(void)
   {
   ZFXMatrix *pProj;
   ZFXMatrix *pView;
   ZFXMatrix *pWorld;

   pWorld = (ZFXMatrix*)&m_mWorld;

   // 2D, perspective, or orthogonal
   if (m_Mode == EMD_TWOD)
      {
      pProj = (ZFXMatrix*)&m_mProj2D;
      pView = (ZFXMatrix*)&m_mView2D;
      }
   else {
      pView = (ZFXMatrix*)&m_mView3D;

      if (m_Mode == EMD_PERSPECTIVE)
          pProj = (ZFXMatrix*)&(m_mProjP[m_nStage]);
      else
          pProj = (ZFXMatrix*)&(m_mProjO[m_nStage]);
      }

   ZFXMatrix *pCombo = (ZFXMatrix*)&m_mWorldViewProj;
```

```
(*pCombo) = ((*pWorld) * (*pView)) * (*pProj);
} // CalcViewProjMatrix
```

Activating View and Projection

Now we have a whole bunch of functions in our render device that can be used to set different projection matrices and adjust the clipping planes to arbitrary valid distances. However, some of these functions are declared only in the implementing class `ZFXD3D` and not in the interface. So, the user has no access to them. To switch these settings, the user needs another trigger function in the interface to set the engine to a certain mode with certain values.

Writing such a function is not complicated from a mathematical point of view. But it's a bit difficult to maintain the internal integrity of the hull ... er, the engine I mean. Note to myself: No more *Star Trek* for this week. If you adjust the clipping planes, you have to recalculate the projection matrix, if you change a projection or view matrix, you have to recalculate the combo matrices, and so on.

Now I will show you the function that lets the user switch between the operational mode of the engine. After that, I will point out what to note. You will see the function call `ForcedFlushAll()` on a new attribute of the `ZFXD3D` class called `m_pVertexMan`. You will get acquainted with this function when the vertex cache manager is discussed later in this chapter. All the things connected to this function take up nearly a third of this chapter because it is an important topic. In addition, Direct3D is horrible at rendering small batches of triangles in one call. Therefore, rendering a thousand triangles in one call is lightning fast but rendering with a thousand calls while rendering a single triangle with each call is very slow.

OpenGL does a much better job rendering single triangles. This is good because it makes life easier for the programmer by skipping the need to batch data together. But it's also a disadvantage because people tend to use this feature a lot. But still, batching triangles together and using fewer calls is faster, and the sooner you get used to this kind of programming for 3D graphics, the better.

Why is OpenGL better in this feature even if it runs on the same hardware? Well, OpenGL relies on the driver you are using that is sorting and batching the render calls. Direct3D uses a more direct approach to the graphics adapter. The bottom line is that graphics adapters are no good at rendering single triangles, and OpenGL provides a helping hand while Direct3D does not. You have to implement such a helping hand in the engine, and that is what the vertex manager (`m_pVertexMan`) is used for. It batches dynamically rendered data together and delays the actual render calls until the frame ends or an important state changes. The change of the engine's mode is such a crucial change, so the caches need to be rendered immediately. That is what this mysterious function call is meant for.

Setting the Mode

Let's have a look at the function:

```
HRESULT ZFXD3D::SetMode(ZFXENGINEMODE Mode, int nStage)
   {
   D3DVIEWPORT9 d3dVP;

   if (!m_bRunning) return E_FAIL;
   if ((nStage > 3) || (nStage < 0)) nStage=0;

   if (m_Mode != Mode)
      m_Mode  = Mode;

   // flush all caches prior to changing mode
   m_pVertexMan->ForcedFlushAll();

   // if 2d use its matrices
   if (Mode==EMD_TWOD) {
      d3dVP.X      = 0;
      d3dVP.Y      = 0;
      d3dVP.Width  = m_dwWidth;
      d3dVP.Height = m_dwHeight;
      d3dVP.MinZ   = 0.0f;
      d3dVP.MaxZ   = 1.0f;

      if (FAILED(m_pDevice->SetViewport(&d3dVP)))
         return ZFX_FAIL;

      if (!m_bUseShaders) {
         if (FAILED(m_pDevice->SetTransform(
                                   D3DTS_PROJECTION,
                                   &m_mProj2D)))
            return ZFX_FAIL;

         if (FAILED(m_pDevice->SetTransform(
                                   D3DTS_VIEW,
                                   &m_mView2D)))
            return ZFX_FAIL;
         }
      }

   // perspective or orthogonal projection
```

```cpp
   else {
      m_nStage = nStage;

      // set viewport
      d3dVP.X      = m_VP[nStage].X;
      d3dVP.Y      = m_VP[nStage].Y;
      d3dVP.Width  = m_VP[nStage].Width;
      d3dVP.Height = m_VP[nStage].Height;
      d3dVP.MinZ   = 0.0f;
      d3dVP.MaxZ   = 1.0f;

      if (FAILED(m_pDevice->SetViewport(&d3dVP)))
         return ZFX_FAIL;

      if (!m_bUseShaders) {
         if (FAILED(m_pDevice->SetTransform( D3DTS_VIEW,
                                             &m_mView3D)))
            return ZFX_FAIL;

         if (m_Mode == EMD_PERSPECTIVE) {
            if (FAILED(m_pDevice->SetTransform( D3DTS_PROJECTION,
                                                &m_mProjP[nStage])))
               return ZFX_FAIL;
            }
         else { // EMD_ORTHOGONAL
            if (FAILED(m_pDevice->SetTransform( D3DTS_PROJECTION,
                                                &m_mProjO[nStage])))
               return ZFX_FAIL;
            }
         }
      CalcViewProjMatrix();
      CalcWorldViewProjMatrix();
      }
   return ZFX_OK;
   } // SetMode
```

Basically this function decides only which mode is requested and then sets the appropriate matrices for the view and the projection transformation as well as the viewport connected to a certain stage, or the whole screen in the case of the 2D mode. This is not complicated, but you need to be aware from which stage you are taking the matrices. Again, the 2D mode of the engine is a bit special because it has no stages at all.

As mentioned previously, the last thing to do is to recalculate the two combination matrices used to extract the view frustum or to transform data manually in vertex shaders. Now you know the whole story about how to switch a mode of the engine to another mode or simply to another stage of the same mode.

Initializing the Mode

You now know how to switch correctly between the modes and the stages, but you don't know how to initialize a stage according to your wishes regarding the viewport and the field of view. The function shown here lets you initialize a stage with these two variables. It then sets the values for the orthogonal and the perspective mode for the appropriate stage:

```
HRESULT ZFXD3D::InitStage(float fFOV, ZFXVIEWPORT *pView, int nStage)
   {
   float fAspect;
   bool  bOwnRect=false;

   if (!pView)
      {
      ZFXVIEWPORT vpOwn = { 0, 0, m_dwWidth, m_dwHeight};
      memcpy(&m_VP[nStage], &vpOwn, sizeof(RECT));
      }
   else
      memcpy(&m_VP[nStage], pView, sizeof(RECT));

   if ( (nStage>3) || (nStage<0) ) nStage=0;

   fAspect = ((float)(m_VP[nStage].Height)) / (m_VP[nStage].Width);

   // perspective projection matrix
   if (FAILED(this->CalcPerspProjMatrix(fFOV, fAspect, &m_mProjP[nStage])))
      {
      return ZFX_FAIL;
      }

   // orthogonal projection matrix
   memset(&m_mProjO[nStage], 0, sizeof(float)*16);
   m_mProjO[nStage]._11 =  2.0f/m_VP[nStage].Width;
   m_mProjO[nStage]._22 =  2.0f/m_VP[nStage].Height;
   m_mProjO[nStage]._33 =  1.0f/(m_fFar-m_fNear);
   m_mProjO[nStage]._43 =  - m_fNear * m_mProjO[nStage]._33;
   m_mProjO[nStage]._44 =  1.0f;
```

```
return ZFX_OK;
} // InitStage
```

This function can be called at any time while an application using the ZFXEngine is running. It sets the values for the matrices of the stage. Changing the orthogonal projection matrix is easy because only a few fields in the matrix are affected by the change. Recalculating the perspective projection is a bit more work, so this is done in an extra function call. Finally, the requested viewport is saved for this stage, if it is given at all. If not, the engine takes the size of the back buffer as the viewport.

Converting from 3D to 2D and Vice Versa

Several situations in a 3D application can require you to do the transformation of points in a 3D space to a 2D space manually. Even the inverted case occurs quite often where you need to calculate 3D data for a given point in a 2D screen space. The graphics card will work for rendering the 3D data to the 2D data, but if you don't want to render data and just want to know the projected position it would have onscreen, you have to do this manually.

One such situation is when you want to mark an object on the heads-up display of the player, such as for a 3D space combat simulation like *Wing Commander* or *Freelancer*. If you target an enemy fighter, it is marked with a flashing rectangle so you can keep an eye on it. Take a look at Figure 6.4 to see what I mean. This is a screenshot from a space fighter demo I wrote some time ago. You can clearly see the rectangle marking the fighter's position that is flying ahead of the player.

This is done by manually projecting the position of the enemy fighter to 2D screen coordinates and rendering a 2D unfilled rectangle around this projected position.

Unfortunately, the graphics adapter hides the secret from us and does not reveal the transformed positions. So there is no way to get the projected data of an object you rendered using the graphics adapter. You therefore have to write a function that can do this transformation from 3D space to 2D space. The next function takes a vector that is given in 3D world coordinates and returns the corresponding point in screen space by applying the currently active transformation matrices to the point:

```
POINT ZFXD3D::Transform3Dto2D(const ZFXVector &vcPoint)
   {
   POINT pt;
   float fClip_x, fClip_y;
   float fXp, fYp, fWp;
   DWORD dwWidth, dwHeight;

   // if 2d mode take the whole screen
```

View and Projection 261

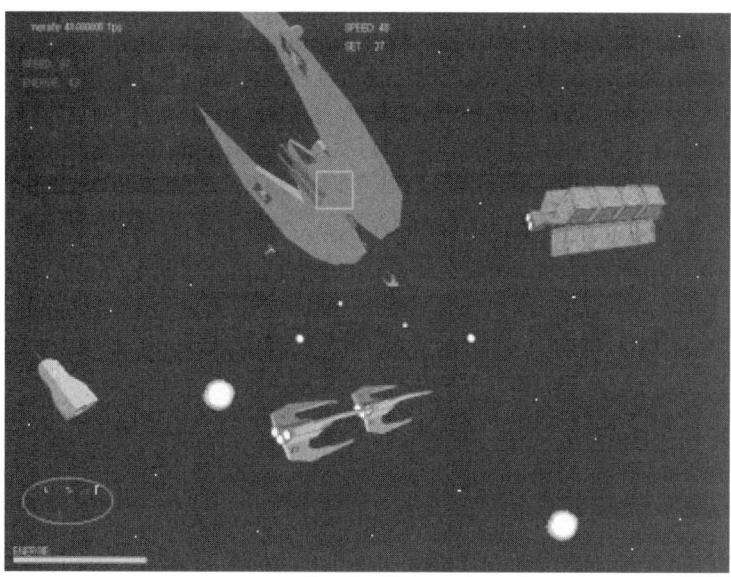

Figure 6.4 A screenshot from *Wing Captain 2* shows a target marker on the projected position of the enemy fighter that tries to escape by pulling straight up.

```
if (m_nMode == EMD_TWOD) {
   dwWidth  = m_dwWidth;
   dwHeight = m_dwHeight;
   }
// else take viewport dimensions
else {
   dwWidth  = m_VP[m_nStage].Width;
   dwHeight = m_VP[m_nStage].Height;
   }
fClip_x = (float)(dwWidth  >> 1);
fClip_y = (float)(dwHeight >> 1);

// transformation & projection
fXp = (m_mViewProj._11*vcPoint.x) + (m_mViewProj._21*vcPoint.y)
    + (m_mViewProj._31*vcPoint.z) + m_mViewProj._41;
fYp = (m_mViewProj._12*vcPoint.x) + (m_mViewProj._22*vcPoint.y)
    + (m_mViewProj._32*vcPoint.z) + m_mViewProj._42;
fWp = (m_mViewProj._14*vcPoint.x) + (m_mViewProj._24*vcPoint.y)
    + (m_mViewProj._34*vcPoint.z) + m_mViewProj._44;

float fWpInv = 1.0f / fWp;
```

```
// converting from [-1,1] to viewport size
pt.x = (LONG)( (1.0f + (fXp * fWpInv)) * fClip_x );
pt.y = (LONG)( (1.0f + (fYp * fWpInv)) * fClip_y );
return pt;
}
```

This function works by multiplying the given vector with the combo matrix built from the view matrix and the projection matrix. After that, the point is already transformed in the correct manner. But there is one catch: After the transformation, the now 2D coordinates must be brought into the viewport coordinate space, which ranges from −1.0f to +1.0f, only to be independent from screen or viewport resolutions. So, the projection matrix is already built to end up in this coordinate range for pixels lying on the screen. After applying the transformation manually, you need to bring the values back from the range −1.0f–1.0f to the actual viewport resolution. You do this by adding 1.0f to the values to bring them to the range 0.0f–2.0f and then multiply them by half the width and half the height of the viewport, respectively.

If the viewport is really the whole screen, you will have the final 2D screen coordinates. You get the screen coordinates minus the offset of the viewport in the window that is used for rendering, and the coordinates are relative to the client area of the window used for rendering.

Now you need to calculate the 3D information from a given 2D information. Many people keep asking how they can calculate the point in 3D space corresponding to a point they have in 2D space, such as a mouse click on the screen. The answer is quite simple: This is just not possible. By projecting a point from 3D space to 2D space, you integrate the depth information into the two other coordinates. But there is no way to transform 2D information like a click with the mouse to a single point in 3D space. How would the mouse possibly know at which exact depth the user wants to have the click take place?

You can transform a point from 2D screen coordinates to 3D world space, but the result is not a point—it's a ray. The ray originates from the viewer's position and runs straight along the viewer's direction vector. The following function calculates the ray in 3D world coordinates from a given point in 2D coordinates:

```
void   ZFXD3D::Transform2Dto3D(const POINT &pt, ZFXVector *vcOrig,
                               ZFXVector *vcDir)
   {
   D3DMATRIX  *pView=NULL, *pProj=NULL;
   ZFXMatrix  mInvView;
   ZFXVector  vcS;
   DWORD      dwWidth,
              dwHeight;
```

```cpp
// 2d mode
if (m_Mode == EMD_TWOD) {
   dwWidth  = m_dwWidth;
   dwHeight = m_dwHeight;

   pView = &m_mView2D;
   }
// else orthogonal or perspective projection
else {
   dwWidth  = m_VP[m_nStage].Width,
   dwHeight = m_VP[m_nStage].Height;

   pView = &m_mView3D;

   if (m_Mode == EMD_PERSPECTIVE)
      pProj = &m_mProjP[m_nStage];
   else
      pProj = &m_mProjO[m_nStage];
   }

// scale to viewport and inverse projection
vcS.x =  ( ((pt.x*2.0f) / dwWidth) -1.0f) / m_mProjP[m_nStage]._11;
vcS.y = -( ((pt.y*2.0f) / dwHeight)-1.0f) / m_mProjP[m_nStage]._22;
vcS.z = 1.0f;

// invert view matrix
mInvView.InverseOf(*((ZFXMatrix*)&m_mView3D._11));

// ray from screen to world coordinates
(*vcDir).x = (vcS.x * mInvView._11) + (vcS.y * mInvView._21)
           + (vcS.z * mInvView._31);
(*vcDir).y = (vcS.x * mInvView._12) + (vcS.y * mInvView._22)
           + (vcS.z * mInvView._32);
(*vcDir).z = (vcS.x * mInvView._13) + (vcS.y * mInvView._23)
           + (vcS.z * mInvView._33);

// inverse translation
(*vcOrig).x = mInvView._41;
(*vcOrig).y = mInvView._42;
(*vcOrig).z = mInvView._43;
```

```
// normalizing
(*vcDir).Normalize();
}
```

To be able to calculate the projection to 3D space correctly, you need to know the viewport's dimension. Using this dimension, you then have to move the point into the coordinate's space of the viewport ranging from −1.0f to 1.0f. After that, the projection is applied in a reverse manner by dividing and not multiplying by the corresponding values from the projection matrix. Finally, you have to apply the inverted view matrix on the point to bring the values into 3D world space.

The origin of the ray is then the position as it appears in the inverted view matrix. Remember that the last row in the view matrix contains the camera position. The direction vector now needs to be normalized, and that's it. Now you can click with the mouse on a point on the rendered image and build a ray into the 3D scene from that point. Such a ray can be used in picking operations—for example, when you want to select objects in the 3D world by clicking them.

Summing Up View and Projection

You've seen a lot of functions in this chapter already. Most of them are related or even connected to each other. Maybe you got the impression of a giant moving along, but we are still dealing only with a pygmy. The ZFXEngine's internal logic takes over a lot of the work now. To demonstrate this, I want to sum up what we've achieved so far and present a code snippet to show you how you can adjust the ZFXD3D device:

```
// inside a ZFXRenderDeviceD3D init function do this:
RECT rcView;
rcView.left   = rcView.top = 0;
rcView.right  = m_dwWidth;
rcView.bottom = m_dwHeight;

m_nMode  = -1;
m_nStage = 0;

IDENTITY(m_mView3D);

SetClippingPlanes(0.1f, 1000.0f);
if (FAILED(InitStage(0.8f, &rcView, 0))) return ZFX_FAIL;
```

The maximum viewing distance is 1000 units, and the minimum viewing distance is 0.1 units. The viewport is initialized to span the whole back buffer, and the field of view is 0.8 radian, which is a reasonable value. A value of 0 for the mode means perspective projection, a value of 1 is the 2D projection, and a value of 2 means the normal orthogonal projection. In this case, the mode is set to −1 indicating that the user has not yet activated a certain mode. So, you can easily use this system with different viewing stages that you can precalculate.

Setting the World Transformation

A 3D pipeline consists of three transformations. One is used to project the data from 3D space to 2D space. Another transforms the 3D data from the world coordinate system to the view coordinate system, which transforms the scene with regard to the camera position and movement. The third transform is used to move 3D data from its local system where it's defined with regard to its local origin to the world coordinate system. Building such a world transformation matrix is easy, especially when employing the matrix class in the math library of the ZFXEngine. A function in the render device interface ZFXRenderDevice lets the user set the world transform.

But before I show you this function, I want to talk about the shaders. If you don't know anything about shaders except that you can do fantastic things by using them, don't worry. The next chapter deals with programming vertex and pixel shaders in depth. However, for now, you need to know only that the fixed function pipeline doesn't perform the transformations for you anymore if you use shaders. So, if you want to use shaders, you have to provide the combination matrix from the world, the view, and the projection matrix to the shader interface. Thus, you don't need to set the world transform for the fixed function pipeline. You will see this in a moment.

The second issue is that we have to take care of the vertex caches, which hold the data rendered from user pointers. If a change in the world matrix occurs, you have to render all the data from the caches before changing the world matrix. Otherwise, the data in the caches is transformed with another world transform, as the user requested. The function ForcedFlushAll() empties all the caches by rendering their contents.

Here is the function for how a user can supply a world matrix that should be activated:

```
void ZFXD3D::SetWorldTransform(const ZFXMatrix *mWorld)
   {
   // last chance check
   m_pVertexMan->ForcedFlushAll();

   // class attribute 'world matrix'
   if (!mWorld) {
      ZFXMatrix m; m.Identity();
      memcpy(&m_mWorld, &m, sizeof(D3DMATRIX));
      }
   else
      memcpy(&m_mWorld, mWorld, sizeof(D3DMATRIX));
```

```
// recalculating depending values
CalcWorldViewProjMatrix();

// if shader set a constant
if (m_bUseShaders) {
   ZFXMatrix mTranspose;
   mTranspose.TransposeOf(
                   *(ZFXMatrix*)&m_mWorldViewProj);
   m_pDevice->SetVertexShaderConstantF(0,
                   (float*)&mTranspose, 4);
   }
else
   m_pDevice->SetTransform(D3DTS_WORLD, &m_mWorld);
} // SetWorldTransform
```

Note the simplicity in usage for the caller of the function. If the user does not provide a pointer to a matrix to be used but provides NULL instead, the function accepts this input as the user's wish to have no world transform. To accomplish this, the function still needs to set the identity matrix for Direct3D because Direct3D isn't that smart. Finally, the combination matrix is recalculated due to the change in one of its components.

Vertex Structures

Unfortunately, there are a few issues that are not that easy to implement in a flexible way. A good example is the vertex format, which describes the components one vertex has. The most common three differentiations of basic vertex formats are

- Untransformed and unlit vertices
- Untransformed and lit vertices
- Transformed and lit vertices

This sounds good, but this is only a rough description of the vertex format. For example, there can be no texture coordinates, one texture coordinate, or two pairs of texture coordinates. There can be additional values used for indexing bones in animated meshes or vectors needed for bump mapping and so on.

The problem is that you must specify the vertex format exactly for Direct3D to be able to work with it. You could build a structure containing all that information that could possibly appear in the vertex format, but this would waste a lot of memory and bandwidth. Furthermore, it would just be ugly. Direct3D uses the flexible vertex format (FVF) that lets you specify which components are present for a certain vertex type. Now I want to concentrate on the engine and not on vertex issues, so I decided to provide different definitions for the vertex format that I will work with in this book. If you need another vertex format in your engine, you have to integrate it in the same way I provided the formats here.

Take a look at the following vertex types that are enumerated and have a structure specifying their components. Some more types are defined in the final rendering engine in this chapter, so take a look at the source code, too. You will find them in the file ZFX.h:

```
// in ZFX.h
typedef enum ZFXVERTEXID_TYPE {
    VID_UU,       // untransformed and unlit
    VID_UL,       // untransformed and lit
    } ZFXVERTEXID;

typedef struct VERTEX_TYPE {
    float   x, y, z;
    float   vcN[3];
    float   tu, tv;
    } VERTEX;

typedef struct LVERTEX_TYPE {
    float   x, y, z;
    DWORD   Color;
    float   tu, tv;
    } LVERTEX;'


// in ZFXD3D.h
#define FVF_VERTEX  ( D3DFVF_XYZ | D3DFVF_NORMAL  | D3DFVF_TEX1 )
#define FVF_LVERTEX ( D3DFVF_XYZ | D3DFVF_DIFFUSE | D3DFVF_TEX1 )
```

If you want to add a certain vertex format to the engine, you just have to add this to the enumerated type, provide a structure for it, and define an FVF definition specifying the contents of the structure. For more information about how you can specify the FVF definition and what kinds of FVF flags are available, take a look at the DirectX documentation to find the complete list.

Shader Support

Vertex shaders and pixel shaders are a strange topic to start with. Most of you will have heard about them. But most of you will not know exactly what a shader is or how to implement one. This is covered in the next chapter, but in this chapter we have to do some groundwork to build an assembly area where the shaders can be equipped and refitted by our engine.

I want to show you how you can load and compile shader programs using Direct3D. You will also learn how to activate a shader so the fixed function pipeline is no longer used until a shader is deactivated.

There are two possibilities when it comes to shaders. You can provide a shader as a program just like a C++ program, but the shader still needs to be compiled. The other option is to use a compiled shader so the engine is not required to compile it, but only to load it and prepare it to be used some time later for rendering. Each of the two options is split up again into loading the shader from a file or providing a pointer to the data in memory if the user specified the shader in her source code.

Of course, the ZFXEngine supports all these options in a single, rather intelligent function.

Prerequisites for using Shaders

In a real-world project, an application would support the fixed function pipeline as well as the *flexible pipeline*, as the use of shaders is called. The samples at the end of this book depend on the use of shaders and don't provide a nice look for the fixed function pipeline. So, I concentrate on shaders, but you should always determine for which generation of graphics adapters you are developing.

I will now show you the member attributes you need in the ZFXD3D class implementing the ZFXRenderDevice interface. There are a number of functions. One private function checks the support of shaders on the current hardware, and five public functions are declared in the interface for the user to access the shader support of our engine. Here are the new members of the class ZFXD3D:

```
private:
   LPDIRECT3DVDECL9        m_pDeclVertex;
   LPDIRECT3DVDECL9        m_pDeclLVertex;

   LPDIRECT3DVSHADER9      m_pVShader[MAX_SHADER];
   LPDIRECT3DPSHADER9      m_pPShader[MAX_SHADER];
   UINT                    m_nNumVShaders;
   UINT                    m_nNumPShaders;

   void     PrepareShaderStuff(void);

public:
   HRESULT CreateVShader(void*, UINT, bool, bool,
                         UINT*);
   HRESULT CreatePShader(void*, UINT, bool, bool,
                         UINT*);
   HRESULT ActivateVShader(UINT, ZFXVERTEXID);
```

```
   HRESULT ActivatePShader(UINT);
   bool    UsesShaders(void) { return m_bUseShaders; }
```

I'll start by showing you the function that checks the hardware capabilities for the shader versions available, if any are. To do this, you need to extract the capabilities structure from the Direct3D device and check its `VertexShaderVersion` and `PixelShaderVersion` fields with the Direct3D macros `D3DVS_VERSION` and `D3DPS_VERSION`, respectively. For the course of this book, I will use shaders only in version 1.1 for vertex shaders and pixel shaders. If you want to provide a separate code path for different shader versions, you should add functions to the render device interface that let the user check the actual version:

```
void ZFXD3D::PrepareShaderStuff(void)
   {
   D3DCAPS9 d3dCaps;

   if (FAILED(m_pDevice->GetDeviceCaps(&d3dCaps)))
      {
      m_bUseShaders = false;
      return;
      }

   if (d3dCaps.VertexShaderVersion<D3DVS_VERSION(1,1))
      {
      m_bUseShaders = false;
      return;
      }

   if (d3dCaps.PixelShaderVersion<D3DPS_VERSION(1,1))
      {
      m_bUseShaders = false;
      return;
      }

   // vertex declaration for vertex shaders
   D3DVERTEXELEMENT9 declVertex[] =
      {
         { 0,  0, D3DDECLTYPE_FLOAT3, D3DDECLMETHOD_DEFAULT,
           D3DDECLUSAGE_POSITION, 0 },
         { 0, 12, D3DDECLTYPE_FLOAT3, D3DDECLMETHOD_DEFAULT,
           D3DDECLUSAGE_NORMAL, 0 },
         { 0, 24, D3DDECLTYPE_FLOAT2, D3DDECLMETHOD_DEFAULT,
           D3DDECLUSAGE_TEXCOORD, 0 },
         D3DDECL_END()
```

```
        };

    D3DVERTEXELEMENT9 declLVertex[] =
        {
            {  0,   0, D3DDECLTYPE_FLOAT3, D3DDECLMETHOD_DEFAULT,
               D3DDECLUSAGE_POSITION, 0 },
            {  0,  12, D3DDECLTYPE_D3DCOLOR, D3DDECLMETHOD_DEFAULT,
               D3DDECLUSAGE_DIFFUSE,   0 },
            {  0,  16, D3DDECLTYPE_FLOAT2, D3DDECLMETHOD_DEFAULT,
               D3DDECLUSAGE_TEXCOORD, 0 },
            D3DDECL_END()
        };

    // Create the vertex declarations
    m_pDevice->CreateVertexDeclaration(declVertex,
                                        &m_pDeclVertex);
    m_pDevice->CreateVertexDeclaration(declLVertex,
                                        &m_pDeclLVertex);
    m_pDevice->SetFVF(NULL);

    m_bUseShaders = true;
    } // PrepareShaderStuff
```

If this function reveals that the current hardware cannot do shaders in version 1.1 for vertex and pixel shaders, it returns `false`. In addition, shader version 1.0 is also available, but the only hardware that can do those old versions is graphics chips for notebooks, such as the GeForce Go from NVIDIA.

But if the hardware can do the requested shader versions, then this function creates the vertex declarations. If you work with the fixed function pipeline, you have to set the FVF to describe the vertex format to Direct3D. Actually, a vertex declaration is the same thing; it's just using another name. You can also use the vertex declaration instead of the FVF for the fixed function pipeline. It's somewhat more complicated to generate, so using the FVF is normally the better choice. But if you are using the flexible pipeline with vertex shaders, you cannot use the FVF—you have to use the vertex declaration.

A vertex declaration is built from an array of `D3DVERTEXELEMENT9` structures, so we better take a look at this structure first:

```
typedef struct _D3DVERTEXELEMENT9
    {
    BYTE Stream;
    BYTE Offset;
    BYTE Type;
```

```
   BYTE Method;
   BYTE Usage;
   BYTE UsageIndex;
} D3DVERTEXELEMENT9;
```

The first field Stream must be set to the index of the input stream from which the data for this element is coming. By calling IDirect3DDevice9::SetStreamSource, you can set a vertex buffer to a certain stream. You can have separate buffers that hold the position data and texture coordinates and set the two buffers to different streams. By building an appropriate vertex declaration, you can then tell Direct3D to take the position data from one stream and the texture coordinate data from the other one. This can be used to morph, or *tween*, between two sets of position data stemming from two different keyframes of the same model. The dolphin sample of the DirectX SDK does exactly this.

The Offset field provides the offset in bytes from the start of a vertex structure to the position where this data element can be found. If the position is the first element with three floating-point values of 32 bit = 4 bytes each, the next element has an offset of 12 bytes if it is coming from the same stream. The Type field is more interesting because it determines what type the data element is. Check the DirectX SDK documentation for a complete list of available types. The Method field is not interesting for us, so we just use the default method here. The Usage is the most interesting one because it determines what this data element is meant for. Table 6.1 lists some possible usage values. The last field, UsageIndex, is interesting only if you have more than one data element with the same usage because this is an index that differentiates the multiple entries. For example, when using two sets of position data in a morphing operation, one set has the index 0 and the other has the index 1. The same applies for multiple sets of texture coordinates.

After you've filled the array of D3DVERTEXELEMENT9 with all the data, you need the last element added, which is the Direct3D macro D3DDECL_END() that marks the end of the array to Direct3D. You can then create a vertex declaration object from this vertex data by using the following function call from Direct3D:

```
IDirect3DDevice9::CreateVertexDeclaration( const LPD3DVERTEXELEMENT9
                                           pVertexElements,
                                           IDirect3DVDecl9 *ppDecl );
```

As the first parameter, you simply supply the function with the array describing how the data in the vertex structure should be expected and interpreted by Direct3D. The second parameter is a reference pointer where the address of the newly created vertex declaration object should be saved. If you are using a vertex declaration, you must not set an FVF but provide NULL for the function IDirect3DDevice9::SetFVF so Direct3D knows you want to use a vertex declaration. This is usually the case when you are working with vertex shaders but, as already mentioned, you can also use a vertex declaration instead of the FVF definition. Because the FVF definition is not able to express that data is coming from different

Table 6.1 Possible Values for D3DDECLUSAGE

D3DDECLUSAGE	Meaning
D3DDECLUSAGE_POSITION	Vertex position data
D3DDECLUSAGE_BLENDWEIGHT	Blending factor
D3DDECLUSAGE_BLENDINDICES	Indices for blending
D3DDECLUSAGE_NORMAL	Vertex normal vector
D3DDECLUSAGE_PSIZE	Point sprite size
D3DDECLUSAGE_DIFFUSE	Diffuse vertex color
D3DDECLUSAGE_SPECULAR	Specular vertex color
D3DDECLUSAGE_TEXCOORD	Vertex texture coordinates
D3DDECLUSAGE_TANGENT	Vertex tangent for bump mapping
D3DDECLUSAGE_BINORMAL	Vertex binormal for bump mapping
D3DDECLUSAGE_TESSFACTOR	Tessellation factor

streams, you are required to use vertex declarations if you want to render from different streams. In this book, we will use just one stream.

Vertex Shader

Again, please let me say that I'm not explaining what vertex shaders are or how to implement them in this chapter. Next, I show you how to load and activate a shader so you can concentrate on developing shaders in the next chapter without wondering about how to make them actually run.

Like I did in the skin manager, the user will not have to deal with vertex shader or pixel shader objects. Instead, the ZFXEngine will keep track of the objects and hand an ID for each created shader object to the user. This ID is then required to activate the shader.

Loading and Compiling the Shader

Resolving the different cases of loading shaders, you end up with four different cases. The user either wants to load a shader program that is not yet compiled from the file or he wants to load an uncompiled shader program from memory. The other two cases are the same for already compiled shaders. For example, you can use the Direct3D command-line compiler to precompile your shaders and save them as a file to the disc. An application could then load this file into its memory and have the engine build a valid shader object for Direct3D with it.

I wrote one function for the engine that can deal with all four types of cases. As a first parameter, it takes a void pointer to the data that might be a filename pointer or a pointer to the memory area where the shader can be found. The second parameter specifies the size in bytes of the first parameter if it happens to be a char array with an uncompiled or compiled shader from memory. Then two bool parameters are used. The first specifies whether the data must be loaded from file, and the second one determines if the shader is already compiled. By twisting the four possible settings with the two boolean values, you can set the function to any of the four possible cases. The function will then return an ID of the created shader object in the last reference parameter.

If the vertex shader is then successfully created, it is saved in the attribute m_pVShader of the class, which is an array of IDirect3DVShader9 interface objects. Now I'll show you the function first and then point out the details of how to create and compile vertex shaders using Direct3D:

```
HRESULT ZFXD3D::CreateVShader(const void *pData, UINT nSize,
                              bool bLoadFromFile, bool bIsCompiled,
                              UINT *pID)
   {
   LPD3DXBUFFER  pCode=NULL;
   LPD3DXBUFFER  pDebug=NULL;
   HRESULT       hrC=ZFX_OK, hrA=ZFX_OK;
   DWORD         *pVS=NULL;
   HANDLE        hFile, hMap;

   // is there storage room for one more?
   if (m_nNumVShaders >= (MAX_SHADER-1))
      return ZFX_OUTOFMEMORY;

   // (1): ALREADY ASSEMBLED SHADER
   if (bIsCompiled) {

      // from file
      if (bLoadFromFile) {
         hFile = CreateFile((LPCTSTR)pData, GENERIC_READ, 0, 0,
                            OPEN_EXISTING, FILE_ATTRIBUTE_NORMAL, 0);
         if (hFile == INVALID_HANDLE_VALUE)
            return ZFX_FILENOTFOUND;

         hMap = CreateFileMapping(hFile,0,PAGE_READONLY, 0,0,0);
         pVS = (DWORD*)MapViewOfFile(hMap, FILE_MAP_READ,0,0,0);
         }

      // from RAM pointer
      else { pVS = (DWORD*)pData; }
```

```cpp
      } // if

   // (2): NEEDS TO BE ASSEMBLED
   else {
      // from file pointer
      if (bLoadFromFile) {
         hrA = D3DXAssembleShaderFromFile((char*)pData, NULL, NULL,
                                          0, &pCode, &pDebug);
      }
      // from RAM pointer
      else {
         hrA = D3DXAssembleShader((char*)pData, nSize-1, NULL, NULL,
                                  0, &pCode, &pDebug);
      }

      // check error
      if (SUCCEEDED(hrA))
         {
         pVS = (DWORD*)pCode->GetBufferPointer();
         }
      else {
         Log("error: AssembleShader[FromFile]()
              failed");
         if (pDebug->GetBufferPointer())
            Log("Shader debugger says: %s", (char*)pDebug->GetBufferPointer());
         return ZFX_FAIL;
         }
      } // else

   // create the shader object
   if (FAILED(hrC=m_pDevice->CreateVertexShader(pVS,
                     &m_pVShader[m_nNumVShaders])))
      {
      Log("error: CreateVertexShader() failed");
      return ZFX_FAIL;
      }

   // save id of this shader
   if (pID) (*pID) = m_nNumVShaders;

   // free resources
   if (bIsCompiled && bLoadFromFile)
```

```
     {
     UnmapViewOfFile(pVS);
     CloseHandle(hMap);
     CloseHandle(hFile);
     }

  m_nNumVShaders++;
  return ZFX_OK;
  } // CreateVShader
```

To compile a shader program, we use the D3DX helper functions. We could also write our own compiler functions. So, we just link the d3dx9.lib library and include its header file, d3dx9.h, and use one of these two functions:

```
HRESULT D3DXAssembleShader(
    LPCSTR              pSrcData,
    UINT                SrcDataLen,
    CONST D3DXMACRO*    pDefines,
    LPD3DXINCLUDE       pInclude,
    DWORD               Flags,
    LPD3DXBUFFER*       ppShader,
    LPD3DXBUFFER*       ppErrorMsgs);

HRESULT D3DXAssembleShaderFromFile(
    LPCSTR              pSrcFile,
    CONST D3DXMACRO*    pDefines,
    LPD3DXINCLUDE       pInclude,
    DWORD               Flags,
    LPD3DXBUFFER*       ppShader,
    LPD3DXBUFFER*       ppErrorMsgs);
```

The parameter pSrcData is a pointer to the data, which represents the uncompiled shader; SrcLenData specifies the length of the data. The second function is already satisfied if you provide it with the name of the file to load containing the shader in the parameter pSrcFile. The next parameters are the same for both functions, but in general, you don't need to use defines, includes, and flags. Please refer to the DirectX SDK documentation if you are interested in what they are meant for. The ppShader parameter is what you are looking for. The data type LPD3DXBUFFER is just a type of general buffer containing all kinds of data. In this case, it contains the assembled (compiled) shader.

The final parameter is one you hope that you will never need because this one gets interesting only if the function call fails. The D3DX shader compiler creates debug error messages and saves them to this buffer. As you can see, the member function GetBufferPointer() of the buffer object can be used to access the data.

However, hopefully everything went all right. Then you have the compiled shader in the buffer and want to create a Direct3D vertex shader object from it. The following function of the `IDirect3DDevice9` interface lets you do this:

```
HRESULT CreateVertexShader( const DWORD *pFunction,
                            IDirect3DVShader9** ppShader);
```

After this call succeeds, you have a valid vertex shader object that you can activate for Direct3D to replace the fixed function pipeline for vertex processing.

To load a shader from a file, you have to use certain WinAPI function calls such as `CreateFile()` to open the file and get a handle to access it. The WinAPI functions `CreateFileMapping()` and `MapViewOfFile()` build a mapped view on the binary file. With this view, you can then build the shader object from the data. This mapping is needed to get the content of the file into the address space of the calling process. If you are a bit rusty on the WinAPI, please refer to the platform SDK or MSDN for more information and the complete parameter lists of the calls. Note that you could also just get the size of the file, allocate a buffer, read the whole file into the buffer, and provide this buffer as string with the shader program.

Activating a Vertex Shader

Now you know how to build vertex shader objects Direct3D can use during vertex processing. But you still do not know how to actually activate such a vertex shader object for the Direct3D device. To activate a vertex shader, you need to do two things. First, you have to call `IDirect3DDevice9::SetVertexDeclaration` to activate the vertex declaration object that is telling Direct3D about the vertex format and the data sources. Then you must call `IDirect3DDevice9::SetVertexShader` with the vertex shader object to activate it. Note that only one (or none) vertex shader can be active. Here is how our engine lets you activate a vertex shader:

```
HRESULT ZFXD3D::ActivateVShader(UINT nID, ZFXVERTEXID VertexID)
   {
   if (!m_bUseShaders) return ZFX_NOSHADERSUPPORT;
   if (nID >= m_nNumVShaders) return ZFX_INVALIDID;

   // write out vertex caches
   m_pVertexMan->ForcedFlushAll();

   // get vertex size and format
   switch (VertexID) {
      case VID_UU: {
         if (FAILED(m_pDevice->SetVertexDeclaration(m_pDeclVertex)))
            return ZFX_FAIL;
```

```
        } break;
    case VID_UL: {
        if (FAILED(m_pDevice->SetVertexDeclaration(m_pDeclLVertex)))
            return ZFX_FAIL;
        } break;
    default: return ZFX_INVALIDID;
    } // switch

if (FAILED(m_pDevice->SetVertexShader(m_pVShader[nID])))
    return ZFX_FAIL;

return ZFX_OK;
} // ActivateVShader
```

Of course, this function is smart enough to evaluate whether the current hardware can use shaders and whether the ID to the vertex shader object provided by the caller refers to a valid shader object. This ID is the one the function call to the vertex shader creator function ZFXD3D::CreateVShader provided the caller with.

Again, you have to take care of rendering all the cached data in the vertex caches because, with the vertex declaration and the vertex shader, it is very likely that the data in the caches used other transformations and vertex formats.

Pixel Shader

The neat thing about pixel shaders is that the implementations regarding pixel shaders are pretty much the same as the ones for vertex shaders. They are even easier than vertex shaders because you don't have to use a certain declaration object or something like that.

Loading and Compiling the Shader

Loading and compiling a pixel shader is similar to loading and compiling a vertex shader. The function ZFXD3D::CreatePShader looks just like the function for the vertex shaders. Interestingly, it uses the same D3DX assembler functions as a vertex shader, so you don't need to change anything there. The most significant difference is that you have to use the function IDirect3DDevice9::CreatePixelShader to create the final shader object. The rest is the same; hence, I don't print this function here. But you can find the implementation of the function on the accompanying CD-ROM.

Activating a Pixel Shader

To activate a pixel shader for Direct3D, just call IDirect3DDevice9::SetPixelShader. This is as easy as it gets. The interface's function secures the availability of shaders on the hardware first and checks whether the ID is valid:

```
HRESULT ZFXD3D::ActivatePShader(UINT nID)
   {
   if (!m_bUseShaders) return ZFX_NOSHADERSUPPORT;
   if (nID >= m_nNumPShaders) return ZFX_INVALIDID;

   // write out vertex caches
   m_pVertexMan->ForcedFlushAll();

   if (FAILED(m_pDevice->SetPixelShader(m_pPShader[nID])))
      return ZFX_FAIL;

   return ZFX_OK;
   } // ActivatePShader
```

Now that you know how to create and activate vertex and pixel shaders, I want to use this short break to point out the advantages of consequent error checking. It is always a good idea to invest a second to use an if statement to check the validity of a pointer or the range of an index to an array. This saves you a lot of trouble while debugging when your code will crash and you don't have a clue as to why.

Activating Render States

Arriving at the halfway point of the chapter, I can say that we are finally approaching the part of the render device where it is actually rendering something. But first I want to talk a bit about an issue tied directly to the rendering—the setting of render states. You probably know about the most important render states and how Direct3D lets you switch render states to certain values.

In this type of functionality, you cannot and should not take control out of the user's hand. So, I defined the following render states that the ZFXEngine can switch to. These are the most common ones; you are welcome to integrate more states if you need them:

```
typedef enum ZFXRENDERSTATE_TYPE
   {
   RS_CULL_CW,         // culling clockwise
   RS_CULL_CCW,        // culling counterclockwise
   RS_CULL_NONE,       // render frontface and backface
   RS_DEPTH_READWRITE,// read and write depth buffer
   RS_DEPTH_READONLY,  // no writes to depth buffer
   RS_DEPTH_NONE       // no reads or writes with depth buffer
   RS_SHADE_POINTS,    // render vertices as points
   RS_SHADE_TRIWIRE,   // render wireframe triangles
   RS_SHADE_HULLWIRE,  // render wireframe polygons
```

```
   RS_SHADE_SOLID      // solid triangles
   } ZFXRENDERSTATE;
```

Over the course of this book, you will also need more render states. So, take these as samples here. You can always recognize the engine's render state enumerations by the prefix RS_.

As opposed to Direct3D, I didn't want to have a single function with thousands of options and three pages of explanations in the reference. So, even if all the render states of the ZFXEngine are in a single enumerated type, a lot of different functions are treated differently from the render states. Here you can see the declaration from the interface of three such methods:

```
// in interface ZFXRenderDevice.h
 ZFXCOLOR        m_clrWire;
 ZFXRENDERSTATE m_ShadeMode;

 virtual void SetBackfaceCulling(ZFXRENDERSTATE)=0;
 virtual void SetDepthBufferMode(ZFXRENDERSTATE)=0;

 virtual void SetShadeMode (ZFXRENDERSTATE, float, const ZFXCOLOR*)=0;
 virtual ZFXRENDERSTATE GetShadeMode (void)=0;
```

Implementing these functions is not a big deal. Each one is a big switch or a big if comparison sorting out the render states it can deal with and making Direct3D as the caller requested. In case of a render state the function is not meant to deal with, it just ignores the call and does nothing. Here are the three implementations:

```
void ZFXD3D::SetBackfaceCulling(ZFXRENDERSTATE rs)
   {
   m_pVertexMan->ForcedFlushAll();
   if (rs == RS_CULL_CW)
      m_pDevice->SetRenderState(D3DRS_CULLMODE,
                                D3DCULL_CW);
   else if (rs == RS_CULL_CCW)
      m_pDevice->SetRenderState(D3DRS_CULLMODE,
                                D3DCULL_CCW);
   else if (rs == RS_CULL_NONE)
      m_pDevice->SetRenderState(D3DRS_CULLMODE,
                                D3DCULL_NONE);
   } // SetBackfaceCulling
/*----------------------*/

void ZFXD3D::SetDepthBufferMode(ZFXRENDERSTATE rs)
   {
```

```cpp
      m_pVertexMan->ForcedFlushAll();
      if (rs == RS_DEPTH_READWRITE) {
         m_pDevice->SetRenderState(D3DRS_ZENABLE,
                                   D3DZB_TRUE);
         m_pDevice->SetRenderState(D3DRS_ZWRITEENABLE,
                                   TRUE);
         }
      else if (rs == RS_DEPTH_READONLY) {
         m_pDevice->SetRenderState(D3DRS_ZENABLE,
                                   D3DZB_TRUE);
         m_pDevice->SetRenderState(D3DRS_ZWRITEENABLE,
                                   FALSE);
         }
      else if (rs == RS_DEPTH_NONE){
         m_pDevice->SetRenderState(D3DRS_ZENABLE,
                                   D3DZB_FALSE);
         m_pDevice->SetRenderState(D3DRS_ZWRITEENABLE,
                                   FALSE);
         }
      } // SetDepthBufferMode
/*----------------------------------*/

void ZFXD3D::SetShadeMode(ZFXRENDERSTATE smd, float f,
                          const ZFXCOLOR *pClr)
   {
   m_pVertexMan->ForcedFlushAll();

   // copy new color if any
   if (pClr)
      {
      memcpy(&m_clrWire, pClr, sizeof(ZFXCOLOR));
      m_pVertexMan->InvalidateStates();
      }

   // no changes in mode
   if (smd == m_ShadeMode)
      {
      // maybe change in size
      if (smd==RS_SHADE_POINTS)
         m_pDevice->SetRenderState(D3DRS_POINTSIZE, FtoDW(f));

      return;
```

```cpp
      }

   if (smd == RS_SHADE_TRIWIRE)
      {
      // real Direct3D wireframe mode
      m_pDevice->SetRenderState(D3DRS_FILLMODE, D3DFILL_WIREFRAME);
      m_ShadeMode = smd;
      }
   else
      {
      m_pDevice->SetRenderState(D3DRS_FILLMODE, D3DFILL_SOLID);
      m_ShadeMode = smd;
      }

   if (smd == RS_SHADE_POINTS)
      {
      if (f > 0.0f)
         {
         m_pDevice->SetRenderState(D3DRS_POINTSPRITEENABLE, TRUE);
         m_pDevice->SetRenderState(D3DRS_POINTSCALEENABLE,  TRUE);
         m_pDevice->SetRenderState(D3DRS_POINTSIZE, FtoDW( f ));
         m_pDevice->SetRenderState(D3DRS_POINTSIZE_MIN, FtoDW(0.00f));
         m_pDevice->SetRenderState(D3DRS_POINTSCALE_A,  FtoDW(0.00f));
         m_pDevice->SetRenderState(D3DRS_POINTSCALE_B,  FtoDW(0.00f));
         m_pDevice->SetRenderState(D3DRS_POINTSCALE_C,  FtoDW(1.00f));
         }
      else {
         m_pDevice->SetRenderState(D3DRS_POINTSPRITEENABLE,FALSE);
         m_pDevice->SetRenderState(D3DRS_POINTSCALEENABLE,  FALSE);
         }
      }
   else
      {
      m_pDevice->SetRenderState(D3DRS_POINTSPRITEENABLE, FALSE);
      m_pDevice->SetRenderState(D3DRS_POINTSCALEENABLE, FALSE);
      }

   // update depending states
   m_pVertexMan->InvalidateStates();
   } // SetShadeMode
/*----------------------------------------*/

ZFXRENDERSTATE GetShadeMode() { return m_ShadeMode; }
```

The function `ZFXD3D::SetShadeMode` seems to be a bit more demanding than just a simple switch. But that is the price of simplicity in usage we have to pay. This function has to take care to make all settings and adjustments to enable a certain shade mode. When I wrote this function, I expected a lot of switching between differently colored wireframe rendering and a filled solid shade mode regarding the level editor tool I implemented in Chapter 14, "Computer-Aided Design Tools." I wanted the engine to switch between filled mode, wireframe mode, and rendering points with a single function call letting the engine take care of the things that need to be adjusted internally then, such as the primitive mode. So, the float parameter in this function is meant to be used only for the point sprite size.

> **Note**
> Point sprites are a special feature that is now widely supported in the hardware of most graphics adapters due to its extensive usage in 3D video games and applications. The user provides only a single point to the graphics adapter—or a list of points—and the graphics adapter automatically extends this point to a screen-aligned rectangle and generates texture coordinates for it. You use this feature for particle systems, such as rain, smoke, and fireworks.

The wireframe mode of the ZFXEngine has two possible options. The first one is the conservative wireframe mode supported by Direct3D. The problem with this approach is that Direct3D then renders each triangle. So, if you have a rectangle and want to render this wireframe mode, the rectangle is no longer a rectangle but two triangles. That's just the way it is on the graphics adapter. But in a level editing tool, it would be nice to see the rectangle as a rectangle because the level designer simply does not care about how the graphics adapter is seeing this rectangle.

OpenGL also provides a mode to render the outline of a polygon, which is what I also wanted to have for my level editor. Direct3D does not provide such a feature, so I added the shade mode `RS_SHADE_HULLWIRE`. This mode does not explicitly use the Direct3D wireframe mode but renders the given polygons as closed line strips. For a rectangle using four vertices [0, 1, 2, 3], you can render these as a closed line strip specifying an index list like so: [0, 1, 2, 3, 0]. This is all you need to do to render only the outline of a polygon even with Direct3D.

Rendering Primitives Efficiently

You have done a great job so far of pushing back the frontier of the ZFXEngine deep into Direct3D's land. The render device `ZFXRenderDevice` now contains a lot of functions whose implementations are a network of interconnected source code that maintains internal integrity. But the functionality of the render device so far is restricted to initialize the rendering API, which is Direct3D in this case, and to adjust some settings for the view and projection as well as for some render states.

Next, I discuss only issues directly connected to rendering graphical primitives to the screen. Just rendering graphical primitives using Direct3D can be done in a single function call, but you would not like to do that, trust me. I will explain why.

Hardware and Performance Foundation

I really like to keep saying that you can bring even the best graphics adapter to its knees by rendering just a few models using just a few thousand polygons. For example, you can just render all models triangle by triangle in one render function call each. Then you can render from back to front and not sort by the textures the triangles are using. Keep following these simple rules and be sure to slow down even the most simple 3D scenes to half a frame each second.

You probably already have some ideas about what you should and should not do to render as efficiently as possible. But I also want to explain why one way is better than the other, or why not. It all starts with knowing your enemy. You have to make the graphics adapter your friend. The next chapter discusses some issues of the 3D pipeline in detail, but I also want to say something about the hardware and its architecture now so you can understand why we spend a whole lot of this chapter on building a vertex cache manager into the engine. So, take a look at Figure 6.5.

Figure 6.5 shows a main board and a graphics adapter connected to this main board. On the right of the main board and below the slots for the RAM, you can see the CPU socket. The graphics adapter is put into the AGP slot, and two banks of VRAM are sitting near the GPU on the graphics adapter. Two command and control centers (CCCs) in this architecture are organizing the communication and issuing orders. The first center is the CPU,

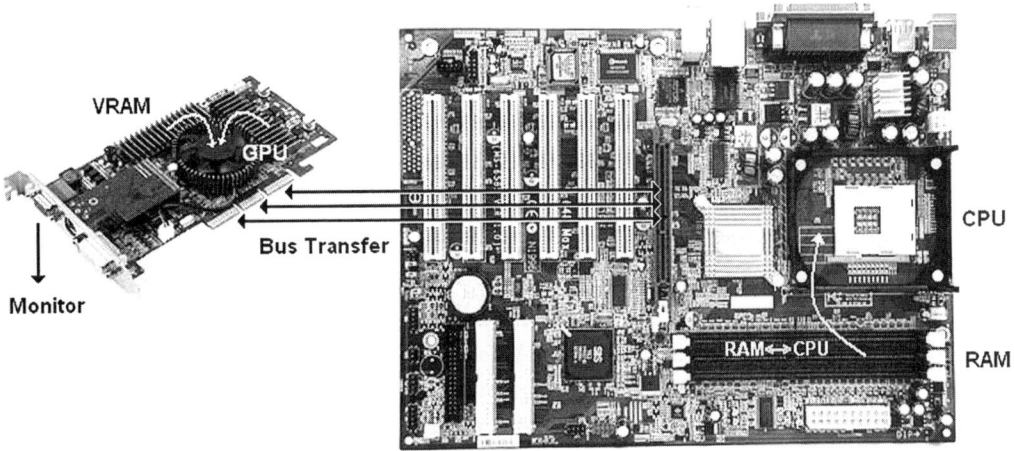

Figure 6.5 A main board and a graphics adapter connected by the bus.

which has to take data from the RAM to process it and then write it back to the RAM. The second CCC is the GPU, which takes data from the VRAM, processes it, and writes it back to the VRAM to be displayed on the screen.

The communication between each CCC and the memory from which it takes its data is very fast and efficient. The data transfer rate is pretty good. But there is a serious bottleneck in this system—the bus. With today's AGP slots and their AGP buses, the data transfer rate on the bus is already faster than the ancient PCI or VESA local systems. But the transfer rates on the bus are still slower than the communication between the memory and its connected processor.

This is the most important point when talking about performance in graphical applications. Each time you have to send data over the bus, it is like pulling the handbrake while flooring the accelerator. The CPU and GPU are trying their best to keep rolling and processing the data as quickly as they can. But the bus is slowly feeding them with new data. In the old days of *Doom* and *Quake*, the bottleneck was the actual process of setting a single pixel to a certain color on the screen. Nowadays, graphics adapters render 140 million vertices per second and the data transfer rate in the VRAM is about 10GB each second. Thus, calculating hidden surface removal on the CPU already takes more time than just rendering all the data by brute force—pixel overdraw or not.

The problem is that the transfer rate on the bus is approximately 1/10 of the VRAM transfer rate for an AGPx4 system. And that is even if the AGP slot is optimized to access the special AGP RAM on the main board. The bottom line is that you have to avoid traffic on the bus as much as possible.

You might ask at which point data is actually transferred over the bus between the main board and the graphics adapter. This is easy to answer: Each time you want to render something, you have to send the vertex and index data from your local memory over the bus to the VRAM to be processed by the GPU. This holds true for textures as well. But the smarter way to do this is to send the data over the bus once and then store it on the graphics adapter in the VRAM for as long as possible. How long that is depends on the amount of data you use during rendering operations in each frame, as well as the amount of VRAM available. So the problem is solved, right?

Well, of course it's never that easy. The VRAM on the average graphics adapter is always limited and is always too small no matter how big it gets. Let's suppose the standard VRAM today is 64MB on graphics adapters. This sounds like a lot, doesn't it? But a simple calculation reveals that this is actually pretty small. The front buffer and back buffer eat up a large part of the VRAM, depending on their resolution and color depth, as well as the number of back buffers or swap chains used.

The same holds true for the graphics used as textures or surfaces. From some commercial titles, you can see they switch between 16-bit and 32-bit textures. Using 16-bit textures saves you about half of the VRAM and avoids bus traffic if your VRAM is too small, thus making the game run faster. However, on alpha-blended triangles, those 16 bits produce a bad visual appearance.

In addition, the vertex and index data packages also want to sit on the graphics adapter's VRAM. Depending on the format of the vertices used, such as multiple texture coordinates, normal vectors, bump mapping vectors, and the like, this also eats up memory. For a rather detailed model, you would need about 10,000–15,000 triangles. Even if each triangle uses only three floating-point values for each of its three vertices to hold their positions, this adds up to about 0.5 MB of data. Now take one pair of texture coordinates and a normal vector, which is usually the least amount of data needed for a single vertex. This nearly triples the storage space needed for this single model. Speaking of a 64MB graphics adapter, the VRAM would be able to hold less than 40 different models at such a resolution in the VRAM. And that is not yet taking texture maps into consideration. Forty models still sounds like a lot, but a single level of a modern first-person shooter has at least 20 different models for characters as well as a lot of geometry used for the level data. Texture maps eat up around 1MB per character for a 512 × 512-sized map with 32 bits of color.

As you can see, all of the numbers add up pretty fast to make the VRAM explode. The point is not that you have to write a manager that deals with loading data into the VRAM as long as there is room enough and exchanging it with data that is used during rendering calls but that does not yet fit into the VRAM. Direct3D takes care of this on its own by managing who's allowed to sit in the VRAM and who has to leave its place for another package of data that is needs to be loaded into the VRAM.

This is the why you should always sort your data as often as possible. If you render your triangles in an arbitrary order, you will likely have to load a certain texture from the RAM over the bus into the VRAM to render a triangle. Later in this frame, this texture gets kicked from the VRAM because other data is needed there. Then a few moments later, another triangle will want to be rendered with this texture, so you have to reload it over the bus into the VRAM. This is a bottleneck you could have avoided by rendering all the triangles together using the same texture in one call or at least in several calls directly following each other to avoid texture switches or, even worse, to avoid texture reloading from the RAM.

Also note that you should always try to keep vertex and index data in the VRAM. Direct3D users typically create a vertex buffer in the VRAM for their model data used for rendering. This is a very good idea, indeed. But they use the same data to do things such as collision detection, which is a bad idea because it requires loading the data back from the VRAM into the RAM over the bus and checking for a collision. A better approach is to keep a copy of the position data from the model in the RAM. What seems to be a waste of RAM by storing redundant data is simply a means of speeding things up because you can let the data stay where it is needed. The whole data set stays in the VRAM to be rendered quickly without bus traffic, while the position data is kept as a copy in the RAM where the CPU can then perform the collision detection without the need for bus traffic. On average, at least 256MB of RAM is widely available on most users' systems, and a lot of games have even more.

I think that was enough of a crash course on how to avoid programming that is just pulling the brakes in your system. However, sometimes it is just not possible to avoid traffic over the bus. So, the issue is to build an efficient system that deals with this kind of dynamic data. This system is, in our case, a vertex cache system.

Caching During Rendering

You could now design and implement some source code that takes care of all the brainwork the application programmer is normally required to do if he wants to get a good performance out of his code rendering 3D graphics. This results in an approach that lets the user render a single triangle individually or sometimes list a bunch of triangles. Then the render device of the engine should collect all of the triangles and build its own internal lists until a frame is presented to the screen. Only then should the device actually render something.

Prior to rendering, the device sorts all the data by texture, switch in matrices, vertex format, and so on. Implementing such a system is not easy, though. As I said previously, a single triangle depends not only on a certain texture, but also on a certain vertex format, world matrix, projection matrix, viewport, and so on. Unfortunately, this list seems to be endless. Just think of two 3D models using the same texture on some of their triangles, but with both requiring the device to be rendered with different world matrices.

It's not easy to decide what is more efficient. You could sort the data by texture and render half of model one and then switch the world matrix and render half of model two. Then you could switch the texture and render the other two halves of the models, which requires resetting the world matrix twice. Or, would it be faster to render one model with its world matrix and switch the texture halfway through? Then you would render the second model with its world matrix and again switch the texture after rendering half of the model. There is no general answer to this question. It depends on too many other things, such as the type of graphics adapter, the driver, the other data calculated and rendered for the 3D scene, and some other factors.

An optimal sorting approach is impossible, and you should not waste your time trying to find one. The user of the engine is still required to have some knowledge about how 3D graphics and adapters work to sort this data before rendering it. But there is one thing we can, should, and will implement for the ZFXEngine.

> **Tip**
>
> Some video games actually use a scheme to render their objects sorted by texture in all odd frames. Then for each even frame, they just invert the sorting starting with the last texture used in the last frame. This prevents some texture moving over the bus because the last used textures are still sitting in the VRAM while the textures used in the first frame are not.

You actually learned something about optimization just now. Before you start optimizing something where you think there is some potential for optimization, you should think about it twice. Let's stick to the vertex data for a moment. Letting the render device sort them does not make much sense because specific applications have specific needs. It would be better to implement certain types of model loaders that have specific and known behaviors of sorting and organizing their data. Instead of letting the user send in triangles, he should send in only whole objects that are already internally optimized.

But I won't go that far in this book. I will show you how to do a basic sorting of single triangles or lists of triangles that are sent to the render device during a frame and which have to go over the bus. It is imperative to cache this data so you can render the triangles with at least some performance. And I really want to be able to render a whole scene of tens of thousands of triangles, sending them one by one to the render device. This makes programming a level editor tool much easier.

Static Versus Dynamic Vertex and Index Buffers

In Direct3D all rendering takes place by using vertex buffers and optionally index buffers. The buffers are nothing more than an encapsulation of a static memory array that can hold arbitrary data. Only the names imply what they should be used for. In the OpenGL language, such buffers are called vertex-arrays. But although OpenGL makes some settings internally, Direct3D allows a lot of flexibility in specifying the buffers and how they should be treated.

It all starts with the creation of such a buffer object where the creator needs to specify where the buffer should be located. You can select a default setting, select the normal RAM, or let Direct3D manage the buffer. There are a lot of advantages in the last option, so this is the one you should use.

Now that you have your buffer, you should copy data into it. This can be done by locking the buffer to get a pointer to the memory address to which you have to copy your data. This act of locking is needed to get this buffer into a state where Direct3D cannot access its contents if you change data in the buffer. If you are done with copying data from or into the buffer, you have to unlock it to make it usable for Direct3D again. If you want to render the primitives you stored in the buffer, you just call the functions `IDirect3DDevice9::DrawPrimitive` or `IDirect3DDevice9::::DrawIndexedPrimitive` after activating the buffers for Direct3D by `IDirect3DDevice9::SetStreamSource` or `IDirect3DDevice9::SetIndices`.

This works well, indeed. However, there are always those nasty little catches. The problem is the performance. Using such buffers is fast if you do not lock them. If the buffers are located in the VRAM and you want to copy data to or from them, they have to travel over the bus. So, the best thing to do is to create a static buffer, fill the data into it at initialization time, and then never touch the contents of the buffer again—just render it when it is visible.

But in many cases, you simply need to access the buffers' data to refresh them. Direct3D also provides flags for the creation of the buffer that makes the speed of rendering with such a buffer slower but makes the speed of filling data into the buffer faster than for the static versions of buffers. Such a buffer is implicitly called a *dynamic buffer*. If such a buffer is flagged as dynamic, Direct3D tries to create it—not in the VRAM or in the normal RAM but in the AGP-RAM, which enables a faster communication with the CPU and which is a shortcut to the entry point of the bus.

If you lock a static buffer and copy its contents, you work from the normal RAM over the CPU and across the bus into the VRAM. If you use a dynamic buffer instead, you are just working inside the fast AGP-RAM with the CPU. If you want to render a dynamic buffer, it is copied from the AGP-RAM with its fast access to the bus and straight into the VRAM. Copying between the AGP-RAM and the VRAM is faster than using the normal RAM instead of the AGP-RAM, and that is the trick behind dynamic buffers.

The disadvantage is that you have to copy them over the bus each time you want to render them whether or not their contents have changed since the last render call. Using static buffers, you have to move them over the bus only if their contents are really changing. We are ignoring the need of freeing space in the VRAM automatically by Direct3D if the VRAM gets too crowded.

> **Note**
>
> I just said that all rendering in Direct3D is done using vertex and, optionally, index buffers. But the `IDirect3DDevice9` interface also provides the functions `DrawPrimitiveUP()` and `DrawIndexedPrimitiveUP()`, which let you provide data to render without a buffer. The *UP* stands for user pointer and specifies where the data is coming from.
>
> This appears to enable you to render without a buffer, but it does not. Direct3D internally creates a dynamic vertex and index buffer that are used to render the data you provided it with.

You should use a static buffer whenever possible, and the user of the engine should work with this buffer as often as possible. The interface of the render device provides the means to create a buffer and fill it with data only one time. After that, the buffer can be destroyed or rendered. However, it does not enable the user to copy data to or from the buffer. Direct3D would allow that, but the ZFXEngine does not due to the reasons of performance mentioned previously.

But to satisfy the need of the users to have a comparably fast way to render dynamic data, the render device of our engine also provides means to do so. Just delegating the function calls to Direct3D's user pointer drawing functions is not optimal because they are slow if you don't batch your data to large packages beforehand. To ensure this, I will show you how to let the engine do this packaging in a rather simple but effective way. The data is then rendered using an explicit dynamic buffer. So, we are actually already talking about a vertex cache manager here.

Interface Definition of a Vertex Cache Manager

Besides the render device and the skin manager, you will now get acquainted with the third interface definition that is sitting inside the render DLL of the ZFXEngine: the vertex cache manager. Just like the skin manager, the vertex cache manager is an attribute of the ZFXD3D class and using its functions is the only way the ZFXEngine provides to render anything. But take a look at the interface definition:

```
class ZFXVertexCacheManager
   {
   public:
      ZFXVertexCacheManager(void) {};
      virtual ~ZFXVertexCacheManager(void) {};

      virtual HRESULT CreateStaticBuffer(
                         ZFXVERTEXID VertexID,
                         UINT  nSkinID,
                         UINT  nVerts,
                         UINT  nIndis,
                         const void *pVerts,
                         const WORD *pIndis,
                         UINT *pnID)=0;

      virtual HRESULT Render(ZFXVERTEXID VertexID,
                         UINT nVerts,
                         UINT nIndis,
                         const void *pVerts,
                         const WORD *pIndis,
                         UINT  SkinID)=0;

      virtual HRESULT Render(UINT nSBufferID)=0;
```

```
   virtual HRESULT ForcedFlushAll(void)=0;

   virtual HRESULT ForcedFlush(ZFXVERTEXID)=0;
}; // class
```

At first glance, the separation of dynamic and static buffers doesn't seem obvious in this interface. The function `CreateStaticBuffer()` creates a static buffer as previously described. Such a buffer can be filled with data at the initialization call, but at no other time. You need to hand over at least a pointer to the vertex data, but the pointer to the index data is optional. There is no such thing as a lock function.

If you then have your static buffer object successfully created, you get an ID to the object that is internally stored. The only thing you can do with this ID is to hand it to the `Render()` function of this interface to request the manager to render the data sitting in this static buffer.

But what about the dynamic buffers? This interface does not seem to provide dynamic buffers. This is right with a point of view located outside the engine. A second render function in this interface definition has a parameter list similar to the function to create a static buffer. Actually, this render function is used to render from user pointers just like the Direct3D user pointer functions. And just like the functions, our engine internally uses dynamic buffers. But it does so in a smarter way because it does not immediately render the contents of the buffer during the function call.

So, we don't need to have any setup functions. The constructor of the class implementing this interface needs to take care of doing all the initialization steps needed for the dynamic rendering to take place. This is not a job the user should be required to perform in order to kick off using a function of the interface, so it is done automatically here.

Finally, you can also see the `ForcedFlush()` and `ForcedFlushAll()` functions the render device was already heavily using each time it changed a crucial setting in the engine, such as the world matrix or a render state. These functions force all cached dynamic data to be rendered immediately no matter what performance says in this moment.

So, why is this interface called the *vertex cache manager*? It's called this because it has to manage something and because it is managing vertex cache objects. Before I show you the class implementing this interface, I want to show you the class for vertex cache objects that is used by this implementation afterward.

Vertex Cache Object

As we all know by now, rendering single triangles at a time produces very poor performance. This depends mostly on the graphics adapters, which don't like small bunches of data to be processed. Each render call comes with a certain overhead of waking up the adapter and getting it ready to perform some action. It is rather disappointing for the adapter to see a single triangle waiting in the pipe.

The purpose of the vertex cache objects is to catch the render calls and delay them. They do this by grabbing the triangles that are supposed to be rendered and storing them in an internal list. Each vertex cache object can take vertices of a single type at a time and is meant to accept triangles that can be rendered together in one call because they are using the same texture, world matrix, and so on. But all this management is done by the manager later.

The vertex cache object is similar to a vertex buffer in Direct3D, but with slightly more features to manipulate its data and render it. No interface exists for these vertex cache objects. There is an implementation in the class ZFXD3DVCache inside the DLL. This is because the user does not need to know about the internal caches and because such a system is unnecessary for OpenGL render devices because OpenGL has a better performance in rendering data triangle by triangle in single calls.

Here is the class declaration:

```
class ZFXD3DVCache
   {
   public:

      ZFXD3DVCache(UINT nVertsMax, UINT nIndisMax, UINT nStride,
                   ZFXD3DSkinManager *pSkinMan, LPDIRECT3DDEVICE9 pDevice,
                   ZFXD3DVCManager *pDad, DWORD dwID, FILE *pLog);

      ~ZFXD3DVCache(void);

      HRESULT Flush(bool bUseShaders);

      HRESULT Add(UINT  nVerts, UINT nIndis, const void *pVerts,
                  const WORD *pIndis, bool  bUseShaders);

      void SetSkin(UINT  SkinID, bool bUseShader);
      bool UsesSkin(UINT SkinID) { return (m_SkinID == SkinID); }
      bool IsEmpty(void)  { if (m_nNumVerts>0) return false; return true; }
      int  NumVerts(void) { return m_nNumVerts; }

   private:
      LPDIRECT3DVERTEXBUFFER9  m_pVB;
      LPDIRECT3DINDEXBUFFER9   m_pIB;
      LPDIRECT3DDEVICE9         m_pDevice;
      ZFXD3DSkinManager        *m_pSkinMan;
```

```
      ZFXD3DVCManager     *m_pDad;
      ZFXSKIN             m_Skin;
      UINT                m_SkinID;
      DWORD               m_dwID;
      FILE                *m_pLog;

      UINT   m_nNumVertsMax;  // max. vertices in the buffer
      UINT   m_nNumIndisMax;  // max. indices in the buffer
      UINT   m_nNumVerts;     // number in buffer
      UINT   m_nNumIndis;     // number in buffer
      UINT   m_nStride;       // stride of a vertex
   }; // class
```

Each instance of this class is a dynamic buffer of its own or even a combination of a dynamic vertex buffer and a dynamic index buffer. You can see the two buffers as attributes in the class declaration. The constructor of this class is used to initialize the Direct3D objects in this class. The Add() function can then be used to append data to the buffer, which can be vertices and indices or just vertices. This function is called by the vertex cache manager if the user calls the ZFXVertexCacheManager::Render function and provides user pointers to the data instead of the ID of a static buffer. The manager then searches for the best-fitting vertex cache object it has at its disposal and appends the data to it instead of rendering it.

The Flush() method in this class is now the interesting one. This is the actual render call, so if you want the contents of a vertex cache object to be rendered on the graphics adapter, you have to call this function.

Actually, these are the most important functions in this class. The other four functions in the declaration are just helper routines to set the skin the data in the cache is using and to query some settings and values from an instance of this class.

What do skins have to do with a vertex cache object? Well, I didn't expect this question to pop up because that should be obvious. For the simple scheme of this engine, I decided to sort dynamic data based on the texture and material they are using. Each time the user sends dynamic data from user pointers to be rendered, we want to cache this data in vertex cache objects and render several of them at a time. But while rendering with a single call, you cannot change the texture or material between this call to Direct3D, so you can batch together triangles using the same texture and material, which is called *skin* in the ZFXEngine.

A vertex cache object is always set to use a certain skin. Only primitive data that is using exactly the same skin object can be appended to a vertex cache object. But note that the skin ID of a vertex cache object can be changed at any time. So, the engine does not create its own vertex cache for each skin the user creates. This would waste memory. Instead, the manager has a certain amount of caches at its disposal, which it can set to certain skins and fill them. But we will see this when I show you the vertex cache manager.

Creating and Releasing a Vertex Cache Object

The constructor of the vertex cache object class does nothing spectacular. It just creates the Direct3D vertex buffer object as well as the Direct3D index buffer object. A cache object also needs to know its relatives, so the pointer to the vertex cache manager owning this vertex cache object is saved in the object, as well as the pointer to the skin manager of the render device and the pointer to the Direct3D device.

The maximum number of data elements that can be stored inside a vertex cache is a crucial setting. The buffers need to be created with a certain size, and data lists using more than the maximum number of possible elements cannot be rendered using the dynamic caches in the ZFXEngine. Rendering too few triangles in a single call is not a good idea; neither is rendering too many triangles in a single call. The optimal amount of triangles in a call depends on the graphics adapter, its manufacturer, and the driver. Typically, graphics adapters like from several hundred triangles to several thousand triangles in a single call.

Here is the constructor of the vertex cache object class:

```
ZFXD3DVCache::ZFXD3DVCache(UINT nVertsMax, UINT nIndisMax,
                   UINT nStride, ZFXD3DSkinManager *pSkinMan,
                   LPDIRECT3DDEVICE9 pDevice, ZFXD3DVCManager *pDad,
                   DWORD dwID, FILE *pLog) {
   HRESULT hr;

   m_pDevice       = pDevice;
   m_pSkinMan      = pSkinMan;
   m_pDad          = pDad;
   m_nNumVertsMax  = nVertsMax;
   m_nNumIndisMax  = nIndisMax;
   m_nNumVerts     = 0;
   m_nNumIndis     = 0;
   m_dwID          = dwID;
   m_nStride       = nStride;
   m_pLog          = pLog;

   memset(&m_Skin, MAX_ID, sizeof(ZFXSKIN));
   m_SkinID = MAX_ID;

   // create the buffer
   m_pVB = NULL;
```

```
    m_pIB = NULL;

    hr = pDevice->CreateVertexBuffer(nVertsMax * nStride, D3DUSAGE_DYNAMIC |
                                     D3DUSAGE_WRITEONLY, 0, D3DPOOL_DEFAULT,
                                     &m_pVB, NULL);
    if (FAILED(hr)) m_pVB = NULL;

    hr = pDevice->CreateIndexBuffer(nIndisMax * sizeof(WORD),
                                    D3DUSAGE_DYNAMIC | D3DUSAGE_WRITEONLY,
                                    D3DFMT_INDEX16, D3DPOOL_DEFAULT,
                                    &m_pIB, NULL);
    if (FAILED(hr)) m_pIB = NULL;
    }
```

Please note the use of the correct Direct3D flags D3DUSAGE_DYNAMIC, as well as D3DUSAGE_WRITEONLY, in the creation functions for the Direct3D buffer objects. The first flag takes care of placing the buffer in the right memory, which should be AGP if it's available. Static buffers, which are implicitly static if the dynamic flag is not given, typically are placed in the VRAM as long as there is enough room for them. The second flag tells Direct3D that we need only to write data to the buffers and will not read back any data. This flag lets Direct3D make some assumptions and do some optimizations under certain circumstances.

The destructor of this class does not have much to do. You need to release the Direct3D objects to avoid memory leaks:

```
ZFXD3DVCache::~ZFXD3DVCache(void)
    {
    if (m_pVB) {
       m_pVB->Release();
       m_pVB = NULL;
       }
    if (m_pIB) {
       m_pIB->Release();
       m_pIB = NULL;
       }
    }
```

You can already see that the vertex cache object isn't very difficult. It doesn't change for the implementation of a single function of this class. The functionality of this class is pretty straightforward, and there is nothing complicated to be done. The logic behind the scenes has to be provided by the vertex cache manager, though.

Setting the Skin for a Vertex Cache Object

The most important factor in deciding whether incoming data is allowed to append itself to a vertex cache object and join its already present content is the skin currently used for the cache object.

You can change the skin that should be used by the vertex cache object at any time. But before you do so, you have to flush the buffer. This means you have to immediately render all its content if it has any because the current content is using the current skin. If you want to set a new skin to this vertex cache object, you must render it first; otherwise, the present data in the cache is rendered with a skin different from the one the user sent it to the render device with.

And you wouldn't want that to happen. So here is the function:

```
void ZFXD3DVCache::SetSkin(UINT SkinID, bool bUseShaders)
   {
   if (!UsesSkin(SkinID)) {
      ZFXSKIN *pSkin = &m_pSkinMan->GetSkin(SkinID);

      if (!IsEmpty()) Flush(bUseShaders);

      memcpy(&m_Skin, pSkin, sizeof(ZFXSKIN));
      m_SkinID = SkinID;

      m_pDad->SetActiveCache(MAX_ID);
      }
   }
```

If this cache object is not already using the skin it should use from now on, it requests a pointer to this skin from the skin manager. Then it flushes its contents to the graphics adapter and copies the new skin into its member attributes afterward. Finally, it tells the vertex cache manager about the currently active vertex cache.

To avoid redundancy in setting skins, stream sources, and such, the vertex cache manager always saves the ID of the active cache. The value of MAX_ID specifies that no cache is currently active. This forces the skin to be set and activated next time any vertex cache is flushed. If the same cache is flushed two times in a row, the Direct3D buffer objects don't need to be set for the Direct3D device, the textures, and the material. However, a new skin exists, so even if the next flush is exactly this cache, the textures and material from the skin must be set at all costs.

Adding Data to a Vertex Cache Object

If the user of the ZFXEngine renders data from user pointers, they are not rendered immediately but appended to a vertex cache object. The following function takes care of appending the data:

```
HRESULT ZFXD3DVCache::Add(UINT   nVerts, UINT  nIndis, const void *pVerts,
                          const WORD *pIndices, bool   bUseShaders)
   {
   BYTE *tmp_pVerts=NULL;
   WORD *tmp_pIndis=NULL;
   int    nSizeV = m_nStride*nVerts;
   int    nSizeI = sizeof(WORD)*nIndis;
   int    nPosV;
   int    nPosI;
   DWORD dwFlags;

   // is buffer size sufficient?
   if (nVerts>m_nNumVertsMax || nIndis>m_nNumIndisMax)
      return ZFX_BUFFERSIZE;

   // cache is full so empty out
   if ( (nVerts+m_nNumVerts > m_nNumVertsMax) ||
        (nIndis+m_nNumIndis > m_nNumIndisMax) ) {
      if ( Flush(bUseShaders) != ZFX_OK)
         return ZFX_FAIL;
      }

   // DISCARD flag if buffer is empty
   if (m_nNumVerts == 0) {
      nPosV = nPosI = 0;
      dwFlags = D3DLOCK_DISCARD;
      }
   // else append with NOOVERWRITE flag
   else {
      nPosV = m_nStride*m_nNumVerts;
      nPosI = sizeof(WORD)*m_nNumIndis;
      dwFlags = D3DLOCK_NOOVERWRITE;
      }

   // lock buffers
   if (FAILED(m_pVB->Lock(nPosV, nSizeV, (void**)&tmp_pVerts, dwFlags)))
      return ZFX_BUFFERLOCK;
```

```
    if (FAILED(m_pIB->Lock(nPosI, nSizeI, (void**)&tmp_pIndis, dwFlags)))
        {
        m_pVB->Unlock();
        return ZFX_BUFFERLOCK;
        }

    // copy vertices
    memcpy(tmp_pVerts, pVerts, nSizeV);

    // copy indices
    int nBase = m_nNumVerts;
    if (!pIndices) nIndis = nVerts;

    for (UINT i=0; i<nIndis; i++)
        {
        if (pIndices != NULL)
            tmp_pIndis[i] = pIndices[i] + nBase;
        else
            tmp_pIndis[i] = i + nBase;
        m_nNumIndis++;
        }

    // increment counter
    m_nNumVerts += nVerts;

    m_pVB->Unlock();
    m_pIB->Unlock();
    return ZFX_OK;
    }
```

As long as enough space is left in the vertex cache object, the buffers are locked and the data is then appended after the existing one. Otherwise, if the vertex cache cannot take the amount of data because it is too full, its content is flushed out. This causes the primitives inside the cache object to be rendered to free up enough room for the new data. Therefore, the task of batching together a certain amount of data is successful.

This appending strategy is a rather simple one, whereas the point sprite/particle sample of the DirectX SDK shows a more complicated scheme of adding data to a dynamic buffer while also rendering from this buffer at the same time. This offers a great boost in performance, but it has a severe drawback. Such a scheme applies only to data consisting of vertices. If indices are also involved, this strategy cannot be applied because you cannot just render a small part of an index list and the vertex list. Well, you could of course, but let's suppose you wanted to render the first 10 triangles from the vertex and index list. You would just copy the first 30 entries of the index list into the index buffer. But then you have to determine how many vertices you need to copy from the vertex list into the vertex buffer. And what if the beginning of the list of vertices contains the vertices that are indexed by the first 30 indices in the index list?

Sure, this problem could be solved, but only at the cost of looping through the index list one time to individually copy the indexed vertices into the vertex buffer and a second time to adjust the index value if indices are present in the buffers. The question is whether this optimization is still faster with all the looping and copying of data element by element.

I decided to use a simpler scheme, the performance of which is adequate. But now I want to revisit the flags you can use in Direct3D while locking a buffer.

Excursion: Using the Appropriate Lock Flags

If you are dealing with dynamic vertex buffers or dynamic index buffers, which is specified during the creation of the buffer using the flag D3DUSAGE_DYNAMIC, you must use the most appropriate flag for the call of the Lock() function. The two available options specific to dynamic buffers are D3DLOCK_DISCARD and D3DLOCK_NOOVERWRITE.

The first flag specifies that the caller will fill data into the whole buffer or that he will at least possibly overwrite existing data in the buffer; hence, the previous contents of the buffer can be thrown away and don't need to be maintained or even copied back into the system RAM for buffer reads. Using this flag results in the assumed loss of all data sitting in the buffer, except for the data that is then written into the buffer. This is unlike locking a static buffer. The Lock() call waits until the buffer is ready to be locked and then doesn't let Direct3D use the buffer until it is unlocked. The Lock() call also waits until a drawing operation from this buffer is finished.

The real boost in performance that makes dynamic buffers faster than static buffers with regard to refilling them is provided by the second flag. By using the D3DLOCK_NOOVERWRITE flag, the caller promises not to overwrite any data sitting inside the buffer since it has been locked with the D3DLOCK_DISCARD flag. This might sound strange at first glance, but it is an important restriction. The reason behind this is that the Lock() call does not have to wait until a drawing operation on this buffer is done. Say you have 1,000 triangles you want to render using a dynamic buffer. Copying all 1,000 triangles to the buffer at the same time would keep the CPU busy while the GPU sat idle. Afterward the CPU would sit idle while the GPU was drawing.

Imagine copying 100 triangles to the buffer, rendering the buffer, getting the next chunk, and locking the buffer using the D3DLOCK_NOOVERWRITE flag. While the GPU is still drawing from this buffer, you could already get the CPU going and append the next 100 triangles to the buffer. There is still an impact due to the data copying over the bus, but now

Rendering Primitives Efficiently 299

you are able to gain some of the lost speed back by already drawing while still copying the data. This is exactly what the point sprite sample in the DirectX SDK does.

The following snippet of pseudo-code shows how you would render many small packages of vertex and index data efficiently using dynamic buffers and the correct flags by dividing them into small batches that are rendered in parallel while the next bunch of data is coming in:

```
for loop()
    {
    if there is space in the buffer
        {
        // append vertices/indices
        pBuffer->Lock(...D3DLOCK_NOOVERWRITE...);
        }
    else
        {
        // Reinitialize
        pBuffer->Lock((...D3DLOCK_DISCARD...);
        }
    Fill few 10s of vertices/indices in pBuffer
    pBuffer->Unlock
    Change State
    DrawPrimitive() or DrawIndexedPrimitive()
    }
```

If you have bigger amounts of data coming in at the same time, the following scheme would be faster. This involves copying all the data into the buffer simultaneously, but it renders them in smaller batches. This lets the copying over the bus take place while the preceding data is still being rendered:

```
for loop()
    {
    // get pointer to memory
    pBuffer->Lock(...D3DLOCK_DISCARD...);

    Fill data (optimally 1000s of vertices/indices, no fewer) in pBuffer

    pBuffer->Unlock

    for loop( 100s of times )
        {
        Change State
```

```
        // tens of packages
        DrawPrimitive() or DrawIndexPrimitives()
        }
   }
```

To wrap up our discussion of dynamic rendering flags, you simply cannot say which solution is the best and fastest one in general. Too many factors are involved that you cannot influence. Even if you found one method to be the fastest in a specific scene, this could look different on another scene or, more annoyingly, with the same scene on another graphics adapter. Only a whole range of test cases on various hardware will reveal whether an average best solution exists for a certain project.

Rendering from a Vertex Cache Object

Rendering from a vertex cache object is what makes it faster than just delegating the user's render call to the `IDirect3DDevice9::Draw(Indexed)PrimitiveUP` function. Now, all this class is lacking is the function that renders the data cached in the object.

We can also gain a boost in performance if we do it the right way. I mentioned previously that the vertex cache manager keeps track of which vertex cache is currently active. If a certain vertex cache object is already active (which means it was the last one used to render something), and if it has not changed its skin, you don't need to set the Direct3D device's stream source, index buffer, texture, or material. This saves some overhead by not switching things such as the vertex format on the Direct3D device that are already switched to the correct settings.

The following function is a bit messy and lengthy at first glance because it needs to evaluate what needs to be set for the Direct3D device and what doesn't. The FVF, for example, needs to be set only if the render device is currently not running with vertex shaders. The wireframe mode is also a special case. Normally, Direct3D renders textured lines. But I didn't really want the wireframe view to be textured; I wanted to use a certain color instead. This can be achieved by setting a material to the color that should be used for the wireframe and which was set by the user beforehand to the render device.

Here it is:

```
HRESULT ZFXD3DVCache::Flush(bool bUseShaders)
   {
   ZFXRENDERSTATE sm;
   HRESULT hr = ZFX_FAIL;
   if (m_nNumVerts <= 0) return ZFX_OK;

   // if this cache is not active
   if ( m_pDad->GetActiveCache() != m_dwID)
      {
```

```cpp
   // no shaders
   if (!bUseShaders) m_pDevice->SetFVF(m_dwFVF);

   m_pDevice->SetIndices(m_pIB);
   m_pDevice->SetStreamSource(0, m_pVB, 0,
                              m_nStride);
   m_pDad->SetActiveCache(m_dwID);
   } // [device->cache]

// if this skin is not yet active
if (m_pDad->GetZFXD3D()->GetActiveSkinID() !=
   m_SkinID) {
   LPDIRECT3DTEXTURE9 pTex=NULL;
   ZFXMATERIAL *pMat = &m_pSkinMan->m_pMaterials[
                                 m_Skin.nMaterial];

   // WIREFRAME-MODE; SPECIAL CASE
   if (!m_pDad->GetZFXD3D()->GetWireframeMode())
      {
      // set the material
      D3DMATERIAL9 mat = {
         pMat->cDiffuse.fR,  pMat->cDiffuse.fG,
         pMat->cDiffuse.fB,  pMat->cDiffuse.fA,
         pMat->cAmbient.fR,  pMat->cAmbient.fG,
         pMat->cAmbient.fB,  pMat->cAmbient.fA,
         pMat->cSpecular.fR, pMat->cSpecular.fG,
         pMat->cSpecular.fB, pMat->cSpecular.fA,
         pMat->cEmissive.fR, pMat->cEmissive.fG,
         pMat->cEmissive.fB, pMat->cEmissive.fA,
         pMat->fPower };
      m_pDevice->SetMaterial(&mat);

      // set the texture
      for (int i=0; i<8; i++)
         {
         if (m_Skin.nTexture[i] != MAX_ID)
            {
            pTex = (LPDIRECT3DTEXTURE9)
                  m_pSkinMan->m_pTextures[m_Skin.nTexture[i]].pData;
            m_pDevice->SetTexture(i, pTex);
            }
         else break;
```

302 Chapter 6 ■ The Render Device of the Engine

```
         } // for
      }
   else {
      ZFXCOLOR clrWire = m_pDad->GetZFXD3D()->GetWireColor();
      // set material
      D3DMATERIAL9 matW = {
       clrWire.fR,clrWire.fG,clrWire.fB,clrWire.fA,
       clrWire.fR,clrWire.fG,clrWire.fB,clrWire.fA,
       0.0f,         0.0f,         0.0f,         1.0f,
       0.0f,         0.0f,         0.0f,         1.0f,
       1.0f };
      m_pDevice->SetMaterial(&matW);

      // no texture for the device
      m_pDevice->SetTexture(0, NULL);
      }

   // activate alpha blending
   if (m_Skin.bAlpha) {
      m_pDevice->SetRenderState(D3DRS_ALPHAREF, 50);
      m_pDevice->SetRenderState(D3DRS_ALPHAFUNC, D3DCMP_GREATEREQUAL);
      m_pDevice->SetRenderState(D3DRS_SRCBLEND, D3DBLEND_SRCALPHA);
      m_pDevice->SetRenderState(D3DRS_DESTBLEND, D3DBLEND_INVSRCALPHA);
      m_pDevice->SetRenderState(D3DRS_ALPHATESTENABLE, TRUE);
      m_pDevice->SetRenderState(D3DRS_ALPHABLENDENABLE, TRUE);
      }
   else {
      m_pDevice->SetRenderState(D3DRS_ALPHATESTENABLE, FALSE);
      m_pDevice->SetRenderState(D3DRS_ALPHABLENDENABLE, FALSE);
      }
   // mark skin as active
   m_pDad->GetZFXD3D()->SetActiveSkinID(m_SkinID);
   } // [device->skin]

// FINALLY RENDER
sm = m_pDad->GetZFXD3D()->GetShadeMode();

// POINT-SPRITES
if ( sm == RS_SHADE_POINTS ) {
   hr = m_pDevice->DrawPrimitive(
                   D3DPT_POINTLIST,
                   0, m_nNumVerts);
```

```
    }
    // LINESTRIP
    else if ( sm == RS_SHADE_HULLWIRE ) {
       hr = m_pDevice->DrawIndexedPrimitive(
                     D3DPT_LINESTRIP,
                     0, 0, m_nNumVerts,
                     0, m_nNumVerts);
    }
    // POLYGONLIST
    else { // RS_SHADE_SOLID || RS_SHADE_TRIWIRE
       hr = m_pDevice->DrawIndexedPrimitive(
                     D3DPT_TRIANGLELIST,
                     0, 0, m_nNumVerts,
                     0, m_nNumIndis/3);
    }

    if (FAILED(hr) return ZFX_FAIL;

    // reset counters
    m_nNumVerts = 0;
    m_nNumIndis = 0;
    return ZFX_OK;
    }
```

At the end of the function, we need to decide which type of primitive should be rendered. For point sprites, there is no sense in using an index list because each vertex in the list is a unique point. Therefore, the index list is ignored by us. Direct3D also refuses to render point sprites with index lists.

Finally, the vertex cache object is now ready to be used. It features a certain amount of gain in performance by caching primitive data up to a threshold and renders the primitives only if it is forced to or if it has collected a certain amount of them. Now it is time to see how the vertex cache manager organizes the rendering and sorting of data into the caches.

Vertex Cache Manager

With the vertex cache object, you have a class that can render primitives from user pointers on the fly. But you should avoid that wherever possible. To get even better performance while rendering dynamic data, I will show you how to build a manager that fills the vertex cache objects in such a way so they are used as quickly as possible. The overall goal is to batch as many triangles together in single render calls as possible.

Besides this task, the vertex cache manager also is responsible for creating and rendering static buffers. You have already seen the interface ZFXVertexCacheManager, so there is no need for further explanations. Looking at a bit of source code sometimes is more effective, so here is the declaration of the class implementing the ZFXVertexCacheManager interface:

```cpp
#define NUM_CACHES 10

class ZFXD3DVCManager : public ZFXVertexCacheManager
   {
   public:
      ZFXD3DVCManager(ZFXD3DSkinManager *pSkinMan,
                     LPDIRECT3DDEVICE9 pDevice,
                     ZFXD3D *pZFXD3D, UINT nMaxVerts,
                     UINT nMaxIndis, FILE *pLog);
      ~ZFXD3DVCManager(void);

      HRESULT CreateStaticBuffer(ZFXVERTEXID VertexID,
                                 UINT nSkinID,
                                 UINT nVerts,
                                 UINT nIndis,
                                 const void *pVerts,
                                 const WORD *pIndis,
                                 UINT *pnID);

      HRESULT Render(ZFXVERTEXID VertexID,
                     UINT nVerts,
                     UINT nIndis,
                     const void *pVerts,
                     const WORD *pIndis,
                     UINT  SkinID);

      HRESULT Render(UINT nSBufferID);
      HRESULT ForcedFlushAll(void);
      HRESULT ForcedFlush(ZFXVERTEXID VertexID);

      DWORD   GetActiveCache(void)       { return m_dwActiveCache; }
      void    SetActiveCache(DWORD dwID) { m_dwActiveCache = dwID; }
      ZFXD3D* GetZFXD3D(void) { return m_pZFXD3D; }

   private:
      ZFXD3DSkinManager *m_pSkinMan;
      LPDIRECT3DDEVICE9  m_pDevice;
      ZFXD3D            *m_pZFXD3D;

      ZFXSTATICBUFFER   *m_pSB;
```

```
    UINT              m_nNumSB;
    ZFXD3DVCache      *m_CacheUU[NUM_CACHES];
    ZFXD3DVCache      *m_CacheUL[NUM_CACHES];
    DWORD             m_dwActiveCache;
    DWORD             m_dwActiveSB;
    FILE              *m_pLog;
}; // class
```

As you can see, the implementation uses only the public functions that were already declared in the interface, except for some accessor methods. This promises to be an easy implementation, or so it seems.

The member attributes of this class are mainly pointers—for example, to the `IDirect3DDevice9` object, which should be used for rendering, or the `ZFXD3D` object, from which this manager comes. Two arrays are used for vertex cache objects, as is a pointer of the type `ZFXSTATICBUFFER`, which is also an array:

```
typedef struct ZFXSTATICBUFFER_TYPE
    {
    int    nStride;
    UINT   nSkinID;
    bool   bIndis;
    int    nNumVerts;
    int    nNumIndis;
    int    nNumTris;
    DWORD  dwFVF;
    LPDIRECT3DVERTEXBUFFER9 pVB;
    LPDIRECT3DINDEXBUFFER9  pIB;
    } ZFXSTATICBUFFER;
```

This structure holds all the data you will need for a static buffer. I even bundled a Direct3D vertex buffer together with an index buffer because, if the user wants to have static data with an index lists, it belongs to just that single object. From the names of the fields, you can already see what all the variables in this structure are used for. I want to let the static buffers be static buffers for now and talk a bit about managing vertex caches.

Creating and Releasing a Vertex Cache Manager

The plan for what the vertex cache manager should be able to do should be clear. The manager should be able to render static objects with very few function calls. It has to save the created objects, such as static buffers in its own member attributes, and provide the caller with only an ID just as the skin manager does.

The second task of the vertex cache manager is rendering primitive lists on the fly so that the user doesn't have to create buffers for them. The vertex cache manager creates the necessary buffer objects internally, but this task takes some time. To avoid doing this at runtime, the vertex cache manager creates two arrays of vertex cache objects on its initialization in the constructor, which looks like this:

```
ZFXD3DVCManager::ZFXD3DVCManager( ZFXD3DSkinManager *pSkinMan,
                                  LPDIRECT3DDEVICE9 pDevice,
                                  ZFXD3D *pZFXD3D, UINT nMaxVerts,
                                  UINT nMaxIndis, FILE *pLog)
   {
   DWORD dwID=1;
   int   i=0;

   m_pSB    = NULL;
   m_nNumSB = 0;

   m_pLog          = pLog;
   m_pDevice       = pDevice;
   m_pZFXD3D       = pZFXD3D;
   m_pSkinMan      = pSkinMan;
   m_dwActiveCache = MAX_ID;
   m_dwActiveSB    = MAX_ID;

   for (i=0; i<NUM_CACHES; i++) {
      m_CacheUU[i] = new ZFXD3DVCache(nMaxVerts, nMaxIndis,
                                      sizeof(VERTEX), pSkinMan, pDevice,
                                      this, dwID++, pLog);

      m_CacheUL[i] = new ZFXD3DVCache(nMaxVerts, nMaxIndis,
                                      sizeof(LVERTEX),
                                      pSkinMan, pDevice,
                                      this, dwID++, pLog);
      } // for
   } // constructor
```

Two arrays of vertex caches are created. Why two arrays? A vertex buffer needs to know how big a single vertex is to allocate enough memory for a number of n vertices. But the various vertex formats the engine provides need to be taken care of. So, for each vertex format in the engine, there is one array of vertex caches. (Actually, there are more than two formats, so the source code on the CD-ROM uses more than just two arrays. I just stripped this version down for ease of understanding.) The two formats used here are the VERTEX and LVERTEX structures, with UU meaning untransformed and unlit and UL meaning untransformed lit.

In the destructor of the `ZFXD3DVCManager` class, you need to delete all the vertex caches from the arrays and free and release the static buffers:

```
ZFXD3DVCManager::~ZFXD3DVCManager(void)
   {
   UINT n=0;
   int  i=0;

   // release the memory in the static buffers
   if ( m_pSB ) {
      for (n=0; n<m_nNumSB; n++)
         {
         if (m_pSB[n].pVB) {
            m_pSB[n].pVB->Release();
            m_pSB[n].pVB = NULL;
            }
         if (m_pSB[n].pIB) {
            m_pSB[n].pIB->Release();
            m_pSB[n].pIB = NULL;
            }
         }
      free( m_pSB );
      m_pSB = NULL;
      }


   // release the vertex cache objects
   for (i=0; i<NUM_CACHES; i++)
      {
      if (m_CacheUU[i]) {
         delete m_CacheUU[i];
         m_CacheUU[i] = NULL;
         }
      if (m_CacheUL[i]) {
         delete m_CacheUL[i];
         m_CacheUL[i] = NULL;
         }
      } // for
   } // destructor
```

Managing Dynamic Render Lists

Welcome to the core of the vertex cache manager and the secret behind the ZFXEngine's ability to render thousands of triangles in single calls at a reasonable speed in real time. Managing the dynamic vertex cache lists requires some implicit logic to deal with single triangles coming in unsorted. Just think of 1,000 triangles using the same vertex format but with five textures. Each one is sent individually in no apparent order by the user. The vertex cache manager should not render the data immediately but cache this to be able to render all 1,000 triangles in five rendering calls (one for each texture).

This might sound complicated, but it is not. As always, there are some minor catches and issues you need to be aware of. The first problem is that you simply cannot know how many skins the user will use for rendering a certain amount of triangles dynamically in one frame. If you cache all the triangles using the same skin and then flush the cache when another skin is used, you won't get a great increase in performance because we suppose the user will render with no regard to sorting data by skins. Thus, you must provide multiple pots into which the manager can dump the triangles. You can do it like this: Each time the user dynamically sends triangles with a new skin the manager has not seen in this frame, the manager opens a new pot and throws the triangles into that one, labeling it with the skin ID.

When the user sends a lot of triangles using many different textures, the manager ends up with several pots filled with triangles, with all the triangles in the same pot using the same skin. If the rendering ends, the manager then activates the skin of the first pot, renders its triangles, activates the skin of the second pot, renders its triangles, and so on.

Naturally, we would not want the manager to create hundreds of pots during runtime. So, I introduced the define `NUM_CACHE`, which is the number of different pots for different skins. In this example, I used 10 as the number of pots. If the user uses an 11th skin during his rendering of dynamic data, there won't be a free pot into which the manager can dump the triangles. The solution to this is simple. If no free pot is available, the manager has to make one of the full pots free by rendering its contents, resulting in a free pot.

Note
The skin is not the only attribute triangles must share to be candidates for the same pot. They must use the same render states, the same world transform, and so on. This is why changing the world matrix, render states, and so on calls the `ZFXD3DVCManager::ForcedFlushAll` function. The manager needs to sort by skin. If another crucial state changes, the data in the caches is rendered no matter how many or few triangles are cached.

The only tricky thing now is to find the best-suited pot into which to sort the incoming data. Just think about it for a moment and you will come up with a heuristic that is pretty easy. There are lots of ways to do this sorting, but the following scheme in pseudo-code is a good option:

```
for (i=0 to all pots ) do
   {
   if ( pot[i] uses the same skin )
       {
       add polygons to pot[i]
       return;
       }
   if ( pot[i] is empty )
       {
       save pot[i] as empty pot
       }
   if ( pot[i] is fuller than the fullest pot found yet )
       {
       save pot[i] as fullest pot
       }
   }
if ( at least one empty pot found )
   {
   set skin for the empty pot
   add polygons to the empty pot
   return;
   }
else
   {
   flush the fullest pot
   set skin to this pot
   add polygons to this pot
   return;
   }
```

Suppose some incoming polygonal data uses a single skin because the user has called the render function for dynamic data. You have a big loop going through all the available vertex caches. If you find a vertex cache that is using the same skin, you are done—you just need to add the new polygons to this pot. Otherwise, you must do two things in each iteration. First, if the current pot is empty, you must save it to a pointer that is meant to point to an empty cache. Note that you save only the last empty cache you found and not all empty caches. Then you compare the current pot to the fullest pot you have found in this loop so far. Next, you save the pointer to the fullest of all caches.

After the loop is over and you are still in the function, you know that no vertex cache occurred using the skin you are looking for because the incoming data uses it. So, you must check whether an empty cache is available. If one is, you set this empty cache to the skin and add the polygonal data to it. Then you are done. But if no empty cache exists, you have to empty out one of the pots. Obviously, you should empty the fullest cache because rendering this one would be better than rendering just a few triangles from the caches that aren't completely full. After the fullest cache has rendered its contents, you set it to the new skin and add the polygonal data.

And now tell me where this is supposed to be difficult at all? Here is the implementation:

```
HRESULT ZFXD3DVCManager::Render(ZFXVERTEXID VertexID, UINT   nVerts,
                                UINT   nIndis, const void *pVerts,
                                const WORD *pIndis, UINT   SkinID)
   {
   ZFXD3DVCache **pCache=NULL,
                *pCacheEmpty=NULL,
                *pCacheFullest=NULL;
   int nEmptyVC   = -1;
   int nFullestVC = 0;

   bool bShaders = m_pZFXD3D->UsesShaders();

   // which vertex type is used?
   switch (VertexID) {
      case VID_UU: { pCache = m_CacheUU; } break;
      case VID_UL: { pCache = m_CacheUL; } break;
      default: return ZFX_INVALIDID;
      } // switch

   pCacheFullest = pCache[0];

   // active buffer gets invalid
   m_dwActiveSB = MAX_ID;

   // SEARCH THE MOST APPROPRIATE POT

   // is there a cache with this skin?
   for (int i=0; i<NUM_CACHES; i++)
      {
      // we got one so add data
      if (pCache[i]->UsesSkin(SkinID))
         {
         return pCache[i]->Add(nVerts, nIndis, pVerts, pIndis, bShaders);
         }

      // save an empty cache
      if (pCache[i]->IsEmpty())
```

```
        {
        pCacheEmpty = pCache[i];
        }

    // save the fullest cache
    if (pCache[i]->NumVerts() > pCacheFullest->NumVerts())
        {
        pCacheFullest = pCache[i];
        }
    }

// no luck finding a cache with the skin, is there an empty one?
if (pCacheEmpty)
    {
    pCacheEmpty->SetSkin(SkinID, bShaders);
    return pCacheEmpty->Add(nVerts, nIndis, pVerts, pIndis, bShaders);
    }

// again no luck so use the fullest cache
pCacheFullest->Flush(bShaders);
pCacheFullest->SetSkin(SkinID, bShaders);
return pCacheFullest->Add(nVerts, nIndis, pVerts, pIndis, bShaders);
} // Render
```

With our functional vertex cache class, this task is done quickly. Now you have successfully built your first primitive data sorting and caching scheme that greatly boosts the performance of rendering single triangles in single render calls. Note that this function is not called something like sort or cache but is called ZFXD3DVCManager::Render instead. As seen from the outside, this function is responsible for rendering the dynamic data and the user does not need to do anything besides send primitive data.

Flushing the Buffers

The vertex cache object has a function called ZFXD3DVCache::Flush that is actually the function that finally renders the data from its shelf using Direct3D. The vertex cache usually takes care of calling this function if more data is added to the cache than it can hold due to its full shelves. But in some situations, the user or the vertex cache manager needs to initiate this rendering process manually. This needs to be done at least once when a frame ends and there is no more data to come. Here are two functions to accomplish this task. The first one flushes all caches using the vertex format, and the second function flushes all vertex caches in the manager:

```
HRESULT ZFXD3DVCManager::ForcedFlush(ZFXVERTEXID VertexID)
    {
```

```
ZFXD3DVCache **pCache=NULL;
HRESULT hr = ZFX_OK;
int i=0;

switch (VertexID) {
    case VID_UU: { pCache = m_CacheUU; } break;

    case VID_UL: { pCache = m_CacheUL; } break;

    // unknown Vertex-Type
    default: return ZFX_INVALIDID;
    } // switch

for (i=0; i<NUM_CACHES; i++)
    if (FAILED( pCache[i]->Flush(
                m_pZFXD3D->UsesShaders()) ))
        hr = ZFX_FAIL;
return hr;
} // ForcedFlush



HRESULT ZFXD3DVCManager::ForcedFlushAll(void)
    {
    HRESULT hr = ZFX_OK;
    bool    bShaders = m_pZFXD3D->UsesShaders();
    int     i;

    for (i=0; i<NUM_CACHES; i++)
       if (!m_CacheUU[i]->IsEmpty() )
          if (FAILED( m_CacheUU[i]->Flush(bShaders) ))
             hr = ZFX_FAIL;

    for (i=0; i<NUM_CACHES; i++)
       if (!m_CacheUL[i]->IsEmpty() )
          if (FAILED( m_CacheUL[i]->Flush(bShaders) ))
             hr = ZFX_FAIL;

    return hr;
    } // ForcedFlushAll
```

The single parameter for the Flush() call specifies whether shaders are currently used by the engine or whether the fixed function pipeline is active.

Creating and Rendering Static Buffers

Besides the dynamic buffers, you can also use static buffers. They are far more important because they should be used by the user of the engine. Their advantage is that they don't need much code to run and produce a good performance. Static buffers reduce the amount of traffic on the bus by keeping the data in VRAM as long as possible. To secure the correct use of such buffers, we will not write any function that lets the user access the static buffer after it is created. The only way to change the contents inside the buffer after that is by destroying the buffer and creating a new one with the changed data.

The two kinds of accesses you could normally perform on a buffer using Direct3D are

- Read access
- Write access

Read access shouldn't be used here because it locks the buffer and copies its contents over the bus to the user pointer where the user can access the data. You might wonder why someone would want to do this. After all, the user is the one who put the data in the buffer in the first place. So, he should keep a copy of what he put in the buffer in his system memory. This copy is better used for things like collision detection instead of copying the whole data each time from the buffer when it's needed.

Write access is needed when the contents of the buffer change, such as when the geometry has been deformed in a way you cannot do with transformation matrices. Character animation, for example, can be done with transformation matrices and does not require changing the buffer's contents. I would not allow accessing a static buffer in the ZFXEngine because this forces the user to keep the data static and to keep his own copy of the contents if he needs it. This results in better performance than just letting the user make changes when he doesn't know changes might affect performance.

A static buffer in Direct3D is created simply by not specifying the D3DUSAGE_DYNAMIC flag; therefore, all buffers in Direct3D are implicitly static. The following function in the vertex cache manager lets the user create a static buffer and add the content to the buffer, which cannot be changed later. For each static buffer it manages, the vertex cache manager uses an instance of the ZFXSTATICBUFFER structure that keeps all data concerning the buffer together in a single variable.

The static buffers are added to a dynamically allocated memory in the vertex cache manager. I always add enough room for 50 new objects in the array if it is full, but there is another object that must be stored:

```
HRESULT ZFXD3DVCManager::CreateStaticBuffer( ZFXVERTEXID VertexID,
                            UINT nSkinID, UINT nVerts,
                            UINT nIndis, const void *pVerts,
                            const WORD *pIndis, UINT *pnID)
```

```cpp
{
HRESULT   hr;
DWORD     dwActualFVF;
void      *pData;

if (m_nNumSB >= (MAX_ID-1)) return ZFX_OUTOFMEMORY;

// allocate memory if needed
if ( (m_nNumSB % 50) == 0)
   {
   int n = (m_nNumSB+50)*sizeof(ZFXSTATICBUFFER);
   m_pSB = (ZFXSTATICBUFFER*)realloc(m_pSB, n);
   if (!m_pSB) return ZFX_OUTOFMEMORY;
   }

m_pSB[m_nNumSB].nNumVerts = nVerts;
m_pSB[m_nNumSB].nNumIndis = nIndis;
m_pSB[m_nNumSB].nSkinID   = nSkinID;

// size and format of the vertices
switch (VertexID)
   {
   case VID_UU: {
      m_pSB[m_nNumSB].nStride = sizeof(VERTEX);
      m_pSB[m_nNumSB].dwFVF = FVF_VERTEX;
      } break;
   case VID_UL: {
      m_pSB[m_nNumSB].nStride = sizeof(LVERTEX);
      m_pSB[m_nNumSB].dwFVF = FVF_LVERTEX;
      } break;
   default: return ZFX_INVALIDID;
   } // switch

// create index buffer if needed
if (nIndis > 0)
   {
   m_pSB[m_nNumSB].bIndis = true;
   m_pSB[m_nNumSB].nNumTris = int(nIndis / 3.0f);

   hr = m_pDevice->CreateIndexBuffer(
                    nIndis * sizeof(WORD),
                    D3DUSAGE_WRITEONLY,
```

```cpp
                              D3DFMT_INDEX16,
                              D3DPOOL_DEFAULT,
                              &m_pSB[m_nNumSB].pIB,
                              NULL);
   if (FAILED(hr)) return ZFX_CREATEBUFFER;

   // fill the index buffer
   if (SUCCEEDED(m_pSB[m_nNumSB].pIB->Lock(
                                     0, 0, (void**)
                                     (&pData), 0))) {
      memcpy(pData, pIndis, nIndis*sizeof(WORD));
      m_pSB[m_nNumSB].pIB->Unlock();
      }
   else return ZFX_BUFFERLOCK;
   }
else {
   m_pSB[m_nNumSB].bIndis = false;
   m_pSB[m_nNumSB].nNumTris = int(nVerts / 3.0f);
   m_pSB[m_nNumSB].pIB = NULL;
   }

// no need for FVF if shaders are used
if (m_pZFXD3D->UsesShaders()) dwActualFVF = 0;
else dwActualFVF = m_pSB[m_nNumSB].dwFVF;

// create vertex buffer
hr = m_pDevice->CreateVertexBuffer( nVerts*m_pSB[m_nNumSB].nStride,
                                    D3DUSAGE_WRITEONLY, dwActualFVF,
                                    D3DPOOL_DEFAULT,
                                    &m_pSB[m_nNumSB].pVB, NULL);
if (FAILED(hr)) return ZFX_CREATEBUFFER;

// fill vertex buffer
if (SUCCEEDED(m_pSB[m_nNumSB].pVB->Lock( 0, 0, (void**) (&pData), 0)))
   {
   memcpy(pData, pVerts, nVerts*m_pSB[
          m_nNumSB].nStride);
   m_pSB[m_nNumSB].pVB->Unlock();
   }
else return ZFX_BUFFERLOCK;

(*pnID) = m_nNumSB;
```

316 Chapter 6 ■ The Render Device of the Engine

```
   m_nNumSB++;
   return ZFX_OK;
   } // CreateStaticBuffer
```

This function appears to be lengthy, but this depends on the switch for the different vertex formats. Keep in mind that there are more vertex formats in the final code on the CD-ROM. After selecting the correct vertex format, you can then build the vertex buffer object of Direct3D in the appropriate size. The function then returns the ID of the newly created buffer to the caller, who should keep track of this ID. It's the only way to access the static buffer again, where *accessing* means rendering in this case.

The vertex cache manager is still missing the implementation of the function that renders the contents of a static buffer. The parameter for this function is the ID of the static buffer. No other parameters are needed because all the data is stored in the static buffer.

If the static buffer uses an index buffer, this is activated by calling the Direct3D function IDirect3DDevice9::SetIndices. After that, the vertex buffer is activated for Direct3D using IDirect3DDevice9::SetStreamSource. Then the function checks whether the skin used by the static buffer is already active. If it is not, it needs to set the materials and all the textures from the skin.

Basically, that is all the function needs to do. Just like the ZFXVCache::Flush function, it then must check for the primitive type that is currently active and call the appropriate Direct3D drawing function:

```
HRESULT ZFXD3DVCManager::Render(UINT nID)
   {
   HRESULT hr=ZFX_OK;

   ZFXRENDERSTATE sm = m_pZFXD3D->GetShadeMode();

   // active vertex cache gets invalid
   m_dwActiveCache = MAX_ID;

   // activate this static buffer if not active yet
   if (m_dwActiveSB != nID)
      {
      // using indices?
      if (m_pSB[nID].bIndis)
         m_pDevice->SetIndices(m_pSB[nID].pIB);

      m_pDevice->SetStreamSource(0, m_pSB[nID].pVB, 0, m_pSB[nID].nStride);
      m_dwActiveSB = nID;
      }
```

```cpp
// skin already active?
if (m_pZFXD3D->GetActiveSkinID() != m_pSB[nID].nSkinID)
   {
   // mark as active now
   ZFXSKIN *pSkin = &m_pSkinMan->m_pSkins[m_pSB[nID].nSkinID];

   // SPECIAL CASE WIREFRAME-MODE
   if (sm == RS_SHADE_SOLID)
      {
      // set material with wireframe color
      ZFXMATERIAL *pMat = &m_pSkinMan->
                  m_pMaterials[pSkin->nMaterial];
      D3DMATERIAL9 mat = {
         pMat->cDiffuse.fR,  pMat->cDiffuse.fG,
         pMat->cDiffuse.fB,  pMat->cDiffuse.fA,
         pMat->cAmbient.fR,  pMat->cAmbient.fG,
         pMat->cAmbient.fB,  pMat->cAmbient.fA,
         pMat->cSpecular.fR, pMat->cSpecular.fG,
         pMat->cSpecular.fB, pMat->cSpecular.fA,
         pMat->cEmissive.fR, pMat->cEmissive.fG,
         pMat->cEmissive.fB, pMat->cEmissive.fA,
         pMat->fPower };
      m_pDevice->SetMaterial(&mat);

      // set texture for the device
      for (int i=0; i<8; i++)
         {
         if (pSkin->nTexture[i] != MAX_ID)
            m_pDevice->SetTexture(i, (LPDIRECT3DTEXTURE9)
                  m_pSkinMan->m_pTextures[pSkin->nTexture[i]].pData);
         }
      }
   else {
      ZFXCOLOR clrWire = m_pZFXD3D->GetWireColor();

      // set material for the device
      D3DMATERIAL9 matW = {
       clrWire.fR,clrWire.fG,clrWire.fB,clrWire.fA,
       clrWire.fR,clrWire.fG,clrWire.fB,clrWire.fA,
       0.0f,          0.0f,       0.0f,       1.0f,
       0.0f,          0.0f,       0.0f,       1.0f,
```

318   Chapter 6 ■ The Render Device of the Engine

```
      1.0f };
   m_pDevice->SetMaterial(&matW);

   // use no texture
   m_pDevice->SetTexture(0, NULL);
   }

// set alpha states if needed
if (pSkin->bAlpha)
   {
   m_pDevice->SetRenderState(D3DRS_ALPHAREF, 50);
   m_pDevice->SetRenderState(D3DRS_ALPHAFUNC, D3DCMP_GREATEREQUAL);
   m_pDevice->SetRenderState(D3DRS_SRCBLEND, D3DBLEND_SRCALPHA);
   m_pDevice->SetRenderState(D3DRS_DESTBLEND, D3DBLEND_INVSRCALPHA);
   m_pDevice->SetRenderState(D3DRS_ALPHATESTENABLE, TRUE);
   m_pDevice->SetRenderState(D3DRS_ALPHABLENDENABLE, TRUE);
   }
else {
   m_pDevice->SetRenderState(D3DRS_ALPHATESTENABLE, FALSE);
   m_pDevice->SetRenderState(D3DRS_ALPHABLENDENABLE, FALSE);
   }

// active skin has changed
m_pZFXD3D->SetActiveSkinID(m_pSB[nID].nSkinID);
} // [device->skin]

// if no shader is used activate the appropriate FVF
if (!m_pZFXD3D->UsesShaders()) m_pDevice->SetFVF(FVF_VERTEX);

// indexed primitives
if (m_pSB[nID].bIndis)
   {
   if ( sm == RS_SHADE_POINTS ) {
      hr = m_pDevice->DrawPrimitive(D3DPT_POINTLIST,0,m_pSB[nID].nNumVerts);
      }
   else if ( sm == RS_SHADE_HULLWIRE ) {
      hr = m_pDevice->DrawIndexedPrimitive( D3DPT_LINESTRIP, 0,
                                     0, m_pSB[nID].nNumVerts,
                                     0, m_pSB[nID].nNumVerts);
      }
   else { // RS_SHADE_SOLID || RS_SHADE_TRIWIRE
      hr = m_pDevice->DrawIndexedPrimitive( D3DPT_TRIANGLELIST, 0,
```

```
                                           0, m_pSB[nID].nNumVerts,
                                           0, m_pSB[nID].nNumTris);
      }
   }
   else
      {
      if ( sm == RS_SHADE_POINTS ) {
         hr = m_pDevice->DrawPrimitive( D3DPT_POINTLIST, 0,
                                        m_pSB[nID].nNumVerts);
         }
      else if ( sm == RS_SHADE_HULLWIRE ) {
         hr = m_pDevice->DrawPrimitive( D3DPT_LINESTRIP,
                                        m_pSB[nID].nNumVerts,
                                        m_pSB[nID].nNumVerts);
         }
      else { // RS_SHADE_SOLID || RS_SHADE_TRIWIRE
         hr = m_pDevice->DrawPrimitive( D3DPT_TRIANGLELIST,
                                        m_pSB[nID].nNumVerts,
                                        m_pSB[nID].nNumTris);
         }
      }
   return hr;
   } // Render
```

Again, you can see here that providing an index list for a static buffer is possible but optional. You can also use the same functions without an index list. The primitive type depends on the render states set in the ZFXD3D class using the render device interface.

The vertex cache manager is now done. The user can have fast static buffers with vertex and optional index buffers. But he can also render data dynamically with good performance. The vertex cache manager is now an attribute of the ZFXRenderDevice interface, so the user can access it in the following way:

```
// pZFXDevice is a valid, initialized object of the type ZFXRenderDevice,
// myID is the id of a static buffer created beforehand
pZFXDevice->GetRenderManager()->Render(myID);
```

Rendering Text, Points, and Lines

We are not done yet. You achieved a great deal of work already, and I will let you go to bed in another dozen pages. But there is one thing we have not done yet. We need to render points, lines, and (most important) text.

The following section of this chapter deals with these issues, but please note that I do not optimize anything for speed here but for comfort in usage. You will not use these features very often in a speed-critical application, such as a video game. But text is useful for debug output, and rendering points and lines is necessary for level editing tools.

Creating Fonts and Rendering Text

Each engine—even a very basic one—needs text output. After all, you want to know about your frame rate without writing it to a log file only, correct? There are a lot of ways to render text or even 3D text. Some of the methods are efficient; others are less efficient. You should implement your own font class specific to your needs.

In the DirectX SDK you will find a class called CD3DFont. If you take a look at it, you can see how to create a font automatically based on some input values, such as size, attributes, and so on. A texture is also created from this font containing all the characters and signs used by the font. While rendering a text string, the characters are taken from the texture and put onto a 3D rectangle. So, the text becomes an object that can be used in a 3D scene to place the text above a player's head, for example.

I recommend you look at this font class, but I don't have the room here to treat this class or a similar implementation. Therefore, I decided to use the class from the extended library called D3DXFont. Internally, this class uses the Windows GDI and therefore is usually not recommended for use because it isn't very fast. Even if the GDI improves, it still requires leaving Direct3D for a second to use another API to render some graphics in between and then switching back to Direct3D. This is all done behind the scenes, so you don't have to deal with the issues. However, it does slow down things, as opposed to a pure Direct3D implementation of your own font.

D3DXFont is still the best choice because it is so easy to use. Now, we need to add the following declarations to the ZFXD3D class:

```
LPD3DXFONT    *m_pFont;        // font objects
UINT          m_nNumFonts;     // number of fonts

HRESULT CreateFont(const char*, int, bool, bool, bool, DWORD, UINT*);
HRESULT DrawText(UINT, int, int, UCHAR, UCHAR, UCHAR, char*,...);
```

We also have to add the two public function calls to the render device interface declaration to enable the users of our engine to access the functions. Before I show you the implementations of the functions, I want to point out that the user of the engine can create as many different fonts as he likes. Just like the skin objects and the static buffers, he then gets an ID to each font to render text with this font later.

Let's create a font. As a first parameter to this function, we need to specify which type of font we want to create—for example Arial or Times New Roman. The next parameter specifies the boldness of the font, where 0 is the default and a value of 700 is a typically bold font. The next settings are three boolean values for italic, underlined, or strikethrough fonts. To close the input parameter list, the caller has to provide a value for the size of the font. The function then creates a font and returns the ID of the new font in the last reference parameter. Here is the function:

```
HRESULT ZFXD3D::CreateFont(const char *chType, int nWeight, bool bItalic,
                           bool bUnderline, bool bStrike, DWORD dwSize,
                           UINT *pID)
   {
   HRESULT hr;
   HFONT   hFont;
   HDC     hDC;
   int     nHeight;

   if (!pID) return ZFX_INVALIDPARAM;

   hDC = GetDC( NULL );
   nHeight = -MulDiv(dwSize, GetDeviceCaps(hDC,
                     LOGPIXELSY), 72);
   ReleaseDC(NULL, hDC);
   hFont = ::CreateFont(nHeight,   // height
                        0, 0, 0,   // average width
                        nWeight,   // thickness
                        bItalic, bUnderline, bStrike,
                        DEFAULT_CHARSET, OUT_DEFAULT_PRECIS,
                        CLIP_DEFAULT_PRECIS, DEFAULT_QUALITY,
                        DEFAULT_PITCH | FF_DONTCARE, chType);
   if (hFont == NULL) return ZFX_FAIL;

   m_pFont = (LPD3DXFONT*)realloc(m_pFont, sizeof(LPD3DXFONT)*(m_nNumFonts+1));

   hr = D3DXCreateFont(m_pDevice, hFont, &m_pFont[m_nNumFonts]);
   DeleteObject(hFont);

   if (SUCCEEDED(hr))
      {
      (*pID) = m_nNumFonts;
      m_nNumFonts++;
      return ZFX_OK;
      }
   else
      {
```

```
        return ZFX_FAIL;
      }
   } // CreateFont
```

This function is pretty straightforward. As I already said, the D3DXFont class uses the WinAPI font objects rendered by the GDI. Hence, this function creates the font object using the WinAPI call CreateFont(). Note the scope operator (::) marking this function as being from the global namespace. This is explicitly not a recursive call of the ZFXD3D::CreateFont method. If you are not familiar with this function from the WinAPI, please refer to the platform SDK or the MSDN for a description of it. If the font construction succeeded, it is then used to build a D3DXFont object.

Now that the user has the ID of his font, he can provide this ID to the ZFXD3D::DrawText function to render text with that font. Besides the ID of the font that should be used, the caller needs to supply the x and y values of the position onscreen where the text should appear. The next three parameters specify the RGB values of the color that should be used for the text. Finally, the last parameter holds a formatting string, such as the fprintf() function, optionally followed by a list of parameters that should be written to the formatting string:

```
HRESULT ZFXD3D::DrawText(UINT nID, int x, int y, UCHAR r, UCHAR g, UCHAR b,
                        char *ch, ...) {
   RECT rc = { x, y, 0, 0 };
   char cch[1024];
   char *pArgs;

   // move optional parameters into the string
   pArgs = (char*) &ch + sizeof(ch);
   vsprintf(cch, ch, pArgs);

   if (nID >= m_nNumFonts) return ZFX_INVALIDPARAM;

   m_pFont[nID]->Begin();

      // calculate bounding rect for the size
      m_pFont[nID]->DrawText(cch, -1, &rc, DT_SINGLELINE | DT_CALCRECT, 0);

      // now draw the text
      m_pFont[nID]->DrawText(cch, -1, &rc, DT_SINGLELINE,
                             D3DCOLOR_ARGB(255,r,g,b));

   m_pFont[nID]->End();
```

```
        return ZFX_OK;
        } // DrawText
```

Note

> The Summer Update of the DirectX 9 SDK introduces some minor changes to the ID3DXFont class. The Begin() and End() functions are obsolete now, and there is an additional first parameter to the DrawText() function, which can be set to NULL here.

To actually render the text, you can use the ID3DXFont::DrawText method. The problem, however, is that you need to hand over a rectangle that bounds the text so Direct3D can calculate the area where the text will be drawn. Calculating such a rectangle is easy because you don't have to. As with some other WinAPI functions, you can use the same function (ID3DXFont::DrawText) to calculate the rectangle. You just have to use the DT_CALCRECT flag, which causes this function to not draw the text but calculate the bounding rectangle and return it in the third parameter. Then you call the function a second time with this rectangle to draw the text. You have to call ID3DXFont::Begin and ID3DXFont::End before and after drawing, respectively.

This is the font supported by the ZFXEngine. Now the user can create as many fonts as he needs—thin ones or thick ones, big ones or small ones, and so on.

Rendering Point Lists

In some situations a 3D video game or application programmer might want to render a list of points. In the context of most graphics APIs such as Direct3D, points are just that—points. Thus, regardless of the resolution of the screen, a point is always the same size as a single pixel on the screen. This is opposed to things that just look like points—for example, point sprites or small billboards. (Note that OpenGL lets you change the size of a point to be greater than a single pixel.)

To let the user render points, the following function is defined in the render device interface from now on:

```
    virtual HRESULT RenderPoints( ZFXVERTEXID     VertexID,
                                  UINT            nVerts,
                                  const void     *pVerts,
                                  const ZFXCOLOR *pClr1)=0;
```

This function takes only the vertex type, the number of vertices, a pointer to an array with the vertices, and the color that should be used for the points.

You probably won't use this function very often because single points are just boring, although you might use it for debug purposes. This is why I leave the function unoptimized using just a call to IDirect3DDevice9::DrawPrimitiveUP.

Chapter 6 ■ The Render Device of the Engine

Actually, that would be enough to render the list of points. But, by just calling this function, you could damage the interacting network of state information in the engine. After rendering a list of points this way, the currently active skin is invalid, as well as the active cache and static buffer. To let the vertex cache manager know about what happened, I introduced the following function:

```
void ZFXD3DVCManager::InvalidateStates(void)
   {
   m_pZFXD3D->SetActiveSkinID(MAX_ID);
   m_dwActiveSB    = MAX_ID;
   m_dwActiveCache = MAX_ID;
   }
```

There is one thing to notice inside the function. If the engine is able to use shaders due to the hardware present, this function activates the vertex shader and the pixel shader with an ID of 0. Upon initialization, the ZFXEngine creates this vertex and pixel shader to perform a basic transformation and create ambient lighting, which is enough for rendering this list of points:

```
HRESULT ZFXD3DVCManager::RenderPoints( ZFXVERTEXID    VID,
                                       UINT           nVerts,
                                       const void     *pVerts,
                                       const ZFXCOLOR *pClr)
   {
   D3DMATERIAL9 mtrl;
   DWORD        dwFVF;
   int          nStride;

   // invalidate active settings
   InvalidateStates();

   memset(&mtrl, 0, sizeof(D3DMATERIAL9));
   mtrl.Diffuse.r = mtrl.Ambient.r = pClr->fR;
   mtrl.Diffuse.g = mtrl.Ambient.g = pClr->fG;
   mtrl.Diffuse.b = mtrl.Ambient.b = pClr->fB;
   mtrl.Diffuse.a = mtrl.Ambient.a = pClr->fA;

   m_pDevice->SetMaterial(&mtrl);
   m_pDevice->SetTexture(0,NULL);

   switch (VID) {
      case VID_UU: {
         nStride = sizeof(VERTEX);
         dwFVF   = FVF_VERTEX;
```

```
      } break;
    case VID_UL: {
       nStride = sizeof(LVERTEX);
       dwFVF   = FVF_LVERTEX;
       } break;
    default: return ZFX_INVALIDID;
    } // switch

// shader or FVF
if ( m_pZFXD3D->UsesShaders() )
   {
   m_pZFXD3D->ActivateVShader(0, VID);
   m_pZFXD3D->ActivatePShader(0);
   }
else m_pDevice->SetFVF(dwFVF);

// finally render list of points
if (FAILED(m_pDevice->DrawPrimitiveUP(D3DPT_POINTLIST, nVerts, pVerts,
                                     nStride)))
   return ZFX_FAIL;
return ZFX_OK;
} // RenderPoints
```

Rendering Line Lists

Just as with rendering points, a function now exists in the engine for rendering lines. This function is not used in performance-critical applications, but it can and will be used to render the grid in a level editor tool. Here is the function declaration from the render device interface:

```
virtual HRESULT RenderLines(ZFXVERTEXID      VertexID,
                            UINT             nVerts,
                            const void       *pVerts,
                            const ZFXCOLOR   *pClrl,
                            bool             bStrip)=0;
```

The implementation of this function is 99 percent the same as the one for lists of points. You need only to change the primitive type on the Direct3D drawing call. However, this function can render lists of lines and line strips. In lists, each pair of vertices forms a line. In a strip, on the other hand, a vertex from the list is used for a line together with its succeeding vertex, thus a strip of lines exists that has no gap in between:

```
HRESULT ZFXD3DVCManager::RenderLines(ZFXVERTEXID   VID,
                                     UINT          nVerts,
```

```cpp
                                        const void     *pVerts,
                                        const ZFXCOLOR *pClr,
                                        bool            bStrip)
   {
   D3DMATERIAL9 mtrl;
   DWORD        dwFVF;
   int          nStride;

   // mark all current states as invalid
   InvalidateStates();

   if (pClr) {
      memset(&mtrl, 0, sizeof(D3DMATERIAL9));
      mtrl.Diffuse.r = mtrl.Ambient.r = pClr->fR;
      mtrl.Diffuse.g = mtrl.Ambient.g = pClr->fG;
      mtrl.Diffuse.b = mtrl.Ambient.b = pClr->fB;
      mtrl.Diffuse.a = mtrl.Ambient.a = pClr->fA;
      m_pDevice->SetMaterial(&mtrl);
      }
   m_pDevice->SetTexture(0,NULL);

   switch (VID) {
      case VID_UU: {
         nStride = sizeof(VERTEX);
         dwFVF   = FVF_VERTEX;
         } break;
      case VID_UL: {
         nStride = sizeof(LVERTEX);
         dwFVF   = FVF_LVERTEX;
         } break;
      default: return ZFX_INVALIDID;
      } // switch

   if ( m_pZFXD3D->UsesShaders() )
      {
      m_pZFXD3D->ActivateVShader(0, VID);
      m_pZFXD3D->ActivatePShader(0);
      }
   else m_pDevice->SetFVF(dwFVF);

   if (!bStrip)
      {
```

```
        if (FAILED(m_pDevice->DrawPrimitiveUP(
                            D3DPT_LINELIST, nVerts/2,
                            pVerts, nStride)))
            return ZFX_FAIL;
        }
    else
        {
        if (FAILED(m_pDevice->DrawPrimitiveUP(
                            D3DPT_LINESTRIP, nVerts-1,
                            pVerts, nStride)))
            return ZFX_FAIL;
        }
    return ZFX_OK;
    } // RenderLines
```

Presenting a Scene

After the dynamic link library project for the render device implementation was enlarged, we need to add some changes to the code. Some more default initializations can be seen from the constructor of the class, as well as some more releases of objects or freeing up memory areas, as can be seen in the destructor.

Notice the changes in the last lines of the ZFXD3D::Go function that is called at the end of a successful device initialization. Now it saves the current resolution and calls a new function:

```
HRESULT ZFXD3D::Go(void)
    {
    // unchanged [...]

    m_dwWidth  = m_d3dpp.BackBufferWidth;
    m_dwHeight = m_d3dpp.BackBufferHeight;
    return OneTimeInit();
    } // ZFXD3D::Go
```

The new function ZFXD3D::OneTimeInit does exactly what its name implies. After initializing the render device, we need to set some values to bring the render device into a state where the user can start rendering without making adjustments to settings such as the projection matrix. The user can do this later or when she wants to use values other than the default ones. But those are chosen to be the average values you would normally use in a simple 3D scene. The function looks like this:

```
HRESULT ZFXD3D::OneTimeInit(void)
    {
```

```cpp
ZFX3DInitCPU();

m_bUseShaders = true;

m_pSkinMan = new ZFXD3DSkinManager(m_pDevice, m_pLog);

m_pVertexMan = new ZFXD3DVCManager( (ZFXD3DSkinManager*)m_pSkinMan,
                                    m_pDevice, this, 3000, 4500, m_pLog);

// activate render states
m_pDevice->SetRenderState(D3DRS_LIGHTING, TRUE);
m_pDevice->SetRenderState(D3DRS_CULLMODE, D3DCULL_CCW);
m_pDevice->SetRenderState(D3DRS_ZENABLE, D3DZB_TRUE);

// create standard-material
memset(&m_StdMtrl, 0, sizeof(D3DMATERIAL9));
m_StdMtrl.Ambient.r = 1.0f;
m_StdMtrl.Ambient.g = 1.0f;
m_StdMtrl.Ambient.b = 1.0f;
m_StdMtrl.Ambient.a = 1.0f;

if (FAILED(m_pDevice->SetMaterial(&m_StdMtrl))) {
   Log("error: set material (OneTimeInit)");
   return ZFX_FAIL;
   }

// activate texture filtering
m_pDevice->SetSamplerState(0, D3DSAMP_MAGFILTER, D3DTEXF_LINEAR);
m_pDevice->SetSamplerState(0, D3DSAMP_MINFILTER, D3DTEXF_LINEAR);
m_pDevice->SetSamplerState(0, D3DSAMP_MIPFILTER, D3DTEXF_LINEAR);

ZFXVIEWPORT vpView = { 0, 0, m_dwWidth, m_dwHeight };
m_Mode   = EMD_PERSPECTIVE;
m_nStage = -1;
SetActiveSkinID(MAX_ID);

// identity matrix for view matrix
IDENTITY(m_mView3D);

// clipping plane values
SetClippingPlanes(0.1f, 1000.0f);
```

```
      // initialize shader stuff
      PrepareShaderStuff();

      // build default shader with ID=0
      if (m_bUseShaders) {
         const char BaseShader[] =
            "vs.1.1                    \n"\
            "dcl_position0 v0          \n"\
            "dcl_normal0   v3          \n"\
            "dcl_texcoord0 v6          \n"\
            "dp4 oPos.x, v0, c0        \n"\
            "dp4 oPos.y, v0, c1        \n"\
            "dp4 oPos.z, v0, c2        \n"\
            "dp4 oPos.w, v0, c3        \n"\
            "mov oD0, c4               \n"
            "mov oT0, v6               \n";

         if (FAILED(CreateVShader((void*)BaseShader,
                                  sizeof(BaseShader),
                                  false, false, NULL)))
            return ZFX_FAIL;

         if (FAILED(ActivateVShader(0, VID_UU)))
            return ZFX_FAIL;
      } // default shader

   // set ambient light level
   SetAmbientLight(1.0f, 1.0f, 1.0f);

   // set perspective projection stage 0
   if (FAILED(InitStage(0.8f, &vpView, 0)))
      return ZFX_FAIL;

   // activate perspective projection stage 1
   if (FAILED(SetMode(EMD_PERSPECTIVE, 0)))
      return ZFX_FAIL;

   return ZFX_OK;
   } // OneTimeInit
```

I don't want to give away too much of what's covered in the next chapter concerning vertex shaders and pixel shaders. However, as you can see, this function already creates the default shaders that can be accessed by an ID of 0 because they are the first ones to be created with the render device. The vertex shader multiplies the combination of the world, the view, and the projection matrix to transform a vertex; then it moves its texture coordinates into the pixel shader, together with the ambient light from the constant register named c4.

Demo Application Using the DLL

To complete this chapter, I've included a demo application. I used the one from Chapter 3 here, so not much needs changing. This is because most of the new settings are taken care of by the ZFXD3D::OneTimeInit function. So, the application does not need to change anything except for using the new features, such as rendering something provided by the render device.

In the following paragraph, I point out only the major changes in the demo application. You can figure out the rest of the code from the CD-ROM.

Multiple Windows with Multiple Viewports

To demonstrate the capabilities of the engine, we will change the demo application to crank up the render device and demonstrate a lot of functionality. Therefore, we'll create four child windows in the main window that are all reported as render windows to the render device, just as we did in Chapter 3. Additionally, we'll create two stages to have two different viewports:

```
ZFXVIEWPORT rc = { 750, 50, 480, 360 };
g_pDevice->InitStage(0.8f, NULL, 0);
g_pDevice->InitStage(0.8f, &rc, 1);
```

The first stage uses the whole screen as the viewport. The second stage uses the same projection field of view angle, but with a viewport sitting in the upper-right corner of the screen.

The new ProgramTick() function is called once each frame to render some objects:

```
HRESULT ProgramTick(void)
    {
    ZFXMatrix mWorld;
    mWorld.Identity();

    // activate first viewport
    g_pDevice->SetMode(EMD_PERSPECTIVE, 0);
    g_pDevice->SetClearColor(0.7f,0.7f,1.0f);

    // clear buffer and start scene
    g_pDevice->BeginRendering(true,true,true);
```

```
   // RENDER-CALLS

// activate second viewport
g_pDevice->SetMode(EMD_PERSPECTIVE, 1);
g_pDevice->SetClearColor(1.0f,0.2f,0.2f);
g_pDevice->Clear(true,true,true);

   // RENDER-CALLS

g_pDevice->EndRendering();
return ZFX_OK;
} // Tick
```

This function sets the first stage where the viewport spans the entire client area. By calling the `BeginRendering()` function, it then clears the contents of the back buffer and starts the scene. It follows this with some render function calls that render a model into this first viewport. Then, the second viewport, which is located in the upper-right corner, is activated. We also need to clear this one to get rid of the pixels sitting in this back buffer. Next, some render calls are rendering into this viewport. Stopping the scene is unnecessary, as you can see.

This function should demonstrate how you can render to different viewports. If you start your window in full-screen mode, you can have as many viewports as you like. But if you start in windowed mode, you can have as many child windows from the operating system as you want and each one can contain as many viewports as you wish.

Next, I want to show you how you can switch between different render windows in the ZFXEngine:

```
int WINAPI WinMain(HINSTANCE hInst, HINSTANCE hPrevInstance,
                   LPSTR lpCmdLine, int nCmdShow)
   {
   [...]

   ZFXVector vR(1,0,0), vU(0,1,0), vD(0,0,1), vP(0,0,0);

   // main loop
   while (!g_bDone) {

      while (PeekMessage(&msg, NULL, 0, 0, PM_REMOVE))
         {
         TranslateMessage(&msg);
         DispatchMessage(&msg);
```

```
            }

    // calculate a frame
    if (g_bIsActive) {

        g_pDevice->UseWindow(0);
        g_pDevice->SetView3D(vR,vU,vD,vP);
        ProgramTick();

        g_pDevice->UseWindow(1);
        g_pDevice->SetView3D(vU*-1.0f,vR,vD,vP);
        ProgramTick();

        g_pDevice->UseWindow(2);
        g_pDevice->SetView3D(vR*-1.0f,vU*-1,vD,vP);
        ProgramTick();

        g_pDevice->UseWindow(3);
        g_pDevice->SetView3D(vU,vR*-1,vD,vP);
        ProgramTick();
        } // if
    } // while

[...]
} // WinMain
```

In the main loop, you switch through all four child windows. You render the same scene into the different windows, so that you are not confused by different scenes and models and can concentrate on the settings for the render device. To prevent this from being too boring, the view is rolled by an additional 90 degrees for each of the four views.

Simple Geometry Loader

With these few changes to the demo application from Chapter 3, you can now test the full power of the ZFXEngine and its render device. This alone would be boring, right? Now it's time to actually see something on the screen other than just a blinking color. The following is a model file loader that loads a 3D model from a custom model format of mine and renders it to the screen using the ZFXEngine. Here is the class declaration:

```
class ZFXModel
    {
    protected:
        ZFXRenderDevice *m_pDevice;
```

```
        UINT    m_nNumSkins;
        UINT    *m_pSkins;
        UINT    m_nNumVertices;
        VERTEX  *m_pVertices;
        UINT    m_nNumIndices;
        WORD    *m_pIndices;
        UINT    *m_pCount;     // indices per material
        UINT    *m_pBufferID;  // static buffer
        FILE    *m_pFile;
        FILE    *m_pLog;
        bool    m_bReady;

        void ReadFile(void);

    public:
        ZFXModell(const char *chFile, ZFXRenderDevice *pDevice, FILE *pLog);
        ~ZFXModell(void);

        HRESULT Render(bool bStatic);
    };
```

In addition to a constructor to initialize things and a render function to render the model, no functionality exists in this class. It just reads in the data from a specific file format and creates vertex and index lists from that data. This class is indeed pretty ugly, and I implemented it in about 1 hour because I was watching TV while doing so.

The only purpose of this class is to make the demo of this application look more interesting. I already got questions from readers who wanted to know which model editors support this file or model format and how they can build their own models in this format. Do me a favor and commit the source code to this model loader to memory and forget about the specification of it. I already did.

I created the sample models for this demo using AC3D with a custom exporter to my s3d format, which I just specified for this chapter. The format is defined in a way that lets me write the data to it and read it out as linearly and as easily as possible. A real file format would have other needs than simplicity, which is why you should not focus on the format in this demo. Please focus on the code of the engine and how the engine is used by the application.

Nonetheless, the entire source code for the model loader can be found on the CD-ROM accompanying this book.

One Look Back, Two Steps Forward

If you got the impression that this chapter would last forever, forgive me.

You have seen a lot of details you won't find in other books. These point out performance optimizations at each stage of this chapter. I hope I made you think about each polygon you use to render, so that now you will ask yourself whether it is really necessary to draw it and if it is drawn in the best (meaning fastest) way possible.

We switch gears for the rest of book and no longer use Direct3D directly. We have what we need, and now everything we want to bring onscreen will use our own render device, the ZFXEngine. From looking at the demo application in this chapter, you will see that you won't have to do much to get the ZFXEngine up and running and that even rendering a model is not a complex task. The engine takes care of most low-level function calls. In this chapter, you created a render device of a sample engine and implemented it using Direct3D in a total encapsulation. Thus, having the DirectX SDK installed is no longer necessary for those developing applications using this engine.

Well, there are two more chapters dealing with DirectX. Chapter 10, "The Audio Interface of the Engine," introduces DirectMusic, and Chapter 9, "The Input Interface of the Engine," the other uses of DirectInput. But regarding our visual outputs we won't talk about DirectGraphics or Direct3D anymore. The next chapter introduces you to programming vertex shaders and pixel shaders.

CHAPTER 7

3D Pipelines and Shaders

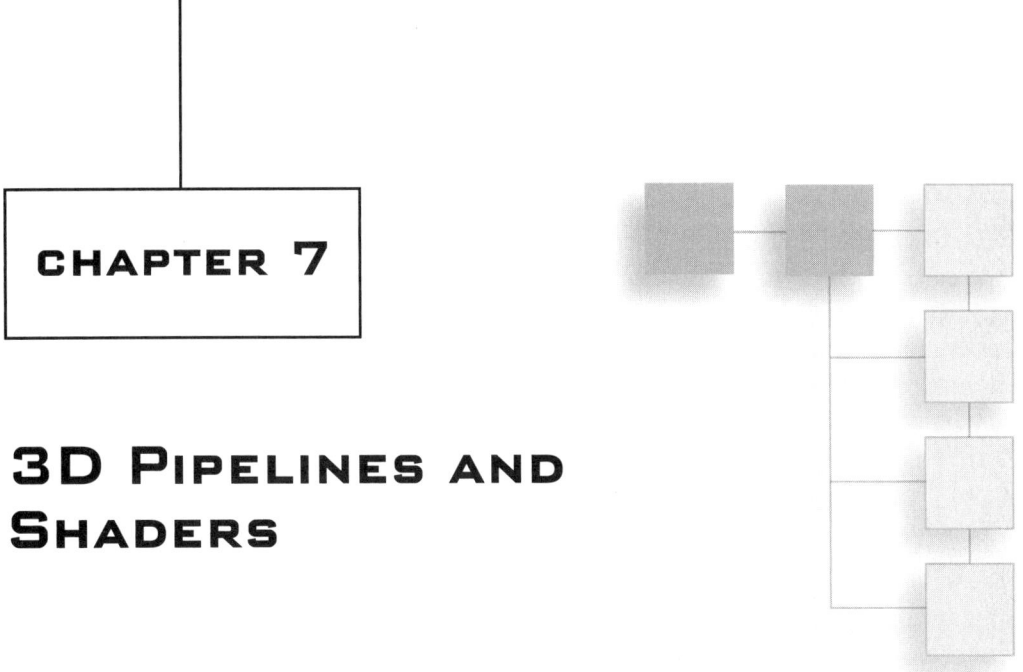

Injustice is backed up by indifference.

H. M. Murdock, Golf-Ball Liberation Army

This chapter covers the topic of shaders. The term *shader* itself is somewhat misleading because vertex shaders have nothing to do with actually shading anything. Simply put, a vertex shader is used to replace the 3D pipeline to manipulate the vertex by transforming and projecting it. A pixel shader is then used to manipulate the color of a pixel the graphics adapter created while rasterizing the primitive. So, perhaps, there is indeed a bit of shading involved.

However, OpenGL uses a better name for the same tool, at least as far as vertex shaders are concerned. OpenGL calls them *vertex programs*, which is closer to the truth. OpenGL calls pixel shaders *fragment programs*, referring to that fragment of a primitive that is processed. Beyond the terms and different naming conventions, you just need to know that you can use shaders with Direct3D and OpenGL. This chapter, however, concentrates on working with Direct3D shaders.

This chapter covers the following objectives:

- The 3D pipeline, operations from the program down to the pixel
- Applications, CPU limited or GPU limited
- Building vertex and pixel shaders from scratch
- Developing some sample chapters
- Performing point light attenuation per pixel
- Calculating tangent space and bump mapping

Shader Basics

Vertex shaders and pixel shaders can be explained easily. In general, shaders are programs that run directly on the graphics processing unit (GPU). In other words, a shader is similar to an assembler program, which enables you to issue instructions to a central processing unit (CPU). In fact, the shader assembly language is very similar to programming assembler. Chapter 4, "Fast 3D Calculus," discussed a special form of assembler called Streaming SIMD Extensions (SSE). You can think of shader programming as a special form of assembler, too, one that is meant to run on the GPU. Simply put, you can program the CPU by using assembler, and you can program the GPU by using vertex and pixel shaders.

Be aware, however, that a few limitations apply, limiting our ability to control the whole 3D pipeline sitting on the graphics adapter. A vertex shader and a pixel shader are used only on certain spots in the 3D pipeline, meaning that certain other parts of the graphics rendering process are still not accessible on current graphics hardware. With each new shader version, however, more features are introduced that further enable shaders to replace more parts of fixed-function pipelines.

3D Pipeline

Now it's about time to talk about the 3D pipeline itself, which means answering the question of what happens to the geometry after you send it to the graphics adapter as lists of vertices and indices. Figure 7.1 shows an image of a 3D pipeline. At the beginning of the pipeline, there is some input in the form of vertex data. This input is sent to the vertex shader if there is one active. If a vertex shader is not active, the input is sent to the transformation and lighting engine, or TnL for short. The TnL is the built-in capability of the graphics adapter to transform the vertex data and calculate the lighting of the vertices. If the hardware is not able to do this, Direct3D will take care of it for us.

Some years ago, a hardware TnL engine on the graphics adapter provided a great boost in speed as compared to the standard TnL done in software up to that point. Today, every graphics adapter should be able to perform TnL functions. This TnL engine is said to be part of the so-called fixed-function pipeline (as opposed to a flexible pipeline). The fixed-function pipeline got its name from the fact that the programmer can set variables to the hardware influencing the outcome of only some of the calculations. This limitation represents a restriction in that there is no free access to the graphics hardware (to write new functions, for example). In contrast, a flexible pipeline in which shaders are used enables you to directly access the GPU instructions and apply any function to the data you can express with a shader as a mathematical formula.

Okay, now let's get back to the movement of the data. The next step for the data during processing in the 3D pipeline is the viewport transformation and the clipping to the viewport size. As mentioned in Chapter 6, "The Render Device of the Engine," the viewport coordinates run from −1.0f to 1.0f, and all projected vertices with greater or smaller coordinates are lying outside the viewport and therefore will be clipped.

The next step also differentiates between the fixed-function pipeline with the so-called multitexturing unit and the flexible pipeline using a pixel shader. This step calculates the current color of the pixel, taking texture colors and per-pixel lighting in pixel shaders into consideration. After this, the 3D pipeline applies the fog color to this color if any fog is active. Only after this are a few tests performed on the pixel (for instance, the alpha test, the stencil test, and the depth test). If the pixel manages to get through all these tests in one piece, the pixel is then blended to the frame buffer.

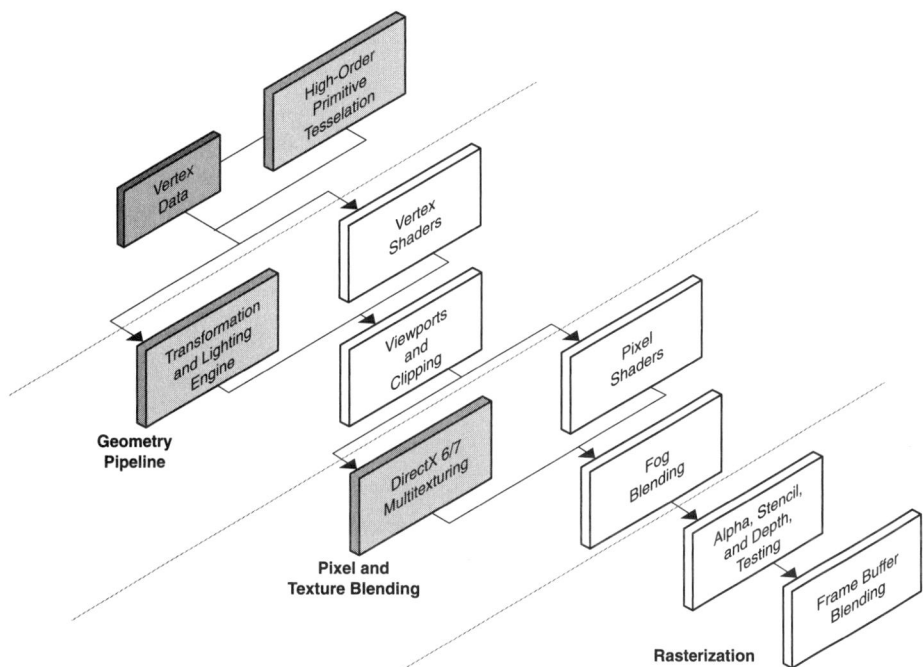

Figure 7.1 The 3D pipeline of Direct3D. (Image courtesy of Microsoft)

In brief, a fixed-function pipeline consists of two elements: the TnL engine and the multitexturing unit. A flexible pipeline replaces those two elements with their respective counterparts: the vertex shader and the pixel shader. As Figure 7.1 shows, the shaders totally replace their counterparts: If you activate a vertex shader, the TnL engine will be switched off; if you use a pixel shader, the multitexturing unit will be switched off. Therefore, if you want to use a vertex shader, for instance, you have to do all the transformations and all the lighting yourself in the vertex shader. There is no way to do just a bit of vertex shading and let the TnL do some of the work, too.

The same applies for the multitexturing unit with respect to the pixel shader. If you use a pixel shader, you must calculate the color of the pixel on your own, including calculating color values from multiple textures into a single color for the pixel. Don't be scared, however; it is not too difficult.

Figure 7.1 shows even more. At most, only one vertex shader can be active. (The same is true of pixel shaders; only one can be active.) There is no way to combine several vertex shaders or pixel shaders in a chain or something like that. There is also no direct way to communicate between a vertex shader and a pixel shader. You can send some data to the pixel shader (for instance, texture coordinates and the like), of course, but only by sending it through the 3D pipeline. It is also impossible to send any data back from the shaders to the application. The 3D pipeline is like a one-way street that ends on the back buffer for valid pixels or in "pixel heaven" for clipped pixels.

Note

As you can see, the 3D pipeline does clipping only in 2D viewport space. That means all primitives are transformed and rasterized before the graphics adapter checks whether they are visible at all. Therefore, clipping or culling in 3D world space is much faster because the graphics adapter doesn't have to transform objects that are not visible at all.

As a final note, remember that some graphics adapters don't have a real fixed-function pipeline anymore. Some just use a built-in shader to emulate a fixed-function pipeline. As you may guess, such shaders must be rather general to deal with all the render state settings. In any case, you should use your own customized shaders that can be specific and therefore perform more efficiently.

Applications, CPU Limited or GPU Limited

Imagine for a moment that you have programmed an important application that uses 3D graphics, one that is not too complex. Imagine further that when you run the application, it runs incredibly slowly. Many reasons may cause an application to run slowly, but all of these potential reasons individually fit into one of two general categories: CPU limited or GPU limited.

CPU limited means that the CPU is doing a lot of work by calculating data and sending it over the bus. Meanwhile, the GPU just idles. In such a scenario, you are ignoring the capabilities of your graphics adapter; in such a scenario, it's fair to say that the application is CPU limited. In this case, you could render some additional 10,000 triangles from the virtual rapid access memory (VRAM) of the graphics adapter without slowing down the frame rate even more. This would result in no impact on the speed because now the GPU would have some work to do while the CPU is still busy.

Some would argue, perhaps, that they own a top-notch graphics adapter and therefore it's fine to just let it do all the dirty work. They perform no culling or clipping calculations on the CPU, but instead render all the data from the VRAM in a brute-force manner. In this scenario, the application will not run any faster. Instead, the GPU is rotating all the time, working hard to comply, while the CPU is just hanging around there being busy doing nothing. In such a scenario, rendering just a few triangles more will bring down the frame rate even more. Your application is therefore GPU limited.

The bottleneck in the GPU-limited scenario could be an overloaded shader. The more instructions and calculations a shader has to perform, the slower it gets. Each vertex shader is run for each vertex, of course, and this shader as well as the TnL of the fixed-function pipeline can become the bottleneck of the application if there are too many vertices. Each pixel shader is run for each pixel from each primitive. Note that the depth buffer check is performed after this calculation has already taken place. Therefore, the fill rate for all those pixels can also be the bottleneck of the application.

Tip

It is hard to detect the exact bottleneck of an application because normally several things are slowing down the application at the same time. If the fill rate is the problem, however, you can evaluate such by using a smaller screen resolution. If the frame rate increases, the fill rate has been the problem (because the frame rate increase means that now each primitive will be rasterized to fewer pixels). If changing the resolution does not influence the frame rate at all, the fill rate has not been an issue. If you are CPU-limited, then a profiler tool could help you find the bottlenecks in your application.

Overusing Shaders

Since the advent of shaders in the computer graphics arena, people have tended to overly rely on shaders as they try to make use of the brand new top-notch graphics adapters. Two examples of this are work with character animation, which is discussed in the next chapter, and shadow volumes, which are covered later in this book. Both deal heavily with vertex data and require lots of calculations. Because all those calculations are done on a vertex level, you can just use a vertex shader and let the top-notch GPU take care of all the calculations.

By doing so, however, you may end up in a situation where your graphics adapter has to do all the character animation, the shadow volume extractions, and the lighting and rendering of absolutely everything in a complex video game level. In such a scenario, you are close to applying a GPU-limited approach (if, in actuality, you're not already applying such). In a real video game application, you also need to access the data of the transformed characters in a specific animation step (for collision detection, for example). If the vertex shader does all the transformations for you, you don't have access to the animated data and would not be able to perform collision detection without running the same calculations a second time on the CPU (perhaps for just involving bounding volumes in a rough approach, but still you see where this is leading).

With regard to the shadow volumes, another problem exists: Vertex shaders work on vertices they get as input, but they cannot generate vertex data. A vertex shader sees exactly one vertex, works on exactly one vertex, and puts out the data from exactly one vertex. They don't even know about the primitive to which this vertex belongs. However, calculating a shadow volume requires you to do something a vertex shader cannot do: add new vertex data to an existing model, depending on the vector of the incoming light to extrude the model away from the light to build the shadow volume. Therefore, to create a shadow volume in a vertex shader, you have to add all potentially necessary vertices beforehand. You must add an additional rectangle for each edge of the model where two polygons touch each other. Depending on the polygon count of a model, this can add up to a lot of additional data. In a worst-case scenario for a closed mesh, you need one additional triangle for each edge of each triangle. So the model you need to build a shadow volume from has four times the number of triangles of the original one. This represents a huge waste of memory, because you will always need just a few of those additional triangles.

There is no magic bullet, no one and best strategy as to how to balance your code. Applications from newbie 3D programmers tend to be CPU limited. That said, don't overcompensate and run GPU-only code; doing so would just produce the opposite problem (a GPU-limited application). Naturally, the best approach is to implement each feature in your application to run on the CPU as well as on the GPU, and then test, test, and test again to determine the best way to go for your application.

Don't Switch

One of the most expensive operations on current graphics adapters is switching the currently active shader. Whether you are switching from the fixed-function pipeline to a custom shader, vice versa, or from a custom shader to a custom shader doesn't matter that much. The bottom line is to avoid such switches wherever possible (perhaps by ordering the primitives you are going to render by the shader they use, for instance).

Of course, you still face the million-dollar question of how to order your primitive data. Order it by texture to avoid texture switches, or by shader to avoid shader switches, and so on. This question does not have a general answer that is true in every case, but it's a question that you should keep in mind as you program.

Vertex Manipulation Using Vertex Shaders

The core of the vertex business is the so-called vertex arithmetic logic unit (ALU). The ALU takes care of all calculations that you want to be done with your vertex shader. The

ALU is the heart and the soul of the vertex processing on the graphics adapter. To calculate anything at all, however, the ALU needs input.

This input can come from one of two sources. On the one hand, there are 16 input vectors (v0 to v15). If you use the fixed-function pipeline, Direct3D specifies via the Flexible Vertex Format (FVF) which vertex component (such as the normal vector), the position, and so on get mapped to which input vector of the vertex ALU. Using a vertex shader, you can, and must do this for yourself; now, however, you can freely decide which one of the 16 registers you want to use.

> **Note**
>
> All registers of the GPU discussed here are 128 bits in size. This size is ample enough to allow 4 floating-point values of 32 bits each to sit in each register. As you can see, this is optimal for 3D graphics (where most of the data comes in 3D and 4D vectors).

The second source of input to the vertex ALU is the constant registers of the vertex ALU. They are named c0, c1, c2.... Those registers are called constant registers because they contain constant values (at least from the vertex shader's point of view). The vertex ALU cannot change the data in constant registers. It can only read the values; it cannot write them. By the way, these input registers cannot be written to. So, the application can set the constant registers to any value they want to. Four of those registers can contain a transformation matrix, for example, or one of them can hold the vector of the incoming light. How many constant registers are available depends on the graphics adapter and can be queried from the D3DCAPS9 structure in the filed MaxVertexShaderConst. In general, there will be at least 96 such registers. This may sound like a lot, but a single matrix will eat up four of those registers. In character animation, each bone needs to come with a transformation matrix, so using 24 bones would already take the constant registers to their limit. But still, 96 will suffice normally.

If a human does some complex calculations, he or she will need a piece of paper (or a new WordPad file for that matter) to make some notes and write down some values. The same holds true for the vertex shader, and thus the vertex ALU offers a bunch of temporary registers that can be written to and read from. The vertex ALU has 12 of those temporary registers (r0 through r11). Each of those registers can take 128 bits of data. After the vertex shader is done, the content of the temporary registers is rendered invalid before the next vertex shader's run can occur. Hence they are called temporary registers.

After a human finishes with his or her calculations, that person takes a ruler and underlines the final result. The vertex ALU is doing more or less the same by moving the outcomes of its work into the output registers. There are two output registers used for the diffuse color of the vertex and the specular color of the vertex respectively, called oD0 and oD1. The transformed position of the vertex should be written to the output register oPos,

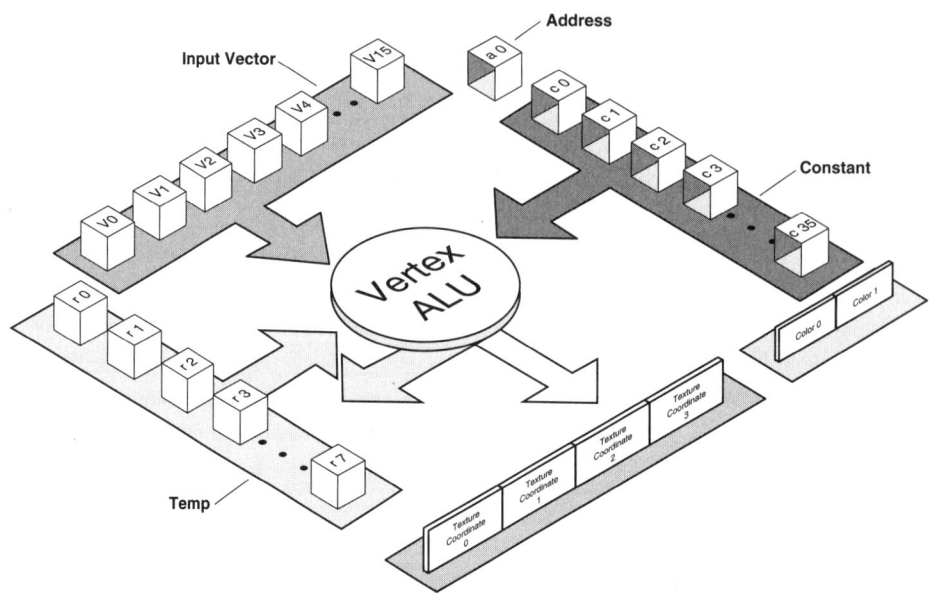

Figure 7.2 The architecture of the vertex ALU. (Image courtesy of Microsoft)

and there are the texture coordinate registers oT0 through oT7 where you can put in up to seven texture coordinates. However, there can be fewer of these output registers (based on the graphics adapter used). The final two output registers can only take a single 32-bit value. The oFog register holds the fog intensity, and the oPts registers will take the size of a point sprite.

After the vertex shader has run, the graphics adapter collects the number of vertices used for a single primitive (three vertices for a triangle, for example). From the output values of those three vertices, the graphics adapter then rasterizes the pixels used to render this triangle. Therefore, the color values and the texture coordinates are interpolated between the output data of the vertices to calculate the final values for each rasterized pixel.

Pixel Manipulation Using Pixel Shaders

Just as there is such a thing as a vertex ALU, there is also an ALU for calculating a pixel shader. Figure 7.3 provides an illustration of one. Its architecture is basically the same as the architecture of the vertex ALU. It has input registers, temporary registers, constant registers, and output registers. The pixel ALU works with those registers to do one thing: calculate the color of the given pixel as an output value. Well, actually it also calculates the depth value rendered to the depth buffer internally.

Caution

As opposed to what most people think when they first hear about pixel shaders, it is not the case that pixel shaders are working as post-rendering processing on the frame buffer. A pixel shader is executed for each pixel from a graphical primitive that is sent to the graphics adapter and that is not clipped in viewport space.

The pixel ALU has exactly two input registers: v0 and v1. Those are the two registers receiving the (now interpolated) content from the vertex ALU registers oD0 and oD1 containing the diffuse and specular colors from the vertex.

The texture registers t0 through t*n* of the pixel ALU are normally used to directly calculate the color of the texture from the appropriate stage, so you won't normally work with the interpolated texture coordinates in the pixel ALU but can directly request the texture color. I write *normally* here because you could as well send any arbitrary data from the vertex shader to the pixel shader through those registers. They don't need to contain texture coordinates.

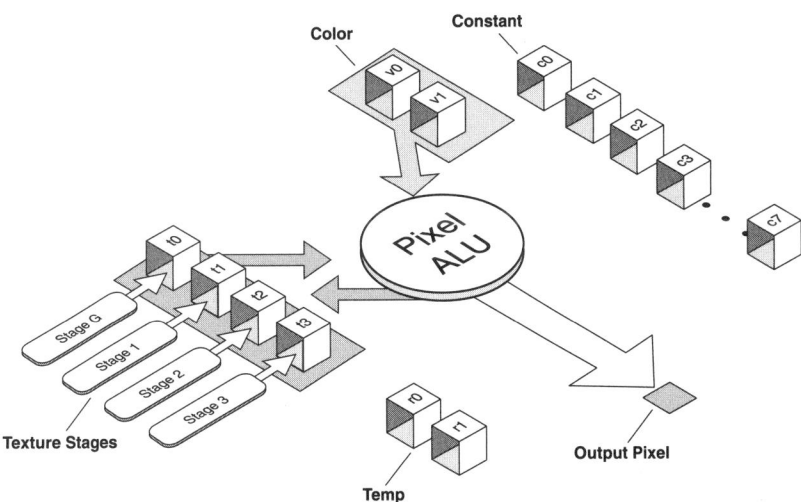

Figure 7.3 The architecture of the pixel ALU. (Image courtesy of Microsoft)

Just as with the vertex ALU, the pixel ALU has several constant registers at its disposal. In contrast to the vertex shader constant registers, however, they can only take four floating-point values, each ranging from −1.0 to +1.0.

Well, now you know a lot about the basic architecture of vertex shaders and pixel shaders and how they relate to the 3D pipeline. Both types of shaders allow for a much greater flexibility than the fixed-function pipeline. All this theory is great, but now it's time to show you a real example of how you can actually program a vertex shader or a pixel shader. The following section provides several shader samples—from basic transformation over multitexturing to bump mapping—to enable you to write your first custom shaders on your own.

Shader Techniques and Samples

Although I'm sure that you have found fascinating the theory of vertex shaders and pixel shaders and why they are good and why they are bad, you still don't know how to actually implement a real shader for your applications. The remainder of this chapter introduces you to the practical aspects and provides you with six real-world samples of vertex and pixel shader pairs.

I must admit that I still use basic assembler code for writing vertex and pixel shader programs, even though there are now several high-level languages out there to implement shaders using a C-like syntax. Such a high-level language may prove beneficial to you later on if you proceed to bigger shaders, but you still should know the assembler codes into which such high-level programs will be translated. These high-level shader languages are still in their early-development stage and sometimes their compilers mess things up a bit. Knowing assembly shaders, you can then take a look at the shaders produced by the high-level language compilers and see whether they do what they should.

Sample 1: Basic Transformations

To begin with, I will introduce you to a very simple pair made up from one vertex shader and one pixel shader that will transform a vertex, including the projection transformation, and will render the triangles with a texture map applied to them. Actually, you have already seen the code for shaders in the last chapter. Just remember the implementation of the `ZFXD3D::OneTimeInit` function. This function was internally creating a character string for a vertex shader and a pixel shader program. Now I will explain the code of this program to you.

Before that, however, here's just a quick mention about vertex shader and pixel shader separation. Most books or tutorials on the Internet start explaining shaders by showing you an application using just a vertex shader and not a pixel shader. This isn't necessarily a good thing. In fact, you should make it a habit not to use a custom vertex shader without a custom pixel shader or vice versa (which would be even more difficult). Some graphics adapters don't even like to combine the fixed-function pipeline with a custom-made shader. So, please don't use a pixel shader if you don't have your own vertex shader, and don't use a vertex shader if you don't have your own pixel shader. Each of the following samples shows a vertex shader and a pixel shader together. That makes sense because they have to work together always.

A Basic Vertex Shader

The following lines are the complete vertex shader source code. If you know a bit of assembler and a bit of 3D graphics in general, there is no question you will understand what's going on there (although I'll still explain in a moment):

```
vs.1.1
dcl_position   v0
dcl_normal     v3
dcl_texcoord   v6
dcl_tangent    v8
m4x4 oPos, v0, c0
mov oD0, c4
mov oT0, v6
```

Cute, isn't it. Actually, this is not the shortest vertex shader you could think of. The "hello world" version of a vertex shader would be much shorter. Because we are all programmers, however, I don't want to insult your intelligence by using this baby-level stuff. This shader is actually not only transforming a vertex, it is also using a texture and some light on it. So let's step through this one line by line.

The first line of a vertex and a pixel shader always contain the shader's version. As you can see, I'm using only version 1.1 here. Later versions add more instructions and different instructions to the arsenal of a shader. (Of course, then you are dependent on hardware that is compatible with the latest shader versions.)

The next lines in the vertex shader program are some declarations prefixed with dcl_. These declarations state which input registers receive which data from the input streams. In this case, we have four data fields coming from the input stream. First there is the position of the vertex in 3D world space, then there is its normal vector and a single texture coordinate set. Finally, the last data element is a tangent vector.

This tangent vector is needed for bump mapping, which is introduced later in this chapter. So that you could use the very same vertex format in all samples from this chapter, however, I decided to define the following structure of a tangent vertex and use it throughout the rest of this chapter:

```
typedef struct TVERTEX_TYPE
    {
    float   x, y, z;
    float   vcN[3];
    float   tu, tv;
```

```
    float vcU[3];
} TVERTEX;
```

There is nothing special about this new vertex structure, except for its support of bump mapping by simply offering an additional vector to store the so-called tangent of the vertex. Hang on a minute; bump mapping is discussed shortly.

Back to the vertex shader at hand. Now we know in which input register we can find what kind of data. In addition, you will recall the combination matrix from the last chapter that is built from the world, the view, and the projection matrix concatenation. The ZFXEngine will store this combination matrix or it is transposed for that matter in the constant register c0 of the vertex ALU. The ambient light value is stored into the constant register c4 by the engine as well. Now about this line:

```
m4x4 oPos, v0, c0
```

The instruction m4x4 is not really an instruction but a macro for vertex shaders. This macro performs a calculation of multiplying a vector in 4D space with a 4x4 matrix. The constant registers are 128 bits in size each, so one register can hold four floating-point values. Therefore, the registers c0, c1, c2, and c3 each contain a row of the transposed transformation matrix. Without using the m4x4 macro, you could do the matrix with vector multiplication as follows:

```
dp4 oPos.x, v0, c0
dp4 oPos.y, v0, c1
dp4 oPos.z, v0, c2
dp4 oPos.w, v0, c3
```

Now dp4 is finally a real instruction of the vertex shader and not only a macro. This instruction performs a dot product operation between the two components listed after the instruction at the end of the line, and the result of the operation is stored into the first parameter following the instruction. After this operation, the output register oPos will contain the transformed position of the vertex.

You may now be wondering why we multiply a vector with a matrix by performing the dot product with the vector on the rows of the matrix and not on the columns as the true formula would require us to. The thing is that such an operation would not be able to perform in a vertex shader using a single instruction. And that is why the matrices we want to use in the shader need to be transposed before we hand them to the shader. This will swap the rows and columns so that we can perform the vector with matrix multiplication as shown above.

The next line in the shader looks like this:

```
mov oD0, c4
```

The `mov` instruction is the very same as the one you already know from assembler programming. So this line is just taking the ambient color value from the constant register c4 and writing it as output for the diffuse color into the output register oD0. You could also calculate a color value here based on light intensity from incoming light rays to perform a per-vertex lighting. But more on that later.

The final line of the vertex shader program is this one:

```
mov oT0, v6
```

This line of code is only moving the incoming texture coordinates into the output register. You could also calculate some texture coordinates in the vertex shader by using arbitrary values. If you use the texture coordinates to apply a texture color to a pixel, however, you would normally stick to just copying the incoming data from the vertex.

So this very basic vertex shader does nothing more than just transform the position of the vertex and delegate the ambient color and the single pair of texture coordinates to the pixel shader. This is really basic stuff, but you could also skip the ambient light values as well as the texture coordinates to keep the shader even more simple. I think you can cope with that one and are happy to see some color on the screen, aren't you?

A Basic Pixel Shader

To provide this vertex shader with a partner in the form of a pixel shader, we don't need to do a lot of work. Look at the following three lines of code that make up a real pixel shader. Note that the first line is again used to name the version of the shader this implementation is using:

```
ps.1.1
tex t0
mul r0, t0, v0
```

Surprisingly short, isn't it? The instruction `tex t0` is used by the pixel ALU to sample the color of a pixel from the texture (called a texel) sitting in the first texture stage of the graphics adapter. Note that the incoming texture coordinates are already interpolated from the vertex to fit this pixel's position in the rasterized primitive.

The last line in this triple is performing a multiplication instruction that multiplies the color of the texel with the color from the input register containing the diffuse vertex color, which is in this case the ambient light from the basic vertex shader above.

The output register labeled r0 is the one that must contain the final color value that the pixel shader wants to set for the pixel. The 3D pipeline of the graphics adapter will then take things over and grab the pixel's color from this register to process it through fogging and frame buffer blending.

348   Chapter 7 ■ 3D Pipelines and Shaders

This pixel shader is also pretty short. However, it is also not the shortest one you could come up with. The texture, for example, is only eye candy, right? So you could just skip the sampling from the texture and just copy the diffuse vertex color into the output register. In addition, you could ignore the diffuse vertex color and just sample the texel from the texture and use this color as output.

The Demo Application

Believe it or not, you have just seen everything you need to make the first test run of your vertex shader and pixel shader. So let's write a demo application that will provide a framework for testing the shader samples from this chapter.

Thanks to the ZFXEngine and its ease of use, we even have the function at hand to compile and activate the shaders. Don't bother with the C style of coding in this application. It is nothing more than just a sandbox for playing around with shaders. Here are the functions of the application:

```
LRESULT   WINAPI MsgProc(HWND, UINT, WPARAM, LPARAM);
HRESULT   ProgramStartup(char *chAPI);
HRESULT   ProgramCleanup(void);
HRESULT   ProgramTick(void);
HRESULT   Render(int);
HRESULT   BuildAndSetShader(void);
HRESULT   BuildGeometry(void);
void      CreateCube(ZFXVector,float,float,float, TVERTEX*,WORD*,bool);
```

As you can see, this application has the typical `WinMain()` function as well as a message procedure for it. Then there are a startup function and a cleanup function. Those two have not changed a lot from the last chapter to this one. The function `CreateCube()` will create . . . well, a cube I would guess. I'm not going to show this function here because creating a cube is not that difficult. Take a look at the code on the accompanying CD-ROM and note that this cube is defined in a way that its surfaces are facing inward (because I want this cube to look like a simple room).

The ZFXEngine is very flexible with regard to the location from where shaders should be created. The sample shaders from this chapter will be written to files using the extensions `*.vsh` and `*.psh`. The following functions take care of creating the shader objects with the engine:

```
UINT g_Base[2] = { 0, 0 };

HRESULT BuildAndSetShader(void)
   {
   if (!g_pDevice->CanDoShaders()) return S_OK;
```

```
   g_pDevice->CreateVShader("base.vsh", 0, true, false, &g_Base[0]);

   g_pDevice->CreatePShader("base.psh", 0, true, false, &g_Base[1]);
   return ZFX_OK;
   } // BuildAndSetShader
```

Now is this easy or not? All the work you did back in the last chapter to encapsulate this whole Direct3D stuff as much as possible is now coming to your rescue. A simple function call to the engine and your shader is ready to rumble. Now, before you start blaming the global variables for being the rogues of the coding world, I want to remind you that this is just our sandbox.

The next function in this sandbox demo application initializes a skin with a single texture applied to it and a room built from a single cube that is stored in a static buffer for efficient rendering:

```
UINT g_sRoom=0;

HRESULT BuildGeometry(void)
   {
   HRESULT hr=ZFX_OK;
   TVERTEX v[24];
   WORD    i[36];
   UINT    s=0;

   memset(v, 0, sizeof(TVERTEX)*24);
   memset(i, 0, sizeof(WORD)*36);

   ZFXCOLOR c = { 1.0f, 1.0f, 1.0f, 1.0f };
   ZFXCOLOR d = { 0.0f, 0.0f, 0.0f, 1.0f };

   g_pDevice->GetSkinManager()->AddSkin(&c, &c, &d,
                                       &c, 1, &s);
   g_pDevice->GetSkinManager()->AddTexture(s,
              "texture.bmp", false, 0, NULL, 0);

   // Geometry for the "Room"
   CreateCube(ZFXVector(0,0,0), 10.0f, 7.0f, 10.0f,
           v, i, true);

   return g_pDevice->GetVertexManager()->
                   CreateStaticBuffer(
                      VID_TV, 0, 24, 36,
                      v, i, &g_sRoom);
   } // BuildGeometry
```

This code doesn't require much analysis. Just create a material for a new skin, add a texture to it, and build the geometry from which to create a static buffer. The only thing you should set is the emissive light to black in the material; otherwise, a white emissive light could influence the color and lighting calculations you are performing in your shader. As of now, no such instructions take the emissive component into account at all. For now just be aware of this issue, but look for such instructions later in this chapter.

The following is the update function of the demo application that is called each frame. It starts and ends the scene while calling the render function in between and writing some text onto the screen:

```
HRESULT ProgramTick(void)
   {
   HRESULT hr = ZFX_FAIL;
   ZFXMatrix mat;
   mat.Identity();

   // Back-Buffer Clear
   g_pDevice->BeginRendering(true,true,true);

   Render(-1);

   g_pDevice->UseShaders(false);
   g_pDevice->DrawText(g_nFontID, 10, 10, 255, 255, 0,
                       "Basic Shader Demo");

   // Flip Back-Buffer
   g_pDevice->EndRendering();
   return hr;
   } // Tick
```

And here is the render function of the demo application. This is also the last function in the framework used in this chapter to demonstrate the shaders in action. This function is more or less the only one that will be changing a bit with each upcoming sample in this chapter:

```
HRESULT Render(int n)
   {
   ZFXMatrix mat;
   mat.RotaY(-0.4f);
   mat._42 -= 0.5f;
   mat._41 -= 1.5f;

   // circulate color of the ambient light
```

```
float fT = GetTickCount() / 1000.0f;
float fR = 0.5f + 0.5f * sinf(fT*1.2f);
float fG = 0.5f + 0.5f * sinf(fT*2.0f);
float fB = 0.5f + 0.5f * sinf(fT*1.7f);

g_pDevice->SetAmbientLight(fR, fG, fB);
g_pDevice->SetWorldTransform(&mat);

g_pDevice->ActivateVShader(g_Base[0], VID_TV);
g_pDevice->ActivatePShader(g_Base[1]);

return g_pDevice->GetVertexManager()->Render(g_sRoom);
} // Render
```

First we are building a rotation matrix and rotate it and translate it so that the viewer of this little scene has a nice look into the room. Then we are calculating the color of the ambient light each frame to make the demo look a bit more interesting. If you would only take random values in this place, the demo would look really jumpy. Luckily, however, we have our three trigonometric friends, which produce a nice smooth curve of values in the range of −1 to +1. So I just used the sine function here to get a smooth change in color.

Then just activate the vertex shader and the pixel shader and render the geometry stored in the static buffer. Now you are ready to run the demonstration of your first vertex shader and pixel shader. Figure 7.4 shows what it looks like. Take a look at this sample program and dig your way through it on the CD-ROM before moving on to the next shaders in this chapter.

Sample 2: Single-Pass Multitexturing

You think this plain old room is way too boring because shaders are supposed to create cool effects? Okay, if so, let's make this one more interesting by rendering it with multiple textures in a single pass by applying an additional detail map to it. If you don't now what a detail map is, don't worry. That is just another texture map that is combined with the normal, diffuse texture map in some way (usually by adding or multiplying the colors of the two textures together). Another name for this is light mapping, but a light map normally contains a grayscale image representing light intensity. A detail map is also usually grayscale, but it shows a structure on it to make the diffuse texture look more interesting.

You'll find this especially useful if you are using a rather small diffuse texture map on a rather big area of geometry and thus significantly stretching the diffuse texture so that it looks like a bunch of messed-up color patches onscreen. An example of this is an area of terrain where a 512-by-512 texture would be used on an area that is 1 square kilometer. To prevent this from looking boringly uniform, you would then add a detail map showing some noise or grass, which is then repeated about 500 times in each direction on the

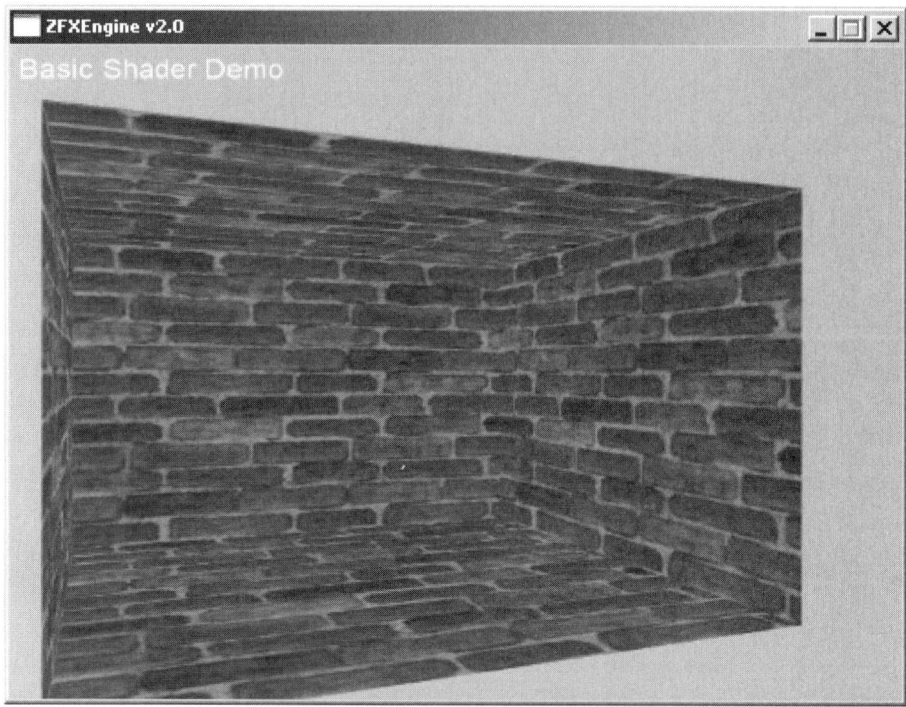

Figure 7.4 A textured room with white ambient light rendered using shaders.

terrain. Simply put, the detail map gives some interesting structure to the terrain while the diffuse map provides variations in color so that the viewer doesn't notice that the same detail map is repeated lots of times (because it comes in different colors all over the place).

Okay, now I want to apply such a detail map to our room. The diffuse texture showing just bricks is also a bit boring if you repeat it several times on a long wall. Figure 7.5 shows an image of the two textures the next sample will use. The left texture map will be used as a detail map, and the texture map on the right will be the diffuse texture map as it was in the preceding sample. But how can you make the detail map put its structure onto the diffuse map at runtime?

The secret is called *multitexturing*. Modern graphics adapters can use four different textures at the same time while rendering a single triangle. That is called single-pass rendering because all textures are used at the same time. This is in contrast to multipass rendering, which is necessary when a graphics adapter can use only two or maybe only one texture during rendering, or when you need to apply more than four textures. To apply more textures, you would then have to render the very same geometry in additional passes using the other textures and blending the output to the result of the preceding pass. This can be done on all hardware, but it is slower than using a single pass (of course).

Figure 7.5 The diffuse texture on the right side and the detail map on the left side.

Multipass rendering isn't discussed here in detail. After all, for this following sample to work, your graphics adapter just has to be able to render two textures in one pass.

Vertex Shader

So let's go. The first thing you need to do is change the vertex shader from the preceding sample by adding the following line to it:

```
mov oT1, v6
```

You should already understand from the previous discussion what this line is supposed to achieve. With this line, the vertex shader not only copies the single pair of texture coordinates into the first texture output register oT0, it also copies it into the second texture coordinate register oT1. This occurs because the sample uses two texture maps, one sitting in the first stage and the second sitting in the second stage (so you have to provide texture coordinates for both stages). Note that now both textures are using the same coordinates. Be aware, however, that you can also put a second pair of texture coordinates into the vertex structure and use this one for the second stage instead.

Pixel Shader

The most amount of work is now done by the pixel shader. But even so, you should still understand what's going on here without too much explanation. Instead of just sampling a single texture, the pixel shader uses the texture coordinates for the first two stages, which are incoming in an interpolated manner, to sample the first two texture stages in order to get the texels.

Again, the pixel shader multiplies the color of the texture with the ambient light sitting in the v0 register where the vertex shader placed it. This time, however, the pixel shader does this multiplication for both sampled texels to modify each texture color with the ambient color separately. The final step in the pixel shader is to combine the two modified colors into a single output color. This is the actual multitexturing step in which both textures are combined. This combining operation can be any formula you want, but most common is the addition or the multiplication of the values. This sample uses multiplication:

```
ps.1.1
tex t0
tex t1
mul r0, v0, t0
mul r1, v0, t1
mul r0, r0, r1
```

If you would have used addition rather than multiplication, you could have used such things as glow maps. If you multiply the two textures together, the pixels from the original diffuse texture can become darker than they are on the texture graphic (see Figure 7.6). If you add the detail map, however, the diffuse map cannot become darker (only brighter). This is what you normally want to achieve by using lightmaps or glow maps.

Demo Framework

There is nothing to change in the demo application source code except for adding a second texture to the skin. Putting the second texture into the second stages is taken care of by the ZFXEngine automatically. You just need to create the new shaders and activate them for rendering. Compare Figure 7.6, which shows this sample in action, with Figure 7.4, which shows the preceding sample. Note the darker but significantly more structured look of the new room.

Sample 3: Directional Lighting per Vertex

Although it is all well and good, ambient light doesn't really produce much of a special effect, does it? All triangles in the scene get the same amount of light intensity shining on them, which is rather boring. The detail map is manipulating (faking it) the light somewhat; still, it looks the same for all the walls of the room.

So it's about time for the directional lighting to float into the room and change the light intensity based on the orientation of the triangles to the incoming light vector. To revisit basic lighting formulas, you know that directional light is streaming from a far distant light source from which all light rays in the scene run parallel. Therefore, the angle of a triangle to this light direction is the only variable influencing the brightness of a triangle except for ambient and emissive light, naturally.

That doesn't sound too bad, does it? The following section shows you how to implement this in a shader. As you will learn, it's surprisingly easy.

Figure 7.6 The same room, but now with a diffuse texture map plus a detail map.

Vertex Shader

This time there is also not much to change in the vertex shader from the preceding sample. However, the changes are crucial and will make this sample look much better than the last one. The application will now have to set the vector of the incoming light into a constant register so that the vertex shader can access it. Then the vertex shader has only to do a dot product between the vertex normal vector and the light direction vector to calculate how much the normal vector is aligned to the light direction. The more it is aligned, the more the vertex (and therefore the triangle it belongs to) looks right into the light. The new line in the vertex shader looks like this:

```
dp3 oD1, v3, -c20
```

The instruction dp3 calculates the dot product for the first three components of the involved registers only. The fourth coordinate, w, is not of any interest in this calculation and is not taken into account. The input register v3 contains the vertex normal, and the constant register c20 holds the light direction vector. However, you must negate or invert the direction of this vector so that it is pointing toward the direction of the light source.

Otherwise, the vertex normal would point toward the opposite direction if the vertex is directly facing the light, and the dot product would produce inverse results.

The result of this operation inputs into the output register oD1, and here you can see that you don't have to use the output register as intended. You can just input any value you want to give to the pixel shader in an interpolated manner. If all normal vectors of a triangle are looking into the same direction, however, there would be no interpolation. In such a case, Gouraud shading would take care of the interpolation.

Pixel Shader

Up to now, the last pixel shader just sampled the texture color for a certain texel and applied the ambient light to it. That was it. Now, however, we have two light values to consider. First there is the ambient light value, of course; but now there is the light value from the parallel light, too. The pixel shader needs to add those two values together because the amount of ambient light in the scene adds up to the diffuse light in the scene, which is in this case the directional light only. Only after this addition is the final light value in the scene multiplied with the color coming from the two textures. Here is the complete pixel shader:

```
ps.1.1
tex t0
tex t1
add r0, v0, v1
mul r0, r0, t0
add r1, v0, v1
mul r1, r1, t1
mul r0, r0, r1
```

You may be asking yourself why you are not already programming shaders (because they're so easy). When you get used to the assembler syntax, it's as easy as eating pancakes.

> **Caution**
>
> The vertex shader and pixel shader samples shown here ignore one important thing: the material. However, the ZFXEngine is implemented in a way that it puts the values of the ambient, diffuse, emissive, and specular reflection into the vertex shader constant registers c1 to c4. To make the shader notice these values, you would have to multiply the final diffuse color for the vertex by the ambient and diffuse color from the material. The specular color would be put into the specular color output register, and the emissive color would simply be added to the diffuse one because it is additional light emitted by the object itself.

Demo Framework

Now we need to adjust the demo application featuring the directional light shader. There is not much to change, but the few changes are important. You should have spotted a serious issue in the preceding shader code. You are multiplying the untransformed vertex normal in the vertex shader with the vector of the directional light. The light vector will normally be given in world space, whereas the vertex is, of course, in its own local system as long as the model it belongs to is not given in world coordinates.

This is like working with apples and bulbs in the same formula, because to get results representing some valid information you have to have all vectors in the very same coordinate system. You might argue that you can transform the vertex normal in the shader using the transposed world transformation matrix. That is totally true, and it will work. Nonetheless, it would be reckless (perhaps even, excuse me, stupid) because for a model with a thousand vertices, you would have to do this calculation a thousand times.

The optimal way is to use only one calculation for all thousand vertices. Or, metaphorically, if the prophet does not come to the mountain, the mountain has to come to the prophet. Instead of transforming all vertex normals, you could just transform the light vector a single time from the world system into the local system of the model. To do this, you just invert the world matrix of the model and apply it to the light vector. Now both components are given in the same coordinate system, and the shader as listed above will work correctly. Here is the new render function of the demo application:

```
HRESULT Render(int n)
   {
   static float fR = -0.4f;

   ZFXMatrix mat, matInv;
   ZFXVector vcLightDir(0.0f, 0.0f, 1.0f);

   // rotate the room
   if (fR < -6.283185f) fR += 6.283185f;

   fR -= 0.02f;

   mat.RotaY(fR);
   mat._42 -= 0.5f;
   mat._41 -= 0.5f;

   g_pDevice->SetAmbientLight(0.2f, 0.2f, 0.2f);
   g_pDevice->SetWorldTransform(&mat);

   // transform light vector to local system
```

358 Chapter 7 ■ 3D Pipelines and Shaders

```
   matInv.InverseOf(mat);
   vcLightDir = matInv * vcLightDir;

   // put light vector to vertex shader constant c20
   g_pDevice->SetShaderConstant(SHT_VERTEX, DAT_FLOAT, 20, 1, &vcLightDir);

   g_pDevice->ActivateVShader(g_Base[0], VID_TV);
   g_pDevice->ActivatePShader(g_Base[1]);

   return g_pDevice->GetVertexManager()->Render(g_sRoom);
   } // Render
```

I added a rotation to the room so that you can see the light intensity changing while the room is rotating and therefore changing its orientation to the constant light vector. Figure 7.7 shows an image of the room. Note the different light intensity on the different walls of the room.

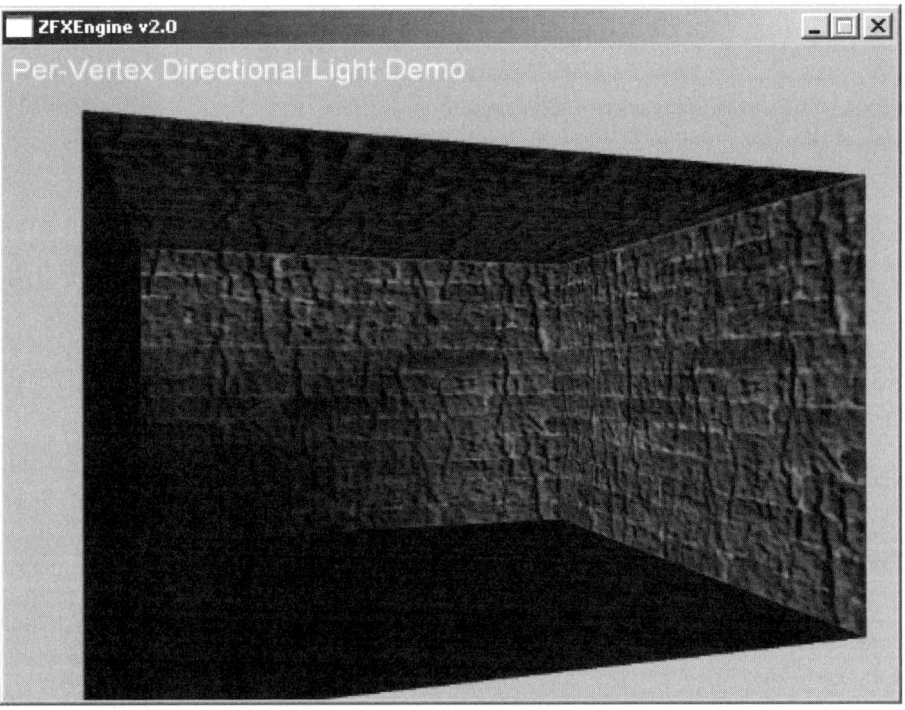

Figure 7.7 The same multitextured room with additional ambient and directional light.

Sample 4: Per-Pixel Omni Lights

Cool. Now you have seen at least some lighting effects done in a vertex shader and a pixel shader. So far, however, the result is not so great looking because we are dealing with vertex lighting only. In most cases, neither the directional light vector nor the room in a first-person shooter level will move at all, so the scene will look boring again. If you have ever heard of shaders before, however, you will most certainly have heard stories about per-pixel lighting.

This section covers how to do per-pixel lighting using a point light source, called an omni light source here (and in most latest-and-greatest first-person shooters). Such light sources evenly emit their light from a single point in space in all directions, thus creating a sphere of light that gets darker on its outer bounds until the range beyond its radius (where it fails to light geometry anymore). This kind of light is actually pretty easy to do, and it looks great. To see what I'm talking about, take a look at Figure 7.8 featuring a screenshot of the sample we are now going to implement. You can clearly see the two bright rectangles in the room, which are the omni light sources. I have removed the directional light because it is quite rare in indoor scenes, except perhaps for some sunlight streaming through windows. Spot lights and point lights are much more common indoors.

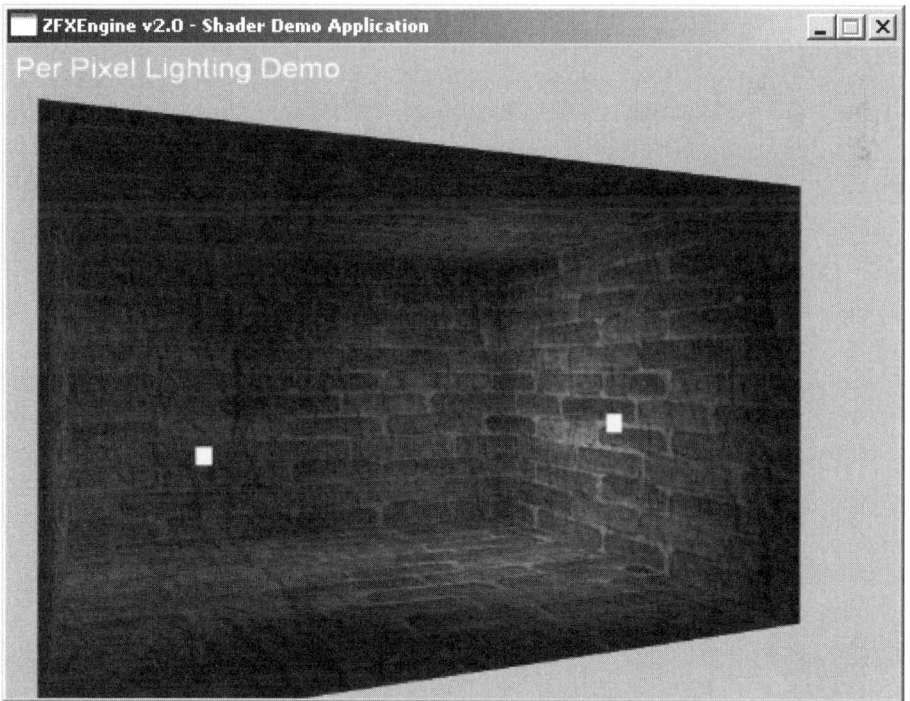

Figure 7.8 The same room again, but this time with two omni lights using different colors.

In the running demo, you can also see that the color of the light is changing and that the light sources are moving around.

If you know your way through the DirectX Software Development Kit (SDK) well, you will wonder what is so special about those moving light sources. The DirectX SDK has a sample called Lighting that does not use vertex and pixel shaders, but instead uses simple hardware lights to achieve the very same effect. So why do we have to make such a noise about our shaders doing the same thing while being more complicated?

Quite simply, the DirectX sample is faking it a bit. When looking at the sample, you could think that this is a valid way to go in a video game, but it is not. To reveal the fake, just switch the DirectX demo to wireframe mode (see Figure 7.9). The big difference is that the room in the DirectX sample is not a room made up of six rectangles. Actually, there are hundreds of rectangles, which are pretty small. The reason behind this is that the hardware lights of the fixed-function pipeline can only do per-vertex lighting. However, this small point light of the sample would not throw light onto a single corner vertex of the room most of the time. Therefore, the light would have no visible effect at all. For vertex

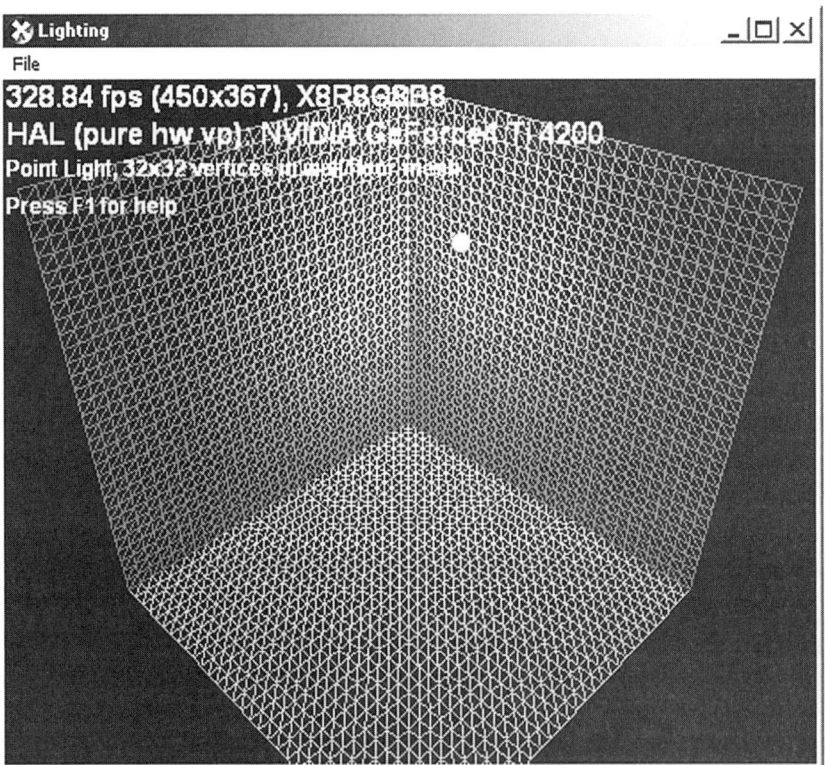

Figure 7.9 The DirectX SDK sample using a hardware point light rendered in wireframe mode.

lighting to look at least a bit realistic, the geometry must be subdivided lots of times, as can be seen in this demo.

Now think of a level in a first-person shooter that has around 50,000 polygons of a reasonable size. Then try to apply this subdivision scheme on this real video game level and you end up with millions of triangles. This is a ridiculous amount of data, which, even in the best case, would slow things down significantly. You would have to come up with an algorithm to subdivide the lit polygons at runtime for each frame in order to subdivide the polygons in the view frustum only. Such an approach is bound to fail, however, due to bad performance.

Actually radiosity is doing something similar by subdividing a scene according to the amount of light shining on a certain polygon. However, radiosity as such is no real-time rendering algorithm, and it is used only in precalculating lighting in the form of static light maps (for *Quake* levels, for example). Another problem besides performance is the subdivision calculation itself, because it is not so easy to subdivide all kinds of geometry without noticeable error.

Calculating the Omni Light Matrix

Before dealing with the vertex and pixel shader for the omni light rendering, you need one more thing: a function for the application using the shaders that will calculate for a given omni light a certain matrix that the vertex shader needs later on to transform the vertices for the lighting calculations. An omni light can be defined by its position and its radius because no other variables influence the lighting calculations. Here is the function that builds such a matrix. Take a look at it (and prepare for the explanation that follows):

```
ZFXMatrix CalcTransAttenNoRot(const ZFXVector &vcPos, float fRadius)
    {
    ZFXMatrix mA, mS, mTL, mB2, mTP, mX;

    float invRad = 0.5f / fRadius;

    mS.Identity();
    mB2.Identity();
    mTL.Identity();

    mS._11 = mS._22 = mS._33 = invRad;
    mTL.Translate(-vcPos.x, -vcPos.y, -vcPos.z);
    mB2.Translate(0.5f, 0.5f, 0.5f);

    mA = mTL * mS;
    mX = mA * mB2;

    mTP.TransposeOf( mX );
```

```
    return mTP;
} // CalcTransAttenNoRot
```

Actually, this matrix does nothing other than move the omni light into the center of the universe. It is doing this by building a matrix that would transform a vertex from its world space position in a way relative to the omni light, and you can think of the omni light as being situated at the origin of the world coordinate system. You can do this by using the matrix mTL in this function.

This function does a second thing, however: It scales the vector to the position of the vertex relative to the light source with a factor such that the sphere of influence around the omni light becomes a unit sphere with the radius 1.0f. To do this, you just have to divide 1.0f by the radius of the omni light and scale the position of the vertex with this factor. You can do this by using the matrix mS in this function. As you can see, however, there is the factor 0.5f involved all of a sudden.

As previously mentioned, inside the pixel shader the registers are clamped to values in the range of 0.0 to 1.0 only. If your omni light influences the space of a unit sphere, the positions inside this sphere would have coordinate values in the range of –1.0f to +1.0. Therefore, you must scale down these values by multiplying them by 0.5f and then adding 0.5f. This will effectively move the values into the range 0.0 to 1.0 while keeping the information inside valid. You can then rebuild the original values by just subtracting 0.5f and multiplying by 2, which equals dividing by 0.5f.

The last thing that is done in the function is multiplying the different matrices together and transposing the information. The multiplication stores all the information in a single matrix, and the transposed matrix is needed only because in this way we can more easily apply the matrix in the vertex shader, just as with the transformation matrix projecting the vertices.

Vertex Shader

Now we have a problem. It is not that easy to run a loop inside a shader with regard to earlier shader versions. However, we want to have a scene that contains lots of omni lights inside, and we have to consider each omni light in the scene while calculating the lighting for the pixels. One solution to this problem is to have different shader versions for different numbers of active omni lights. In this scenario, however, the engine would limit itself to a certain number of lights (just as with the hardware TnL engine and its eight hardware lights). On the other hand, the number of instructions for a shader is also limited, in general, so we cannot write shaders with uncounted instructions. The second option, which is much better, involves rendering the scene with ambient light only. After that, we activate additive rendering and render the scene again, this time without ambient lighting but with only a single omni light active. There are as many additional render passes as there are different active omni lights in the scene. So for each omni light, the scene is rendered one time plus one additional pass for the ambient light.

This sounds pretty slow, doesn't it? But it is not. In the ambient pass, the depth buffer gets filled and therefore the writing to the depth buffer can be switched off for the following passes. Therefore, the render passes for the omni lights don't eat up fill rate to the depth buffer. They just read values back from the depth buffer to check whether they are allowed to render a pixel. More importantly, the feature called Early-Z-Culling of modern graphics adapters can then take effect and save a whole lot of calculations on pixels that are not visible.

BuzzWord

> The Early-Z-Culling feature is a very helpful feature for modern graphics adapters. As you know from Chapter 6, the depth test that removes pixels from the 3D pipeline if they are already behind another rendered pixel occurs only at the end of the whole pipeline. This is not optimal because the pixel has by that point already eaten up a lot of calculation time for texture sampling, fog calculations, and so on.
>
> Currently, and as of the nVidia GeForce 3/4, the triangle setup of modern graphics adapters performs this depth test right after the pixel is generated, during rasterization prior to all other calculations on the pixel, thus saving all further calculation on this pixel if it is already bound to lose the depth test in the end.

If you have a completely filled depth buffer after the ambient pass, the Early-Z-Culling feature will ensure that each following pass only calculates each pixel on the screen one time at a maximum and won't produce any overdraw. This makes rendering additional passes pretty fast indeed. Rendering a scene of thousands of triangles with dozens of omni lights using this method can be done on average hardware in real time. No problem. This is also because such lights don't have a very large radius normally. Therefore, each omni light will only shine on several hundred polygons, so each additional pass is just dealing with several hundred polygons.

So back to the shaders at hand. You actually need two vertex shaders and two pixel shaders for this sample. The first pair of shaders is the basic shader pair from the first sample of this chapter. They are used to render the ambient pass of the scene. The second pair of shaders is the one that is used for each pass of an omni light. Here is the vertex shader for the omni light:

```
vs.1.1
dcl_position0 v0
dcl_normal0   v3
dcl_texcoord0 v6
m4x4 oPos, v0, c0
```

```
mov    oT0, v6
m4x4   oT1, v0, c20
```

Oh no, this is boring stuff again. There is nothing happening that you would not already know. The position of the vertex is transformed using the combined world, view, and projection matrix from the constant register c0, and the texture coordinates are just copied to the output register. Then the original position of the vertex is again transformed, this time using the omni light matrix from the constant register c20. The result is stored in the second texture coordinate output register. There is simply no other way to bring data from the vertex shader to the pixel shader. Note that this transformed position will be interpolated for the pixels of the triangle just as the texture coordinates and the normal position are.

Pixel Shader

Until now I have only used the texture instruction `tex` in the pixel shader to get the texel from the texture map according to the interpolated texture coordinates from the input register. So this instruction is already doing a lot of things in the background. If the data sitting in the texture coordinate input registers of the pixel shader are explicitly not texture coordinates, this instruction is useless. In such a case, the vertex shader puts the vertex position relative to the omni light into the texture coordinate register.

Another instruction enables the pixel shaders to access the data in the register directly and not take values from a texture map. This instruction is called `texcoord`, and the pixel shader for the omni light will use it to access the transformed vertex position relative to the unit sphere omni light. Here is the pixel shader:

```
ps.1.1
tex        t0
texcoord   t1
dp3_sat    r0, t1_bx2, t1_bx2
mul        r0, c0, 1-r0
mul        r0, r0, t0
```

The line containing the dot product calculation is the core of the whole omni light pixel shader. Because the omni light is treated as sitting in the world system's original by the omni light matrix, and because the vertex position transformed with this matrix is treading the vertex position as being a vector from the origin to the vertex position inside or outside the unit sphere omni light radius, the value extracted from the register t1 is a 3D vector from the omni light's center to the current pixel.

Before going on, you need to understand the suffixes _bx2 and _sat used in this shader. The suffix _bx2 is doing nothing more than a bias on the values, which is just subtracting 0.5f from it. The x2 in the suffix means that the value is multiplied by two. So this is how you can bring back the position of a pixel from the clamping range 0.0 to 1.0 to the range

−1.0f to +1.0. Note that the clamping on the pixel shader registers takes place only at the beginning and at the end of the shader. In between, you can store values of this range in its registers, too. The suffix _sat is then saturating the result, which means to clamp it back to the range 0.0 to 1.0. This may seems ridiculous because you just brought the values back to include the negative range as well. But, after all, this line of the pixel shader will multiply the vector by itself and thus effectively eliminate all negative signs of its components, of course. So the saturation is done only to cut off values greater than one, because those would be invalid lighting values in the pixel shader.

At the end of this dot product instruction, the register r0 contains the squared magnitude (called D^2 for squared distance from now on) of the vector from the omni light to the pixel in its first three fields.

The next line in the pixel shader multiplies the value $1 - D^2$ by the value sitting in the pixel shader constant register c0, which is, of course, the color of the omni light. Effectively, this is the formula that reduces the brightness of the light with the square of the distance from the light source. This is usually called *fall off* or *attenuation*. We now finally have the light color and light intensity calculated for the pixel. This values needs to be multiplied with the color from the diffuse texture, and, then, there you are: the final output color for this pixel, which is lit by an omni light.

Figure 7.10 shows another approach that can be used to calculate the attenuation of an omni light: an attenuation map. Attenuation maps are used to reflect the light intensity in the range from 0.0 to 1.0, with a fall off over the squared distance as well. The approach shown above got rid of the attenuation map because it uses the omni light matrix,

Figure 7.10 On the left side, the 2D-attenuation map; on the right side, the 1D-attenuation map, which is stretched vertically to make it more visible.

building a unit sphere around the omni light. Using attenuation maps would involve blocking one texture stage and sampling the attenuation map in the pixel shader. There is a two-dimensional texture to reflect the attenuation sphere on the x and y axes and an additional one-dimensional texture for the z axis.

Demo Application

Now that you know everything there is to know about per-pixel omni lights, you can put as many per-pixel omni lights into your applications as your graphics adapter can handle. You have seen a screenshot of the application earlier in this chapter, in Figure 7.8. In the demo application, however, you must make a few changes, of course. The first thing you need to rewrite is the `ProgramTick()` function. It should look like this now:

```
// geometry
UINT g_sRoom=0;
UINT g_sLight=0;

// shaders
UINT g_Base[2] = { 0, 0 };
UINT g_Omni[2] = { 0, 0 };

// light attribute
ZFXVector g_vcL[2];
ZFXCOLOR  g_clrL[2] = { {1.0f,1.0f,1.0f,1.0f},
                       {1.0f,1.0f,1.0f,1.0f} };

HRESULT ProgramTick(void)
   {
   HRESULT hr = ZFX_FAIL;
   ZFXMatrix mat;
   mat.Identity();

   // calculate values depending on time
   float fT = GetTickCount() / 1000.0f;

   // move light position smoothly
   g_vcL[0].Set( sinf(fT*2.0f) + 2.0f, cosf(fT*2.5f), sinf(fT*2.0f) );

   g_vcL[1].Set( cosf(fT*2.5f)-4.0f, sinf(fT*1.8f)*2.0f, sinf(fT*2.3f)+2.0f);

   // change light color smoothly
   g_clrL[0].fR = 0.5f + 0.5f * sinf(fT*2.0f);
   g_clrL[0].fG = 0.5f + 0.5f * sinf(fT*2.35f);
```

```
g_clrL[0].fB = 0.5f + 0.5f * sinf(fT*2.7f);

g_clrL[1].fR = 0.5f + 0.5f * cosf(fT*2.0f);
g_clrL[1].fG = 0.5f + 0.5f * sinf(fT*1.8f);
g_clrL[1].fB = 0.5f + 0.5f * sinf(fT*2.0f);

g_pDevice->BeginRendering(true,true,true);

RenderLight(g_vcL[0].x, g_vcL[0].y, g_vcL[0].z);
RenderLight(g_vcL[1].x, g_vcL[1].y, g_vcL[1].z);
Render(-1);  // ambient Pass
Render(0);   // Light-0-Pass
Render(1);   // Light-1-Pass

g_pDevice->UseShaders(false);
g_pDevice->DrawText(g_nFontID, 10, 10, 255, 255, 0, "PerPixel Light Demo");
g_pDevice->EndRendering();
return hr;
} // Tick
```

In this case, our three trigonometric friends will not only help us in smoothly changing the color over the course of time while this application is running, but also by changing the position of the two omni lights present in this scene. The function RenderLight() is used only to render the geometrical objects representing the light sources. However, I used only a small cube without a texture for each omni light object, so I'm not going to print this function here. The new Render() function of the demo application is far more interesting because this is where the actual rendering of the lit scene takes place:

```
HRESULT Render(int n)
  {
  ZFXMatrix mat, matA;
  mat.RotaY(-0.4f);
  mat._42 -= 0.5f;
  mat._41 -= 1.5f;

  g_pDevice->SetAmbientLight(0.5f, 0.5f, 0.5f);
  g_pDevice->SetWorldTransform(&mat);

  // ambient pass
  if (n<0) {
     g_pDevice->ActivateVShader(g_Base[0], VID_TV);
     g_pDevice->ActivatePShader(g_Base[1]);
     }
```

```
    // additive pass one per each omni light n
    else {
        matA = CalcTransAttenNoRot( g_vcL[n], 6.0f );

        g_pDevice->SetShaderConstant(SHT_VERTEX,
                                     DAT_FLOAT, 20,
                                     4, (void*)&matA);

        g_pDevice->SetShaderConstant(SHT_PIXEL,
                                     DAT_FLOAT, 0, 1,
                                     (void*)&g_clrL[n]);

        g_pDevice->ActivateVShader(g_Omni[0], VID_TV);
        g_pDevice->ActivatePShader(g_Omni[1]);
        g_pDevice->UseAdditiveBlending(true);
    }
    HRESULT hr = g_pDevice->GetVertexManager()->Render(g_sRoom);
    g_pDevice->UseAdditiveBlending(false);
    return hr;
} // Render
```

The ambient pass is not so interesting because you just need to activate the correct shaders, which are the very basic shaders. The parameter of this function will also receive a parameter that is an index to the omni light that is to be used in this call, where a negative value means that the ambient pass should take place.

If the function should render a pass for an omni light, it first calculates the omni light matrix with a radius of 6.0f for the omni light. Then it puts the variables into the shader registers, activates that shader, and switches additive rendering on. This results in the pixels of this pass being added to the back buffer and not overwritten.

That is all there is to say about rendering omni lights in multiple passes. Now you should run the demo and play around with it a bit. Try to skip the ambient pass from the system and see what happens. The scene will be totally dark, except for the pixels where the light of the omni lights falls.

Note that the omni light matrix expects the light position to be in the same coordinates space as the geometry you want to render later on using this omni light matrix. If you want to move or rotate the room, you must move the light vector into the local system of the room.

Sample 5: Grayscale Filter

If you now think that you can only use pixel shaders to apply lighting effects on rendered triangles, you are wrong. You can simply apply each color operation on the pixel output of the graphics adapter that you can express as a mathematical formula. Such a formula might be as follows:

```
NewColor = { 0.30*OldColor.R, 0.59*OldColor.G, 0.11*OldColor.B };
```

You just take each component of the RGB color and modify it with a certain factor. Note that the factors add up to 1.0f, thus keeping the color in a valid range if it has been beforehand. Some of you might know this formula and guess from the section heading what it is used for. With those factors, you can build a grayscale color from an arbitrary color value. By implementing this formula in a pixel shader, you can write a grayscale filter for your application to render the whole image in grayscale.

For the basic pixel shader with multitexturing, you can add a grayscale filter as follows:

```
ps.1.1
def c1, 0.30, 0.59, 0.11, 1.0
tex t0
mul r1, t0, c3
mad r0, t0, v0, r1
dp3 r0, r0, c1
```

The instruction `def` defines a four-dimensional vector for a constant register in the shader, so there is no need for the application to put values into the constant register. Note, however, that this might decrease performance because you will use this define each time the pixel shader is executed, whereas setting the values from the application into the constant registers can be done prior to each rendering for a single time (letting the values stay there).

The last line in the pixel shader program then multiplies the grayscale factors with the color components. Note that the constant register c3 is also multiplied to the color value. The ZFXEngine will put the emissive color value from the current material into this register, so by adjusting this value in the material you can brighten up the rendered geometry even without having a light source shining on it. Such an effect is needed for the geometry of a bulb, for example, where the geometry should be as bright as possible (something unachievable if you just let the lighting calculations do the job alone).

The sample on the CD-ROM for this section uses the room with the two omni lights to calculate the scene, but it is rendered as a grayscale image.

Sample 6: Bump Mapping

The omni light shaders enable an application to bring very detailed lighting onto flat, nonsubdivided surfaces without the need for helper vertices only needed to make vertex lighting look good. However, there is a problem with this per-pixel lighting type. If there is a detail map or a detailed diffuse map sitting on a surface, the omni lights can create a realistic light spot on that surface, but the surface is still lit as if it is flat, because it is flat. Even if the texture shows the image of a rough surface, there will be no variations in light intensity such as shadows or darker areas that such a roughness would create in reality.

The bottom line is that you have to build your geometry very detailed to compensate for this or you have to use another per-pixel lighting technique. One other such technique is the so-called bump mapping, and it is even supported by all current graphics adapters in hardware for the fixed-function pipeline. This section briefly discusses the concept of bump mapping and shows you how to implement it using a vertex shader and a pixel shader.

To calculate the intensity of light shining onto a vertex, you perform a dot product operation of the vertex normal with the light vector. You can do the very same thing on a per-pixel level by defining a normal for each pixel. The huge advantage behind this simple idea is that the normal is then no longer depending on the vertices and you don't need to have lots of vertices to have lots of normals with which to calculate the lighting. That also means that you can have weird normals pointing in all directions across a triangle. By defining the normals per pixel, you can simulate the existence of a detailed geometry on a single flat triangle.

Due to the realistic lighting, the surface would look like real, detailed geometry. A viewer can see the fake only if he looks at the silhouette of an object. When the viewer is looking more or less directly on, however, the object will look like high poly.

Now the big question is from where do you get the per-pixel normal vector. A vertex normal can be stored in the vertex structure, of course. However, there is no such thing for a pixel, right? Luckily that is not totally true. To provide information on a per-pixel basis, you can use a texture map. Take a look at Figure 7.11. On the top, it shows the diffuse texture map used for this sample. Below there is another texture map that represents a heightmap. This is like looking at rough terrain from above. The bright spots are places that are rather high; and the darker the color of the heightmap gets, the flatter the geometry is in this location.

The purpose of a heightmap is to define how the detailed geometry on a flat surface should look. From this texture map, which is pretty easy to generate, you can then calculate a single normal for each pixel. This is pretty much like precalculating the lighting of a terrain. From three pixels in this heightmap, you can build two vectors spanning an imaginary triangle. Of course, you can then build the cross product of the two-edge vectors to get the normal vector of this triangle, which is the normal vector for the pixel where you started the operation in the first place.

Shader Techniques and Samples

Figure 7.11 The diffuse texture on the top of the image and the heightmap texture below it.

You will see the code that enables you to do this in a moment. For now, let me add that you will then encode this normal vector as an RGB color value and save this value into a texture map. When you have finished this process, this texture map contains a normal vector for each pixel and is called a normal map afterward. Figure 7.12 shows such a normal map. In real-world colors, those normal maps are blue and red toned.

If you still cannot really see where this is leading, consider the two images in Figure 7.13. You can see two rectangles there using the diffuse texture shown above. At first glance, the image looks as if the rectangle is using an additional detail map to put a bumpy structure on it. But look again. The small bright rectangles on the upper-left corner and the lower-right corner are light sources. Now take a look at the shadow on the rectangle and see that it is different on both triangles, being correct with respect to the light source belonging to the rectangle. As the light moves up and down, so does the shadow.

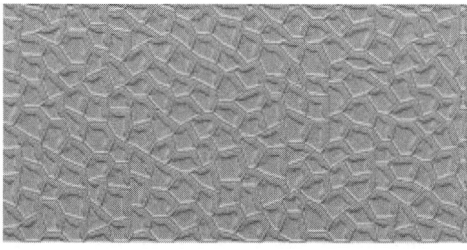

Figure 7.12 The normal map calculated from the heightmap.

372 Chapter 7 ■ 3D Pipelines and Shaders

Figure 7.13 Appearance of a bump-mapped wall. On the left side, the light source is at the upper-left corner; on the right side, it is in the lower-left corner. Note the change in shading on the flat rectangle.

In the running demo, you will see that the shadows give you the impression that the rectangles are not real rectangles, but that there are lots of geometrically modeled bumps on the surface. Awesome, isn't it? With no more than the lighting techniques discussed thus far, you can create realistic shadows on a flat surface representing the faked geometry on this surface with respect to a moving light source. And this, ladies and gentlemen, is bump mapping, which we are going to implement now.

Convert a Heightmap to a Normal Map

As mentioned previously, during the implementation of the skin manager for the ZFXEngine, the following function is in the interface:

```
virtual HRESULT AddTextureHeightmapAsBump(UINT nSkinID, const char *chName)=0;
```

Now you understand its purpose. If you want to have bump mapping, you have to provide a heightmap that represents a grayscale top-down view of the geometry you want to appear on a flat surface. Then you create a skin for the bump-mapped object and add the diffuse texture map and then the heightmap, using this function to build a normal map from it.

After you load the heightmap as texture, the conversion to the normal map takes place. To do this, you must lock the texture, loop through all pixels of the texture, and then save a normal vector for each pixel whose coordinates are expressed in a DWORD value (just as an

ARGB color would be). As mentioned previously, the color of a pixel in the heightmap can be taken as a point in 3D space, as follows:

```
ZFXVector vcPoint( x, y, color );
```

The values x and y express the position of the pixel in the texture map, and the color value is interpreted as the third missing dimension, which is the height of the point above the ground level. Therefore, a color value of 0x00 = black would mean no height at all, and a white color 0xffffffff would mean the maximum height possible.

To build a normal vector for a pixel, just see this pixel as point v0 in 3D space. Then take the pixel on the right side of this point along with the pixel below its right neighbor and call them points v1 and v2, respectively. Now you have a triangle made out of the three points v0, v1, and v2. If you build two edges of the triangle (for instance, e0=v1–v0 and e1=v2–v0), you can then calculate the cross product of those two edges. The result is the normal vector for this triangle, which you take as the normal vector for the point v0. Actually, this is also the normal vector for the pixel you used to start the whole calculation, of course. And it is actually as easy as it sounds here.

Understand, however, that the variable value for the height of the pixel is the factor deciding the direction of the normal, and this is saved in the z component of the vector. So what you call an unperturbed normal in tangent space is a vector in the form (0,0,1) running along the positive z axis. Each other vector in tangent space is called a perturbed normal and leads to a light intensity for a pixel that differs from the surface's light intensity if you calculate the light intensity based on the surface's normal.

Okay, here is the function from the skin manager that builds a normal map out of a given heightmap:

```
HRESULT ZFXD3DSkinManager::ConvertToNormalmap(ZFXTEXTURE *pTexture)
   {
   HRESULT hr=ZFX_OK;
   D3DLOCKED_RECT   d3dRect;
   D3DSURFACE_DESC desc;
   LPDIRECT3DTEXTURE9 pTex = ((LPDIRECT3DTEXTURE9) pTexture->pData);
   pTex->GetLevelDesc(0, &desc);

   if (FAILED(pTex->LockRect(0, &d3dRect, NULL, 0)))
      return ZFX_BUFFERLOCK;

   // pointer on pixel data
   DWORD* pPixel = (DWORD*)d3dRect.pBits;

   // build normal vector for each pixel
```

```
         for (DWORD j=0; j<desc.Height; j++)
            {
            for (DWORD i=0; i<desc.Width; i++)
               {
               DWORD color00 = pPixel[0];
               DWORD color10 = pPixel[1];
               DWORD color01 = pPixel[d3dRect.Pitch
                                      / sizeof(DWORD)];

               // use only the red component from ARGB,
               // shift to the right side in 32 bit DWORD
               // to get it as value in the range 0 to 255
               // scale with 1/255 to get the range 0.0 to 1.0
               float fHeight00 = (float)( (color00 & 0x00ff0000) >>16 ) / 255.0f;
               float fHeight10 = (float)( (color10 & 0x00ff0000) >>16 ) / 255.0f;
               float fHeight01 = (float)( (color01 & 0x00ff0000) >>16 ) / 255.0f;

               // build the edges
               ZFXVector vcPoint00(i+0.0f,j+0.0f,fHeight00);
               ZFXVector vcPoint10(i+1.0f,j+0.0f,fHeight10);
               ZFXVector vcPoint01(i+0.0f,j+1.0f,fHeight01);
               ZFXVector vc10 = vcPoint10 - vcPoint00;
               ZFXVector vc01 = vcPoint01 - vcPoint00;

               // calculate the normal
               ZFXVector vcNormal;
               vcNormal.Cross(vc10, vc01);
               vcNormal.Normalize();

               // save normal as RGB values
               *pPixel++ = VectortoRGBA(&vcNormal, fHeight00);
               }
            }
   pTex->UnlockRect(0);
   return ZFX_OK;
   } // ConvertToNormalmap
```

After that lengthy explanation earlier and the number of comments in this code, you should understand what is going on in this function. However, let's review the important details of the implementation. To build the normal vector, this function takes only the red component of the heightmap colors. A heightmap must be given in grayscale, so the values for each component should be exactly the same. The pixel of the heightmap is then given in the form 0xAARRGGBB so that the bit mask 0x00ff0000 will cut off all bits from the color that are not part of the red component. Finally, this value is then shifted 16 bits to the right side to make the red part of this value sit in the first 8 bits of the variable. This leaves the variable with a value between 0 and 255, where 255 would stream from a white color and means the maximum possible height value. To scale this to a range of 0.0 to 1.0, the variable is then cast into a float and divided by 255. And now you can calculate the normal vector as discussed earlier.

Then, if you have the normal at hand, you have to save it. So you encode the normal as a 32-bit value and write it back to the texture on the pixel you used to generate it in the first place. Because the normal vector is normalized, it is in the range of –1.0 to +1.0. Now you scale this to the range of 0 to 255 to make it a color value. To do this, you only have to multiply the values by half of the maximum value and then add half of the maximum value. The alpha component will hold the scaled height value that is given in the range 0.0 to 1.0. The following function encodes a vector as a 32-bit ARGB color value:

```
DWORD VectortoRGBA(ZFXVector *vc, float fHeight)
   {
   DWORD r = (DWORD)( 127.0f * vc->x + 128.0f );
   DWORD g = (DWORD)( 127.0f * vc->y + 128.0f );
   DWORD b = (DWORD)( 127.0f * vc->z + 128.0f );
   DWORD a = (DWORD)( 255.0f * fHeight );

   return( (a<<24) + (r<<16) + (g<<8) + (b<<0) );
   } // VectortoRGBA
```

That's all you need to do to build a normal map from a heightmap. Tools such as Adobe Photoshop have plug-ins that will create normal maps for you. (However, I like to work with cheaper tools in the hobby arena and build my own normal maps.) D3DX would also be able to build a normal map for you, but I think it is more interesting to see how this works under the hood. Note that the ZFXEngine will save the last normal map created as the file `normal.bmp`, so you can have a look at it.

Opening Up the Tangent Space

The so-called tangent space is an interesting thing. If you have ever heard of bump mapping or using normal maps before, you will have heard about the tangent space, of course, and you will have asked yourself what it is (or more importantly, how to calculate it). You can always take the easy way out and use something like the D3DX library for this calculation. However, even the function of the D3DX library must be implemented somehow so that this is really possible.

To clarify the question as to what the tangent space is, it is even more important to ask the question of why do we need the tangent space at all. In the previous samples, you have seen that you have to transform the light vector into the same coordinate system where the normal vector of the vertex is defined. So the lighting was calculated in the local model space. In bump mapping, you don't work with the vertex normal, but with the normal of the pixels stored in the texture map. This is another space than the local model space. The per-pixel normal vectors are sitting in the texture, and the coordinate space of the texture is called . . . no, not texture space, but tangent space, of course. Therefore, you need the tangent space to transform the light vector from the object space to the coordinate system where the per-pixel normals are stored.

You could transform the normals into the local space of the model as well, but a calculation would be needed for each pixel rendered. The bigger the screen resolution, the worse the performance. Transforming the light vector into tangent space requires just a single calculation per model, so this is preferable.

To transform something into tangent space, you need the three base vectors opening up the tangent space, similar to the three vectors spanning the world coordinate system. From these three vectors, you can build a rotation matrix that will transform objects into the tangent space. Take a look at Figure 7.14, which shows these three vectors. The vector U is called the tangent vector, the vector V is called the binormal, and the vector UxV is the cross product of those two vectors, which is also called the tangent normal. Note that each vertex has its own tangent space. The name stems from the fact that the vectors U and V are a tangent to the vertex. They do not lie in the plane of the triangle to which the vertex belongs.

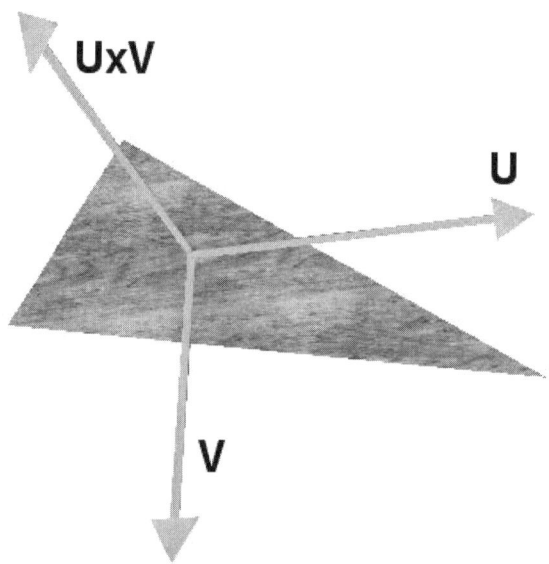

Figure 7.14 The three basis vectors of the tangent space. The U vector is the tangent vector, V is the binormal, and UxV is the tangent normal calculated as the cross product of U and V.

If you have any questions, hold on to them; they'll most likely be answered shortly. For now, roll up your sleeves and pull your keyboard a bit closer. First, you need a structure for a vertex to save the results of the tangent space base vector calculations. The ZFXEngine should stay as independent from vertex formats as possible, so I do not use a real rendering vertex format here. The following structure will serve our needs:

```
typedef struct TANGENTVERTEX_TYPE
   {
   ZFXVector  vcPos;   // vertex position
   ZFXVector  vcN;     // vertex normal
   float      fu;      // vertex u-coordinate
   float      fv;      // vertex v-coordinate
   ZFXVector  vcU;     // new tangent vector
   ZFXVector  vcV;     // new binormal vector
   ZFXVector  vcUxV;   // new tangent normal
   } TANGENTVERTEX;
```

The final three vectors in this structure are the outputs the calculations should reveal for us. The other fields are inputs from the vertex for which we want to calculate the tangent space. Actually, if you want to calculate the tangent space for a model, however, you have to loop through all triangles of the model and build a TANGENTVERTEX object for all three vertices of a triangle. You need to use all three vertices of a triangle to calculate the direction of the increasing texture coordinate values u and v. So, actually, you save the tangent space base vector after the successful calculation in the vertices of the model.

To be more exact, you need to save only one of the three vectors. You don't need all three of them. It would be a very accurate method to save all three of the vectors, but keep in mind that they are orthogonal to each other. Therefore, you can just save two of the vectors and rebuild the second one later by doing the cross product. However, you can ignore even one more of the three vectors. The tangent normal will normally only be slightly different from the triangle normal, which is stored in the vertex as the vertex normal. So, finally, it is enough to store the tangent vector only. Then you can use the vertex normal as the tangent normal and rebuild the binormal by performing the cross-product operation. This saves the vertex structure used for rendering from storing 2 vectors with 12 bytes each. For a single model with 5000 vertices, you save more than 100 kilobytes of memory, which would otherwise probably keep your bus busy from time to time.

But now what exactly are the tangent, the binormal, and the tangent normal with regard to a vertex they are valid for? In most books, you will find descriptions like this: "The partial derivatives of u and v will be calculated in relation to x, y, and z in world coordinates." With such a description, you'll be just as clever as before. Think back to your last math class, however. The derivative of a function describes the change of the function over a strictly defined interval. In bare-boned simplicity, you can say that the tangent vector U is pointing in the direction in which the u texture coordinate will increase along the triangle. The binormal vector V is pointing in the direction in which the v texture coordinate will increase along the triangle. The tangent normal is just the vector sitting orthogonal to those two. So, ignoring the tangent normal for now and concentrating on the tangent and the binormal, you will also remember from your math class that you can define the partial derivatives of U and V as follows:

```
U = [ du/dx, du/dy, du/dz ]
V = [ dv/dx, dv/dy, dv/dz ]
```

The vectors U and V are also called the gradients of the texture because a gradient keeps the partial derivatives of a function or a system of functions as its components. From school, you might know the variables only in the form f(x) and its derivative f'(x), which can be written as df/dx also. The second form describes that the change of the function f is described in dependency of the change of the variable x. If you are in n space with n variables in a function rather than only the one x, then you can only calculate partial derivatives, treating all variables except for one as constants. In such a case, each of the partial derivatives describes the change of the function with respect to a single variable:

```
f(x1, ..., xn) with the partial derivatives:
     fx1 = df/dx1
     ...
     fxn = df/dx
```

The gradient of a function with n variables is therefore a vector field of partial derivatives. Now looking at the texture gradients U and V, you can see that they just describe the change in one of the texture coordinates, depending on the change of the variables x, y, and z. And here is the implementation of this fancy math stuff, which will calculate the texture gradients for three given vertices:

```
void CalcTangentSpace(TANGENTVERTEX *tv1, TANGENTVERTEX *tv2,
                      TANGENTVERTEX *tv3)
   {
   ZFXVector vc, vcA, vcB;

   float fu21 = tv2->fu - tv1->fu,
         fv21 = tv2->fv - tv1->fv,
         fu31 = tv3->fu - tv1->fu,
         fv31 = tv3->fv - tv1->fv;

   vcA.Set(tv2->vcPos.x - tv1->vcPos.x, fu21, fv21);
   vcB.Set(tv3->vcPos.x - tv1->vcPos.x, fu31, fv31);
   vc.Cross(vcA, vcB);
   if (vc.x != 0.0f) {
```

```
      tv1->vcU.x = -vc.y / vc.x;
      tv1->vcV.x = -vc.z / vc.x;
      }

   vcA.Set(tv2->vcPos.y - tv1->vcPos.y, fu21, fv21);
   vcB.Set(tv3->vcPos.y - tv1->vcPos.y, fu31, fv31);
   vc.Cross(vcA, vcB);
   if (vc.x != 0.0f) {
      tv1->vcU.y = -vc.y / vc.x;
      tv1->vcV.y = -vc.z / vc.x;
      }

   vcA.Set(tv2->vcPos.z - tv1->vcPos.z, fu21, fv21);
   vcB.Set(tv3->vcPos.z - tv1->vcPos.z, fu31, fv31);
   vc.Cross(vcA, vcB);
   if (vc.x != 0.0f) {
      tv1->vcU.z = -vc.y / vc.x;
      tv1->vcV.z = -vc.z / vc.x;
      }

   // normalize U and V Vector
   tv1->vcU.Normalize();
   tv1->vcV.Normalize();

   tv2->vcU = tv3->vcU = tv1->vcU;
   tv2->vcV = tv3->vcV = tv1->vcV;

   // calculate tangent vectors and make sure that they are pointing
   // roughly to the same direction as the triangle normal
   tv1->vcUxV.Cross(tv1->vcU, tv1->vcV);
   if ( ( tv1->vcUxV * tv1->vcN) < 0.0f )
      tv1->vcUxV *= -1.0f;

   tv2->vcUxV.Cross(tv2->vcU, tv2->vcV);
   if ( ( tv2->vcUxV * tv2->vcN) < 0.0f )
      tv2->vcUxV *= -1.0f;

   tv3->vcUxV.Cross(tv3->vcU, tv3->vcV);
   if ( ( tv3->vcUxV * tv3->vcN) < 0.0f )
      tv3->vcUxV *= -1.0f;
   } // CalcTangentSpace
```

As you can see, the tangent space vectors are the same for three vertices of a triangle. That implies that the three given vertices must stem from the same triangle lying in the same plane. Otherwise, the tangent vectors for the vertices would be different. So you must not use the very same vertex for another polygon, which also means that a single vertex must not be shared by multiple triangles. The following calculations would then overwrite the preceding ones, making the vertex contain wrong data for all other polygons it belongs to except for the last one where we calculated the tangent space. However, this is just the same as a vertex normal. Normally, you don't want a vertex to be shared by multiple polygons, because then the normal would be valid only for one polygon, of course.

Vertex Shader

The vertex shader used for bump mapping will now finally be a shader that is a bit more complex than those you have seen so far. At the beginning of the vertex shader, there are those standard lines defining the version of the shader, declaring where the data comes from, and transforming the vertex position to viewport space by applying the combination matrix of the world, the view, and the projection matrix via constant register c0 to the vertex position:

```
vs.1.1
dcl_position   v0
dcl_normal     v3
dcl_texcoord   v7
dcl_tangent    v8
m4x4 oPos, v0, c0
```

Now you have to take into consideration again that all vectors you want to use in a certain calculation need to be represented in the same coordinate system. It does not matter which coordinate space you are using (the world space, the model space, or the tangent space). However, it is recommendable to use the space where you would have to do not so many transformations. In the case of bump mapping, it would be difficult to bring the normals from the normal map to another space than the tangent space in which they are already defined. As for the vertex normal and the vertex tangent, they are given in local object space so we transform to the world space by applying the transposed world matrix sitting in the constant register c31, as follows:

```
m3x3 r5.xyz, v8, c31    ; rotate tangent (U)
mov  r5.w, c30.w
m3x3 r7.xyz, v3, c31    ; rotate vertex normal
mov  r7.w, c30.w
```

Take care, though, because direction vectors must not be translated, but just rotated. You can do this by using the m3x3 macro, which will only multiply the 3 × 3 rotational part of the matrix, ignoring the translation vector now sitting in the fourth column of the matrix.

The rotated vectors are saved to the temporary registers r5 and r7 using the .xyz suffix to indicate that only the first three values of the vector result from the multiplication with the matrix. The fourth component of the two vectors is then set manually to a value of 1.0 from the constant register c30 containing the vector (0.5, 0.5, 0.5, 1.0) as a helping hand. You could also have used the def instruction to declare this helper vector in the vertex shader, but then this instruction would be executed each time the shader is run.

The next step is to build the binormal vector. This is easy because the binormal is orthogonal to the tangent vector that is given in the vertex structure and orthogonal to the normal vector. To build such a vector being orthogonal to two given vectors, you just have to calculate the cross product between those two:

```
mul r0, r5.zxyw, -r7.yzxw;
mad r6, r5.yzxw, -r7.zxyw, -r0;
```

Tip
The vertex shader version 2.0 introduced a "crs" instruction for the cross product.

As you can see, you don't have to execute an operation in a shader component by component, but you can use suffixes to name the ordering in which the components of a register should be used in this operation. Now, looking on to those two lines bringing some output vector to the temporary register r6, you will see that they are doing the exact calculations needed to build a cross product:

$$A \times B = \begin{matrix} A_y B_z - A_z B_y \\ A_z B_x - A_x B_z \\ A_x B_y - A_y B_x \end{matrix}$$

If you have never heard of the mad instruction before, this is just an instruction combining a mul and an add instruction at the same line. First you name the destination register for the result, followed by two registers that will be multiplied first, and finally a register that is added to the result of the multiplication. These two lines will clear things up for you if you prefer to see formulas rather than explanations:

```
mad destination, factor1, factor2, summand
=> destination = (factor1 * factor2) + summand
```

Now let's recap what the vertex shader has done so far, except for transforming the vertex position. Here is what the temporary registers contain so far. All three vectors are given in the world space of the model belonging to the primitive the shader is working at:

- r5 tangent vector
- r6 binormal
- r7 tangent normal

That made clear, the shader now has to calculate a vector running from the vertex position to the light source in model space. The position of the light source in model space is saved by the demo application into the vertex shader register c25. Now the shader calculates the vector to the light source by subtracting the position of the vertex from the position of the light source. Then this vector is transformed to the tangent space using the three-basis vector of the tangent space for this vertex:

```
sub r2, c25, v0
dp3 r8.x, r5.xyz, r2
dp3 r8.y, r6.xyz, r2
dp3 r8.z, r7.xyz, r2
```

The resulting vector is transformed using the rotational part of a matrix built from the three vectors defining the tangent space. Therefore, the vector from the vertex to the light is now given in tangent space. For this vector to be useful in a dot product calculation, however, it needs to be normalized, so the vertex shader also takes care of this:

```
dp3 r8.w, r8, r8
rsq r8.w, r8.w
mul r8.xyz, r8, r8.w
```

To normalize a vector in a vertex shader, the dot product for the first three components is calculated—(x*x + y*y + z*z), which equals the squared magnitude of the vector. The result of this operation is saved in the fourth component of the vector. Now to normalize a vector, you would have to draw the square root from this value and divide each component of the vector by this square root. The shader does the same operation, but by multiplying with the reciprocal square root (1/(square root(x))), which is the very same operation.

Now the shader is almost done. The temporary register r8 now contains the normalized vector from the vertex to the light given in tangent space. The problem now is that this vector uses the range −1.0 to +1.0 for its components, but the pixel shader registers would clamp this to 0.0 to 1.0 when they receive this vector. So again we take care of this by multiplying 0.5 to the components of the vector and adding 0.5 afterwards using the constant values from the helper vector in c30:

```
mad oD0.xyz, r8.xyz, c30.x, c30.x
mov oT0.xy, v7.xy
mov oT1.xy, v7.xy
```

Finally, the vertex shader moves the vector to the light into the register meant for the diffuse color value to send it to the pixel shader. The texture coordinate set is put into the output registers for the first two texture stages because the same coordinates are used for the diffuse texture map as well as for the normal map. To sum up, the challenge for the vertex shader was to calculate the vector from the vertex to the light in tangent space. It's just that easy to express, even if it is not that easy to calculate. We're now done with that one, and it's about time for the pixel shader to take over.

Pixel Shader

After this extensive vertex shader, the pixel shader for the bump mapping effect is surprisingly short. After all, why should it be lengthy? After all, all the calculations are already done in the vertex shader. Now the program has all the information it needs, including the vector pointing to the light source sitting in the input register v0 as well as the normal vector of the pixel, so we can sample from the normal map in the texture stage t1. Both are defined in tangent space luckily, so we can perform operations between them delivering valid information. The only thing the pixel shader needs to do is build the dot product between those two vectors, which will result in the light intensity value shining onto this pixel and which is totally independent from the vertex normals of a triangle.

This intensity value is then multiplied with the color of the light from the constant register c0 and again with the sampled texel from the diffuse texture map. After these three steps, the pixel shader has calculated the lighting on a per-pixel basis as color output:

```
ps.1.1
tex t0
tex t1
dp3 r1, t1_bx2, v0_bx2
mul r0, c0, r1
mul r0, t0, r0
```

As previously mentioned, we have to bring the vector to the light back to a valid range by biasing and multiplying by two so that it is again in the range −1.0 to + 1.0. The same applies for the values taken for the pixel normal from the normal map. While building the normal map out of a heightmap, you have seen that those values were brought to the range of 0.0 to 1.0 to comply with the shader registers orders to be clamped this way.

Finally, the diffuse texture on the triangles is no longer used to fake geometrical details anymore. The only reason such a texture is needed now is really the diffuse color. The geometrical detail is faked much more effectively by using bump mapping, which makes the flat polygon look as if it is really built out of several polygons (based on the change of shading with respect to moving light sources). Diffuse textures with detail maps would maintain a constant look even under moving light. However, bump mapping only makes real sense if the bump-mapped object is moving with respect to a light source or vice versa. If both remain static, the bump mapping is a waste of processing time because a detail map could then achieve the same visual result.

Chapter 7 ■ 3D Pipelines and Shaders

> **Caution**
>
> Due to the interpolation of the pixel normals during the sampling process from the normal map, the vector you work with in the pixel shader is not guaranteed to be of unit length and therefore normalized any longer. Only the later pixel shader versions enable you to renormalize vectors in the pixel shader. To get around this problem, you would use a so-called normalizing cube map containing information to normalize vectors in a pixel shader. Take a look at the DirectX SDK documentation or search the Internet to find out more about those special cube maps.

Demo Application

This time we will also use an omni light in our demo application, but this omni light will not send out a light sphere surrounding it with attenuation, but it will be used to set the position of the light source to calculate the bump mapping and define the color of the light. The geometrical object for the light source itself will again be rendered as a single cube in the scene. Then the actual render function is called. Look for yourself:

```
HRESULT ProgramTick(void)
   {
   HRESULT hr = ZFX_FAIL;
   ZFXMatrix mat;
   mat.Identity();

   // move the light
   float fT = GetTickCount() / 1000.0f;
   g_vcL[0].Set( 2.5f, cosf( fT*2.5f) * 3.0f -0.5f, 1.0f );

   // change light color
   g_clrL[0].fR = 0.5f + 0.5f * sinf(fT*2.0f);
   g_clrL[0].fG = 0.5f + 0.5f * sinf(fT*2.35f);
   g_clrL[0].fB = 0.5f + 0.5f * sinf(fT*2.7f);

   g_pDevice->BeginRendering(true,true,true);

   RenderLight(g_vcL[0].x, g_vcL[0].y, g_vcL[0].z);
   Render( g_vcL[0] );

   g_pDevice->UseShaders(false);
   g_pDevice->DrawText(g_nFontID, 10, 10, 255, 255, 0,
                       "Bump-Mapping PS Demo");
   g_pDevice->EndRendering();
   return hr;
   } // Tick
```

The `Render()` function will now receive the position of the light source as a parameter. This position is put into a constant register of the vertex shader as well as the helper vector containing the constants 0.5f and 1.0f (implicitly set for the coordinate w). The shader also needs to know about the world matrix of the room, so this one is set to a constant register as well. Then the shaders are switched on, and the scene is rendered:

```
HRESULT Render(ZFXVector vcLight)
   {
   ZFXMatrix mat, matInv, matT;
   ZFXVector vcHalf(0.5f,0.5f,0.5f);
   mat.Identity();
   mat._42 -= 0.5f;

   matInv.InverseOf(mat);
   vcLight = matInv * vcLight;

   g_pDevice->SetAmbientLight(0.5f, 0.5f, 0.5f);
   g_pDevice->SetWorldTransform(&mat);

   g_pDevice->SetShaderConstant(SHT_VERTEX, DAT_FLOAT, 25, 1, (void*)&vcLight);

   g_pDevice->SetShaderConstant(SHT_VERTEX, DAT_FLOAT, 30, 1, (void*)&vcHalf);

   matT.TransposeOf(mat);
   g_pDevice->SetShaderConstant(SHT_VERTEX, DAT_FLOAT, 31, 4, (void*)&matT);

   g_pDevice->SetShaderConstant(SHT_PIXEL, DAT_FLOAT, 0, 1, (void*)&g_clrL[0]);

   g_pDevice->ActivateVShader(g_Bump[0], VID_TV);
   g_pDevice->ActivatePShader(g_Bump[1]);

   return g_pDevice->GetVertexManager()->Render(g_sRoom);
   } // Render
```

Because of the changing color of the light, you might not see the bump-mapping effect very well in the demo. This is especially true for pretty dark color values of the light. So to see the pure bump mapping without disturbances, you should skip the change in the color of the light and set it to plain old white instead. Go ahead and start this sample now and play around with it a bit.

One Look Back, Two Steps Forward

This chapter has been a race through topics that can fill whole books, and there are indeed some books about shader programming out there. Of course, I cannot go in depth about shaders in this book because this is not what you came for. If you are more interested in shaders (and you should be as a video game application programmer for that matter), open up your favorite Internet browser and use a search engine to find some tutorials about shader programming.

Many more assembly shaders are out there than just those shown here. There are the high-level languages C for Graphics (Cg) and Direct3D's High Level Shader Language (HLSL) as well as one from OpenGL in the next major release. However, I hope I gave you a good introduction into the topic while enabling you to develop some shaders you can use. Later in this book, I use the omni light shader again to bring light to the 3D indoor levels the ZFXEngine will render.

This chapter also provided a basic introduction to bump mapping, a subject you should educate yourself more about in whatever ways possible. There are lots of interesting extensions to the very basic bump-mapping approach covered in this chapter. For example, there is bump mapping with a self-shadowing term as in the DirectX sample. You should also combine bump mapping with other kinds of lighting, such as omni lights. And, finally, there is the specular highlighting for metallic surfaces and reflections on mirroring surfaces. Actually, you can do an infinite number of effects using shaders, but then you can also break down your application by using way too heavy shaders that are executed on way too many pixels.

And now for something completely different. The next chapter introduces you to the art and magic of character animation—that is, how you can make humans, monsters, and other models move and behave like living creatures. You could also do this animation using shaders, but this is not recommended in general because in certain situations it makes life more complicated. Therefore, in this engine, I will not use shaders for the character animation, but more on that in the next chapter.

Now you should start the demo applications of this chapter and play around with them a bit; try to twist their parameters and manipulate the shader programs.

CHAPTER 8

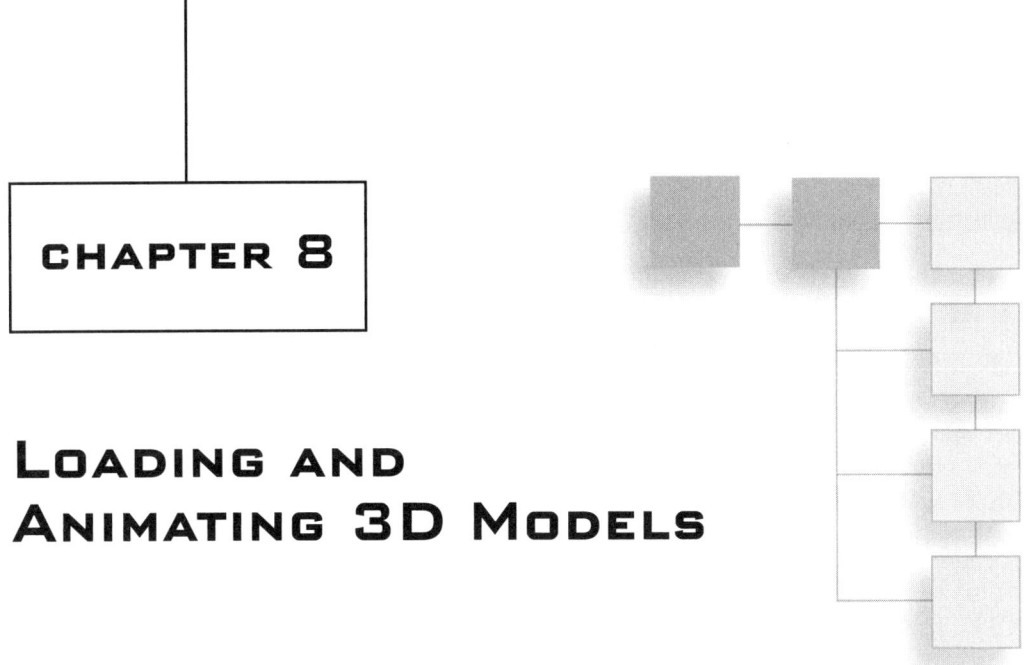

LOADING AND ANIMATING 3D MODELS

Humans overcome obstacles to find calmness and silence. Only to think then that nothing is as unbearable as silence.

Henry Brooks Adams

In the past few years, video game character model animation techniques have changed significantly. In the early years of video games, character and object animation was stored as two-dimensional image files, which were then drawn to the screen as so-called "sprites." As you might remember, games such as *Doom 1* and *Doom 2* as well as *Dark Forces* and *Duke Nukem 3D* used this technique to great effect. In each frame, another image of the animation cycle was shown on the sprite, thus creating the appearance of a real animated object.

Quake 1 was the first video game that introduced real 3D models that were used for weapons, items, and, of course, for characters. On average hardware at that time, the game demanded every cycle the central processing unit (CPU) could expend, and only top-notch hardware could cope with that video game. A technique of key-framed animation was used in which the different poses of the animation cycles were saved as separate models, and during the animation phase the game interpolated between two of those key frames.

Nowadays, most 3D video games use a technique called skeletal animation, which is also called skin 'n bones every now and then. Games such as *Half Life* and *Half-Life 2* as well as *Far Cry* and *Doom 3* use this technique.

This chapter covers the following topics:

- Different animation techniques
- Loading and parsing files (*.cbf*)

- Skeletal animation
- Implementing a viewer for animated characters

Triumphant Advance of Skeletal Animation

Mother Nature took her time, and after several millions of years she came up with an animation system for humans and animals that is indeed very good. Like always, the best ideas are pretty simple, and in this case the system involves bones that are connected to each other by joints. Those bones are moved by muscles and tendons. When you read about skeletal character animation in a moment, you will see the parallels to Mother Nature's approach.

Some years ago, 3D graphics (and all the data that required processing) really shook the CPU. Therefore, the key frame animation system was used for characters because it was faster to calculate (although it consumed more memory). Nowadays, the CPU is much faster and the graphics processing unit (GPU) can do animation in shaders as well.

Key Frame Animations

The md2 file format was used for the first time in the video game *Quake 2*. The animation system used by this format was key frame animation. For an animated model, each frame saved in the file was a certain pose of the model. Actually, each pose of the model was saved with all its vertices; so if the model contained 650 vertices, all 650 vertices were saved for each pose of the model in their transformed positions. Those poses are called key frames.

To put life into the model, the animation was accomplished by looking at the two poses the model was supposed to be in between right at a given moment. Then the positions of each vertex were interpolated from the two key frames marking the start and the end of an animation between two different poses. As you can see, this system does not allow for arbitrary animations defined upon an application's execution. The 3D artist would have to define and save the key frames in a precalculation step. This makes it very difficult, to say the least, to link this animation technique to a physics system.

Figure 8.1 shows a model in two different poses, each of them one key frame of the model. All vertices of the two key frames are saved in the file containing the model. The key frame on the left side shows the model in a standing pose, and the key frame on the right side shows the model in a jumping position. To run a jumping animation with this model, you would only have to interpolate between those two key frames. With each key frame, however, the size of the model file grows by x bytes, where x is the size in bytes of the model without animation.

Triumphant Advance of Skeletal Animation

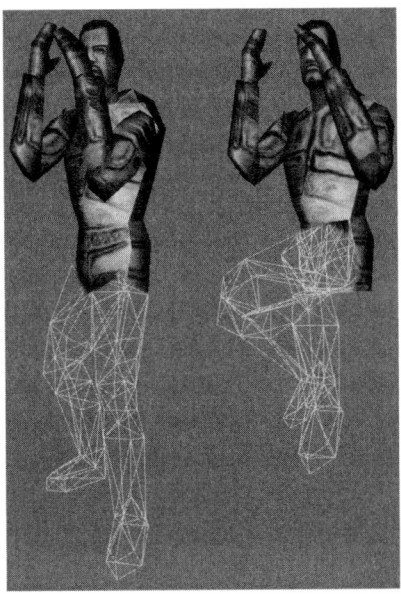

Figure 8.1 Two different key frames of a 3D model. Interpolating between those poses would make the model jump.

BuzzWord

Key Frame Animation

Keep in mind the following attributes of key frame animation, as opposed to the skeletal animation:

1. It is memory consuming.
2. It is inflexible due to predefined poses needed.
3. Connection to a physics system is difficult, to say the least.
4. It is easy to implement.

To sum up, you can think of key frame animation as an ancient technique that is not really used anymore in current or upcoming video games across all platforms.

For the animated characters in this book, I use a custom format called the Chunk-Based Format (CBF), which is discussed later in this chapter. As opposed to the ancient key frame animation, this format uses the more modern skeletal animation, which is also known as skin 'n bones or even as skinned meshes. All three names refer to the very same method.

Skeletal Animation and Skinned Meshes

The idea behind skeletal animation is taken from nature, as many technical methods are. Take a look at your hand. It is connected to the lower arm by a joint, and the lower arm in turn is connected to the shoulder by another joint. Now bend your arm at the elbow. As you can see, your hand also moves, even if the joint at the hand is not rotated. Not very surprising, is it? In fact, you have just revealed the secret behind a hierarchical skeletal animation system. Figure 8.2 demonstrates this principle with two pictures showing this scene.

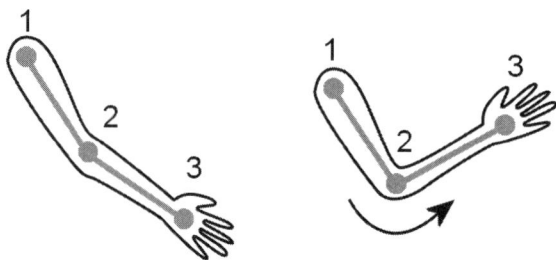

Figure 8.2 The illustration shows an arm with three joints. To bend the arm as seen on the right side, you need to rotate joint number 2 only. However, that movement also influences the subordinated joint number 3, which has moved to a new position.

In skeletal animation, the joints connecting the bones are always organized in a hierarchy. There is a so-called root joint that is the parent of the whole skeleton. In Figure 8.2, this root joint is the shoulder joint number 1. At the next-lower hierarchical level, there is the elbow joint number 2, and on the lowest level the hand joint number 3. A rotation or translation of a joint is always influencing all succeeding joints on lower hierarchy levels. So if you rotate the hand joint, no other joints are influenced because, in this case, the hand is the lowest level in the hierarchy. If you go one level up and rotate the elbow joints, however, this rotation applies to all succeeding elements (bones and joints) in the hierarchy where the elbow joint is the pivot point.

The same holds true for the shoulder joint, of course. If you rotate each of the three joints, the shoulder joint is influenced by its own rotation only. The elbow joint will see the same rotation with the shoulder joint as the pivot point, then additionally its own rotation around its own position. At the hand joint, you already have three rotations around three different pivot points taking place.

So where are the bones in this scenario? The simple answer is that there are no bones.

Bones in Skinned Meshes

The connection between two joints is called a bone (not surprisingly, the same naming scheme used to describe natural skeletons). Nature requires those limy things you build up by drinking milk to keep the joints in the position they are meant to hold to keep the body in shape. In skinned meshes, however, it's much easier: You just place the joint where it should be, period. There is no such thing as gravity or other impacting forces that will make the joints lose their position.

As just mentioned, you need the bones to hold the natural skeleton in its position. Therefore, normally, you cannot translate a joint, you can only rotate it. In computer graphics and skinned meshes, of course, you can translate a joint. However, this would lead to distorted meshes, which is why nature does not let you do this to your own body. Therefore, as a basic rule for skeletal animation, remember that you should only rotate the joints, not translate them. By those rotations, you can model each and every physically possible pose of an animated character, so there is no need for translations.

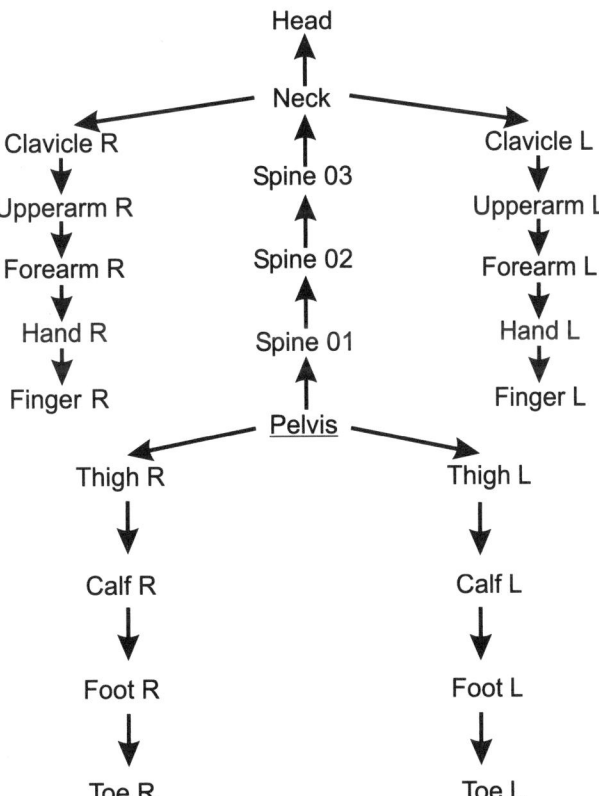

Figure 8.3 The anatomy of a biped. The pelvis serves as the root joint and is underlined here.

As previously mentioned, joints and their connected bones are organized in a hierarchical structure in a skinned mesh. Each joint has exactly one parent and an arbitrary number of children (which, of course, can also be zero). The only exception is the root joint, which must not have a parent joint.

Figure 8.3 shows a biped (well, its skeleton, for that matter). As you can see, many joints are involved, but you don't need to use all the joints for simple animations. Here you can see the root joint as well. The pelvis does not have a parent. If you want to rotate the biped around on the y axis, you only have to rotate the pelvis because the same rotation around this pivot point is applied to all other joints in the hierarchy. Pretty easy, isn't it?

And now you know exactly what joints are and how they apply their attributes to the succeeding joints in the hierarchy. So by influencing the joints—namely, by rotating them—you can animate the skeleton. That would look really good for a scary video game featuring skeletons rising from their graves to rule the world by fear. To make animated characters look more like realistic humans or aliens, however, you need a real model to be animated and no skeleton, right? So the 3D artist just creates the model for the character along with a skeleton of joints connected by bones. Then the artist connects each vertex of the character model with at least one joint of the skeleton.

Thus you know which joints influence which vertices. If you rotate a joint in an animation sequence of the skeleton, you have to rotate the vertices connected to this joint as well. And that is why this animation technique is also called skin 'n bones or skinned mesh. You have a skeleton that defines the animations, and then you have a hull of vertices and polygons that is put onto this skeleton just like a human skin. The skin itself does not really contain animation information. It just defines to which points of the animated skeleton it is attached, and that is enough to animate this skin sitting on the skeleton.

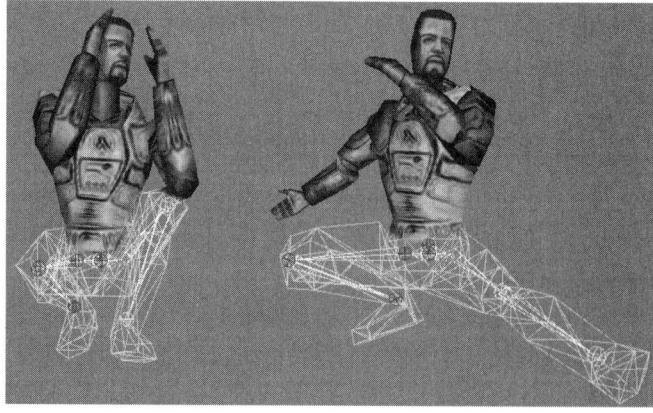

Figure 8.4 Here you can see a model using the skeletal animation technique. The joints and bones can be seen inside the wireframed legs.

Figure 8.4 also shows lots of vertices and polygons for the animated character. Now, however, you don't need to save the vertices redundantly for each key frame position. Instead, the skeleton or its joints are saved in key frame positions. For each pose of the model, you just need to know the rotation value of all joints to bring the skeleton to this pose. Compare the data overhead of saving key frames for each vertex for a 10,000-vertices animated mesh to just saving the key frames for about 24 joints for the same model. Obviously, with the latter method you save a significant amount of data overhead. The figure shows the joints and the bones connecting them in the wireframe legs.

It is of the utmost importance that the model be loaded initially in a so-called bind position. That means all joints, and therefore the implicit bones, are in the exact position that connects the vertices to the joints.

Perhaps you know the position from some screenshots. It's what you can call the Jesus position: The model is standing upright with its arms stretched to both sides. This pose makes it very easy for the artist to select vertices and connect them to the joints without overlapping definitions. Normally, you lay a sphere or cylinder of influence around each joint. If the model were in a position where its arms were close to the body, for example, the pelvis' sphere of influence might also include the hand joints (making the hand joints children of the pelvis). This would result in strange animations.

That should be enough of an introduction to skeletal animation. As you can see, the theory is not that difficult. Now let's start with the praxis part of this chapter.

BuzzWord

Skeletal Animation

Keep in mind the following attributes of skeletal animation, as opposed to the key frame animation of the md2 style:

1. Skeletal animation is saving (virtual) rapid access memory (V)RAM by not storing redundant data.
2. Arbitrary animations are possible, but normally predefined.
3. Connecting an animated model to a physics system is possible.
4. It is more complex to implement.

For the latest commercial video games, the third attribute mentioned is probably the most important one. Video games such as *Max Payne 2* and the brand new *Half Life 2* use the so-called rag doll technique, which means connecting an animated model to the physics system in order to let bodies be rocked by bullet impacts and the like.

The CBF File Format

For the use of skeletal animation with the ZFXEngine, I developed a custom format to let you see the skeletal animation being implemented from scratch. This file format is called the Chunk-Based Format (CFB). To enable you to build your own animated models, there is also a converter provided that converts *.ms3d files from the low-poly, low-price modeler called Milkshape into the CBF format. You can find this on the CD-ROM accompanying this book.

The loader for this file format is a class called CZFXModel, which contains all the necessary information to deal with a CBF model from start to finish. In an application, you just have to build an instance from this class and provide the name of a model to load during the initialization process.

The structures for this class to store all the needed information such as joint data and so on are stored in member attributes of the class. Here are the most important attributes of the class CZFXModel from its declaration:

```
class CZFXModel
{
protected:
   CVERTEX      *m_pVertices;        // vertices
   CVERTEX      *m_pVertices_Orig;   // vertices
   LPFACE       m_pFaces;            // faces
   LPMESH       m_pMeshs;            // meshes
   LPMATERIAL   m_pMaterials;        // materials
   LPJOINT      m_pJoints;           // joints
   LPANIMATION  m_pAnimations;       // animations
   CHUNKHEAD_S  m_sHeader;           // model header
   ... to be continued
```

Of course, there are some more, but I will show you the contents of this class step by step. Be sure to check out the code on the CD-ROM. Note the vertex format CVERTEX, which is contained in the ZFXEngine now and is used for animated characters only (more on that later). As you can see, only the member attribute for the header is a variable. The other attributes are pointers of a specific type only. The following sections explore, step by step, the implementation of this class and the meaning of its member.

What Is a Chunk?

The name CBF already gives away that this format is chunk based. Even if you have never heard of this before, I'm still sure that you know the concept behind chunks. A chunk is just a block of specific data contained in the file. Each type of chunk has a specific identifier that is called the chunk ID, and a specific type of chunk contains a specific structure of data. Take a look at Figure 8.5 to see a file holding two chunks.

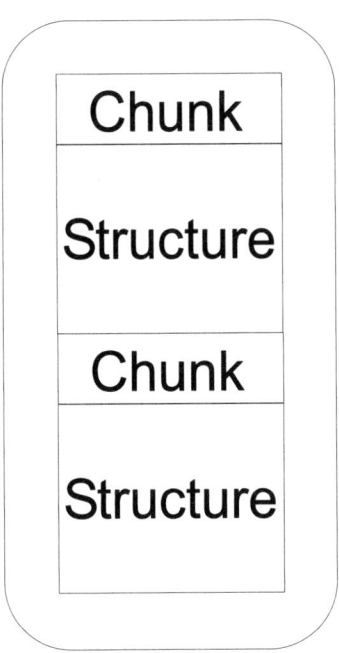

Figure 8.5 This is how the data is stored in the file. Chunk by chunk. Each chunk contains a structure with data or again just another chunk.

The structures inside a chunk can have an arbitrary length. Therefore, a definition for a chunk needs to hold two pieces of information, and the chunk structure itself is just something like a header you know from other file formats. Besides the chunk ID, which is unique for each type of a chunk and not for each chunk instance, a field (following right after the chunk header) holds the size (in bytes) of the data belonging to this chunk.

You can now read a file by reading the first chunk header from the file. If you know the chunk ID, you know what kind of data is following after the chunk header, and you can read the data or ignore it. If you want to ignore this kind of data or if you don't know the chunk ID, you can just skip the number of bytes defined in the chunk header. This effectively lets you jump to the next chunk in the file. And here is the structure for a chunk header:

```
// --- Chunk ---
typedef struct _CHUNK {
    WORD    wIdentifier;
    ULONG   ulSize
} CHUNK_S;
typedef CHUNK_S* LPCHUNK;
```

The idea behind chunks should be obvious by now. You can extract the information you really want to have from the file and can skip contents of the file you don't want to have or you don't recognize at all. This is important if you have different versions of a file format where each new version is adding new chunk types to the file format. The old loaders will then still work because the unknown chunks can just be ignored.

The following chunk types are defined for version 1.0 of the CBF file format:

```
#define V1_HEADER              0x0100 // Header
#define V1_VERTEX              0x0200 // Vertices
#define V1_FACE                0x0300 // Faces
#define V1_MESH                0x0400 // Meshes
#define V1_MATERIAL            0x0500 // Material
#define V1_JOINT               0x0600 // Joints
#define V1_JOINT_MAIN          0x0610 // Joints Main
#define V1_JOINT_KEYFRAME_ROT  0x0620 // Keyf.-Rotation
#define V1_JOINT_KEYFRAME_POS  0x0630 // Keyf.-Position
#define V1_ANIMATION           0x0700 // Animation
#define V1_END                 0x9999 // End-Chunk
```

For each of those chunk types, there will be one structure to read all the data in the correct order, so things are pretty simple. To load the data from a CBF file, follow these steps:

1. Read the chunk header structure.
2. Identify the chunk ID.
3. Decide whether to read the data or skip it.
4. Call a subroutine to read the data if you are not ignoring it.
5. Repeat the process until the end of the file.

Reading a Chunk

The main routine to keep the whole file reading process running is the function to read a chunk header from the file. As you can see, this function does nothing except read data from the file sized as a chunk header structure:

```
// -----------------------------
// Name: GetNextChunk( CHUNK_S &pChunk )
// Info: Reads the next ChunkID
// Return     = (WORD)     next chunk id
// pChunk     = (CHUNK_S&) Pointer to Chunk
// -----------------------------
WORD CZFXModel::GetNextChunk( CHUNK_S &pChunk )
{
   // read the next chunk
```

```
  fread( &pChunk, sizeof( CHUNK_S ), 1, m_pFile );

  // return chunk id
  return pChunk.wIdentifier;
}
// -----------------------------
```

The data is read from the current read-write head position in the file and is returned using a reference parameter. The chunk ID is separately returned a second time using the return value of the function. This enables you to use this function as a parameter for a switch instruction, for example.

The Main Function

This section covers the main function that is used to read the known contents of a whole file. Note the chunk ID V1_END that marks the end of the data in the CBF file as well as the end of each chunk. The function runs in a loop until the chunk marking the end of the file is found. Finally, this function checks whether joints were found in the file. If not, there are no animations for this model, and so the function deletes the memory allocated for one of the vertex arrays that is only needed for an animated model:

```
// -----------------------------
// Name: CheckForChunks( void )
// Info: Checks for Chunks
// Return      = (HRESULT)    Status
// -----------------------------
HRESULT CZFXModel::CheckForChunks( void )
{
   bool    bLoop = true;

   // loop until end chunk is found
   do{
      // seek the next Chunk
      switch( GetNextChunk( m_sChunk ) ){
         case V1_HEADER:      ReadHeader();     break;
         case V1_VERTEX:      ReadVertices();   break;
         case V1_FACE:        ReadFaces();      break;
         case V1_MESH:        ReadMesh();       break;
         case V1_MATERIAL:    ReadMaterials();  break;
         case V1_JOINT:       ReadJoints();     break;
         case V1_ANIMATION:   ReadAnimations(); break;
         case V1_END:         bLoop = false;    break;
         default: break;
```

```
        }
    }while( bLoop );

    // are there animations at all?
    if( m_sHeader.uiNumJoints == 0 )
    {
        // if not we don't need this member
        delete [] m_pVertices_Orig;
        m_pVertices_Orig = NULL;
    }

    // return OK
    return S_OK;
}
// -------------------------------
```

> **Note**
>
> Remember that I'm leaving out error checking to make the code simpler. What you see above can't handle thing like invalid model files. Instead of using the break instruction, you should move the read head for the size of the unknown chunk and proceed with reading the following chunk.

Each chunk ID that this loader can handle then results in an appropriate loading function call to read the actual data. Note that the `CZFXModel::GetNextChunk` function gets the chunk structure only, not the data belonging to the chunk.

Reading the Header

You can normally find the header at the head of the file (hence its name). Do not mistake this file header for the chunk structure, wherein every chunk has a header. The header discussed here relates to the whole file, providing us general information about the model or the file and its creator. The structure for the file header looks like this:

```
// --- Header ---
typedef struct _CHUNKHEAD{
    UCHAR  ucIdentifier[ 4 ];  // identifier
    UCHAR  ucName[ 32 ];       // name
    UCHAR  ucAuthor[ 32 ];     // author
    UCHAR  ucEmail[ 32 ];      // E-mail
    UCHAR  ucType;             // type
    UCHAR  ucVersion;          // version
    ULONG  ulNumVertices;      // number vertices
    ULONG  ulNumIndices;       // number indices
    ULONG  ulNumFaces;         // number faces
```

```
    ULONG   ulNumMeshs;         // number meshes
    UINT    uiNumMaterials;     // number materials
    UINT    uiNumJoints;        // number joints
    float   fAnimationFPS;      // FPS
    float   fCurrentTime;       // current time
    UINT    uiNumFrames;        // number frames
    UINT    uiNumAnimations;    // number animations
} CHUNKHEAD_S;
typedef CHUNKHEAD_S* LPCHUNKHEAD;  // Chunk-Header
```

Reading the header data into a structure from a file is as easy as it gets. Note that the function writes a debug string into a log file. This is really helpful if you want to track down errors in the code. Then the function clears the memory of the m_sHeader attribute of the class, where the header is then stored. After reading the data, the function is still not done with its work. I also let it check for the existence of the end chunk. Without the end chunk, the file would not be valid and would be treated as if it were corrupted or incompletely written in the first place. Therefore, each CBF file must have a valid end chunk at the end of each chunk, otherwise it cannot be processed:

```
// ---------------------------
// Name: ReadHeader( void )
// Info: Reads header from open file
//
// Return                = (HRESULT)    Status
// ---------------------------
HRESULT CZFXModel::ReadHeader( void )
{
    // write to log file
    LOG( 20, false, "Reading Header..." );

    // clear memory area
    ZeroMemory( &m_sHeader, sizeof( CHUNKHEAD_S ) );

    // read the header
    fread( &m_sHeader, sizeof( CHUNKHEAD_S ), 1, m_pFile);

    // seek the end chunk
    if( GetNextChunk( m_sChunk ) == V1_END ) {
        LOG( 20, true, " OK" );       // logit
        return S_OK;                  // bye
    }

    // no end chunk found
    LOG( 1, true, " FAILED [Header]" );
```

```
// return
return E_FAIL;
}
// ---------------------------
```

Reading the Vertices

The function to read in the vertex data from the model file is a bit lengthy compared to the preceding one. However, the principle used here is again the same. First, a bunch of temporary variables are declared. Then there is a bit of logging data to a log file to track down bugs, and the memory for the attributes holding the vertex data is allocated and initialized if no error occurred.

However, now we are dealing with different vertex formats. This class uses another structure to load the vertex data into, as the ZFXEngine does to render the vertices later on. The engine uses the CVERTEX format, which is briefer and therefore better suited than the vertex format used inside this class to extract the animation information.

> **Tip**
>
> All structures that are meant for use with a certain chunk ID as data packages can be found in the file zfxModelStructs.h on the accompanying CD-ROM.

The vertex structure used by CZFXModel is called _VERTEX and is defined like this:

```
// --- Vertex---
typedef struct _VERTEX{
    float       fXYZ[ 3 ];      // coordinates
    float       fUV0[ 2 ];      // texture coordinates 1
    float       fUV1[ 2 ];      // texture coordinates 2
    ZFXVector   fNormal;        // normal vector
    USHORT      usReferences;   // references
    UINT        uiBoneID_A;     // bone-ID 1
    float       fWeight_A;      // weight 1
    UINT        uiBoneID_B;     // bone-ID 2
    float       fWeight_B;      // weight 2
    BYTE        byFlags;        // flags
} VERTEX_3F_S;
typedef VERTEX_3F_S* LPVERTEX_3F;
```

From the comments behind the fields and from the field names, you can guess what most of the fields are used for. By adding up the bytes burned by this structure, you can already guess that it is not a good idea to use this structure in the render device. The following vertex format, CVERTEX, will be used in the render device to render an animated model. As you can see, it's much briefer than the preceding format:

```
typedef struct CVERTEX_TYPE {
   float   x, y, z;
   float   vcN[3];
   float   tu, tv;
   float   fBone1, fWeight1;
   float   fBone2, fWeight2;
   } CVERTEX;
```

Those formats are different for good reason: Different applications have different needs. A video game, for instance, needs to see only the relevant information for rendering and animating. In contrast, a tool used to build or animate a model needs other information as well.

The following function first reads the vertices from the file to a temporary variable. After that, the vertices are converted to the format used by the engine and stored in an attribute of the class. Finally, after all the vertices have been read, the function checks for the end chunk marking the end of this chunk to confirm this is a valid CBF file that has not been corrupted. This checking enables you to detect irregularities from early on in the file, reducing the possibility of moving the file pointer beyond its valid boundaries.

Here is the function to read in the vertex data:

```
// -----------------------------
// Name: ReadVertices( void )
// Info: reads vertices from the open file
//
// Return      = (HRESULT)    Status
// -----------------------------
HRESULT CZFXModel::ReadVertices( void )
{
   // initialize the variables
   ULONG    ulNumVertices = m_sHeader.ulNumVertices;
   LPVERTEX_3F pVertices = NULL;

   LOG( 20, false,"Read Vertices [%d]", ulNumVertices );

   // allocate memory
   pVertices = new VERTEX_3F_S[ ulNumVertices ];
   if( !pVertices ){
      LOG( 1, true, " FAILED [VERTICES]" );   // log it
      return E_FAIL;                           // bye
   }
```

```cpp
// read all vertices
fread( pVertices, sizeof( VERTEX_3F_S ),
       ulNumVertices, m_pFile );

// allocate memory
m_pVertices      = new CVERTEX[ ulNumVertices ];
m_pVertices_Orig = new CVERTEX[ ulNumVertices ];
ZeroMemory( m_pVertices,      sizeof( CVERTEX ) *
            ulNumVertices );
ZeroMemory( m_pVertices_Orig, sizeof( CVERTEX ) *
            ulNumVertices );

// convert the vertices
for( ULONG ulCounter = 0; ulCounter <
     m_sHeader.ulNumVertices; ulCounter++ )
{
    // copy the vertices
    memcpy( &m_pVertices[ ulCounter ].x, &pVertices[ ulCounter ].fXYZ,
            sizeof( float ) * 3 );
    memcpy( &m_pVertices[ ulCounter ].vcN, &pVertices[ ulCounter ].fNormal,
            sizeof( float ) * 3 );
    memcpy( &m_pVertices[ ulCounter ].tu, &pVertices[ ulCounter ].fUVO,
            sizeof( float ) * 2 );
    m_pVertices[ ulCounter ].fBone1   =
            (float) pVertices[ ulCounter ].uiBoneID_A;
    m_pVertices[ ulCounter ].fWeight1 =
            (float) pVertices[ ulCounter ].fWeight_A;
    m_pVertices[ ulCounter ].fBone2   =
            (float) pVertices[ ulCounter ].uiBoneID_B;
    m_pVertices[ ulCounter ].fWeight2 =
            (float) pVertices[ ulCounter ].fWeight_B;
}
// free memory
delete [] pVertices;

// search the end chunk
if( GetNextChunk( m_sChunk ) == V1_END ) {
    LOG( 20, true, " OK" );    // logit
    return S_OK;               // bye
}

LOG( 1, true, " FAILED [VERTICES]" );
return E_FAIL;
```

}
// ------------------------------

Reading Faces

A triangle, also called a face in this context, consists of three vertices. But, no, that is not really true. Actually, a triangle consists of three indices into the vertex list. So reading the face data from a model file is pretty easy. You just have to allocate enough memory for the member attribute that should hold the incoming data. The number of faces is information you can find in the header of the model. Then the fread() function gets the data into the member attribute and you are done.

The structure to hold the data of a single face looks like the following one. Note that a face in this context will always be a triangle with three indices:

```
// --- Face ---
typedef struct _FACE{
   ULONG        ulIndices[ 3 ];    // indices
   ZFXVector    fNormal;           // normal vector
   ULONG        ulMeshID;          // mesh-ID
   UINT         uiMaterialID;      // material-ID
   BYTE         byFlags;           // flags
} FACE_S;
typedef FACE_S* LPFACE;
```

After the data is stored into an array of _FACE elements, the function loading the data from the face chunk checks for the end chunk as usual. This is no big deal. Actually, the function just looks like the ones shown earlier. As you can see, the only thing that is really changing is the structure used to get that data:

```
// ------------------------------
// Name: ReadFaces( void )
//
// Return       = (HRESULT)   Status
// ------------------------------
HRESULT CZFXModel::ReadFaces( void )
{
   ULONG    ulNumFaces = m_sHeader.ulNumFaces;// temp Var

   LOG(20, false, "Reading Faces [%d]...", ulNumFaces );

   // allocate memory
   m_pFaces = new FACE_S[ ulNumFaces ];
   if( !m_pFaces ){
      LOG( 1, true, " FAILED [FACES]" );
```

```
        return E_FAIL;
    }

    // read all faces
    fread(m_pFaces, sizeof( FACE_S ),ulNumFaces,m_pFile );

    // read end chunk
    if( GetNextChunk( m_sChunk ) == V1_END ) {
        LOG( 20, true, " OK" );
        return S_OK;
    }

    LOG( 1, true, " FAILED [FACES]" );

    return E_FAIL;
}
// ---------------------------
```

Reading the Mesh

Reading the data for a mesh is now done the very same way. You just have to define a structure for the mesh data and read the data into the member attribute m_pMeshs. But what exactly is a mesh? A mesh is an arbitrary bunch of faces that belong together because they form a separate part of the model, such as a submodel, or the whole model itself. Therefore, a mesh consists of several faces, has a specific name, and uses a specific material. Therefore, in this scheme, all faces belonging to a mesh have to use the same material.

This is the structure I use for a mesh in the loader:

```
// --- Mesh ---
typedef struct _MESH {
    char    cName[ 32 ];    // name
    WORD    wNumFaces;      // number of faces
    PWORD   pIndices;       // face index
    UINT    uiMaterialID;   // material ID
    BYTE    byFlags;        // flags
} MESH_S;
typedef MESH_S*   LPMESH;
```

Reading the data is now nothing new to you. First, get the number of objects to read, then allocate the memory, read the data, and check for the end chunk. After this function call, you will then have extracted the mesh information from the model file:

```
// -----------------------------
// Name: ReadMesh( void )
```

```
//
// Return        = (HRESULT) Status
// ----------------------------
HRESULT CZFXModel::ReadMesh( void )
{
   ULONG   ulNumMesh = m_sHeader.ulNumMeshs;

   LOG( 20, false, "Reading Meshs [%d]...", ulNumMesh );

   // allocate memory
   m_pMeshs = new MESH_S[ ulNumMesh ];
   if( !m_pMeshs ){
      LOG( 1, true, " FAILED [MESH]" );
      return E_FAIL;
   }

   // clear memory
   ZeroMemory( m_pMeshs, sizeof( MESH_S ) * ulNumMesh );

   // read the whole mesh
   fread(m_pMeshs,sizeof( MESH_S ),ulNumMesh, m_pFile );

   // check for end chunk
   if( GetNextChunk( m_sChunk ) == V1_END ) {
      LOG( 20, true, " OK" );                  // logit
      return S_OK;                             // bye
    }

   LOG( 1, true, " FAILED [MESH]" );

   return E_FAIL;
}
// ----------------------------
```

Reading the Material

The next function that reads in the material information is, yet again, the very same thing. You define an appropriate structure to extract the information from the file and then just read it in. Again, the following algorithm is used:

1. Get the number of materials from the header.
2. Allocate memory for the attribute m_pMaterials.

3. Read materials from the file.
4. Return S_OK if end chunk is found, otherwise E_FAIL.

Chapter 5, "Materials, Textures, and Transparency," covered materials, so you already know about the four color values a material contains. For the model format, however, we will store some more information in a material, such as two texture names, and a name for the material itself, as well as some flags and a transparency value:

```
// --- Material ---
typedef struct _MATERIAL{
   char       cName[ 32 ];         // name
   float      fAmbient[ 4 ];       // ambient color
   float      fDiffuse[ 4 ];       // diffuse color
   float      fSpecular[ 4 ];      // specular color
   float      fEmissive[ 4 ];      // emissive color
   float      fSpecularPower;      // specular power
   float      fTransparency;       // transparency
   char       cTexture_1[ 128 ];   // texture name
   char       cTexture_2[ 128 ];   // texture name
   BYTE       byFlags;             // flags
} MATERIAL_S;
typedef MATERIAL_S*   LPMATERIAL;
```

Hang on for one more function. This is the last one that uses the same old teabag. Just get the material out of the file and move on to the next paragraph. This will be much more interesting. I promise:

```
// ---------------------------
// Name: ReadMaterials( void )
//
// Return      = (HRESULT)    Status
// ---------------------------
HRESULT CZFXModel::ReadMaterials( void )
{
   UINT    uiNumMat = m_sHeader.uiNumMaterials;

   LOG(20,false, "Reading Materials [%d]...",uiNumMat );

   // allocate memory
   m_pMaterials = new MATERIAL_S[ uiNumMat ];
   if( !m_pMaterials ){
      LOG( 1, true, " FAILED [MATERIALS]" );
      return E_FAIL;
   }
```

```
    // read the materials
    fread( m_pMaterials, sizeof( MATERIAL_S ), uiNumMat, m_pFile );

    // check for end chunk
    if( GetNextChunk( m_sChunk ) == V1_END ) {
        LOG( 20, true, " OK" );
        return S_OK;
    }

    LOG( 1, true, " FAILED [MATERIALS]" );
    return E_FAIL;
}
// ----------------------------------
```

Reading the Joints

Now it's finally time for something really interesting. We will read all the joint data from the file. This is where you will start to realize that a chunk-based system, in which a chunk can also contain another chunk as its data, really proves helpful to bring some structure into the data and to save it in a simple way.

You know that the chunk id V1_JOINT will have brought you to the function that should then read in the joints (namely, CZFXModel::ReadJoints). However, now you will not just read a structure for the joints from the file as with all the other functions so far. This function handles one joint at a time. However, the information for one joint is coming from different subchunks in the joint chunk. Therefore, this function is in fact using other functions for reading certain chunks that are contained in the chunk for a joint. The structure will clear up any questions you may have.

A joint needs lots of information, and the structure to hold the joint is rather large. Even so, it contains two pointers to other structures that will come in a subchunk of the joint chunk, as mentioned previously. Those two structures are KF_ROT_S and KF_POS_S:

```
// --- Joints ---
typedef struct _JOINT{
    char        cName[ 32 ];        // descriptor
    char        cParentName[ 32 ];  // parent descriptor
    WORD        wParentID;          // parent-ID
    ZFXVector   vRotation;          // rotation
    ZFXVector   vPosition;          // position
    WORD        wNumKF_Rotation;    // number of rotations
    WORD        wNumKF_Position;    // number of positions
    LPKF_ROT    pKF_Rotation;       // key frame rotations
```

```
    LPKF_POS    pKF_Position;        // key frame positions
    bool        bAnimated;           // animated or not
    BYTE        byFlags;             // flags
    ZFXMatrix   sMatrix;             // matrix
    ZFXMatrix   sMatrix_absolute;    // matrix absolute
    ZFXMatrix   sMatrix_relative;    // matrix relative
} JOINT_S;
typedef JOINT_S*   LPJOINT;
```

At the end of the structure, you can see three matrices, which are used during the animation calculation to get the joint's final translation matrix. As you remember, a joint has to take its parent's transformation into account as well. The two structures contained in this one will be filled by two other functions because their data is coming from two other chunks (namely, V1_JOINT_KEYFRAME_ROT and V1_JOINT_KEYFRAME_POS). A third chunk is also involved, V1_JOINT_MAIN. Actually, the V1_JOINT chunk will only contain subchunks but no other data. So the following function has just to sort out which chunk is found inside the chunk and call the appropriate method to load this one. Here you go:

```
// ---------------------------
// Name: ReadJoints( void )
//
// Return      = (HRESULT)    Status
// ---------------------------
HRESULT CZFXModel::ReadJoints( void )
{
    bool    bLoop = true;
    UINT    uiLoop = 0;
    UINT    uiNumJoints = m_sHeader.uiNumJoints;
    LPJOINT pJoint = NULL;

    LOG(20,false,"Reading Joints [%d]...",uiNumJoints );

    // allocate memory
    m_pJoints = new JOINT_S[ uiNumJoints ];
    if( !m_pJoints ){
        LOG( 1, true, " FAILED [JOINTS]" );
        return E_FAIL;                    // bye
    }

    // loop until end chunk found
    do{
        // find the next chunk
        switch( GetNextChunk( m_sChunk ) )
        {
```

```
            case V1_JOINT_MAIN:
                pJoint = &m_pJoints[ uiLoop ];
                ReadJoint_Main( pJoint );
                uiLoop++;
                break;

            case V1_JOINT_KEYFRAME_ROT:
                ReadJoint_KeyFrame_Rot( pJoint ); break;

            case V1_JOINT_KEYFRAME_POS:
                ReadJoint_KeyFrame_Pos( pJoint ); break;

            case V1_END:
                bLoop = false;                          break;
            }

        }while( bLoop );

        // check for end chunk
        if( !bLoop ) {
            LOG( 20, true, " OK" );
            return S_OK;
        }

        LOG( 1, true, " FAILED [JOINTS]" );
        return E_FAIL;
}
// ------------------------------
```

This function reads all the joints stored in a V1_JOINT chunk, which should be all joints present in the file. After allocating the memory for all those chunks, we just start a loop until we find the V1_END marker that indicates that there is no more chunk data to be read. Most of the data is sitting in the chunk called V1_JOINT_MAIN, whereas the information about the rotation and position key frames is stored in the separate chunks called V1_JOINT_KEYFRAME_POS and V1_JOINT_KEYFRAME_ROT.

Of course, each of these three chunk types has again its own function to load the information from the model file. However, there is no separate structure for those three. As you can see, a reference pointer to the joint from the master array will be given to the functions in order to store the data there.

The following three sections introduce you to the three functions used here: ReadJoint_Main(), ReadJoint_KeyFrame_Rot(), and ReadJoint_KeyFrame_Pos().

Reading the Main Joint

This section shows the function to read the main parts for the structure JOINT_S from the file. Or, to put it straight forward, it reads the whole structure, of course, but the pointers to the two other structures contained inside are not initialized and are set to zero. So this function is pretty easy indeed:

```
// -----------------------------
// Name: ReadJoint_Main( LPJOINT pJoint )
//
// Return      = (HRESULT)    Status
//
// pJoint      = (LPJOINT)    Parent-Joint
// -----------------------------
HRESULT CZFXModel::ReadJoint_Main( LPJOINT pJoint )
{
    // log start
    LOG( 20, false, "Reading Joint " );

    // read joints
    fread( pJoint, sizeof( JOINT_S ), 1, m_pFile );

    // check for the end chunk
    if( GetNextChunk( m_sChunk ) == V1_END ) {
        LOG( 20, true, " OK" );
        return S_OK;
    }

    LOG( 1, true, " FAILED [JOINT_MAIN]" );
    return E_FAIL;
}
// -----------------------------
```

Note that this function, in contrast to the majority of its predecessors, works on an already valid area of memory. Therefore, it does not have to allocate any memory; it just has to fill in the data for the given reference pointer.

There will be only one chunk for the main joint data inside a joint chunk. At least this should be the case, and there is no test to determine whether a joint chunk has more than one subchunk for its main data. However, if you don't trust your model files, such a test would be easy to integrate.

As always, the consistency is checked by testing for the chunk marking the end of the current data package. If this is not found, something is definitely wrong.

Reading the Key Frame Rotations

The core of the skeletal animation is the rotation applied to the joints of the skeleton, which will also influence the attached skin, which is the actual model the viewer will perceive on the screen. The animation is saved in a skinned mesh as key frames (of the bones in certain poses) that are the start and the end point of an animation cycle. If a model's arm is just hanging down in frame 5, but you want the model to bend its elbow, for instance, you might save the angle of, let's say, 23 degrees in frame 6.

It is as easy as it sounds. Therefore, to be able to know about this data, each joint has a list of key frame poses that are stored in the field wNumKF_Rotation of the structure JOINT_S. All of those rotation key frame values are now saved to an array of the following type of structure:

```
// --- Keyframe-Rotation ---
typedef struct _KF_ROT{
   float        fTime;           // time
   ZFXVector    vRotation;       // rotation
} KF_ROT_S;
typedef KF_ROT_S*   LPKF_ROT;
```

As you can see, a vector is used to store the rotation angles. Now this is no fancy part of a quaternion or a rotational axis or something like that. The vector will just contain the angles for the x, the y, and the z axis in its components.

After this short break from the old-fashioned data-loading style, we are now back on the track of reading the data from the file just like in all the other functions shown earlier (allocating memory and reading in an array of our custom structure). There is a slight difference this time, however: The function does not directly use a member attribute of the class to store the data; it uses the reference parameter instead. However, after all, this is also a field of a structure in a member attribute array:

```
// -------------------------------
// Name: ReadJoint_KeyFrame_Rot( LPJOINT pJoint )
//
// Return    = (HRESULT)    Status
//
// pJoint    = (LPJOINT)    Parent-Joint
// -------------------------------
HRESULT CZFXModel::ReadJoint_KeyFrame_Rot( LPJOINT pJoint )
{
   UINT   uiNumKeys = pJoint->wNumKF_Rotation;

   LOG(20,false,"Reading KF Rot. [%d]...", uiNumKeys );
```

```
    // allocate memory
    pJoint->pKF_Rotation = new KF_ROT_S[ uiNumKeys ];
    if( !pJoint->pKF_Rotation ){
        LOG(1,true,"FAILED [JOINT_KEYFRAME_ROTATIONS]" );
        return E_FAIL;
    }

    // clear memory
    ZeroMemory( pJoint->pKF_Rotation, sizeof( KF_ROT_S )
                * uiNumKeys );

    // read the rotations
    fread( pJoint->pKF_Rotation, sizeof( KF_ROT_S ), uiNumKeys, m_pFile );

    // check for the end chunk
    if( GetNextChunk( m_sChunk ) == V1_END ) {
        LOG( 20, true, " OK" );
        return S_OK;
     }

    LOG( 1, true, " FAILED [JOINT_KEYFRAME_ROTATIONS]" );
    return E_FAIL;
}
// ----------------------------
```

Again, don't miss the security check to determine whether the end marker of this chunk is set as intended. Otherwise, the file would be treated as invalid.

Reading the Key Frame Positions

Reading the positions of the joints for all key frames is not exactly the same as reading the rotation, as we just did. If you look at the structure, you can see that it is basically the same as the structure used for the rotations. However, the name of the vector field is different, as is the name of the structure:

```
// --- Keyframe-Position ---
typedef struct _KF_POS{
    float       fTime;                  // time
    ZFXVector   vPosition;              // position
} KF_POS_S;
typedef KF_POS_S*    LPKF_POS;
```

No big surprise then that even the function looks pretty much the same. The only difference here is that the memory allocation and the reading function use the name for the new structure to calculate the size to be read or allocated, respectively:

```
// -------------------------
// Name: ReadJoint_KeyFrame_Pos( LPJOINT pJoint )
//
// Return      = (HRESULT)    Status
//
// pJoint      = (LPJOINT)    Parent-Joint
// -------------------------
HRESULT CZFXModel::ReadJoint_KeyFrame_Pos( LPJOINT
                                                 pJoint )
{
   UINT   uiNumKeys = pJoint->wNumKF_Position;

   LOG( 20, false, "Reading KeyFrame Positions [%d]...", uiNumKeys );

   // allocate memory
   pJoint->pKF_Position = new KF_POS_S[ uiNumKeys ];
   if( !pJoint->pKF_Position ){
      LOG(1,true," FAILED [JOINT_KEYFRAME_POSITIONS]" );
      return E_FAIL;
   }

   // clear memory
   ZeroMemory( pJoint->pKF_Position, sizeof( KF_POS_S ) * uiNumKeys );

   // read the positions
   fread( pJoint->pKF_Position, sizeof( KF_POS_S ), uiNumKeys, m_pFile );

   // check for the end chunk
   if( GetNextChunk( m_sChunk ) == V1_END ) {
      LOG( 20, true, " OK" );
      return S_OK;
   }

   LOG( 1, true, " FAILED [JOINT_KEYFRAME_POSITIONS]" );
   return E_FAIL;
}
// -------------------------
```

Read the Animations

Finally, we are pretty close to having read all the data from the model file. However, we still lack one function to read the last of the necessary data information from the file: the information about the animation. We need to know which animation is running from which key frame to which other key frame. The following structure gathers all this data, including a name for the animation:

```
// --- Animations ---
typedef struct _ANIMATION{
    char        cName[ 64 ];        // name string
    float       fStartFrame;        // start frame
    float       fEndFrame;          // end frame
    bool        bActive;            // active or not
} ANIMATION_S;
typedef ANIMATION_S*   LPANIMATION;
```

In the converter that reads Milkshape files and converts them into the CBF, you always need a plain-text file describing and defining the animation sequences that will be used in the model. The syntax of this text file is pretty simple. It all starts with the number of animation sequences present in the file. This is followed by the corresponding number of lines, with each line defining one animation sequence.

The first part of a line names the start key frame of an animation sequence, and the middle part names the key frame that is the end pose for this animation cycle. Finally, a text description appears at the end of each line:

```
// animation.txt
// this files contains all animations for the model
//-----------------------------
Number: "14"
S: "001" E: "001" D: "Bind position"
S: "002" E: "020" D: "Walk Cycle 1"
S: "022" E: "036" D: "Walk Cycle 2"
S: "038" E: "047" D: "Zombie being attacked 1"
S: "048" E: "057" D: "Zombie being attacked 2"
S: "059" E: "075" D: "Blown away onto his back"
S: "078" E: "088" D: "Still lying down and twitching
                      (offset)"
S: "091" E: "103" D: "Die and fall forward"
S: "106" E: "115" D: "Kick attack"
S: "117" E: "128" D: "Punch/grab attack"
S: "129" E: "136" D: "Head butt :-)"
S: "137" E: "169" D: "Idle 1"
S: "170" E: "200" D: "Idle 2"
```

The converter uses this animation file to extract the animation data and write it to the CBF file itself to get rid of an additional file. When all the data is inside the CBF model file, you can extract the animation's data from the file after spotting the according chunk by using this function:

```
// ----------------------------
// Name: ReadAnimations( void )
//
// Return       = (HRESULT)  Status
// ----------------------------
HRESULT CZFXModel::ReadAnimations( void )
{
    UINT    uiNumAnim = m_sHeader.uiNumAnimations; //tmp

    LOG( 20, false, "Reading Animations [%d]...", uiNumAnim );

    // allocate memory
    m_pAnimations = new ANIMATION_S[ uiNumAnim ];
    if( !m_pAnimations ){
        LOG( 1, true, " FAILED [ANIMATIONS]" );
        return E_FAIL;
    }

    // clear memory
    ZeroMemory( m_pAnimations, sizeof( ANIMATION_S ) * uiNumAnim );

    // read the animations
    fread( m_pAnimations, sizeof( ANIMATION_S ), uiNumAnim, m_pFile );

    // check for the end chunk
    if( GetNextChunk( m_sChunk ) == V1_END ) {
        LOG( 20, true, " OK" );
        return S_OK;
    }

    LOG( 1, true, " FAILED [ANIMATIONS]" );
    return E_FAIL;
}
// ----------------------------
```

You have now finished loading the complete model. All data from the file is now stored in an instance of the class CZFXModel and waits to be animated and displayed onscreen.

Set the Scaling of the Model

Before you learn the actual secrets of how to run the animation sequences of the loaded model, you need to be aware of another nasty little detail. If you have ever worked with files from different 3D artists (for example, if you have downloaded free model files from the Internet), you will most certainly have encountered scaling problems. Each artist is used to his own style, and that style includes building models in a certain size relative to the dimensionless units of the modeling tool.

To compensate for that and scale a model that you have loaded into the memory, you have to write another function. This function will take one input parameter: a scaling factor describing how the model should be scaled after loading. The final scaling factor is then calculated from the actual size of the model according to its bounding box by the following formula:

```
fScaling = ( m_sBBoxMax.y - m_sBBoxMin.y ) / fScale;
```

This final scaling factor is then used to scale all the vertices and joints in the model so that the model will have the requested size when the function finishes with it. Here is the scaling function:

```
// -----------------------------
// Name: SetScaling( float fScale /* = 0.0f  */ )
//

// -----------------------------
void CZFXModel::SetScaling( float fScale /* = 0.0f  */ )
{
    ULONG      ulCounter   = 0;       // Counter
    ULONG      ulInner     = 0;       // Counter
    CVERTEX    *pVertex    = NULL;    // temporarily
    float      fScaling    = 0.0f;    // scaling
    LPJOINT    pJoint      = NULL;    // Joint

    // do we need to scale?
    if( fScale == 0.0f ) return;

    // calculate bounding box
    m_sBBoxMin.x = 999999.0f; m_sBBoxMax.x = -999999.0f;
    m_sBBoxMin.y = 999999.0f; m_sBBoxMax.y = -999999.0f;
    m_sBBoxMin.z = 999999.0f; m_sBBoxMax.z = -999999.0f;

    // calculate the bounding box
    for( ulCounter = 0; ulCounter < m_sHeader.ulNumVertices; ulCounter++ )
```

```
    {
        pVertex     = &m_pVertices[ ulCounter ];

        // enlarge box if needed
        m_sBBoxMax.x = MAX( m_sBBoxMax.x, pVertex->x );
        m_sBBoxMax.y = MAX( m_sBBoxMax.y, pVertex->y );
        m_sBBoxMax.z = MAX( m_sBBoxMax.z, pVertex->z );
        m_sBBoxMin.x = MIN( m_sBBoxMin.x, pVertex->x );
        m_sBBoxMin.y = MIN( m_sBBoxMin.y, pVertex->y );
        m_sBBoxMin.z = MIN( m_sBBoxMin.z, pVertex->z );
    }

    // scale bounding box
    fScaling = ( m_sBBoxMax.y - m_sBBoxMin.y ) / fScale;

    // scale the vertex data
    for( ulCounter = 0; ulCounter < m_sHeader.ulNumVertices; ulCounter++ )
    {
        pVertex     = &m_pVertices[ ulCounter ];

        pVertex->x  /= fScaling;
        pVertex->y  /= fScaling;
        pVertex->z  /= fScaling;
    }

    // copy to back up array if animation is present
    if( m_sHeader.uiNumJoints > 0 )
       memcpy( m_pVertices_Orig, m_pVertices, sizeof(CVERTEX ) *
               m_sHeader.ulNumVertices );

    // scale the bones
    for( ulCounter = 0; ulCounter < m_sHeader.uiNumJoints; ulCounter++ )
    {
        pJoint      = &m_pJoints[ ulCounter ];

        pJoint->vPosition.x   /= fScaling;
        pJoint->vPosition.y   /= fScaling;
        pJoint->vPosition.z   /= fScaling;

        // scale key frame positions for this bone
        for( ulInner = 0; ulInner < pJoint->wNumKF_Position; ulInner++ )
        {
```

```
                pJoint->pKF_Position[ ulInner ].vPosition.x /= fScaling;

                pJoint->pKF_Position[ ulInner ].vPosition.y /= fScaling;

                pJoint->pKF_Position[ ulInner ].vPosition.z /= fScaling;
            }

        // build ZFXEngine aabb
        m_sAabb.vcMin.x = m_sBBoxMin.x;
        m_sAabb.vcMin.y = m_sBBoxMin.y;
        m_sAabb.vcMin.z = m_sBBoxMin.z;
        m_sAabb.vcMax.x = m_sBBoxMax.x;
        m_sAabb.vcMax.y = m_sBBoxMax.y;
        m_sAabb.vcMax.z = m_sBBoxMax.z;
        m_sAabb.vcCenter.x = ( m_sBBoxMax.x - m_sBBoxMin.x ) / 2;
        m_sAabb.vcCenter.y = ( m_sBBoxMax.y -   m_sBBoxMin.y ) / 2;
        m_sAabb.vcCenter.z = ( m_sBBoxMax.z -   m_sBBoxMin.z ) / 2;
        }
    }
// -----------------------------
```

The tasks to be fulfilled by this function are twofold. On the one hand, the bounding box of the model will be calculated. Then, after determining the final scaling factor, the scaling is applied to the data of the model and then finally to the bounding box as well.

If there are animations defined for the model, which is the case when there are any joints at all, this function will also copy the vertices into the master array m_pVertices_Orig. This master array then holds a copy of the nonanimated, original mesh in its initial bind position. This position is needed during the animation process; it's something like the vertices defined in local coordinates. After an animation sequence has been applied in a certain frame, the vertices from the normal vertex array will not be in this position anymore, which would in turn make it impossible to run a correct animation sequence even one frame after.

But I'm already talking about doing the animations. I better leave this topic to a section of its own, which is, in fact, the following section.

Processing the Data in the Memory

After loading the whole model into the memory, we can now start processing the data, doing the animation and things like that. Then the model can be rendered featuring animations using the ZFXEngine, of course. The class CZFXModel contains a function called Prepare() that is used to preprocess the data for this purpose.

Preparing the Data

After loading the data, you need to sort all the data in the appropriate buffers or skin objects of the ZFXEngine one time to make rendering possible. The first step toward optimization here is to sort all faces by the material they are using. Because we will have to recalculate the vertices later on, it is necessary to render them dynamically with each frame. Even if the internal pipeline of the ZFXEngine will sort the data, it is always a good idea to keep track of such things for yourself.

The second main task of this function is to create the needed skins using the engine and add the necessary textures to those skin objects. The function is rather lengthy, even though it isn't necessarily complicated. It's shown here part by part so that you can concentrate on what is going on line by line. Here is the first part of the function:

```
// -----------------------------
// Name: Prepare( void )
//
// Return       = (HRESULT)     Status
// -----------------------------
HRESULT CZFXModel::Prepare( void )
{
    // Variablen init
    ULONG       ulNumIndices   = 0;
    ULONG       ulNumVertices  = 0;
    UINT        uiCurrentMat   = 0;
    PWORD       pIndex         = NULL;       // Index
    ULONG       ulCounter      = 0;
    LPMATERIAL  pMaterial      = NULL;
    char        cTexture[256]  = { 0 };
    PCHAR       pcSeperator    = NULL;
    ULONG       ulIndexCount   = 0;

    // 1. setup of the bones
    SetupBones();

    LOG( 20, false, "Sort Indices by Material [%d]", m_sHeader.uiNumMaterials );

    // calculate maximum memory needed
    m_sHeader.ulNumIndices = m_sHeader.ulNumFaces * 3;
    pIndex         = new WORD[ m_sHeader.ulNumIndices ];

    m_ppIndices    = new PVOID[m_sHeader.uiNumMaterials ];
    ZeroMemory( m_ppIndices, sizeof( PVOID ) *
                m_sHeader.uiNumMaterials );
```

```
m_pIndices     = new WORD[ m_sHeader.ulNumIndices ];
ZeroMemory( m_pIndices, sizeof( WORD ) *
            m_sHeader.ulNumIndices );

m_puiNumIndices = new UINT[m_sHeader.uiNumMaterials];
ZeroMemory( m_puiNumIndices, sizeof( UINT ) *
            m_sHeader.uiNumMaterials );

m_puiSkinBuffer = new UINT[m_sHeader.uiNumMaterials];
ZeroMemory( m_puiSkinBuffer, sizeof( UINT ) *
            m_sHeader.uiNumMaterials );

// to be continued ...
```

Actually, this first part of the function does nothing more than allocate some memory areas and clean them up. There is also a call to a function that will set up the bones' data. The pointer attributes for where memory is allocated have the following meaning:

- `pIndex`: temporary array used to copy the index data
- `m_ppIndices`: array with pointers to the real index arrays
- `m_pIndices`: array for all indices of the model
- `m_puiIndices`: array with the number of indices for each of the index arrays

Okay, it goes like this: First, the temporary pointer `pIndex` gets the memory to hold all index data for the model from the file. Second, the index data is sorted into this temporary array according to the material ID of the faces, which is stored in the field `uiMaterialID` of the face structure. In addition, all indices will be stored into the class's index array `m_pIndices` in the same sorted order. This array is only meant for a fast access to the complete index data (if you want to get a grip on the index data from outside the class, for example).

If all indices using the same skin are stored in the temporary array `pIndex`, the function will allocate the memory for a new index list in the pointer array `m_ppIndices`. Then the complete list of indices using the same skin is copied from the temporary array to this new array, and the number of those indices is stored in the counter array `m_puiIndices`.

So after going through all faces and their materials, you will have an array of arrays in the attribute `m_ppIndices`. Each array in this array is a list of indices that are using the very same skin. The according counter in `m_puiIndices` will indicate how many indices are stored in such an array:

```
// ... continued
```

```cpp
    // sort all faces into the index array
    do{

      ZeroMemory( pIndex, sizeof(WORD) * m_sHeader.ulNumIndices );

      // reset counter
      ulNumIndices = 0;

      // loop trough all faces
      for( ulCounter = 0; ulCounter <
           m_sHeader.ulNumFaces; ulCounter++ )
      {
         // still the same material
         if( m_pFaces[ ulCounter ].uiMaterialID ==
             uiCurrentMat )
         {
             m_pIndices[ ulIndexCount++ ] =
             pIndex[ ulNumIndices++ ]     =
             (WORD)m_pFaces[ ulCounter ].ulIndices[ 0 ];

             m_pIndices[ ulIndexCount++ ] =
             pIndex[ ulNumIndices++ ]     =
             (WORD)m_pFaces[ ulCounter ].ulIndices[ 1 ];

             m_pIndices[ ulIndexCount++ ] =
             pIndex[ ulNumIndices++ ]     =
             (WORD)m_pFaces[ ulCounter ].ulIndices[ 2 ];
         }
      }
      // enough indices?
      if( !ulNumIndices )
      {
          // new material
          uiCurrentMat++;

          LOG( 1, true, "STOP Error: Not enough
                          Indices..." );
          continue;
      }
      m_puiNumIndices[ uiCurrentMat ] = ulNumIndices;
      m_ppIndices[ uiCurrentMat ]= new WORD[ulNumIndices];
      memcpy( m_ppIndices[ uiCurrentMat ], pIndex, sizeof(WORD) * ulNumIndices );
// to be continued ...
```

After sorting all the index data by skin to make the dynamic rendering as smooth as possible, we still have to create the skin objects with the skin manager of the ZFXEngine. Note that the CZFXModel class has a pointer to the current render device stored in m_pRenderDevice, which was saved there in the constructor of this class. Then we can simply get the skin manager from the render device and create the skin objects by assigning textures to materials.

The colors from the model structure must then be cast to the ZFXCOLOR structure, but then they will contain the data in the expected manner. And here is the final part of the function that prepares the model after loading the data:

```
// ... continued

    // set current material
    pMaterial = &m_pMaterials[ uiCurrentMat ];

    // read material
    if( FAILED( m_pRenderDevice->
                GetSkinManager()->AddSkin( (ZFXCOLOR*)&pMaterial->fAmbient,
                                           (ZFXCOLOR*)&pMaterial->fDiffuse,
                                           (ZFXCOLOR*)&pMaterial->fEmissive,
                                           (ZFXCOLOR*)&pMaterial->fSpecular,
                                           pMaterial->fSpecularPower,
                                           &m_puiSkinBuffer[ uiCurrentMat ])))
    {
       LOG( 1, true, " FAILED [LOAD SKIN %d]", uiCurrentMat );
    }

    // prepare textures
    ZeroMemory( cTexture, sizeof( char ) * 256 );
    pcSeperator = strchr(strrev(strdup(m_pcFileName)), '/' );

    if( !pcSeperator )
       pcSeperator = strchr( strrev( strdup( m_pcFileName ) ), 92 );

    if( pcSeperator )
       strcpy( cTexture, strrev( pcSeperator ) );

    strcat( cTexture, pMaterial->cTexture_1 );

    // load textures
    if( FAILED( m_pRenderDevice->GetSkinManager()->AddTexture(
                                           m_puiSkinBuffer[ uiCurrentMat ],
```

```
                                          cTexture, false, 0, NULL, 0 ) ) )
   {
      LOG( 1, true, " FAILED [LOAD TEXTURE %s]", pMaterial->cTexture_1 );
   }

   // new material
   uiCurrentMat++;

   }while( uiCurrentMat != m_sHeader.uiNumMaterials );

   // clean up
   delete [] pIndex;

   LOG( 20, true, " done" );

   return S_OK;
}
// ---------------------------
```

This part of the function is just a big loop through the materials present in the attributes. As you can see, a model must contain some material. There has to be at least one material to get the indices sorted and placed into the appropriate member attribute used for rendering later on. Keep this in mind when supplying custom models.

Finally, don't forget to free the memory allocated for the temporary index. You don't want to offend your memory by smashing leaks into it, right?

Setting Up Bones for the Skeletal Animation

While preparing the model data for the first time, you need to set up the bones as well. This function will effectively calculate the position of the vertices used in the first animation frame. To understand what will happen now, you need to know about the meaning of the three matrices in the JOINT_S structure:

- pJoint->sMatrix_relative:
  This matrix stores the rotation and the translation that a joint has on its own. That means those transformations are relative to the parent joint of this joint. That means if a character bends its elbow by x degrees, this rotation is stored as a relative transformation of the elbow joint.

- pJoint->sMatrix_absolute:
  The relative matrix is needed to apply a certain rotation and translation to a joint. Because of the hierarchy system in the skeletal animation, however, each joint has to take its parent transformation into account as well. If the shoulder of the character is rotated by y degrees, this will also influence the elbow's position. To get the

absolute matrix for a joint, you have to multiply its relative matrix by the absolute matrix of its parent.

- **pJoint->sMatrix:**
  This field contains the final matrix, which is used to transform all vertices that are connected to this joint. To get this matrix, you only need to transpose the absolute matrix of the joint.

And here comes the first part of the function. It is used to calculate the three matrices for each joint based on the joint's initial rotations:

```
// -----------------------------
// Name: SetupBones( void )
//
// Return      = (HRESULT)   Status
// -----------------------------
HRESULT CZFXModel::SetupBones( void )
{
    // Variablen
    LPJOINT    pJoint       = NULL;       // joint
    ULONG      ulCounter    = 0;          // counter
    UINT       uiLoop       = 0;          // counter
    UINT       uiParentID   = 0;          // parent ID
    ZFXVector  sVector_A;                 // vector
    ZFXVector  sVector_B;                 // vector
    CVERTEX    *pVertex     = NULL;       // temporary
    ZFXMatrix  matTemp; matTemp.Identity();// temporary

    // are there bones at all?
    if( m_sHeader.uiNumJoints == 0 ) return S_OK;

    // build the matrix
    for( ulCounter = 0; ulCounter <
         m_sHeader.uiNumJoints; ulCounter++ )
    {
        // get the joint
        pJoint = &m_pJoints[ ulCounter ];

        // set rotation to matrix
        pJoint->sMatrix_relative = CreateRotationMatrix( &pJoint->vRotation );

        // set position to matrix
        pJoint->sMatrix_relative._14 = pJoint->vPosition.x;
```

```
        pJoint->sMatrix_relative._24 = pJoint->vPosition.y;

        pJoint->sMatrix_relative._34 = pJoint->vPosition.z;
// to be continued ...
```

Don't forget to check whether there are any joints at all in this model. A CBF file is also valid if there is no animation at all, so be sure to check first. If joints are present, the function loops through all of them and calculates the relative matrix that is representing the joint's own rotation.

After having the rotation integrated into the relative matrix, the function sets the position of the joint into the matrix by using the fields _14, _24, and _34. Those fields are concerned because we are working with a transposed matrix so far where columns and rows are switched.

The next part of the function searches the parent of the joint if there is one, and then it calculates the absolute matrix for the joint:

```
// ... continued

        // find the parent...
        for( uiLoop = 0; uiLoop < m_sHeader.uiNumJoints; uiLoop++ )
        {
            // remember parent id
            uiParentID = 255;

            if( strcmp( m_pJoints[ uiLoop ].cName, pJoint->cParentName ) == 0 )
            {
                // found
                uiParentID = uiLoop;
                break;
            }
        }

        // remember found id
        pJoint->wParentID = uiParentID;

        // is there a parent
        if( uiParentID != 255 )
        {
            // parent found so we need to multiply its absolute matrix with
            // the relative matrix of this joint to get its absolute matrix
            pJoint->sMatrix_absolute = m_pJoints[ uiParentID ].sMatrix_absolute
                                * pJoint->sMatrix_relative;
```

```
        } else {
            // no parent found so relative matrix equals absolute matrix
            pJoint->sMatrix_absolute = pJoint->sMatrix_relative;

        }

        // final matrix
        pJoint->sMatrix.TransposeOf( pJoint->sMatrix_absolute );

        // transposed matrix
        matTemp = pJoint->sMatrix_relative;
        pJoint->sMatrix_relative.TransposeOf( matTemp );
    }
// to be continued ...
```

To find the parent, a loop goes through all the joints in the model and compares their names to the name of the parent that is saved in the current joint. If the parent is found, its ID is saved. Then the absolute matrix of the parent is multiplied with the relative matrix of the current joint to build the current joint's absolute matrix. If no parent is found, the relative matrix is the absolute matrix as well. Finally, the final matrix is calculated by transposing the absolute matrix of the current joint. And that's it.

Caution

> Note that the parent's absolute matrix has to be calculated before you can process its children and calculate their matrices. Due to the simple bone system used here this is always the case, but in more general models you would need to ensure this by using a flagging system, for example.

The last part of the function will then only transform all the vertices in the model by using the joint to which a vertex is connected. This is done the following way:

```
// ... continued

    // vertices Setup
    for( ulCounter = 0; ulCounter <
         m_sHeader.ulNumVertices; ulCounter++ )
    {
        // get the current vertex
        pVertex = &m_pVertices_Orig[ ulCounter ];

        // continue only if there is a bone
        if( pVertex->fBone1 != 255.0f )
```

```
            {
                // get current matrix
                matTemp.Identity();
                matTemp = m_pJoints[ (UINT)pVertex->fBone1 ].sMatrix;

                // 1. rotate vertices
                sVector_A.x = pVertex->x;
                sVector_A.y = pVertex->y;
                sVector_A.z = pVertex->z;
                sVector_A -= matTemp.GetTranslation();
                sVector_A.InvRotateWith( matTemp );
                pVertex->x = sVector_A.x;
                pVertex->y = sVector_A.y;
                pVertex->z = sVector_A.z;

                // 2. rotate normals
                sVector_A.x = pVertex->vcN[ 0 ];
                sVector_A.y = pVertex->vcN[ 1 ];
                sVector_A.z = pVertex->vcN[ 2 ];
                sVector_A.InvRotateWith( matTemp );
                pVertex->vcN[ 0 ] = sVector_A.x;
                pVertex->vcN[ 1 ] = sVector_A.y;
                pVertex->vcN[ 2 ] = sVector_A.z;
            }
        }
    return S_OK;
}
// -----------------------------
```

Oh well. Is there something going wrong here? As you can see, this function will not transform the vertices with the transformation matrix of the connected joint, but it will do an inverse transform by adding the inverse position and applying the inverse rotation. Note that the translation is not done for direction vectors, such as the normal vectors.

Rest assured, however, that this inverse transformation is correct. Actually, the start frame of the model has all vertices in the position they should have relative to their joints. In the joints, however, there is the transformation matrix stored to bring the vertices into this position in the first place. So now we have to move the vertices away from this position because the joint will later on apply this transformation to the vertices. By transforming the vertices inverse, you move them into an initial position. During the animation, you then transform all vertices with the joint's transformation matrix, and this moves the vertices to the correct position relative to the joint.

Now all the one-time setup work is done, and you can start the calculations that need to run each frame to animate the model. Let's go.

Animating the Model

To animate the model, you need to calculate the position of all vertices in each frame because the joints will move between certain key frame positions. While the joints are moving, however, they should take their connected vertices with them. Hence we will run through the complete vertex list each frame and take the absolute matrix of the joint connected to a vertex to transform this vertex.

Here is the first part of the function that will do some checks as to whether calculating an animation is even necessary:

```
// -------------------------------
// Name: Animation( void )
//
// Return      = (HRESULT)    Status
// -------------------------------
HRESULT CZFXModel::Animation( void )
{
    float       fElapsed    = -1.0f;    // time
    float       fStart      = -1.0f;    // start
    float       fEnd        = -1.0f;    // end
    LPANIMATION pAnimation  = NULL;     // animation

    // is there an animation at all?
    if( m_sHeader.uiNumJoints == 0 )
        return S_OK;

    // run only once?
    if( m_bAnimationRunOnce && m_bAnimationComplete && !m_bAnimationChanged )
        return S_OK;
// to be continued ...
```

At the end of this part, three Boolean variables are checked. They are used to enable running the animation only once. If this is the case, the function exits if the animation sequence is completed or if the animation sequence has changed. You can set the animation sequence as well as the run-once flag by using the public function `CZFXModel::SetAnimation`.

If the function evaluates that it still has work to do and needs to calculate the animation, however, it moves on. The next part of the function calculates the elapsed time first. Based on the elapsed time, the function checks the start and the end point of the animation and interpolates the time between those points where the animation is currently positioned. This value is stored in the attribute m_fFrame, which is used for interpolating between the start and the end pose of the current animation cycle:

```
// ... continued

    // check time
    m_fTime = (float)GetTickCount();

    // if new then this is the new start time
    if( m_fStartTime == -1.0f )
        m_fStartTime = m_fTime;

    // calculate elapsed time
    fElapsed = m_fTime - m_fStartTime;

    // get current animation
    pAnimation = &m_pAnimations[ m_uiCurrentAnimation ];

    fStart = pAnimation->fStartFrame;
    fEnd   = pAnimation->fEndFrame;

    // calculate frame position
    m_fFrame = fStart + (m_sHeader.fAnimationFPS / 2048) * fElapsed;

    // set new start frame
    if( m_fFrame <= fStart ) m_fFrame = fStart;

    // animation ended?
    if( m_fFrame >= fEnd )
    {
        m_fStartTime = m_fTime;
        m_fFrame     = fStart;
        m_bAnimationComplete= true;
    }
    else
    {
        // prepare animation
        AnimationPrepare();

        // setup vertices
        AnimationVertices();
        m_bAnimationComplete= false;      // set Flag
```

```
          m_bAnimationChanged = false;
       }
   return S_OK;
}
// -------------------------------
```

As you can see, this function is not really doing the animation of the model; instead, it delegates the workload to two other functions. First, the call to the member function `CZFXModel::AnimationPrepare` prepares the animation. (This function is discussed momentarily.) The call to `CZFXModel::AnimationVertices` then calculates the vertex positions according to the interpolated animation pose that the model currently has.

Note that the Boolean variable `m_bAnimationComplete` is set to `true` if the end frame of the animation is reached. This will cause the animation to stop when the other Boolean flag `m_bAnimationRunOnce` is set. Otherwise, the animation will continue in the next frame; it will then jump to the start frame again and set the flags back to `false`.

Prepare the Animation

The preparation for an animation is done by calculating the correct position between the start-pose frame and the end-pose frame. Even though it's been pretty simple to get to this point, you still have a lot of work to do.

Actually, calculating the correct position between the two poses involves building new absolute transformation matrices for each joint by interpolating between the two key frame positions. After this function has gone through all the data, the final matrix for all joints will be set for the current animation position. This matrix can then be used to transform the vertices later on.

But back to the task at hand. The first part of the function declares a bunch of local variables needed during the function. Then it starts a loop for all joints in the model and gets the key frame index for the rotation and the translation of the current joint. Here we go:

```
// -------------------------------
// Name: AnimationPrepare( void )
//
// Return      = (HRESULT)     Status
// -------------------------------
HRESULT CZFXModel::AnimationPrepare( void )
{
   // Initialize Variables
   LPJOINT    pJoint     = NULL;     // joint
   ULONG      ulCounter  = 0;        // counter
   UINT       uiLoop     = 0;        // counter
   ZFXVector  sPosition;             // vector
```

```
ZFXVector   sRotation;                  // vector
UINT        uiKeyPos    = 0;            // key-position
UINT        uiKeyRot    = 0;            // key-position
LPKF_ROT    pLastRot    = NULL;         // rotation
LPKF_ROT    pThisRot    = NULL;         // rotation
LPKF_ROT    pKeyRot     = NULL;         // rotation
LPKF_POS    pLastPos    = NULL;         // position
LPKF_POS    pThisPos    = NULL;         // position
LPKF_POS    pKeyPos     = NULL;         // position
float       fScale      = 0.0f;         // scaling
ZFXMatrix   matTemp; matTemp.Identity();
ZFXMatrix   matFinal; matFinal.Identity();

// clip the animation
if( m_fFrame > m_sHeader.uiNumFrames ) m_fFrame = 0;

// calculate matrix
for( ulCounter = 0; ulCounter < m_sHeader.uiNumJoints; ulCounter++ )
{
    // get current joint
    pJoint   = &m_pJoints[ ulCounter ];

    // get data
    uiKeyPos = pJoint->wNumKF_Position;// position
    uiKeyRot = pJoint->wNumKF_Rotation;// rotation
// to be continued ...
```

Wow, there are really a lot of declarations here. Leaving everything else alone, you already need three variables each for the rotation and the position. That makes six variables. Here is what they are used for:

- pKeyPos, pKeyRot:
  You need these variables to set the current frame's joint position and joint rotation for the given animation sequence.
- pLastPos, pLastRot:
  These variables hold the last known rotation and position, respectively. This can be thought of as the previous frame.
- pThisPos, pThisRot:
  And, finally, these two variables hold the rotation and the position of the next frame of the animation sequence.

The next part of the function then checks whether a recalculation is even necessary. This is the case if the current key frame is not zero.

Chapter 8 ■ Loading and Animating 3D Models

Then the function loops through all key frame positions for the given position of the joint and tries to find one that is valid for the current position and the current frame time:

```
// ... continued

        // recalculation necessary?
        if( ( uiKeyRot + uiKeyPos )  != 0 )
        {
            // yes new position or rotation
            pLastPos = NULL;
            pThisPos = NULL;
            pKeyPos  = NULL;

            for( uiLoop=0; uiLoop < uiKeyPos; uiLoop++ )
            {
                // get current position
                pKeyPos = &pJoint->pKF_Position[uiLoop];

                // check time
                if( pKeyPos->fTime >= m_fFrame )
                {
                    pThisPos = pKeyPos;

                    break;
                }
                // nothing found
                pLastPos = pKeyPos;
            }
// to be continued ...
```

After running this loop, the function has the current position saved in the variable pThisPos, and the preceding position in the animation sequence is stored in pLastPos. The current position in the animation sequence is the first one that has a greater time index than the current time elapsed since the animation started, so it's actually the next key frame position that is following in the animation sequence.

Now you have found the two positions preceding and succeeding the position in time the animation is currently at. To calculate the correct position of the model in between those two key frames, you must interpolate between the position of the skeleton in those two frames, of course. The following part of the function accomplishes this:

```
// ... continued

        // interpolate the two positions
```

```
if( pLastPos && pThisPos )
{
    // calculate scaling
    fScale = ( m_fFrame - pLastPos->fTime )/
             ( pThisPos->fTime - pLastPos->fTime );

    // interpolation
    sPosition = pLastPos->vPosition + ( pThisPos->vPosition -
                                        pLastPos->vPosition ) * fScale;
} else if( !pLastPos )
{
    // copy the position
    sPosition = pThisPos->vPosition;
} else {
    // copy the position
    sPosition = pLastPos->vPosition;
}
// to be continued ...
```

The factor fScale then holds the value of how one position should be scaled to apply the interpolation. As you can see, the function also checks for valid pointers of the current position pThisPos and pLastPos and works with the valid data only. If one of the pointers is not set, the animation cycle is right at the start frame or at the end frame for the sequence (hence no need to calculate an interpolation between two positions, naturally).

Here is the next part of the function, which is doing the very same thing for the rotations. The preceding parts have just used the same calculation, but for the positions of the key frames only:

```
// ... continued

            // apply the rotation
            pLastRot = NULL; pThisRot = NULL;
            pKeyRot  = NULL;

            for( uiLoop=0; uiLoop < uiKeyRot; uiLoop++ )
            {
                // get current rotation
                pKeyRot = &pJoint->pKF_Rotation[uiLoop];

                // check time
                if( pKeyRot->fTime >= m_fFrame )
                {
                    pThisRot = pKeyRot;
```

```
            break;
    }
    // nothing found
    pLastRot = pKeyRot;
} // all Rotations

// interpolate the rotations
if( pLastRot && pThisRot )
{
    sRotation = pLastRot->vRotation + ( pThisRot->vRotation -
                                pLastRot->vRotation ) * fScale;
} else if( !pLastRot )
{
    // copy rotation
    sRotation = pThisRot->vRotation;
} else {
    // copy rotation
    sRotation = pLastRot->vRotation;
}
// to be continued ...
```

Now the local variables `sPosition` and `sRotation` contain the value for the interpolated position and rotation that must now be taken into consideration for the two possible key frame positions. From those interpolated values, you can calculate the final matrices for the current joint:

```
// ... continued
            // joint matrix setup
            matTemp.SetTranslation( sPosition );
            matTemp.Rota( sRotation );

            // calculate relative matrix
            matFinal = matTemp * pJoint->sMatrix_relative;

            // is there a parent
            if( pJoint->wParentID != 255 )
            {
               // take parent matrix into account
               pJoint->sMatrix = matFinal * m_pJoints[
                                 pJoint->wParentID ].sMatrix;

            } else {
```

```
                pJoint->sMatrix = matFinal;
            }
        } else {

            // no new matrix, copy old one
            pJoint->sMatrix = pJoint->sMatrix_relative;
        }
    }
    return S_OK;
}
// -----------------------------------------
```

Using these two interpolated values, you build a temporary matrix containing the interpolated position and rotation as a transformation matrix. That is exactly how the current joint must additionally be transformed to be in the right position between two key frame positions. When this matrix is ready, you have to multiply it with the relative matrix of the joint to move it into the new temporary relative position for this animation step.

To move the joint into its final position with regard to the whole model, you have to multiply the temporary relative matrix with the joint's parent's absolute matrix. If there is no animation concerning a current joint, you just copy its relative matrix as the final matrix.

And that's it. Now each joint of the model has a final matrix stored that is valid to transform the connected vertices into the right position according to the animation running currently and to the interpolated position in this animation sequence.

Animating the Vertices

The good news is that the preceding function that prepares the animation by calculating the current transformation matrices valid for each joint is by far the most complex function of the animation process. The rest is rather easy. The following function loops through all vertices in the model and transforms its positions according to the joint to which they are connected.

To be able to calculate a correct collision detection, this function also rebuilds the bounding box accordingly to include the whole new model. If the character will extend its arms all the way upward, the old bounding box ranging to the top of the head is no longer valid.

Here is the first part of the function, which starts the loop:

```
// -----------------------------------------
// Name: AnimationVertices( void )
//
// Return      = (HRESULT)     Status
// -----------------------------------------
```

```
HRESULT CZFXModel::AnimationVertices( void )
{
    // Variablen init
    ULONG       ulCounter     = 0;        // counter
    CVERTEX     *pVertex      = NULL;     // temporary
    CVERTEX     *pVertex_Orig = NULL;     // temporary
    ZFXVector   sVector_A, sVector_B;     // vector

    // reset bounding box
    m_sBBoxMin.x =  999999.0f;m_sBBoxMin.y =   999999.0f;
    m_sBBoxMin.z =  999999.0f;m_sBBoxMax.x =  -999999.0f;
    m_sBBoxMax.y = -999999.0f;m_sBBoxMax.z =  -999999.0f;

    // setup the vertices
    for( ulCounter = 0; ulCounter < m_sHeader.ulNumVertices; ulCounter++ )
    {
        // get current vertex
        pVertex      = &m_pVertices[ ulCounter ];
        pVertex_Orig = &m_pVertices_Orig[ ulCounter ];
// to be continued ...
```

And, finally, you can see the reasoning behind the master array of vertices. The member attribute m_pVertices_Orig contains the original nonanimated positions of the vertices. We have to keep this copy because we will always build the animated skin from scratch. So the animated, and therefore transformed, vertices for a certain frame are then saved to the array m_pVertices, which is then used for rendering, and the original vertex data is used in the next frame to rebuild the array m_pVertices to reflect the new position in an animation cycle:

```
// ... continued

        // only do this if a bone is found
        if( pVertex->fBone1 != 255.0f )
        {
           // 1. get original (non-animated) vertex
           sVector_A.x = pVertex_Orig->x;
           sVector_A.y = pVertex_Orig->y;
           sVector_A.z = pVertex_Orig->z;

           // 2. rotate the vertex
           sVector_A.RotateWith( m_pJoints[
             (UINT)pVertex_Orig->fBone1 ].sMatrix );
```

```
            // 3. get position
            sVector_A  += m_pJoints[ (UINT)pVertex_Orig
                            ->fBone1 ].sMatrix.GetTranslation();

            // 4. calculate new position
            pVertex->x = sVector_A.x;
            pVertex->y = sVector_A.y;
            pVertex->z = sVector_A.z;

            // 5. animate the normals
            sVector_A.x = pVertex_Orig->vcN[ 0 ];
            sVector_A.y = pVertex_Orig->vcN[ 1 ];
            sVector_A.z = pVertex_Orig->vcN[ 2 ];
            sVector_A.RotateWith(m_pJoints[(UINT)pVertex_Orig->fBone1].sMatrix);
            pVertex->vcN[ 0 ] = sVector_A.x;
            pVertex->vcN[ 1 ] = sVector_A.y;
            pVertex->vcN[ 2 ] = sVector_A.z;
// to be continued ...
```

To find the joint to which a vertex is connected, you can just take a look at the field `fBone1` in the vertex structure. Note that this animation technique here only allows a single vertex to be connected to exactly one joint. (Other approaches do allow a vertex to be connected to more bones.) If a vertex is connected to two bones, for example, there have to be two weights in the vertex structure, too. Each weight will then express to which degree the vertex is depending from each joint to which it is connected. Of course, the weights must add up to 1.0.

Don't forget about the normal vectors here, too. Or as the professionals would say, "You have to skin the normals as well." By applying the rotation to the normals (don't translate them, as you remember), you will ensure their correct direction according to the animated model in order to be able to do lighting calculations reflecting the current model's position and rotation.

The final part of the function deals with rebuilding the bounding volume of the model. After that, you know all you need to know to make the model run with its animation sequences at runtime. Take a look at it:

```
// ... continued

            // 6. calculate bounding box
            m_sBBoxMax.x = MAX(m_sBBoxMax.x,pVertex->x);
            m_sBBoxMax.y = MAX(m_sBBoxMax.y,pVertex->y);
            m_sBBoxMax.z = MAX(m_sBBoxMax.z,pVertex->z);
            m_sBBoxMin.x = MIN(m_sBBoxMin.x,pVertex->x);
```

```
                    m_sBBoxMin.y = MIN(m_sBBoxMin.y,pVertex->y);
                    m_sBBoxMin.z = MIN(m_sBBoxMin.z,pVertex->z);
            }
     }
     // 7. create aabb
     m_sAabb.vcMin.x = m_sBBoxMin.x;
     m_sAabb.vcMin.y = m_sBBoxMin.y;
     m_sAabb.vcMin.z = m_sBBoxMin.z;
     m_sAabb.vcMax.x = m_sBBoxMax.x;
     m_sAabb.vcMax.y = m_sBBoxMax.y;
     m_sAabb.vcMax.z = m_sBBoxMax.z;
     m_sAabb.vcCenter.x =(m_sBBoxMax.x-m_sBBoxMin.x) / 2;
     m_sAabb.vcCenter.y =(m_sBBoxMax.y-m_sBBoxMin.y) / 2;
     m_sAabb.vcCenter.z =(m_sBBoxMax.z-m_sBBoxMin.z) / 2;
     return S_OK;
}
// ----------------------------
```

Using the Animated Model

Okay, you can load, process, and animate the model from a CBF file. That is already the biggest part of this chapter. Now you only need to have some other functions handy to actually use the model and render it. The best animation sequence calculation is wasted if you don't see a single thing on the screen. That is now what this section is all about. Of course, for your convenience, I include functions to render the normals and the bones as well so that you can see what is going on.

Updating the Model

The single most important thing for calculating the animation is knowing about the current time that has passed since the last frame. That is because the interpolation is based on the elapsed time. So we will call the following functions from the main routine using an animated CBF model:

```
    m_pModel->Update( fDeltaTime );
    m_pModel->Render();
```

Well, updating the model is now a trivial task because it is delegating the workload to the function calculating the animation. Additionally, it will only save the time given to the instance by the main application:

```
// ----------------------------
// Name: Update( float fTime )
//
```

```
//  fTime        = Deltatime
//
//  Return       = (HRESULT)    Status
// -----------------------------
HRESULT CZFXModel::Update( float fTime )
{
    // set the time
    m_fTime = fTime;

    // do the animation
    return Animation();
}
// -----------------------------
```

Rendering the Model

As always, rendering something is by far the most trivial task (especially with a good engine at hand that handles all the gritty details for you). Note that this function renders the animated model by using the dynamic rendering method of supplying user pointers with the data to the engine. Unfortunately, this is necessary because we have to recalculate the vertex positions and orientations each frame when an animation takes place.

The only way to avoid the submission of the whole model vertex and index data over the bus is by using a vertex shader to do the skinning. However, that is a topic of its own for another book. So, for the remainder for this book, we stick to calculating the animation on the CPU:

```
// -----------------------------
// Name: Render( void )
//
// Return       = (HRESULT)    Status
// -----------------------------
HRESULT CZFXModel::Render( void )
{
    UINT    uiCounter = 0;

    // set culling
    m_pRenderDevice->SetBackfaceCulling(RS_CULL_CCW);

    // render vertex buffer
    for( uiCounter = 0; uiCounter < m_sHeader.uiNumMaterials; uiCounter++ )
            if( FAILED( m_pRenderDevice->GetVertexManager()->Render(
                    VID_CA,
```

440 Chapter 8 ■ Loading and Animating 3D Models

```
                            m_sHeader.ulNumVertices,
                            m_puiNumIndices[ uiCounter ],
                            m_pVertices,
                            (PWORD)m_ppIndices[ uiCounter ],
                            m_puiSkinBuffer[ uiCounter ] ) ) )
            LOG( 1, true, "ERROR Failed to Render VB:
                            %d [%d]", m_puiSkinBuffer[
                            uiCounter ], uiCounter );

    // render other data if requested
    if( m_bRenderBones )   RenderBones();  // bones
    if( m_bRenderNormals ) RenderNormals();// normals
    return S_OK;
}
// ---------------------------
```

As you can see in the final lines, this function also calls the render methods to display the bones and the normals for debugging purposes. The main application enables you to switch the flags for whether or not to render those parts.

Rendering the Bones

You remember that the bones are not really contained in the model data read from the file. However, the bones are implicitly there because the bones are just a visual connection between two joints where a parent-child(ren) relationship must be given between those two. Figure 8.6 shows a model with the bones rendered on top of it.

And here is the function that calculates the bones and renders them in the form of a simple triangle for each bone. This is not meant as eye candy, but only for debugging:

Figure 8.6 Here you can see the bones rendered on top of the model with a deactivated depth buffer. The bone between the legs is very interesting. This can be used to throw the model to the ground in a smooth animation. (Source for the free model: http://www.psionic3d.co.uk)

```cpp
// -----------------------------
// Name: RenderBones( void )
//
// fTime        = Deltatime
//
// Return       = (HRESULT)    Status
// -----------------------------
HRESULT CZFXModel::RenderBones( void )
{
    UINT    uiCounter = 0;              // counter
    LVERTEX pLine[3];                   // joints
    WORD    pIndis[3] = { 0, 1, 2 };    // indices
    DWORD   dwColor   = 0x00ffff;       // color

    // are there bones at all
    if( m_sHeader.uiNumJoints == 0 ) return S_OK;

    m_pRenderDevice->SetBackfaceCulling(RS_CULL_NONE);
    m_pRenderDevice->SetDepthBufferMode(RS_DEPTH_NONE);

    // render the bones
    for( uiCounter = 0; uiCounter <
         m_sHeader.uiNumJoints; uiCounter++ )
    {
       // first vertex
       pLine[0].x = m_pJoints[ uiCounter ].sMatrix._41;
       pLine[0].y = m_pJoints[ uiCounter ].sMatrix._42;
       pLine[0].z = m_pJoints[ uiCounter ].sMatrix._43;
       pLine[0].Color = dwColor;

       if( m_pJoints[ uiCounter ].wParentID != 255 )
       {
          // second vertex
          pLine[1].x = m_pJoints[ m_pJoints[
          uiCounter ].wParentID ].sMatrix._41;
          pLine[1].y = m_pJoints[ m_pJoints[
          uiCounter ].wParentID ].sMatrix._42;
          pLine[1].z = m_pJoints[ m_pJoints[
          uiCounter ].wParentID ].sMatrix._43;
          pLine[1].Color = dwColor;

          // third vertex
```

```
                pLine[2].x     = pLine[1].x + 1.0f;
                pLine[2].y     = pLine[1].y + 1.0f;
                pLine[2].z     = pLine[1].z + 1.0f;
                pLine[2].Color = dwColor;

                // render
                m_pRenderDevice->GetVertexManager()->
                    Render(VID_UL, 3, 3, pLine, pIndis, 0);
            }
        }
    m_pRenderDevice->SetDepthBufferMode(RS_DEPTH_READWRITE);
    m_pRenderDevice->SetBackfaceCulling(RS_CULL_CCW);
    return S_OK;
}
// ----------------------------------------
```

As usual, there is the test to determine whether there are any joints at all (because without joints there can't be bones). Then the function switches off the backface culling because there is just a triangle built for each bone without taking the facing of the model into consideration. By switching off backface culling, you ensure that the viewer can always see the triangle from both of its sides.

Then two vertices are built from the parent joint, and a third vertex is added to complete a triangle from the current joint. Then this triangle representing the bone between the current joint and its parent is rendered.

Rendering the Normals

While debugging, it is also useful to take a look at the normal vectors of an animated model. If you have the impression that the lighting is calculated wrongly for an animated model, it might be as well due to the fact that the normals are not skinned or that they are wrongly skinned. To verify this, you would like to see them, and you don't want to use a pen and a paper and start drawing pictures from numbers on the screen.

Take a look at Figure 8.7 to get an impression of how an animated model looks if you render the normal vectors of the vertices.

Here is the function rendering the vertices. The normal is drawn as a line running in the same direction as the normal vector for a certain fixed size. The line starts at the position of the vertex it belongs to and is then rendered right away. Although this might not be fast, it is not meant for performance, just for debugging:

```
// -------------------------------------
// Name: RenderNormals( void )
//
```

Using the Animated Model 443

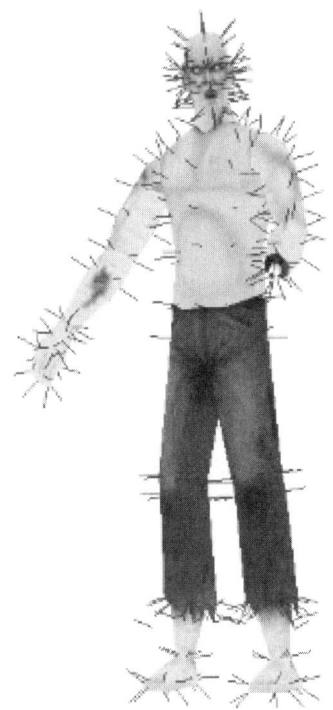

Figure 8.7 This is the zombie model in its new hedgehog outfit. The spikes of the model are the rendered normals. (Source for the free model: http://www.psionic3d.co.uk)

```
// fTime       = Deltatime
//
// Return      = (HRESULT)    Status
// -----------------------------
HRESULT CZFXModel::RenderNormals( void )
{
    ULONG    ulCounter = 0;
    float    fStart[3] = { 0,0,0 };
    float    fEnd[3]   = { 0,0,0 };
    ZFXCOLOR sColor    = { 1.0f, 0, 0, 0 };
    CVERTEX* pVertex   = NULL;

    // render the normals
    for( ulCounter = 0; ulCounter < m_sHeader.ulNumVertices; ulCounter++ )
    {
        // get current vertex
        pVertex = &m_pVertices[ ulCounter ];
```

```
            // set starting point
            memcpy( fStart, &pVertex->x,sizeof(float) * 3 );

            // set end point
            fEnd[0] = fStart[0] + (pVertex->vcN[0] * 2.0f);
            fEnd[1] = fStart[1] + (pVertex->vcN[1] * 2.0f);
            fEnd[2] = fStart[2] + (pVertex->vcN[2] * 2.0f);

            // render normal vector
            m_pRenderDevice->GetVertexManager()->RenderLine(fStart, fEnd, &sColor);
        }
    return S_OK;
}
// ----------------------------
```

Thanks to the ZFXEngine, we have an efficient rendering function to bring lines on the screen with an arbitrary color. This saves you from dealing with render state settings and calling render functions in the application.

One Look Back, Two Steps Forward

This chapter covered how to implement a so-called skinned mesh using a skeletal animation system. Even though the focus in this chapter was on animating characters, this is not the only use for such a method. Of course, it is the most common one, and the one people like to use when talking about animations. However, there are other animated models in a 3D graphics application, such as a video game. You can build animated machineries, for examples, with moving parts inside. You could also define a moving lift platform as an animated model. However, that is usually an easier task because such linear movements are faster to calculate by using normal transformation matrices.

On the accompanying CD-ROM, you will find an application that shows the class CZFXModel in action by loading and displaying an animated object. You should now open this project space and start digging your way through the code until you are sure you understand everything going on. The cursor keys enable you to switch through the different animation sequences and toggle rendering of the normals and the bones.

The next chapter will now be a bit . . . how should I say . . . a bit less action packed. We still have to add components to the engine, which will make life easier later on (and, after all, you are here to learn about programming an engine). The next chapter shows you how to use DirectInput and how to encapsulate it to abstract the input interface from the engine away from DirectX.

PART III

SUPPORT MODULES FOR THE ENGINE

CHAPTER 9
The Input Interface of the Engine 447

CHAPTER 10
The Audio Interface of the Engine 483

CHAPTER 11
The Network Interface of the Engine 503

CHAPTER 12
Timing and Movement in the Engine 569

CHAPTER 13
Scene Management 585

CHAPTER 9

THE INPUT INTERFACE OF THE ENGINE

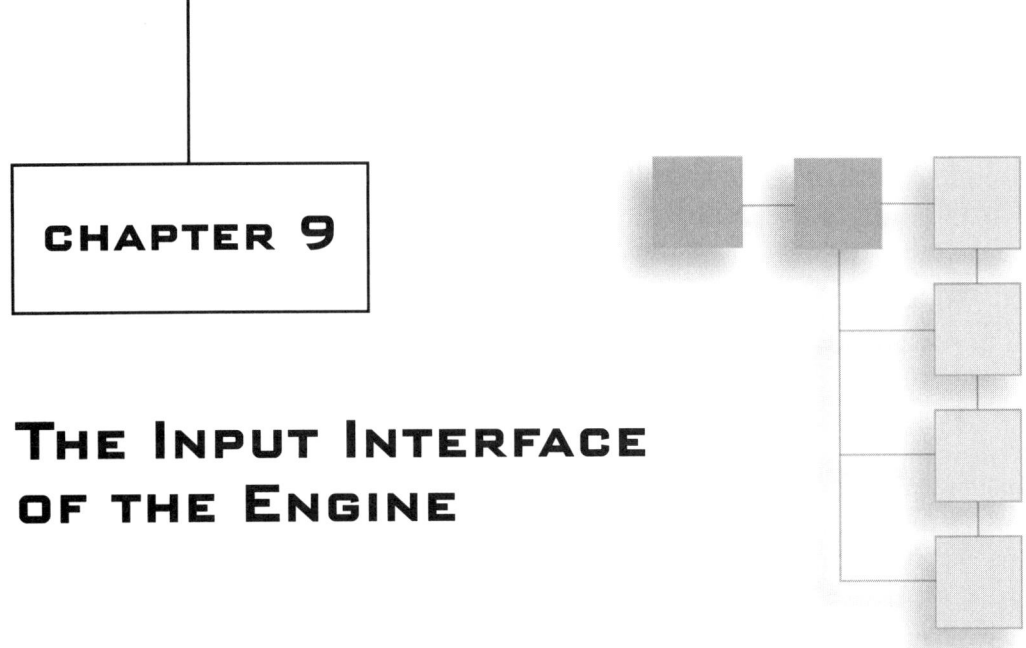

One ought to be ashamed to make use of the wonders of science embodied in a radio set, while appreciating them as little as a cow appreciates the botanical marvels in the plant she munches.

Albert Einstein

As Einstein said, we really should be ashamed if we are just going to use a technical miracle without understanding it at all (or at least trying to). Some may argue that a person using a tool does not really need to know *why* the tool works, that the tool should be designed in such a way that the user can benefit from its utility without necessarily understanding its inner workings. In contrast, I have always liked to understand my tools (user interfaces, for example), and especially appreciate those that are self-explanatory; but my search for understanding hasn't always been supported. For instance, I actually had university professors who encouraged me to use the phrase *using interfaces* rather than *user interfaces*; their reasoning held that a user should not be used and therefore has no interface. Ridiculous then, ridiculous now (in my opinion).

To be realistic, we must admit that we are at the middleware end of the line. The engine we are developing here is a tool for the end users. However, we are the ones developing this tool, so we should indeed understand the inner workings of the tool. This chapter introduces you to DirectInput and explains how to encapsulate it to abstract the ZFXEngine's input device away from DirectX.

This chapter covers the following topics:

- Initializing DirectInput
- Implementing a DLL to encapsulate input issues

- Querying the keyboard, mouse, and joystick for input
- Adding a new component to the ZFXEngine

Good Old Interface Design

In this chapter, we will add another component to the ZFXEngine. The component is meant to deal with input issues, so we use the same scheme as in Chapter 3, "Engineering the Engine," where we defined an interface structure for a device and implementation for this interface, now residing inside a dynamic link library (DLL) that is loaded by a static library. The basic architecture of this project is the very same that you learned about in Chapter 3. In this case, however, the project containing the static library is called ZFXInput, and the project with the DLL is called ZFXDI, where DI stands for DirectInput. The following list identifies the files you need to add to the two new projects, respectively.

Files used for ZFXInput:

- ZFXInput.h and ZFXInput.cpp
- ZFXInputDevice.h
- ZFX.h
- ZFX3D.h

The first two files from this list contain the implementation of the static library, and ZFXInputDevice.h is the definition of the input device interface. The header ZFX.h is our big rummage counter for all global exported symbols, structures, and the like. ZFX3D.h is the header of our math library from Chapter 4, "Fast 3D Calculus." We don't need the math stuff here, but the ZFX.h header does contain some structures from the math library, so we have to include its header as well.

It's unnecessary in this chapter to review all the code of the static library implementation. The system used to load the DLL is the very same as in Chapter 3, where it was discussed thoroughly. However, you will find the whole source code for this chapter on the CD-ROM accompanying this book.

Files used for ZFXDI:

- ZFXDI.def, ZFXDI.h, and ZFXDI.cpp
- ZFXKeyboard.cpp
- ZFXMouse.cpp
- ZFXJoystick.cpp

The first three of these files contain mainly the implementation of the interface ZFXInputDevice from the according file in the static library project (as discussed in detail later in this chapter). The other three files give the secret away: that we will define separate

Interface Definition for an Input Class

The interface for the input class is an abstract class that contains only pure virtual functions and, therefore, cannot be instantiated. This interface will abstract the most common tasks of querying input from the hardware away from DirectX or another application programming interface (API) such as SDL or whatever you decide to use for the real implementation. When we have finished with the implementation of this interface, the user needs nothing more than our engine to work with input devices.

We start by defining an enumeration for the three kinds of input devices the ZFXEngine is going to support in this chapter: the keyboard, the mouse, and a joystick with several buttons. In a real-world engine, you might also want to support force-feedback devices to rock and shake the player:

```
// in ZFX.h
typedef enum ZFXINPUTDEV_TYPE
   {
   IDV_KEYBOARD,
   IDV_JOYSTICK,
   IDV_MOUSE
   } ZFXINPUTDEV;
```

The interface for working with input is now ridiculously easy. There are no more than three functions to query for input events, and there is no decline in functionality. Those three functions suffice to check for all keys, mouse and joystick button, and movements of the joystick and the mouse. See for yourself:

```
// in ZFXInputDevice.h
class ZFXInputDevice
   {
   protected:
      HWND        m_hWndMain;
      HINSTANCE   m_hDLL;
      bool        m_bRunning;

   public:
      ZFXInputDevice(void) {};
      virtual ~ZFXInputDevice(void) {};

      virtual HRESULT Init(HWND, const RECT *, bool)=0;
      virtual void Release(void)=0;
```

```
            virtual bool    IsRunning(void)=0;
            virtual bool    HasJoystick(char*)=0;
            virtual HRESULT Update(void)=0;

            // works with mouse and joystick only
            virtual HRESULT GetPosition(ZFXINPUTDEV, POINT*)=0;

            // works with keyboard, mouse, and joystick
            virtual bool IsPressed(ZFXINPUTDEV, UINT)=0;

            // works with keyboard, mouse, and joystick
            virtual bool IsReleased(ZFXINPUTDEV, UINT)=0;
      }; // class
```

The idea behind this is that the functions to query for certain inputs are very similar. After all, it does not matter much whether you ask for a keyboard button or a mouse button to be pressed, right? That is why the interface does not provide a separate object for a keyboard, a mouse, and a joystick. You don't have to initialize and update three different objects and query the input from three different objects. This architecture would be of no concern to most users because the three devices would essentially provide the same methods.

Whereas the ease of use is the focus of the engine's front end, the back end is more interested in defining real objects for the different devices. That is why internally the DLL works with three different classes for keyboards, mice, and joysticks. Even then, however, you cannot ignore the similarity of those three input devices, and that is why the three of them are derived from a common base class.

Base Class for Input Devices

A mouse is a mouse is a mouse. Or not? In its component called DirectInput, the DirectX package only recognizes the interface IDirectInputDevice8, which is a device used for wiring an application with a real hardware input device (more or less via the driver, at least). Whether this device is a keyboard, a mouse, or a joystick is of no concern to DirectInput. During initialization, you must supply some different parameters, and, later on, querying the data from the device differs somewhat.

Users must remember for themselves which device was initialized as the keyboard, which one as the mouse, and which one as the joystick. That's not so difficult. However, I still like to differentiate inside the engine to make the differences clear. However, all those things common to all types of DirectInput devices will be implemented in a base class encapsulating DirectInput that looks like this:

```
class ZFXDIDevice
   {
```

```cpp
public:
   ZFXDIDevice(void)  { /*nothing*/; }
   virtual ~ZFXDIDevice(void) { /*nothing*/; }

   // base functions
   virtual void    Create(LPDIRECTINPUT8, HWND, FILE*);
   virtual void    Release(void);
   virtual HRESULT CrankUp(REFGUID rguid, LPCDIDATAFORMAT lpdf);

   // accessor functions
   virtual void    GetPosition(POINT *pPoint) { (*pPoint).x = m_lX;
                                                (*pPoint).y = m_lY; }

   // pure virtual functions
   virtual HRESULT Init(void)=0;
   virtual HRESULT Update(void)=0;

protected:
   virtual HRESULT GetData(ZFXINPUTDEV Type, void *pData, DWORD *dwNum);

   LPDIRECTINPUTDEVICE8  m_pDevice;
   LPDIRECTINPUT8        m_pDI;
   HWND                  m_hWnd;
   long                  m_lX;
   long                  m_lY;
   FILE                  *m_pLog;
}; // class
```

The constructor and the destructor of this class are not needed because we will not create an instance of this call. Actually, you cannot instantiate an object from this class because there are pure virtual functions, making this class abstract or an interface itself. Later on, we will derive three classes for the keyboard, the mouse, and the joystick from this call implementing the pure virtual functions.

The functions Create(), CrankUp(), and Release() are, line by line, the same for the different types of input devices as far as DirectInput is concerned. So those functions are implemented in the base class, and there is no need to overwrite them. The GetPosition() function provides the joystick's or the mouse's position to the caller, but for keyboard devices this is meaningless, of course.

The function GetData() then retrieves the current status of an input device and its buttons or keys, which are then saved to certain structures. This function is nearly identical for the joystick and the keyboard and very similar for the mouse. That is why it is also sitting with its implementation in the base class.

Chapter 9 ■ The Input Interface of the Engine

That's not too difficult to understand, is it? So, let's get started with implementing the base class' functions before we move on to the derived classes.

Creating and Destroying an Input Device

As always, the creation and the destruction of an instance from a certain class is an easy task. The most important thing is to set all pointers to NULL. If you fail to do so, it is not so dramatic in a debug compilation where the compiler will jump in with a helping hand. In a release version, however, the program will crash because the memory the pointer is pointing to will contain some old data that is interpreted as an object (and, of course, a call to this object will result in jumps to memory we are not allowed to work in).

Therefore, be kind to your memory and keep it from being trashed by our application screwing it up. Here is the Create() function's implementation:

```
void ZFXDIDevice::Create(LPDIRECTINPUT8 pDI, HWND hWnd, FILE* pLog)
   {
   m_pLog    = pLog;
   m_hWnd    = hWnd;
   m_pDI     = pDI;
   m_pDevice = NULL;
   }
```

This function needs a pointer to a valid object of the type IDirectInput8. You need this object to be able to create DirectInput device objects. Therefore, this function saves the pointer for later access in its member attribute. I know you have not yet seen how to create this object, but hang on for a moment. For now, just take it for granted that this object exists.

The Release() function of the ZFXDIDevice class has nothing else to do than just call the IDirectInputDevice8::Unacquire function that will disconnect the wire that DirectInput has drawn from this object to the input hardware object's driver. Thus the device knows that we don't need it any longer. Then the object can be released, and the releasing function of our class has finished:

```
void ZFXDIDevice::Release(void)
   {
   if (m_pDevice)
      {
      m_pDevice->Unacquire();
      m_pDevice->Release();
      m_pDevice = NULL;
      }
   } // Release
```

Making It Run

Now that you know how to initialize and release an instance of our own render device class, I will now show you how to initialize an instance of the IDirectInputDevice8 interface. It does not matter whether you want this object to be connected to a keyboard, to a mouse, or to a joystick later on. The initialization process is always the same, and it uses the following three functions. Note that the type of the input device (keyboard, mouse, or joystick) is decided by the parameters of the first two functions:

```
IDirectInput8::CreateDevice(REFGUID rguid, LPDIRECTINPUTDEVICE8 *ppDevice,
                            LPUNKNOWN *pUnkOuter);

IDirectInputDevice8::SetDataFormat(LPCDIDATAFORMAT lpdf);
IDirectInputDevice8::SetCooperativeLevel(HWND hwnd, DWORD dwFlags);
```

The first of the three functions wants to see a reference (REF) to a so-called globally unique identifier (GUID), which is a 128-bit number. This number contains an ID that should identify a certain device connected to the system. You can enumerate the attached input devices, for example, to get the GUID of each device. For a keyboard and for a mouse, however, this is unnecessary because they are basically mandatory for Windows anyway. So, we have GUID_SysKeyboard and GUID_SysMouse defined as default values for the keyboard and the mouse, and there is no need for enumeration as far as those two are concerned.

The second function enables you to set a certain data format for the input device object. This feature is necessary because if you want to retrieve the input data from this device later on, DirectInput needs to know in what format the data should be. An application can then define its own instance of the structure DIDATAFORMAT and sets its fields accordingly. However, DirectInput has already done this with typical settings in its global variables called c_dfDIKeyboard, c_dfDIMouse, and c_dfDIJoystick, which you can use.

The third function enables you then to set the cooperative level for Windows and provide the handle of the window whose focus is treated as the focus for the input devices. The second parameter takes a number of flags defining how this device should cooperate with Windows. For example, you could ask for exclusive rights on using the requested input device so that no other application can get access to it at the same time while your application is running. In general, however, it is recommended to adopt a more cooperative approach by using the flags DISCL_FOREGROUND and DISCL_NONEXCLUSIVE, which enable you to use the input device if your application has the focus.

Okay, you just enjoyed a crash course in using DirectInput. If you still feel a bit unsure about DirectInput, head for the good tutorials in the DirectX Software Developer's Kit (SDK) documentation to learn about this in more depth. If you think you're ready, however, let's move on and initialize our own input device:

```cpp
HRESULT ZFXDIDevice::CrankUp(REFGUID rguid, LPCDIDATAFORMAT pdf)
   {
   DWORD dwFlags = DISCL_FOREGROUND | DISCL_NONEXCLUSIVE;

   // if already existing destroy it
   if (m_pDevice)
      {
      m_pDevice->Unacquire();
      m_pDevice->Release();
      m_pDevice = NULL;
      }

   // 1. Step: create the device
   if ( FAILED(m_pDI->CreateDevice(rguid, &m_pDevice, NULL)))
      return ZFX_FAIL;

   // 2. Step: define the right data format
   if ( FAILED(m_pDevice->SetDataFormat(pdf)))
      return ZFX_FAIL;

   // 3. Step: set the cooperative level
   if (FAILED(m_pDevice->SetCooperativeLevel(m_hWnd, dwFlags)))
      return ZFX_FAIL;

   return ZFX_OK;
   } // CrankUp
```

This function enables you to create all types of input devices discussed so far. You need to provide only the corresponding GUID and the data format structure to this function. Note that this class is used inside the dynamic link library only. In the interface of the ZFXEngine, you are not required to handle DirectInput types, of course.

Querying the Input

Just like cranking up the different types of input devices in DirectInput, querying the data is done the very same way for all different types of input devices. There is only a single function to get the data about the current input status of a device. You can only differentiate the device types such as keyboard, mouse, and joystick by providing certain parameters to the very same DirectInput function. So again, we can encapsulate this function the same way as initializing the devices. That means the base class can fulfill this task, and the derived classes do not need to overwrite this function.

To query the data from an input device in DirectInput, there are two methods, because you can run an input device in two modes. First, there is a so-called buffered data mode. That already implies the second possible mode, which is, of course, the nonbuffered data mode. A buffer for an input device just means that all input events occurring on the devices are cached and saved into a buffer for this device. Using this method, you can guarantee that you do not miss a single input event until the buffer is full and the stored events are dropped one by one to accept new ones.

Without a buffer, you could sometimes get the impression that an application is gulping some key hits and does not react to them (so you have to press the key twice). Such a situation happens with nonbuffered data—because if you do not query an input device each frame, the input event is not stored but lost.

In DirectInput, you can use a buffer for all input devices because they are all stemming from the same interface class. Normally in a video game, however, buffered input data is not of very much importance. If you miss a W-key event or a press of the left mouse button, that won't hurt much because while moving the player is pressing the W key all the time anyway. The same applies for the fire button, which is the left mouse button normally.

To demonstrate the use of buffered data as opposed to immediate data, however, I will implement the buffered technique here for the mouse device, leaving the keyboard and the joystick with nonbuffered data.

The two different modes must be queried by DirectInput with two different functions. If you are working with a buffered input device, you have to call a function that returns the buffered data to you by the means of a structure and clears the buffer if requested. If you are using a nonbuffered input device, you can only query the current state of the device. DirectInput offers the following two functions to do this:

```
IDirectInputDevice8::GetDeviceData(DWORD    cbObjectData,
                                   LPDIDEVICEOBJECTDATA rgdod,
                                   LPDWORD pdwInOut,
                                   DWORD    dwFlags);
IDirectInputDevice8::GetDeviceState(DWORD cbData, LPVOID lpvData);
```

The first parameter of the first function wants to know the size in bytes of the structure supplied in the second parameter, which is in turn an array of DIDEVICEOBJECTDATA structures. Each element of the array will then receive a single input event that is stored in the device's buffer. The third parameter names the number of incoming elements in the array when supplied by the user. The function then changes this parameter to the value of events stored into the array. The most common flag for the third parameter is DIGDD_PEEK, which will say that none of the queried input events should be deleted from the buffer to clear it up. In general, you would not want to use this flag.

456 Chapter 9 ■ The Input Interface of the Engine

The second function is easier to use than the first one because not that many multiple events can occur. The first parameter again wants to know the size in bytes of the structure supplied for the second parameter. For the second parameter, you provide a structure that can hold the data depending on the type of the device. For keyboards, a simple array of the type `char` will do. For joysticks, DirectInput offers a data structure meant for this purpose.

Now take a look at how to use those functions in the real source code. The code "says" more than a thousand words of explanation. Here is how you can get the current status and buffer data from the input devices:

```
HRESULT ZFXDIDevice::GetData(ZFXINPUTDEV Type, void *pData, DWORD *pdwNum)
   {
   HRESULT hr=ZFX_FAIL;
   size_t size=0;

   // is this a mouse or a keyboard/joystick?
   if (Type == IDV_MOUSE)
      {
      size = sizeof(DIDEVICEOBJECTDATA);

      hr=m_pDevice->GetDeviceData(size,(DIDEVICEOBJECTDATA*)pData,pdwNum,0);
      }
   else
      {
      if (Type==IDV_KEYBOARD) size = sizeof(char)*256;
      else size = sizeof(DIJOYSTATE);

      hr = m_pDevice->GetDeviceState(size, pData);
      }

   // query failed?
   if (FAILED(hr)) {
      // device acquired at all?
      if ( (hr==DIERR_NOTACQUIRED) || (hr==DIERR_INPUTLOST) )
         {
         hr = m_pDevice->Acquire();
         while (hr==DIERR_INPUTLOST)
            hr = m_pDevice->Acquire();

         // another application has priority!
         if (hr==DIERR_OTHERAPPHASPRIO) return ZFX_OK;
```

```
         // we got it back
         if (SUCCEEDED(hr)) {
            if (Type == IDV_MOUSE)
               hr=m_pDevice->GetDeviceData(size, (DIDEVICEOBJECTDATA*)pData,
                                           pdwNum, 0);
            else
               hr = m_pDevice->GetDeviceState(size, pData);
            }
         // another error
         if (FAILED(hr)) return ZFX_FAIL;
         }
      // another error
      else return ZFX_FAIL;
      }
   return ZFX_OK;
   } // GetData
```

First, this function needs to decide what type of input device is concerned: a keyboard, a mouse, or a joystick. For the keyboard and the joystick, we use the function to get the immediate device state, whereas the mouse is a buffered input device.

Of uppermost importance are the security checks of the return values here. To get hardwired to a certain input device, DirectInput has to call the parameterless function IDirectInputDevice8::Acquire. Only if this call succeeds can DirectInput get data from this device. If the call to get the data or the state of a device results in the error DIERR_NOTACQUIRED, however, the device is not yet acquired or it is no longer acquired. If you get the error DIERR_INPUTLOST, your application has lost the rights to access the input device, which can happen if another application has got the focus or exclusive rights on the input devices.

To get the device back, we start calling the acquiring function in a loop until there is another return value. If this happens to be the error DIERR_OTHERAPPHASPRIO, another application has the focus or the exclusive rights to this device, so there is no chance to get it back right now. In this case, just return without an error report (because, in fact, this doesn't usually indicate a crucial error). So, the program should not terminate itself because of this loss of input devices. However, you should give some thought to including a flag that indicates that we cannot get any input as of right now. In essence, the application should pause until this can be changed.

If the function manages to get the device back, however, it tries again to get the input data or the device states. If this fails again for a second time, there must be something wrong. That is why the function is in this case returning with an error.

Now the basic functionality of our DirectInput device object encapsulation is complete. We can start deriving the three classes for keyboards, mice, and joysticks from this one and implement the missing functionality. Luckily, due to our efforts in the base class, the derived classes will be rather short and simple.

Getting Down to the Keys

Now that you have already completed all this work, implementing a class for a keyboard will require just a matter of seconds. You do have to take care of some little details, but this section shows you how. The base class ZFXDIDevice is now the workhorse of the input system; that is why the keyboard, the mouse, and the joystick classes have only some very specific tasks to do, as discussed in the following subsections.

ZFXKeyboard Class

The first class derived from the base class in our engine module dealing with the input issues is the class ZFXKeyboard used for keyboards. The base class names some pure virtual functions that we are forced to implement now in order to be able to instantiate objects from the new keyboard class. The functions Input() and Update() must be implemented here. In addition, I added the functions IsPressed() and IsReleased() to this class; these are used to determine whether a certain key is pressed at the time of the call and whether a certain key was pressed during the last call and is now released.

Here is the definition of the new class for keyboards:

```
class ZFXKeyboard : public ZFXDIDevice
   {
   public:
      ZFXKeyboard(LPDIRECTINPUT8, HWND, FILE*);
      ~ZFXKeyboard(void);

      HRESULT Init(void);
      HRESULT Update(void);

      bool    IsPressed(UINT nID);
      bool    IsReleased(UINT nID);

   private:
      char    m_Keys[256];
      char    m_KeysOld[256];
   }; // class
```

This class has only two attributes, which will hold the status of the 256 available keys in DirectInput. Normally you can query only if a certain key is pressed, and that is why this class will save the status of the last frame in the array m_KeysOld before updating the array m_Keys with the data for the current frame. This enables you to test whether a certain key was pressed in the last frame but is not pressed in this frame (which would mean that the key was just now released by the user).

For most actions in games, the evaluation of whether a key is released is far more important than if a key is pressed. It is impossible for a human to press a key for such a short amount of time that the input system will interpret that only in a single frame as a pressed key. It is more likely that this will be recognized as a pressed key for several frames. If this key were to change the magazine of a weapon, for example, and a user were to press this key for just half a second, the application would interpret this as 20 key presses and change 20 magazines. For such an action, it is therefore better to check whether the key was released in a certain frame. After all, this event (the release) can occur only once until the key is pressed again.

Initializing and Releasing

Initializing and releasing an instance of this keyboard class is done totally by the functions of the base class. Therefore, in the constructor and the destructor of the keyboard class, you only have to call the appropriate functions of the base class and let them take care of all the necessary work:

```
ZFXKeyboard::ZFXKeyboard(LPDIRECTINPUT8 pDI, HWND hWnd, FILE* pLog)
   { Create(pDI, hWnd, pLog); }
ZFXKeyboard::~ZFXKeyboard(void) { Release(); }
```

You still have to define the Init() function in this class, however, which has a little more workload than the constructor (not much more, but it is responsible for cranking up the DirectInput device object using the correct settings):

```
HRESULT ZFXKeyboard::Init(void)
   {
   if (FAILED(CrankUp(GUID_SysKeyboard, &c_dfDIKeyboard)))
      return ZFX_FAIL;

   // clear memory
   memset(m_Keys, 0, sizeof(m_Keys));
   memset(m_KeysOld, 0, sizeof(m_KeysOld));

   // acquire the device
   m_pDevice->Acquire();
   return ZFX_OK;
   } // Init
```

The real workload is done by the base class function `ZFXDIDevice::CrankUp`. Take a look at the parameters handed to the function that are identifying the device as a keyboard with the appropriate DirectInput values. Then you just clear out the two member arrays of the class and acquire the device.

Updating

Updating the keyboard is ridiculously simple. You could also do this using the base class, but note that there are differences in the keyboard as opposed to the mouse and the joystick. That is why the updating function is left for implementation to the derived classes. Note that the keyboard is used as a nonbuffered DirectInput device, so you need to get its data as a single structure into the key state array:

```
HRESULT ZFXKeyboard::Update(void)
   {
   memcpy(m_KeysOld, m_Keys, sizeof(m_Keys));

   // query status
   if (FAILED(GetData(IDV_KEYBOARD, &m_Keys[0], NULL)))
      return ZFX_FAIL;
   return ZFX_OK;
   } // Update
```

Before querying the current state of the keyboard, however, the old state is saved so that you can always compare the current state with the last known state to decide whether a certain key has been released.

Querying the Input

After updating the device information by getting the state of all the 256 available keys from the keyboard, you can then query the input for a certain key state. The DirectInput header `dinput.h` from the DirectX SDK defines several hexadecimal values that are the scan codes used in Windows to check for the keys. I just copied the scan codes and defined custom values for them so that the user can query those keys. Here are a few examples of what those new definitions look like:

```
#define ZVK_ESCAPE          0x01
#define ZVK_TAB             0x0F
#define ZVK_SPACE           0x39
#define ZVK_RETURN          0x1C
```

The numbers given as hexadecimal values are nothing more than the indices into the array with the 256 key states. To check for a certain key press, you just check the high bit at the according index in the array. If this high bit is actually set, the key was pressed at the time of updating the input information from the hardware:

```
bool ZFXKeyboard::IsPressed(UINT nID)
   {
   if (m_Keys[nID] & 0x80)
      return true;

   return false;
   } // IsPressed


bool ZFXKeyboard::IsReleased(UINT nID)
   {
   if ( (m_KeysOld[nID]&0x80) && !(m_Keys[nID]&0x80) )
      return true;

   return false;
   } // IsPressed
```

As you can see from the second function, you can just compare the current state with the last known state from the immediately preceding process. If the key was pressed down in the last update and it is now not pressed any longer, the key was released some time during the last update and this one. It's just that easy. You just have to call the update very frequently. In a video game, this should be done each frame anyway so that the update process occurs about 30 times a second at the least.

Now the whole implementation for the keyboard class is ready and can be used internally in the ZFXEngine. Therefore, it's time to switch our attention to the next derived class dealing with the best friend of the computer: its rodent.

The Pied Piper of Redmond

I guess you know the story about the Pied Piper of Hamelin. Interestingly, it is called something like the "Rat Catcher of Hamelin" in my native tongue (German). I must admit that we are not dealing with rats here, but with mice (but what's the difference really besides hair on the tail?). Nowadays, almost every computer has a mouse (the computer's best friend) sitting beside the keyboard. However, I can still remember when not so long ago working with a computer meant hacking things into the keyboard on text-based operating systems such as MS-DOS. Today, the only thing you need a keyboard for is to write letters or programs. You can run most other applications by just using the mouse for a majority of the functionality.

462 Chapter 9 ■ The Input Interface of the Engine

Well, enough of the introductory chitchat. After all, this section is where you start using the mouse for the engine. Just remember, computers will continue to develop over time. The mouse that we know now, and that most of today's youngsters have grown up with (even though I still occasionally encounter computers without a mouse), may not be the most common input device we will be using in 10 years' time. Perhaps you will even tell your kids about the old days when people used mice to do their input.

ZFXMouse Class

To get control over a rodent in the old days of Hamelin, you needed a flute. Today, however, it suffices to have a DirectInput at hand to tame that mouse. After all, dealing with a mouse is as easy as the keyboard class. Here is the class that we are using internally in the ZFXEngine to work with a mouse device:

```
class ZFXMouse : public ZFXDIDevice
   {
   public:
      ZFXMouse(LPDIRECTINPUT8, HWND, FILE*);
      ~ZFXMouse(void);

      HRESULT Init(void);
      HRESULT Update(void);

      void SetCage(RECT rcCage)   { m_rcCage = rcCage; }

      bool IsPressed(UINT nBtn)   { if (nBtn<3) return m_bPressed[nBtn];
                                    return false; }
      bool IsReleased(UINT nBtn)  { if (nBtn<3) return m_bReleased[nBtn];
                                    return false; }
   private:
      HANDLE              m_hEvent;
      bool                m_bPressed[3];
      bool                m_bReleased[3];
   }; // class
```

The number of buttons on this mouse is restricted to three. You can query the state of the buttons by using the appropriate function that is implemented inside the class declaration. How you can set the values for the button state is discussed later along with the examination of the Update() function.

Another interesting thing to note here is that there is a so-called mouse cage. Perhaps you can already understand what this is used for, but its use is discussed later on. For now, however, let's initialize a mouse.

Initializing and Releasing

The constructor and the destructor of the new mouse class are as easy and boring as the class for the keyboard (but then that was the reasoning behind implementing a base class that takes care of all the workload common to the input devices). Here are the constructor and the destructor:

```
ZFXMouse::ZFXMouse(LPDIRECTINPUT8 pDI, HWND hWnd, FILE* pLog)
   { Create(pDI, hWnd, pLog); }

ZFXMouse::~ZFXMouse(void) { Release(); }
```

Luckily, initializing the mouse is a bit more interesting than the initialization of the plain old keyboard. Besides calling the base class function CrankUp(), you have to create the buffer for the buffered input as well. Because you can do this after creating the DirectInput device object, however, you don't have to change the initialization routine of that one. Such a mouse buffer is of the structure type DIPROPDWORD, which you can set for a certain property of the DirectInput device. Using IDirectInputDevice8::SetProperty, you can activate this buffer for the device:

```
#define BUFFER_SIZE 16

HRESULT ZFXMouse::Init(void)
   {
   // clear memory
   memset(m_bPressed,  0, sizeof(bool)*3);
   memset(m_bReleased, 0, sizeof(bool)*3);
   m_lX = m_lY = 0;

   if (FAILED(CrankUp(GUID_SysMouse, &c_dfDIMouse)))
      return ZFX_FAIL;

   // event notification
   if (!(m_hEvent = CreateEvent(NULL, FALSE, FALSE, NULL)))
      return ZFX_FAIL;

   if (FAILED( m_pDevice->SetEventNotification(m_hEvent)))
      return ZFX_FAIL;

   // build mouse buffer
   DIPROPDWORD dipdw;
   dipdw.diph.dwSize       = sizeof(DIPROPDWORD);
   dipdw.diph.dwHeaderSize = sizeof(DIPROPHEADER);
   dipdw.diph.dwObj        = 0;
```

```
dipdw.diph.dwHow       = DIPH_DEVICE;
dipdw.dwData           = BUFFER_SIZE;

if (FAILED( m_pDevice->SetProperty(DIPROP_BUFFERSIZE, &dipdw.diph)))
   return ZFX_FAIL;

m_pDevice->Acquire();
return ZFX_OK;
} // Init
```

Only after setting all properties such as the buffer in this are you allowed to acquire the device. If you were to acquire the device beforehand, setting the property to it might fail. Now, however, the device for the mouse is ready to get input data from the real hardware device.

Updating

The final function that we need for our implementation of the `ZFXMouse` mouse class is `ZFXMouse::Update`. By using the base class function `ZFXDIDevice::GetData`, we can query the data from the buffer of the mouse using an array of the `DIDEVICEOBJECTDATA` structure from DirectInput.

After that, you still have to interpret the data to see what the user did to the cute little mouse in the meantime. (For instance, the user may have clicked it or just moved it around on the desk.) The third parameter of the function needs to supply the number of elements in the array to retrieve the buffer's data, and this variable will hold the number of returned events, which is equal to the elements in the array that are now filled with data.

The field `dwOfs` of the `DIDEVICEOBJECTDATA` structure will then contain one of the following enumerated definitions identifying what kind of input event occurred:

```
typedef enum
   {
   DIMOFS_BUTTON0,
   DIMOFS_BUTTON1,
   DIMOFS_BUTTON2,
   DIMOFS_BUTTON3,
   DIMOFS_BUTTON4,
   DIMOFS_BUTTON5,
   DIMOFS_BUTTON6,
   DIMOFS_BUTTON7,
   DIMOFS_X,
   DIMOFS_Y,
```

```
            DIMOFS_Z
        } Mouse Device;
```

Because those values are self-explanatory, let's just move on to the function querying the events from the mouse. You just need to call the function to get the data and then run a loop over the number of retrieved input events. Then you save the position of the mouse if it changed and, of course, you save the button states (that is, whether a button is pressed or not). The function to do this is as follows:

```
HRESULT ZFXMouse::Update(void)
    {
    DIDEVICEOBJECTDATA od[BUFFER_SIZE];
    DWORD dwNumElem = BUFFER_SIZE;

    // read data from the mouse buffer
    if (FAILED(GetData(IDV_MOUSE, &od[0], &dwNumElem)))
        return ZFX_FAIL;

    m_bReleased[0] = m_bReleased[1] = m_bReleased[2] = false;

    // now we have dwNum mouse events to process
    for (DWORD i=0; i<dwNumElem; i++)
        {
        switch (od[i].dwOfs)
            {
            // MOVEMENT
            case DIMOFS_X: {
                m_lX += od[i].dwData;
                if (m_lX < m_rcCage.left)
                    m_lX = m_rcCage.left;
                else if (m_lX > m_rcCage.right)
                    m_lX = m_rcCage.right;
                } break;

            case DIMOFS_Y: {
                m_lY += od[i].dwData;
                if (m_lY < m_rcCage.top)
                    m_lY = m_rcCage.top;
                else if (m_lY > m_rcCage.bottom)
                    m_lY = m_rcCage.bottom;
                } break;

            // MOUSE-KEYS
```

```
            case DIMOFS_BUTTON0: {
               if (od[i].dwData & 0x80) {
                  m_bPressed[0] = true;
                  }
               else {
                  if (m_bPressed[0])
                     m_bReleased[0] = true;
                  m_bPressed[0] = false;
                  }
               } break;

            case DIMOFS_BUTTON1: {
               if (od[i].dwData & 0x80)
                  m_bPressed[1] = true;
               else {
                  if (m_bPressed[1])
                     m_bReleased[1] = true;
                  m_bPressed[1] = false;
                  }
               } break;

            case DIMOFS_BUTTON2: {
               if (od[i].dwData & 0x80)
                  m_bPressed[2] = true;
               else {
                  if (m_bPressed[2])
                     m_bReleased[2] = true;
                  m_bPressed[2] = false;
                  }
               } break;
         }; // switch
      } // for
   return ZFX_OK;
   } // Update
```

As you can see now, the mouse is helplessly trapped in a cage that is restricting its movement. The hardware mouse itself knows nothing about the desktop or certain resolutions. Therefore, the mouse will not give you a position but rather movement values. As far as the hardware mouse is concerned, the user can move the mouse toward the very same direction for an infinite amount of time and space. It will then continually send the according movement information to the user. Therefore, the user is responsible for displaying the cursor image on a certain position on the screen, and thus the movement of the mouse can be restricted to a rectangle of valid data. Such a rectangle might be the desktop area, for example.

That is all you need to know about the mouse and how to tame it. Now we can move on to the final input device handled in this book: the joystick.

No Joy Without a Joystick

Now that you understand the classes for the keyboard and the joystick, we can make this a quick journey through the new class for a joystick. The only difference this time is that a joystick requires you to enumerate all attached devices, because you cannot just say that there is a joystick, of course. However, the enumeration is fairly easy (although a bit more complicated if you want to determine whether the attached joystick is a force-feedback device or not). The following class just takes the first attached joystick found on the system and doesn't care whether it is a device that could support force feedback or whether it is a joypad or anything else.

ZFXJoystick Class

Of course, we implement a new class for the joystick derived from the ZFXDIDevice base class. (Again, we're using the same old teabag.) Be aware, however, that some special issues are unique to joysticks. The function JoystickFound() lets the caller know whether a joystick is attached to the current system. After all, you won't find a gamer's computer without a keyboard and a mouse, but joysticks are not that common anymore. Games such as *Freelancer*, for example, have replaced joystick control with mouse control, even for flying space-combat vessels.

To examine the attached joysticks (if there are any), the class uses the function EnumJoyCallback(), which is handed to DirectInput as a callback routine for devices that look like a joystick. Finally, the function GetName() delivers the name of the joystick device if one is found and could be initialized:

```
class ZFXJoystick : public ZFXDIDevice
   {
   public:
      ZFXJoystick(LPDIRECTINPUT8, HWND, FILE*);
      ~ZFXJoystick(void);

      HRESULT Init(void);
      HRESULT Update(void);

      bool JoystickFound(void) { return m_bJoyFound; }
      BOOL EnumJoyCallback(const DIDEVICEINSTANCE *pI);
      void GetName(char *pJoyName) {memcpy(pJoyName,m_Name,sizeof(char)*256);}
```

```
            bool IsPressed(UINT nBtn) {
                              if (nBtn<m_dwNumBtns) return m_bPressed[nBtn];
                              return false; }

            bool IsReleased(UINT nBtn) {
                              if(nBtn<m_dwNumBtns) return m_bReleased[nBtn];
                              return false; }
   private:
      GUID                    m_guid;
      char                    m_Name[256];
      bool                    m_bJoyFound;
      bool                    m_bPressed[12];
      DWORD                   m_dwNumBtns;
   }; // class
```

Now look at the member attribute m_guid. In contrast to the standard GUID values for the keyboard and the mouse supplied by DirectInput, you now have to get a real GUID unique to a certain joystick manufacturer and type. This GUID can be found by the enumeration callback routine, as you will see in a moment.

Initializing and Releasing

The construction and the release of an instance of the joystick class are not at all different from the two you have already learned. Just call the appropriate functions from the base class and provide the corresponding values:

```
ZFXJoystick::ZFXJoystick(LPDIRECTINPUT8 pDI, HWND hWnd, FILE* pLog)
   { Create(pDI, hWnd, pLog); }
ZFXJoystick::~ZFXJoystick() { Release(); }
```

Initializing a joystick will require a bit more work. As previously mentioned, it is quite possible that no joystick is attached to the system the application is running. Of course, there may also be more than one joystick attached. For these reasons, you must enumerate all attached joysticks and use a callback function to examine them. Again, however, putting a callback function into a class is not that easy. Therefore, I chose the same solution as in Chapter 3, where we enumerated the graphics adapters on the system by declaring a global pointer pointing to the instance of the class and a global callback function that just relates the call to the member function.

Note
DirectInput has only one class of input devices besides keyboards and mice: the game controller class. This class includes joysticks as well as joypads, and there is no real difference as to the exact type of a game controller the actual hardware device is.

No Joy Without a Joystick 469

To get a list of all the attached joysticks, you just call the DirectInput enumeration function IDirectInput8::EnumDevices. As is common for enumeration functions, you can hand a pointer to a callback function, which is then called for each enumerated element.

If this enumeration process finds a valid device that can be used as a joystick, the function ZFXDIDevice::CrankUp is called to get it ready. After that occurs, which will take place in the callback function, you have to set certain properties on the joystick device, such as the numeric range of the axis. Here is what the initialization routine looks like:

```
ZFXJoystick *g_pThis=NULL;

BOOL CALLBACK gEnumJoyCallback( const DIDEVICEINSTANCE* pInst, void* pUserData)
   { return g_pThis->EnumJoyCallback(pInst); }


HRESULT ZFXJoystick::Init(void)
   {
   DIPROPRANGE diprg;
   DIDEVCAPS   diCaps;

   // some initializations
   memset(m_bPressed, 0, sizeof(m_bPressed));
   memset(m_bReleased, 0, sizeof(m_bReleased));
   m_bJoyFound = false;
   m_lX = m_lY = 0;
   g_pThis     = this;

   // enumerate attached joysticks
   m_pDI->EnumDevices(DI8DEVCLASS_GAMECTRL, (LPDIENUMDEVICESCALLBACK)
                      gEnumJoyCallback, &m_guid, DIEDFL_ATTACHEDONLY);

   // none found?
   if (!m_bJoyFound)
      return ZFX_FAIL;

   // final settings
   diprg.diph.dwSize = sizeof(DIPROPRANGE);
   diprg.diph.dwHeaderSize = sizeof(DIPROPHEADER);
   diprg.diph.dwHow = DIPH_BYOFFSET;
   diprg.lMin = -1000;
   diprg.lMax = +1000;

   diprg.diph.dwObj = DIJOFS_X;
```

```
m_pDevice->SetProperty(DIPROP_RANGE, &diprg.diph);

diprg.diph.dwObj = DIJOFS_Y;
m_pDevice->SetProperty(DIPROP_RANGE, &diprg.diph);

// number of buttons
if (SUCCEEDED(m_pDevice->GetCapabilities(&diCaps)))
   m_dwNumBtns = diCaps.dwButtons;
else
   m_dwNumBtns = 4;
return ZFX_OK;
} // Init
```

The following code shows you the callback function that we jump to for each device that the enumeration function of DirectInput finds attached to the system. The function tries to crank up the device as a joystick, which will fail if the device is not a joystick and no other input devices can be treated similarly. Upon failure of this attempt, the function returns DIENUM_CONTINUE to the enumeration process to proceed with it.

If the device is indeed a valid "joystickable" object, however, the function returns DIENUM_STOP to hold and abort the enumeration process because we found what we were looking for. See for yourself:

```
BOOL CALLBACK gEnumJoyCallback(const DIDEVICEINSTANCE* pInst,
                               void* pUserData)
   {
   return g_pThis->EnumJoyCallback(pInst);
   } // gEnumJoyCallback


BOOL ZFXJoystick::EnumJoyCallback(const DIDEVICEINSTANCE *pInst)
   {
   // try to crank up this one
   if (SUCCEEDED(CrankUp(pInst->guidInstance, &c_dfDIJoystick)))
      {
      m_bJoyFound = true;
      strcpy(m_Name, (char*)pInst->tszProductName);
      return DIENUM_STOP;
      }
   return DIENUM_CONTINUE;
   } // EnumJoyCallback
```

Updating

As with all DirectInput devices, getting the data from the hardware device is a really trivial task. Especially for joysticks, the function `IDirectInputDevice8::Poll` is provided by DirectInput. For some joysticks, you have to call this function so that the DirectInput device gets the data from the joystick. However, some joysticks and game pads do not require you to call this function and actually fail on this call and return an error. You can ignore this error, however, because it will not hurt the device at all.

After the polling call to the hardware device, you can call the `GetData()` function to retrieve the input data from the joystick device. This time, however, you use the structure `DIJOYSTATE` to be filled with information about the current stick position as well as the state of the firing buttons. This data is then saved into the class's attributes (thus allowing easy access). Here is the function:

```
HRESULT ZFXJoystick::Update(void)
   {
   DIJOYSTATE js;

   // poll the joystick
   m_pDevice->Poll();

   // get the data from the joystick
   if (FAILED(GetData(IDV_JOYSTICK, &js, NULL)))
      return ZFX_FAIL;

   // joystick buttons
   for (DWORD i=0; i<m_dwNumBtns; i++)
      {
      m_bReleased[i] = false;

      if (js.rgbButtons[i] & 0x80)
         m_bPressed[i] = true;
      else {
         if (m_bPressed[i]) m_bReleased[i] = true;
         m_bPressed[i] = false;
         }
      }

   // position of the stick
   m_lX = js.lX;
   m_lY = js.lY;
```

```
    return ZFX_OK;
    } // Update
```

That was the last function of the last class that the ZFXEngine is using internally to differentiate between the three types of input devices. We still lack the class implementing the interface though. That is what the next section is all about.

Implementing the Interface

The real implementing class, ZFXDI, which uses the interface ZFXInputDevice, will not surprise you. The declaration of the class looks exactly like the interface definition, and no additional member functions are needed. However, we do need four additional member attributes: one for the DirectInput main object and one for each type of input device that might be attached to the system. Those attributes are, of course, the three derived classes we developed in the preceding few pages:

```
class ZFXDI : public ZFXInputDevice
   {
   public:
      ZFXDI(HINSTANCE hDLL);
      ~ZFXDI(void);

      HRESULT Init(HWND, const RECT *, bool);

      void    Release(void);
      bool    IsRunning(void) { return m_bRunning; }
      bool    HasJoystick(char *pJoyName);

      HRESULT Update(void);

      bool    IsPressed(ZFXINPUTDEV idType, UINT nID);
      bool    IsReleased(ZFXINPUTDEV idType, UINT nID);
      HRESULT GetPosition(ZFXINPUTDEV idType,
                          POINT *pPt);

   private:
      LPDIRECTINPUT8   m_pDI;
      ZFXKeyboard      *m_pKB;
      ZFXMouse         *m_pMouse;
      ZFXJoystick      *m_pJoy;
   }; // class
```

Initializing and Releasing

The constructor is again fairly standard work; you just set each attribute to the initial value, which is NULL for all pointers. The destructor is calling the release method, which will clean up after the party has ended:

```
ZFXDI::ZFXDI(HINSTANCE hDLL)
   {
   m_hDLL      = hDLL;
   m_pDI       = NULL;
   m_pLog      = NULL;
   m_bRunning  = false;
   m_pKB       = NULL;
   m_pMouse    = NULL;
   m_pJoy      = NULL;
   }

ZFXDI::~ZFXDI()
   {
   Release();
   }

void ZFXDI::Release()
   {
   if (m_pKB) {
      delete m_pKB;
      m_pKB = NULL;
      }
   if (m_pMouse) {
      delete m_pMouse;
      m_pMouse = NULL;
      }
   if (m_pJoy) {
      delete m_pJoy;
      m_pJoy = NULL;
      }
   if (m_pDI) {
      m_pDI->Release();
      m_pDI = NULL;
      }
   }
```

After the user of our ZFXEngine input DLL has created a ZFXInputDevice object, he has to call the Init() function of this interface to crank up this object and enable it to query

474 Chapter 9 ■ The Input Interface of the Engine

for input from the hardware. So the function call starts by building the DirectInput main object. If this succeeds, the function proceeds by creating the three objects for the keyboard, the mouse, and the joystick and initializes them.

If initializing the joystick fails, that isn't really an error because we can interpret this as no joystick being attached to the system. If the keyboard or the mouse fails, however, the function ends with an error message to the caller.

Here is the function to get the input devices of the ZFXEngine ready:

```
HRESULT ZFXDI::Init(HWND hWnd, const RECT *rcMouseCage, bool bSaveLog)
   {
   HRESULT hr;
   m_hWndMain = hWnd;

   // create DirectInput main object
   if (FAILED (hr = DirectInput8Create(m_hDLL, DIRECTINPUT_VERSION,
                                       IID_IDirectInput8, (void**)&m_pDI,
                                       NULL)) )
      return ZFX_FAIL;

   // create all input device objects
   m_pKB    = new ZFXKeyboard(m_pDI, hWnd, m_pLog);
   m_pMouse = new ZFXMouse(m_pDI, hWnd, m_pLog);
   m_pJoy   = new ZFXJoystick(m_pDI, hWnd, m_pLog);

   // initializing all input device objects
   if (FAILED( m_pKB->Init() )) {
      if (m_pKB) delete m_pKB;
      m_pKB = NULL;
      return ZFX_FAIL;
      }

   if (FAILED( m_pMouse->Init() )) {
      if (m_pMouse) delete m_pMouse;
      m_pMouse = NULL;
      return ZFX_FAIL;
      }
if(rcMouseCage)m_pMouse->SetCage(*rcMouseCage);

   if (FAILED( m_pJoy->Init() )) {
      if (m_pJoy) delete m_pJoy;
      m_pJoy = NULL;
      }
```

```
   m_bRunning = true;
   return ZFX_OK;
   } // Init
```

Besides the handle of the main window used by the application requesting an input device, the user has to provide a RECT structure. This structure is used for the dimension of the mouse cage discussed earlier. It is imperative that a cage for the mouse be provided by the caller.

Note that I stripped some of the logging functions from this class and that the code on the companion CD-ROM contains a bit more error handling than the source code printed in this book. I want to keep things simple in the text so that you can easily grasp what's going on. In a real project, however, you should pay a lot more attention to the error-checking and, even more importantly, to the error-tracking methods you want to use.

Updating the Input

This updating function is nothing more than a big catchall function that is just requesting all three input devices to update themselves. So the final updating call of the input device in our engine looks like this:

```
HRESULT ZFXDI::Update(void)
   {
   HRESULT hr;

   if (!IsRunning()) return ZFX_FAIL;

   if (m_pKB) {
      if ( FAILED( hr=m_pKB->Update() ) )
         return hr;
      }
   if (m_pMouse) {
      if ( FAILED( hr=m_pMouse->Update() ) )
         return hr;
      }
   if (m_pJoy) {
      if ( FAILED( hr=m_pJoy->Update() ) )
         return hr;
      }
   return ZFX_OK;
   } // Update
```

Querying the Input

Now internally all the derived classes can already query the input data from the hardware. However, the user of the interfaces has no access to the subclasses, nor does he even know about them. Therefore, the ZFXDI class implementing the engine's input device provides four functions for the user to get access to the input data.

The first of those functions enables the user to ask the input device whether a joystick device is available and ready to be queried for input:

```
bool ZFXDI::HasJoystick(char *pJoyName)
   {
   if (m_pJoy)
      {
      if (pJoyName) m_pJoy->GetName(pJoyName);
      return true;
      }
   return false;
   } // HasJoystick
```

The second function dealing with input is the one that enables the user to query the position of the input device. Naturally, this function only makes sense for devices that can have different positions (such as the mouse and the joystick). Of course, you could also reposition your keyboard on your desk, but that won't result in an input event for current keyboards. Don't laugh about that. Future keyboards might just provide this feature.

For a mouse, this function returns the position of the mouse inside the given cage. For a joystick, the returned values are the amount of the extend on both axes of the stick:

```
HRESULT ZFXDI::GetPosition(ZFXINPUTDEV idType, POINT *pPt)
   {
   if (idType == IDV_MOUSE) {
      m_pMouse->GetPosition(pPt);
      return ZFX_OK;
      }
   else if (idType==IDV_JOYSTICK) {
      if (m_pJoy)
         m_pJoy->GetPosition(pPt);
      else {
         (*pPt).x = 0;
         (*pPt).y = 0;
         }
      return ZFX_OK;
      }
   else return ZFX_INVALIDPARAM;
   } // GetPosition
```

The remaining two functions deal with buttons. You can use those functions with all three types of input devices and just delegate the call to the according function of the appropriate input device object.

For a mouse, there can be three different buttons, for a joystick the engine can cope with four different buttons, and a keyboard has, of course, 256 keys, which are also called buttons in this case. Here are the two functions:

```
bool ZFXDI::IsPressed(ZFXINPUTDEV idType, UINT nBtn)
   {
   if (idType == IDV_MOUSE)
      return m_pMouse->IsPressed(nBtn);
   else if (idType==IDV_KEYBOARD)
      return m_pKB->IsPressed(nBtn);
   else if ( (idType==IDV_JOYSTICK) && (m_pJoy) )
         return m_pJoy->IsPressed(nBtn);
   else
      return false;
   } // Pressed


bool ZFXDI::IsReleased(ZFXINPUTDEV idType, UINT nBtn)
   {
   if (idType == IDV_MOUSE)
      return m_pMouse->IsReleased(nBtn);
   else if (idType==IDV_KEYBOARD)
      return m_pKB->IsReleased(nBtn);
   else if ( (idType==IDV_JOYSTICK) && (m_pJoy) )
      return m_pJoy->IsReleased(nBtn);
   else
      return false;
   } // Released
```

We have now finished implementing the brand new component of our engine. The new DLL and its loading static library comprise the new input component of the ZFXEngine.

Demo Application

This little demo application, which demonstrates the use of the new input component of the engine, is meant to be as small as possible to let you see the use of this new component in the simplest environment. Basically, it shows a big dialog box and reacts to certain input events by means of printing numbers or text to the screen as well as making some information dialog boxes pop up.

Besides the standard `WinMain()` function and the message callback procedure, only a few lines of code are necessary to build the framework for this demo application. Note that it is not a problem to mix the Windows input event notification in the form of messages while also using DirectInput at the same time. Remember that we are in a nonexclusive mode with our DirectInput implementation.

By now you should be very familiar with the `ProgramStartup()` function of our demo applications. For this chapter, I stripped out all details concerning the render device acquisition from the ZFXEngine. Those calls are now replaced with calls to get the input device up and running. As you can see, however, there is no big difference in those two components of the engine regarding the initialization process. You can find the complete code for this demo application on the CD-ROM accompanying this book. In this section, I just show you the interesting details (while assuming you are familiar with creating controls and windows using the WinAPI):

```
HRESULT ProgramStartup(void)
   {
   RECT rcCage = { 0, 0, 0, 0 };

   HDC hdc = GetDC(NULL);
   rcCage.right  = GetDeviceCaps(hdc, HORZRES) - 1;
   rcCage.bottom = GetDeviceCaps(hdc, VERTRES) - 1;
   ReleaseDC(NULL, hdc);

   // create the ZFXInput object
   g_pInput = new ZFXInput(g_hInst);

   // create the ZFXInputDevice object
   if (FAILED( g_pInput->CreateDevice() ))
      return ZFX_FAIL;

   // get a pointer to the device
   g_pDevice = g_pInput->GetDevice();
   if(g_pDevice == NULL) return E_FAIL;

   // initialize the device
   if (FAILED(g_pDevice->Init(g_hWnd, rcCage, true)))
      return ZFX _FAIL;

   return ZFX_OK;
   } // ProgramStartup
```

As a mouse cage, this function is using the dimensions of the desktop. Smaller values than zero are not tolerated for the mouse pointer (cursor); neither are coordinates that are greater than the according value from the desktop resolution. You need to be aware, however, of some small issues in the code of this demo application. The first thing is that the mouse coordinates displayed in the dialog box are not corresponding to the cursor that Windows displays. There are several reasons for this mismatch between the Windows cursor coordinates and the coordinates supplied by DirectInput for the mouse hardware device.

One of those reasons is the mouse's speed, which you can configure in a great range for Windows. Therefore, it is rather complex to mix the Windows input events with DirectInput as far as the mouse is concerned in windowed applications. In such a case, you should use the Windows events exclusively and save DirectInput for your full-screen or video game applications.

Another apparent problem seems to be the joystick coordinates, which are fluttering in a certain range even if the joystick is not moved at all. This can happen if the joystick is, even in its resting position, not calibrated at 100 percent or if it is just an old one that has seen a lot of hard dogfights. In such cases, instead of being as calm as you perceive it, the joystick sends minimal but rapidly changing input signals over its wire. Therefore, you should process the input coming from a joystick as real input you want to interpret as user commands only if a certain absolute value is exceeded by the incoming signal. If there is no fluttering when you run the application with your joystick, you can rest assured that your joystick is in really good shape . . . or irreparably broken already.

The function `ProgramTick()` in the demo application queries certain inputs from the three different devices and shows their status in the window. I don't list the whole function here because it is a rather lengthy function consisting of lots of more or less redundant lines dealing with the left mouse button, the right mouse button, and then the joystick buttons and so on. You will be able to grasp what's going on at a glance. If you release a mouse button or a joystick button, the code lets a message box pop up as a reaction to this event.

The following lines of code are an example of how this is done in the function:

```
#define MSGBX(a) MessageBox(NULL, a, "ZFXEngine report",
                            MB_OK|MB_ICONINFORMATION);

   if (g_pDevice->IsPressed(IDV_MOUSE, 0))
      {
      SetWindowText(hMouseBtn0, "1");
      }
   else
      {
      SetWindowText(hMouseBtn0, "0");
```

```
    if (g_pDevice->IsReleased(IDV_MOUSE, 0))
       MSGBX ("mouse button 0 released");
}
```

Other inputs queried by the application are the following keyboard keys: Return, backspace, spacebar, and the right Shift key. The first two keys mentioned here create a reaction from the program if they are pressed, the other two when they are released.

The following lines of code demonstrate how you can achieve such a behavior by using the input device of the ZFXEngine:

```
if (g_pDevice->IsPressed(IDV_KEYBOARD, ZVK_RETURN))
   MSGBX("RETURN key was pressed");
if (g_pDevice->IsPressed(IDV_KEYBOARD, ZVK_BACK))
   MSGBX("BACKSPACE key was pressed");
if (g_pDevice->IsReleased(IDV_KEYBOARD, ZVK_SPACE))
   MSGBX("SPACEBAR was released");
if (g_pDevice->IsReleased(IDV_KEYBOARD, ZVK_RSHIFT))
   MSGBX("RIGHTSHIFT key was released");
```

Finally, take a look at Figure 9.1, which shows a screenshot of the demo application from this chapter. Then put the CD-ROM accompanying this book into your drive and check out the code for yourself.

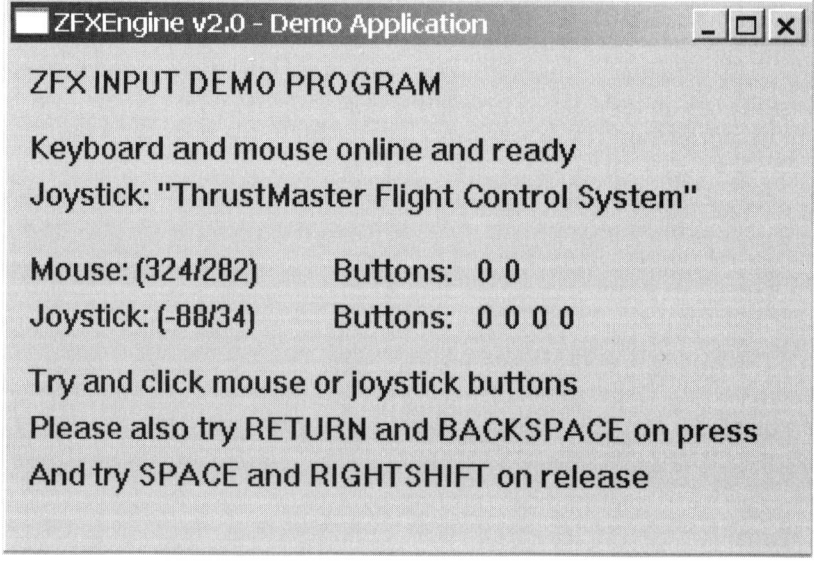

Figure 9.1 Screenshot of the running demo.

One Look Back, Two Steps Forward

DirectInput is fairly easy to handle, isn't it? It just took us about 30 pages to deal with DirectInput and to encapsulate it and make it a part of our engine by defining a smart interface that is as easy as possible while still letting you query all information you could want to know from an input device.

Now the `ZFXInputDevice` object is the second component of the ZFXEngine besides the all-mighty `ZFXRenderDevice` object. Both objects follow the same design scheme, and you can initialize them from the engine by doing more or less exactly the same steps. This is in important fact in the design of an engine because it encourages an intuitive and positive user learning curve. If users know how to initialize a render device, they will also know how to initialize the input device and vice versa.

Because this was only a crash course in DirectInput (and dealing with input in general), there is a lot of room for improvement left for you to explore. The most interesting topic not covered here is force-feedback devices. Such devices are steering wheels or joysticks with little engines inside that can make the device vibrate, shake, or create pressure against movement. If you have access to such a force-feedback device, you can program simulated turbulence for a flight simulator, a bumpy road for a racing game, and other such effects. If you are interested in those topics, review the DirectX SDK documentation. Then you should be able to add a new derived class for a force-feedback joystick inheriting from the `ZFXJoystick` class. It is worth the effort for the added realism in video games. After all, people who invest in force-feedback devices want to see something for their money.

Another area with room for improvement is the fixed set of input types known to the engine. There are certain predefined values for the keys a user can press, of course. However, there is no encapsulation of the action-mapping feature DirectInput provides. After all, a video game is not interested in the fact that the user pressed the left mouse button or the spacebar. It is interested in the fact that the user wants to fire a weapon or make the avatar jump up in the air. So the whole input system should be flexible and programmable. You should be able to map certain commonly used user commands to arbitrary keys or buttons or let the user decide which keys should generate what kind of command to the system.

As a reminder, you just added an important part to the ZFXEngine. In the next chapter, the set of device interfaces will see a new interface that adds another component to the engine to transform it into something you could really call a small game engine by the end of this book. In the next chapter, you integrate a simple audio engine into the ZFXEngine, one that can play sound effects and music. So switch your audio system online and keep reading.

CHAPTER 10

THE AUDIO INTERFACE OF THE ENGINE

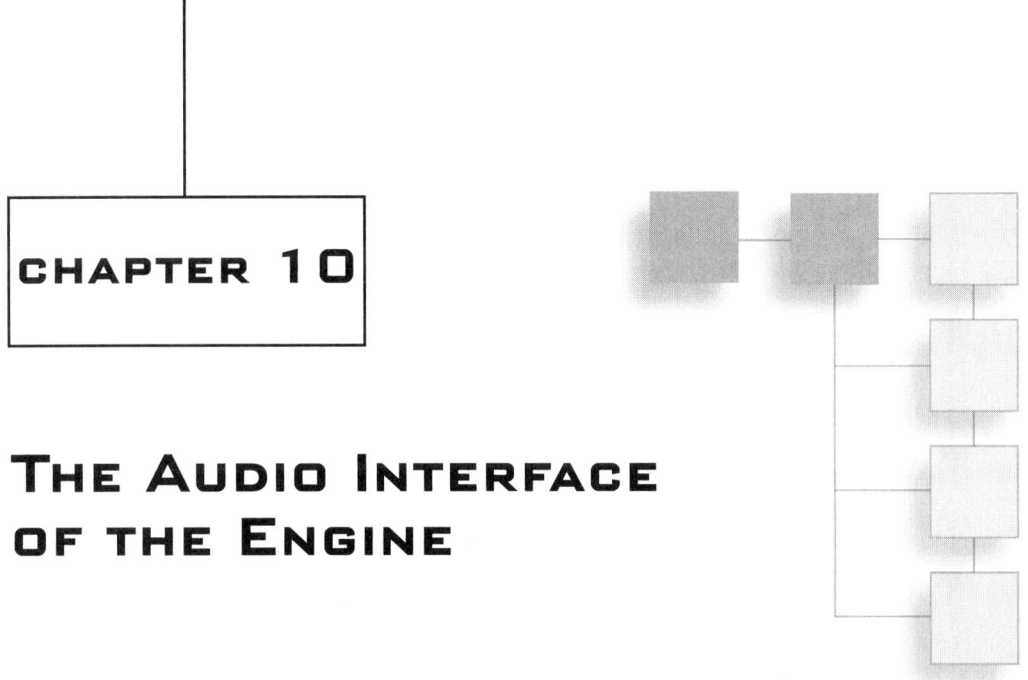

Who is all ears does not hear.

Moritz Heimann

A video game engine definitely needs supporting audio output, of course. Because it's unnecessary to go into detail about audio programming, however, this chapter is rather short. You should be able to see lots of parallels to the preceding chapter because the architecture of the audio component of the ZFXEngine is the same as for the other two components you know already: the `ZFXInputDevice` and the `ZFXRenderDevice`. Therefore, this chapter introduces you to the `ZFXAudioDevice`, which is used to play sound files and music to create an appropriate atmosphere in your game using the engine. The implementation of this device will be accomplished using DirectMusic internally.

This chapter covers the following topics:

- Initializing DirectMusic
- Encapsulating the audio implementation with a DLL
- Loading and playing sound effects files
- Creating and positioning 3D sound sources in the scene

Quick and Painlessly

Throughout this chapter, I use DirectMusic and DirectSound to implement the `ZFXAudioDevice`, but this chapter does not explain the DirectX components and their usage. To learn more about DirectMusic and DirectSound, refer to documentation (a book or tutorial) specific to these applications (the DirectX Software Developer's Kit

[SDK], for instance). You will see all the code needed to initialize and use those components here, but my explanations focus on building the new component for our own engine (and not on DirectMusic, for that matter). I do hope you have some experience using DirectMusic or that you are a quick learner. If you think you do need more information than what is provided in this chapter, refer to the DirectX SDK documentation and read the tutorials about DirectMusic there. They are pretty good.

Caution

In this chapter, I assume that you are familiar with the design reasoning behind the ZFXEngine. If you are not, go back to Chapter 2, "Designing the Engine," to refresh your memory. I also assume that you know by now how to set up a project with two project spaces, where one is a dynamic link library (DLL) implementing an interface and the other is a static library defining the interface and loading a DLL implementing the interface. If you don't, go back to Chapter 3, "Engineering the Engine," to see how this is done in detail.

The Same Old Interface

Just like the other two main components of the engine we have already completed (the render device and the input device), the implementation of the audio device will be done inside a DLL that is loaded using a separate static library. The static library project is called ZFXAudio, and the DLL project is called ZFXDA for DirectAudio. Note that you can exchange the DLL with any implementation you like (for example, SDL or OpenAL).

Note

In DirectX, you will find the two audio components DirectSound and DirectMusic. DirectMusic is a more comprehensive library geared toward professional audio programmers, and this component is also using the interfaces of DirectSound in some cases. So sometimes you will hear people talking about DirectAudio when meaning DirectMusic and DirectSound, but there is no such real component in DirectX (at least as of now).

The following list identifies which files are needed for the static library project and what they are used for. You can also take a look at the companion CD-ROM to see the project setup and the files contained in the projects.

Files used for ZFXAudio:

- ZFXAudio.h and ZFXAudio.cpp
- ZFXAudioDevice.h
- ZFX.h
- ZFX3D.h

As always, the first two files are used for the implementation of the static library with the class definition and the function implementations. The header `ZFXAudioDevice.h` contains the interface definition for the audio device. The catchall header `ZFX.h` is also integrated here because it takes all the needed structures, enumerations, and the like. That is why we also need the header of the static math library here, because the catchall header uses some of the classes from the math library.

However, this time we will also use some of the math classes for the audio device itself. At least the vector class is needed here when we are talking about three-dimensional sounds, where you can set a position for the sound and for the listener. I won't show the implementation of the static library here because there are no changes in it except for the class name, the name of the DLL to load, and easy things like that.

Files used for `ZFXDA`:

- `ZFXDA.def`
- `ZFXDA.h` and `ZFXDA.cpp`

The actual DLL project does not contain very much, as you can see from this short list of files. Not much effort is needed to load a sound file and to play it using DirectMusic. Even three-dimensional sound can be done quickly. Note, however, that the audio component of our engine is rather rudimentary and in a real-world engine you would need to enrich such an audio device by adding more functionality (such as appending sound files together, adding certain effects and similar things, and, in general, enhancing the overall atmosphere of the application). This book, however, principally concentrates on graphics and networking issues.

Interface Definition for an Audio Class

Before exploring the land of DirectMusic, we need a plan of action. The big questions are what our audio device should be able to do for us and how it should be operated by the user with regard to the function calls needed to make things run.

These questions lead us to the interface design of the first generation. Normally, you would want to define the interface, and then discuss it in meetings with your fellow programmers and move on to the next iteration of the interface definition. For the sake of simplicity, however, let's stick to the first version we come up with here. The following class is the interface definition for the rather simple audio device used in the ZFXEngine.

```
class ZFXAudioDevice
   {
   protected:
      HWND        m_hWndMain;     // main window
      HINSTANCE   m_hDLL;         // DLL handle
      bool        m_bRunning;     // init done
```

```cpp
public:
   ZFXAudioDevice(void) {};
   virtual ~ZFXAudioDevice(void) {};

   virtual HRESULT Init(HWND, const char*, bool)=0;
   virtual void    Release(void)=0;
   virtual bool    IsRunning(void)=0;

   // stop all audio output
   virtual void StopAll(void)=0;

   // load a sound file from disc
   virtual HRESULT LoadSound(const char*, UINT*)=0;

   // play a certain sound
   virtual void PlaySound(UINT, bool bLoop)=0;

   // stop a certain sound
   virtual void StopSound(UINT)=0;

   // listener parameters
   virtual void SetListener(ZFXVector vPos, ZFXVector vDir,
                            ZFXVector vUp,  ZFXVector vV)=0;

   // parameters of the sound source
   virtual void SetSoundPosition(ZFXVector, UINT)=0;
   virtual void SetSoundDirection(ZFXVector, ZFXVector vV, UINT)=0;
   virtual void SetSoundMaxDist(float, UINT)=0;
}; // class
```

As you can see, there is nothing more in this interface than just the initialization of the component and the shutdown and the loading and playing of sound files, naturally. So the front end of the engine's audio device is rather small and does not provide lots of functions. But then, that is the whole idea behind building engines to encapsulate functionalities that are provided by application programming interfaces (APIs) such as DirectX. The fewer the functions, the easier it is to use are the component (even if it is missing some functionality). The trick is to evaluate which functionality is really needed for a video game project and which is not.

Tip

The motto of the former Soviet airplane construction bureau MIG was that "a system that is not built into an airplane is a system that is guaranteed not to fail during flight operations." The same applies to programming complex software. The fewer the functions provided by the interface, the fewer the possible spots for bugs.

Of course, this philosophy put into practice decreases the functionality of the software (or the MIG, for that matter). So, again, you are dealing with the two concurrent targets of greatest possible ease of use and greatest possible flexibility. Nothing is as valuable as your own experience in this regard concerning what you think you need and what can be skipped. As a bottom line, however, you can stick to the KISS principle: Keep It Simple, Stupid.

Implementing the Interface

With that slim interface at hand, we can now start to implement the interface to build the audio component of the ZFXEngine. Throughout the remainder of this chapter, you will learn a bit about DirectMusic on the fly, but don't expect a detailed explanation. You should concentrate on the implementation of the audio component only, and you will hopefully see some similarities to the engine's components we have in stock already.

As with textures, we also need to manage and control the sound files loaded by the user. Therefore, the engine also takes care of storing the loaded files for the user.

ZFXDA Class

Before learning about the class `ZFXDA`, which is implementing the interface `ZFXAudioDevice`, you need to be aware of another detail. Because this chapter deals with audio programming, you will encounter audio files sooner or later when working on this implementation. To be prepared for that encounter, you need a structure at hand to use to store a single sound file in this implementation. Here it is:

```
typedef struct ZFXSOUND_TYPE
   {
   char                    *chName;
   bool                    bChanged;
   IDirectMusicSegment8    *pSegment;
   IDirectMusicAudioPath8  *p3DPath;
   IDirectSound3DBuffer8   *p3DBuffer;
   } ZFXSOUND;
```

This is the famous DirectMusic, with its little brother DirectSound. Besides the field for the name of the sound file and a Boolean flag indicating whether the sound file has changed, there are three fields of DirectX types. The flag is needed for 3D sounds only when their position or their direction and speed has changed, for example.

To understand the DirectX fields, you need to know a bit more about how DirectMusic works. In DirectMusic, just about nothing is going on without a so-called audio path. This audio path is not a path pointing to a file on your disc; it is the path all the audio data is floating through inside DirectMusic. You can think of this as a channel in DirectMusic where all audio data is managed and processed and that ends on the sound adapter of the hardware system. Such an audio path is present in each and every DirectMusic application. You can create your own audio paths, but there is always an implicit one called the default audio path.

A real musician can now do a hell of a lot of things with such an audio path. Remember that DirectMusic is not really targeting video game developers, but professional audio programmers and musicians. For our purposes, we do not need to access the audio path in most cases. In one case, however, we have to get a pointer to the audio path to get access: when creating and processing a 3D sound effect. Even still, the default audio path will suffice.

DirectSound takes care of the three-dimensional calculations needed for those sounds. You are only required to set the position, the range, and the orientation of a 3D sound in the virtual 3D world. To do this, you need a pointer to an IDirectSound3DBuffer8 interface object. As no big surprise, the only way to get such an object from DirectMusic is by requesting one from the default audio path.

However, you still have not saved your sound to any structure, right? Each and every sound you want to work with or you just want to play needs to be stored in a DirectMusic object called a segment. Such a segment is a structure that is used by DirectMusic to save the sound data; so when you are loading a sound from disc, you have to store it in such a segment. That's basically all you need to know about DirectMusic.

If you have already worked with DirectMusic's little brother DirectSound, you know the principle of the primary and the secondary sound buffer. The same idea applies to the DirectMusic sound segments. You can only play a single sound segment at a given time and not multiple ones. The segment that is played is called the primary segment. That would be rather boring if there could not be multiple sounds at the same time. So, normally you store your sounds as secondary segments. You can then play as many secondary segments at the same time as you like. DirectMusic takes all active secondary segments and mixes them together so that they are actually a single segment. This single segment is then played as the primary segment.

You've probably had just about enough theory by now, so here is the declaration of the class that the engine uses to implement the audio device interface:

```
class ZFXDA : public ZFXAudioDevice
   {
   public:
      ZFXDA(HINSTANCE hDLL);
      ~ZFXDA(void);
```

```
    HRESULT Init(HWND, const char*, bool);

    // interface functions
    void    Release(void);
    bool    IsRunning(void) { return m_bRunning; }

    void    SetListener(ZFXVector, ZFXVector, ZFXVector, ZFXVector);

    HRESULT LoadSound(const char*, UINT*);
    void    PlaySound(UINT nID, bool);
    void    StopSound(UINT nID);
    void    StopAll(void)    { if (m_pPerformance)
                                 m_pPerformance->Stop(NULL,NULL,0,0); }

    void    SetSoundPosition(ZFXVector,UINT);
    void    SetSoundMaxDist(float,UINT);
    void    SetSoundDirection(ZFXVector, ZFXVector, UINT);

 private:
    IDirectMusicLoader8      *m_pLoader;
    IDirectMusicPerformance8 *m_pPerformance;
    IDirectSound3DListener8  *m_pListener;
    IDirectMusicAudioPath8   *m_pDAPath;
    DS3DLISTENER              m_dsListener;
    DS3DBUFFER                m_dsBuffer;
    ZFXSOUND                 *m_pSounds;
    UINT                      m_NumSounds;
 }; // class
```

This class does not need any additional functions. Instead, it is only declaring the functions that the interfaces want to see from it. There are, however, a number of attributes that this class needs in order to work with DirectMusic. Except for the last two attributes, all of them are coming from DirectMusic or DirectSound. Here you can already see the pointer that is meant to point to the default audio path. It is good to keep that one handy so that you don't have to call a function to gain access to it each time you need it later on.

You can also see a DirectMusic loader. The name already gives away that this object is used to load sound files. Using DirectMusic, you don't have to bother with sound file formats because this loader object knows all the common formats and loads the data for you.

You can also see the DirectMusic performance object. This one is the workhorse in the DirectMusic component. In contrast to Direct3D and DirectInput, there is no such thing as an `IDirectMusicDevice8` interface in DirectMusic. Most of the tasks that you would expect from such an interface are done by the performance object.

The final two attributes stemming from DirectMusic (or DirectSound, for that matter) are a listener object and a sound buffer. The listener object is needed if you are dealing with 3D sounds because this sets the position of the viewer (or listener in this case) in the virtual 3D world.

Now that you know a bit more about implementing audio with DirectMusic and DirectSound, you're ready to see the constructor and the destructor of the class:

```
ZFXDA::ZFXDA(HINSTANCE hDLL)
   {
   m_hDLL          = hDLL;
   m_pLoader       = NULL;
   m_pListener     = NULL;
   m_pPerformance  = NULL;
   m_pSounds       = NULL;
   m_pLog          = NULL;
   m_bRunning      = false;

   // initializing structures
   m_dsListener.dwSize = sizeof(DS3DLISTENER);
   m_dsBuffer.dwSize   = sizeof(DS3DBUFFER);
   } // constructor

ZFXDA::~ZFXDA()
   {
   Release();
   } // destructor
```

The only interesting thing to point out here is that you have to set the field `dwSize` in the two DirectSound structures because those fields have to be initialized with the correct size; otherwise, your attempt to use them will fail.

Initializing and Releasing

Another thing that differs in DirectMusic is that there is no such thing as a `Create...()` function to get an object of DirectMusic as you would with Direct3D or DirectInput. So there is a little inconsistency involved in DirectX in this case. You actually have to implement such a function for yourself. That's a good thing, however, because then you can see what is going on inside those functions. The only thing you need to do is to initialize COM and query the appropriate interface object from it. The other create functions for DirectX components don't do this any differently.

> **Note**
>
> COM is an acronym for Component Object Model, a binary standard for interoperable software modules. The first software pieces that used the COM specification were the object linking and embedding (OLE) elements. The OLE controls (OCX) were added later on. The whole technology was renamed ActiveX in 1996, only to be renamed COM in 1997.

This probably sounds worse than it actually is. To initialize the COM system, you just have to call the parameterless function `CoInitialize()` of the WinAPI. This function then cranks up the COM system if it is not yet working. Then you can use the function `CoCreateInstance()` to create an instance of any COM-based object by providing the identifier for those objects as well as the interface name.

We will do this for the DirectMusic loader object as well as for the DirectMusic performance object. After building those objects, you can start working with them. The first step is to initialize the objects (as discussed later). For now, however, take a look at the following function. It starts by initializing the COM systems and creating the two DirectMusic objects:

```
HRESULT ZFXDA::Init(HWND hWnd, const char *chPath,
                    bool bSaveLog) {
   HRESULT hr;
   WCHAR   wPath[MAX_PATH];

   m_hWndMain = hWnd;
   g_bLF      = bSaveLog;

   // COM initialization
   CoInitialize(NULL);

   // create an instance of the loader object
   hr = CoCreateInstance(CLSID_DirectMusicLoader, NULL, CLSCTX_INPROC,
                    IID_IDirectMusicLoader8, (void**)&m_pLoader);
   if (FAILED(hr)) return ZFX_FAIL;

   // create an instance of the performance object
   hr = CoCreateInstance(
         CLSID_DirectMusicPerformance,  // Class-ID
         NULL,                          // aggregating the object
         CLSCTX_INPROC,                 // context
         IID_IDirectMusicPerformance8,  // reference ID
         (void**)&m_pPerformance);      // address
```

```
       if (FAILED(hr)) return ZFX_FAIL;

       // default path for sound files
       if (MultiByteToWideChar(CP_ACP, 0, chPath, -1, wPath, MAX_PATH)==0)
          return ZFX_FAIL;

       if ( FAILED ( hr = m_pLoader->SetSearchDirectory(GUID_DirectMusicAllTypes,
                                                       wPath, false)))
          return ZFX_FAIL;

       // initializing the performance object
       if ( FAILED ( hr = m_pPerformance->InitAudio( NULL, NULL, hWnd,
                                      DMUS_APATH_SHARED_STEREOPLUSREVERB,
                                      64, DMUS_AUDIOF_ALL, NULL)))
          return ZFX_FAIL;

       // pointer to default audio path
       if (FAILED(m_pPerformance->GetDefaultAudioPath(&m_pDAPath)))
          return ZFX_FAIL;

       // get pointer to listener in path
       if (FAILED(m_pDAPath->GetObjectInPath(0, DMUS_PATH_PRIMARY_BUFFER,
                                0, GUID_NULL, 0,
                                IID_IDirectSound3DListener8,
                                (void**)&m_pListener)))
          return ZFX_FAIL;

       m_bRunning = true;
       return ZFX_OK;
       } // Init
```

After retrieving the two DirectMusic objects from the COM system, you have to set the default search directory path, to which the sound files path is relative, by calling the IDirectMusicLoader8::SetSearchDirectory function of the loader object. However, DirectMusic is programmed to work with wide chars (WCHAR) only, so you have to convert your strings into wide chars by using the WinAPI function MultiByteToWideChar(). Check the Microsoft Developer Network (MSDN) or the platform Software Developer's Kit (SDK) documentation to learn more about that.

Before you can start using DirectMusic to play any sound effects or music at all, you must initialize the audio system of DirectMusic. So far, you have only created the objects; now you have to call IDirectMusicPerformance8::InitAudio to crank up the performance object of DirectMusic. The call in the preceding function is a standard call with standard parameters. I don't want to explain all the possible options here, so be sure to check the DirectMusic tutorial of the DirectX SDK.

After the successful initialization process of the `IDirectMusicPerformance8` interface object, you call `IDirectMusicPerformance8::GetDefaultAudioPath` to get the default audio path object. In this case, you need the default audio path to get the listener object by calling the `IDirectMusicAudioPath8::GetObjectInPath` function. You should remember this function from now on pretty well because it is used to get all kinds of objects from the audio path that are inside this big black box. As mentioned previously, the audio path is some kind of a channel from the sounds stored in the random access memory (RAM) over the bus to the sound adapter of the system. Therefore, in this path there are all the objects you have to accomplish the task of playing a sound.

That was quite a lengthy initialization process. At the end of the lifetime for an audio device object, you just need to call the destructor, which in turn calls the `Release()` function of the class. This function then releases and destroys all objects that were created during the lifetime of the audio device object to prevent memory leaks from occurring (most of the objects you have seen just now in the initialization process). However, the member attribute m_pSounds was not filled yet. We will do this in a moment, though, so you have to clean this up as well.

Anyway, here is the function releasing all attributes of this class:

```
void ZFXDA::Release()
   {
   if (m_pSounds)
      {
      for (UINT i=0; i<m_NumSounds; i++)
         {
         if (m_pSounds[i].pSegment)
            {
            m_pSounds[i].pSegment->Unload(m_pPerformance);
            m_pSounds[i].pSegment->Release();
            m_pSounds[i].pSegment = NULL;
            delete [] m_pSounds[i].chName;
            m_pSounds[i].chName = NULL;
            }
         }
      free(m_pSounds);
      }

   if (m_pLoader)
      {
      m_pLoader->Release();
```

```
            m_pLoader = NULL;
            }
      if (m_pListener) {
         m_pListener->Release();
         m_pListener = NULL;
         }
      if (m_pPerformance)
         {
         m_pPerformance->Stop(NULL,NULL,0,0);
         m_pPerformance->CloseDown();
         m_pPerformance->Release();
         m_pPerformance = NULL;
         }

      // shutting down COM
      if (m_bRunning) CoUninitialize();
      m_bRunning = false;
      } // release
```

Before you are allowed to cleanly release a DirectMusic performance object, you have to stop all sounds that are currently running on your instance of this performance object. Then you have to make a `IDirectMusicPerformance8::CloseDown` function call to stop all internal processes running in the performance objects, such as mixing and the like. Only then can you release the object smoothly without the fear of creating any errors or leaks.

Do not forget to shut down the COM system. This is done by the parameterless function `CoUninitialize()`. If no other application is using COM at the moment, the COM system is put back to sleep by this call.

Loading and Playing Sounds

Besides enabling you to play sound effects and music, another important feature of DirectMusic is that it can load sound files of all common formats (which means you don't have to write those loaders for yourself). The function `IDirectMusicLoader8::LoadObjectFromFile` enables you to order the DirectMusic loader object to load a sound file for you. Thus, you can load files, such as those in the wave format, without writing a single line of custom code.

Because we are encapsulating DirectMusic here with our own API, however, we have to do a bit more work before using this neat function the loader objects provides. The first task at hand is that you have to convert the given char string with the name of the sound file to load into a wide character string. You already saw how this works in the initialization function of this class.

After that, the loading function loops through all loaded sound files stored in the member variable `m_pSounds` and compares the name string to the ones of the already loaded sounds. This is the same thing we did for the materials and the textures, and the same reasoning applies: We do not need to load a sound file twice.

Another catch is that the pointer `m_pSounds` is not initialized at first. So, if there is no sound loaded yet, you have to allocate memory for the pointer. Again, I always allocate enough memory for the storage of 50 objects. If the storage fills up, another 50 slots will be allocated and so on. After you have found a valid storage space into which the new sound can be loaded, you copy the name string into the structure and load the sound file, finally.

After you have made DirectMusic load the file, you must complete three more steps before you can use the loaded sound effect. First you have to call the DirectMusic function `IDirectMusicSegment8::Download`. This downloads all instruments used in the sound effect from the DirectMusic performance object. The second step after loading the sound file is to create an audio path for this sound. The third and final step is to retrieve a DirectSound 3D sound buffer from this newly created audio path.

You need to know that there are basically two different methods to store sound effects or music in a file. The first one is by using digitalized samples, and the second one is by using instruments. The first method just saves the final wave of the sound in a digital form directly to the file. The drawback of this method is that it consumes a lot of memory. The advantage is that you don't have to process the data after it is loaded. You can just play the wave. The second method is just saving the types of instruments used to generate the sound along with information about which instrument has to become active at which time interval with which volume and so on (as if you were not storing the sound itself, but the composer himself along with the commands he issues). This consumes less memory, but you have to process the data after the sound has been loaded to generate the wave.

The DownLoadable Sounds format (DLS), which is used by DirectMusic as well, combines both methods. At runtime, the necessary instrument information is generated and you have to get that information to your segment by calling the above-mentioned `IDirectMusicSegment8::Download` function. You have to do this only one time, after the segment is filled with a sound file.

That's all you have to do to make the segment ready. If you are dealing with 3D sound, however, you face two more issues. Generally, you only have to use the default audio path. If you use 3D sound effects, however, you must create a separate audio path object for each and every 3D sound effect you are loading. So, the second step after loading the sound file is to create an audio path for this sound.

The third and final step is to retrieve a DirectSound 3D sound buffer from this newly created audio path. You need this sound buffer in order to have access to the functions that enable you to set the parameters of the 3D sound (such as its position, for example).

Here is the function:

```cpp
HRESULT ZFXDA::LoadSound(const char *chName, UINT *nID)
   {
   WCHAR    wName[MAX_PATH];
   HRESULT  hr;

   if (MultiByteToWideChar(CP_ACP, 0, chName, -1, wName, MAX_PATH)==0)
      return ZFX_FAIL;

   // is this sound file already loaded?
   for (UINT i=0; i<m_NumSounds; i++)
      {
      if (strcmp(chName, m_pSounds[i].chName)==0)
         {
         *nID = i;
         return ZFX_OK;
         }
      } // for

   // 50 new slots for the sounds
   if ( (m_NumSounds%50) == 0 )
      {
      int n = (m_NumSounds+50)*sizeof(ZFXSOUND);
      m_pSounds = (ZFXSOUND*)realloc(m_pSounds, n);
      if (!m_pSounds) return ZFX_OUTOFMEMORY;
      }

   m_pSounds[m_NumSounds].chName = new char[strlen(chName)+1];
   memcpy(m_pSounds[m_NumSounds].chName, chName, strlen(chName)+1);

   m_pSounds[m_NumSounds].bChanged = false;

   // load the file
   if (FAILED(hr=m_pLoader->LoadObjectFromFile(
                               CLSID_DirectMusicSegment, // class
                               IID_IDirectMusicSegment8, // interface type
                               wName,                    // name
                               (void**)&m_pSounds[m_NumSounds].pSegment)))
                                                         // address
      {
      if ((hr==DMUS_E_LOADER_FAILEDOPEN) || (hr==DMUS_E_LOADER_FAILEDCREATE))
         return ZFX_FILENOTFOUND;
```

```
        else if (hr==DMUS_E_LOADER_FORMATNOTSUPPORTED)
            return ZFX_INVALIDPARAM;
        else if (hr==E_OUTOFMEMORY)
            return ZFX_OUTOFMEMORY;
        return ZFX_FAIL;
        }

    // download instruments
    if (FAILED(pSeg->Download(m_pPerformance)))
        {
        pSeg->Release();
        pSeg = NULL;
        return ZFX_FAIL;
        }

    // create an audio path
    m_pPerformance->CreateStandardAudioPath( DMUS_APATH_DYNAMIC_3D,
                                             64, TRUE,
                                             &m_pSounds[m_NumSounds].p3DPath);

    m_pSounds[m_NumSounds].p3DPath->GetObjectInPath(
          DMUS_PCHANNEL_ALL,          // performance channel
          DMUS_PATH_BUFFER,           // stage in path
          0,                          // index in path
          GUID_NULL,                  // class
          0,                          // index
          IID_IDirectSound3DBuffer,   // type
          (void**)                    // address
          &m_pSounds[m_NumSounds].p3DBuffer);

    m_NumSounds++;
    return ZFX_OK;
    } // LoadSound
```

Now the requested sound file should be loaded and stored, ready to be played by the application using this audio device object of the ZFXEngine. Playing such a sound segment is then rather easy, as you can see from the following function:

```
void ZFXDA::PlaySound(UINT nID, bool bLoop)
    {
    if (nID >= m_NumSounds)
        return;
```

```
   // any changes?
   if (m_pSounds[nID].bChanged)
      {
      m_pListener->CommitDeferredSettings();
      m_pSounds[nID].bChanged = false;
      }

   if (bLoop)
      m_pSounds[nID].pSegment->SetRepeats(DMUS_SEG_REPEAT_INFINITE);

   // play as secondary buffer
   m_pPerformance->PlaySegment(m_pSounds[nID].pSegment, DMUS_SEGF_DEFAULT |
                               DMUS_SEGF_SECONDARY, 0, 0);
   } // PlaySound
```

If the user requests the function to play this sound in a loop, it will do so. Therefore, you also must provide a stop function to get rid of this noise. The DirectMusic function IDirectMusicSegment8::SetRepeats enables you to adjust the loop settings. You can play the sound then by calling IDirectMusicPerformance8::PlaySegment. The first parameter of this function is a pointer to the segment you want to play. The second parameter is a bunch of flags, and we can ignore the final two parameters. For our simple purposes of playing sound segments, the two flags shown in the code will do. The first parameter indicates that the flags and attributes of the segment itself should be used (for example, its own audio path rather than the default audio path). The second flag states that this segment is a secondary segment to be mixed into the primary segment.

You can also see the call to IDirectSound3DListener8::CommitDeferredSettings. You will learn a bit about this later, but for now you just need to know that DirectSound needs to recalculate the 3D sounds if some of their attributes have changed. If the position or the direction of a sound changes, for instance, it will just sound different, requiring DirectSound to recalculate that on the central processing unit (CPU) or maybe on the processor of a modern sound adapter if one is present. Those calculations take time, however; so DirectSound can be told to hold off until you call this function, allowing you to make as many changes as you want to the sound without it being recalculated each and every time.

The following section covers those recalculations and how to withhold them.

For now, here is the function that enables you to stop a running sound:

```
void ZFXDA::StopSound(UINT nID)
   {
   if (nID >= m_NumSounds)
      return;
```

```
m_pPerformance->Stop(m_pSounds[nID].pSegment, 0, 0, 0);
} // StopSound
```

Listener and Source for 3D Sounds

Actually, sound effects in a game are a very good thing. For a player to get the real, immersive multimedia experience, however, 3D sound effects are a must. Because you've made it this far, I suppose you already have some general knowledge of virtual 3D worlds, so I'm probably not writing anything here you don't already understand about the value of 3D sound effects. That said, DirectMusic and DirectSound provide all necessary functions and calculations to enable 3D sound.

You must do just two things to make this system work. First, you have to set the position of the listener in the virtual world because this position is part of the calculations, of course. The second thing you have to do is tell DirectMusic the position of each 3D sound effect you have playing in your scene. Besides that information, DirectMusic also needs to know about the direction and the speed of the listener. From that information, DirectMusic and DirectSound can then calculate the volume with which a certain sound effect has to be played as well as on which channels in a surround system, thus giving the player the impression of being in a real three-dimensional world.

The following function enables the user of the audio device to set the needed values for the listener, which should be taken from the current camera or viewer object, of course:

```
size_t g_szoff3 = sizeof(float)*3;

void ZFXDA::SetListener(ZFXVector vPos, ZFXVector vDir,
                        ZFXVector vUp, ZFXVector vSpeed)
   {
   m_pListener->GetAllParameters(&m_dsListener);

   memcpy(&m_dsListener.vPosition, &vPos, g_szoff3);
   memcpy(&m_dsListener.vOrientFront, &vDir, g_szoff3);
   memcpy(&m_dsListener.vOrientTop, &vUp, g_szoff3);
   memcpy(&m_dsListener.vVelocity, &vSpeed, g_szoff3);

   if (m_pListener)
      m_pListener->SetAllParameters(&m_dsListener, DS3D_IMMEDIATE);
   } // SetListener
```

At first you query the appropriate data of the current listener in DirectMusic by calling the function `IDirectMusic3DListener8::GetAllParameters`. Then you could check whether there are any changes at all. Then copy the new data into the listener object member attribute of the class and write the structure back to DirectMusic to activate the changes.

500 Chapter 10 ■ The Audio Interface of the Engine

If you use the flag `DS3D_IMMEDIATE`, DirectMusic will recalculate all 3D sound effects immediately.

In a 3D video game where the player will live in a rather action-loaded world, you can expect the listener position to change each frame as well as the camera the viewer uses. That is why you should let DirectMusic recalculate the 3D sound immediately. As you learned earlier in this chapter, you can set the attributes of the 3D sounds as well (for instance, their position and range). You will call those methods, especially for moving sounds, quite often (even several times each frame) for all sound objects. Therefore, it would be rather stupid to request immediate calculations on those calls because of the resultant large number of redundant calculations per frame.

Instead, you use the flag `DS3D_DEFERRED` to withhold the recalculations until the DirectMusic function `CommitDeferredSettings()` is called (as in `ZFXDA::PlaySound`). Finally, here are the functions that enable you to set the parameters for 3D sound effects:

```
void ZFXDA::SetSoundPosition(ZFXVector vPos, UINT nID)
   {
   IDirectSound3DBuffer8 *p3DBuffer;
   if (nID >= m_NumSounds) return;

   p3DBuffer = m_pSounds[m_NumSounds].p3DBuffer;
   m_pSounds[m_NumSounds].bChanged = true;

   p3DBuffer->GetAllParameters(&m_dsBuffer);

   m_dsBuffer.dwMode = DS3DMODE_NORMAL;
   memcpy(&m_dsBuffer.vPosition, &vPos, g_szoff3);

   p3DBuffer->SetAllParameters(&m_dsBuffer, DS3D_DEFERRED);
   } // SetSoundPosition


void ZFXDA::SetSoundDirection(ZFXVector vDir, ZFXVector vV, UINT nID)
   {
   IDirectSound3DBuffer8 *p3DBuffer;
   if (nID >= m_NumSounds) return;

   p3DBuffer = m_pSounds[m_NumSounds].p3DBuffer;
   m_pSounds[m_NumSounds].bChanged = true;

   p3DBuffer->GetAllParameters(&m_dsBuffer);
```

```
   m_dsBuffer.dwMode = DS3DMODE_NORMAL;
   memcpy(&m_dsBuffer.vVelocity, &vV, g_szoff3);
   memcpy(&m_dsBuffer.vConeOrientation,&vDir,g_szoff3);

   p3DBuffer->SetAllParameters(&m_dsBuffer, DS3D_DEFERRED);
   } // SetSoundDistance


void ZFXDA::SetSoundMaxDist(float fDis, UINT nID)
   {
   if (nID >= m_NumSounds) return;
   IDirectSound3DBuffer8 *p3DBuffer;
   if (nID >= m_NumSounds) return;

   p3DBuffer = m_pSounds[m_NumSounds].p3DBuffer;
   m_pSounds[m_NumSounds].bChanged = true;

   p3DBuffer->GetAllParameters(&m_dsBuffer);

   m_dsBuffer.dwMode = DS3DMODE_NORMAL;
   m_dsBuffer.flMaxDistance = fDis;

   p3DBuffer->SetAllParameters(&m_dsBuffer, DS3D_DEFERRED);
   } // SetSoundMaxDist
```

Demo Application

As fitting for a short chapter such as this, the little demo program of this chapter is also short. After initializing the audio device component of the ZFXEngine, the demo application just uses an open-file-dialog box of the WinAPI to enable the user to select a sound file. This sound file is then loaded and played in an infinite loop until another sound is loaded.

This demo application is rather boring because there is no visual output. Later on, however, if you use the sound in a virtual 3D world, it will make a big difference in the experience the players get from the virtual world you build for them.

One Look Back, Two Steps Forward

You have now seen the third main component of the ZFXEngine come to life. This component also used the static-library-loading-a-DLL scheme, to keep the interface independent from a specific API (such as DirectMusic and DirectSound, for example). Our engine is now pretty close to being some kind of multimedia engine: After all, we now have visual output by 3D graphics, audio output of sound effects and music, and the ability to query the user's input from the input hardware devices.

Actually, only one main component you would like to have in an engine is left: the network component (discussed in the next chapter). Nowadays players demand (and developers and manufacturers comply) that video games be connectable over a local or even a worldwide network (such as the Internet). This network connectability enables users to play their games not only by themselves, but also with others likewise connected (be that a neighbor next door or even someone on the other side of the world).

Check out the demo application of this chapter, and then move on to the next chapter to learn what all this networking stuff is about.

CHAPTER 11

THE NETWORK INTERFACE OF THE ENGINE

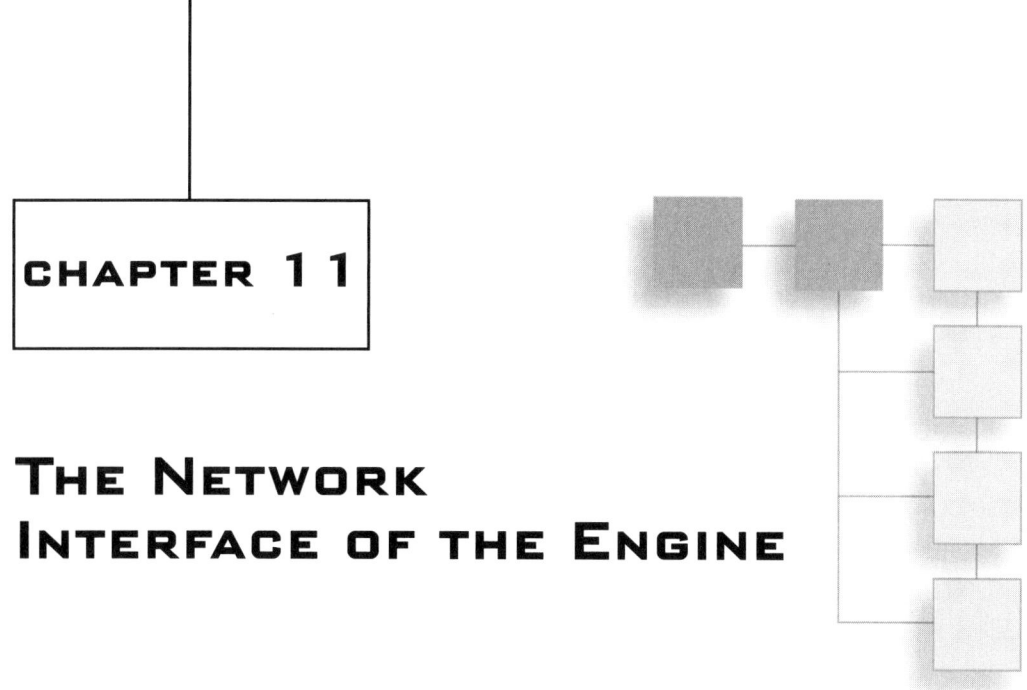

Don't put me to the test like a weak boy or an old woman who knows nothing about war.

Hector, Homer's Iliad

Today, you cannot take a video game on the PC platform to market if it does not offer a network mode to let multiple players play together in the same virtual game world. Even the console platforms have become connected by networks in the past few years. Such network connections are not limited to systems reachable by network cables in your home—you can now use the Internet to get connected to other systems all over the world.

Such a game can be a simple death match first-person shooter in which the players are asked to get as many *frags* as possible, meaning you should wipe out as many opposing players as possible. But even complex games such as *Ultima Online, Diablo 2,* and *Star Wars Galaxies* are completely based on playing online and, in most cases, don't support single-player modes at all. These games feature vast virtual worlds where the gamers can live an online life. In some cases, virtual objects such as equipment or whole video game characters become real-life values. The first level-70 fighter character of the game *Diablo 2* was sold on eBay for about $5,000, and you can get several thousand virtual credits for nearly all current online games for a few hundred bucks on eBay.

This chapter introduces you to networking architectures. We will add a new main component to the ZFXEngine that enables the programming of network applications with the engine.

This chapter covers the following topics:

- The various types of network games
- The basic technical infrastructure of networks
- Peer-to-peer and client/server architectures
- Implementing a network DLL for the ZFXEngine
- Programming a chat and file transfer application

Network Games

Let's start by discussing some general topics and important keywords you need to know. There are two basic kinds of network games. Both of them differ in their architectures as well as in the goal they aim to achieve. The two types are

- Session-based video games
- Persistent virtual worlds

Session-Based Video Games

In a *session-based* environment, each player has a client on his computer that is used to keep track of the player and display the game situation to him. This approach is mostly used for strategy games such as *GalaxyWars* or even a simple chess game. In a session, the player can make his move, send it to the other players, and wait until they make their moves. If one turn completes, the necessary information is put into a network package and is then sent to all the clients participating in the same game session or, even better, to a server analyzing the turn and issuing the necessary events to let the game react to the turn.

In play by email (PBEM) games, it takes several days at least to complete a full turn of all the players and update the scenario accordingly. Simple card games such as MS Hearts, for example, or board games are similar. However, in these types of games, it takes each player just a few moments to make his turn, so the game session can be completed within minutes, or at least within hours.

The predecessors of such games are, of course, the ancient mail role-playing games in which the players had to send their turn instructions to the game master or game host by snail mail. In such games, typically only up to two turns were possible each month.

In addition, many games are available in which all the players can make their turns at the same time and the players don't have the impression of a turn-based game at all. One example of such a game is a simple first-person shooter match.

The most important attribute of session-based games is that the game lasts only until a certain goal is reached (or until all players have gotten fed up and quit). Then the game ends and can be restarted. But no persistent information or data is stored on a server, except simple high-score lists. If the player starts a game, the game has no relationship to other gaming sessions the player has experienced before. No player states are saved, such as health, ammunition, inventory, weapons, and so on.

Death Match Scenarios

A *death match scenario* is hosted by a server that runs the game by starting a map or level and lets a number of players play in this map until the map's goal is reached or a certain amount of time has passed. The players start the game and connect as *clients* to the server. If they get access to the server, they appear as players in the game level and can start playing. The server can also run a number of bots in the level or on the map. A *bot* is a player that is controlled by the computer and that acts automatically by employing artificial intelligence. The goal of a death match is simply to collect as many kills of other players as possible (a kill is also called a *frag*). The game ends after a certain period of time, normally ranging from 5 minutes up to 1 hour. But the game can also terminate either when all the players except one are fragged and spawning is impossible or when a defined number of maximum frags is reached by a certain player. Games such as *Quake Arena* and *Unreal Tournament* are the most famous examples of such games.

Team and Cooperative Games

In a *team game* or a *cooperative mission*, a server runs in the background. Players from all over the world can log in to the server and participate in the game just like in a death match scenario. The only difference is that the players are divided into a number of opposing teams so they don't have to just kill each other. A similar mode is cooperative play, in which all players play on the same team and the opposing team is made up of bots controlled by the computer. The most famous example of such team-based games is *Battlefield 1942*. In this game, a player can operate a tank, jeep, ship, submarine, and plane; operate the tank's main gun and coaxial machine gun; or just walk through the game. In team death matches, the goal is still to wipe out as many enemies as possible; other forms of team games, such as capture the flag, are also possible.

One disadvantage in team games is the presence of *t'kers*, or team killers. These are players who kill their teammates out of frustration, because they're undercover players from the opposing team, or just because they don't know how the game works or who is or isn't a teammate. This can be very annoying; therefore a lot of network games include the option to deactivate friendly fire. Then a player's weapon fire does not affect his team members. This, however, results in some unrealistic situations where teammates can raid enemy positions with heavy fire without putting each other in danger. Another option is to let the friendly fire stay activated but to kick team killers from the server. That means a human administrator running the game removes any player who has too many team kills from the server and locks his account. This can also be done automatically by the program itself.

Still, team kills can occur in heavy combat, so the maximum number of team kills allowed before being kicked off should take this into consideration. In the previously mentioned *Battlefield 1942*, a common problem is that people like to kill their teammates to get a certain vehicle before their teammates can reach the vehicle and use it. Also, some players like to blow up any of their own team vehicles that they do not control as driver to enforce a respawn of the vehicle so they can then grab it.

Capture the Flag

In this game mode, players are organized into teams. Each team has a number of flags or flagpoles it has to guard, and the task of the players logging in to the server and taking part in the game is to steal the flag of the opposing team and carry it to their own flagpole. Each time a player manages to steal a flag and take it to his home flagpole, the team gets points. If the player carrying the flag is losing virtual life, the flag can be picked up by any player, including those on his team and those on the opposing team.

This kind of game ends after a certain period of time or when the number of available flags that can be stolen is reached. Several versions of this type of game exist, including capture the hill in the *Delta Force* series as well as capture the Ysalamiri in *Jedi Knight*. One negative issue connected to this type of game is the *camping effect*, in which players don't try to get points but instead camp at a certain position in the game. They hide behind a hill, for example, and guard the enemy flagpole. Each time an enemy player tries to bring a stolen flag in, the hiding player opens fire on him.

Such behavior is not what the game is meant to create because these campers are not actively trying to get points but just want to prevent the other team from scoring. This is a valid playing strategy, but most players don't like or tolerate such behavior on their servers.

Persistent Worlds

A virtual home is provided to video game players in *persistent worlds*. A database server manages all the players registered to play a certain game. To register for such a game, you usually are required to pay a subscription fee of $5–$15 a month. Then you are allowed to play the game 24 hours a day all month long. The real human players settle whole cities, continents, or even planets in the persistent virtual worlds and experience interesting adventures, or *quests*, together. As in real life, there are political systems as well as economic systems or hierarchies in which the players can live.

These differ from session-based games in that, in a persistent world, the data about a player (such as his character's attributes, health, equipment, and so on) are stored each time he leaves the game. When he enters the game a few hours, days, or even weeks later, he will find his character in the same state as it was when he left the game. The only difference is that the world itself might have advanced on its timeline, but this enhances only the impression of a real world.

Leveling

Leveling games typically feature characters with a smart system of abilities and attributes that a player can improve by doing certain things in the game. Balancing all of these abilities and attributes to certain character classes is a time-consuming task. Soon after the launch of a new game, patches are released that correct the balance and affect how the player's behavior influences its abilities. If you improve your character's abilities by successfully fulfilling quests, this is called *leveling* your character because the abilities raise you to the next level. The more a character has leveled, the more complicated but rewarding the missions that he can accept and try to accomplish in the persistent virtual world. The setting of persistent game worlds can be anything from ancient knight tales to fantastic wizard worlds to alien space simulations.

Persistent Data

If the player leaves the virtual world, all the abilities of his character are saved. A hardware server saves all the data in a database on disk. As long as the server is up and running and its hard disk is unharmed, all the game data is persistent. Therefore, if a player leaves the virtual world for a while, the virtual world continues to exist and evolve because thousands of other people are still playing the game. The problem with this is that a more casual player needs more time to achieve the same level as someone who plays for several hours each day.

This can be frustrating for players who do not or cannot play as often. Currently, some games try to get around this problem by using several approaches. One such approach is that the character can also develop its abilities with slower speed if the human player is not online but still paying its subscription. Other games offer players virtual credits or virtual objects and abilities in exchange for real-world money.

RPG Versus MMORPG

Role-playing games (RPGs) have typically been played in the offline world. But the worldwide availability of such persistent virtual worlds has added many new dimensions and possibilities to these games, resulting in what are called massive multiplayer online role-playing games (MMORPGs).

Handling millions of players who are playing an internationally successful title is not so easy. The more people who are online on a single server, the more complex the task of managing them if the game runs at considerable speed or performance. That is why a single game doesn't usually run on a single server. Many strategies are used to split this task into manageable parts, but the most common approach is to have multiple instances running on multiple servers, where players cannot take their characters from one server to another.

The virtual universe therefore exists several times in separate instances of the game, which are not connected to each other. If you want to play online with your buddies, you have to make sure all of them are using the same server. You can usually select the server you want to play on while creating a character for the game. Another splitting strategy involves dividing the game into different continents or planet systems, where each part of the world runs on its own server. This leads to a short loading and processing time when a player leaves one part of the world or planet system and moves into another one. In the background, the data of her character is then transferred from one server to another. The advantage of this approach is that all the players around the world are in the same virtual universe.

Lag

The final buzzword you need to know about multiplayer games is "*Lag.*" If you have ever played an online action game, you will most likely know the term because many people use it over the messaging function of the game. Lag refers to a slow connection to the server, and the more *A*s used, the worse the situation. If someone types, "laaaaaaaaaaag," he's pointing out that his connection to the server is very slow. Because of the slow connection, small pauses occur in the game or the player's position and location must be reset every few seconds because the client's estimations of the movements are not exactly what the server calculated.

The term lag stems from *latency*, which is the time a data package needs to travel from the server to the client. The only way to get rid of lag is getting your own Internet or network connection. Most of lag stems from client connections that are too slow. If there is one slow client on a peer-to-peer system, all the players will suffer. However, lag can also occur due to an overloaded server with too many clients. In this case, changing the server can help.

Network Architecture

The basic architecture of the network systems can be divided into two categories: the peer-to-peer and client/server. This has nothing to do with the physical connection of the computers in the network but how they communicate with each other. Even on a single hardware machine like your Windows computer, you can run peer-to-peer or client/server systems with multiple players without using multiple hardware systems.

The single entities that connect to the network are just programs, so a client as well as a server or a peer is nothing more than a piece of software. You can start two instances of a network first-person shooter on your computer and theoretically play against yourself using two monitors.

Peer-to-Peer

In a *peer-to-peer* network, each client is connected to all other clients in the system. That means each client can directly communicate with the others. No server is needed to handle communication between the clients. Figure 11.1 shows such a peer-to-peer architecture.

The advantage of peer-to-peer networks is as follows:

- Each member of the network can disconnect without causing the whole communication to fail

The disadvantages of peer-to-peer networks are as follows:

- They have a lot of traffic because, to broadcast a message to all the clients on the system, each client needs to send the message to each other client.
- They decentralize the control, as there is no obvious place to store high-score lists, ban lists, game settings, and the like.
- They are normally limited to a maximum number of peers due to high traffic.

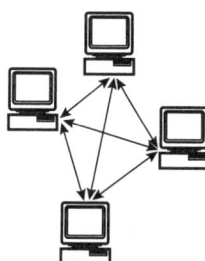

Figure 11.1 Representation of a peer-to-peer network. All the computers in the system are connected to each other.

Client/Server Networks

In client/server networks, one entity is a server and it hosts the game or whatever network application should be run on the network. Other entities that want to be part of the network can connect to the server and, if they get access, become clients in this network. If a message needs to be processed between the clients, a client is not allowed to send the message to another client directly. This is impossible because the client does not have a connection to the other clients in the system. Instead, all messages are sent to the server and the server broadcasts the message to all the clients or to the clients that should receive it.

In the case of a video game, the server does not even have to run the visual part of the game itself. The server can be an instance of the game that is started only to host a game and not to let the players play it. Therefore, the server doesn't need to calculate the graphics output; it can instead concentrate on transmitting messages and calculating collision detection and things like that for the clients to prevent them from having to calculate this and also to prevent them from cheating by tweaking the collision detection, for example. Such a server is called a *dedicated server*.

You can also let the server provide the visual output of the game. In that case, the server owner can also play on the same instance of the game running.

The client/server technology is normally used in video games, especially in huge network games such as MMORPGs. The server handles all the requests made to the database and deals with the persistent data because clients should never be allowed to access that data directly. After all, hackers can mess up the code of the client to do things they should not be able to do. Figure 11.2 shows such a client/server architecture.

The advantages of client/server networks are as follows:

- They're well suited for huge network games using databases.
- Each client talks only to a single entity in the system (the server).
- They have a centralized communication with clients.
- They allow you to offload much of the processing in your game onto the server—which you can set up as extremely high-power hardware—instead of dumping it on the client.
- They are secure—clients can't touch the central game data.

The disadvantages of client/server networks are as follows:

- They have a single point of failure (if the server is down, the whole network stalls).
- Separate hardware is needed for the server.
- The server hardware needs to be powerful.

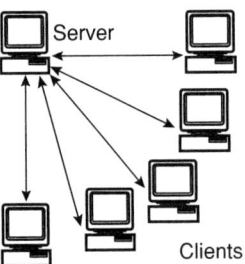

Figure 11.2 Representation of a client/server architecture. Note that each client has only one connection in the system.

Network Technology

Basically, the systems sitting on a network communicate with each other using copper or glass fiber cables. This is similar to the way a telephone call is sent over wires. Your voice is processed and transmitted to the telephone exchange that relays the call to the person to whom you are talking. Such a system works only if the receiving part of the systems knows what kind of format the data is in, for example modulated audio data as opposed to digital signals. The same applies for a computer network that uses a network protocol. This protocol defines how the incoming data is organized and what the data contains in which order.

The most famous network protocols are `IPX/SPX`, `NETBEUI`, and `TCP/IP` (which is used on the Internet). The elder generations of fraggers who have played *Doom 1* over a network will still remember how the endorphins flooded their veins when IPX was finally configured and found your mate's computer. Many other protocols are used. We will get to this topic shortly, but let's first talk about the OSI model on which the IP part of the TCP/IP protocol is based.

The OSI Model

Open System Interconnection (OSI) is a model of communication processes developed in the late 1970s by the International Organization for Standardization (ISO). The OSI model is based on seven layers that build on each other. A communication process always starts in the topmost layer and then works its way down through all the other layers to the bottom—the data goes through all seven layers.

After being sent over the network, the data arrives at its destination where it has to go through all seven layers again, only in reverse order this time. When it reaches the topmost layer, it then gets to the application that is expecting it. During this process, each layer works with the data to serve its needs. A very important decision is made at the fourth layer, when it is decided whether the data should be sent as a User Datagram Protocol (UDP) package or as a Transmission Control Protocol (TCP) package. Figure 11.3 shows the OSI model.

Layer 7: Application

The application layer is the layer where the users of the communication highways are sitting. These applications are programs such as your email tool, FTP clients, and Internet browsers. Each application uses a network protocol to exchange data over a network.

Layer 6: Presentation

This layer takes care of the presentation of the data, meaning whether it is encrypted for transportation on the network, whether it is compressed, and so on. Outgoing data is

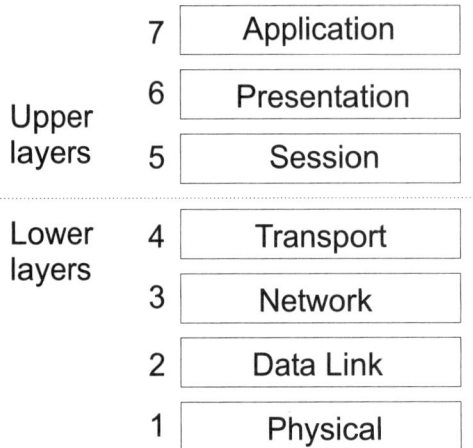

Figure 11.3 Illustration of the OSI model layers. Refer to the text for further explanations.

encrypted and compressed, if necessary, while incoming data is decrypted and decompressed if necessary.

Layer 5: Session

A *session* defines how a connection between a client and a server can be started or ended. This layer also takes care of the synchronization of the network communication and enables an application to send data over an existing connection.

Layer 4: Transport

On the transport layer, the data that should be sent is checked for errors and packed in a way that makes it fastest and easiest to transmit. Additionally, this layer checks whether the current status of the network allows for the correct sending and receiving of packages. The selection of UDP or TCP influences the packaging in this layer.

Layer 3: Network

For the packets to find their destinations on the network, this layer equips them with an address where the destination can be found. At this layer, the codes and signals that are laid down by the Internet Protocol (IP) are generated.

Layer 2: Data-Link

The data-link layer is the level of the network hardware's driver that processes the data. Another consistency check secures the validity of each packet prior to sending it. This layer also prepares the connection between two real hardware points in the network and breaks the data packets into small pieces that can be sent individually.

Layer 1: Physical

Finally, the physical layer is the layer that actually sends the small pieces of data over the network cable by transforming them into Hi/Lo signals the cable can deal with. The bits are physically transmitted to the destination by electrical (or light) signals. Data at this level is said to be "on the wire."

Protocols

Without protocols, the communication on a network wouldn't be possible. Take, for example, Star Fleet protocols that describe a certain behavior and course of action which Star Fleet officers have to follow to secure the best possible communication on first contacts.

The same applies for human voice communication. If you talk to your friend, you might use a protocol called "English language" or "German language," where this protocol defines the syntax, grammar, and vocabulary of the language you use. If you don't know the protocol that contains the grammar, syntax, and vocabulary, you will be lost. Ever tried to talk to a Klingon?

The very same problem arises in network communication. A computer sees the incoming data, but if it doesn't know the protocol used, it cannot interpret the data. It must know how to put the pieces of a package together, so it must know the protocol used to split the package into pieces in the first place. If the same protocol is not used for sending and receiving the data, the hardware cannot put the bits and bytes together to form the message that was originally sent over the network.

As already mentioned, many protocols are used, but I want to focus on the two most important ones: UDP and TCP.

UDP

UDP, unlike TCP, is a connectionless way of sending data. That means that there is no permanent connection between the members of the network. Thus, the destination of the data must be named each time a package is sent. This is also a non-guaranteed protocol because, after sending the data, the link between the source and the destination is cut off and no feedback is checked to see whether the package sent made it to the destination and arrived safely and completely.

The advantage of skipping delivery and consistency checks is increased speed. In a video game where you send the position of each moving object about 20 times per second, it simply doesn't matter if you lose two or three of these packages. The client can use the last known position for the fragment of a second. This prevents a lot of network traffic that would have to be used for delivery and integrity checks to ensure the arrival of each package. You can also implement such a security check while using UDP. When sending a package, you can either use the non-guaranteed method for less important messages, such as position data, or use the secure method, which needs feedback from the destination for important messages such as a character being hit by a bullet. Such a secure method could be implemented as a guaranteed delivery mechanism over UDP or even by using a separate TCP implementation for the important data.

TCP/IP

The Transmission Control Protocol (TCP) is a connection-oriented protocol. It lets you send data over the network only if a stable connection between the source and the destination is established. The connection is then maintained until it is explicitly terminated when you close it. Thus, the connection is permanent as long as the program is running and no error occurs in the hardware. TCP is a guaranteed protocol because each package sent is internally acknowledged by the destination in the form of a feedback packet. If this feedback does not arrive within a certain amount of time after sending the data, the sender automatically sends the packet again.

TCP therefore features a guaranteed delivery. No package can be lost because, if it is lost in the network, a copy is sent again. If the lost package then makes its way to the destination as well, no error occurs because all redundant packages are simply skipped. Another advantage of TCP is that the order in which the pieces of a package are received does not matter because they are ordered automatically prior to rebuilding the whole package at the destination point.

As you can already see, the amount of work handled internally by the driver and the protocol eats up time. This time slows down the network and creates additional traffic. But TCP does ensure that important messages aren't lost.

Network APIs

You don't have to implement all seven layers of the OSI model because most of this is already handled by the hardware, the drivers, or certain APIs. The following paragraph lists the most important APIs that provide easy access to network hardware.

Berkeley Sockets

Berkeley Sockets was the first API ever used to implement the TCP/IP definition. In 1986, this API was available on various operating systems—mostly Unix derivates. In 1991, version 4.3 of the Berkeley Sockets API was used as a starting point for the developers of the Windows Sockets API, which is why both APIs are more or less compatible in their main parts. Even today, Berkeley Sockets is the most widely used API on Unix and Linux systems as the standard API for programming network applications.

Windows Sockets (WinSock)

The Windows Sockets API (WinSock) is an integral part of the Windows operating system. Currently, version 2.0 of this API is available and, similar to its predecessors, implements the same standards as the Berkeley Sockets API. So, if you write your network application encapsulating one of these network APIs, it should also be able to be compiled with the other API.

The WinSock API provides a few features not found in Berkeley Sockets, aimed at making network programming easier under Windows. One such enhancement is message loop-based asynchronous sockets, which is a mechanism through which sockets notify you of events (such as the arrival of new data) through your window's message procedure. WinSock is also the API we will use in this chapter to implement the ZFXNetwork DLL. The WinSock API is very efficient and easy to use. But like all low-level APIs, you should encapsulate its low-level functions and standardize frequently used calls to get a simpler, higher-level API.

DirectPlay

As a component of the DirectX package, the DirectPlay API is the library that Microsoft has come up with to support the development of network applications with a focus on video games. There is a lot of high-level functionality in this library, such as a lounge or lobby used as a login area for a network game, a message router, and different connectors. If you take a look at its documentation, you can see that it is comprehensive and offers more functionality than needed for the purpose of simple first-person shooters or for this book.

One drawback is that DirectPlay is available only on Windows machines and servers hosting MMORPGs are usually not run on Windows machines but on Linux or Unix servers. So, if you use the DirectPlay API, you have to implement a separate server application using another networking API or use only Windows servers. It is also worth mentioning that DirectPlay uses a proprietary protocol, so trying to communicate between DirectPlay clients and non-DirectPlay servers is extremely difficult.

In this book we will use the WinSock API. It is similar to the Berkeley Sockets API, so you should be able to quickly port this code to a Linux version. Once you get used to working with socket objects, it is not that complicated. Most of the functions are identical in both APIs, so there is no need to apply a lot of changes.

Implementing a Network Library

Now that you've learned about networks, network protocols, network architecture, and application programming interfaces, let's implement a network library using a low-level API. I decided to use WinSock here to stay as close to the hardware as possible without introducing another level of abstraction (as we would do with using DirectPlay). Each additional level of abstraction would just slow things down.

The Same Old Interface Tea

You have seen the render device, input device, and audio device, which are all main components of the engine implemented using the same scheme of an interface in a static library used to load an implementation of the interface from a dynamic link library. The network device we are going to develop now will also be a main component of the engine implemented using the same scheme. You can also exchange the implementation in the DLL with a DirectPlay or Berkeley Sockets implementation. Here are the files you need in your two new projects for the ZFXEngine's network component starting with the static library project.

Files used for ZFXNetwork:

- ZFXNetwork.h and ZFXNetwork.cpp
- ZFXNetworkDevice.h
- ZFX.h
- ZFX3D.h

The first two files are used for the implementation of the static library's class ZFXNetwork, which provides access to a network device. The header ZFXNetworkDevice contains the interface definition for a network device of our engine. Again, we need the two headers containing the enumerations, structures, and the like from the whole engine as well as the header from the math library, which is needed for the general header.

The second project used for the DLL with a class implementing the network interface is structured like this:

Files used for ZFXWS:

- ZFXWS.def
- ZFXWS.h and ZFXWS.cpp
- ZFXSocketObject.h and ZFXSocketObject.h
- ZFXQueue.h and ZFXQueue.cpp

Besides the definition file naming the exported function and the files implementing the class ZFXWS, which provides the functionality requested by the interface, two more classes are inside this project. One class encapsulates a socket object used as a connection point for a link into the network. The other class, ZFXQueue, is a simple first in first out (FIFO) queue. This is a data structure similar to a linked list, but in this case you can append new elements only at the end of the list. If you want to remove an element from the list, you have to take the element from the head of the list and you cannot take one from the middle or from the end. This means you can take elements from the list only in the same order in which they were put into it.

Server Versus Clients

The basic principle of a client/server architecture is not new to you because we already covered its theory. With regard to the application, you normally implement a separate program for the client as well as for the server to keep them strictly separate. But with this network component, I don't want to move that far away from the low-level network programming. So, I'll leave this task of separation to the application using the network library. The ZFXNetworkDevice will implement both types of objects into one class that is easy to use. An application that wants to use the library later can then just get two instances of the ZFXNetwork object and initialize one of them as a server and one of them as a client if both functionalities are needed.

If an application wants to be only a server or a client, it would get one object of the interface definition and work with just that one. The interface is easy to use because you can crank it up as a server or client with a single function call. The application featuring a simple video game at the end of this book shows you how to implement a session-based first-person shooter where the server is also a player and is not dedicated.

Packing Packages

Programming network applications involves simply providing the ability for the application to pack data packages and send them over a network connection. The suitable design and layout of such a package is important because it directly affects the amount of traffic created by the application and therefore influences the performance of the final program.

Note

The word "packet" is a more common term to describe the same objects that I call "packages" here.

In a best-case scenario, the packages should be as small as possible. However, if you have a large chunk of data you need to send, sending it as a single large package instead of several smaller ones can be quicker in some situations. For example, if you need guaranteed delivery, a single large packet means you only have to send one time-consuming receiving-notification. A good network engine design should therefore be flexible with regard to the package size. The network component of the ZFXEngine is based on the ZFXPACKAGE structure that defines the only package type that can be processed by the engine:

```
typedef struct ZFXPACKAGE_TYPE
   {
```

```
    UINT   nLength;   // length of pData in bytes
    UCHAR  nType;     // message type id
    UINT   nSender;   // sender id where 0 is the server
    void   *pData;    // actual data in this package
    } ZFXPACKAGE;
```

The structure contains some fields that should be part of every network package. The most important field is nLength because it specifies the length of the data that is unique to this package and which is stored in the last field of the structure. It also contains a field to specify the type of the message contained in the package as an ID. An application can name its own ID values, but some values are reserved because they are internally used by the engine itself. The third field requires the ID of the sender, which is 0 for the server; otherwise, it's the ID a client got from the server after its connection request was granted. Finally, the pData field contains a pointer to the data that is the actual message of nLength bytes.

Here are the reserved values for the different packages' type IDs, which are used internally in the engine itself:

- 0: The first message a client receives from the server after it connects. The data field of the structure contains the client's ID as unsigned int value.
- 1: A message from the server to each client that a new client is accepted into the network. The data field contains the ID of the new client.
- 2: A message from the server to all clients that one client is disconnected from the network. The data field contains the ID of the new client.

As you can see, you can define your own message IDs starting from number 3 and connect them to certain messages, such as PLAYER_FIRING or PLAYER_TURNING. The pData field can then be used to store a structure that contains the actual data members used for the message, such as the player's position, its rotational values, and so on.

The predefined package type is not the real message that delivers the information a certain application needs. It just wraps around that information; such structures are also called *carrier messages* because they carry only the real data that you are after.

Waiting Queues

Let's get down to the code. Now that you know that doing the network dance is all about sending and receiving packages, it should be obvious that the network implementation of our engine has to provide a means to manage all of the messages. If a client has to report something, it sends a package to the server. The server should then send this package to all the other clients to inform them about what's going on. So, even the clients must be ready to receive messages.

Please note that the network dynamic link library we will write is on an abstraction level not too close to the application using the network device. Internally, the DLL is more or less just able to manage a number of clients for a server and to send data packages. What needs to be done to react correctly to such a package is left up to the application. The DLL knows nothing about the various packages except for the three ones listed previously, which are just basic notifications from the server.

A problem does exist, though. If a package arrives over the network connection, it is just virtually sitting on the network hardware card in some kind of temporary buffer. If the application does not react to the event of incoming messages, the buffer will become full at some point. This results in a loss of messages. To prevent this from happening, the network device receives all the messages for the application, causing it to have to store the messages somewhere until the application finally is ready to request its messages.

The network device receives the messages and puts these messages into an inbox of the application owning the network device object. The application is not really requesting the messages waiting at the network connection point; it's requesting them from its inbox, where the network device has placed them. This inbox is of the type ZFXQueue. If an application wants to send a package, it is sent directly to the server over the network connection. But if an application wants to receive a message, it does not receive it from the network connection, which would be the normal way to do it. The network device has already taken care of this process so the application instead checks its inbox to see whether there are messages waiting.

The following shows the classes implementing this inbox:

```
class ZFXQueueElem
   {
   public:
      ZFXQueueElem(const char *pData, unsigned int nSize);
      ~ZFXQueueElem(void);

      ZFXQueueElem *m_pNext;
      char         *m_pData;
      unsigned int  m_nSize;
   };

class ZFXQueue
   {
   private:
      ZFXQueueElem *m_pHead;
      ZFXQueueElem *m_pTail;
      unsigned int  m_Count;
```

```
public:
    ZFXQueue(void);
    ~ZFXQueue(void);

    void Dequeue(void);
    void Enqueue(const void *pData, unsigned int nSize);
    void Front(void *pData, bool bDequeue);

    unsigned int GetCount(void) { return m_Count; }

    unsigned int GetFrontSize(void)
       {
       if (m_pHead) return m_pHead->m_nSize;
       else return 0;
       }
    };
```

One element of the queue needs a pointer to the data it contains as well as a member variable to hold the size in bytes of the data it stores. Each time you put an object into the queue, the new element copies the data into its own member variable so that the caller can release its copy of the object. The pointer m_pNext in the class is used to point to the following element in the queue, if any exists. The concept of a queue is similar to a linked list; the only difference is that a queue is simpler to implement.

The class for the queue itself is as easy as it gets. There aren't even a lot of functions in this class. The member attributes are just a pointer to the head, which is the object you can remove from the queue, and a pointer to the tail, which is the last element in the queue where you can append new elements. A counter holds the number of elements in the queue.

To add an element to the queue, you just call the ZFXQueue::Enqueue function, like so:

```
void ZFXQueue::Enqueue(const void *pData, unsigned int nSize)
    {
    ZFXQueueElem *pNew = new ZFXQueueElem( (const char*)pData, nSize);

    // this is the first element
    if (m_Count == 0)
       {
       m_pHead = pNew;
       m_pTail = pNew;
       }
    // there is already one element
    else if (m_Count == 1)
```

```
   {
   m_pHead->m_pNext = pNew;
   m_pTail = pNew;
   }
  else
   {
   m_pTail->m_pNext = pNew;
   m_pTail = pNew;
   }
  m_Count++;
  } // Enqueue
```

The function is straightforward. You just need to handle three separate cases to adjust the two pointers of the class accordingly. Copying the data is done by the ZFXQueueElem class.

To remove an element from the queue, you need a parameter-less function because you can remove only the head of the queue. Note that the element is lost after calling this function:

```
void ZFXQueue::Dequeue(void)
  {
  ZFXQueueElem *pTemp;

  // already empty
  if (m_Count == 0) return;

  // one element left
  else if (m_Count == 1)
    {
    delete m_pHead;
    m_pHead = NULL;
    m_pTail = NULL;
    }
  else
    {
    pTemp = m_pHead;
    m_pHead = m_pHead->m_pNext;
    delete pTemp;
    }
  m_Count--;
  } // Dequeue
```

Again, you have to take care to set the two pointers accordingly. The purpose of the queue is normally to hold data you can access later. For this reason, the class offers the following function to get a copy of the data sitting in the head element. Also, a boolean parameter is available that you can set if you want the object to be removed from the queue, which then calls the dequeue function of the class:

```
void ZFXQueue::Front(void *pData, bool bDequeue)
   {
   if (pData)
      {
      if (m_pHead)
         {
         memcpy(pData, m_pHead->m_pData, m_pHead->m_nSize);
         }
      }
   if (bDequeue) Dequeue();
   } // Front
```

As you can see, the function wants to see a pointer from the caller which is pointing to a valid memory area that can take all the data from the element. But to let the user know how much memory he needs to allocate beforehand, the ZFXQueue::GetFrontSize function is used. It returns the size in bytes needed to store the element.

These are all functions you need to implement for the queue class. The class for an element of the queue is even simpler because it needs only a constructor and a destructor:

```
ZFXQueueElem::ZFXQueueElem(const char *pData, unsigned int nSize)
   {
   m_pData = NULL;
   m_pNext = NULL;
   m_pData = new char[nSize];
   m_nSize = nSize;
   memcpy(m_pData, pData, nSize);
   } // constructor
/*----------------------------*/

ZFXQueueElem::~ZFXQueueElem(void)
   {
   if (m_pData)
      {
      delete [] m_pData;
      m_pData = NULL;
      }
   m_pNext = NULL;
   } // destructor
```

If you create a new instance of this class, the constructor allocates enough memory to store the given object. Then it copies the object into its member attribute. If the instance is deleted and the destructor is called, the memory is freed again.

With these two simple classes, we now have a comfortable message inbox that the network device can use to store incoming messages and free the socket object's small buffer that is holding the incoming packages on the network hardware card.

Socket Objects

The foundation of all communication processes using a network connection in the Berkeley Sockets or WinSock API is the socket object. You can think of a *socket* as an imaginary object marking the two end points of a connection line between a client and server. Each client in a network has exactly one socket object, which is its connection to the server. If the client wants to send data, it sends it over this socket object. And if the client receives data, the data comes on this socket object.

The server in a network has multiple socket objects. First, it needs the *master* socket object, which is used by the server to monitor the network. Each time a new client wants to connect to the network, the server hears that on its master socket. Additionally, the server has exactly one socket object for each client accepted into the network. If the server wants to talk to a specific client, it needs to use the specific socket connected to this client or to this client's own socket object on the other end. If the server wants to send data to all the clients connected to it, it has to send the data over each of its socket objects, except for the master socket of course.

This means that each time a client wants to connect to a network, it needs to ask the server to accept it. Once it is accepted, two things happen. First, the server creates a new socket object for the new client that is its exclusive data-link to this client. Second, the client opens a socket that leads to the new socket the server created for it. Now both of them are connected by a hot wire.

What exactly such a socket object is and how the server recognizes a certain socket are technical issues that are treated by the OSI model and the WinSock API implementation. For our purpose, this simply does not matter. We will next implement a class encapsulating a WinSock API socket object. The encapsulation is more or less equal if you use the Berkeley Sockets API. Table 11.1 shows all the tasks a socket object has to fulfill and also lists the public functions our socket object class will provide. The underlying sockets API will also provide similar functions, but in a functional way of programming without using objects. Table 11.1 also shows which tasks are used by the server and which are meant for a client socket object.

Table 11.1 Functions of the ZFXSocketObject Class

Function	Task	Server	Client
CreateSocket()	Initializing a socket object	x	x
Bind()	Naming the server master socket	x	-
Listen()	Server listening for new clients	x	-
Accept()	Server accepts new client	x	-
Connect()	Client wants access to server	-	x
Send()	Sends data over the network	x	x
Receive()	Receives data over the network	x	x
Disconnect()	Frees socket by closing connection	x	x

ZFXSocketObject Class

The following class simplifies the work with the socket object of the WinSock API and should also encapsulate certain processes. The internal socket object of the WinSock API is of the type SOCKET, which is defined inside the WinSock API. It is just an identifier for the connection used on the network hardware. Our class will also be used later to send data over the socket's connection or to receive data no matter whether the socket object represents a socket on the server's or on the client's side of the world:

```
class ZFXSocketObject
   {
   public:
      ZFXSocketObject(FILE *pLog);
      ~ZFXSocketObject(void);

      bool    IsRunning(void) { return m_bRunning; }

      // socket MISC functions
      HRESULT CreateSocket(void);
      HRESULT Bind(int nPort);
      HRESULT Listen(void);
      HRESULT Accept(SOCKET *skToNewClient);
      HRESULT Connect(char *chServer, int nPort);
      void    Disconnect(void);

      // send and receive data
      int     Send(const char*,UINT);
      int     Send(const char*,UINT,SOCKET);
      HRESULT Receive(SOCKET sk);
```

```
        // get information
        SOCKET  GetSocket(void) { return m_skSocket; }

        // information about the inbox
        bool    IsPkgWaiting(void)   { return (m_pInbox->GetCount() > 0); }
        UINT    GetNextPkgSize(void) { return (m_pInbox->GetFrontSize()); }
        HRESULT GetNextPkg(ZFXPACKAGE*);

    private:
        ZFXQueue    *m_pInbox;
        SOCKET      m_skSocket;
        char        *m_Buffer;
        bool        m_bRunning;
    }; // class
```

This class offers many functions for us to work comfortably with the internal SOCKET object. We will go through each function step by step in a moment. But please note that all the functions listed below the MISC comment are used only during the initialization phase of the socket object. Also, a client uses other functions from the MISC part as a server. We'll discuss that later when you see the network class working with this socket class.

Next, functions are used to send and receive data. The function to receive the data then saves the incoming data into the inbox, which is an instance of the queue class we just implemented. There are also functions to get access to the inbox, such as querying the size of the next package in the inbox, getting the next package, and checking whether a package is waiting.

Let's start at the beginning with the constructor and destructor:

```
ZFXSocketObject::ZFXSocketObject(FILE *pLog)
    {
    m_skSocket   = INVALID_SOCKET;
    m_bRunning   = false;
    m_pInbox     = NULL;
    m_Buffer     = NULL;
    } // constructor
/*----------------------------------*/

ZFXSocketObject::~ZFXSocketObject(void)
    {
    if (IsRunning())
        {
```

```
         Disconnect();
         m_bRunning = false;
         }
      if (m_pInbox)
         {
         delete m_pInbox;
         m_pInbox = NULL;
         }
      if (m_Buffer)
         {
         delete [] m_Buffer;
         m_Buffer = NULL;
         }
      m_skSocket = INVALID_SOCKET;
      } // destructor
```

As you can see, there is not much going on besides initializations to default values. The destructor calls the function to disconnect this object from the network so that no socket object is deleted while its connection is still open.

Creating a Socket

Before you can start using a socket object, it needs to be initialized. For the socket objects on the clients as well as for the master socket, you use the following WinSock function. Note that the socket objects a server builds for each client are created in another way:

```
SOCKET socket(int af, int type, int protocol);
```

The first parameter is the address family of the socket object. Several parameters can be used, such as AF_INET for TCP/IP, AF_IPX for IPX, or AF_APPLETALK for AppleTalk. The second parameter sets the type of the socket, which is either SOCK_STREAM or SOCK_DGRAM. Here, SOCK_STREAM is used for TCP and SOCK_DGRAM is used for UDP. The third parameter is more or less obsolete because the second parameter already names the protocol you want to use.

The return value of this function is INVALID_SOCKET if an error has occurred. If it's successful, the function returns a valid socket object. Here is what our class adds to the story:

```
HRESULT ZFXSocketObject::CreateSocket(void)
   {
   if (m_skSocket != INVALID_SOCKET) Disconnect();

   m_skSocket = socket(AF_INET, SOCK_STREAM, 0);
   if (m_skSocket==INVALID_SOCKET)
      {
```

```
      return ZFX_FAIL;
      }
   m_pInbox = new ZFXQueue();
   m_Buffer = new char[65536];
   memset(m_Buffer,0,65536);
   return ZFX_OK;
   }
```

Naming a Socket

Naming a socket is also called *binding*. This connects the socket object to a certain *port*, which is similar to a hole in the computer where data can slip through into the network. As Table 11.1 shows, this binding is needed only for the master socket of the server. You can also bind a client socket object, but this is unnecessary. Here is the WinSock function to do this:

```
int bind(SOCKET s, const struct sockaddr FAR* name, int namelen);
```

The first parameter is the socket object you want to bind. The second object is a structure that contains the necessary data, and the third parameter is the length of the structure you provide. The length is needed because the structures are different in the Berkeley Sockets API and the WinSock API but the function declaration is the same. The structure sockaddr returns repeatedly even if it covers itself behind the name sockaddr_in. In version 2.0 the new structure is also accepted by this function, so we will work with only this one:

```
struct sockaddr_in
   {
   short    sin_family;
   u_short  sin_port;
   struct   in_addr sin_addr;
   char     sin_zero[8];
   };
```

The first field of this structure needs to be AF_INET because we are working with TCP/IP. The second field takes the port number the server's master socket works on, and the third field takes the IP address of the server. But you can also put the value INADDR_ANY here to cause the API to get the address on its own from the system. The last field in this structure is only needed to bring the structure to the same size as the original sockaddr.

Here is our interpretation of the binding process:

```
HRESULT ZFXSocketObject::Bind(int nPort)
   {
   sockaddr_in saServerAddress;

   memset(&saServerAddress, 0, sizeof(sockaddr_in));
   saServerAddress.sin_family      = AF_INET;
```

```
        saServerAddress.sin_addr.s_addr = htonl(INADDR_ANY);
        saServerAddress.sin_port        = htons(nPort);

        if ( bind(m_skSocket, (sockaddr*)&saServerAddress, sizeof(sockaddr))
           == SOCKET_ERROR)
           {
           Disconnect();
           return ZFX_FAIL;
           }
        return ZFX_OK;
        } // Bind
```

To get the meaning of the `htonl()` and `htons()` functions, you should read the following excursion about byte ordering and endians.

Excursion: Byte Ordering and Endians

For the design of computers or CPUs, there are basically two different approaches of how to store the data: Big Endian and Little Endian. An Intel processor, for example, uses the Little Endian approach, whereas Motorola chips work with the Big Endian method.

The difference between these two approaches is whether the data is saved and read beginning with the most significant bit (MSB) or with the least significant bit (LSB). In the Little Endian method, you save the data beginning with the little end, which is on the right side. The value 0x1234 would be saved in memory as [0x34 0x12], for example. The Big Endian method does things exactly the opposite way and stores this value as [0x12 0x34].

In the network context, you separate the byte ordering used by the host (the computer) and the byte ordering used by the network API. The WinSock API works with the Big Endian method as network byte order. In our program for Intel-compatible processors, we use the Little Endian approach instead as host byte order. So, if you hand over addresses or ports to the network API, you have to convert the values first. To do this, the WinSock API offers the following functions:

```
// host to network (short = 16 Bit)
u_short htons(u_short hostshort);

// network to host (short = 16 Bit)
u_short ntohs(u_short netshort);

// host to network (long = 32 Bit))
u_long htonl(u_long hostlong);

// network to host (long = 32 Bit)
u_long ntohl(u_long netlong);
```

Speech Is Silver, Listening Is Golden

After you have created and named a socket object for a server, this socket object is up and running, ready to take the workload waiting for it. But the master socket of a server does not have to send or receive data that the clients are transmitting—at least, no data that is meant for the network application layer to receive. This master socket has only one purpose—informing the server when a new client wants access to the network. A client tells this to the network by calling the connect() function of the WinSock API. But to enable the server to hear this call it or its master socket has to listen for such a call. Here is the declaration of the function that lets you switch a socket into listening mode:

```
int listen(SOCKET s, int backlog);
```

The first parameter is the socket object that is put to guard. In a client/server architecture, this is always the master socket of the server. The second parameter is the number of clients that can start a connection call at the same time. The following is our encapsulation of this functionality:

```
HRESULT ZFXSocketObject::Listen(void)
   {
   if (listen(m_skSocket, 32) != 0)
      return ZFX_FAIL;

   m_bRunning = true;
   return ZFX_OK;
   } // Listen
```

Accepting Clients

Now that the server's master socket has heard something, you know that a new client wants to get into the network. If there are no reasons not to let it connect, you should accept this new client into the network by calling the appropriate function. But the server needs to open a separate socket object for each client in the network. With that in mind, take a look at the following function that lets a server's master socket allow a client into the network:

```
SOCKET accept (SOCKET s, struct sockaddr FAR* addr, int FAR* addrlen);
```

The first parameter of this function is the socket that heard the new client knocking and which is used to accept the client. Again, this is the server's master socket. The second parameter is an optional structure you can provide for this function if you want the function to fill it with the address data of the new client. The third parameter is the size of the structure in bytes.

The return value of this function is the new socket object that is the server's data-link to the new client. Here is our encapsulation of the function:

```
HRESULT ZFXSocketObject::Accept(SOCKET *skToNewClient)
   {
   sockaddr_in saClientAddress;
   int         nClientSize = sizeof(sockaddr_in);

   (*skToNewClient) = accept(m_skSocket, (sockaddr*) &saClientAddress,
                             &nClientSize);

   if ((*skToNewClient) == INVALID_SOCKET)
      return ZFX_FAIL;

   return ZFX_OK;
   } // accept
```

As you can see, the address where the new socket should be stored is an input parameter of this function. This is a slot in an array of all the connected clients a server object will have.

Connecting to the Server

All the previously shown functions just deal with tasks the server's master socket has to fulfill. The client sockets also want some functionality, however. So, here it is. If a client wants to connect to a network, you have to call the following function:

```
int connect (SOCKET s, const struct sockaddr FAR* name, int namelen);
```

The first parameter is the socket object you want to connect to the network and which should call for the master socket. This socket object has to be a free one that is not yet connected. The second parameter is the name and address of the server to which you want to connect, and the third parameter holds the size of the second parameter in bytes.

To be able to connect to a server, you need to know the IP address and the port of the server. A client can also be connected to a server running on the same IP as itself on the same computer. Here is our encapsulation of this functionality, where the IP address and the port number are inputs to the function:

```
HRESULT ZFXSocketObject::Connect(char *chServer, int nPort)
   {
   sockaddr_in saServerAddress;
   LPHOSTENT   pHost=NULL;

   // try to find the server
```

```
    memset(&saServerAddress,0,sizeof(sockaddr_in));
    saServerAddress.sin_port      = htons(nPort);
    saServerAddress.sin_family    = AF_INET;
    saServerAddress.sin_addr.s_addr=inet_addr(chServer);

    if (saServerAddress.sin_addr.s_addr==INADDR_NONE)
       {
       pHost = gethostbyname(chServer);

       if (pHost != NULL)
          {
          saServerAddress.sin_addr.s_addr = ((LPIN_ADDR)pHost->h_addr)->s_addr;
          }
       else
          return ZFX_FAIL;
       }

    // connect to server address
    if (connect(m_skSocket, (sockaddr*)&saServerAddress, sizeof(sockaddr))
        == SOCKET_ERROR)
       {
       Disconnect();
       return ZFX_FAIL;
       }

    m_bRunning = true;
    return ZFX_OK;
    } // Connect
```

The IP address provided as a parameter can take one of two representations. You can define the IP address as a series of four 8-bit numbers separated by a period, such as 192.168.0.128. The WinSock function inet_addr() then changes this string into a value that can be used for the s_addr field in the sockaddr_in structure. Optionally, you can also provide the server name instead of the address. Then the call to inet_addr() fails and you can run the function gethostbyname(). This resolves the server name (but no IP address) in such a way that the return value HOSTENT contains the appropriate data.

Disconnecting from the Server

If a socket object wants to be disconnected from the network because a client or even the server is leaving, you need to shut down the open socket object. This is done by the function shutdown() of the WinSock API. After that, you still have to call the function closesocket() to ensure that the socket is cleanly switched off:

```
void ZFXSocketObject::Disconnect(void)
   {
   if (m_skSocket != INVALID_SOCKET)
      {
      shutdown(m_skSocket, SD_BOTH);
      closesocket(m_skSocket);
      m_skSocket = INVALID_SOCKET;
      }
   } // Disconnect
```

The second parameter of the shutdown() function ensures that in this case no more data is sent over this socket and that no more data can be received over this socket. Alternatively, you can also specify that already received data can be accessed over the socket objects from its internal buffer prior to shutting down. But this makes no sense in our case. If the client wants to leave the game or even the server, you just let it go.

Sending Data

Finally, let's see how you can send data over the network. After the correct initialization of a socket object, you can start sending data over the socket object. This can be done with the following WinSock API function, which is called send():

```
int send(SOCKET s, const char FAR * buf, int len, int flags);
```

The first parameter is again the socket that is used to send the data. For a client, this is the single socket object a client owns. In the case of a server, this is the socket object leading to the client that was accepted into the network by the accept() call, which also returned the socket object leading to the client that must be used here to talk to this client. The second parameter is a pointer to the data that should be sent, and the third parameter is the size of the data in bytes. The last parameter can be a flag indicating the type of the data transmission, but you usually don't need this. The return value of the function is either SOCKET_ERROR or the number of bytes that were actually sent.

TCP/IP ensures that you have a guaranteed delivery of the packages at the destination. But this does not protect you from a case where the send() function is not able to send all the data in the first place. This can be the case if the buffer taking the incoming data of the socket object you want to send the data to is already full.

If this situation occurs, you can see from the return value how many bytes were actually sent over the network. If this is smaller than the number of bytes you intended to send, you have to call this function repeatedly until all the data is finally sent. Here is the encapsulation that does this. Note that an overloaded version of this function takes the receiving socket object as a parameter. This is used for the server that hands over the socket object leading to a certain client; the first version of the function will do for clients because the socket object inside the class itself is the socket that should receive the data to send it:

```
int ZFXSocketObject::Send(const char *pPkg, UINT nSize)
   {
   UINT nSent=0;
   UINT n=0;

   while (nSent < nSize)
      {
      n = send(m_skSocket, pPkg+nSent, nSize-nSent, 0);
      if (n==SOCKET_ERROR)
         return n;
      else nSent += n;
      }
   return nSent;
   } // Send
/*----------------------------*/


int ZFXSocketObject::Send(const char *pPkg, UINT nSize, SOCKET skReceiver)
   {
   UINT nSent=0;
   UINT n=0;

   while (nSent < nSize)
      {
      n = send(skReceiver, pPkg+nSent, nSize-nSent, 0);
      if (n==SOCKET_ERROR)
         return n;
      else nSent += n;
      }
   return nSent;
   } // Send
```

Receiving Data

You might think that working with sockets is simple, but some problems can arise, such as when receiving data over a socket. First, take a look at the function that lets you receive data:

```
int recv(SOCKET s, char FAR* buf, int len, int flags);
```

The first parameter is the socket object over which the data is incoming. The second parameter is the pointer to a buffer where the received data should be stored; the third parameter tells the function how many bytes fit into this buffer. The final parameter meant for flags is not used here. The return value of the function is an error message or the number of bytes that were actually received by this call of the function.

The first and foremost problem is that you know nothing about the amount of data waiting to be received at the internal buffer of the socket object. Are there only a few bytes, some kilobytes, or even megabytes? You simply cannot set up the receiving buffer in a size that would take all the possibly waiting data. The most obvious solution is to run the function in a loop until no more data is waiting, which is indicated by the return value of 0.

In each iteration of this loop, you have then read a number of bytes into your buffer that represent the received data. So, you can extract all the packages from this buffer before you go on to the next iteration to receive the next bunch of data. The received packages are then put into the inbox of this socket object. Note that this class supposes that all packages received are of the type ZFXPACKAGE.

But now you have another problem. If you are unlucky, one call to the recv() function might receive some bytes containing some of the packages. However, you cannot receive all the waiting data, which is why one package is split. The first part is received into the end of your buffer, and the other part of the package is still waiting to be received. After one iteration, you might not have five or so data packages inside your buffer but five and a half. To solve this problem, you must go through your buffer in each iteration and put all the complete packages into the inbox. If you encounter an incomplete package, you copy it to the start of the buffer. Then you start the next iteration and receive the next bunch of data—but not to the start of the buffer, to the offset where this split package ends in the buffer. This then puts the split package back together.

That sounds like an interesting task, doesn't it? Here is the implementation:

```
int g_PkgSize=sizeof(ZFXPACKAGE);

HRESULT ZFXSocketObject::Receive(SOCKET sk) {
   HRESULT hr          = ZFX_OK;
   UINT    nSize       = 65536;   // max bytes for each read call
   UINT    nBytesRead  = 0;       // gelesene Bytes
   UINT    nReadHead   = 0;       // Position in m_Buffer
   UINT    n           = 0;       // verbleibende Daten
   bool    bDone       = false;   // fertig?

   ZFXPACKAGE *pPkg          = NULL;
   UINT       nPkgSizeTotal  = 0;
```

Implementing a Network Library 535

```
// read up to 65.536 Bytes in each call
// loop until no more data is waiting
while (!bDone)
   {
   nBytesRead = recv(sk, &m_Buffer[n], nSize-n, 0);

   if (nBytesRead == SOCKET_ERROR) {
      int WSAError = WSAGetLastError();

      // ignore harmless messages
      if ( (WSAError != WSAEMSGSIZE) && (WSAError != WSAEWOULDBLOCK) )
         {
         hr = ZFX_FAIL;
         bDone = true;
         break;
         }
      }

   // now we have nBytesRead bytes ii m_Buffer
   if (nBytesRead <= 0) bDone = true;
   else
      {
      // take care of old data in the buffer
      nBytesRead += n;

      // loop until complete header is found
      while ( (nBytesRead-nReadHead) > g_PkgSize )
         {
         // next bunch of data
         pPkg = (ZFXPACKAGE*)&m_Buffer[nReadHead];
         pPkg->pData = &m_Buffer[nReadHead] + g_PkgSize;

         nPkgSizeTotal = g_PkgSize + pPkg->nLength;

         // did we get the whole package?
         if ( (nBytesRead-nReadHead) >= (nPkgSizeTotal) )
            {
            m_pInbox->Enqueue(pPkg, nPkgSizeTotal);
            nReadHead += nPkgSizeTotal;
            }
         // no back to recv()
         else {
```

```
                    // copy half package to the start of the buffer
                    memcpy(m_Buffer, &m_Buffer[nReadHead], nBytesRead-nReadHead);
                    n = nBytesRead-nReadHead;
                    break;
                    }
               } // while

          // now we got all data waiting for us
          if (nBytesRead < nSize) bDone = true;
          }
     } // while
   return hr;
   } // Receive
```

Alternatively, you can just receive a bunch of data until your buffer is full. Then you can reallocate more memory for your buffer and receive the next bunch of data. You can repeat this scheme until there is no more data to be received. Then you will have a complete list of complete packages that were waiting at the socket object.

But there are two problems with this solution. The first problem is that you would have to allocate memory during runtime and would have to copy the data after you allocate a new memory area for it. This is pretty slow. But even worse is the second problem. A lot of data can be coming in, forcing you to allocate and move a lot of memory, which is never a good idea at all.

So, the approach shown previously might seem a bit unconventional and complicated without any kind of basic elegance. But it is the most stable version you can get.

Querying the Inbox

Now we are just one step away from completing the class for socket objects. We've given each socket object its own inbox to store its data until the application comes along and picks it up, but we still need a function to access this inbox. You have already seen the class ZFXQueue, which handles data packages. Here is the function that lets a user get a package from the inbox. Note that the queue function awaits a linear memory array where it can store its head element. So, you cannot just provide it with a ZFXPACKAGE object because there is no room for the data inside the carrier message in this structure. You have to get the package into the linear buffer of the socket object that is also used to receive the incoming data over the network:

```
int g_PkgSize=sizeof(ZFXPACKAGE);

HRESULT ZFXSocketObject::GetNextPkg(ZFXPACKAGE *pPkg)
   {
```

```
   // anything at all?
   if (m_pInbox->GetCount() > 0)
      {
      // draw data into the buffer
      m_pInbox->Front(m_Buffer, true);

      // fill structure
      memcpy(pPkg, m_Buffer, g_PkgSize);
      memcpy(pPkg->pData, m_Buffer+g_PkgSize, pPkg->nLength);
      return ZFX_OK;
      }
   return ZFX_FAIL;
   } // GetNextPkg
```

This function requires the parameter to come with a structure where the `pData` member is already pointing to a valid memory area. The user must allocate memory before calling this function.

Finally, we have a functional and easy-to-use class that encapsulates the WinSock (and Berkeley Sockets) `SOCKET` object pretty well. But as you know from the first part of this chapter, the `ZFXSocketObject` class is used only inside the dynamic link library implementing the network device interface. This class is therefore invisible to the user outside the DLL. That is because only the `ZFXWS` class that implements the network device interface `ZFXNetworkDevice` uses this socket object. Let's move on and take a look at this class.

Interface Definition for a Network Class

With that comfortable socket object class, we can now start implementing the network device, which is the only class the user has access to using the interface definition. Even if the socket object class is a bit complex with all its functions, the user won't be distracted by that complexity because she cannot even see it. In fact, the class that handles all these socket objects is pretty simple in its interface.

If an application wants to use a network communication, it is only required to call a single function. Whether it wants to be a server or just a client does not matter. The dynamic link library takes care of all the rest. After this single function call, the application can start sending data with one other function call or check its inbox with another function.

Here is the interface definition for the `ZFXNetworkDevice`:

```
#define WM_ZFXSERVER (WM_USER + 1)
#define WM_ZFXCLIENT (WM_USER + 2)

typedef enum ZFXNETMODE_TYPE
   {
```

```
       NMD_SERVER=0,
       NMD_CLIENT=1,
       } ZFXNETMODE;

class ZFXNetworkDevice
    {
    protected:
       HWND       m_hWndMain;          // window handle
       HINSTANCE  m_hDLL;              // DLL handle
       bool       m_bRunning;
       int        m_nPort;             // port number
       char       m_pIP[256];          // IP address
       UINT       m_nMaxSize;          // buffer size

    public:
       ZFXNetworkDevice(void) {};
       virtual ~ZFXNetworkDevice(void) {};

       // init and release
       virtual HRESULT Init(HWND,ZFXNETMODE,int Port,char *IP,UINT Size, bool)=0;
       virtual void    Release(void)=0;
       virtual bool    IsRunning(void)=0;

       // message procedure
       virtual HRESULT MsgProc(WPARAM, LPARAM)=0;

       // sending and receiving
       virtual HRESULT SendToServer(const ZFXPACKAGE*)=0;
       virtual HRESULT SendToClients(const ZFXPACKAGE*)=0;

       // information about the inbox
       virtual bool    IsPkgWaiting(void)=0;
       virtual UINT    GetNextPkgSize(void)=0;
       virtual HRESULT GetNextPkg(ZFXPACKAGE*)=0;
    }; // class
```

Most of the functions in this interface definition should reveal their functionality by their names. I just want to add some words about the ZFXNetworkDevice::MsgProc function. You have already seen a lot of functions that can receive data from the network or send data into the network. The question is how do you call these functions and how do you know that data is waiting at a socket to be received?

All these tasks can be done using the WinSock API by the means of messages. You can register certain events for the WinAPI so that your application gets a message notification if a network event occurs. Then you have to check this message to see which kind of event happened to react accordingly. In this case, we defined the messages WM_ZFXSERVER and WM_ZFXCLIENT, which are sent to your application if something occurs in the network. I will show you this in detail later.

WinSock API Encapsulation

After defining the interface for the network device, the following paragraph deals now with actually implementing the interface. This implementation uses the WinSock API as well as our ZFXSocketObject class. You will see that most of the encapsulation of the WinSock API is already done in our socket object class, so there is not much left to this class except for managing the socket objects.

ZFXWS Class

Let's start with a look at the class declaration ZFXWS, which is the class that implements the interface ZFXNetworkDevice. This declaration sticks to the interface definition as close as possible, so there are just a few additional functions that are not part of the public interface:

```
class ZFXWS : public ZFXNetworkDevice
   {
   public:
     ZFXWS(HINSTANCE hDLL);
     ~ZFXWS(void);

     // interface functions
     HRESULT Init(HWND, ZFXNETMODE, int, char*, UINT, bool);
     void    Release(void);
     bool    IsRunning(void) { return m_bRunning; }
     HRESULT MsgProc(WPARAM wp, LPARAM lp);
     HRESULT SendToServer(const ZFXPACKAGE*);
     HRESULT SendToClients(const ZFXPACKAGE*);
     HRESULT ServerUpdate(void);
     bool    IsPkgWaiting(void)           {return m_pSockObj->IsPkgWaiting();   }
     UINT    GetNextPkgSize(void)         {return m_pSockObj->GetNextPkgSize();}
     HRESULT GetNextPkg(ZFXPACKAGE *pPkg){return m_pSockObj->GetNextPkg(pPkg);}

   private:
     ZFXSocketObject *m_pSockObj;
     ZFXNETMODE      m_Mode;
     ZFXCLIENT       m_Clients[256];
     char            m_ClCount;
     UINT            m_ClID;
```

```
char           *m_Buffer;

// initializing ZFXSocketObject
HRESULT CreateServer(ZFXSocketObject **ppSkObject);
HRESULT CreateClient(ZFXSocketObject **ppSkObject);

// message processing
HRESULT OnAccept(void);
HRESULT OnReceive(SOCKET skReceiving);
HRESULT OnDisconnect(SOCKET skDisconnecting);
}; // class
```

Most of the attributes in this class are needed only for a server instance. Still, I think there is no need to separate this interface into two different interface types—one for a server and one for a client. These are treated internally, so the user does not have to worry about initialization. The only things a client needs to use are the socket object, the mode it is running in, and the buffer to receive incoming data.

The other attributes are used by the server to build a list of connected clients. The member m_ClID is an ID given to each new client connected to the system. This is a simple counter that is incremented for each new client in the network. m_ClCount is a counter that counts how many clients are active at a given time. As opposed to the ID member, this counter is decremented each time a client disconnects. This is a char variable, so no more than 256 clients can be active at the same time; this should be more than enough for non-persistent session-based games.

The array m_Clients contains information about all the connected clients active in the network. The array uses the following structure:

```
typedef struct ZFXCLIENT_TYPE
   {
   SOCKET skToClient;
   UINT    nID;
   } ZFXCLIENT;
```

The SOCKET object is opened by the accept() call of the server's master socket object. It is the socket the server has to use to communicate with the newly connected client. The nID field is the ID the server has given to the client.

To start the network device object, you have to call the initialization function, which gets a parameter of the type ZFXNETMODE, saying whether it should be a client or server. Two private create functions exist in this class and are called depending on the network mode the user has requested. As you saw in Table 11.1, a client and a server have different steps to follow during the initialization process on their socket objects.

The remaining three private functions are called by the ZFXWS::MsgProc function, depending on the event given in the message. Before we start implementing the functions of this class, we should write the constructor and the destructor. The only interesting thing there is that the m_ClID field is initialized with a value of 1 and not 0 because the ID 0 is reserved as the ID for the server:

```
ZFXWS::ZFXWS(HINSTANCE hDLL)
   {
   m_hDLL       = hDLL;
   m_pSockObj   = NULL;
   m_Buffer     = NULL;
   m_nPort      = 0;
   m_ClID       = 1;        // 0 reserved for server
   m_ClCount    = 0;
   m_bRunning   = false;
   } // constructor
/*------------------------*/

ZFXWS::~ZFXWS()
   {
   Release();
   } // destructor
/*------------------------*/

void ZFXWS::Release()
   {
   if (m_Mode == NMD_SERVER)
      {
      for (int i=0; i<m_ClCount; i++)
         {
         shutdown(m_Clients[i].skToClient,0x02);
         closesocket(m_Clients[i].skToClient);
         m_Clients[i].skToClient = INVALID_SOCKET;
         }
      }
   if (m_pSockObj)
      {
      delete m_pSockObj;
      m_pSockObj = NULL;
      }
   if (m_Buffer)
      {
      delete [] m_Buffer;
```

```
      m_Buffer = NULL;
      }
   WSACleanup();
   m_bRunning = false;
   }
```

During the clean-up operation, you should not forget to release all the clients and close their sockets if this instance of the class was used as a server. This involves calling `shutdown()` and `closesocket()` from the WinSock API. A server does not save the socket objects to the connected clients as `ZFXSocketObject` instances, but as raw WinSock sockets only.

Then a server and a client must delete their socket objects, which are instances from our own sockets class. The buffer for the incoming messages must also be freed to avoid memory leaks. Then you have to shut down the WinSock API by calling the `WSACleanup()` functions. So let's take a look at how you crank the WinSock API up in the first place.

Initializing the Network

The first step in initializing the network device is cranking up the WinSock API by using the `WSAStartup()` function. The first parameter is the version of the API you want to use. We are using version 2.0 here. The second parameter is the structure `WSADATA`, which is filled by the function with information about the real implementation of the requested version. This information is not of any relevance to us.

The last step in initializing an instance of the class `ZFXWS` is the initialization of its socket object attribute. Depending on what the caller has requested, this is done using the `ZFXWS::CreateServer` function or the `ZFXWS::CreateClient` function.

The source code is as follows:

```
HRESULT ZFXWS::Init(HWND hWnd, ZFXNETMODE nmd, int nPort, char *pIP,
                    UINT nMaxPkgSize, bool bSaveLog)
   {
   WSADATA  wsaData;
   UINT     nEvents=0;
   WORD     wVersion;
   int      nRes;

   m_nMaxSize  = nMaxPkgSize;
   m_Buffer    = new char[m_nMaxSize];
   m_hWndMain  = hWnd;
   m_nPort     = nPort;
   m_Mode      = nmd;
   g_bLF       = bSaveLog;
```

```
   if (pIP) sprintf(m_pIP, "%s", pIP);

   wVersion = MAKEWORD(2,0);

   if ( (nRes = WSAStartup(wVersion, &wsaData)) != 0)
      return ZFX_FAIL;

   // create master socket object listening
   if (m_Mode==NMD_SERVER)
      {
      if ( FAILED( CreateServer(&m_pSockObj) ))
         return ZFX_FAIL;
      }
   // create socket object as client
   else if (m_Mode==NMD_CLIENT)
      {
      if (strcmp(m_pIP, "")==0)
         sprintf(m_pIP, "LOCALHOST");

      if ( FAILED( CreateClient(&m_pSockObj) ))
         return ZFX_FAIL;
      }
   else return ZFX_INVALIDPARAM;

   m_bRunning = true;
   return ZFX_OK;
   } // Init
```

A server only needs to know the number of the port the user wants to use for the network communication. A client needs to know the same port number as well as the address of the server. If you run a client on the same computer as the server, you can hand over LOCALHOST as the server name instead of the IP address.

Creating a Server

If you take another look at Table 11.1, you can see which steps are necessary to crank up a server socket object (I've repeated the steps here). To initialize a socket object as a server, you have to call the following functions on the socket object:

- CreateSocket()
- Bind()
- Listen()

Chapter 11 ■ The Network Interface of the Engine

In the real implementation, a fourth step is involved, but before we come to that, I want to look at the code:

```
HRESULT ZFXWS::CreateServer(ZFXSocketObject **ppSkObject)
   {
   UINT nEvents=0;

   (*ppSkObject) = new ZFXSocketObject(m_pLog);

   if (!(*ppSkObject))
      return ZFX_FAIL;

   // 1. Step: create a socket object
   if (FAILED( (*ppSkObject)->CreateSocket() ))
      return ZFX_FAIL;

   // 2. Step: bind to port
   if (FAILED( (*ppSkObject)->Bind(m_nPort) ))
      return ZFX_FAIL;

   // 3. Step: set to listening guard
   if (FAILED( (*ppSkObject)->Listen() ))
      return ZFX_FAIL;

   nEvents |= FD_READ | FD_WRITE | FD_CONNECT | FD_ACCEPT | FD_CLOSE;

   // 4. Step: set Windows notification
   if ( WSAAsyncSelect((*ppSkObject)->GetSocket(), m_hWndMain, WM_ZFXSERVER,
                       nEvents) == SOCKET_ERROR)
      {
      m_pSockObj->Disconnect();
      return ZFX_FAIL;
      }

   // set all clients as invalid
   for (int i=0; i<256; i++)
      {
      m_Clients[i].skToClient = INVALID_SOCKET;
      m_Clients[i].nID = 0;
      }
   return ZFX_OK;
   } // CreateServer
```

Basically, the WinSock API separates two communication modes: synchronous and asynchronous. In synchronous mode, some functions of the WinSock API block calls. That means if you call such a function, it stops the program until the function is either successful or fails. The program cannot proceed until this is complete. An example of such a call is the accept() function. This stops the program as long as a client is connecting to the network. If this occurs, no other client is heard in its request to connect as well as long as you do not call the function again because doing so stops the program again until a new client connects.

This sounds as ugly as it is. The way out of this crisis on multitasking systems is to use a separate thread for each new client process. This involves another bunch of problems with thread-safe programming.

If you develop under a Windows system, you can use the asynchronous mode of the sockets API. This is based on the callback procedure method instead of blocking calls. You don't have to wait for an event to occur; instead, you let the event notify you when it occurs. Then you decide whether to react to it. This is a smarter way to do things, and if you have this possibility at your disposal, you should use it. This is the option we will use.

If you want to use asynchronous mode, you have to call the function WSAAsyncSelect() of the WinSock API. In the first parameter of this function, you have to provide the socket for which this notification scheme should be used. The second parameter is a handle of the main window of the application that should receive the notification if there is something going on in the network. The third parameter is the message that should be sent.

The fourth parameter states which kind of events this message should be generated for. The following options can be chosen:

- FD_READ: There is incoming data waiting to be received.
- FD_WRITE: Data was sent over the network.
- FD_CONNECT: A client was accepted by the server in the network.
- FD_ACCEPT: A new client wants to be accepted into the network.
- FD_CLOSE: A client is closing.

A server needs to deal with more of these events than a client does. The server is informed in the case of FD_CONNECT and FD_WRITE, but it doesn't react on the notifications in this example. Now we can discuss how to initialize a client.

Creating a Client

With the server doing several tasks on its initialization to adjust its master socket, dealing with a client is fairly easy. The following two steps are the only ones that are needed to bring a client socket object up online:

- CreateSocket()
- Connect()

You have to adjust the notification process of asynchronous communication to let your application know when something is going on in this socket:

```
HRESULT ZFXWS::CreateClient(ZFXSocketObject **ppSkObject)
   {
   UINT nEvents=0;

   (*ppSkObject) = new ZFXSocketObject(m_pLog);

   if (!(*ppSkObject))
      return ZFX_FAIL;

   // 1. Step: create socket object
   if (FAILED( (*ppSkObject)->CreateSocket() ))
      return ZFX_FAIL;

   if (m_pIP == NULL)
      gethostname(m_pIP, 10);

   // 2. Step: try to connect
   if (FAILED( (*ppSkObject)->Connect(m_pIP, m_nPort) ))
      return ZFX_FAIL;

   nEvents |= FD_READ | FD_CLOSE;

   // 3. Step: set Windows notification
   if (WSAAsyncSelect( (*ppSkObject)->GetSocket(), m_hWndMain, WM_ZFXCLIENT,
                       nEvents) == SOCKET_ERROR) {
      m_pSockObj->Disconnect();
      return ZFX_FAIL;
      }
   return ZFX_OK;
   } // Create Client
```

Unlike a server socket object, a client does not have to process many events. A client doesn't get a notification if another client wants to connect, for example. The only important events are when the server has closed its socket, which effectively terminates the connection. The second important event is the notification that data is waiting to be received.

You've now seen what you need to do to initialize the network, a server, and an arbitrary number of clients. So, it is time to look at the functions that enable you to send data over the network.

Sending Data to the Server

As you can see from the declaration of the two functions provided by the class to send data, you can send packages only of the type ZFXPACKAGE. This structure is just a carrier message and can contain an arbitrary message inside. You should be careful when doing this, though. The data inside this package is provided in the form of a void pointer that points to the place in memory where the data is, which differs from where the ZFXPACKAGE structure is located in memory.

The send() function requires that all the data to be sent sit in a linear array in memory with no gaps in between. Otherwise, the function sends the wrong part of the memory, which results in nonsense or problems in your program or another program that's running.

The solution to this is to serialize the data before you send it from the ZFXPACKAGE structure. The following function takes the incoming package and copies the structure into the linear buffer of the ZFXWS class. Then the data that is the pointer to the package is copied directly behind the package structure in the buffer. All the data that should be sent over the network then sits in a row in the memory and can be sent. Here's the code:

```
int g_PkgSize=sizeof(ZFXPACKAGE);

HRESULT ZFXWS::SendToServer(const ZFXPACKAGE *pPkg)
   {
   int nBytes=0;
   int nSize=g_PkgSize+pPkg->nLength;

   if (m_Mode != NMD_CLIENT) return ZFX_FAIL;
   if (nSize > m_nMaxSize) return ZFX_OUTOFMEMORY;

   // data serialization
   memcpy(m_Buffer, pPkg, g_PkgSize);
   memcpy(m_Buffer+g_PkgSize, pPkg->pData, pPkg->nLength);

   nBytes = m_pSockObj->Send(m_Buffer, nSize);
   if ( (nBytes==SOCKET_ERROR) || (nBytes<nSize) )
      return ZFX_FAIL;
   return ZFX_OK;
   } // SendToServer
```

Sending Data to the Clients

The same steps need to be performed by the function that lets a server send data to all the clients. The only difference here is that the server has to loop through all the connected clients and send the package to each of the clients. This is opposed to a client instance of this class, which only sends the package of the one socket object it owns, which leads to the server:

Here is the function for the server:

```
HRESULT ZFXWS::SendToClients(const ZFXPACKAGE *pPkg)
   {
   HRESULT hr=ZFX_OK;
   int     nBytes=0;
   int     nSize=g_PkgSize+pPkg->nLength;

   if (m_Mode != NMD_SERVER) return ZFX_FAIL;
   if (nSize > m_nMaxSize) return ZFX_OUTOFMEMORY;

   // data serialization
   memcpy(m_Buffer, pPkg, g_PkgSize);
   memcpy(m_Buffer+g_PkgSize, pPkg->pData, pPkg->nLength);

   for (UINT i=0; i<m_ClCount; i++)
      {
      if (m_Clients[i].skToClient != INVALID_SOCKET)
         {
         nBytes = m_pSockObj->Send(m_Buffer, nSize, m_Clients[i].skToClient);

         if ( (nBytes==SOCKET_ERROR) || (nBytes<nSize) )
            hr = ZFX_FAIL;
         }
      }
   return hr;
   } // SendToClients
```

The function reports an error to the caller if sending the data to at least one client fails; however, it still tries to send the package to all the other clients in the list. So, it does not critically affect the whole network if one client is lost due to an error or a disconnection.

Message Procedure

Because we are working with asynchronous socket objects, the application using our network device DLL receives the two Windows messages WM_ZFXSERVER and WM_ZFXCLIENT into its normal Windows message queue to process them in their own message procedure. In this case, the procedure gets the event that occurred from the lower part of the LPARAM of the message, whereas the WPARAM of the function contains the socket object on which the event occurred.

This class implementation of the network device interface offers a message procedure function that must be called with the appropriate parameters if one of the two messages occurs. The function looks like this:

```
HRESULT ZFXWS::MsgProc(WPARAM wp, LPARAM lp)
   {
   WORD  wEvent, wError;

   wError = HIWORD(lp);
   wEvent = LOWORD(lp);

   // evaluate which event occurred
   switch (wEvent) {
      // new client is accepted
      case FD_CONNECT: break;

      // new clients is knocking
      case FD_ACCEPT:  { return OnAccept(); } break;

      // there is data to be received
      case FD_READ:    { return OnReceive(wp); } break;

      // a socket is closing
      case FD_CLOSE:   { return OnDisconnect(wp); } break;

      // after sending data
      case FD_WRITE:   break;

      }
   return ZFX_OK;
   } // MsgProc
```

The two events `FD_CONNECT` and `FD_WRITE` are left unprocessed by this function because we simply don't want to react to them. For the other three events, we will implement certain functions in this class that are called in case of the according event so we can keep this functioning.

Connecting Clients

If we run a server, the `FD_ACCEPT` event will occur frequently. This event shows the server that a new application wants to enter the network as a new client and has therefore called the function `connect()` on its socket object. The server reacts and accepts the new client into its network.

The server has to build a new socket object for the new client to be able to communicate with it. Only two tasks are left after that. First, the server has to inform the client about the ID under which the client will be known in the network. To let the client know its ID, the server sends a package with the message ID 0, which is used for this type of message to a new client.

The second task is to inform all the other clients that a new client has connected. To do this, the server changes the type ID of the package sent to the new client and sends this package to all the other connected clients. The new type ID is 1.

Here is the function in our class:

```
HRESULT ZFXWS::OnAccept(void)
   {
   int nSize=0, nBytes=0, i=m_ClCount;

   if (m_ClCount >= 255) return ZFX_OUTOFMEMORY;

   if ( FAILED( m_pSockObj->Accept(
                      &(m_Clients[i].skToClient) )))
      return ZFX_FAIL;

   // SEND THE ID TO THE NEW CLIENT:
   ZFXPACKAGE *pPkg = (ZFXPACKAGE*)m_Buffer;
   pPkg->pData = &m_Buffer[g_PkgSize];
   pPkg->nLength = sizeof(UINT);
   pPkg->nType   = 0;   // ID Msg
   pPkg->nSender = 0;   // Server
   memcpy(pPkg->pData, &m_ClID, sizeof(UINT));

   // increase counter
   m_Clients[i].nID = m_ClID;
   m_ClCount++;
   m_ClID++;

   nSize = g_PkgSize + pPkg->nLength;
   nBytes = m_pSockObj->Send(m_Buffer, nSize, m_Clients[i].skToClient);
   if ( (nBytes==SOCKET_ERROR) || (nBytes<nSize) )
      return ZFX_FAIL;

   // INFORM ALL OTHER CLIENTS ABOUT THE NEW GUY IN TOWN
   pPkg->nType = 1;
   SendToClients(pPkg);
   return ZFX_OK;
   } // OnAccept
```

Disconnecting Clients

If a player decides that he has had enough of the video games played on a network and wants to leave the network, the server receives notification. This happens, for example, if the ZFXNetworkDevice the client was using is deleted by the application that initialized it.

As soon as the server knows that a client wants to disconnect, it has to react with the appropriate steps. First, it searches for the client that wants to go offline in its list of all the sockets leading to the clients in the network. If it finds the concerned socket, it closes it. The other end of this line is already dead because the client is already gone. Now all the required work is actually done. But the server also quickly packs a package to inform the other clients about the client who left the network. So, if the application wants to process this message, it could print a message to the screens of the players telling them that a player has left the game.

Here is the function:

```
HRESULT ZFXWS::OnDisconnect(SOCKET skDisconnecting)
   {
   ZFXPACKAGE Pkg;
   UCHAR      i=0;

   if (skDisconnecting==INVALID_SOCKET) return ZFX_FAIL;

   if (m_Mode==NMD_SERVER)
      {
      // delete from list
      for (i=0; i<m_ClCount; i++)
         {
         if (m_Clients[i].skToClient == skDisconnecting)
            break;
         }
      if (i>=m_ClCount)
         return ZFX_FAIL;

      // close the socket
      shutdown(m_Clients[i].skToClient,0x02);
      closesocket(m_Clients[i].skToClient);
      m_Clients[i].skToClient = INVALID_SOCKET;

      // INFORM THE OTHERS
      Pkg.pData   = &m_Buffer[g_PkgSize];
      Pkg.nLength = sizeof(UINT);
      Pkg.nType   = 2;    // ID disconnecting Message
```

```
        Pkg.nSender = 0;    // Server
        memcpy(Pkg.pData, &m_Clients[i].nID,
               sizeof(UINT));

        SendToClients(&Pkg);

        // copy last entr to free positon
        memcpy(&m_Clients[i], &m_Clients[m_ClCount-1], sizeof(ZFXCLIENT));
        m_ClCount--;
        }
    else
        {
        shutdown(m_pSockObj->GetSocket(),0x02);
        closesocket(m_pSockObj->GetSocket());
        }
    return ZFX_OK;
    } // OnDisconnect
```

Even a client is able to receive and process a disconnect message. In this case, it has to close its own socket object to clean up behind itself.

Receiving Packages over the Network

We are now pretty close to completing the new network component of the engine. Believe it or not, these few pages are enough to get a network engine up and running. The DLL offers basic networking tasks that an application can utilize to build a chat program, a file transfer tool, or even a video game with a network mode.

The only function missing in the class now is the one that starts the process of receiving incoming data after the message procedure has been informed about that event. Here it is:

```
HRESULT ZFXWS::OnReceive(SOCKET skReceiving)
    {
    if (m_bRunning)
        return m_pSockObj->Receive(skReceiving);
    else
        return ZFX_FAIL;
    } // OnReceive
```

As a parameter for the receive function of the socket object class, the receiving socket object is given. This is the object that reported the incoming data. In the case of a server, you don't have to check which of the socket objects leading to different clients is concerned. But, for this reason, it is helpful that our packages contain the IDs of the sender so the server can identify the client who sent the data without needing to loop through its list and compare addresses. In the case of a client, the socket that receives the data is the one that leads to the server.

The network component of the ZFXEngine is finally complete. There might still be some little details missing such as a lobby for huge online games and support for UDP traffic. But all these are things you can add on your own. The last chapter of the book builds a video game with network capabilities based on this network engine. But first, let's see how a chat works or a file transfer application.

Demo Application

Before we proceed to the test of the network component in the video game at the end of this book, I want to show you two sand boxes you can use to test the network component of the ZFXEngine. You will see how the engine's new network component works in an isolated Windows application to accomplish two tasks.

The first demo application is a simple chat tool to which an arbitrary number of clients can connect. The WinAPI is used for the graphical user interface, and the ZFXEngine network component is used for the data transfer over the network connections. The second example for this chapter is a file transfer program that lets you send files from your hard disk over the network connection to another client.

Chat Application

A *chat* is the hello world application of the network world. The base code for this is the same as for all the other demos with the three DLL components our engine contains so far. This is why I won't show the full source code of the demo here. Just take a look at the code on the companion CD-ROM. The initialization process of this component is straightforward. You just have to build an object of the `ZFXNetwork` static library class and query a `ZFXNetworkDevice` object from this object. If one application wants to create a client and a server in the same instance, you use two separate `ZFXNetwork` objects:

```
HRESULT ProgramStartup(ZFXNETMODE nmd)
   {
   g_pNetwork = new ZFXNetwork(g_hInst);

   if (FAILED( g_pNetwork->CreateDevice() ))
      return E_FAIL;

   g_pDevice = g_pNetwork->GetDevice();

   if (FAILED( g_pDevice->Init(g_hWnd, nmd, g_nPort,
                              g_chIP, 5000, 64, true) ))
      return E_FAIL;
```

```
return ZFX_OK;
} // ProgramStartup
```

The first parameter of the initialization function is the handle to the application's main window. In this case, it is a global variable. The other two global variables are used for the port number and the string containing the IP address. This information is needed if you want to create a client. If you want to run the application as a server, you only need to name the port number it should work on.

Tip

> The DOS application `ipconfig.exe` delivers the IP address of the computer you are working on. If you want to test this program on a single computer, you have to start an instance from it as a server. Then you run the `ipconfig.exe` program and look for your IP. Finally, you start another separate instance and select to run it as a client using the IP address of the server, which is the address you got from this DOS command. For the port number, you can use a value of 6000.

The values for the IP address and the port number make their way into the global variables via a dialog that the application shows on startup because it is called from the function `ProgramStartup()`. Figure 11.4 shows this dialog. The two buttons to start the application are disabled first. As soon as you enter a port number, you can start the application as a server. If you enter a valid IP address, you can select whether to start as a server or client.

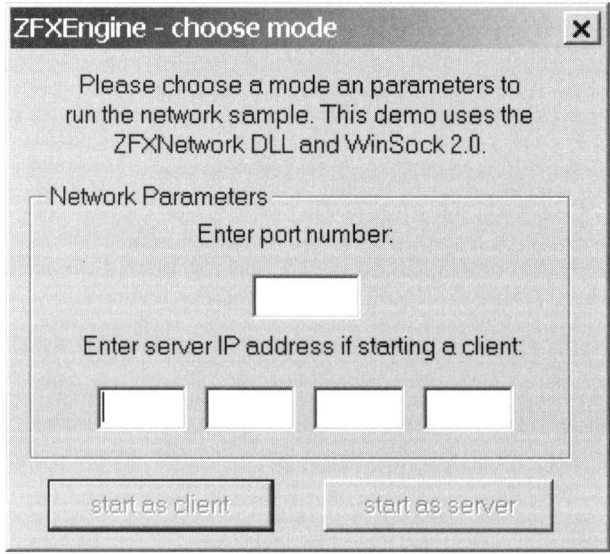

Figure 11.4 The startup dialog of the chat program.

I won't describe how to build a dialog here or how to write its callback function. This is just basic WinAPI programming and isn't very complex. Look at the sources provided for this chapter for help. I will show you the code needed to run the chat itself and transmit the chat messages. Figure 11.5 shows the chat after you've started the program from the dialog.

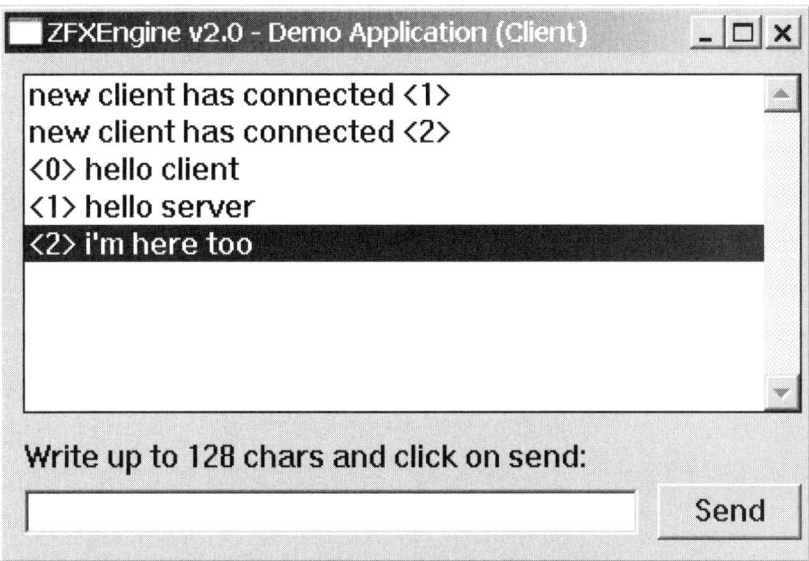

Figure 11.5 The chat running with the server and two connected clients.

Sending Messages

To implement the chat, two things are needed after the initialization of the network component in the application. First, you need a changed Windows procedure; second, you have to adjust the main loop of the program. The changed procedure is necessary because you have to react to the WM_ZFXSERVER and WM_ZFXCLIENT messages. In both cases, you simply have to delegate the incoming messages to the message procedure of the ZFXNetworkDevice object. This function then processes the incoming messages as shown previously. The only thing you need to take care of is sending the data.

This is done in the message procedure of this application because it takes place in the chat when the user hits a button and generates a Windows event you can intercept in the message procedure. The handle of this SEND button is IDC_hBtn. If this event happens, the application gets the text string from the text field and then puts this string into a ZFX-PACKAGE object to be sent.

Chapter 11 ■ The Network Interface of the Engine

There are some differences in the implementation path for a server and a client. Normally, a server is not meant to act in the chat itself—at least not in the general client/server architecture. The server should only process the workload given to it by the clients and then distribute the results into the network to all the clients. But in the case of the chat, the server should also be able to participate in the chat session to prevent the user from starting a separate instance just to chat. In the case of a server, the application puts the chat text string directly into the list box used for displaying all the chat messages. But it also is sent to all the connected clients, instead of putting it into the list box directly:

```
case WM_ZFXSERVER: case WM_ZFXCLIENT:
   {
   g_pDevice->MsgProc(wParam, lParam);
   } break;

case WM_COMMAND:
  {
  switch (LOWORD(wParam)) {
    case IDC_hBtn: {
       ZFXPACKAGE       msgPkg;
       char             buffer[128],buf[200];
       msgPkg.pData = buf;

       GetWindowText(hText, buffer, 128);
       SetWindowText(hText, "");

       if (strcmp(buffer, "exit")==0)
          {
          g_bDone = true;
          PostMessage(hWnd, WM_CLOSE, 0, 0);
          }
       else
          {
          sprintf((char*)msgPkg.pData, "<%d> %s", g_ID, buffer);

          // +1 for terminating 0 character
          msgPkg.nType    = 3;
          msgPkg.nSender  = g_ID;
          msgPkg.nLength  = strlen((char*)msgPkg.pData)+1;

          // SERVER-CODE
          if (g_nmd==NMD_SERVER)
             {
             SendMessage(hLbx, LB_ADDSTRING, 0, (LPARAM)msgPkg.pData);
```

```
            int n = SendMessage(hLbx,LB_GETCOUNT,0,0);

            SendMessage(hLbx,LB_SETCURSEL,(WPARAM)n-1,0);

            g_pDevice->SendToClients(&msgPkg);
            }
         // CLIENT-CODE
         else g_pDevice->SendToServer(&msgPkg);
         }
      return 0;
      } break;
   } // switch [CMD]
   return 0;
   } break; // WM_COMMAND
```

The server needs to be taken care of in a special-case decision. Normally, the server is not a part of the visual output of the program, so you could have skipped the server case from this program. The clients would then be able to chat like they do now. The only drawback would be that the server would not show the incoming chat messages in its list box and would also not be able to send messages.

Receiving Messages

The message procedure of this application can now create messages and send them to the server, which should then send them to the inboxes of the ZFXNetworkDevice objects of all the connected clients. The only thing that remains for the application is actually receiving the messages from the network. This task is done in the main loop of the application:

```
ZFXPACKAGE      msgPkg;
char            buffer[5000], temp[300];
msgPkg.pData = buffer;

// MAIN LOOP
while (!g_bDone) {
   while (PeekMessage(&msg, NULL, 0, 0, PM_REMOVE))
      {
      TranslateMessage(&msg);
      DispatchMessage(&msg);
      }

   while ( g_pDevice->IsPkgWaiting() )
      {
      g_pDevice->GetNextPkg(&msgPkg);
```

```
        // client gets ID from server
        if (msgPkg.nType == 0)
           g_ID = *((UINT*)msgPkg.pData);

        // a new client is around
        else if (msgPkg.nType == 1)
           {
           sprintf(temp, "new client connected <%d>", *((UINT*)msgPkg.pData));
           SendMessage(hLbx,LB_ADDSTRING,0,(LPARAM)temp);
           }

        // a client left the network
        else if (msgPkg.nType == 2)
           {
           sprintf(temp, "client <%d> disconnected", *((UINT*)msgPkg.pData));
           SendMessage(hLbx,LB_ADDSTRING,0,(LPARAM)temp);
           }

        // else its a chat message
        else
           {
           SendMessage(hLbx, LB_ADDSTRING, 0, (LPARAM)msgPkg.pData);

           if (g_nmd==NMD_SERVER)
              g_pDevice->SendToClients(&msgPkg);
           }
        int n = SendMessage(hLbx,LB_GETCOUNT,0,0);
        SendMessage(hLbx, LB_SETCURSEL, (WPARAM)n-1, 0);
        } // while msg incoming
     } // main loop
```

How this main loop works should be clear. In each iteration of the main loop, we start a new loop inside that is running as long as there are messages in the inbox of the `ZFXNetworkDevice` object of the application. After extracting such a message from the inbox of the object, a case decision takes place to differentiate between the various message types that can arrive. The client and the server need to know which types of messages can occur.

In this simple chat program, only four types of messages can be processed, so for the sake of simplicity, we do this inside the main loop. One message is the ID that is sent to the client by the server after a new client has entered the network. If a new client is connected or an old one is disconnected, the program writes a text string to the list box so the user knows what has happened. The final case is treated as a chat message that was received and which is then displayed in the list box.

If this instance of the application is a server and not only a client, it is not enough to output the chat message into the application's list box. The server has to handle all communication between the clients as well, so this message is also broadcast by sending it to all the connected clients. The client path of the application explicitly does not output a message that its own user made on the keyboard. It just sends this message to the server and displays it in its list box only if the message comes back from the server's broadcast. So, this application sticks to the rule that the clients should work only with data coming from the server. This enables the server to perform security checks to prevent cheating.

That's all it takes to write a chat application that can communicate with up to 256 clients over a TCP/IP connection.

File Transfer Application

The second part of the demo application code accompanying this chapter is used to send data files between a client and a server. This application can be run as a server or as a client, as the chat can, and you can select the mode after starting the program. If the connection between the client and server is up and running, you can exchange files over the network connection. The dialog to control this program is kept simple, as you can see in Figure 11.6.

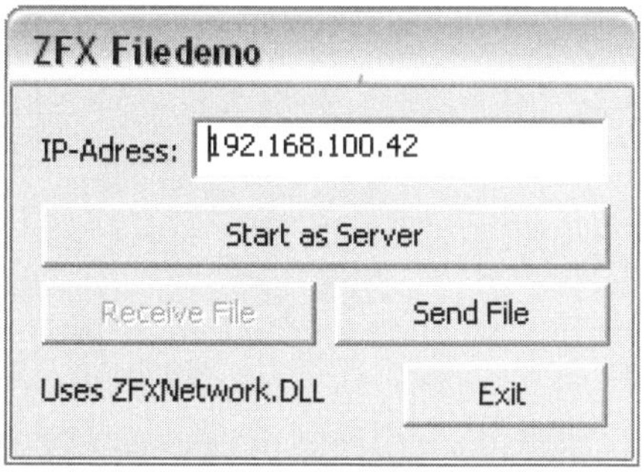

Figure 11.6 Dialog to choose the file that should be sent.

Again, the framework for this demo application is similar to the one used in the preceding chapter. The start of the application takes place in the Init() function where all the necessary work is done to crank up the program, which in this case is the initialization of the ZFXEngine's network component:

```
HRESULT Init( void )
    {
```

```
    g_ofn.lStructSize       = sizeof(OPENFILENAME);
    g_ofn.hwndOwner         = g_hWnd;
    g_ofn.lpstrTitle        = g_szAppName;
    g_ofn.hInstance         = g_hInst;
    g_ofn.lpstrFilter       = TEXT("All Files(*.*)\0*.*\0\0");
    g_ofn.lpstrCustomFilter = NULL;
    g_ofn.nMaxCustFilter    = 0;
    g_ofn.nFilterIndex      = 0;
    g_ofn.nMaxFile          = MAX_PATH;
    g_ofn.nMaxFileTitle     = MAX_PATH;
    g_ofn.lpstrInitialDir   = NULL;
    g_ofn.nFileOffset       = 0;
    g_ofn.nFileExtension    = 0;
    g_ofn.lpstrDefExt       = TEXT( "*.*" );
    g_ofn.lCustData         = 0L;
    g_ofn.lpfnHook          = NULL;
    g_ofn.lpTemplateName    = NULL;

    g_pNetwork = new ZFXNetwork( g_hInst );
    if( FAILED( g_pNetwork->CreateDevice() ) )
        return E_FAIL;

    g_pDevice = g_pNetwork->GetDevice();
    if( g_pDevice == NULL ) return E_FAIL;

    g_sData.nSender = 0;
    g_sData.nType   = 0;
    g_sData.pData   = new BYTE[ MAX_PACKAGE_SIZE ];
    ZeroMemory( g_sData.pData, MAX_PACKAGE_SIZE );
    return S_OK;
    } // Init
```

To make the selection of the files to be transferred as easy as possible, this application uses the `OpenFileName` dialog from the WinAPI. This is the standard Windows dialog that is used to let users browse the directories on the computer to search for files they want to work with. To make this dialog do what you want, you must adjust some settings in the structure. In this case, the dialog is adjusted to let users open many types of files with no special file type.

The next step in the `Init()` function is the initialization of the network engine from the DLL. Finally, the standard package variable is initialized because it is reused each time a file is sent. The `MAX_PACKAGE_SIZE` constant is defined in the header and set to 65535. So, the files you can send with this application must not be bigger than 64KB.

Demo Application

In the message procedure `DLGProc()`, the application processes all the messages meant for the application's dialog. The most important buttons here are the ones to select which data to send or to receive:

```
case WM_COMMAND:
   switch( LOWORD( wParam ))
      {
      // Session beenden?
      case IDCANCEL:
         Destroy();
         PostQuitMessage( 0 );
         return 0;
      // File versenden?
      case IDC_SENDFILE:    FileSend();    break;
      // File empfangen?
      case IDC_RECEIVEFILE: FileReceive(); break;
      // Als Server starten?
      case IDC_BESERVER:
         g_nmd = NMD_SERVER;
         g_iID = 1;
         NetworkInit();
         break;
      } // switch
   } // WM_COMMAND
```

If the user wants to send or receive a file and presses the appropriate button, another function is called that does the receiving and sending. If the user hits the button to start the application as a server, the appropriate global variables are set to identify a server. Then the initialization of the network is called. The client is treated at another point in the program, which is where a file is about to be received.

This message procedure also has to process the ZFXEngine messages `WM_ZFXCLIENT` and `WM_ZFXSERVER`, which indicate network activity:

```
case WM_ZFXCLIENT:
case WM_ZFXSERVER:
   {
   // process message
   g_pDevice->MsgProc( wParam, lParam );

   // update application
   NetworkReceive();

   } break;
} // Messages
```

562 Chapter 11 ■ The Network Interface of the Engine

The two messages from the network DLL are processed. The only thing you need to do is call the message procedure of the network device because these two messages indicate that something is occurring in the network, such as an incoming data package that must be handled.

Next, we will look at the function that cranks up the network. This is the same process as the one used for the chat application:

```
HRESULT NetworkInit( void )
   {
   // network online?
   if( !g_bNetOK ) {
      // start as client?
      if( g_nmd == NMD_CLIENT )
        {
        GetWindowText(GetDlgItem(g_hWnd,IDC_IPADRESS), g_cIPADRESS,16);
        }
      else {
        SetDlgItemText(g_hWnd,IDC_IPADRESS," ...waiting for files");
        }

      // start the network device
      if( FAILED( g_pDevice->Init(g_hWnd, g_nmd, g_iPort, g_cIPADRESS,
                                  MAX_PACKAGE_SIZE, true ) ) )
         {
         MessageBox(g_hWnd,"Network init failed", "error", MB_ICONERROR );
         return E_FAIL;
         }
      g_bNetOK = true;

      EnableWindow(GetDlgItem(g_hWnd,IDC_BESERVER), false );
      EnableWindow(GetDlgItem(g_hWnd,IDC_IPADRESS), false);
      }
   return S_OK;
   }
```

After evaluating whether to start as a client or server, the function takes the necessary data from the global variables and starts the network device. If all is okay, the button to start the application as a server is deactivated, similar to the field in which you had to enter the IP for a client.

Note that the application uses port 10042, which is set in a global variable. If you have a firewall, you should open this port or allow the application to get through your firewall to do its job. After recompiling the project, you always must reallow the application access through the firewall because the firewall will know that the executable has changed and might therefore be dangerous to your computer.

As a server, the program now sits and waits for clients to connect to it so they can start to exchange files. As a client, the program has loaded a file that the user wants to submit and tries to reach the server with the given IP. Now we will look at the code for the client.

Suppose the user has entered a valid IP in the appropriate field of the dialog and clicked Send File. The FileSend() function is called:

```
HRESULT FileSend( void )
   {
   FILE* pFile = NULL;

   g_ofn.Flags       = OFN_HIDEREADONLY | OFN_CREATEPROMPT;
   g_ofn.lpstrTitle  = TEXT("Send a File");
   g_ofn.lpstrFile   = (PTSTR)&g_szFile;

   // open file dialog
   if( !GetOpenFileName( &g_ofn ) ) return S_OK;

   if( !g_bNetOK )
      {
      if( FAILED( NetworkInit() ) )  return E_FAIL;
      }
// to be continued ...
```

First, the function adjusts the parameters of the open file dialog structure because you have to supply an instance of this structure to open the dialog. After everything is in place in this structure, you call the GetOpenFileName() function from the WinAPI, which pops up the dialog for the user to select the file he wants to send. After getting this name, the call is made to initialize the network system. This is the place where a client begins the initialization process of the ZFXEngine's network component.

If everything went okay, the client should now have the path to a file that should be transferred, as well as a valid connection to a server in this network:

```
// ... continued
   pFile = fopen( g_szFile, "rb" );
   if( pFile == NULL ) return E_FAIL;

   g_sData.nLength = _filelength( _fileno( pFile ) );

   // check file size
   if( g_sData.nLength > MAX_PACKAGE_SIZE )
```

```
    {
    fclose( pFile );
    MessageBox( g_hWnd, "Unexpected filesize", "error", MB_ICONERROR );
    return E_FAIL;
    }

// clear buffer
ZeroMemory( g_sData.pData, MAX_PACKAGE_SIZE );

// read data into buffer
fread( g_sData.pData, sizeof(BYTE), g_sData.nLength, pFile );

    fclose( pFile );
// to be continued ...
```

The name of the file as well as the whole path to its location (where it's waiting for the transmission) is now stored in the variable g_szFile. The function tries to open this file. Then the function checks how many bytes the file contains and whether it is below the 64KB limit for this application. You can also decide to support files of unlimited size, but then you must break the file into pieces and send the pieces individually. This prevents the socket's buffer from overflowing before the network has a chance to extract some data from the socket's buffer and store it in its inbox. This simple program refuses to send the file if it is too big.

Then you can close the file handle after the data is read from the file, and it can be sent from local memory. This is done in the remainder of the function:

```
// ... continued
    g_sData.nSender    = g_iID;
    g_sData.nType      = 0;

    // client or sever?
    if( g_nmd == NMD_CLIENT )
        {
        // send package
        if (FAILED(g_pDevice->SendToServer(&g_sData))) {
            MessageBox( g_hWnd, "Sending data failed", "error", MB_ICONERROR );
            return E_FAIL;
            }
        }
    else {
        if (FAILED(g_pDevice->SendToClients(&g_sData))) {
            MessageBox( g_hWnd, "Sending data failed", "error", MB_ICONERROR );
            return E_FAIL;
```

```
      }
    }
    return S_OK;
    } // FileSend
```

The data package finally gets the ID of the client that is ending it as well as the package type, which is 0 in this case. Then you have to separate the cases of being a client or being a server. A client needs to send its data to the server, whereas the server sends its data to all the clients. In this simple implementation, all the files from clients are sent to the server only and all the files from the server are sent to all the connected clients. You can enlarge the program to let a client select one of the connected clients to send the file to exclusively.

This is the most complex function of the program. The rest of the demo is easy. To check whether the network activity indicated by the messages WM_ZFXCLIENT or WM_ZFXSERVER has provided this instance of the application with data to process, we need a function that checks the inbox of the connected network device and that gets the data from the inbox if there is any. Here it is:

```
HRESULT NetworkReceive( void )
   {
   if( !g_bNetOK ) return E_FAIL;

   // check for package
   while( g_pDevice->IsPkgWaiting() )
      {
      if (FAILED(g_pDevice->GetNextPkg(&g_sData)))
         {
         MessageBox( g_hWnd, "GetNextPkg() failed", "error", MB_ICONERROR );
         return E_FAIL;
         }
      else
         {
         if( (g_sData.nType == 0) && ( g_iID != g_sData.nSender ) )
            {
            // enable save button
            EnableWindow( GetDlgItem( g_hWnd, IDC_RECEIVEFILE ), true );
            }
         }
      } // while
   return S_OK;
   } // NetworkReceive
```

If the network should not be initialized at this time, the function reports an error, but this should normally not happen. If everything is okay, you just check this instance's inbox in the network device by calling `IsPkgWaiting()`; if this is the case, you extract the package by calling `GetNextPkg()`. As a parameter, you hand over a reference to the global package used in this application and it is then filled with the waiting data.

Now the application should have received a file over the network if the message ID is 0. If the message was not sent by this instance of the program, the application enables the receive button in the GUI dialog so the user can save the file to her hard disk if she wants to accept it.

Hitting this button starts the appropriate Windows event, which in turn is processed by our message procedure that calls the following function to actually receive the file. The open filename dialog is used again, but this time, it names a path where the incoming file should be saved:

```
HRESULT FileReceive( void )
   {
   FILE* pFile = NULL;

   // set open file dialog
   g_ofn.Flags       = OFN_OVERWRITEPROMPT;
   g_ofn.lpstrTitle  = TEXT("Receive a File");
   g_ofn.lpstrFile   = (PTSTR)&g_szFile;

   // check for data
   if( g_sData.nLength == 0 ) return S_OK;

   // open file dialog
   if( !GetOpenFileName( &g_ofn ) ) return S_OK;

   // now we have the path
   pFile = fopen( g_szFile, "wb" );

   if( pFile == NULL )
      return E_FAIL;

   // write file into data stream
   fwrite( g_sData.pData, sizeof(BYTE), g_sData.nLength, pFile );

   fclose( pFile );

   // show that file was saved
   EnableWindow( GetDlgItem( g_hWnd, IDC_RECEIVEFILE ),
                 false );
```

```
return S_OK;
} // FileReceive
```

Just as in the `FileSend()` function, you have to adjust the structure used by the open file dialog. After doing a cross-check of whether a package was received, this dialog is then called to let the user choose the location for the file and give it a name. This whole string is then placed in the variable `g_szFile`. Then you can open the file using this string in a write binary (wb) mode. Note that the file is created by this function if it does not exist. Writing the actual data from the package to the new file takes only a single call to `fwrite()`. Finally, the function cleans up behind it by closing the open file and disabling the receive button because the current file that was just received is now saved to disk so there is no need to receive it again. The button is enabled again only if there is a new file incoming.

Ideas for Improvements

We are already at the end of this chapter. But first I want to give you some ideas of how you can improve this program. As already mentioned, this application can send only 64KB of data in a single file transfer. This is the limit the network DLL of the ZFXEngine can handle internally, and it should be enough to work with in game messages. But to send large files, you have to write a function that splits large files into small batches and sends them individually. The receiving application is then required to put these pieces together to get the complete file.

The next improvement is to build a package containing the name of the file so that the user receiving a file also gets the name of the file from the sender. Even if the name is not that important, the file type indicated by the filename ending would be important to know, wouldn't it?

Next, you can also enable the application to transmit more than one file at the same time. Currently, the application is only working with a single instance of the network package type. You would only need a list of these package types to receive a bunch of them at the same time. This will only make sense for larger files that take more time to transmit than 64KB.

One Look Back, Two Steps Forward

Aren't you always surprised how easily most things can be implemented once you get a grip on them? There are still some things you need to be aware of in networks, such as synchronizing everything, but now you have a head start on learning about these topics.

In this chapter, we added a fully functional, new, main component to the engine, and this component can now handle all network communication issues. A video game running in a network is nothing more than just a normal game sending data packages instead of directly calling functions. The processing of the packages results in function calls to be made. Furthermore, you have seen two sample programs in this chapter using the WinAPI to write a chat program as well as a file transfer program. These samples also showed you how you can use the network component of the ZFXEngine as a standalone component without using the render, input, and audio component.

I will also show you how to use all the engine's components together in a simple 3D network video game. But before we start working on this, we need to talk about some data structures and algorithms you will need when developing 3D video games. The next chapter introduces you to the concept of cameras used to view 3D scenes in computer graphics. This chapter was the last one that added a main component to our engine.

Chapter 12

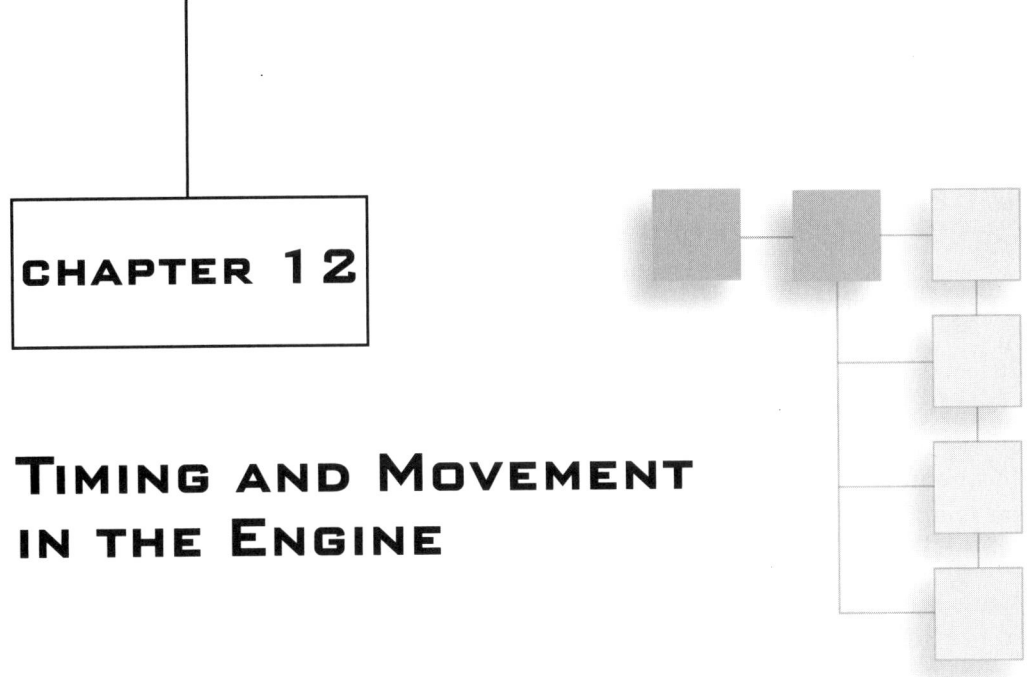

Timing and Movement in the Engine

The iron pot would with a silver prong / Be lifted from the furnace—to imagine Itself a silver vase.

Nathan the Wise, Gotthold Ephriam Lessing

This short chapter deals with an additional helper library provided for the ZFXEngine that lets you accomplish two tasks that are necessary for each video game, but that are not part of the four main components. These two tasks are the camera's movement and timing issues.

This new static library project is called `ZFXGeneral.lib` and it is totally independent of the main parts of the engine, though it uses the math library for 3D calculations. In this library, you will find a class that lets you do the timing in the engine, and you will find classes that let the viewer move around in the virtual 3D world. Review the timer class source code on the CD-ROM that accompanies this book. In this chapter, I focus on the more complicated camera issue.

The following objectives are covered in this chapter:

- Calculating the movement of the viewer in a 3D scene
- Transforming camera objects with six degrees of freedom
- Implementing a base class for cameras
- Programming a free camera and a first-person camera
- Developing an additional static helper library for the ZFXEngine

Different Camera Modes

Some of you might think that the term camera is a bit misplaced in the context of discussions about 3D computer graphics. Although it sounds strange and although most textbooks refer to the camera as the viewer or viewer object, I would like to stick with this term.

A camera in our context means that an object sits at a certain location and watches the scene at a certain angle. As you might gather from the term scene for the virtual world, computer graphics programmers like to draw comparisons to the movie business. And those comparisons are not wrong. After all, you can see the projected image of the scene on your monitor just as you can watch a movie on the television screen.

In conclusion, the camera is the correct term to describe the location of a viewer in a 3D scene. Just as you can in movies, you can have several cameras and switch between them to watch a scene from different positions and angles. The one advantage in 3D graphics is that you can control the camera by moving it through the scene. This is like working a handheld camcorder you would film with.

After all, you already have an implicit camera. Even if you cannot move through the scene yet, it is still filmed and projected onto your screen, isn't it?

Free Cameras

A totally free camera is one that is not possible in reality. It flies in a gravity-free space. This is a camera object that has what we call six degrees of freedom. Such a camera can rotate on its three local axes and it can be moved on three axes. The combined local axes and the three movable axes are the six degrees of freedom. There are no physical limits to this type of camera and no restricted movement on a certain axis. Conversely, a human cannot roll around his z-axis for 360 degrees, for example. All he can do is tilt his head a bit. So such a camera type is mostly interesting for space-combat simulations, for environments with zero gravity, or in tools used to build virtual worlds.

Don't forget about the human debugger. A programmer or a level designer would want to switch to such a free mode, ignoring even collision detection to track down errors in the code, in the level, or even just to watch the final level without the need to maneuver through a difficult set of rooms, walls, and traps. Note that there is this nasty gimbal lock effect that can occur if you do not plan ahead. If you don't know what the gimbal lock is then please refer to Chapter 4, "Fast 3D Calculus," for more information on quaternions.

The First-Person Camera

The most famous type of camera for 3D video games is the first-person camera that is used in most action shooters, which are also called first-person shooters. With such a camera type, the player can perceive the virtual world as if he were viewing it through the eyes of his own character/avatar.

These cameras are normally restricted in their movement. For example, you can rotate for a full 360 degrees on the y-axis. Looking up or down on the local x-axis of the camera is only possible in a range from about –88 degrees to about +88 degrees. Most programs do not allow for angles equal to or greater than 90 degrees for the sake of preventing gimbal lock. The rotation on the z-axis is also restricted, even if it is possible, to a small range of about 30 degrees in each direction (to sneak around a corner, for example).

The Third-Person Camera

Because the famous female Indiana Jones clone Lara Croft has fought her way into the hearts of video game players and movie fans with the *Tomb Raider* series and the *Lara Croft* movies, you should know what a third-person camera is.

This camera type does not allow you to see the scene through the virtual eyes of your avatar in the virtual world, but you see the scene from a camera perspective focusing on your avatar from outside. Normally, such a camera is located behind and above the avatar so that you can see the avatar and the area in front of it.

This kind of camera needs to be more intelligent because it has to avoid collisions with the world's geometry. In some situations, there are locations of the camera where you can see the avatar but not the area in front of the avatar because the camera has to move to the side to avoid collisions. This happens, for example, when you let your avatar stand with its back close to a wall. There is no room for the camera behind the avatar because the camera gets situated inside of the solid wall. This is the disadvantage of the third-person camera. The player has no control where the camera looks. The player gains control by moving its avatar. With a first-person camera, you control the camera directly by moving the avatar because the camera is positioned in the eyes of the avatar. For fighting scenes, the third-person camera can be annoying because while you try to evade enemy bullets and aim at your opponents, the camera can swing around and change its angle and location, even if you are moving in straight lines, thus making it harder to get a clear shot.

A big advantage of the third-person camera is that it does not cause as much motion sickness as a first-person camera. For whatever reason, it seems that Japanese video game players tend to get motion sickness when using first-person action games so those games sell poorly in Japan. Although using a first-person shooter title in Japan is common, it is more common to switch the system to a third-person camera. Japanese gamers also prefer consoles for playing video games and first-person shooters are only now starting to become widely available for consoles (they were not common in Japan).

The Fixed Camera

The final type of camera I want to talk about is the fixed camera. Just like its name implies, this camera does not move; however, it can also refer to the fact that the camera is not allowed to rotate, but can move.

Applications that don't allow for camera movement, such as the *Tetris* games, use the cameras. You can also employ them to show cut scenes or to play a dialogue between two characters in which one player cannot walk away from the dialogue.

Finally, these cameras are used in real-time strategy games with an isometric perspective. In this situation, you normally see the world from slightly above it with an angle of about 50 degrees.

Movement by a ZFXMovementController

If you think about the concept of a camera in 3D computer graphics, you will quickly see that this concept contains more than just a position and an angle from which the viewer looks at a scene. It is about the movements of the camera to get to a certain angle, a certain position, or to move the camera object according to the inputs of the player. In the remainder of this chapter, I discuss how to implement the functionality of certain camera types by means of so called movement controllers that can react to the user's input.

What Is a Movement Controller?

The idea of a movement controller is that each object can potentially be used as a location for the camera and therefore has one such controller as an attribute. These objects include, for example, soldiers or vehicles in the player's fighting unit in which he as a commander can switch from unit to unit and see its view on the screen.

The idea behind the movement controller is more complex because each object that can move with regard to the virtual 3D world needs the same calculations as a first-person camera. These objects must move and rotate on their own local axis system, similar to a camera. So it is recommended that you build these movement controllers to build the view matrix, and to reuse it for the object connected to it as well to extract the current local axes of this object.

I show you how to implement a base class for a movement controller that contains pure, virtual functions. Just like the base class for input devices in the input device component of the ZFXEngine, you cannot instantiate an object from this class. So the idea of this base class is that you simply derive all types of cameras you need from this class to provide some basic functionality, which is the same for all types of cameras or which can be overwritten for that matter.

Implementing the Base Class

The base class, called `ZFXMovementController`, defines a set of attributes and member functions that you will need for the tasks explained in the previous section. In this section, I show you the basic implementation of a movement controller and two derived camera types that we will need later in Chapter 15, "Deathmatch Shooter," for example. These two derived classes also sit inside the `ZFXGeneral.lib` library; however, there is no reason why the user of our engine should not implement his own derived classes if the two implementations do not serve his needs.

ZFXMovementController Class

This section assumes that you have programmed a camera object and that you know which functions are necessary for the task of creating your own view matrix.

The base class needs to provide the four vectors used to build a view matrix. These four vectors are based on the local axis of the camera and its position. Other attributes hold the current rotation angles, the rotation speed on the three axes, and the moving speed of the camera.

Here is the base class for all of the movements:

```
class ZFXMovementController
   {
   public:
      ZFXMovementController();
      virtual ~ZFXMovementController();

      virtual void Update(float fElapsedTime)=0;

      // Accessor-Methods
      ZFXVector GetPos(void)       { return m_vcPos;   }
      ZFXVector GetRight(void)     { return m_vcRight; }
      ZFXVector GetUp(void)        { return m_vcUp;    }
      ZFXVector GetDir(void)       { return m_vcDir;   }
      ZFXVector GetVelocity(void)  { return m_vcV;     }

   protected:
      ZFXVector m_vcPos;      // position
      ZFXVector m_vcRight;    // right vector
      ZFXVector m_vcUp;       // up vector
      ZFXVector m_vcDir;      // direction vector
      ZFXVector m_vcV;        // speed vector
      ZFXQuat   m_Quat;       // quaternion for rotation
```

```
    // rotation speed on local axis
    float     m_fRollSpd;
    float     m_fPitchSpd;
    float     m_fYawSpd;

    float     m_fRollSpdMax;
    float     m_fPitchSpdMax;
    float     m_fYawSpdMax;

    // rotation angle on local axis
    float     m_fRotX;
    float     m_fRotY;
    float     m_fRotZ;

    float m_fThrust;

    // methods
    virtual void RecalcAxes(void);
    virtual void Init(void);
};
```

The function `ZFXMovementController::Update` is declared as virtual and not defined. This is because each derived class needs its own update function to update the values for the movement and the rotation on its own. This update is the main thing defining the behavior of a certain camera type. The derived class will therefore overwrite this function, which is why it is not implemented in this class.

Note that the velocity is also part of this class. You might wonder why this is the case. As I said previously, I don't want to use this class to get the view matrix only, but also to calculate the movement of movable objects.

Setting the Attributes

The constructor and the destructor of this base class are empty. The constructor calls the `ZFXMovementController::Init` function, which sets the default values. Note that the destructor is declared as virtual, just as it should be. This destructor should not be called, as we will only work with the derived classes. Following are the constructor, the destructor, and the `Init()` function of the base class.

```
ZFXMovementController::ZFXMovementController(void)
   {
   Init();
   } // constructor
/*----------------------------------------*/
```

```
ZFXMovementController::~ZFXMovementController(void)
   {
   } // destructor
/*------------------------------*/

void ZFXMovementController::Init(void)
   {
   m_vcPos.Set(0.0f, 0.0f, 0.0f);
   m_vcRight.Set(1.0f, 0.0f, 0.0f);
   m_vcUp.Set(0.0f, 1.0f, 0.0f);
   m_vcDir.Set(0.0f, 0.0f, 1.0f);
   m_vcV.Set(0.0f, 0.0f, 0.0f);
   m_fRotX = m_fRotY = m_fRotZ = m_fThrust = 0.0f;
   m_fRollSpd = m_fPitchSpd = m_fYawSpd = 0.0f;
   m_Quat.x = m_Quat.y = m_Quat.z = 0.0f;
   m_Quat.w = 1.0f;
   } // constructor
```

Recalculating the Axis

In addition to the accessor methods to get access to the member variables and the startup function ZFXMovementController::Init, there is only one function remaining in this base class. This function recalculates the local axis of the camera depending on the rotation angles that are set in the class at a given time.

This function first checks the rotation values stored in the member attributes and ensures that they do not exceed a value of 360 degrees, which equals 2 PI in radian. This is done because although if they were to exceed 360 degrees they wouldn't affect the sine or cosine functions, left unchecked for too long the values could become too large and overflow. This situation reminds me of a time when I was in the armed services. During his introduction to the unit tanks, one of the recruits happened to ask whether or not the turret would come out of the chassis if you rotated it in a single direction for too long.

If you keep the rotation value to its bounds, the function will build a new quaternion from those rotation angles and it will add the rotation from this quaternion to the member quaternion that holds the overall rotation values for the movement controller. This is done by multiplying the quaternions, not by adding them to each other. Finally, you can extract the current view matrix from the quaternion to get the local axis of the object from this matrix. Here is the code:

```
void ZFXMovementController::RecalcAxes(void)
   {
   ZFXQuat    qFrame;
```

```
    ZFXMatrix   mat;

    static float f2PI = 6.283185f;

    // keep to range of 360 degree
    if (m_fRotX > f2PI) m_fRotX -= f2PI;
    else if (m_fRotX < -f2PI) m_fRotX += f2PI;

    if (m_fRotY > f2PI) m_fRotY -= f2PI;
    else if (m_fRotY < -f2PI) m_fRotY += f2PI;

    if (m_fRotZ > f2PI) m_fRotZ -= f2PI;
    else if (m_fRotZ < -f2PI) m_fRotZ += f2PI;

    // build new quaternion for this rotation
    qFrame.MakeFromEuler(m_fRotX, m_fRotY, m_fRotZ);

    // add to current rotation by multiplying quaternions
    m_Quat *= qFrame;

    // extract local axis
    m_Quat.GetMatrix(&mat);

    m_vcRight.x = mat._11;
    m_vcRight.y = mat._21;
    m_vcRight.z = mat._31;

    m_vcUp.x    = mat._12;
    m_vcUp.y    = mat._22;
    m_vcUp.z    = mat._32;

    m_vcDir.x   = mat._13;
    m_vcDir.y   = mat._23;
    m_vcDir.z   = mat._33;
    } // RecalcAxes
```

The quaternions are used instead of rotating the local axis because this avoids the gimbal lock discussed in Chapter 4. If you use quaternions, you cannot get trapped in a situation in which you mess up the axis due to the gimbal lock. This base class can be operated as a six-degrees-of-freedom camera without any restriction. You simply need to derive a class and implement the ZFXMovementController::Update function to set the new rotation values. The function to recalculate the axis would then do the rest of the work for you.

If you do not want to use quaternions in your derived class, you need to overwrite the `ZFXMovementController::RecalcAxes` function.

Coupling to the View Matrix

We must set the view matrix to the render device to take the camera's position and orientation into account. The engine user can get this matrix by simply using the accessor functions to get the local axis and the position of the controller to set the view matrix.

You can also enrich this base class by providing the necessary function to get a complete view matrix from this `ZFXMovementController` base class. To do this, you also have to add a function to the render device object that accepts a complete matrix as view matrix. Currently, only the function that requests the local axis and the position is capable of this. You have some homework to do to make this work.

Deriving a Free Camera

Because of the nice base class, there is not much to do to derive a camera class for a free camera with six degrees of freedom. The most complicated part is the recalculation of the axis. Following is the declaration of the class `ZFXMCFree` derived from the base class `ZFXMovementController`:

```
class ZFXMCFree : public ZFXMovementController
   {
   public:
     ZFXMCFree(void) {ZFXMovementController::Init();}
     virtual ~ZFXMCFree(void) { /*nothing to do*/ }

      virtual void Update(float fElapsedTime);

      void AddRotationSpeed(float x, float y, float z);
      void SetRotationSpeed(float x, float y, float z);
      void SetRotationSpeedX(float f) {m_fPitchSpd=f;}
      void SetRotationSpeedY(float f) {m_fYawSpd  =f;}
      void SetRotationSpeedZ(float f) {m_fRollSpd =f;}
      void AddThrust(float f)         {m_fThrust += f;}
      void SetThrust(float f)         {m_fThrust  = f;}

      void SetRotation(float rx, float ry, float rz);
      void SetPos(ZFXVector &vc)
          { memcpy(&m_vcPos, &vc, sizeof(ZFXVector)); }
      void SetRight(ZFXVector &vc)
          { memcpy(&m_vcRight, &vc, sizeof(ZFXVector));}
      void SetUp(ZFXVector &vc)
```

```
        { memcpy(&m_vcUp,  &vc, sizeof(ZFXVector)); }
    void SetDir(ZFXVector &vc)
        { memcpy(&m_vcDir, &vc, sizeof(ZFXVector)); }
}; // class
```

Adjusting the Rotations

Controlling the movement of the free camera should not explicitly take place by setting the rotation angles on the three axes manually. Of course, this is possible, but it is not appropriate, especially if you start to integrate a physics system. An application should set the rotation speed to the movement controller only when there is a steady rotation on the three local axes.

From those rotation speeds, the class will calculate based on the elapsed time since the last update and by how many degrees or radians the movement controller has rotated on the three axes.

Following are the three functions that let the user set the appropriate values for both methods of applying a rotation to a movement controller. You can also see why setting the absolute rotation value for the axis is less efficient. Each time you set these values, you have to call the function to recalculate the axis, which is again called in the Update() function.

```
void ZFXMCFree::SetRotation(float x, float y, float z)
   {
   m_fRotX = x;
   m_fRotY = y;
   m_fRotZ = z;
   RecalcAxes();
   } // SetRotation
/*------------------------------*/

void ZFXMCFree::AddRotationSpeed(float sx, float sy, float sz)
   {
   m_fPitchSpd += sx;
   m_fYawSpd   += sy;
   m_fRollSpd  += sz;
   } // AddRotationSpeed
/*------------------------------*/

void ZFXMCFree::SetRotationSpeed(float sx, float sy, float sz)
   {
   m_fPitchSpd = sx;
   m_fYawSpd   = sy;
   m_fRollSpd  = sz;
   } // SetRotationSpeed
```

Updating the Camera

Updating the free camera is a trivial task given the base class. Assuming that the user has stored the rotation speed in the appropriate member variables, you simply have to add these values to the current rotation angles after multiplying them with the elapsed time since the last frame. This calculation is the rotation speed defined in radians per second.

Also calculate the velocity vector based on the current speed of the object and update the position of the movement controller by adding the velocity vector to the position after it has been scaled with the elapsed time.

Finally, call the function for recalculating the axis from the base class, which will then build the new local axis of the movement controller based on the current rotation angles of the controller. Note that the corresponding function is not overloaded in this class. Therefore, the function from the base class using the quaternions is called instead.

```
void ZFXMCFree::Update(float fET)
   {
   // adding rotation speed
   m_fRotX = (m_fPitchSpd * fET);
   m_fRotY = (m_fYawSpd   * fET);
   m_fRotZ = (m_fRollSpd  * fET);

   // recalc speed vector
   m_vcV = m_vcDir * m_fThrust * fET;

   // move position
   m_vcPos += m_vcV;

   // recalc axis
   RecalcAxes();
   } // Update
```

Those few lines are really the first fully functional derived class that will enable the viewer to move through the virtual space. And, as noted, they let the user experience six degrees of freedom without suffering from gimbal lock.

Deriving a First-Person Camera

The second class I derive from the base class for movement controllers is a class that can be used as camera for a first-person scenario. Most of the function calls are explained in the class declaration, and you should immediately notice that the function ZFXMovementController::RecalcAxes is overwritten by this class. Thus, we need to provide another implementation for recalculating the axis without quaternions using the Euler angles instead.

First, take a look at the class declaration:

```
class ZFXMCEgo : public ZFXMovementController
   {
   public:
     ZFXMCEgo(void);
     virtual ~ZFXMCEgo(void);

      virtual void Update(float fElapsedTime);

      void       GetRotation(float*X,float*Y,float*Z);
      ZFXVector  GetRotation(void);

      void SetRotationSpeedX(float f) {m_fPitchSpd=f;}
      void SetRotationSpeedY(float f) {m_fYawSpd  =f;}
      void SetSpeed(float a)          {m_fSpeed   =a;}
      void SetSlideSpeed(float a)     {m_fSlide   =a;}

      void SetRotation(float rx, float ry, float rz);
      void SetPos(ZFXVector &vc)
         { memcpy(&m_vcPos, &vc, sizeof(ZFXVector)); }
      void SetRight(ZFXVector &vc)
         { memcpy(&m_vcRight, &vc, sizeof(ZFXVector));}
      void SetUp(ZFXVector &vc)
         { memcpy(&m_vcUp,   &vc, sizeof(ZFXVector)); }
      void SetDir(ZFXVector &vc)
         { memcpy(&m_vcDir,  &vc, sizeof(ZFXVector)); }

   private:
      float m_fSpeed;
      float m_fSlide;
      void RecalcAxes(void);
   };
```

Adjusting the Rotations

The implementation of the functions to adjust the rotation angles and to get their values is now rather simple. Here are the three functions:

```
void ZFXMCEgo::SetRotation(float rx, float ry, float rz)
   {
   m_fRotX = rx;
   m_fRotY = ry;
   m_fRotZ = rz;
```

```
    RecalcAxes();
    } // SetRotation
/*------------------------*/

void ZFXMCEgo::GetRotation(float *pfX, float *pfY, float *pfZ)
    {
    if (pfX) *pfX = m_fRotX;
    if (pfY) *pfY = m_fRotY;
    if (pfZ) *pfZ = m_fRotZ;
    } // GetRotation
/*------------------------*/

ZFXVector ZFXMCEgo::GetRotation(void)
    {
    return ZFXVector( m_fRotX,
                      m_fRotY,
                      m_fRotZ );
    } // GetRotation
```

Recalculating the Axis

There is a problem with the function that calculates the rotation using quaternions to rebuild the local axis. This problem is that the rotations are really applied totally free (without restrictions). Thus, the player can move the camera into a position where he cannot control it. Assume that the player rotates the movement controller to the left and then up. If you rotate back to the right, you are doing a rotation on the local up axis of the controller, which does not really point up due to the rotation done earlier. This is okay for a space combat simulator, but for a first-person camera, it is not a good thing.

In a first-person scenario, you need a restricted camera. The first restriction, of course, is that the most common rotation in this scenario is always done on the world axis. Of course the most common rotation is the rotation around the y-axis. The difference is that by rotating on the x-axis, the player moves only his head or eyes, and his body still points up along the world axis. In a free camera scenario, it is assumed that the object is rotated upward (an example is a space fighter such as *Cobra MK III*). Then the up axis should be rotated.

I think you get the point. The following function implements a recalculation of the axis for a first-person scenario. The local axis of the controller is initialized as the world axis for each frame. Then the rotation on the y-axis is performed and therefore takes place around the world's up vector. To make the following rotation around the x-axis, use the new, rotated x-axis of the controller. Then rotate the x-axis and the z-axis of the controller to confirm validation after the rotation on the y-axis. You can then safely perform the rotation on the local x-axis of the controller, which will allow the player to look up and down.

Again, you have to rotate the other two axes to comply with this new rotation so that the local axis system maintains its orthogonal integrity. Finally, these rotations can distort the orientation and the normalization of the axis vectors, and therefore, you need to rebuild them. Following is the code:

```
void ZFXMCEgo::RecalcAxes(void)
   {
   ZFXMatrix   mat;

   static float f2PI = 6.283185f;

   // keep in range of 2 PI = 360 degree
   if (m_fRotY > f2PI) m_fRotY -= f2PI;
   else if (m_fRotY < -f2PI) m_fRotY += f2PI;

   // up/down max 80 degree
   if (m_fRotX > 1.4f) m_fRotX = 1.4f;
   else if (m_fRotX < -1.4f) m_fRotX = -1.4f;


   // initializing axis
   m_vcRight = ZFXVector(1.0f, 0.0f, 0.0f);
   m_vcUp    = ZFXVector(0.0f, 1.0f, 0.0f);
   m_vcDir   = ZFXVector(0.0f, 0.0f, 1.0f);

   // rotate around y-axis
   mat.RotaArbi(m_vcUp, m_fRotY);
   m_vcRight = m_vcRight * mat;
   m_vcDir   = m_vcDir * mat;

   // rotate around x-Axis
   mat.RotaArbi(m_vcRight, m_fRotX);
   m_vcUp  = m_vcUp * mat;
   m_vcDir = m_vcDir * mat;

   // correct rounding errors
   m_vcDir.Normalize();
   m_vcRight.Cross(m_vcUp, m_vcDir);
   m_vcRight.Normalize();
   m_vcUp.Cross(m_vcDir, m_vcRight);
   m_vcUp.Normalize();
   } // RecalcAxes
```

As you can see, we do not allow for a rotation on the z-axis. This means the player cannot sneak around corners; of course, you can add this behavior if you want. The rotation on the x-axis is restricted to 80 degrees. This prevents gimbal lock effects and it reflects some of the natural boundaries of human heads.

You also have to do the rotation around the y-axis before you do other rotations. As explained previously, you can end up with a rotated y-axis after the first rotation; therefore, the player cannot correctly turn his body to the left or the right. You do not want this.

Updating the Camera

Updating the movement controller is done the very same way as the update of the free camera movement controller. However, this time there is a new member variable called m_fSlide. This variable is used to store the speed with which the user of the movement controller wants to move sideways. Such a movement is especially important for the first-person shooter because it allows the object to slide out of the way of incoming bullets or particle beams. Skip this feature and see what the reaction of the players is.

```
void ZFXMCEgo::Update(float fET)
   {
   ZFXVector vcS;
   // add rotation speed
   m_fRotX += (m_fPitchSpd * fET);
   m_fRotY += (m_fYawSpd   * fET);
   m_fRotZ += (m_fRollSpd  * fET);

   // calculate axis
   RecalcAxes();

   // calculate speed vector
   m_vcV = m_vcDir * m_fSpeed * fET;
   vcS   = m_vcRight * m_fSlide * fET;

   // move position
   m_vcPos += m_vcV + vcS;
   } // Update
```

The second derived movement controller is done. You can now implement a first-person style camera as well as a free camera. This should be enough to introduce you to the concept of movement controllers, allowing you to derive your own class with a customized camera without a problem. You also know how to use quaternions to build a camera, and you know that those quaternions are not as complicated to use as people might think.

Demo Application

Of course there is a demo application for this chapter so that you can test the functionality of the movement controllers. Do you belong to the group of people that doesn't believe something until they have seen it with their own eyes? The demo application features a free camera so that the user can move freely through the 3D space. With the exception of the camera, the application is like the demo for Chapter 6, "The Render Device of the Engine." You will see 3D models in the scene, and you can move around to take a look at them from all positions and angles.

Check out the dome on the accompanying CD-ROM for this book.

One Look Back, Two Steps Forward

Well, the look back at this chapter can be rather brief because building a camera is an easy task if you know about things such as the gimbal look. I think the most interesting thing with gimbal lock is the use of quaternions for the camera as opposed to the Euler angles version most are familiar with. Also, the approach to build certain camera types from a base class by deriving new classes from it is a new way of doing the camera dance. As homework, try to implement a derived class for a third-person camera.

After this short ride in easier territories, you should now put your helmet back on and put on your bulletproof jacket. In the next chapter, you have to prepare to work at full power, as Chapter 13 is a demanding chapter. It deals with scene management issues and it teaches you the nasty details of what a binary space partitioning tree is, why John Carmack liked BSP trees, what an octree is, and what a portal engine is. I bet those keywords get you fired up. So let's go. You take point.

CHAPTER 13

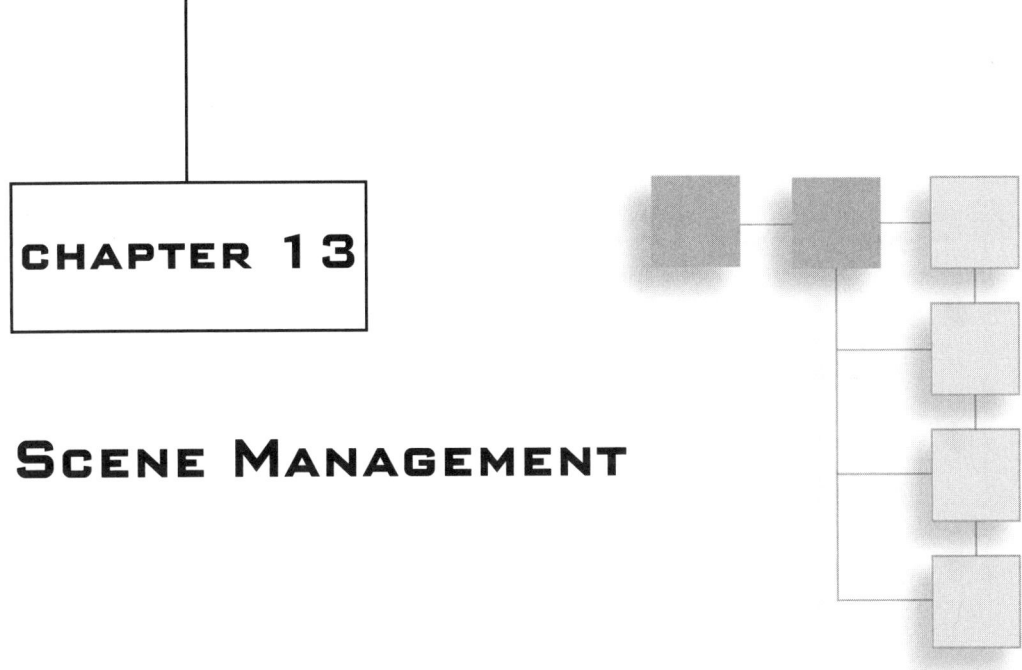

SCENE MANAGEMENT

The smart man can be recognized by the answers he gives. The wise man by the questions he asks.

Chinese Saying

Just like the old, wise Chinese, we want to ask the right questions in this chapter. The very first question of this chapter is, of course: Why don't video games get automatically faster with each new generation of graphics adapters so that you do not have to worry about performance and how to write code that can be executed quickly? The hardware is not far from a time when a gain in performance cannot be reached by speeding up the vertex processing (3D pipeline) or by using the current technologies and approaches. It will be quite some time before we can develop computers that transmit bits through quantum tunneling.

On a current graphics adapter, you can render a whole level of the *Quake III* video game from id Software in brute force without any kind of scene management. This task was impossible when the game was first published. In those days, very complex scene management algorithms had to be used to run the game on an average machine in real time with a decent frame rate. Why do we need a chapter about scene management if you can render such a level brute force? We need it because modern games get even slower when it comes to modern graphics adapters. This is because the video game developers and the players want to use more and more effects for every single triangle they render. Each pixel is not only set with the color from its texture, but it is set with effects such as spot lights, bump maps, shadow maps, specular reflection, shadow volumes, mirroring effects, transparency, depth of field, motion blur, and blending.

This is why scene management is as important as it was many years ago. The way you do scene management has changed and takes advantage of the capabilities of modern graphics adapters.

This chapter covers the following objectives:

- Learning the concepts of scene management
- Understanding quadtrees and terrain rendering
- Using BSP trees and octrees for collision detection
- Understanding what a portal engine is
- Implementing a BSP tree and an octree
- Using the code in the demo application

The Concept of Scene Management

Scene management is still a valid and important instrument if you want to do more than just present ten thousand triangles on the screen. If you work with levels that consist of hundreds of thousands of polygons that are rendered with multiple effects on them, you will mess up a GeForce FX graphics adapter faster than you can say *gosh*. The term *scene management* describes algorithms and methods that let you select only the polygons that are needed for a certain location and orientation of the viewer out of the whole set of a hundred thousand polygons of the level. Most of those polygons are not visible to the user.

The removal of polygons that cannot be seen from a certain position and orientation of the viewer (because they are completely hidden behind other polygons) is called *hidden surface removal*, or HSR. Another term for this is *occlusion culling*. There are some slight differences between HSR and occlusion culling. Although HSR typically does its calculations on the level of a single polygon, the occlusion culling will work with a more shotgun-like approach (culling whole objects consisting of several hundreds of polygons).

For occlusion culling, you will normally check a bunch of polygons or surfaces that make up a certain entity, such as a character, a whole room, or something similar. You will then test this set of polygons simultaneously to see if it is totally occluded or not. If it is only partially occluded, you don't need to use single surfaces from the object that might be occluded; instead, just render the whole object. To calculate whether such an object is occluded, you need to define the occluders. These are big static objects in the scene, such as a skyscraper, a hill, or a big piece of machinery. Several algorithms do the occlusion calculation. For example, you can use occlusion frustums, which is similar to an inverted view frustum culling in world space, or you can use a hierarchical occlusion map (HOM), which works in the screen space.

Do not mistake occlusion culling and HSR as the removal of polygons that the viewer can only see the (normally invisible) back side of because they are oriented away from the user's view. This is called *backface culling* or backface removal and is done on the graphics adapters automatically if you adjust the according render state.

The third type of culling is the *view frustum culling* you should already be familiar with. This is also called object culling or just culling. This refers to removing objects from the calculations and rendering for a certain frame outside the space that the viewer can see. This happens for objects behind the viewer or for those that are too far to the right of the viewer, making it impossible for him to see without turning.

With this set of basic scene management terms, we can now dive into the theoretical part of this chapter. I introduce you to some of the most important algorithms and data structures used for scene management in a large 3D scene and especially in video games. After we cover the theoretical aspects of scene management, you will be able to implement two of the techniques used for large 3D, indoor environments.

Scene Management Techniques

The first thing you need to know is that you should always separate your algorithms in terms of the setting in which they should be used. You can differentiate between indoor games, outdoor games, and what I like to call no-door games. I guess the indoor games are obviously the games played mostly in closed environments in which a lot of polygons sit with great angles with respect to each other. In such a scene, the viewing distance is limited, but the need for efficient collision detection is high. There are scene management algorithms that deal specifically with these kinds of environments.

The outdoor games should also be clear. These are games that play in vast-free areas under the sky and on a surface such as a terrain. The most obvious problem here is that the viewing distance is normally straight up to the horizon if there are not too many mountains. The need for collision detection is drastically reduced here, but to render a terrain with a suitable amount of detail for several square kilometers is a demanding task. Thus, you need to use special scene management algorithms that take these issues into account. The good news is that in outdoor environments most problems can be simplified to two-dimensional solutions. That is because the third dimension, which is in this case the height of the level geometry (which is the terrain), is somewhat unimportant. Its dimensions are on the two axes—width and depth; the height of the terrain is rather flat and can be ignored as well.

The other category is the no-door games category. These are the games in 3D space that do not fall into one of the other two categories. Space simulations, such as *Freelancer* or *Homeworld*, should come to mind. The scene management is very easy for these games because there is no such thing as a level geometry. There are, of course, some issues, such as planets moving around, space stations, and a huge number of space ships that continually move around in the scene, that make it hard to easily manage the scene. This gets more interesting if you want to enrich your space simulation by letting a player approach a planet's space by landing on the terrain. That is another story.

In the following sections, I introduce you to the most important data structures and algorithms that deal with scene management and I explain which ones are suited for which type of game.

No Solution Is Also a Solution

The basic method of scene management is the brute force approach. This means that you don't apply any culling techniques at all. At first glance, you might not think this is a good idea, but it is a valid technique that has its own right of existence if you know how to employ it correctly.

Such brute force methods are used in outdoor games that feature a number of small buildings. There is no special indoor scene management applied for houses with six or seven rooms, and so on. The same holds true for the first-person shooter games in which outdoor scenes are needed. In this case, the outdoor terrain is a brute force-rendered heightmap without scene management. But note that the brute force approach is used in conjunction with proper scene management for the main part of the scene.

In conclusion we can say not only that brute force is fast enough for such small scenes, but also that using a brute force scheme will save you a lot of development time and headaches. This is why brute force is an option you should consider.

Continuous and Discrete Level of Detail

Asked what your goal is in terms of scene management your answer might be to remove surfaces or whole objects from the scene to speed up rendering. This is somewhat true, but there is more you can do with scene management. It is not only about removing whole objects from the scene.

So do not immediately resort to removing objects from the scene. Of course, you want to speed up the performance of your application as much as possible. Removing objects in the scene is one way to achieve this goal, but it is not always feasible. For example, you cannot remove objects that are still inside the view frustrum and should therefore be visible to the viewer. For such objects, you can also gain performance by reducing the complexity of visible objects. This is exactly what the level of detail approach (or LOD) aims to do.

Think about the situation in an outdoor game in which you want to simulate tank battles. The gunner of a tank reports a moving vehicle two miles ahead. The commander looks through his optics to get an image of the battlefield, which is magnified fifteen times. However, even in the bright daylight and good weather conditions, he will not be able to make out details from the vehicle because the distance is too long and the vehicle is too small. All details, such as unit signs, number of antennas, the shape of the hull and the turret, and so on, melt together to form a single, moving dark point or sphere. Is it the commander's friend or foe?

The problem is that even if you build a detailed model with about ten thousand vertices for a tank, the projection of the computer graphics pipeline will create a 2D image of this tank. This image takes about 15 x 15 pixels on the screen. As in reality, this set of pixels is not enough to identify the details of the objects. So you must let the commander come closer to the scene. The main cannon of a tank can engage vehicles over a range of about two miles so if it is an enemy, the artificial intelligence will take its shot on the commander if you let him get closer than one and a half kilometers. However, even at a distance of about 1500 virtual meters, the vehicle is too small in its projected image to justify the 10,000 polygons rendered for it. Using a model with less detail costs about 500 polygons and will look the same at such a distance.

This is exactly what the level of detail approach will do. Instead of using only one model for an object, such as a tank, you build three or more models. The first detail level is very detailed and uses the 10,000 polygons. The next level of detail uses 2000 polygons, whereas the third level uses 500 polygons. The more distant a model is from the viewer, the fewer polygons you need. At the lowest detail level, you can use a billboard or an imposter.

The method just described using certain distinct models is called *discreet level of detail* (DLOD). It involves a model designer or 3D artist who is required to build certain level of detail stages for its models. There is also an LOD variant that is called *continuous level of detail* (CLOD). This algorithm starts from the most detailed version of the model and calculates a less detailed version on-the-fly and this is based on certain algorithms. The CLOD approach is suited for big, complex objects for which the exact shape is not as important, such as with a huge terrain area. However, you can also apply CLOD to static models, such as the progressive mesh method by Hugues Hoppe. The precalculated models, such as the DLOD approach, have a better visual quality (due to the artist's total control over what the LOD models look like), and more importantly, they are much faster because there is no need for calculations during runtime. But one visual drawback of the DLOD method is the so-called "popping." When switching from a low-detail representation of a model to a higher level of detail, vertices and polygons will be added to the model. This will obviously change the appearance of the model due to details suddenly popping into the view. A CLOD method will also suffer from this effect but not quite as much as a DLOD method.

Figure 13.1 shows a model of a Cessna aircraft, which is calculated at various, distinct CLOD stages using the progressive mesh method from Hoppe. Of course you can also program a tool that uses CLOD to calculate DLOD levels.

Figure 13.1 Calculating a low detail version of a Cessna model using Hugues Hoppe's progressive mesh method. The number indicates the triangle count of the model. (Source: SIGGRAPH, 1996 slides from Hugues Hoppe, http://research.microsoft.com/~hoppe/#pm)

Applying a DLOD scheme should be clear now. For the more complex CLOD approach, I just gave you a sample here. For the next scene management technique, I discuss how to render huge, outdoor terrains.

Quadtrees

You have seen the approach that can reduce the amount of details for a 3D objects, which will ultimately speed up the application. I next show you a technique that lets you decide which objects are visible. You already know the frustum culling text. This culling test has a disadvantage—that is, you have to test each object in the game. A hierarchical approach is better because with it, the whole level or game world is divided into a hierarchy for which you can check certain nodes of the hierarchy against the view frustum to check their visibility. If a node in the tree is not visible, then all the nodes underneath it are not visible either, and you can skip checking them.

General Quadtrees

One of the easiest data structures for such a hierarchical approach is the quadtree. Let me add here that the quadtree is suited to tread 2D problems. Don't let this fool you if you want to stick to 3D worlds only. I previously mentioned that you can simplify working with 3D terrains to 2D problems in most cases because the height of the terrain is not of primary concern when your character has to fight in the terrain. The same is true for games that play on the very same level in which the third coordinate is missing, such as in bird view games.

The name quadtree is derived from the fact that it is a treelike data structure in which each node of the structure has exactly four or zero children. It is better to explain quadtrees with an example of how you can use them. Take a look at Figure 13.2.

Scene Management Techniques 591

Figure 13.2 A 3D scene of a village, seen from above.

To speed things up, scene management for the village shown in Figure 13.2 can occur in two locations in the program. The first location is, of course, in the rendering where you render only the parts that are visible. The second place is in the collision detection where you want to test the player's character against as few of the houses as possible. Even if you can see the village from a bird's eye view in this scene, suppose the game is played in first-person view with the player walking around in the village. You need to ensure that the player does not walk through the walls of the houses via collision detection. The most naïve way to do this is with brute force. This means you check the player's character model against each house of the village by testing the bounding volumes for intersection. This works well indeed. However, it is also very slow.

You must bring the quadtree into the game. As mentioned previously, the quadtree is a tree structure with nodes; each node of the tree has four or zero child nodes. A node without children is called a leaf of the tree. The uppermost node has no parent node because it is the child of no other node. It is called the root node. In this case, the root node of the quadtree is a 2D rectangular area that spans the entire village as a bounding rectangle.

The algorithm starts from the root node by subdividing the big rectangle into four rectangles (if there are objects included in the rectangle). This process goes on continually by subdividing each of the subdivided rectangles until a certain condition is satisfied. This condition can be two-fold. One option is to subdivide for a given number of steps without taking care of the geometry involved. The better option is to subdivide each branch of the tree as long as there is a certain number of objects inside the leaves.

For example, I chose the condition that a leaf must not contain polygons from more than a single house. If you apply the quadtree algorithm to the village, the output looks like what is shown in Figure 13.3.

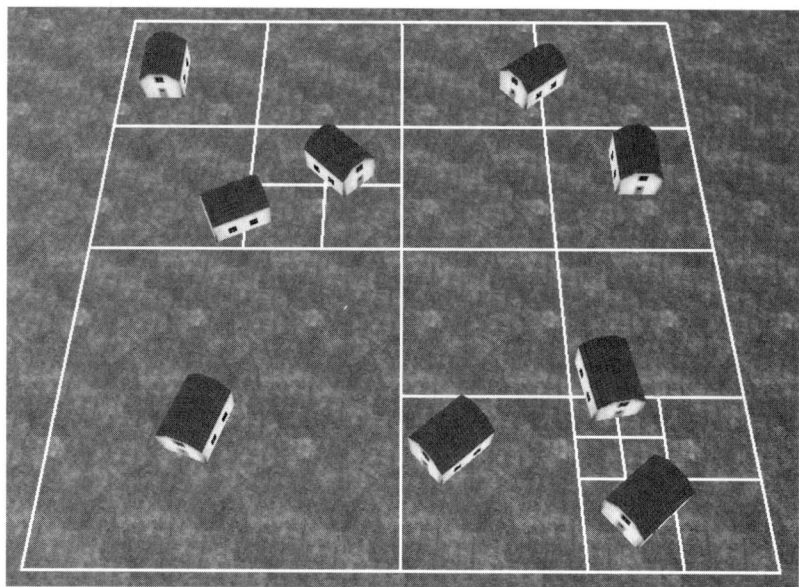

Figure 13.3 The quadtree for the village, whereby each leaf of the tree must not contain parts from more than one single house.

The quadtree subdivides the 2D rectangles so that each leaf only contains one house at the maximum or just parts of one house. The big advantage of this is that you can simplify the collision detection to a 2D problem. You take the position of the player as a 2D value, and you ignore the player's height. The houses are at the same height as the player (assuming, of course, that he cannot fly). You put this position information into the root of the tree. At each node, you decide in which of the children the player stands and you push the position down the appropriate branch. This is done until the position finally reaches a leaf. There you are, you now have one player against one single object that you need to test for collision. In each step, you can successfully skip three quarters of the remaining game world in the collision test by simply applying this very simple test, which assumes that a 2D point is inside a 2D rectangle.

You can also boost rendering by skipping objects that are not visible. This is similar to the view frustum test. A quadtree is not that efficient for frustum culling. Normally, you would put a bounding box around each house in the village and test the bounding box against the view frustum, if it is totally outside the frustum. You do not need to process this house for rendering. You store a bounding box at each node of the quadtree in which the box is large enough to contain the geometry that is in the nodes and leaves in the four underlying branches of the tree. If the view frustum culling test reveals that the bounding box of a node of the tree is totally outside the view frustum, you do not need to test the single houses in the underlying leaves. You can just skip the branch from this node downward.

If you have the ideal situation in which the player stands in a quarter of the village and looks to the closest border where the village ends, the view frustum culling test under the root node would reveal that three of the children are not visible. By using four bounding box checks, you skip three quarters of the houses in the village that you don't need to process for this frame. This does assume that the houses are evenly distributed in the village.

You can see that the quadtree is a great data structure that helps a great deal in doing culling calculations.

Excursion into Heightmap Foundations

Of course, the quadtree approach is not spectacular across the board; however, it is very popular. This popularity stems from the terrain rendering fraction in the computer graphics, which uses quadtrees extensively in combination with special CLOD techniques. In addition, many famous academic papers discuss the rendering of vast outdoor areas that are implemented using quadtrees.

Tip

For a comprehensive list of papers on terrain rendering algorithms, refer to the website www.vterrain.org/LOD/Papers/index.html. You will find many papers and open source implementations.

Before I go into more detail about using a quadtree in a CLOD approach for terrain rendering, I want to discuss the details of rendering terrains on the screen using heightmaps. Such a heightmap is the most common way to represent the data of a terrain, and it is actually nothing more than a 2D array or a 1D array that is interpreted as having two dimensions. The following 9 x 9 array is s sample heightmap I use for explanation purposes:

```
UCHAR hMap[9*9] = { 1, 5, 6, 3, 4, 6, 8, 5, 6,
                    3, 4, 6, 5, 4, 5, 6, 4, 5,
                    2, 3, 5, 6, 5, 7, 8, 6, 4,
                    3, 5, 7, 4, 5, 8, 9, 7, 5,
                    4, 4, 5, 3, 4, 7, 8, 7, 6,
                    3, 5, 4, **2**, 3, 6, 7, 6, 5,
                    2, 3, 4, 3, 5, 5, 6, 5, 4,
                    4, 4, 6, 4, 3, 4, 5, 4, 3,
                    3, 3, 4, 3, 4, 3, 3, 3, 2
                  };
```

This heightmap provides you with information about the height of a terrain at certain points on the x- and the z-axis, which are the width and the depth of the terrain area. At position x = 3 and z = 5, the terrain has a height of 2 units. Note that you start the count at column 0 and row 0 because these are the indices in an array. The position is underlined in the previous array. Note that the data in the heightmap is specified without a particular unit. You can interpret them in feet, meters, miles, or whatever you like.

If you build a mesh for this terrain, you would start in the upper left corner and take the four vertices of the first square to build the first 3D rectangle of the terrain mesh using the vertex coordinates (0;1;0), (1;5;0), (0,3,1), and (1,4,1). If you do this for the whole heightmap, you will end up with 8 x 8 rectangles; this is equal to 128 triangles. The general formula for the number of triangles is $2(n-1)^2$ where n is the dimension of one edge of the array, which is of the size n^2. To get a suitable resolution in the detail of the terrain, assume the measurable units are in meters. You want a nice playground, so take a 2000 m^2 area of terrain. You need eight million triangles to build the mesh for this area. Recall that a tank can fire over a distance of roughly 2000 meters. So a terrain piece the size 2000 x 2000 meters is not that much. Even if you employ a smart view frustum culling algorithm, there are too many triangles to render in real-time with good performance.

It is also very stupid to try to render that many triangles because several hundreds of thousands of triangles get melted together to the size of 20 x 20 pixels on the screen, or even less. As mentioned previously, you simply cannot perceive the resolution of a mesh build meter-by-meter over a distance of several hundred meters. This is where the CLOD approach offers its help. To render terrain, you must deal with the issue of how to adjust the mesh needed for a certain position and orientation of the viewer, and you must do this in a way to allow for more details. The more distant part of the terrain mesh is from the viewer, the less detail it gets. Another criterion can influence the level of detail of a piece of terrain. Take a look at the following excerpt from an arbitrary heightmap:

```
3, 4, 3, 4, 3, 4,
4, 3, 2, 2, 2, 3,
5, 3, 2, 2, 2, 4,
4, 3, 2, 2, 2, 3,
5, 3, 3, 3, 3, 3,
```

You can see that the inner area of three square units has the very same height of 2 units. It is rather stupid to generate four rectangles with eight triangles. You can achieve the same result by using only one rectangle with two triangles. It gets even better. If the viewer happens to be very far away, he cannot perceive the difference of one unit in the height so if you look at the surrounding height values, which are mostly 3, you can expand this single rectangle of the mesh to cover the areas without changing the optical result perceived by the viewer.

This is the big secret behind using CLOD algorithms for terrain rendering. All of the approaches aim for the smartest algorithm that can dynamically adjust the resolution of the mesh in real-time depending on the current position and orientation of the viewer.

Caution

There are a lot of smart approaches, but most of them were meant for the last generation of video adapters. So if you stumble across terrain papers that are two or three years old, they aren't ideal for the current hardware.

Quadtrees for Terrain Rendering

You now know how a CLOD approach relates to the efficiency of an algorithm that can render a terrain mesh with good performance for large data sets. How do the quadtrees fit into this picture? This section explains the theory of applying quadtrees to terrain rendering.

Assume the root of a quadtree is laid down to span the heightmap data you want to cover with the quadtree. The root node of the quadtree basically represents the whole terrain. You then start the quadtree algorithm to subdivide the bounding rectangle in each iteration. You do this until a situation is reached where a node of the quadtree spans a 3 x 3 area of the heightmap and becomes a leaf of the quadtree. For the 9 x 9 heightmap shown previously, this is a very short process because after the second iteration, this situation is reached.

An area of 3 x 3 height values from a heightmap is called a terrain block. One leaf of the quadtree is equal to one terrain block.

Figure 13.4 shows you the complete quadtree structure for a 9 x 9 heightmap. In this illustration, you can see straight down the root of the quadtree. In the center of the illustration is the root of the tree with index 0. There are four children to the root with indices 1, 2, 3, and 4. Each of these has four children of its own with the matching indices. The stop condition of the algorithm is hit because each node covers only a 3 x 3 block of the terrain and hence, they become the children of the quadtree. In this scheme, you can also calculate the indices of children or of parents by very basic formulas without being inside a certain object, and you can follow a certain pointer to a child or a parent. Thus, you can store each node and leaf of a quadtree in a linear array and you can access them without traveling through the whole data structure from the root.

Here are the formulas to calculate the indices to relatives of a given object:

```
P := parent index
N := index of any node
Upper Left  Node = 4*P + 1
```

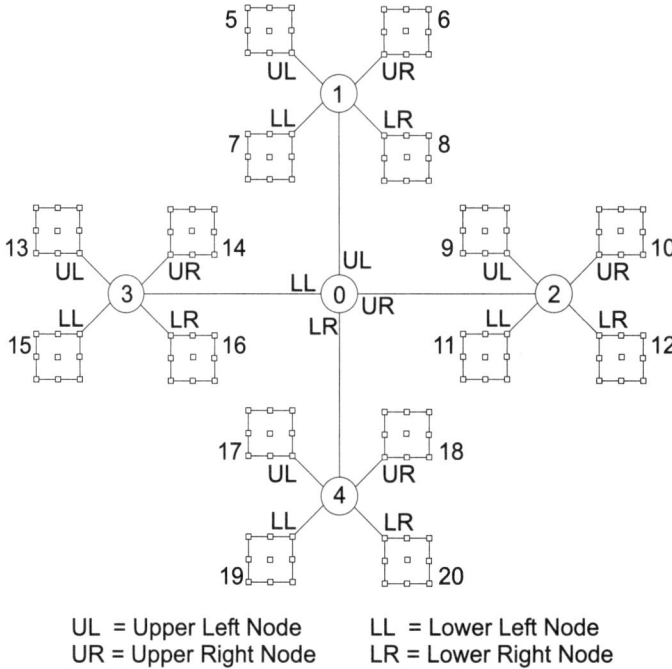

Figure 13.4 Illustration of a complete quadtree for a 9 x 9 heightmap. The circles represent nodes of the quadtree while the rectangles are leaves / blocks with 3 x 3 vertices each. The numbers indicate the indices of the nodes and leaves.

```
Upper Right Node = 4*P + 2
Lower Left  Node = 4*P + 3
Lower Right Node = 4*P + 4
P of N = floor( (N-1)/4 )
```

You now have a heightmap divided into a quadtree. There is no gain in performance because you separated some pieces of data, which makes it even more difficult to render the whole mesh. The secret lies in the fact that the terrain mesh needs to be rebuilt each time the camera moves its position significantly. Then you make the journey down the quadtree starting from the root.

While traveling through the quadtree, perform normal view frustum culling with the nodes bounding boxes, as explained earlier. If a node is not inside the view frustum, you can ignore it and all of its child nodes. But if a node *is* inside the view frustum, you need to decide if you want to proceed with its children at all. Note that each node of the tree has attached a low-res geometry representing a CLOD level of the underlying terrain. You already know the two criteria for deciding whether to go down one more level. First, you look at the distance of the viewer to the center of the node you are currently in. Second, you look at the differences in height that will be added if you go down one level. If the viewer is very far away from this node, or if the underlying terrain is just a bit rough or even plain flat, there is no need to subdivide even more because the gain in detail (if any) cannot be perceived by the viewer.

Suppose you have a big chunk of terrain and you are somewhere in the quadtree covering an area of 20 height values. Your two criteria say that there is no need to subdivide. So you stop and render a single rectangle of two triangles covering this whole area of 20 x 20 meters. If you had walked down to the lowest level and had rendered a rectangle between each group of four vertices in the heightmap, it would have required no less than 722 triangles. This is great stuff, isn't it? Using such a quadtree can save a lot of triangles as opposed to the brute force approach.

This sounds too good to be true—or at least very simple. Unfortunately, this is correct. A great deal of processing time in such approaches is wasted (or spent) on closing the cracks that appear in the terrain. Figure 13.5 shows a screenshot of what I mean. The problem is that you normally decide at each quadtree node whether you should subdivide it or not. However, this decision ignores one fact. The fact is the subdivision level of the neighboring quadtree nodes. As you can see in Figure 13.5, there are two neighboring nodes of a

Figure 13.5 Cracks occur in the terrain mesh due to different levels of subdivision in two neighboring nodes of the quadtree.

quadtree. The one in the background is heavily subdivided whereas the one in the foreground is subdivided only once. The ugly result of this difference in subdivision levels is the cracks that occur on the edge where the two quadtree nodes touch each other.

Fortunately, there are ways to deal with those cracks in the quadtree approach. A block, which is the leaf of a quadtree in which you don't subdivide but that you want to render, not only contains four border vertices, but nine vertices in total. So you have five helper vertices that are used to prevent the cracks. Four helper vertices sit in the middle of each edge of the block while the fifth one is in the center of the block. These five helper vertices can be activated or deactivated if necessary. Furthermore, you can enforce the neighboring blocks to be subdivided to the same level plus or minus one level, which is more or less detailed, respectively. To prevent a crack, you have to activate or deactivate the helper vertex on the appropriate edge where a block touches a neighboring block that is on a different level of detail.

There are seven possible configurations for a block depending on which helper vertices are activated. Figure 13.6 shows an illustration of these different configurations. When all four neighboring blocks of this block are subdivided to the same level of detail, you don't have to activate any of the helper vertices. This situation equals the sixth configuration in Figure 13.6.

Figure 13.7 shows an example of the very same terrain block in two different configurations. On the left side, there are three helper vertices active and on the right side, all five helper vertices are active.

Figure 13.8 shows an example of how a small 9 x 9 heightmap is subdivided by a quadtree algorithm. You can see in this illustration how the inserted helper vertices take care of the

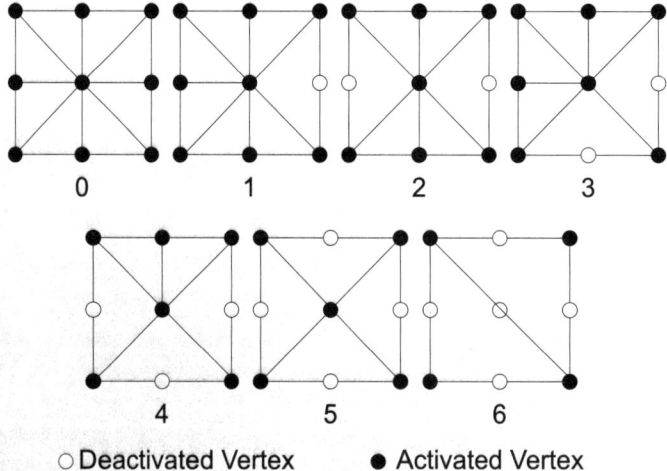

Figure 13.6 The seven different resolutions of a terrain block showing the triangulation.

Scene Management Techniques 599

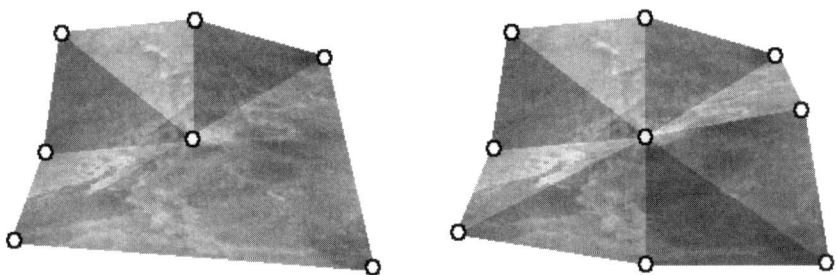

Figure 13.7 Two different resolutions of the same terrain block. On the right side, the most detailed resolution of the type 0, and on the left side, type 3 resolution.

fact that connected edges of neighboring quadtree blocks do not use a different number of triangles that would result in cracks.

Because this is a programming game book, I didn't include a terrain rendering example in this chapter. If you are interested in different programming techniques for outdoor scenes, do not miss the ultimate terrain source for papers and implementations, which is located at http://www.vterrain.org/LOD. At this site, you will see new and old papers.

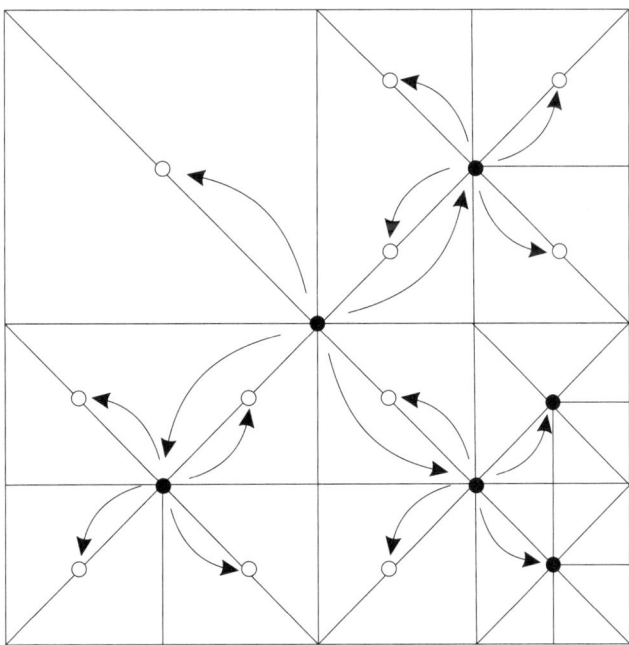

Figure 13.8 An example for the subdivision of a 9 x 9 heightmap. The arrows indicate parent-child relationships in the quadtree. Only the central helper vertices are being shown. (Based on: Röttger et al: "Real-Time Generation of CLOD for Height Fields," Paper delivered at WSCG '98 conference, Page 2, Figure 1).

Unfortunately, most papers still deal with techniques that were designed for the previous generation of graphics adapters. As you can see from the approach shown previously, the CLOD method depends on rebuilding the mesh for almost every frame, which in turn means that you have to send the data over the bus. You might think this is a bad idea, and I would agree with you. More and more research and papers on the topic concentrate on how to make better use of the current hardware. Look for papers such as the one mentioned above on geometrical mip-mapping or ROAM version 2.0, which will be more suited for current hardware.

Octrees

At some point, quadtrees started to strive for more and left their well-known home of 2D to boldly go where no quadtree has gone before: to the 3D world. The same thing that you do with quadtrees in 2D can be done in 3D. Octrees enrich the concept of the quadtree with yet another additional dimension. There is no need to explain a lot. Just take the bounding rectangle of a quadtree and add a height for the third dimension. The rectangle will then become a cube.

If you want to subdivide a cube into smaller units, where each unit has the same size, you end up with eight little cubes that sit inside their parent cube. The rest of the algorithm remains untouched. You start the algorithm by defining a bounding cube around the geometry you want to cover with the octree. Then you subdivide the cube recursively as long as a certain stop condition is not fulfilled. A node of the octree can have exactly zero or eight children, hence the name octree.

The stop condition is basically the same as in the quadtree. You can go on until you reach a certain number of subdivisions in each branch. However, you can also go on until only a certain number of polygons or objects is left in the octree. There is no strict rule that you must obey. Figure 13.9 illustrates a part of a corridor from an indoor level that was dumped into an octree. This shot was taken from the demo application for this chapter.

You will stumble into an interesting topic that is connected to subdivision algorithms. That is, what do you do with level geometry such as polygons that do not fit completely into one node of a structure because the strict subdivision on fixed bounds in space will most likely intersect a lot of triangles in the geometry? There are two solutions for the situation of when an object will not fit completely into one single node. The first option is to cut the objects into two separate objects on the line or plane of intersection. Then, each smaller part will fit into one of the two nodes concerned. The drawback of this method is that you can end up with very, very small objects. This is not a good approach for rendering.

The second option is not to cut those objects but to store them only on the node where their center point lies. Doing this alone would be wrong so there must be a list of objects

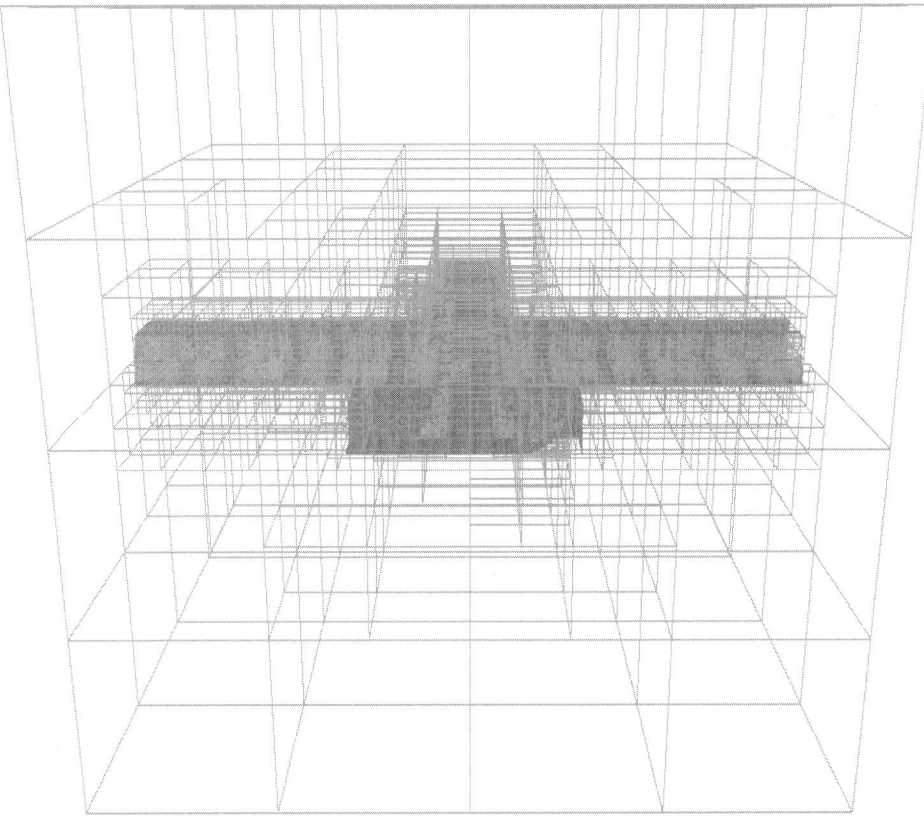

Figure 13.9 A visualized octree for a little piece of a corridor. You can clearly recognize the high subdivision depth in areas with a lot of polygons.

in each node that does not belong to the node but that is partly inside of it. You can call the objects visitors, guests, temporary objects, or whatever you like. Additionally, each object needs a flag. If you use the structure for rendering, you must flag the object you previously rendered in each frame to avoid rendering it again if you come to a neighboring node in which this object is also partly inside.

Which one of the two options you choose is up to you and depends on the purpose you want to use the data structure for. At the end of this chapter, we implement an octree and use the method of cutting objects into small pieces to fit them into subdivision nodes. This prevents error-prone handling of touching object lists. You will also learn how to use the octree for doing collision detection and not for rendering. In this situation, the number of polygons does not matter as much because of the hierarchical culling of the collision query in the upper nodes. If you want to use the octree for rendering, use the option with the neighboring or touching objects list.

Finally, moving objects is an issue in subdivision algorithms. The biggest problem is when a lot of things move inside this structure and you have to do a lot of sorting of the moving objects in the tree which slows things down. There is also the problem of touching objects or objects that cross borders between nodes. There is a lot of management involved, and again, you have two approaches for moving objects in an octree. First, you can pump down each object until its center point is sorted into the octree node where it belongs. Other nodes can be used for the moving object depending on how small you want the leaves to be.

The other approach is to push the moving objects only to the deepness in the octree where they fit into a complete cube of a node, but also where they would have to be split on the next lower level in the octree. In this approach, you use a list of objects at nearly each node of the octree where moving objects are stored. This appears to be the better and easier way to go.

Well, you can already read between the lines. The octree can be used for a lot of things. You can use it for rendering in its basic configuration without neighboring lists, although it is not recommended. You can also use it for collision detection of the player with the static level geometry. You can integrate the collision detection of moving objects with the player and with each other easily. The nice thing about octrees is that they are really easy to implement, especially with a good math library at your disposal, which the engine has of course. You will see this at the end of the chapter.

Note

Interestingly, there are U.S. patents on scene management algorithms and their data structures. The utilization of quadtrees for use with space partitioning in accordance with hidden surface removal can be found under the U.S. patent number 3602702. U.S. patent 4694404 involves speeding up the representation of solid, 3D models using a hierarchical subdivision based on an octree. See http://www.uspto.gov/patft/index.html for more examples and information.

Binary Space Partitioning Trees

The octree you are now familiar with is used to partition the space in a regular manner that is also axis-aligned to the world axis. This is why you can use the axis-aligned bounding boxes in this type of scene management, especially with regard to the comprehensive AABB class in the math library. The binary space partitioning trees, or BSP trees, are a totally generalized approach to the space partitioning scheme. There are also kd trees, which are pretty much the same as BSP trees, except that the splitting planes are axis-aligned and not arbitrary as they are in BSP trees.

The BSP tree can partition the space or the geometry that occupies space using arbitrary partitioning planes. The subdivision of the space is therefore not given by the space itself but by the geometry. The advantage of this approach is that you do not need to split as many polygons. In fact, you can even adjust the algorithm's heuristic to avoid splits.

Before discussing the BSP tree, it is important to discuss why I dedicate so much space in this chapter to the technique. Video game products at id Software, such as *Doom, Quake,* and *Castle Wolfenstein,* are among the top sellers in the first-person shooter genre. This is mostly due to their groundbreaking technology that always pushes hardware to its limits while rendering with quality that others cannot reproduce. The name of the technical director of this company, John Carmack, made its way into the honor rolls of video game programmers. These products are always on the cutting edge, such as when they offered the first among first-person shooters and when they made the first shooter 3D. They were the first to feature real 3D models to represent enemies, weapons, and power ups as well.

A few years ago it was revealed that the secret behind *Doom* was a BSP tree that enabled the program to run in real-time even while using comparably large, detailed 3D indoor levels. The BSP tree is a long-known data structure in informatics and computer science. However, with *Doom,* this data structure was used to speed up rendering of computer graphics in a video game for the first time. And it was quite successful. The BSP tree was actually the scene management structure behind id Software games and engines. Only since *Doom 3* the BSP tree is no longer used for rendering levels. Let's have a look at how the BSP tree works.

The three letters BSP mean binary space partitioning. So the algorithm should take care of partitioning the space in a binary way, splitting the space into two areas for each iteration. The BSP tree is a data structure that stores the result of the BSP algorithm, which can be used for 2D problems and 3D problems. Of course we concentrate on the 3D scenario in this chapter because we do not want to redo *Doom.* Take a look at Figure 13.10, which shows the small level of a 3D room that we will partition with the BSP algorithm. For the sake of better visibility, I removed the ceiling's polygons and displayed the culled back faces of the walls. To differentiate the back faces from the actual polygons, I put a texture with diagonal stripes on them.

The primary goal of the BSP tree is to partition the geometry into convex groups of polygons. Figure 13.11 shows a convex polygon on the left side as opposed to a concave polygon on the right side. A convex polygon is simply a polygon that does not have a dent. A concave polygon can have dents whereby the inner angles inside the polygon can be greater than or equal to 180 degrees. You can take this definition and move it to 3D objects, such as a room or a level. A more technical definition says that in a convex polygon or volume, you can trace a line between any two vertices and that line will always be completely within the polygon or volume. If there is any place where it goes outside, the polygon or volume is concave.

604 Chapter 13 ■ Scene Management

Figure 13.10 A small 3D level. Note that the back faces are rendered using a texture with diagonal stripes.

A collection of polygons in 3D space is convex when you can go into each position inside the convex and look in each direction. No part of the geometry of a convex group is even partly occluded from another part in the group. In a concave group of polygons, you can move into a position where one part of the group occludes your view of the other parts of the group. You can slide into a dent, for example, and hide there to avoid being eaten by a monster.

You probably understand now why BSP trees were important historically. By dividing a complex 3D level into a lot of convex groups, you can render a whole level without the need for a depth buffer. As you know, the polygons of the convex groups would not occlude each other at all. So the only thing you need to do to render the scene without error in the occlusions is to order the convex groups by their distance to the viewer. Then you can simply render the most distant groups first, then the closer ones, and so on. You end up with a scene in which no errors in the overlapping depth occur, even without a depth buffer.

It gets even better. The convex groups are stored inside the BSP tree in a way that orders them by their depth or in a way that you can traverse the tree and collect them already sorted. If you don't understand why this was so important, you might if you know that *Doom* and *Quake* were played without a depth buffer available on the graphics adapter hardware as we have today. The memory was too slow and too small to implement your own depth buffer functionality.

Figure 13.11 A convex polygon on the left side opposed to a concave polygon on the right side.

> **Note**
>
> If you render without a depth buffer or if you render (semi-) transparent polygons, you still need to render back-to-front to prevent visual artifacts. This means you have to order the polygons starting with the most distant ones in the scene. On modern graphics adapters, the depth buffer is usually faster than sorting your polygons back-to-front. The depth buffer will be even faster if you render your scene front-to-back starting with the closest one first. They will then fill the depth buffer and the early z culling will effectively cull away pixels that are occluded anyway. This will avoid overdraw.

BSP Algorithm

This section looks at how to build a BSP tree step-by-step using a real level. The B in the acronym BSP means binary. Binary trees are nothing spectacular in computer science. The trees are a data structure in which each inner node of the tree has exactly two children as opposed to a quadtree, which has four children or a linked list with one child. The root of the tree has no parent node, but this is the place where the whole tree starts. It is not a secret that you can store a 3Dlevel in a BSP tree so you can think of the root of the tree to as the whole level. You also have two children of the root so you have to split your level into two parts to partition the space.

Finally, when you reach a situation in which you cannot split the geometry in a node, the node becomes a leaf of the tree. So the question is, "How do you split the geometry at each node and how do you know when you cannot split the geometry?" You probably know the answer to the second half of this question. The BSP algorithm should split the level data into convex groups. As soon as the geometry in a node is a convex group, you have reached a leaf. One question remains. How do we do the splits at each node to end up in convex groups without trial-and-error approaches? Take a look back at Figure 13.10. This is the level you should dump into the BSP algorithm.

The BSP algorithm uses a very smart way to get down to the convex groups. At each node, it selects a polygon from the geometry of the node to use as the so-called splitter whose plane is then used as a partitioning plane in space. The polygons that are on the back side of this plane are stored in one child of this node, which is called the backlist. All polygons on the front side of the splitting plane are stored in the other child of this node, which is called the frontlist. If a polygon is intersected by the splitting plane, then it is cut into two pieces. Each piece is then sorted into the appropriate list. If a polygon is positioned on the plane, then look at its normal vector. If it points into the same direction as the splitting plane's normal, then you sort it into the frontlist. Otherwise, it goes to the backlist.

This is the complete BSP algorithm. There is nothing more to it. Look at Figure 13.12. The picture shows the first iteration of the algorithm. Here, the small polygon on the left wall in the small corridor was used as splitter. The L-shaped part of the level in the foreground is the group of polygons that is in the frontlist of the BSP tree's root. The backlist contains the remaining polygons, which form two open cubes that are not connected with each other, which is not a requirement.

The game goes on and on. Each child of a node is treated separately using the same algorithm by selecting a splitter and then splitting the group of polygons. This game will stop only if you cannot find a polygon at a node that can be used as a splitter. This is how the convexity of the leaves is ensured. A polygon from a node can be used as splitter only if

Figure 13.12 The first iteration of the BSP algorithm. The polygon in the center of the image was used as the splitter.

there is at least one polygon in each of the resulting lists. If all polygons are in the frontlist or if all are in the backlist, you cannot split the group. In a convex group you cannot find a splitter because each polygon is in front of the other. Thus, if the polygon of a node can be used as a splitter, the geometry at the node forms a convex group.

Figure 13.13 shows you the complete BSP tree for our simple level. The left branch at each node is the front list whereas the right branch is the backlist. The polygon that was selected as the splitter is marked by a bright circle. By chance, we ended up with a balanced tree. This means that all the branches of the tree have the same depth. This is not a requirement, but it is a nice effect because the search times in the tree are stable. Otherwise, you have differences depending on how deep the branch is.

History of the BSP Tree in Video Games

The algorithm we know of today as the BSP algorithm and that leads to the BSP tree was originally developed in the end of the 1970s at the University of Texas at Dallas. At Texas,

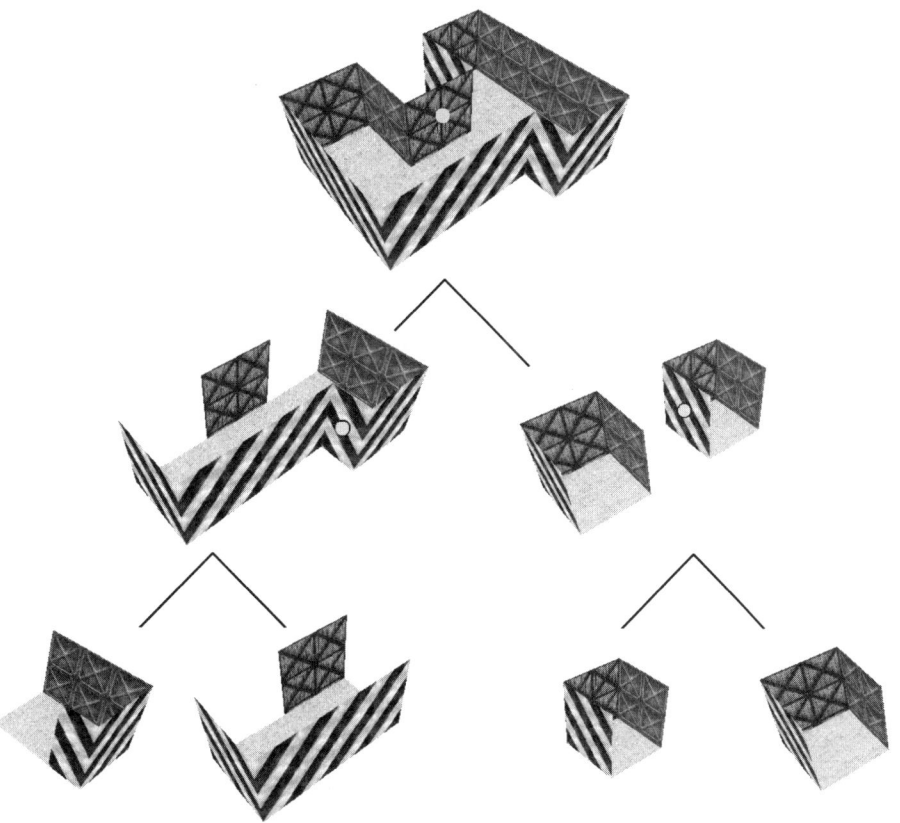

Figure 13.13 The complete BSP tree of the level. The frontside polygons are in the left branch whereas the backside polygons are in the right branch. The used splitters are marked with a bright circle.

Henry Fuchs and Zvi Kedem were teachers, and they noted a promising student named Bruce Naylor who was looking for a topic for his Ph.D. thesis. The rest of the story is history and the cooperation of these three guys was documented in the following three publications concerning BSP trees:

- Fuchs, Kedem, Naylor, "Predeterming Visibility Priority in 3D Scenes," SIGGRAPH '79, pp 175-181.
- Fuch, Kedem, Naylor, "On Visible Surface Generation by A Priori Tree Structures," SIGGRAPH '80, pp 124-133.
- Bruce F. Naylor, "A Priori Based Techniques for Determining Visibility Priority for 3D Scenes," Ph.D. Thesis, University of Texas at Dallas, May 1981.

In December 1993, the first video to use a BSP tree for scene management and rendering was published. The graphic artist Adrian Carmack, the game designer Tom Hall, and the programmers John Romero and a certain John Carmack did, of course, create *Doom 1* (see Figure 13.14). (Note that the two Carmacks of this team are not related to each other.)

Doom 1 was not the first video game of these developers. The predecessors, such as *Hovertank* and *Wolfenstein 3D* (see Figure 13.15), had also been little sensations due to what they could do on hardware in those days. However, these games had to put some severe restrictions on the level design and make a lot of assumptions and simplifications to calculate the HSR in real-time. In the game *Wolfenstein 3D,* all rooms of a level must

Figure 13.14 A screenshot of *Doom 1* by id Software.

have the same height for the ceilings and the floors, respectively. Furthermore, each wall had to be positioned in ninety degree angles to each other and had to stand vertical on the even floors. Of course the floors and ceilings had to be horizontal.

Figure 13.15 A screenshot of *Wolfenstein 3D* by id Software.

In the game *Doom 1*, the team wanted to get rid of these restrictions, but had to find another way of doing the HSR to avoid overdraw and to render without a depth buffer. John Carmack stumbled across the BSP tree, which was already used in *Bell Labs* to represent 3D objects. For use in a real-time environment, hardware was too slow. This is why *Doom 1* uses a 2D BSP algorithm and BSP tree. The walls in this game used arbitrary angles and the floors and ceilings had different heights in different rooms. The walls still needed to be vertical and the floors and ceilings had to be horizontal. However, this was a great success because the game looked more real than anything else available at the time.

The restriction of vertical walls and horizontal floors and ceilings is easily explained. From a bird's eye view, the level looks like a 2D drawing. The ceilings and the floors will not split the space in their respective rooms and can be ignored for the BSP calculations because it is guaranteed that there is no geometry above a ceiling polygon or below a floor polygon. Because the walls are vertical, they boil down to lines when seen from above. So the BSP algorithm that works in *Doom 1* and *Doom 2* had only a 2D BSP algorithm that partitions 2D lines and are nothing like a 3D polygon.

Splitting 2D lines was possible in real-time even then, as opposed to splitting polygons in 3D space. That is why everyone talks about *Doom* being 2.5D instead of 3D. The next step in the evolution of the BSP algorithm in video games was the game *Quake 1* by id Software (see Figure 13.16), which was released in June 1996. This was the first video game that used a real 3D BSP algorithm without restrictions and with arbitrary geometry. It even featured real 3D models to represent enemies.

Figure 13.16 A screenshot of *Quake 1* by id Software.

Ever since Doom 1, the BSP tree has been used as a data structure, which can be found in most major first-person 3D action games. On current hardware, there is no advantage to using a BSP tree for rendering. However, a BSP tree is a great tool for collision detection so it is still around.

Finding the Best Splitter

The BSP algorithm is not very complicated. It is very simple. As is the case with all tree-like data structures that build a BSP tree, the source code is easy because you can use a single, recursive function. You still need to get the answer to one question before you can program a BSP tree. The secret of the algorithm is to select one of the polygons at each node as splitter to divide the list of polygons into two smaller lists. Which polygon do you choose as a splitter? Must certain conditions be fulfilled? Interestingly, there is not a condition that must be met by the splitter, except that there has to be at least one polygon on either side of it.

There is, of course, a heuristic to find the best splitter out of a list of polygons. There are two attributes that each splitter will have. The first attribute shows how many polygons get cut by a certain splitter. If you split a single polygon to make two out of it on either side of the splitter, this will take time, which adds up to the amount of polygons in the lists. So a good splitter plane should intersect as few polygons as possible. The second attribute is the balance of the tree. Each splitter will force a number of polygons into its backlist and a number of polygons into the frontlist. The goal is to keep both numbers pretty much the same to achieve a balanced tree.

From these two attributes, you can now build a heuristic that allows you to evaluate each polygon of a list. The more points a polygon gets from the heuristic, the less suited it is to be the best splitter of this list:

```
Score = abs( NumFront - NumBack ) + ( NumSplits * 3 )
```

The variables `NumFront` und `NumBack` are the number of polygons in the backlist and the frontlist with regard to the given splitter, and `NumSplits` is the number of polygons that get clipped. The constant weight of 3 is used here to add more penalty for each split the splitter enforces. If you want the selected splitter to use as few splits as possible, increase this number even more. The greater the score becomes for a certain polygon, the less is its value as a splitter.

If you stand at a node of the BSP tree with a list of polygons and split them, you loop through the list of polygons and calculate the heuristic for each of the polygons. Then you have the score for each polygon if it is used as a splitter, and you simply choose the one with the lowest value. This is then your best splitter, and you really split the list into a frontlist and a backlist.

Here is the pseudo-code to do this:

```
PLANE FindBestSplitter(polygonlist) {
   PLANE BestSplitter, CurrentSplitter;
   int   nClass=0, nFront=0,
         nBack=0,  nSplits=0
         nBestScore=99999,
         nCurrentScore=0;

   for ( i < num polygons at node )
      {
      CurrentSplitter = Polygon[i].GetPlane();
      for ( j < num polygons in node )
         {
         if ( i == j ) continue;

         nClass = CurrentSplitter.Classify(Polygon[i]);
```

```
            if      (nClass == BACKSIDE)  nBack++;
            else if (nClass == CLIPPED)   nSplits++;
            else if (nClass == FRONTSIDE) nFront++;
            else
               {
               if ( NormalsSameDirection(Plane,Polygon[i]) ) nFront++;
               else nBack++;
               }

            nCurrentScore = abs(nFront - nBack) + (nSPlits*3);

            if (nCurrentScore < nBestScore)
               {
               BestSplitter = CurrentSplitter;
               nBestScore   = CurrentScore;
               }
            } // for
         } // for

      return BestSplitter;
      } // function
```

In summary, you now realize why you implement the functions for classifications and splits into the comprehensive math library. The actual code for this function is similar to this pseudo-code version because a lot of things are already implemented in the class `ZFXPlane` and `ZFXPolygon`. At the end of this chapter, we implement a class for a BSP tree.

BSP Tree Variants

If you dig deeper into the topic of BSP trees, you will find three variants of the algorithm, resulting in different versions of the BSP tree. These three major versions are the node-based BSP tree, the leafy BSP tree, and the solid BSP tree (this is also known as a solid leaf tree). These three versions apply only minor changes to the algorithm and are mostly about where you store the polygonal data.

Node-Based BSP Trees

The most simple variant of the BSP tree is the node-based BSP tree. It is called this because all of the polygons of the level are stored in each node of the tree. If you split the list of polygons at a certain node, you can save the polygon that was used as splitter at this node and hand down the other polygons to the children. You do this until you are left with a leaf in which a convex group of polygons sits. Then you select an arbitrary polygon from this group to serve as the splitter. The polygon is saved in this node and the other polygons go down into the frontlist branch. The backlist will remain empty because the group is already convex. You then set the pointer to the backlist to NULL. With the frontlist, you proceed this way until there is only one polygon left, which then forms a leaf of the tree.

The motivation behind this idea is to do collision detection without doing any kind of calculation. You can differentiate between the empty space, for which it is valid for an entity to be there, and the solid space for which an entity cannot be at any time. The empty space is the space inside the convex group of polygons whereas the solid space is indicated by the NULL pointers in the BSP tree. As soon as an entity tries to move over the border a splitter provides and where the backlist is empty, it simply means that the entity is trying to move through a wall.

You can simply dump the position of an entity into the root of the BSP tree. This position gets classified at each node—whether it is on the front side or on the back side of the splitter—which is stored at the node. If the point ends up in solid space indicated by a NULL pointer, the entity is not at a valid location inside the level. If it is a moving entity, it has to run into a wall. If the point ends up in empty space, which is a leaf with a polygon of the BSP tree, everything is fine.

Leafy BSP Tree

The leaf-based or leafy BSP tree does not save the polygons of the splitters at each node of the tree. Instead, it saves the plane that is used as a partitioning plane and as the plane of the selected splitter. The polygon that was used as the splitter is marked by a flag because a polygon cannot be used as splitter more than once. The splitter polygon is then sorted into the frontlist.

If you cannot find a polygon in the tree that has not already been used as splitter, you have a convex group. In this case, you simply save the list of polygons in this group at the leaf. The disadvantage of the node-based BSP tree is that you have solid information for collision detection, but you do not have convex groups of polygons you can use for rendering. The leafy BSP tree overcomes this problem by storing the convex groups of polygons together in the leaves, making it optimal for rendering. The disadvantage is that you do not retain the solid information. If the point you want to test for collision ends up in a leaf, do a polygon-by-polygon test again.

Solid Leaf BSP Tree

The solid leaf tree combines both of the advantages of the approaches into a single BSP tree. First, you build the leaf-based BSP tree for a set of polygons. Then you move down like you did in the node-based BSP tree and take each polygon from the convex list as a splitter to build the frontside branch of the former leaves. Of course the backlists from this node onward are always NULL as it was in the node-based BSP tree. If the polygons from the convex group had been used as the splitter, you would be done. However, the whole group of convex polygons sits in the leaf of the tree, but the final tree levels just before the leaf now contain the solid information about invalid space.

Portal Engines

When John Carmack introduced the BSP algorithm and tree into the high video game developer society, there was another scene management approach working its way into the industry. This was called the portal engine, and it was used for the first time in the video game hit *Duke Nukem 3D* by 3D Realms. *Duke Nukem 3D* was not completely 3D because there sprites were used for enemies and weapons, but it was already more 3D than *Doom 1* and *Doom 2*. The most obvious difference was that players could look up and down and that the floors and ceilings were at steep angles. In addition, to a certain degree, the game featured rooms that were located above each other, which was not possible in *Doom*. The final eye candy was the mirrors, which were seen for the first time in games. This game was revolutionary in the 3D world, and its secret was the portal engine ticking inside.

> **Note**
>
> I still remember sitting for hours and hours in front of this `build` editor while constructing levels for *Duke Nukem 3D*. After awhile, I could really push this tool beyond its limits and do things to the engine that even the commercial game did not offer. I built a level that had an outdoor part, which was modeled after Hadley's Hope colony on LV426 from the movie *Aliens*. You could enter the complex of the colony, which had two stories off the main part of the complex and which were located above each other. Each story had the same layout of rooms. From the upper story, you could not only look out of the windows, but you could also jump down the outdoor scene from which you started.
>
> This isn't anything special in today's games because you can build arbitrary geometry. However, back in those days, no other commercial game could provide such an experience. One of the restrictions of the `BUILD` tool was that you could not build rooms above each other creating a situation whereby the player could look into both rooms at the same time from the outside, for example. This could mess up the rendering of the early portal engine. There were still good `BUILD` tool tricks for building a level.

The Idea of the Portal Engine

How could the portal engine realize something that no other tool could at that time? To understand what is going on in a portal engine, look at Figure 13.17, which presents the bird's eye view of a simple 3D level in which two rooms are connected by a bent corridor.

A scene management algorithm needs to know how to detect the polygons inside the view frustum of the viewer given a set of arbitrary polygons that form a game level. The BSP tree is meant to be walked through while collecting the visible polygons. The portal engine involves a totally different approach in that it is not a tree structure. The Figure 13.18 shows the level that was processed by a portal processor. If you look carefully, you can see that the level is suddenly broken into convex parts in which a portal sits where two parts touch. Portal engineers call these convex groups of polygons sectors, cells, or areas.

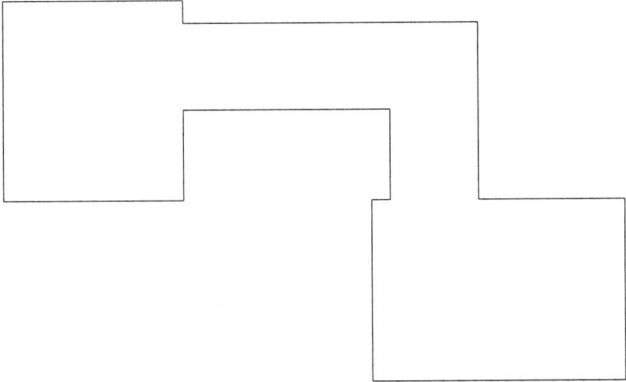

Figure 13.17 A simple 3D level seen from the bird's eye view in which there are two rooms and a corridor.

The funny thing is that sectors that are adjacent from the player's point of view don't need to actually be adjacent in the level data. You are required to store only the sectors and their polygons and the portals that sit in this sector. Such a portal is always two-sided and each of the two sides belongs to a different sector. This is the connection between two sectors that do not need to be physically correct. You can think of a portal as being a Stargate like the one in the movie or an entry to a wormhole. One side is located in one sector and the other side is located in another sector. If both sectors happen to touch each other, such as when a portal sits in a door frame, this is fine. However, if they do not touch each other because one sector is here on earth and the other is on another planet, then . . . it's still fine. It is not a problem for the algorithm.

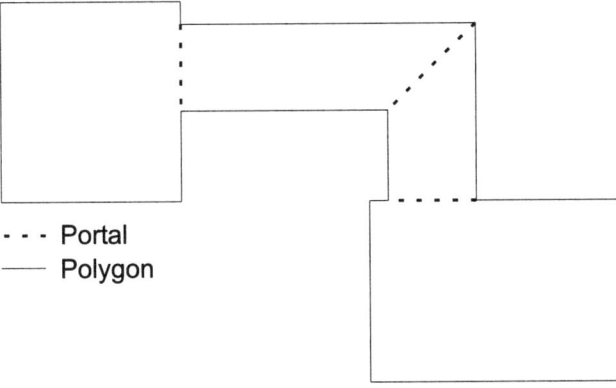

Figure 13.18 The same level is now in convex pieces (called sectors, cells, or areas) that are connected by portals.

The only thing you need to know is the sector in which the player starts. Then you render this sector. After that, you loop through the portals saved in this sector. For each portal, you go into the sector to which the portal leads, you render the sector, you loop through its portals, and so on. The trick is that each time the render function crosses a portal, the view frustum is clipped to fit exactly through the portal if it is greater than the portal. Of course you process only portals that are inside the modified frustum in neighboring sectors.

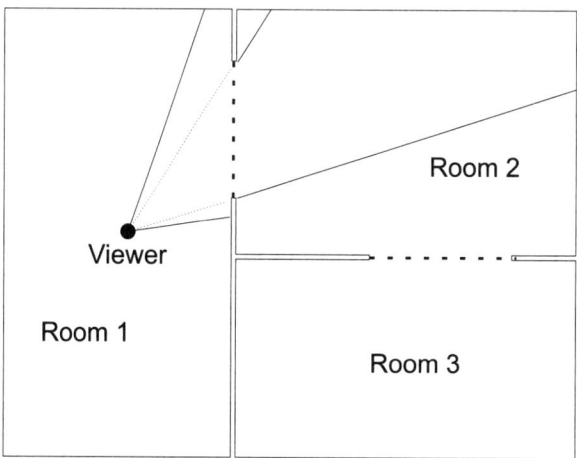

Figure 13.19 The view frustum and a smaller frustum clipped to fit through a portal.

Figure 13.19 shows a small level with three rooms from a bird's eye view. The player is in room 1 so this room is rendered. The portal that connects room 1 and room 2 is inside the view frustum of the player. Room 2 will also be rendered and its portals will be checked; however, before this happens, the view frustum is clipped so that it is no bigger than the portal allows. Render room 2 and take a look at the portal of this room. The portal that connects room 2 and room 3 is not inside the frustum so room 3 is not rendered or processed. The algorithm would come to the portal that connects room 2 and room 1, and this is inside the frustum. So you have to render room 1 again and then you would be caught in an infinite loop. Of course, each sector has a flag that indicates if it was already visited in the current frame to prevent this from happening.

Note that if the portal that connects room 2 and room 3 had been in the clipped view frustum, then the previously clipped view frustum would have been clipped again to be no bigger than the portal that leads to room 3.

Zero Overdraw

This sounds fairly simple and of course it is. However, you might ask what the advantage is and why this can be used in a time where no depth buffer is available. With no depth buffer, rendering the scene from front to back, so sectors that are more distant from the viewer are rendered later, would result in distant sectors "overdrawing" the nearer sectors that were already rendered. The BSP tree overcomes this problem by rendering its convex pieces back-to-front to prevent a false overdraw from taking place.

The big trick of the portal engine comes in now. The logic behind clipping the view frustum to each portal it crosses is not only to cull away more invisible portals that are inside the original frustum and that are occluded by walls, but also to clip the level geometry. What I didn't mention previously was that you do not just render the sector where a visible portal leads. You first take the list of polygons from this sector and clip this list to fit exactly into the clipped view frustum. This involves the need to clip each polygon that intersects the frustum. When this process is over, you have a list of polygons that are totally inside the clipped view frustum and all parts of the sector are outside of the clipped frustum. You then render the clipped polygons, and the projected pixels will be rendered only in places of the back buffer that were not yet touched because they represent the hole the projected portal of the last sector left in the back buffer.

This is the secret of the portal engine: You have exact zero overdraw. This means that each pixel on the back buffer is written exactly one time or not at all. This is why you don't need to worry about the depth values.

The Portal Engine Versus the BSP

Portal engine scene management sounds like the perfect plan, doesn't it? But video game developers have been debating portal engine versus the BSP tree ever since both methods were first used in games. The criticism of the BSP algorithm is that it has a lot of potential overdraw. This means there are no visible artifacts even without a depth buffer due to rendering convex groups of polygons ordered from back to front. But the problem with the hardware some years ago was the slowness of the pixel setting operation. So lots of overdraw equals slow rendering.

The criticism of the portal engine is that it involves a lot of clipping operations. Normally a view frustum has six planes. Using arbitrarily shaped portals, a clipped view frustum can have an unusually high number of planes. This leads to huge overhead. Even with relatively simple viewing volumes, there is a lot of clipping on the CPU, and as you might guess, the CPUs of that time before the advent of real hardware accelerators were slow because the CPU also had to do the other tasks of rendering.

The bottom line is that there is no such thing as the optimal approach. Currently, there are hardware implementations of a depth buffer so rendering with zero overdraw is still nice for boosting the performance; however, the impact isn't significant. I do not discuss the criticisms in detail because they are outdated.

Do not mistake this chapter as a lesson in historical importance, but as one that covers obsolete approaches. With a few adjustments and using modern hardware, both approaches are very useful in large, 3D indoor projects. The BSP tree should not be used for rendering, although it is a good structure for collision detection. The portal engine, on the other hand, is a very good tool for rendering if you skip the polygon clipping. If you render front-to-back, this is an advantage because of early z culling. Therefore, you can just render the sector where the player is, and then go through the visible portals to render the attached sectors in a brute force manner. It is very efficient and fast. The transformation on the hardware, together with the early z culling, is much faster than the CPU if it clipped a few thousand polygons per sector to an n-sided frustum.

Note that the convexity of the sectors is no longer a requirement for a portal engine if you do not use a strict portal system, which is the original approach involving polygon clipping. If you render with a depth buffer, the sectors can also be concave.

In this chapter, we implement only a leafy BSP tree and an octree. You will see the portal engine prepared in Chapter 14, "Computer-Aided Design Tools," and implemented in Chapter 15, "Deathmatch Shooter."

Special Effects with Portals

As opposed to the BSP tree, a portal engine has one very big advantage. There are a lot of special effects that can be natively built using a portal engine. The most important concept is that the sectors that are connected between portals do not need to physically touch each other. You can leave as much space and geometry of other sectors between them as you like. The algorithm just travels from one end of the portal to the other. The BSP tree awaits the level data to be physically connected. In a portal engine, you can even save each room in a separate file.

You can create an effect for the portals, such as mirrors. If a mirror portal is inside the view frustum, the render function will not look for a neighboring sector, but it will render the same sector where the position and orientation of the portal is used as viewer. For example, you can render the scene onto a texture that is put onto the mirror. This is tricky because you have to render some sectors twice so you need another flag that indicates that this sector can be rendered again, even if it has already been rendered. The second catch is that two mirrors that see each other can then create an infinite loop. This can be prevented by putting a mirror-rendering counter that is incremented each time a mirror is rendered in a certain frame and limit this value to four or five times.

You might want a fun house level with a labyrinth. When you start the level, the game will randomize which portal leads to which one. Each time you play the level, a door will lead to another room. It is difficult to transform this approach into a good game; however, it is still possible and even useful for certain effects. You can also build a list of destination portals that is cycled through by each portal. Imagine standing in front of a Star Gate and imagine seeing another exit on a different planet every five seconds. A Star Gate can internally use a fluctuating wormhole that jumps between approximately five locations. This gets interesting, doesn't it?

You can also build portals that lead to the same sector. The player leaves the room through one door and enters the room through another door. Or maybe he enters through the same door through which he left. It is also possible to build things that are physically not possible. There was one *Enterprise* episode in which Captain Archer found a small escape pod in space. This pod was a few meters long and about two meters in diameter. Inside this small pod was a hatch leading to a large corridor ending in a big machinery section. Of course all these rooms would not have fit into the small pod if there hadn't been an artificially created anomaly inside the pod.

Automatic Generation of Portals

One question remains. You have a level split into sectors, and the sectors are connected by portals. That is good, but how can you define these sectors and portals? There are two ways to do this. The first way is to implement a level editing tool that allows for arbitrary portal placement and sector definitions. This is the most bullet-proof variant because the level designer has total control of how the sectors are organized and how special effect portals can be placed.

Of course you can also automatically generate portals. There are indeed methods for doing this, but the drawback is that such automated procedures generate way too many portals in such a level. You also end up with too many sectors that are too small. This is not what the current hardware likes to see and it would not be very quick at rendering from such a system.

You should know how this method works. Keep in mind, however, that you are encouraged to come up with a more modern version that allows for concave sectors. The convex sector of the strict portal engine should remind you of another thing that has convex groups of polygons. Have you ever heard of the leafy BSP tree? The idea is that you dump the level geometry into a BSP tree and let the leafy BSP tree create the convex sectors right into its leaves. You then just have the task of building the portals between the leaves of the BSP tree. Each polygon that was used as a splitter can be a portal because the splitters are in fact the polygons that connect the convex groups, which were the ones that divided them into separate groups.

The idea is that you create a rectangular *initial portal* for each node of the leafy BSP tree that is not a leaf. This initial portal needs to be processed. Therefore you dump this initial portal from its node down the tree. The size of the initial portal must be large enough to span the whole bounding box of this node, which includes the underlying geometry. After you have this initial portal in place, send it down the tree and classify it at each node's partitioning plane. Following is how you must react to the result of this classification:

- FRONT
  Send the portal down the frontlist of this node.
- BACK
  Send the portal down the backlist of this node.
- PLANE
  Send the portal down the frontlist. As a return value, you will get a list of clipped portals that you need to send down the backlist one-by-one.
- CLIP
  Clip the portal and send each of the two new portals down the list, depending on which side of the splitter it is located.

During its journey down the tree, an initial portal gets clipped and separated into a number of fragments. Such a fragment then arrives at a leaf. This is the first place at which a decision is made about whether or not this portal is allowed to stay. Such a fragment has the potential to become a real portal if it is located inside the convex group of this leaf. You have to loop through the list of polygons of the leaf. The portal fragment must not intersect any of the polygons and it must not lay on the back side of a polygon in this convex group. It must be located inside the bounding box of this group. If all three conditions are true, you save this fragment as a possible portal. Otherwise, you can delete it because it is in solid space.

After you do this process for the initial portals, you have a list of potential portals. Not all of them are valid portals. The list will still contain two types of black sheep that you have to find. A valid portal must belong to exactly two leaves. So you look through the list and remove the candidates that do not exist in two different leaves with the same vertices and an inverted normal vector. The second type of black sheep is a redundant portal candidate. The algorithm described previously will generate valid portals that are located at the same location in space but with a different size. You go through the list again and if you find two pairs of portals that connect the same two leaves, one of the pairs can be removed because the convex leaves can be connected only by one valid pair of portals. You should remove the smaller one.

Now you have a list of portals for which each portal has two sides and each side belongs to another leaf of the BSP tree. You can copy the leaves into your sector structures and save the portal along with them. However, as I already mentioned, there are a lot of small sectors and a lot of portals created by this approach. People like to think of portals as doorframes or holes in the wall that lead into another room. This approach creates portals all over the level, where a lot of portals will sit in a single room at arbitrary angles and positions.

Now you can decide on your own if you want to invest the work to automatically create a portal. I recommend hand-placed portals with greater sectors to comply with the wishes of your graphics adapter.

Potential Visibility Set

A trivial, but iron-clad rule of computer game development says that you should precompute everything you can to avoid slow calculations at run time. This was the rule during the time of *Quake*'s programming. In the article series *Inside Quake*, Michael Abrash, who was one of the programmers, explains the early stages of the BSP tree engine. He describes how the engine suffered a severe performance problem in huge open areas in which a lot of the level geometry could be seen. The frame rate was too low so John Carmack rewrote the engine numerous times. After a long weekend, he had another idea implemented. Of the changes, Michael Abrash says:

> *The first time John showed me his working prototype, I went to the most complex scene I knew of, a place where the frame rate used to grind down into the single digits, and spun around smoothly, with no perceptible slowdown.*

After John Carmack tried to improve the direct BSP approach (this took him an entire weekend) an idea came to him while laying in bed. The reduction in the frame rate resulted from the slow traveling down the whole BSP tree (which is rather long for a complete level). The second problem was that a lot of pixel overdraw was going on for leaves that were rendered but finally occluded by others.

The idea was to precalculate which leaves could potentially be seen from each other. Think of a convex room with two doors into other convex rooms on opposing walls, whereby each room is a leaf of the BSP tree. The player can look through only one of the doors at a time. However, the BSP tree still renders both leaves behind both doors. Even worse, if in those rooms there are other doors leading to other rooms, they would also be rendered (and then overdrawn) even if the viewer could not see those doors because they are not visible through the door frame.

So the idea was two-fold. In a precalculation step, you build a list for each leaf. This list contains all other leaves that can potentially be seen from each position and orientation in the leaf. During runtime, you would not walk through the level and render everything. You just need to find the leaf the viewer is in and then render the list of potentially visible leaves—the potential visibility set or short PVS. A frustum culling does the second optimization for these leaves and renders only the ones inside the view frustum.

This sounds good enough; however, the big catch is that the PVS is not very easy to calculate. Interestingly, it involves building the portals for the level. Therefore, the strict portal engine cannot live without the BSP whereas the strict BSP tree with PVS cannot live without the portal engine. I do not recommend using a PVS for a BSP tree because there are too many issues starting with the restriction on the level geometry (search the Internet for "illegal geometry"), the floating point precision problems that end up in infinite loops, or the PVS compiler crashes.

Implementing a BSP Tree

You now know a lot about the theory behind scene management. However, you have yet to implement such a system in real life code. In the following section, I discuss the implementation of a BSP tree, which will be a new part of the math library of the ZFXEngine. I use the leafy variant of the BSP tree in this example. It is not too difficult to make this a node-based tree, if you think you need it. That is why I use the leafy version. You can easily downgrade this to the node-based variant, but you can also update it to the solid leaf variant.

At the end of this chapter, I also implement a simple demo application that uses the BSP tree and the octree. I point out details about the performance faults of the demo application. For now, you need to know that you should keep a separate vertex list and index list in static buffers on the graphics adapter, and keep a BSP tree or an octree in the system memory that represents the same geometry. This tree is then used for collision detection, and this approach will be the quickest one you can use.

In this chapter, we also use a tree for rendering. To do this, the math library needs another helper class because it does not know of a render device, which is why you cannot simply dump a render device into the root of the tree and ask it to render all visible polygons. Instead, we query a list of visible polygons from the tree and render the list. We also convert the extracted data into real vertices. The following helper class is just a half stack that can take polygons. It is a half stack because you can delete only the whole list and not single elements from it.

Here is the list of polygons for which the traversing of the tree stores the visible polygons:

```
class ZFXPolylist
   {
   public:
     ZFXPolylist(void);
     ~ZFXPolylist(void);
     bool          AddPolygon(const ZFXPolygon&);
     void          Reset(void);
     ZFXPolygon*   GetPolylist(void){return m_pPolys;}
     unsigned int  GetNum(void)     {return m_Num;    }
   private:
     ZFXPolygon    *m_pPolys;
     unsigned int  m_Num;
     unsigned int  m_Max;
```

```
      bool        CheckMem(void);
   }; // class
/*----------------------------*/

ZFXPolylist::ZFXPolylist(void)
   {
   m_pPolys = NULL;
   m_Num    = 0;
   m_Max    = 0;
   } // constructor
/*----------------------------*/

ZFXPolylist::~ZFXPolylist(void)
   {
   if (m_pPolys) {
      free(m_pPolys);
      m_pPolys = NULL;
      }
   } // destructor
/*----------------------------*/

bool ZFXPolylist::AddPolygon(const ZFXPolygon &Poly)
   {
   if ( !CheckMem() ) return false;
   m_pPolys[m_Num].CopyOf( Poly );
   m_Num++;
   return true;
   } // AddPolygon
/*----------------------------*/

void ZFXPolylist::Reset(void)
   {
   if (m_pPolys) {
      free(m_pPolys);
      m_pPolys = NULL;
      }
   m_Num = 0;
   m_Max = 0;
   } // Reset
/*----------------------------*/

bool ZFXPolylist::CheckMem(void)
```

```
       {
       if (m_Num < m_Max) return true;
       m_Max += 100;
       int nSize = sizeof(ZFXPolygon)*m_Max;
       m_pPolys = (ZFXPolygon*)realloc( m_pPolys, nSize );
       memset(&m_pPolys[m_Num], 0, sizeof(ZFXPolygon)*100);
       return (m_pPolys != NULL);
       } // Reset
/*------------------------*/
```

As has been implied, this class is not designed for elegance or performance. It is designed only to work for the purposed of this chapter. With this helper class, we can move on to the BSP tree implementation.

Class Declaration

BSP trees seem complex at this point, correct? There are frontlists and backlists and splitter polygons and partitioning planes. Don't let the fancy terms fool you. A few data structures are easier to implement than tree-like data structures. In all such tree-based structures, traversing the tree in order to do something inside the tree or while building the tree in the first place involves just a single, simple function. The magic word in this context is "recursion." As a programmer, you should know about recursion.

Recursion means that a function calls itself until a certain stop condition is met. Examples are in the class for the BSP tree and in the class for the octree. Look at the class declaration for the BSP tree class so that you can see how simple it is:

```
class ZFXBspTree
   {
   public:
      ZFXBspTree(void);
      virtual ~ZFXBspTree(void);

      void      BuildTree(const ZFXPolygon*, UINT);
      void      TraverseBtF(ZFXPolylist*, ZFXVector,
                            const ZFXPlane*);
      void      TraverseFtB(ZFXPolylist*, ZFXVector,
                            const ZFXPlane*);

      ZFXAabb   GetAabb(void) { return m_Aabb;   }

      bool      LineOfSight(const ZFXVector&, const ZFXVector&);

      bool      TestCollision(const ZFXRay&, float, float*, ZFXVector*);
```

```
    private:
       ZFXAabb      m_Aabb;          // bounding box
       ZFXPlane     m_Plane;         // splitting plane
       ZFXBspTree *m_pBack;          // backlist
       ZFXBspTree *m_pFront;         // frontlist
       ZFXBspTree *m_pRoot;          // root node
       ZFXBspTree *m_pParent;        // parent node
       ZFXPolygon *m_pPolys;         // if leaf node
       UINT         m_NumPolys;      // if leaf node

       static UINT m_sNum;           // final poly count

       void CreateChilds(void);
       bool FindBestSplitter(void);
       void AddPolygon(const ZFXPolygon&);
       void CalcBoundingBox(const ZFXPolygon*, UINT);
       void SetRelationship(ZFXBspTree *R, ZFXBspTree *D) { m_pParent = D;
                                                            m_pRoot = R;}
       bool IsLeaf(void) {return (m_pFront==NULL)&&(m_pBack==NULL);}
    }; // class
```

This class is what you need to implement a BSP tree. Some people separate the design into two classes; one class is a carrier class for the access to the BSP tree, and the other class is for a node of the tree. The second class is an overkill and serves no real purpose. This is why I use only a single class. As you will see shortly, this class does not have many lines.

Most class names are self-explanatory. I do not show the implementations of the `ZFXBspTree::CalcBoundingBox` and `ZFXBspTree::AddPolygon` functions. You should know how to calculate a bounding box for a given number of polygons. Adding a polygon to a node of the tree is also easy. The polygon is stored in the member attribute `m_pPolys`, which is dynamically allocated to the number of polygons at the node. The two traverse functions are used to traverse the tree. One of the functions traverses the tree in back-to-front order and the other in front-to-back order. We discuss this later when we implement the functions.

Creating and Releasing Instances

Constructing and destroying an instance of the class `ZFXBspTree` is done in a similar way to other classes. The attributes are set to default values in the constructor and memory that is dynamically allocated is freed. There are two functions of the BSP tree class. Note that the dynamic memory needs to be adjusted at runtime when building the tree, and due to the lack of a custom memory manager, uses the old C-style memory allocation functions, as shown in the following:

```
ZFXBspTree::ZFXBspTree(void)
   {
   m_NumPolys = 0;
   m_pBack    = NULL;
   m_pFront   = NULL;
   m_pRoot    = NULL;
   m_pParent  = NULL;
   m_pPolys   = NULL;
   } // constructor
/*------------------------*/

ZFXBspTree::~ZFXBspTree(void)
   {
   m_NumPolys = 0;

   SAFE_FREE(m_pPolys);
   SAFE_DELETE(m_pFront);
   SAFE_DELETE(m_pBack);
   } // destructor
/*------------------------*/
```

Recursive Creation of the Tree

Because an instance of the class itself is used for all the nodes of the BSP tree and the root objects represent the whole tree to an external viewer, the class contains a separate function to kick off the recursive creation process of the tree. If you want a BSP tree, you must provide a list of polygons and the number of polygons in this list. The class ZFXBspTree will then create the whole tree.

The ZFXBspTree::BuildTree function then allocates the memory in the node object, which is the root, to take the whole polygon list and it copies the list from the parameter to its attribute. Note that the ZFXPolygon class also uses dynamically allocated memory, and therefore, you cannot simply copy the memory area of the list. You must copy the whole list polygon-by-polygon.

Then the recursive creation process is started by calling the private function ZFXBspTree::CreateChilds. This creates the tree based on the node from which it is called using this node's polygon list, as shown in the following:

```
void ZFXBspTree::BuildTree(const ZFXPolygon *pPolys, UINT Num)
   {
   m_pRoot   = this;
   m_pParent = NULL;
```

```
    if (Num<1) return;

    // allocate memory
    int nSize = sizeof(ZFXPolygon)*Num;
    m_pPolys = (ZFXPolygon*)malloc(nSize);
    memset(m_pPolys, 0, nSize);
    m_NumPolys = Num;

    for (UINT i=0; i<Num; i++) m_pPolys[i].CopyOf( pPolys[i] );

    // start recursion
    CreateChilds();
    } // BuildTree
```

The first thing you need to do for a node is calculate its bounding box by going through its polygon list and calculating its extends on the world axis. Then the function ZFXBspTree::FindBestSplitter is called to find the best splitter out of the list of polygons of this node. If this returns false, a splitter might not have been found and you can end the recursion in the branch because the geometry in the node's list is convex. In other words, the node is a leaf. If the function returns true, the best splitter has been found, its marker has been used as a splitter and is set, and the attribute m_Plane of the node is filled with the plane from the polygon used as the splitter. You must then divide the list of polygons into a frontlist and a backlist. This means you must create two new objects for the attributes m_pFront and m_pBack; these objects are the two children of this node.

Dividing the list of polygons is fairly easy. You just have to loop through the list of polygons and classify each polygon with respect to the plane of the splitter. If a polygon is located on the front side of the plane, it goes to the frontlist child; if it is located on the back side, it goes to the backlist child. If it lies in the plane, check the angle between its normal and the plane's normal. If this angle is zero, both normals are looking in the same direction and the polygon is sorted into the frontlist child, or it is sorted into the backlist child. The last possibility is that the polygon intersects the plane. If this is the case, clip the polygon into two pieces on the front side and on the back side of the plane, and then sort them into the appropriate lists.

This is all you need for the events that must be handled for a node of the BSP tree. You can then delete the list of polygons in this node if it is not a leaf. The node saves only the splitting plane, whereas the polygons are now temporarily saved in the node's two children. The function is called recursively on both children to proceed with the tree generation. That's all there is to it.

```
void ZFXBspTree::CreateChilds(void)
    {
    float      fDot=0.0f;
```

628 Chapter 13 ■ Scene Management

```cpp
ZFXPolygon plyFront, plyBack;
int        nFront=0, nBack=0, nClass=0;

CalcBoundingBox(m_pPolys, m_NumPolys);

// if no splitter found, this is a leaf
if ( !FindBestSplitter() )
   {
   ZFXBspTree::m_sNum += m_NumPolys;
   return;
   }

// create objects for the two children
m_pFront = new ZFXBspTree;
m_pBack  = new ZFXBspTree;
m_pFront->SetRelationships(m_pRoot, this);
m_pBack->SetRelationships(m_pRoot, this);

// sort polygons into the children
for (UINT i=0; i<m_NumPolys; i++)
   {
   nClass = m_Plane.Classify( m_pPolys[i] );

   if (nClass == ZFXFRONT)
      {
      m_pFront->AddPolygon( m_pPolys[i] );
      }
   else if (nClass == ZFXBACK)
      {
      m_pBack->AddPolygon( m_pPolys[i] );
      }
   else if (nClass == ZFXCLIPPED)
      {
      // split polygon at the splitting plane
      m_pPolys[i].Clip(m_Plane, &plyFront, &plyBack);

      m_pFront->AddPolygon( plyFront );
      m_pBack->AddPolygon( plyBack );
      }
   else if (nClass == ZFXPLANAR)
      {
      fDot = m_Plane.m_vcN * m_pPolys[i].GetPlane().m_vcN;
```

```
        if ( fDot >= 0.0f )
           {
           m_pFront->AddPolygon( m_pPolys[i] );
           }
        else {
           m_pBack->AddPolygon( m_pPolys[i] );
           }
        }
   } // for

// delete polygon list on inner leaves
SAFE_FREE(m_pPolys);

// RECURSION
m_pFront->CreateChilds();
m_pBack->CreateChilds();
} // CreateChilds
```

This function does not use a parameter because recursive functions will pump all of their parameters on the stack continually for each recursive call until the recursion ends in a branch finally. Only then are the parameters' values removed from the stack one after the other. If the recursion runs for too long and if you have too many parameters that are too big in size, you risk a stack overflow. Note that the same holds true for the local variables. You can use static attributes of the class for the integer counters and the two helper polygons, for instance. This optimization is up to you.

We are not yet done with creating the tree because we still have not seen the function to select the best splitter out of a list of polygons. We have seen only how to do this in pseudo code.

Selecting the Best Splitter

With a list of polygons, you can find the best splitter for the BSP algorithm as follows. Loop through the list of polygons in an outer loop. For each iteration of the loop, select the current polygon from the list and assume that it is used as splitter. Start an inner loop that also loops through the polygons in the list and classifies each polygon with respect to the polygon that is currently acting as the splitter. Count how many of the polygons are on the front side, on the back side, and how many polygons get split. When the inner loop is done, calculate the score for the polygon that is supposed to be the splitter and compare that score to the best (lowest) score you have found. Keep a pointer to the polygon with the lowest score because the greater the score, the worst off the polygon is to act as the splitter.

630   Chapter 13 ■ Scene Management

At the end of the function, you need to check if there is at least one splitter and if there is at least one polygon on either side of this splitter. If this is not the case, then you have not found a valid splitter and the geometry in the list of this node is convex. If a splitter is found, save its plane into the appropriate attribute of the node. Here is the complete function to find the best splitter:

```
bool ZFXBspTree::FindBestSplitter(void)
   {
   ZFXPolygon *pBestSplitter=NULL, *pSplitter=NULL;
   ZFXPlane    Plane;
   LONG     lFront  = 0,     // how many polygons lay in
            lBack   = 0,     // front, back, and planar
            lPlanar = 0,     // or spanning with regard
            lSplits = 0;     // to each possible splitter
   int      nClass;
   LONG     lScore, lBestScore = 1000000;
   bool     bFound = false;

   for (UINT i=0; i<m_NumPolys; i++)
      {
      pSplitter = &m_pPolys[i];
      Plane     = pSplitter->GetPlane();

      // reset counters
      lFront = lBack = lPlanar = lSplits = 0;

      // has been used as splitter already?
      if ( pSplitter->GetFlag() == 1 ) continue;

      // test all polygons as splitter
      for (UINT j=0; j<m_NumPolys; j++)
         {
         if (i==j) continue;

         nClass = Plane.Classify( m_pPolys[j] );
         if      ( nClass == ZFXFRONT  ) lFront++;
         else if ( nClass == ZFXBACK   ) lBack++;
         else if ( nClass == ZFXPLANAR ) lPlanar++;
         else                            lSplits++;
         } // for

      // CALCULATE SCORE
      lScore = abs(lFront - lBack) + (lSplits * 3);
```

```
      if (lScore < lBestScore)
         {
         if ( ((lFront > 0) && (lBack > 0)) || (lSplits > 0) )
            {
            lBestScore = lScore;
            pBestSplitter = pSplitter;
            bFound = true;
            }
         } // if [ulScore]
      } // for

   // no splitter can be found
   if ( !bFound ) return false;

   // mark polygon, save splitter plane
   pBestSplitter->SetFlag(1);
   m_Plane = pBestSplitter->GetPlane();
   return true;
   } // FindBestSplitter
```

Note that you can adjust the heuristic used here. If you want a strictly balanced tree to keep the search times steady, you have to ignore the number of splits. However, if you want to ignore the balance of the tree and still keep the tree smaller by avoiding splits, you have to increase the penalty factor.

Traversing the Tree

The BSP tree is ready for action now. As discussed previously, you need a function that traverses the tree and collects a list of polygons from the tree that can be used for rendering in this case. In addition to a list in which the collected polygons are stored, the function for the traversal takes the position of the viewer and the view frustum as parameters. The view frustum is needed to do a view frustum culling with the bounding boxes stored at each node of the tree to skip non-visible parts of the tree as soon as possible, which is the task of scene management. The position of the viewer is necessary to sort the polygons collected from the BSP tree. As I said previously, the BSP tree already stores the data in a specific way. That is not strictly true, but while traversing the tree you can traverse it in a certain order to get the output list sorted.

You can sort polygons in one of two ways. You can traverse the tree in a back-to-front manner. The resulting list of polygons you extract from the tree is ordered starting with the most distant polygons first. Because of the convexity of the leaves, you will get the polygons to render without a depth buffer. This is not that important, but it does have a nice effect on BSP trees if you need to sort a model using transparency effects that must be sorted back-to-front to avoid flaws in the transparency effect when rendering more distant polygons after the closer ones.

On the other hand, the front-to-back ordering is currently better suited for faster rendering because early z culling will drop hidden pixels quickly.

First, I show you how to do the front-to-back traversal of the BSP tree. At each node, you start with the frustum culling. If the node is not totally outside of the view frustum, test if the node is a leaf. If it is a leaf, store all polygons from the leaf in the polygon list provided as a parameter. If it is not a leaf, things will get interesting. It is important to decide with which child you will continue the traversal first because this influences the sorting of the polygons in the final list. Classify the position of the viewer with regard to the splitting plane of the node. If the position is located on the back side of the plane, nothing on the front side of the plane can occlude anything on the back side of the plane. Thus, you will continue the traversal in the child that holds the list with polygons on the same side as the view position to have a front-to-back ordering.

The case of a planar classification of the position with regard to the splitting plane can be handled arbitrarily. In this case, you treat it as analogous to the front side case:

```
void ZFXBspTree::TraverseFtB(ZFXPolylist *pList, ZFXVector vcPos,
                              const ZFXPlane *Frustum)
   {
   // frustum culling for this node
   if (m_Aabb.Cull(Frustum,6 ) == ZFXCULLED) return;

   // leaves contain polygons
   if ( IsLeaf() )
      {
      for (UINT i=0; i<m_NumPolys; i++)
         pList->AddPolygon( m_pPolys[i] );
      }
   else
      {
      int nClass = m_Plane.Classify( vcPos );

      if (nClass == ZFXBACK) {
         m_pBack->TraverseFtB(pList, vcPos, Frustum);
         m_pFront->TraverseFtB(pList, vcPos, Frustum);
         }
      else {
         m_pFront->TraverseFtB(pList, vcPos, Frustum);
         m_pBack->TraverseFtB(pList, vcPos, Frustum);
```

```
        }
      }
    } // TraverseFtB
```

The other function that does a back-to-front traversal is now not very hard to write. The only thing you need to change is the order in which you continue the traversal at the child nodes. You need to order the more distant polygons first in the list. If the viewer is located on the front side of the plane, you can continue with the back list of the node because nothing on the front side list will be overdrawn by the polygons on the back side.

```
void ZFXBspTree::TraverseBtF(ZFXPolylist *pList, ZFXVector vcPos,
                             const ZFXPlane *Frustum)
   {
   // frustum culling for this node
   if (m_Aabb.Cull(Frustum,6 ) == ZFXCULLED) return;

   // leaves contain polygons
   if ( IsLeaf() )
      {
      for (UINT i=0; i<m_NumPolys; i++)
         pList->AddPolygon( m_pPolys[i] );
      }
   else
      {
      int nClass = m_Plane.Classify( vcPos );

      if (nClass == ZFXBACK) {
         m_pFront->TraverseBtF(pList, vcPos, Frustum);
         m_pBack->TraverseBtF(pList,  vcPos, Frustum);
         }
      else {
         m_pBack->TraverseBtF(pList,  vcPos, Frustum);
         m_pFront->TraverseBtF(pList, vcPos, Frustum);
         }
      }
   } // TraverseBtF
```

Collision Detection

If you use the BSP tree to store the data of a 3D, indoor level, you should also provide some functions to do a collision detection with the tree because that is the most important usage of BSP trees nowadays. The following function takes an instance of the ZFXRay class and checks the BSP tree to see if the ray collides with a polygon of the geometry inside the tree at a given length. Note that this function assumes that the origin of the ray is inside the empty space of the BSP tree.

The only place where such a collision can happen in the BSP tree is a leaf because that is the place where the geometry of the tree is stored. The algorithm is fairly easy because it works as if you are sorting a polygon into the tree. You dump the ray into the root node of the BSP tree and classify the ray at each node with the node's splitting plane. If the ray intersects the plane at its given length, you cut the ray into two separate rays with one in front of the plane and one in the back. Then dump the rays into the child of the node. If the ray does not intersect the plane, dump it into the child as it is. This is the whole algorithm. If a ray arrives in a leaf node, test all polygons in this leaf for a collision with the ray using the function of the ray class. If one of the polygons is hit by the ray, you can conclude that the ray has collided with the level geometry.

```
bool ZFXBspTree::TestCollision(const ZFXRay &Ray,
                               float fL, float *pfD,
                               ZFXVector *pvcN) {
   ZFXRay rayFront, rayBack;
   int    nFront=0;

   // THIS IS A LEAF
   if ( IsLeaf() )
      {
      for (UINT i=0; i<m_NumPolys; i++)
         {
         // collision with a polygon?
         if ( m_pPolys[i].Intersects(Ray,false,fL,0) )
            {
            if (pvcN)
               *pvcN = m_pPolys[i].GetPlane().m_vcN;
            return true;
            }
         } // for
      return false;
      }

   // ELSE THIS IS AN INNER NODE
   int nClass = m_Plane.Classify( Ray.m_vcOrig );

   // ray intersects split plane?
   if ( m_Plane.Clip(&Ray, fL, &rayFront, &rayBack) )
      {
      // search in front-to-back order
```

```
      if ( nClass == ZFXBACK )
         return m_pBack->TestCollision(rayBack,  fL, pfD, pvcN)
             || m_pFront->TestCollision(rayFront, fL, pfD, pvcN);
      else
         return m_pFront->TestCollision(rayFront, fL, pfD, pvcN)
             || m_pBack->TestCollision(rayBack,   fL, pfD, pvcN);
      }
   else
     {
     if ( nClass == ZFXBACK )
        return m_pBack->TestCollision(Ray,fL,pfD,pvcN);
     else
        return m_pFront->TestCollision(Ray,fL,pfD,pvcN);
     }
   } // TestCollision [ray]
```

Note that it is imperative to keep an eye on the order of traversal here. The point behind the collision detection is to find the collision point (if any) that is closest to the origin of the ray. Do the traversal into the children in the front-to-back order to find the closest leaf that collides.

With this function—which checks for a collision of the geometry in the BSP tree with a ray—you can also write a line of sight function. This can be used to check whether a monster can see a player inside the level or vice versa. This is most important for artificial intelligence, for example, because if the line of sight between two entities is occluded, they should not behave as if they can see each other. The exception to this case is when they have seen each other a moment before and still remember the event, of course. This is a matter of artificial intelligence implementation.

The following function checks to see if there is a free line of sight between two points:

```
bool ZFXBspTree::LineOfSight(const ZFXVector &vcA, const ZFXVector &vcB)
   {
   ZFXRay Ray;

   // ray from A to B
   ZFXVector vcDir = vcB - vcA;
   vcDir.Normalize();
   Ray.Set( vcA, vcDir );

   // test for collision
   return !TestCollision(Ray,vcDir.GetLength(),0,0);
   } // LineOfSight
```

You calculate the vector between the two points and take its length as the length for a ray and the normalized vector as the direction vector for the ray. Then just call the collision detection function using the ray to check to see if this ray collides with the level geometry. If this is the case, the hit polygon occludes the view between these two points. Note that if you want to check if a monster can see the player, it might not be enough to check the line of sight between the monster's eye point and the player's center point. If the player is, for example, partly hidden behind a box, its center will be occluded from the view but the monster will see the player's head. It is better to shoot rays to three or four points on the player to get a better result.

Implementing an Octree

Now that we've cultivated the BSP tree, we are pretty close to becoming master gardeners. Let's put our green thumb to the test yet again. This time I want you to plant an octree into the math library of the engine. Then, I show you a sample application that uses the BSP tree and the octree for collision detection and rendering.

In the first part of this chapter, you heard a lot about scene management and about the octree. In this part, we implement an octree; however, note that the octree I show you here is mainly designed for collision detection that uses scene management in a smart way. It is not designed to organize polygons to find optimal sets of primitives for rendering a given frame. This would involve sending vertex lists or triangle lists over the bus, which we want to avoid.

As you already know, an octree has eight children for each node, or no children for each leaf. The class we implement uses an array for eight children. It is unusual (and ugly) to use the indices 0 to 7 for these children so I want them to have names. Here is a list of the children with their names:

```
#define UP_NE  0       // upper north east
#define UP_NW  1       // upper north west
#define UP_SE  2       // upper south east
#define UP_SW  3       // upper south west
#define LW_NE  4       // lower north east
#define LW_NW  5       // lower north west
#define LW_SE  6       // lower south east
#define LW_SW  7       // lower south west
#define POLYS_PER_LEAF 10
```

A geometry is ordered into an octree by splitting the geometry into the children again and again until . . . until what? There are two popular ways to define the stop condition for this algorithm. First, you can stop it if you have a certain depth for the tree that equals the number of subdivisions you did. Second, you can stop it if the number of objects reaches a certain maximum value in a node. I chose to let the octree stop at a given number of polygons that are allowed in a leaf and this is what the define POLYS_PER_LEAF is for. You can always adjust this value and play around with it because the depth of the tree and the necessary cuts influence the performance.

The deeper the octree gets, the longer the search times in the tree until you reach a certain node (for example, in collision detection). On the other hand, the geometry contained in the octree is always the same. However, the smaller the leaves, the more polygons you will have because you need to clip big polygons until they fit into a certain leaf. Play around with this stop condition and see how the performance develops with changes in the values.

Class Declaration

This section shows you the class declaration for the octree. A few public functions indicate the simplicity of this class. In addition to the constructor and the destructor, there are two functions for collision detection and a traversing function that walks through the tree and collects the visible polygons. This is used like the BSP tree class implementation to collect a list of polygons that you need to render a given frame.

You should not use the octree for rendering polygons, especially not those polygons cut into pieces by the octree. It is still beneficial to include a render function for debugging purposes and to have a visual output in this chapter's demo application. Following is the class declaration:

```
class ZFXOctree
   {
   public:
      ZFXOctree(void);
      virtual ~ZFXOctree(void);

      void      BuildTree(const ZFXPolygon*, UINT);
      void      Traverse(ZFXPolylist*, ZFXPolylist*,
                         const ZFXPlane*);
      ZFXAabb   GetAabb(void) { return m_Aabb; }

      bool      GetFloor(const ZFXVector&, float*, ZFXPlane*);
      bool      TestCollision(const ZFXAabb&, ZFXPlane*);
      bool      TestCollision(const ZFXRay&, float, float*);
   private:
      ZFXAabb     m_Aabb;            // bounding box
      ZFXPolygon *m_pPolys;          // if leaf
      UINT        m_NumPolys;        // if leaf
      ZFXOctree  *m_pChild[8];       // 8 children
```

```
        ZFXOctree  *m_pRoot;     // root node
        ZFXOctree  *m_pParent;   // parent node
        int        m_Pos;        // NO, NW, ...

        void CalcBoundingBox(const ZFXPolygon*, UINT);
        void InitChildObject(int ChildID, ZFXOctree *pP);
        void ChopListToMe(ZFXPolygon*, UINT);
        void CreateChilds(ZFXOctree *pRoot);
        void GetAabbAsPolygons(ZFXPolylist*);
        bool IntersectsDownwardsRay(const ZFXVector&, float);

        bool IsLeaf(void) { return (m_pChild[0]==NULL); }
        void SetBoundingBox(const ZFXAabb &Aabb) { memcpy(&m_Aabb, &Aabb,
                                                  sizeof(ZFXAabb)); }
    }; // class
```

There aren't a lot of attributes in this class. There is an axis-aligned bounding box, a list of polygons together with a counter for the number of polygons contained in this list, and an array of the eight child nodes. The polygon list attribute will only be used by leaf nodes, while the child node attributes will only be used by non-leaf nodes. You can also see that this class does not implement a carrier class COctree and a class for its elements, such as COctreeNode. You can also use such a design, but it is not necessary because the octree acts as the root node object from which you can access the entire tree, and the creation process of the tree can be kept natively simple by using recursive functions as a member of this class. Note the attribute m_Pos in which a node stores the ID of its position relative to its parent.

What these private functions are for is revealed in the following sections. Each octree node has exactly eight children or none. If there is none, this node is a leaf of the tree. So you can check any of the child pointers you want to check. If it is NULL, the node is definitely a leaf.

Creating and Releasing Instances

The construction of an instance of the ZFXOctree class is as boring as the destructor, which is called for the deletion of the instance. The constructor sets default values to the attributes and the destructor cleans up attributes by releasing dynamically allocated memory. For the leaf nodes, this is a list of polygons, and for all other nodes in the octree, you have to delete the object created for their children.

```
ZFXOctree::ZFXOctree(void)
   {
   m_NumPolys = 0;
   m_Pos      = -1;
```

```
   m_pPolys   = NULL;
   m_pRoot    = NULL;
   m_pParent  = NULL;

   for (int i=0; i<8; i++) m_pChild[i] = NULL;

   memset(&m_Aabb, 0, sizeof(ZFXAabb));
   } // constructor
/*----------------------------------*/

ZFXOctree::~ZFXOctree(void)
   {
   m_NumPolys = 0;

   SAFE_DELETE_A(m_pPolys);

   for (int i=0; i<8; i++) {
      SAFE_DELETE(m_pChild[i]);
      }
   } // destructor
```

Initializing a Child Node

Before we start the implementation of the octree creation process and a helper function for the collision detection, I want to show you a function of this class. This function initializes a certain child of a node from the octree where most of the initialization necessary deals with the creation of the bounding box for this child. Because of the even separation of a node into eight cubes of the same size, you can calculate that part of the node's bounding box for a specific child.

Following is the function that takes the ID of the concerned child and a pointer to the parent:

```
void ZFXOctree::InitChildObject(int ChildID, ZFXOctree *pParent)
   {
   ZFXAabb aabb;

   float xmin = m_Aabb.vcMin.x, xcen = m_Aabb.vcCenter.x,
         xmax = m_Aabb.vcMax.x;

   float ymin = m_Aabb.vcMin.y, ycen = m_Aabb.vcCenter.y,
         ymax = m_Aabb.vcMax.y;

   float zmin = m_Aabb.vcMin.z, zcen = m_Aabb.vcCenter.z,
```

```
            zmax = m_Aabb.vcMax.z;

   switch(ChildID)
      {
      case UP_NW:
         aabb.vcMax = ZFXVector(xcen, ymax, zmax);
         aabb.vcMin = ZFXVector(xmin, ycen, zcen);
         break;
      case UP_NE:
         aabb.vcMax = m_Aabb.vcMax;
         aabb.vcMin = m_Aabb.vcCenter;
         break;
      case UP_SW:
         aabb.vcMax = ZFXVector(xcen, ymax, zcen);
         aabb.vcMin = ZFXVector(xmin, ycen, zmin);
         break;
      case UP_SE:
         aabb.vcMax = ZFXVector(xmax, ymax, zcen);
         aabb.vcMin = ZFXVector(xcen, ycen, zmin);
         break;
      case LW_NW:
         aabb.vcMax = ZFXVector(xcen, ycen, zmax);
         aabb.vcMin = ZFXVector(xmin, ymin, zcen);
         break;
      case LW_NE:
         aabb.vcMax = ZFXVector(xmax, ycen, zmax);
         aabb.vcMin = ZFXVector(xcen, ymin, zcen);
         break;
      case LW_SW:
         aabb.vcMax = m_Aabb.vcCenter;
         aabb.vcMin = m_Aabb.vcMin;
         break;
      case LW_SE:
         aabb.vcMax = ZFXVector(xmax, ycen, zcen);
         aabb.vcMin = ZFXVector(xcen, ymin, zmin);
         break;
      default: break;
      }

   aabb.vcCenter = (aabb.vcMax + aabb.vcMin) / 2.0f;

   m_pChild[ChildID] = new ZFXOctree();
```

```
m_pChild[ChildID]->SetBoundingBox(aabb);
m_pChild[ChildID]->m_Pos     = ChildID;
m_pChild[ChildID]->m_pParent = pParent;
} // InitChildObjects
```

Recursive Creation of the Tree

Now we can build the tree. Surprisingly, the functions to create the tree recursively are simple; this is true for all algorithmically created, tree-like data structures. I'll try to make it more complicated so that you won't get offended by how easy it is.

The following function has to be called a single time for the root node of the octree and it is the kick-off point for the tree creation process. The application that needs to have an octree will provide a list of polygons to this function along with the number of polygons contained in this list. The root node copies the list into its own attribute and then builds the tree by calling the ZFXOctree::CreateChilds function. This is the workhorse function, which results in the recursive creation of the tree. It is best to separate these two calls because the recursive function will then be easier without differentiation for the root node as kick-off point.

```
void ZFXOctree::BuildTree(const ZFXPolygon *pPolys, UINT Num)
   {
   m_pRoot = this;

   if (Num<1) return;

   // calculate AABB for the root node
   CalcBoundingBox(pPolys, Num);

   m_pPolys = new ZFXPolygon[Num];
   m_NumPolys = Num;

   for (UINT i=0; i<Num; i++)
      m_pPolys[i].CopyOf( pPolys[i] );

   // calculate the children
   CreateChilds(this);

   SAFE_DELETE_A(m_pPolys);
   } // BuildTree
```

The address of the root node is taken through the whole tree without changing it. Then each node needs a pointer to the root. This is not actually needed, but it does not hurt to store this piece of information just in case. Then the function ZFXOctree::CreateChilds checks the stop condition for the creation process, which is the number of polygons in a leaf. If there are too many polygons, you need to build another eight children for this node. Here is how you would do that:

- Initialize the eight child objects.
- Clip the polygon list to the child nodes.
- Recursively create the children of the child nodes.

You treated the initialization of the children previously. The only thing you need to do is set up the bounding box as part of its parent node's box. The third step is also trivial because this is the only recursive call of the same function. The second step clips the list of polygons to a child node.

Following is the function that builds the octree in a recursive process until the stop condition is met and a leaf is built:

```
void ZFXOctree::CreateChilds(ZFXOctree *pRoot)
   {
   // save address of the root node
   m_pRoot = pRoot;

   // go on?
   if ((pRoot == this) || (m_NumPolys > POLYS_PER_LEAF))
      {
      // initialize children
      for (int i=0; i<8; i++)
         {
         InitChildObject( i, this );

         // build polygonlist for the child
         m_pChild[i]->ChopListToMe(m_pPolys, m_NumPolys);
         m_pChild[i]->CreateChilds(pRoot);
         }

      SAFE_DELETE_A(m_pPolys);
      }
   // no, this is a leaf
   else return;
   } // CreateChilds
```

Again this function is not the stuff that makes up the octree. The most interesting part is the ZFXOctree::ChopListToMe function. This function cuts the polygons or the partial polygons from the list of the given node, which fits into the bounding box of the eight children respectively. As you can see, the function deletes the list at each node after its children are done with it. These lists are not needed because only the leaves will keep their lists and provide the geometry for collision tests. So you just have to remove the redundant data.

Clip the Polygon List to a Node

If a node should select only those polygons from a list that are included inside its bounding box, then there are two very easy cases to be dealt with. If a polygon from the list is totally outside of the box, it is ignored. If it is inside the box, it is added to the list of the node in question. However, if a polygon intersects the box and is partially inside, you have to use one out of two different strategies. The first one might include this polygon in the node's main list, but only if its center is in the node. Otherwise, store it as a visitor if its center is not inside this node. The second strategy is to cut the polygon so that it fits exactly into the node's bounding box. Then save it for the node.

This is how the octree in the following code works. The geometrical data is multiplied by introducing more polygons than the number in the original list. It is still easier to do collision detection this way. The 3D math library of the ZFXEngine is great because it contains the objects and methods you need to do this:

```
void ZFXOctree::ChopListToMe(ZFXPolygon *pList, UINT Num)
   {
   ZFXPolygon ChoppedPoly;
   int nClass=0;

   if (Num < 1) return;

   // better safe than sorry ...
   SAFE_DELETE_A(m_pPolys);
   m_NumPolys = 0;

   ZFXPolygon *TempMem = new ZFXPolygon[Num];

   // loop through the list
   for (UINT i=0; i<Num; i++)
      {
      if (pList[i].GetFlag() == 1) continue;

      ChoppedPoly.CopyOf( pList[i] );

      nClass = ChoppedPoly.Cull(m_Aabb);

      // polygon outside the AABB
      if (nClass == ZFXCULLED) continue;
```

```
         // polygon contain in or intersecting the AABB
         else {
            // flag if contained
            if ( nClass != ZFXCLIPPED) pList[i].SetFlag(1);

            // else clip polygon
            else ChoppedPoly.Clip(m_Aabb);

            // add to temporary list
            TempMem[m_NumPolys].CopyOf(ChoppedPoly);
            m_NumPolys++;
            }
         }

      // copy temporary list to this node
      m_pPolys = new ZFXPolygon[m_NumPolys];

      for (UINT j=0; j<m_NumPolys; j++) m_pPolys[j].CopyOf( TempMem[j] );

      delete [] TempMem;
      } // ChopListToAabb
```

As a parameter, you provide the list of polygons to this function, which comes from the parent node. The function then loops through the list of polygons and builds a copy of the current polygon. It also does a culling test for this polygon. If the polygon is outside of this node's bounding box, the next polygon is tested. If it is inside, it is added to a temporary list and its flag is set to 1. With this flag set, the neighboring nodes (which are children of the same parent and get the same list) can then ignore these polygons without additional tests. If the culling test reveals that the polygon is only partially inside of the box, clip the copy of the polygon so that it fits in the box. This clipped polygon is then added to the temporary list. Luckily, this clipping is implemented in the math library of the engine so the code of this function is still short and straightforward.

At the end of the function, the temporary list is copied into the list of the node. Now this node contains this part of the geometry that fits into its bounds. However, copying this list is an annoying task because the class `ZFXPolygon` uses dynamically allocated memory so you cannot simply copy the entire list at one time. You have to loop through the list and copy each element; this in turn results in more memory allocations. This process is rather slow, especially for a lot of geometry. It is worth a thought to revisit the polygon class and to look at it to use a static array for its data. This limits the number of points a polygon can have and it will waste the memory of polygons that are smaller than the maximum number. But this will speed up creating instances of the class.

Collision Detection in the Octree

One of the most important uses for the octree class is collision detection. We have to implement functions for this purpose. To start, I show you how to implement a function that checks for whether or not a given bounding box in world coordinates collides with geometry stored in the octree. To do this you first dump the bounding box into the root of the octree. At each node, you have to test the bounding box to see if it intersects the node's bounding box. If it does not intersect, you can leave this branch alone because collision cannot occur in the geometry of its leaves. If a collision occurs, you have to check the eight children of the node to see which ones are involved. This can be done by calling the function recursively on the child nodes.

If the box that is checked for collision arrives at a leaf of the octree, you have to test all polygons that sit inside the leaf to see if one of them collides with the bounding box. If a collision is found, the function will end its test and return true to the caller. Note that this does not find the closest point of intersection, but a bounding box can collide with a huge number of polygons depending on the size of the box and on the size of the polygons. The question is, "What is the first point of collision and which polygon is the one that is intersected?" You must use other methods to evaluate this, such as shooting a ray into the octree.

Following is the function for the bounding box collision:

```
bool ZFXOctree::TestCollision(const ZFXAabb &aabb, ZFXPlane *pP)
   {
   // test collision in this node
   if (this != m_pRoot) {
      if (!m_Aabb.Intersects(aabb))
         return false;
      }

   // no geometry, just a node
   if ( !IsLeaf() ) {
      for (int i=0; i<8; i++)
         {
         // check children for collision
         if ( m_pChild[i]->TestCollision(aabb, pP) ) return true;
         } // for

      // none of the children collided either
      return false;
      } // if [!leaf]

   // this is a leaf with geometry
```

```
      else {
        if (!m_pPolys) return false;

        // test all polygons for collision
        for (UINT i=0; i<m_NumPolys; i++)
           {
           if (m_pPolys[i].GetAabb().Intersects(aabb))
              {
              if (pP) *pP = m_pPolys[i].GetPlane();
              return true;
              }
           }
        // no collision in this leaf
        return false;
        }
     } // TestCollision [aabb]
```

The second collision detection function we want to implement is the one between the octree geometry and a ray. You can use this function, for example, to calculate whether the line of sight is occluded or not. Such a check is important when evaluating if a bot can see the player inside the level. You shoot a ray from the eye point of the bot to the position of the player (the center of its bounding box) and test to see if any of the geometry inside the octree blocks the ray.

This function looks similar to the one for the collision detection that uses bounding boxes, discussed previously. However, there is a small and important difference. If you manage to get to a leaf with the ray, you have to search the closest one with regard to the ray's origin. Do not just take the first collision that occurs. You can take any leaf, but you should take the polygon that is closest to the ray origin if you want to use the function for other things later, such as painting bullet hole decals onto levels walls.

```
bool ZFXOctree::TestCollision(const ZFXRay &Ray, float fL, float *pfD)
   {
   bool   blnCollision=false;
   float  _fD=0.0f;

   // collision in this node
   if (this != m_pRoot)
      {
      if ( !m_Aabb.Intersects(Ray, fL, pfD) &&
           !m_Aabb.Contains(Ray, fL) )
         return false;
      }
```

```
// no geometry, just a node
if ( !IsLeaf() ) {
   for (int i=0; i<8; i++)
      {
      // check the children
      if ( m_pChild[i]->TestCollision(Ray, fL, pfD) ) return true;
      } // for

   // none of the children collided
   return false;
   } // if [!leaf]

// this is a leaf with geometry
else {
   if (!m_pPolys) return false;

   // test all polygons for collision
   for (UINT i=0; i<m_NumPolys; i++)
      {
      if (m_pPolys[i].Intersects(Ray,false,fL,&_fD))
         {
         blnCollision = true;
         if (!pfD) return true;

         // get the closes collision point
         if ( (*pfD<=0.0f) || (_fD < *pfD))
            *pfD = _fD;
         }
      }
   return blnCollision;
   }
return false;
} // TestCollision [ray]
```

Player's Height in the Octree

A special problem addressed with collision detection is finding the closest polygon below a given position in 3D space. The position can be the position of a player in the level. If you want to get the height of a player in the level, you need to start a ray that originates at the player's head from its current position and fire the ray down. If you find the closest polygon hit in the octree by this ray, you have found the polygon on which the player is or should be standing. This function can set the player to the correct height regardless of whether or not he walks down stairs or if he is on a ramp or on flat ground.

Chapter 13 ■ Scene Management

Obviously, this special ray goes straight down. This is a good simplification of the problem because you don't need to do a full ray versus a bounding box intersection test. You can just check if the given position where the ray originates is outside the box on the x- or the z-coordinate. If this is the case, the ray cannot hit the box. In addition, if the y-coordinate of the position is already under the box, the downward ray cannot hit the box either.

If the checks are negative, the ray must hit the bounding box. If only one of the conditions is true, the ray cannot hit the box, and you can skip the node for further tests. The following helper function encapsulates this simple check and evaluates with cheap calculations or even just comparisons whether or not the ray hits the box.

```
bool ZFXOctree::IntersectsDownwardsRay(const ZFXVector &vcOrig, float f)
   {
   // ray origin below this node
   if (vcOrig.y < m_Aabb.vcMin.y) return false;

   // on x-axis outside this node
   if (vcOrig.x < m_Aabb.vcMin.x) return false;
   if (vcOrig.x > m_Aabb.vcMax.x) return false;

   // on z-axis outside this node
   if (vcOrig.z < m_Aabb.vcMin.z) return false;
   if (vcOrig.z > m_Aabb.vcMax.z) return false;

   // minimal possible distance to this node is already
   // greater than current intersection found in "f"
   if (f < (fabs(m_Aabb.vcMax.y - vcOrig.y)))
      return false;

   return true;
   } // IntersectsDownwardsRay
```

With the helper function, you can write a function that is called with the root of an octree and that returns the height for a given position in the octree. This means that for a position in 3D space, you can determine the closest point of the level geometry stored in the octree. Here you are only interested in the closest point right below the given point. Of course you will use this function to get the height at which an object stands as it moves inside the geometry (the player or a monster, for example).

This function is similar to `ZFXOctree::TestCollision`, but you can apply some simplifications. You still do a collision detection using a ray from the given point. However, you know that this ray always points vertically down. A minor difference is that you cannot return from the function after the first point of collision is discovered. You must find the

Implementing an Octree

closest point under the given position so you have to loop through all children. And here is the code for this function.

```cpp
bool ZFXOctree::GetFloor(const ZFXVector &vcPos, float *pf, ZFXPlane *pPlane)
   {
   float   fAabbDist=0, fHitDist=0;
   bool    bHit=false;
   ZFXAabb aabb;
   ZFXRay  Ray;

   // if this is the root node
   if ( this == m_pRoot) *pf = 99999.0f;

   // no geometry just a node
   if ( !IsLeaf() ) {
      for (int i=0; i<8; i++)
         {
         // is ray intersecting any child at all?
         if ( m_pChild[i]->IntersectsDownwardsRay(vcPos, *pf) )
            {
            // intersection closer than current one?
            if (m_pChild[i]->GetFloor(vcPos, pf, pPlane))
               bHit = true;
            }
         } // for
      return bHit;
      } // if [!leaf]

   // this is a leaf with geometry
   else {
      if (!m_pPolys) return false;

      Ray.Set(vcPos, ZFXVector(0.0f,-1.0f,0.0f));

      for (UINT i=0; i<m_NumPolys; i++)
         {
         aabb = m_pPolys[i].GetAabb();

         // quick-test ray besides the polygon
         if ((Ray.m_vcOrig.x < aabb.vcMin.x) ||
             (Ray.m_vcOrig.x > aabb.vcMax.x) ||
             (Ray.m_vcOrig.z < aabb.vcMin.z) ||
             (Ray.m_vcOrig.z > aabb.vcMax.z) ||
```

```
                (Ray.m_vcOrig.y < aabb.vcMin.y) )
                continue;

            // full blown collision test
            if (m_pPolys[i].Intersects(Ray, true, *pf, &fHitDist))
                {
                *pf = fHitDist;
                bHit = true;
                }
            } // for
        return bHit;
        }
    } // GetFloor
```

You only need to build the ray that you do the collision test with to get the height in a leaf. Thanks to quick checking, if a downward ray does intersect the bounding box of a node at all, you can decide whether or not to check the children. At a leaf, you check the leaf's bounding box. If this still reports an intersection, you can loop through the polygons of the leaf and do a full collision test between the ray and the polygons. This results in a polygon that is hit and returns the point on which the polygon is hit. Note that the function will still loop through the rest of the polygons because there could be other polygons that get hit by the ray. Again, you need to find the one that is closest to the origin of the ray.

The octree is ready to be used in collision detection for a 3D geometry application that features indoor levels.

Traversing the Tree

The BSP tree class's traversing of the tree to collect the visible polygons for rendering is exciting in terms of front-to-back or back-to-front ordering. The function for the octree class is boring by comparison. If a current node is totally outside the view frustum, you can leave the current branch. If it is at least partially visible, go down to the eight children of the node by calling the function recursively until you finally reach a leaf of the tree.

In the BSP tree, you can see the space partitioning only by watching the cuts through the level geometry. In the octree, however, you can also render the bounding boxes of the leaves, which are the visualization of the octree itself. For the function to collect the polygons from the octree, provide an additional list to collect the polygons that make up the leaf's bounding boxes:

```
void ZFXOctree::Traverse(ZFXPolylist *pList, ZFXPolylist *pAabbList,
                        const ZFXPlane *pFrustum)
    {
    if (m_Aabb.Cull(pFrustum, 6) == ZFXCULLED) return;
```

```
   if ( IsLeaf() ) {

      if (pList)
         {
         for (unsigned int i=0; i<m_NumPolys; i++)
            pList->AddPolygon(m_pPolys[i]);
         }
      if (pAabbList) GetAabbAsPolygons(pAabbList);
      }
   else {
      m_pChild[0]->Traverse(pList, pAabbList, pFrustum);
      m_pChild[1]->Traverse(pList, pAabbList, pFrustum);
      m_pChild[2]->Traverse(pList, pAabbList, pFrustum);
      m_pChild[3]->Traverse(pList, pAabbList, pFrustum);
      m_pChild[4]->Traverse(pList, pAabbList, pFrustum);
      m_pChild[5]->Traverse(pList, pAabbList, pFrustum);
      m_pChild[6]->Traverse(pList, pAabbList, pFrustum);
      m_pChild[7]->Traverse(pList, pAabbList, pFrustum);
      }
   } // Traverse
```

Building a cube out of an axis-aligned bounding box instance is a bit of work, but it is not complicated. You know the center point of the box and its extensions on the three axes. With this information, it is not a problem to define the eight points in space that are the vertices for the cube. You can build the six rectangles that make up the six sides of the cube:

```
void ZFXOctree::GetAabbAsPolygons(ZFXPolylist *pList) {
   ZFXPolygon   Poly;
   ZFXVector    vcPoints[24];
   unsigned int nIndis[6] = { 0, 1, 2, 2, 3, 0 };

   float fW = m_Aabb.vcMax.x - m_Aabb.vcMin.x;
   float fH = m_Aabb.vcMax.y - m_Aabb.vcMin.y;
   float fD = m_Aabb.vcMax.z - m_Aabb.vcMin.z;

   // top rectangle
   vcPoints[0].Set( m_Aabb.vcCenter.x - (fW / 2.0f),
                    m_Aabb.vcCenter.y + (fH / 2.0f),
                    m_Aabb.vcCenter.z - (fD / 2.0f) );
   vcPoints[1].Set( m_Aabb.vcCenter.x - (fW / 2.0f),
                    m_Aabb.vcCenter.y + (fH / 2.0f),
```

```
                              m_Aabb.vcCenter.z + (fD / 2.0f) );
vcPoints[2].Set( m_Aabb.vcCenter.x + (fW / 2.0f),
                 m_Aabb.vcCenter.y + (fH / 2.0f),
                 m_Aabb.vcCenter.z + (fD / 2.0f) );
vcPoints[3].Set( m_Aabb.vcCenter.x + (fW / 2.0f),
                 m_Aabb.vcCenter.y + (fH / 2.0f),
                 m_Aabb.vcCenter.z - (fD / 2.0f) );
Poly.Set( &vcPoints[0], 4, nIndis, 6 );
pList->AddPolygon( Poly );

// right rectangle
vcPoints[4] = vcPoints[3];
vcPoints[5] = vcPoints[2];
vcPoints[6].Set( m_Aabb.vcCenter.x + (fW / 2.0f),
                 m_Aabb.vcCenter.y - (fH / 2.0f),
                 m_Aabb.vcCenter.z + (fD / 2.0f) );
vcPoints[7].Set( m_Aabb.vcCenter.x + (fW / 2.0f),
                 m_Aabb.vcCenter.y - (fH / 2.0f),
                 m_Aabb.vcCenter.z - (fD / 2.0f) );
Poly.Set( &vcPoints[4], 4, nIndis, 6 );
pList->AddPolygon( Poly );

// left rectangle
vcPoints[8] = vcPoints[0];
vcPoints[9] = vcPoints[1];
vcPoints[10].Set( m_Aabb.vcCenter.x - (fW / 2.0f),
                  m_Aabb.vcCenter.y - (fH / 2.0f),
                  m_Aabb.vcCenter.z + (fD / 2.0f) );
vcPoints[11].Set( m_Aabb.vcCenter.x - (fW / 2.0f),
                  m_Aabb.vcCenter.y - (fH / 2.0f),
                  m_Aabb.vcCenter.z - (fD / 2.0f) );
Poly.Set( &vcPoints[8], 4, nIndis, 6 );
pList->AddPolygon( Poly );

// backside rectangle
vcPoints[12] = vcPoints[2];
vcPoints[13] = vcPoints[1];
vcPoints[14] = vcPoints[10];
vcPoints[15] = vcPoints[6];
Poly.Set( &vcPoints[12], 4, nIndis, 6 );
pList->AddPolygon( Poly );
```

```
   // frontside rectangle
   vcPoints[16] = vcPoints[0];
   vcPoints[17] = vcPoints[3];
   vcPoints[18] = vcPoints[7];
   vcPoints[19] = vcPoints[11];
   Poly.Set( &vcPoints[16], 4, nIndis, 6 );
   pList->AddPolygon( Poly );

   // bottom rectangle
   vcPoints[20] = vcPoints[7];
   vcPoints[21] = vcPoints[6];
   vcPoints[22] = vcPoints[10];
   vcPoints[23] = vcPoints[11];
   Poly.Set( &vcPoints[20], 4, nIndis, 6 );
   pList->AddPolygon( Poly );
   } // GetAabbAsPolygons
```

I'm a little ashamed of this function. The amount of dynamically allocated memory is reason enough to never call this function at runtime. We still have to call this function, however, for each visible leaf of the octree. Therefore, keep in mind that this function is slow and it is used only to implement the functionality that allows you to visualize the octree. This functionality is not needed in a real application of course.

We can finally write a demo application that features an octree and a BSP tree for rendering and collision detection.

Demo Application: Octree and BSP Tree

Let's be clear about what we want to demonstrate for this application. Recall that we now have the classes ZFXBspTree and ZFXOctree inside the math library of our ZFXEngine. Both can be used to build the tree from a list of arbitrary polygons, which form a level. This tree can then be used for collision detection.

The demo application loads the data from a simple level file and builds an octree and a BSP tree from the geometry; it will also render the geometry on the screen. The viewer can then move around in the level using a free camera movement controller. The walls, floors, and ceilings of the level will block the player's movement if he collides with them. Rendering the geometry is done by the Traverse...() function of the tree that is currently active. As you will see from the frame rate, this method is not generally recommended.

At runtime, you can also switch the demo between three modes. The first mode uses the octree for rendering and collision detection. The second and the third option use the BSP tree for both whereas one option will render the BSP tree front-to-back and the other will render back-to-front. In the back-to-front sorting, the depth buffer will be switched so that you can see the BSP tree can do without it. Finally, there are two more options for rendering. One is the solid textured mode and the other is the wireframe mode. For the octree, the bounding boxes of the nodes from the tree are rendered so that you can see how the octree looks.

There is a small problem with texturing the level data. Because we do not save vertex lists with texture coordinates and texture files, but just polygons, which know nothing about normals or texture coordinates (they know only the position of their points in 3D space), there is no way to place good textures on the rendered output. Rendering without a texture is also not a good idea because the polygons would have the same color, and due to the lack of the normals, they would also have the same shading intensity making it impossible to see the shape of the geometry, except for the outline. We revisit this issue when we calculate simple, restorable texture coordinates on-the-fly in Chapter 14.

Rendering ZFXPolygon Instances

Let's start with rendering a list of polygons that are instances of the ZFXPolygon class. You will find the source code for this chapter on the CD-ROM; thus, I skip the WinMain() function and the message procedure callback in this section.

> **Caution**
>
> The demo application features an ugly and slow renderer. It takes the class ZFXPolygon, which is not designed to be used for rendering, and it builds a vertex list and an index list for the polygons. Each frame sends the polygons one-by-one to the renderer. Take this as an example of how it should not be done and how you can ruin a top-notch graphics adapter with just a few thousand polygons.

The following function lets you render a list of polygons in which a boolean flag says whether you should render in Wireframe mode or not.

```
void RenderPolylist(ZFXPolylist &List, bool bWired, const ZFXCOLOR *pClr)
   {
   ZFXPolygon  *pCP = NULL;
   UINT        i=0, j=0;
   ZFXAabb     aabb;
   float       fMaxX=0.0f, fMaxY=0.0;
   ZFXPolygon  *pPolys = List.GetPolylist();
   UINT        Num = List.GetNum();
   VERTEX      Verts[256];
   WORD        Indis[256];

   for (UINT p=0; p<Num; p++) {
      pCP = &pPolys[p];
```

```
         aabb = pCP->GetAabb();
         fMaxX = aabb.vcMax.x - aabb.vcMin.x;
         fMaxY = aabb.vcMax.y - aabb.vcMin.y;

         for (i=0; i<pCP->GetNumPoints(); i++) {
          memset(&Verts[i], 0, sizeof(VERTEX));
          Verts[i].x = pCP->m_pPoints[i].x;
          Verts[i].y = pCP->m_pPoints[i].y;
          Verts[i].z = pCP->m_pPoints[i].z;

          // TEXTURE-COORDINATES
          Verts[i].tu = Verts[i].x - aabb.vcMin.x / fMaxX;
          Verts[i].tv = Verts[i].y - aabb.vcMin.y / fMaxY;
          }

      if (!bWired) {
          g_pDevice->SetBackfaceCulling(RS_CULL_CCW);
          g_pDevice->SetShadeMode(RS_SHADE_SOLID,0,NULL);

          for (j=0; j<pCP->GetNumIndis(); j++)
             Indis[j] = pCP->m_pIndis[j];
          }
      else {
         g_pDevice->SetBackfaceCulling(RS_CULL_NONE);
         g_pDevice->SetShadeMode(RS_SHADE_LINES,0,pClr);

         for (j=0; j<pCP->GetNumPoints(); j++) {
           Indis[(j*2)] = j;
           Indis[(j*2)+1] = j+1;

           if (j==(pCP->GetNumPoints()-1))
              Indis[(j*2)+1] = 0;
          }
         j = 2 * pCP->GetNumPoints();
         }
      g_pDevice->GetVertexManager()->Render(VID_UU, i, j, Verts, Indis, 0);
      } // for
  } // RenderPolylist
```

Following is how it works: First you copy the position of the points from the polygon into the vertices. Then the texture coordinates are calculated on-the-fly for those vertices by using a very primitive form of planar texturing on the XY plane. When you implement the level editor in the next chapter, I show you how to do the planar texturing for all three possible world planes. The problem is that a polygon in the XY plane gets only the first row of pixels from the texture. These are then stretched over the polygon along the Z-axis. This isn't pretty, but it works for our purposes. The textures are used only to recognize and differentiate the single polygons of the geometry, which would otherwise have the same color, making it thereby impossible to see their actual shape.

After this is done, generate a list of indices to render the polygons. In the wireframe mode, the index list is built in a way to render the polygons as a closed line strip.

Loading the Level Data

You might ask where the test data comes from. Normally, people tend to hack simple .txt files that contain handcrafted simple models, and they leave it to the reader to build more complex models. I use a file with a data format that is not yet known to you. For the purpose of this demo application, you can find the file named TestLevel.pbp on the CD-ROM in the directory for this chapter. It contains a small corridor that is small because the renderer of this chapter is slow. The file itself is a Prefab file from the level editor you will implement in the next chapter, where you will also learn about the data format used.

This editor has a graphical user interface, and you can build static models or whole levels with the tool. The editor supports two data formats in its current version. The first format is the level format in which the spawn points, portals, information about the textures, and so on are saved in addition to the geometry. The second format is a simpler one that is used for Prefabs that contains only information about the geometry and the skin used for the polygons of the Prefab.

The file format of the Prefab is designed in a way that makes it very easy for the level editor to load the data. The binary file starts with the number of polygons in the file. The polygons follow one-by-one in the file. However, before each polygon starts, there is another number and a string without the zero terminating \0 sign. The number is the length of the string and the string contains the name of the graphics file that is used as texture for the polygon that will follow right after it. The texture is not used in this sample for the sake of simplicity. Note that this demo is not meant for visual appeal, but to demonstrate how to use the BSP tree and the octree for collision detection.

This is the function that lets you load a Prefab file *.pbp:

```
bool LoadLevel(const char *chFile)
   {
   ZFXPolygon *pList=NULL, Poly;
   char       buffer[2048];
   UINT       Num=0, n=0;

   FILE *pFile = fopen(chFile, "rb");
```

```
    if (!pFile) return false;

    // read number of polygons
    fread(&Num, sizeof(UINT), 1, pFile);
    if (Num == 0) return false;

    pList = new ZFXPolygon[Num];

    // load all polygons
    for (UINT i=0; i<Num; i++) {

       // read name of the texture
       fread(&n, sizeof(UINT), 1, pFile);
       fread(buffer, n, 1, pFile);
       buffer[n] = '\0';

       // load polygon from the file
       LoadPolygon(pFile, &Poly);
       pList[i].CopyOf( Poly );
       } // for

    // build BSP tree
    g_pBSPTree = new ZFXBspTree;
    g_pBSPTree->BuildTree(pList, Num);

    // build octree
    g_pOctree = new ZFXOctree;
    g_pOctree->BuildTree(pList, Num);

    fclose(pFile);
    if (pList) { delete [] pList; }
    return true;
    } // LoadLevel
```

After the polygons are loaded into the list, you have to build two trees that are from the list. First, you want to use a BSP tree that represents the same geometry with binary space partitioning and then you want to use the same geometry represented in an octree. The demo application can then switch between both at runtime. As you can see, the instances of the classes ZFXBspTree and ZFXOctree are global variables.

You still have not seen how to load the data for a single polygon from the file. This functionality is encapsulated in the function LoadPolygon(). This single polygon in the file first defines pieces of information similar to a header. The following information is at the head of each polygon:

- UINT   - number of vertices
- UINT   - number of indices
- UINT   - not used here (id of skin)
- ZFXAabb   - not used here
- bool   - not used here
- float[4]   - not used here (texture repeat/offset)

The vertices of the type VERTEX and the indices of the type WORD are next in the file and then there is a second index list. This second index list is the list of interfaces used to draw a closed triangle strip for the outline wireframe mode of the polygon. Direct3D can render only triangles in wireframe mode, not the outline of a polygon.

Following is the function that extracts the data for a polygon from the file and stores it in a ZFXPolygon instance. Note that this class is not meant for rendering; this is used to demonstrate the BSP and the octree.

```
void LoadPolygon(FILE *pFile, ZFXPolygon *pPoly)
   {
   UINT    NumVerts=0, NumIndis=0, ID=0;
   bool    bln=false;
   ZFXAabb aabb;
   float   f[4] = { 0.0f,0.0f,0.0f,0.0f };

   // read counters
   fread(&NumVerts, sizeof(UINT),    1, pFile);
   fread(&NumIndis, sizeof(UINT),    1, pFile);
   fread(&ID,       sizeof(UINT),    1, pFile);
   fread(&aabb,     sizeof(ZFXAabb), 1, pFile);
   fread(&bln,      sizeof(bool),    1, pFile);
   fread(f,         sizeof(float),   4, pFile);

   // allocate memory
   VERTEX *pvVerts = new VERTEX[NumVerts];
   WORD   *pwIndis = new WORD[NumIndis];
   WORD   *pDummy  = new WORD[NumVerts*2];

   ZFXVector *pvcPoints = new ZFXVector[NumVerts];
   UINT      *pnIndis   = new UINT[NumIndis];

   if ( !pvVerts  || !pwIndis || !pvcPoints || !pnIndis ) return;
```

```
// read data
fread(pvVerts, sizeof(VERTEX), NumVerts,   pFile);
fread(pwIndis, sizeof(WORD),   NumIndis,   pFile);
fread(pDummy,  sizeof(WORD),   NumVerts*2, pFile);

// convert vertices to vectors
for (UINT i=0; i<NumVerts; i++)
   pvcPoints[i].Set(pvVerts[i].x, pvVerts[i].y, pvVerts[i].z);

// convert WORD to UINT
for (UINT j=0; j<NumIndis; j++)
   pnIndis[j] = pwIndis[j];

// set data for the polygon
pPoly->Set( pvcPoints, NumVerts, pnIndis, NumIndis );

delete pvVerts;
delete pwIndis;
delete pvcPoints;
delete pnIndis;
delete pDummy;
} // LoadPolygon
```

You have successfully loaded the simple level data. Note that I use the term level generously here. What is actually here is a bunch of polygons that are ordered to look like a level of a first-person, indoor shooter. There isn't such a thing as spawn points, power ups, moving entities, doors, and so on, which would be needed for a real level. You will encounter a real level in Chapter 14.

Calculating a Frame

Now that you have saved the data for the simple level file in two trees, you can bring interactivity into the application. The application will use the Windows API for the user's input so the WinProc() function is used. A movement controller from the helper library is used to comply with the user's input commands.

The application will do the following: The movement controller will stay put in its position as the Update() function is called. Save the current position of the movement controller first, and then make the function call. Apply the collision detection by drawing a ray from the old position to the new one and call the TestCollision() function of the scene management tree, which is either the octree or the BSP tree.

The global variable g_bBSP controls whether the octree or the BSP tree should be used. The player can use the E key to toggle between the three variants because in addition to the octree, there are two BSP tree versions. To toggle between the front and back, render the global variable g_bFtB.

If the scene management tree reports back that a collision occurred with the ray between the old position and the new position, the player runs into a wall. You can put the movement controller back in the old position, ignoring the user's input. Then you set the position and orientation of the movement controller for the render device and start rendering. You have to traverse the active tree and collect the visible polygons from it. Finally, you render this list with the RenderPolygonlist() function, which was shown earlier in this chapter.

Following is the complete function to do this frame update:

```
HRESULT ProgramTick(void)
   {
   ZFXPlane    Frustum[6];
   ZFXPolylist List, AabbList;
   ZFXMatrix   mWorld;
   static ZFXCOLOR clrR = {1.0f, 0.3f, 0.3f};
   static ZFXCOLOR clrG = {0.0f, 0.7f, 0.0f};

   mWorld.Identity();

   g_pTimer->Update();

   // get current position
   ZFXVector vcOld = g_pMCEgo->GetPos(), vcNew(0,0,0);

   // update movement controller
   g_pMCEgo->Update( g_pTimer->GetElapsed() );

   // reset movement controller
   g_pMCEgo->SetSpeed(0.0f);
   g_pMCEgo->SetSlideSpeed(0.0f);
   g_pMCEgo->SetRotationSpeedX(0.0f);
   g_pMCEgo->SetRotationSpeedY(0.0f);

   // get new position
   vcNew = g_pMCEgo->GetPos();
   ZFXRay Ray; Ray.Set(vcNew, g_pMCEgo->GetDir());
```

```
   // if collision, then back to old position
   if ( g_bBsp ) {
      if (g_pBSPTree->TestCollision(Ray, 0.5f, 0, 0))
         g_pMCEgo->SetPos(vcOld);
   }
   else {
      if (g_pOctree->TestCollision(Ray, 0.5f, 0))
         g_pMCEgo->SetPos(vcOld);
   }

   // set position of the viewer
   g_pDevice->SetView3D(g_pMCEgo->GetRight(), g_pMCEgo->GetUp(),
                        g_pMCEgo->GetDir(), g_pMCEgo->GetPos());

   // get current view frustum
   g_pDevice->GetFrustrum( Frustum );

   // get polygonlist from the BSP tree
   if ( g_bBsp ) {
      if (g_bFtB)
         g_pBSPTree->TraverseFtB( &List, g_pMCEgo->GetPos(), Frustum );
      else
         g_pBSPTree->TraverseBtF( &List, g_pMCEgo->GetPos(), Frustum );
   }
   else {
      g_pOctree->Traverse( &List, &AabbList, Frustum );
   }

   g_pDevice->BeginRendering(true,true,true);
   mWorld.Translate(0.0f, 0.0f, 0.0f);
   g_pDevice->SetWorldTransform(&mWorld);

   if (g_bBsp) RenderPolylist(List,g_bWired,&clrR);
   else {
      RenderPolylist( List, g_bWired, &clrR );
      if (g_bWired) RenderPolylist(AabbList, g_bWired, &clrG);
   }
   return g_pDevice->EndRendering();
} // Tick
```

Figure 13.20 shows a screenshot of the demo application in action. Here, it currently renders the scene using the BSP tree. If you switch your attention from the cruel texture mapping to the wireframe representation of the scene, which is rendered as overlay, you can

Figure 13.20 A screenshot of the demo application using the BSP tree. The black lines show the scene in wireframe mode. You can see how arbitrarily the BSP algorithm cuts the level into pieces.

clearly see the arbitrary cuts through the scene that were introduced by the BSP tree (for example, look on the ceiling in the foreground of the screenshot).

Remarkable Things in the Demo

Now you have the demo up and running; what can you do with it? You can hit the E key to cycle through both BSP tree modes and the octree mode of the demo. From the textures, which look very ugly because of the weird texture coordinates, you can see the polygons and where cuts have been introduced. If you switch between the octree and the BSP tree, you can see jumps in the textures. The octree has clipped the polygons in a way that is different from the BSP tree.

The second observation you can make in the demo is the performance. Aside from the overall bad frame-rate and performance for this small geometry, you will see that the octree is much slower than the BSP tree. Look at the polygon counter displayed in the rendered image. The octree represents the same scene with three times as many polygons as the BSP tree. This is due to the fact that the octree introduces cuts through the geometry with respect to the world axis, as opposed to the BSP tree, which selects the partitioning planes based on the orientation of the geometry and which can be adjusted to avoid cuts. The BSP tree is still a very intelligent approach.

Note that the bad performance results from the bad rendering of the geometry. As you can see from the frame rate, the graphics adapter doesn't like it this way.

If you click the W button, you can toggle the wireframe mode rendering. In the BSP tree variants, you can clearly see the arbitrary cuts that run through the level. You would not believe from this representation of the scene that it is more optimal than the partitioning along the world axis; however, this is the case. It would be even better if you could render each polygon with a different color or if you could render each leaf of the BSP with a different color. You can also try to implement this in the demo.

Take a look at the wireframe mode rendering with the octree. You can spot the small cubes of the octree, and you can see that the more geometry there is in a location in space, the smaller the boxes you will see. The depth of the octree is deeper in spaces with more geometry versus less geometry.

One Look Back, Two Steps Forward

I talk about scene management for hours and cover several pages. We didn't even cover scene graphs in this chapter, which is an interesting and demanding topic due to the complexity of current video games and the question of how to sort geometry an optimal way. I also wanted to talk more about terrain rendering, which is a challenge to do even on current hardware. I hope this chapter provided enough information to help you learn more about scene management techniques.

The only rule for scene management is that you should not use only algorithm X or data structure Y because a great programmer will do this as well. If you get the ideas behind the algorithms and the data structures, you can customize them to fit your own project.

In the remaining two chapters of this book, I show you how to implement a level-editing tool and a simple network deathmatch game that uses the octree class from this chapter to do the collision detection. The functions for doing the collision detection are enough for the purpose of this book and the demo game. However, they could be better. You can enrich them to get the plane of collision to bounce the player and things like that. Based on the normal vector of the collision plane, you could also apply real physics to the colliding object.

Another thing you can test is building an octree for which the leaves are not too small, such as ten square meters in size. You can then put a BSP tree into each of the octree leaves and use BSP trees for the collision detection. The octree is better suited to include moving objects whereas the BSP tree is better and faster in collision detection. I cannot tell if such a hybrid approach is faster than a pure octree or a pure BSP tree version. It is up to you to test this and get ideas for hybrid approaches. In other words, think beyond the borders of well-known and proven methods.

In the next chapter, you learn how to implement a low-polygon level editor that you can also use to build low-polygon models.

PART IV
Black Art of Game Programming

Chapter 14
Computer-Aided Design (CAD) Tools 667

Chapter 15
Deathmatch Shooter 787

CHAPTER 14

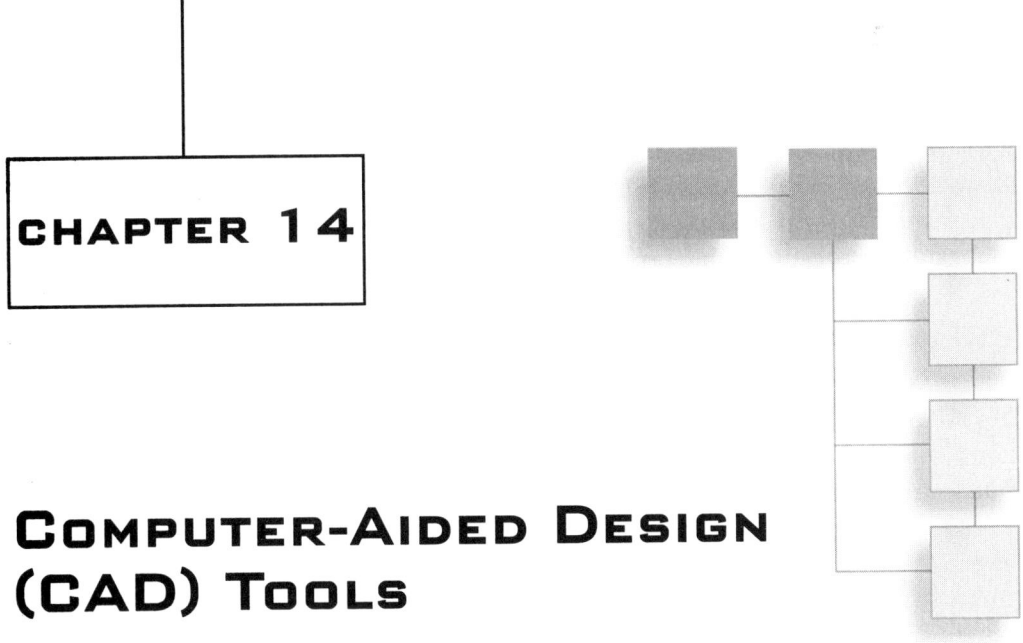

Computer-Aided Design (CAD) Tools

Pity is for free, but envy must be earned.

Old Chinese saying

Video game developers used to have to hack weird coordinates into text files to describe positions in three-dimensional space that would finally come together to form a nice-looking 3D model (a spaceship, a tank, or a ship, for example). In those times past, the graphics adapters and the central processing unit (CPU) were relatively limited, and so the models were not very complex. A detailed model used only a few dozen triangles, which made it easy to draw the model on a piece of paper to calculate the necessary vertices used for it. Those days of hard-coding are long gone. Models now are significantly more complex. Those early hard-coders don't have to feel any pity for today's programmers, however, because programmers today can use a low-polygon editor with a graphical user interface (GUI) to deal with those complex models. This chapter covers the following objectives:

- Level-editing tools
- The structure and design of CAD applications
- Implementing a low-polygon editor

Using CAD Tools

Although this is a book about game engines, a game engine is only one tool you need to develop a video game. Other important tools include editors to create game content. Therefore, this chapter covers a really usable level-editing tool that you could also adjust to be a model editor. You may be wondering whether it is worth the effort to implement a custom model-editing tool. After all, most 3D artists use commercial programs, such as Maya. What you learn in this chapter will be useful, however, because even with a commercial program you still need to have a tool to build your level (even if you use it only to place and arrange models built with another tool).

Engineer, Architect, and Game Developer

At the first glance, you may think that the professions of engineer, architect, and game developer have few, if any, things in common. However, they do have at least one thing in common: Each of these professions uses CAD tools. The acronym CAD stands for computer-aided design and refers to the support of human work in designing objects by software tools. Architects who work with pencil and paper are a vanishing species. Today, architects use CAD tools to develop their work on the computer. One famous architectural program is *ArchiCAD*, from Graphisoft. Engineers have been using CAD software for quite some time. One of the most prominent applications in this sector is *AutoCAD*, from Autodesk. And, of course, video developers use CAD tools. 3D artists use CAD software to develop 3D models that are then used in video games or even in Hollywood movies. A popular program in this sector is *3D Studio Max*, from Discreet (a division of Autodesk). The various CAD tools used in these professions offer similar functionality. Today, video game CAD tools are as full-featured as engineering CAD tools. Those tools have certainly come a long way. The first video game level-editing tools—*wadedit* for *Doom*, for instance, and *BUILD* for *Duke Nukem 3D*—offered limited functionality. For instance, users had to settle for a two-dimensional, top-down view of the level under construction.

Level-Editing Tools

The first level-editing tools were nothing more than just plain text-editing programs. You could adjust some values and attributes for variables used in the game. Even the simple layout of a level for an early video game could be fitted into a text file. Of course, this was not a very comfortable way to edit game data (such as levels), and this method has essentially gone the way of MS-DOS. The next evolutionary step was the two-dimensional editors that enabled developers to build levels from a bird's eye view of the virtual world and to place walls, doors, and objects with just a click. The two programs previously mentioned used this method. If you ever used the *BUILD* editor yourself, however, you know that the *Duke Nukem 3D* engine actually allowed for some three-dimensional construction, but it wasn't easy to use this editing tool to make use of that functionality (for instance, to place rooms above one other). In a simple top-down view on such a level, you would get lost in overlapping colored lines pretty fast.

The next evolutionary step of level-editing tools takes us to the ones available today. Those are level editors that look like professional CAD tools used by architects and engineers. One very famous example is the *Hammer* editor, by Valve, which was formerly known as

WorldCraft. Figure 14.1 shows this professional video game editing tool. By using such editors, the level designer now has total control in all three dimensions. In-game editors represent another interesting approach. In such an editor, you can walk or fly in a first-person view through the virtual game world featuring a terrain or just empty space. By clicking some interface buttons or just by pressing some keys, you can insert models and move them around. This interesting approach is the most intuitive one, but it is not suited for building huge indoor levels with a lot of detail. Although interesting, the concept isn't exactly new. Some years ago, the glorious *3D Construction Kit*, by Domark, enabled users to do exactly this. Basically, it worked by enabling you to place simple predefined shapes such as a rectangle, a sphere, or a cube in the virtual world. Then you could select the object and loop through the vertices of the object, which could then be translated. This system, which is just like deformable Lego cubes, enables users to build complex shapes, models, and even whole levels.

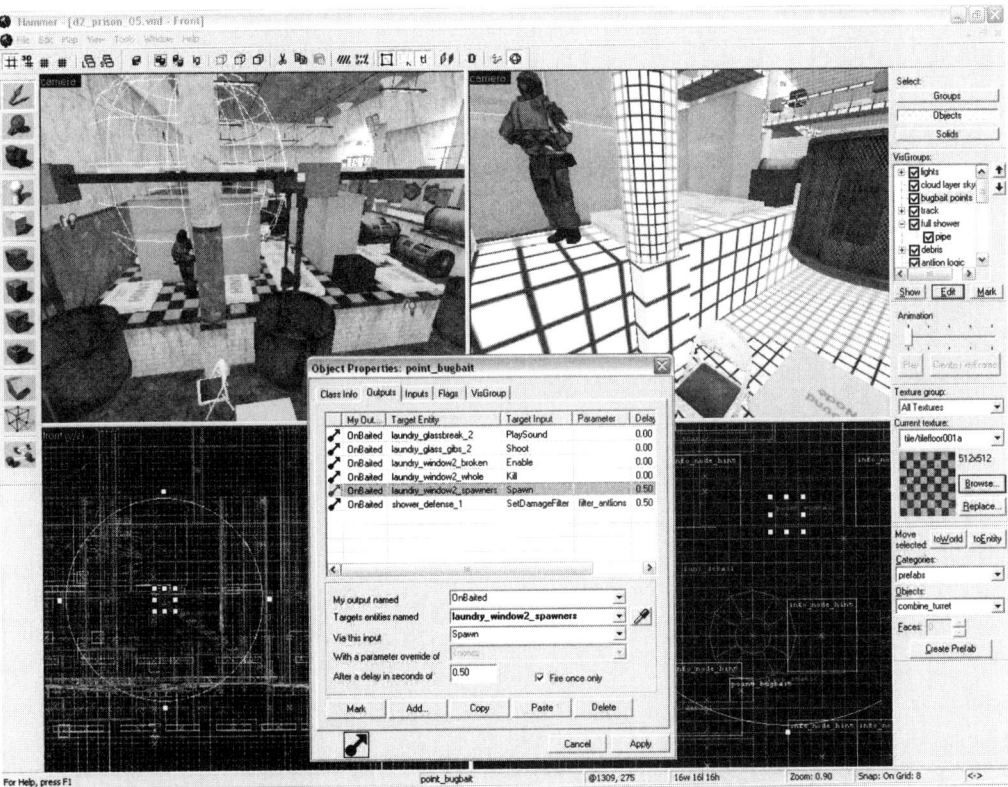

Figure 14.1 The Valve *Hammer* editor. You can see the typical layout using several child windows to display orthogonal and perspective views on the level under construction.

Low-Polygon Editor: *PanBox-Edit*

From the first chapter of this book onward, you have been reading about implementing a full-blown level-editing tool. Now this chapter introduces you to professional CAD software and video game level-editing tools. You may be thinking a single chapter can't possibly cover the integration of such tools. Think again; this chapter is longer than most in order to provide such coverage. Read on and you will find that it is possible to implement a low-polygon editing tool with a GUI. Don't worry, though; as with most things related to computer graphics, *complexity* does not necessarily translate to *complicated*.

This chapter is long, but by the end of it you will have the tool. Although it won't be of commercial quality, it will provide a platform to which you can add all kinds of desired functionality. By the end of this chapter, you will have a fully functional level editor that you can even use as a model editor. Although it will still lack features such as polygon reduction, animating objects, and things such as that, you can use it to build fully textured levels with custom lighting through a comfortable GUI. Figure 14.2 shows what the final tool will look like by the end of this chapter.

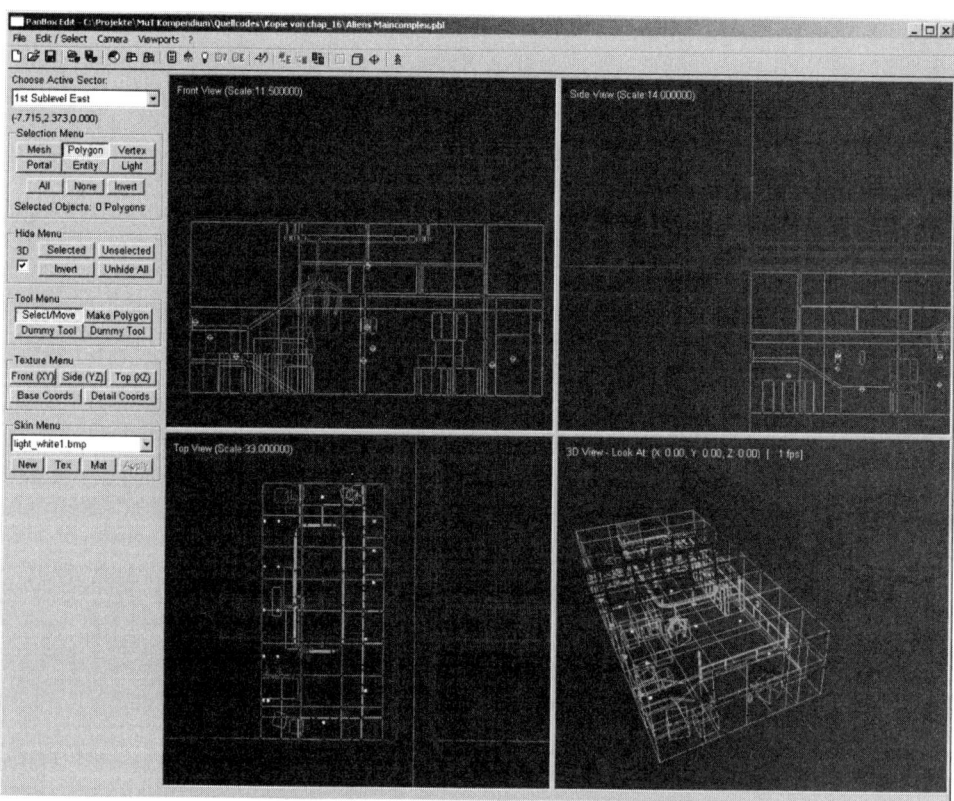

Figure 14.2 The *PanBox-Edit* tool implemented in this chapter.

PanBox-Edit Capabilities

The preceding section identified some functionality limitations that differentiate this tool from commercial CAD software. Whether those functionalities are integral for a level-editing tool is a debate for another venue. This chapter instead focuses on the features relevant to this tool. The tool implemented in this chapter is not limited to use with the ZFXEngine only, nor is it bound to (and therefore limited to) a certain video game project. Instead, the application is a standalone program that is not part of the engine, but that does use the engine for the rendering. As mentioned previously, *PanBox-Edit* is not equivalent to a commercial program; however, you can implement additional functionality into it. That said, by the end of this chapter, *PanBox-Edit* will enable us to build a textured 3D indoor level with light sources and usable doors and shadow-casting objects and to edit, save, and load this level. Those task generalities are achieved through specific subtasks, which are more or less a feature list for the editor, as follows:

- Create polygons and simple geometrical objects
- Edit polygons and objects down to the level of the vertices
- Delete and copy objects
- Select and hide objects
- Group geometry to a mesh
- Edit texture coordinates
- Load and save a level
- Load and save parts of the geometry as prefab
- Define spawn points for players in the game
- Set and edit point-light sources
- Flag objects that should throw shadow
- Define portals for the scene management

Tip

A *prefab* (from the word *prefabricated*) is a prebuilt object that you can place inside a virtual world by just loading it into a level. For instance, every office needs a desk. Therefore, you could build a detailed object representing a desk (maybe even with some pencils and papers on it). You could save this model as a prefab and use it each time you build a new office (by just loading it into the office). Prefabs are a time-saver, and you can enhance editing tools by providing a library of ready-to-use prefabs.

Although the preceding list may not identify every specific task, it provides a good starting point for this discussion. As you can see from this list, the level files will follow a portal-engine approach to scene management. Actually, this scene-management approach works well for the purposes of this chapter, and starts to get "interesting" only when you start implementing an application that is meant to display the levels as interactive environments (as in video games, for instance). Even still, the editor does enable the level designer to set portals if necessary. You may decide to ignore this feature altogether, or you may decide just to ignore the portals until you are loading the level into your game later on. The video game developed in Chapter 15, "Deathmatch Shooter," uses the portal information to perform scene management.

WinAPI Framework

This book is meant for advanced programmers, which means that you have to be familiar with, at a minimum, the WinAPI. The full source code of the editor is not listed in this book, but this chapter does cover the code relevant to 3D graphics. Also, be aware that this chapter skips the details of building WinAPI control elements such as buttons, combo boxes, menus, toolbars, and other similar things.

If you don't feel "up to speed" with the WinAPI, don't panic. The companion CD-ROM contains the entire source code. If you are a quick learner and know your way through the platform Software Developer's Kit (SDK) documentation that came with Visual C++, you should be able to figure this out on your own. If you need more information than that, however, consider finding a book that provides WinAPI exhaustive coverage. The authoritative book on this topic is *Programming Windows*, by Charles Petzold (Microsoft Press, 1998). This chapter covers the most interesting part of the editor: creating polygons, grouping them into meshes, and editing single vertices of a whole level. Now it's time to roll up your sleeves.

Class Design of the Tool

This section examines the design of the editor. That is, how the level data is stored and managed. You need to understand this because there are at least as many ways to do this as there are Elvis imitators. For instance, you could store the whole geometry in a big list of vertices with a big list of indices referencing it. Alternatively, you could use vertex buffers to hold the data. And so on, and so on, and so on. Before you start creating the biggest vertex buffer the world has ever seen, hold on a second. Although it is true that a static vertex buffer offers the best possible performance for your geometrical data, an editor is only an editor, not a video game. It simply doesn't matter that much whether the rendering is fast in the editor. It has to be only fast enough to handle big levels. The most important thing in an editor is not that you can render fast, but that you have fast and (most importantly) easy access to all the geometrical data down to the level of a single vertex you want to select and translate. If you were to use a static vertex buffer such as those Direct3D offers, you would have to lock the buffer and get its contents each time the level designer changes any of the geometry (something level designers do frequently in the level editor). Therefore, this editor uses a very different approach to dealing with this data.

Instead of storing all vertices in vertex buffers and accessing them all the time, the lowest level of the editor works with a class for a polygon that contains all its own vertices in a simple memory array of vertex structures. This method provides the easiest access to the data, and, as you will see by the end of this chapter, it is still fast enough to render even complex levels without noticeable slowdown in the frame rate.

Note

The class `ZFXPolygon` in the ZFXEngine's math library is meant just for mathematical calculations and collision detection. It stores only the position and normal vector information for the polygon. Therefore, we need a custom class for a polygon in the level editor that can handle a list of vertices and that can be rendered more easily.

During the rendering operation of the level, the editor sends each polygon one by one down the bus to be rendered by the graphics adapter. Normally, this is a declaration of war on the graphics adapter. If you were to use OpenGL, however, the driver would take care of the performance by batching the data together for fewer rendering calls. In our case, we are using our custom engine, which does the same thing with its vertex caches. Now you're probably pleased that you spent all that time writing the vertex cache manager. You can try to make a call to the `ForcedFlushAll()` function in the editor after each render call of a polygon. You'll then see the frame rate dying and note how Direct3D would fail to support you in this task (in contrast to OpenGL, which would support you).

Basic Structure of a Level

On the topmost layer of a level set, there is an object for the level itself. Therefore, we will have a class for such a level object within our code as well. In actuality, however, this class will be very boring because it does not contain much. You may find this surprising. After all, shouldn't the level contain the whole data set for a level of the game? Well, indeed it does, but only after the introduction of another layer, which is the workhorse in our application: the layer of sectors. Each sector is a part of the level with arbitrary size and shape. A sector can be a single room or it can be a bunch of rooms or a whole story. Although that is not important for managing the objects it contains, it is important for the performance in the video game you develop for the level data.

Sectors for Performance

Although Chapter 13, "Scene Management," covered scene management, it's important for you to remember several important points about scene management. Several years ago, old-fashioned scene-management algorithms such as binary space partitioning (BSP) were meant to find the exact pixel set that had to be rendered in a given frame. With current hardware, however, it is more important to find the set of triangles that are most likely (or even just potentially) visible.

The approach covered in Chapter 15 concentrates on visible sectors. Sectors are evaluated only when they are visible, and then the whole sector gets rendered along with all objects it contains without further culling of the geometry. Well I guess now it is time to duck in order to avoid the incoming stones being thrown upon me. Although you may be familiar with BSP and want to stick to what's familiar, it's really just a waste of time to do this strict BSP thing with current hardware. (And, hey, don't shoot the messenger!) The graphics adapter transforms and rejects hidden objects faster than a CPU can calculate culling. That last statement isn't absolute, however. Many algorithms enable you to find potential visibility sets, and that might be a reasonable approach to take (especially when you are using a lot of effects or render passes on each triangle you will output to the screen).

However, the bottom line is that you should let the graphics processing unit (GPU) do as much work as it can. And that is a lot.

The culling should take place at the topmost levels in a hierarchical system, and it should be switched off if you cross a certain boundary while heading downward through the geometry. Culling away single objects is still a good idea under certain conditions (if those objects are detailed, animated, shadow-casting characters, for example). However, it is not ideal to try and cull away single walls from a big room of an indoor level. You would find it faster just to render the whole room after you have evaluated that the room is at least partially visible.

As you might expect from this discussion, the approach the game in the next chapter takes is to check just the visibility of a sector. If the sector object is visible, it gets rendered with all its geometry. Still, however, you can control the level of culling by making the sector big or small in the editor, but it is recommendable not to make them too small. (A single room is fairly small in this context.)

Level Objects in a Sector

All objects contained inside a level are level objects, except for the management layer of the sector objects. Such objects are polygons or light sources, for example. Because the sectors are meant as management layers, however, those objects are not stored in the level class. An instance of the level class has only a list of sectors. The sectors in turn have a list of level objects that are inside the sector. The following list shows the kinds of level objects implemented in the level editor:

- Polygons
- Meshes
- Light sources
- Portals
- Entities
- Spawn points
- (Vertices)

Polygons, in this context, are self-explanatory. A mesh, which should be called polymesh if we want to stick to a strict mathematical language, is just a bunch of polygons grouped together to form something like a model. The only type of light source supported in the editor is omni lighting done by shaders (which you learned about earlier in this book). Besides that, there will only be ambient light. The use of the portals should also be clear by now, and you might already know a bit about entities. The only type of entity implemented here is a sliding door. The spawn points are the points where a player can enter the level or where a bot is placed.

The category Vertices appears in this list in parentheses because there is no separate explicit class for them. Vertices are used here only as structures, and a list of vertices is an attribute of the polygon class. However, still they are editable, of course. The following sections examine in detail the implementation of all those level objects. Because they share a common base of functionality, a base class for them is introduced first.

The Foundation of All Existence: CLevelObject

Because the editor will work a lot with the base class type, I wanted to have a function for each instance of a derived class that provides an ID of this object so that a user can check which type it is. So the following list contains a number of defines that are meant for the different level object types. As you can see, those level objects are all LOBs here:

```
#define LOB_NONE        0
#define LOB_ALL         2
#define LOB_SECTOR      4
#define LOB_MESH        8
#define LOB_POLYGON     16
#define LOB_PORTAL      32
#define LOB_ENTITY      64
#define LOB_LIGHT       128
#define LOB_SPAWNPOINT  256
```

And now for the mother of all LOBs: a class called CLevelObject. This class contains a set of pure virtual functions that must be implemented by each derived class. However, the class is not a pure interface because there are already some basic functions implemented. Most of them just toggle some flags of an instance of the class (perhaps for those heavily used by the editor for selecting a level object, for example). Such a base class is really helpful, as you will see when we start to insert or delete level objects into a sector or from a sector, respectively.

Here is the class declaration:

```
class CLevelObject {
   public:
      CLevelObject(void) { /* nothing */ }
```

```cpp
            virtual ~CLevelObject(void) { /* nothing */ }

            // virtual interface stuff
            virtual void Init(void)=0;
            virtual void Release(void)=0;
            virtual void Save(FILE*)=0;
            virtual bool Load(FILE*)=0;
            virtual void Translate(const ZFXVector&)=0;
            virtual void CopyOf(CLevelObject*)=0;
            virtual bool Picked(const ZFXRay&, float*)=0;
            virtual bool Intersects(const ZFXAabb&,ZFXAXIS)=0;
            virtual void Render(ZFXVertexCacheManager*, bool)=0;

            virtual void Reset(void)   { Release(); Init(); }

            // all small helpers
            bool     IsOfType(DWORD dw){return(m_Type==dw);}
            DWORD    GetType(void)      {return m_Type;      }
            UINT     GetNumVerts(void) {return m_NumVerts; }
            UINT     GetNumIndis(void) {return m_NumIndis; }
            UINT     GetNumPolys(void) {return m_NumPolys; }
            ZFXAabb  GetAabb(void)     {return m_Aabb;     }
            void     DeSelect(void)    {m_bSelected=false; }
            void     Select(void)      {m_bSelected=true;  }
            bool     IsSelected(void)  {return m_bSelected;}
            void     UnHide(void)      {m_bHidden=false;   }
            bool     IsHidden(void)    {return m_bHidden;  }
            void     Hide(void)        {m_bHidden=true;
                                        m_bSelected=false; }

        LPVOID* InitMem(LPVOID*, UINT, int);
        LPVOID* CheckMem(LPVOID*, UINT, int);

    protected:
        UINT     m_NumVerts;      // number of vertices
        UINT     m_NumIndis;      // number of indices
        UINT     m_NumPolys;      // number of polygons
        bool     m_bSelected;     // currently selected?
        bool     m_bHidden;       // currently hidden
        DWORD    m_Type;          // LOB_MESH, ...
        ZFXAabb  m_Aabb;          // bounding box
    }; // class
typedef class CLevelObject *LPLEVELOBJECT;
```

Note that there are also functions that enable the caller to hide or unhide a level object. This proves quite helpful when you are editing a huge level with a lot of geometry. Even in the three orthogonal views, the image gets fairly crowded, which makes it difficult for the level designer to select the part of the geometry he really wants to edit. With these functions, you can just hide arbitrary parts of the level so that they do not display.

The pure virtual functions of this class are mostly self-explanatory. The function CLevelObject::Picked enables you to check whether the object was hit by a given pick ray. This functionality is needed for picking, which refers to the task of selecting an object by clicking it (with the mouse) in the perspective view of the editor. The function CLevelObject::Intersects is also meant for some kind of selection process. However, it checks whether the bounding box of the object is intersecting the given rectangle on the given axis. That is needed if the level designers open a selection rectangle with the mouse in one of the three orthogonal views.

Then there are two functions that are neither purely virtual nor implemented inside the class declaration. Those functions deal with the memory allocation, and they are allocating memory dynamically on the given pointer for the given number of slots, where each slot has a given size. For example, a mesh could contain an arbitrary number of polygons. There is no way to tell ahead of time what the maximum number will be. I remember the good old *BUILD* engine, which was limited to a maximum number of 1024 sectors. If you started building complex and detailed levels, you could reach this limit very fast and had to skip a lot of details then to avoid this limit.

Here are the two implementations:

```
LPVOID* CLevelObject::InitMem(LPVOID *ppMem, UINT Slots, int Stride)
    {
    if (Slots==0) return NULL;
    int n = ((int)(((float)Slots)/50)+1)*50;
    ppMem = (LPVOID*)malloc(Stride*n);
    return ppMem;
    }
/*-------------------------*/

LPVOID* CLevelObject::CheckMem(LPVOID *ppMem, UINT Slots, int Stride)
    {
    if ( (Slots%50) == 0 )
        ppMem = (LPVOID*)realloc(ppMem, Stride*(Slots+50));
    return ppMem;
    }
```

The first function allocates the memory for the first time, and the second function enlarges the memory area. Note that both functions allocate enough memory for 50 objects, even if fewer are needed. If more than 50 objects should fit into the memory, the given number is rounded up to the next additional 50 elements. This prevents the function from allocating memory over and over again.

This process doesn't represent optimal memory management. After all, there is no management involved here. Therefore, you should implement a custom memory manager that serves your needs and that performs the tasks you want it to in a secure and debuggable way. But that is beyond the scope of this book.

At the Lowest Level: CPolygon

The first class we will derive from the CLevelObject base class is the class CPolygon for polygons forming the level geometry, mainly. Because the levels that you can build with the *PanBox-Edit* level-editing tool are polygon oriented, the class for a polygon is rather comprehensive. The level designer can also edit single vertices in the level; as you will see quite soon, however, this is also done using the class for polygons (which are the instances that store the vertices, after all).

The only functionality the polygons are missing so far is the deleting operation for vertices. You can obviously understand how important it is to delete a single vertex from a polygon. This operation is not too complex to do, and after you have seen the polygon class you should be able to integrate it into the editor if you think you need it.

Note

Besides the polygon-based approach to level editing, there is a competing approach that is not based on setting polygons into a level but on using brushes instead. You can insert brushes only into a level such as a cube or a cube with the faces looking inward so that this cube is a starting point for a room. If you want to have a doorframe in a wall, for instance, you would not build the polygons for the wall and save the space for the door. Instead, you would add a cut brush to the level, which is again a shape like cube. The difference is that this shape is not added as geometry to the level; instead, it is subtracted from the level geometry to create the hole in the wall. Such operations (adding or subtracting from other level geometry, for instance) are called constructive solid geometry (CSG).

Class Declaration

The class for a polygon is by far the most complex of all classes derived from the base class CLevelObject. The reason for this is that a polygon is something like the atom in our editor. The polygon is used for nearly everything in the editor (starting from the level geometry of free polygons to groups of meshes and even to portals, which are also rendered as a polygon). Most of the functions in this class are trivial (setting the skin ID for the polygon, for instance). Others are more complex (calculating the texture coordinates using planar texture mapping, for instance). All these functions are covered here, however.

Here is the class declaration:

```cpp
class CPolygon : public CLevelObject
   {
   public:
      CPolygon(void);
      virtual ~CPolygon(void);

      void     CopyOf(CLevelObject*);
      bool     CreatePortal(CPortal*);
      void     SetVertices(const VERTEX*, UINT);
      void     SetIndices(const WORD*, UINT);

      void        SetSkinID(UINT ID) { m_SkinID = ID;    }
      UINT        GetSkinID(void)    { return m_SkinID; }
      CPolymesh*  GetParent(void)    { return m_pDad;   }
      bool        IsPartOfMesh(void) {return m_bPartOfMesh;}

      void     GetTexOff(float *pU, float *pV) {
               if (pU) *pU = m_fTexOff[0];
               if (pV) *pV = m_fTexOff[1]; }
      void     GetTexRep(float *pU, float *pV) {
               if (pU) *pU = m_fTexRep[0];
               if (pV) *pV = m_fTexRep[1]; }

      void     Render(ZFXVertexCacheManager*,bool);
      void     Translate(const ZFXVector&);
      void     Rotate(ZFXAXIS,  const ZFXVector&, float);
      void     Mirror(ZFXAXIS,  const ZFXVector&, float);
      bool     Picked(const ZFXRay&, float*);
      bool     Intersects(const ZFXAabb&, ZFXAXIS);
      void     GetIntersectingVerts(const ZFXAabb&,CSelectionBuffer*,ZFXAXIS);
      void     InsideOut(void);
      void     SetAsPartOfMesh(CPolymesh *p);
      void     Triangulate(void);
      void     CalcBoundingBox(void);
      void     CalcNormals(void);
      void     CalcTextureCoords(ZFXAXIS,const ZFXAabb*);
      void     TransTextureCoords(float ftU, float ftV, float frU, float frV);
      void     GetTextureTrans(float*,float*,float*,float*);
      void     Save(FILE*);
      bool     Load(FILE*);
```

```
    private:
        VERTEX      *m_pVerts;          // vertices
        WORD        *m_pIndis;          // indices
        WORD        *m_pLineIndis;      // polyline indices
        CPolymesh*  m_pDad;             // if part of a mesh
        UINT        m_SkinID;           // skin ID
        bool        m_bPartOfMesh;      // part of a mesh?
        float       m_fTexOff[2];       // texture offset
        float       m_fTexRep[2];       // texture repeat

        void        Init(void);
        void        Release(void);
    }; // class
typedef class CPolygon *LPPOLYGON;
```

Two things about this class should immediately attract your attention. The first thing is the object CSelectionBuffer, which is used in a function here. The second thing is that a polygon can have a parent, apparently, which is of the type CPolymesh. Such a polymesh is normally just called a mesh, and it is nothing more than a group of polygons. The parent of a polygon is then the group of polygons it belongs to, if there are any. The selection buffer gives away its purpose by its name. If you select anything in the editor, the selected object will be put in the selection buffer (as discussed later in this chapter).

The accessor functions of this class are self-explanatory, so let's move on and look at the constructor and the destructor:

```
CPolygon::CPolygon(void)  { Init();    }
CPolygon::~CPolygon(void) { Release(); }
```

As you can see, not much is going on in the constructor and the destructor of this class, except for calling an initialization and a releasing function, respectively. By separating those functionalities from the constructor and destructor you can easily reuse an existing object without the need to recreate it, which would be time consuming. Here are those two functions:

```
void CPolygon::Init(void)
    {
    m_NumVerts    = 0;
    m_NumIndis    = 0;
    m_NumPolys    = 1;
    m_SkinID      = 2;       // default texture
    m_fTexOff[0]  = 0.0f;
    m_fTexOff[1]  = 0.0f;
    m_fTexRep[0]  = 1.0f;
    m_fTexRep[1]  = 1.0f;
```

```
    m_bSelected   = false;
    m_bHidden     = false;
    m_bPartOfMesh = false;
    m_pDad        = NULL;
    m_pVerts      = NULL;
    m_pIndis      = NULL;
    m_pLineIndis  = NULL;
    m_Type        = LOB_POLYGON;
    memset(&m_Aabb, 0, sizeof(ZFXAabb));
    } // Init
```

Note that some of the attributes set here stem from the base class. The most important thing in the Init() function is setting the type of the level object so that the query to the ID of the object will be valid. Note that the ID for the skin of this polygon is set to 2, not to an initial 0. Skins 0 and 1 are meant for other purposes (as discussed later). Normally, the level designer will name a skin that the polygon should use; if not, the default skin is number 2.

If you want to delete a polygon or if you just want to reset it, you first have to call its function CPolygon::Release. This is done in the destructor of the class, too, and it will clean up all the memory that was allocated in this class:

```
#define SAFE_DELETE(p)   {if(p!=0){delete(p);(p)=0;}}
#define SAFE_DELETE_A(p) {if(p!=0){delete[](p);(p)=0;}}
#define SAFE_FREE(p)     {if(p!=0){free(p);(p)=0;}}

void CPolygon::Release(void) {
    SAFE_DELETE_A(m_pVerts);
    SAFE_DELETE_A(m_pIndis);
    SAFE_DELETE_A(m_pLineIndis);
    }
```

Creating an Instance

If you want to fill an instance of the polygon class with data, you must supply the vertices and the indices to this instance. Doing so requires two separate functions. Therefore, you can change only the index list without changing the vertex list, for example. Setting the vertices also results in a recalculation of the bounding box that includes the polygon, whereas setting the indices involves the calculation of the normal vector, which depends on the winding order indicated by the index list.

Here are the two functions to feed the polygon with data:

```
void CPolygon::SetVertices(const VERTEX *pVerts, UINT NumVerts)
    {
```

```
   SAFE_DELETE_A(m_pVerts);
   SAFE_DELETE_A(m_pLineIndis);

   m_pVerts = new VERTEX[NumVerts];
   m_pLineIndis = new WORD[NumVerts*2];

   if ( !m_pVerts || !m_pLineIndis ) return;

   memcpy(m_pVerts, pVerts, sizeof(VERTEX)*NumVerts);
   m_NumVerts = NumVerts;

   for (UINT i=0; i<NumVerts; i++) {
      m_pLineIndis[(i*2)] = i;
      m_pLineIndis[(i*2)+1] = i+1;

      if (i==NumVerts-1) m_pLineIndis[(i*2)+1] = 0;
      }

   CalcBoundingBox();
   } // SetVertices
/*----------------------------*/

void CPolygon::SetIndices(const WORD *pIndis, UINT NumIndis)
   {
   SAFE_DELETE_A(m_pIndis);
   m_pIndis = new WORD[NumIndis];
   if (!m_pIndis) return;
   memcpy(m_pIndis, pIndis, sizeof(WORD)*NumIndis);
   m_NumIndis = NumIndis;

   CalcNormals();
   } // SetIndices
```

In this function, it is interesting that we build the index list in the attribute `m_pLineIndices` automatically when the vertices are set. This is needed because if you want to render the polygon as an outline in the wireframe mode, Direct3D is not really able to do this. So you have to render the polygon as a closed-line strip. Otherwise, Direct3D would render the polygon as wireframe triangles, which is not what we want in the editor. Take a look at Figure 14.3. This figure shows a polygon rendered as a solid texture, as an outline using a line strip, and as a triangulated wireframe.

If a level designer were to see the polygon he just created as a triangulated wireframe view, he would wonder what exactly it was. After all, this isn't what he created. Another drawback of this method is that it adds a number of lines to the orthogonal views, which will already be very crowded with all kind of lines (even for a moderate-size level).

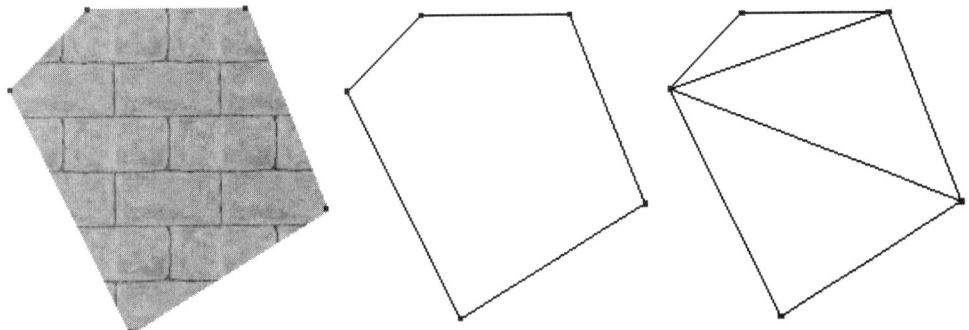

Figure 14.3 Image of a polygon filled and with a texture, in outline wireframe mode, and in triangulated mode (from left to right.).

Loading and Saving a Polygon

The editor would be of no use if it were impossible to save the data at the end of a level-designing session. Therefore, we need to have functions to load and save each of the level objects, as required by the pure virtual functions in the base class. You'll understand the level format we are using here when we discuss the level class. As you can see from the base class, however, each level object has to take care of itself when it comes down to loading and saving.

Here is how a polygon saves and loads itself to and from a file:

```
void CPolygon::Save(FILE *pFile)
   {
   if (!pFile) return;

   fwrite(&m_NumVerts,    sizeof(UINT),    1, pFile);
   fwrite(&m_NumIndis,    sizeof(UINT),    1, pFile);
   fwrite(&m_SkinID,      sizeof(UINT),    1, pFile);
   fwrite(&m_Aabb,        sizeof(ZFXAabb), 1, pFile);
   fwrite(&m_bPartOfMesh, sizeof(bool),    1, pFile);
   fwrite(m_fTexOff,      sizeof(float),   2, pFile);
   fwrite(m_fTexRep,      sizeof(float),   2, pFile);

   fwrite(m_pVerts, sizeof(VERTEX), m_NumVerts, pFile);
   fwrite(m_pIndis, sizeof(WORD), m_NumIndis, pFile);
   fwrite(m_pLineIndis,sizeof(WORD),m_NumVerts*2,pFile);
   fflush(pFile);
```

```cpp
   } // Save
/*------------------------------*/

bool CPolygon::Load(FILE *pFile)
   {

   if (!pFile) return false;

   fread(&m_NumVerts,    sizeof(UINT),    1, pFile);
   fread(&m_NumIndis,    sizeof(UINT),    1, pFile);
   fread(&m_SkinID,      sizeof(UINT),    1, pFile);
   fread(&m_Aabb,        sizeof(ZFXAabb), 1, pFile);
   fread(&m_bPartOfMesh, sizeof(bool),    1, pFile);
   fread(m_fTexOff,      sizeof(float),   2, pFile);
   fread(m_fTexRep,      sizeof(float),   2, pFile);

   if (m_NumVerts == 0)
      {
      return false;
      }
   else {
      m_pVerts    = new VERTEX[m_NumVerts];
      m_pIndis    = new WORD[m_NumIndis];
      m_pLineIndis = new WORD[m_NumVerts*2];

      if ( !m_pVerts || !m_pIndis || !m_pLineIndis)
         return false;
      }

   fread(m_pVerts, sizeof(VERTEX), m_NumVerts,   pFile);
   fread(m_pIndis, sizeof(WORD),   m_NumIndis,   pFile);
   fread(m_pLineIndis,sizeof(WORD),m_NumVerts*2,pFile);

   CalcNormals();
   return true;
   } // Load
```

Copying an Instance

Just as with the functions to load and save a polygon, each derived class of the level object base class needs to provide a function that copies an instance into another instance. After all, we are dealing a lot with those level objects (such as inserting copies of geometrical objects). I don't like to overwrite the = operator, however, because I prefer having a real function for this purpose. Of course, if you prefer, you can also use the = operator or the copy constructor:

```
void CPolygon::CopyOf(CLevelObject *pLob)
   {
   if ( !pLob->IsOfType(m_Type) ) return;

   LPPOLYGON pPoly = (LPPOLYGON)pLob;

   Reset();
   SetVertices(pPoly->m_pVerts, pPoly->m_NumVerts);
   SetIndices(pPoly->m_pIndis, pPoly->m_NumIndis);
   m_SkinID = pPoly->m_SkinID;
   m_Aabb   = pPoly->m_Aabb;

   m_fTexOff[0] = pPoly->m_fTexOff[0];
   m_fTexOff[1] = pPoly->m_fTexOff[1];
   m_fTexRep[0] = pPoly->m_fTexRep[0];
   m_fTexRep[1] = pPoly->m_fTexRep[1];
   } // CopyOf
```

The attributes that make up a unique polygon are copied from the instance of the polygon class that is provided as a parameter, and they are copied into the attribute of the this object. A small security check evaluates whether the given instance is of the same type. Note that some attributes are automatically set and need not be copied, such as the bounding box that is calculated in the call that sets the vertices for the polygon.

Collision Detection

You may be wondering just what is collision detection for polygons in a level editor? Well, consider this from another angle. This is not about finding collisions between the level geometry and moving objects. This collision detection is meant for the level designer to enable him to select parts of the geometry. There are two ways for the level designer to do this kind of selection. It can take place in one of the three orthogonal views if the level designer clicks and opens a two-dimensional selection rectangle by dragging the cursor. The other option is to click an object in the perspective view.

Now you need some functions to check for collisions or intersection between such a selection rectangle and the level geometry. This is very easy because the problem is purely two-dimensional. The axis of the view direction in the orthogonal view does not matter at all, so it can be ignored. If you want to know whether a polygon is partially inside the selection rectangle you only need to loop through its vertex list and check whether any of the vertices are inside the rectangle on the two concerned axes. The missing third coordinate, which is the distance of the vertex to the projection plane, does not matter at all:

```
bool CPolygon::Intersects(const ZFXAabb &aabb, ZFXAXIS axis)
   {
   if (!m_Aabb.Intersects(aabb)) return false;

   for (UINT i=0; i<m_NumVerts; i++) {

      // simplify to 2d problem
      if (axis == X_AXIS) {
         if ((m_pVerts[i].y < aabb.vcMax.y) &&
             (m_pVerts[i].y > aabb.vcMin.y) &&
             (m_pVerts[i].z < aabb.vcMax.z) &&
             (m_pVerts[i].z > aabb.vcMin.z))
            return true;
         }
      else if (axis == Y_AXIS) {
         if ((m_pVerts[i].x < aabb.vcMax.x) &&
             (m_pVerts[i].x > aabb.vcMin.x) &&
             (m_pVerts[i].z < aabb.vcMax.z) &&
             (m_pVerts[i].z > aabb.vcMin.z))
            return true;
         }
      else if (axis == Z_AXIS) {
         if ((m_pVerts[i].y < aabb.vcMax.y) &&
             (m_pVerts[i].y > aabb.vcMin.y) &&
             (m_pVerts[i].x < aabb.vcMax.x) &&
             (m_pVerts[i].x > aabb.vcMin.x))
            return true;
         }
      } // for
   return false;
   } // Intersects
```

By using this function, you can evaluate whether a polygon is inside the selection rectangle and should therefore be flagged as selected. Now, however, we also want to be able to select single vertices from a polygon without selecting the polygon itself. To do this, we write a quite similar function to check the single vertices of the polygon. But then how should you flag a vertex as being selected?

Normally, the level object offers a function that returns true or false for the selection case, flagging the objects as being selected. The return value is then used on another layer above the polygons in the program. This is not possible for vertices, so we need to come up with another solution. For this case, I have jumped ahead a bit. Near the end of this chapter, we will implement the class CSelectionBuffer, which is used to store all selected objects. It will also be able to store selected vertices, so we provide this selection buffer to the function that lets you select vertices from a polygon. Each selected vertex is then added to the selection buffer as a reference pointer:

```
void CPolygon::GetIntersectingVerts(const ZFXAabb &aabb, CSelectionBuffer *pSB,
                                    ZFXAXIS axis)
   {
   for (UINT i=0; i<m_NumVerts; i++)
      {
      // simplifying to 2d problem
      if (axis == X_AXIS) {
         if ((m_pVerts[i].y < aabb.vcMax.y) &&
             (m_pVerts[i].y > aabb.vcMin.y) &&
             (m_pVerts[i].z < aabb.vcMax.z) &&
             (m_pVerts[i].z > aabb.vcMin.z))
            pSB->AddVertex(&m_pVerts[i], this);
         }
      else if (axis == Y_AXIS) {
         if ((m_pVerts[i].x < aabb.vcMax.x) &&
             (m_pVerts[i].x > aabb.vcMin.x) &&
             (m_pVerts[i].z < aabb.vcMax.z) &&
             (m_pVerts[i].z > aabb.vcMin.z))
            pSB->AddVertex(&m_pVerts[i], this);
         }
      else if (axis == Z_AXIS) {
         if ((m_pVerts[i].y < aabb.vcMax.y) &&
             (m_pVerts[i].y > aabb.vcMin.y) &&
             (m_pVerts[i].x < aabb.vcMax.x) &&
             (m_pVerts[i].x > aabb.vcMin.x))
            pSB->AddVertex(&m_pVerts[i], this);
         }
      }
   } // GetIntersectingVerts
```

This is enough to handle the selection processes in the orthogonal views. That leaves the perspective view. A click in 2D screen space will translate to a ray in 3D space because you cannot say anything about the depth value of the click. Hence you build a ray in 3D space that originates at the camera position and passes through the point that the user clicked on (which is on the near plane of the perspective projection matrix). Then you check whether the ray hits an instance of the polygon class. If so, you return this result to the caller and provide the distance to the point where the ray intersected the polygon. This is the distance from the viewer to the concerned polygon. Here is the function:

```
bool CPolygon::Picked(const ZFXRay &Ray, float *pfD)
   {
```

```
   ZFXVector vc0, vc1, vc2;
   WORD     I0, I1, I2;

   for (UINT i=0; i<m_NumIndis; i+=3)
      {
      I0 = m_pIndis[i];
      I1 = m_pIndis[i+1];
      I2 = m_pIndis[i+2];

      vc0.Set( m_pVerts[I0].x, m_pVerts[I0].y, m_pVerts[I0].z );
      vc1.Set( m_pVerts[I1].x, m_pVerts[I1].y, m_pVerts[I1].z );
      vc2.Set( m_pVerts[I2].x, m_pVerts[I2].y, m_pVerts[I2].z );

      if ( ((ZFXRay)Ray).Intersects(vc0, vc1, vc2, true, pfD) )
         return true;
      }
   return false;
   } // Picked
```

You just need to loop through the triangulation of the polygon and check each triangle for a collision with the ray. However, it is sufficient for a triangle just to be intersected by the ray; so if you find one collision, you can return from the function.

Rendering an Instance

Rendering an instance of the polygon class is done using our own render device interface. To access its render functions, you must provide a pointer to the vertex cache manager of the render device as a parameter to the function. A second parameter says whether the polygon should be rendered even if it is hidden. The flag m_bHidden of the base class says whether this object is hidden. If it is, it won't get drawn in the orthogonal modes; however, you can still select in the editor if you want the hidden objects to be shown in the perspective view:

```
void CPolygon::Render(ZFXVertexCacheManager *pVCM, bool bHide)
   {
   if (m_bHidden && bHide) return;

   bool bAsLine = (pVCM->GetShadeMode() == RS_SHADE_LINES);
   if (bAsLine) {
      pVCM->Render(VID_UU, m_NumVerts, m_NumVerts*2,
                   m_pVerts, m_pLineIndis, m_SkinID);
      }
   else {
      pVCM->Render(VID_UU, m_NumVerts, m_NumIndis,
```

```
         m_pVerts, m_pIndis, m_SkinID);
      }
   } // Render
```

The actual process of rendering using the render device interface should not require more explanation here. The only remarkable thing is the query whether the device is currently in line-drawing mode. If it is, the polygons are rendered as a line strip to show up as a wireframe outline. Otherwise, the polygons are rendered using the normal index list. Take a look at Figure 14.3 again to compare the different render modes.

Transformations for Polygons

Now we'll really start to edit polygons, by transforming them. The transformations are simple enough. However, there are a few catches here and there that could lead to unwanted results if you don't watch out for them. Don't worry, though; this section shows you how to avoid all obstacles:

```
void CPolygon::Translate(const ZFXVector &vcT)
   {
   for (UINT i=0; i<m_NumVerts; i++) {
      m_pVerts[i].x += vcT.x;
      m_pVerts[i].y += vcT.y;
      m_pVerts[i].z += vcT.z;
      }
   m_Aabb.vcCenter += vcT;
   m_Aabb.vcMax    += vcT;
   m_Aabb.vcMin    += vcT;

   if (m_bPartOfMesh) m_pDad->CalcBoundingBox();
   } // Translate
```

Of course, we are smart enough to translate the polygon's own bounding box along with the polygon itself. And we are even smart enough to take care of our relatives, which means that we ask the mesh to recalculate its bounding box if the polygon is part of a mesh. It would not be enough to translate the bounding box of the mesh, because only a single part of the mesh was translated. Therefore, you must recalculate it from scratch.

The next operation is to rotate the polygon. That is not as easy as it might look at first glance. Think back to your first lesson ever in computer graphics. Remember that an object will also be translated if you rotate it around another pivot point other than its own center? The coordinates of our polygons are given in world space, and hence the pivot point for the rotation formulas is the world's origin. Normally, however, you want to rotate an object around its own center point. To overcome this problem, you must translate the object back to the world origin first, then you rotate it, and finally you translate it back to its original position:

```
void CPolygon::Rotate(ZFXAXIS axis, const ZFXVector &vcPos, float a)
   {
   ZFXMatrix mat;
   ZFXVector vc;

   if (axis == X_AXIS) mat.RotaX(a);
   if (axis == Y_AXIS) mat.RotaY(a);
   if (axis == Z_AXIS) mat.RotaZ(a);

   for (UINT i=0; i<m_NumVerts; i++) {
      // retranslate to the origin
      vc.x = m_pVerts[i].x - vcPos.x;
      vc.y = m_pVerts[i].y - vcPos.y;
      vc.z = m_pVerts[i].z - vcPos.z;

      // rotate
      vc = mat * vc;

      // back to its position
      m_pVerts[i].x = vc.x + vcPos.x;
      m_pVerts[i].y = vc.y + vcPos.y;
      m_pVerts[i].z = vc.z + vcPos.z;
      }

   CalcBoundingBox();
   if (m_bPartOfMesh) m_pDad->CalcBoundingBox();
   } // Rotate
```

As the vector for the translation, you could just use the vector running from the world's origin to the center of the bounding box of the polygon and invert that one. This would effectively translate the polygon to the world's origin, of course. However, there's a reason why we are not doing this: You can only rotate an object you have selected. If you select one polygon, this would be okay. If you were to select multiple polygons, such as a whole mesh, however, you would still rotate each polygon on its own axis, because a different pivot point is used for each polygon. This is normally not what you want to have, as you can see in Figure 14.4. Instead, you can supply a separate translation vector to this function. This is normally the center of the bounding box, which includes all selected objects.

Another kind of transformation for polygons is the mirroring of a polygon on one of the three world axes. This proves especially useful when constructing symmetrical objects inside your level. If you build a very complex corridor that is using several pipes and columns on either side of the corridor's walls, for instance, you need to build this geom-

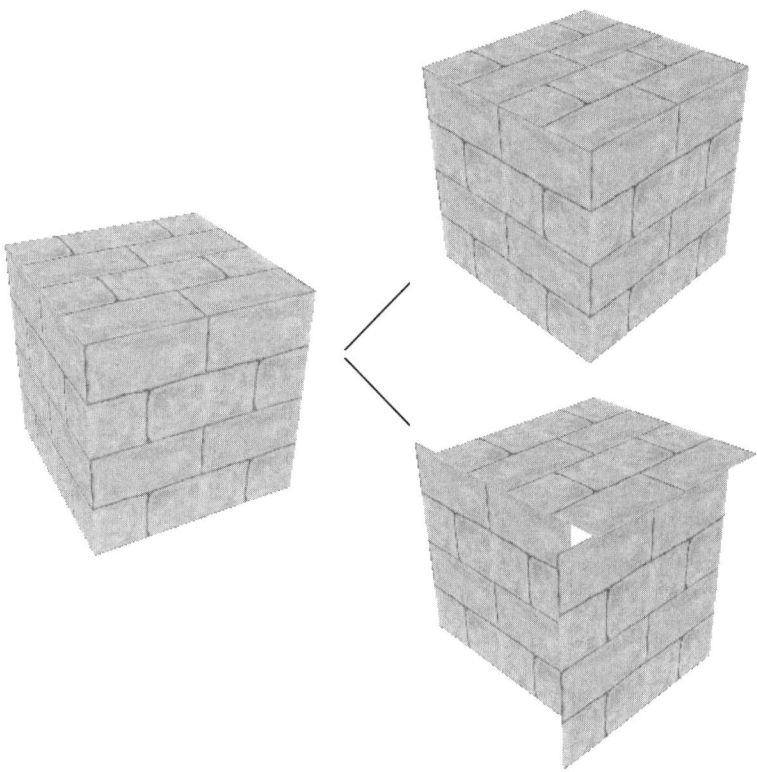

Figure 14.4 Rotating the single polygons of a cube around the same pivot point (upper right) and around the center of each polygon (lower right).

etry only for one side. Then you can select it, copy it, and mirror it to serve as the opposing side of the corridor:

```
void CPolygon::Mirror(ZFXAXIS axis, const ZFXVector &vcPos)
   {
   for (UINT i=0; i<m_NumVerts; i++) {
      m_pVerts[i].x -= vcPos.x;
      m_pVerts[i].y -= vcPos.y;
      m_pVerts[i].z -= vcPos.z;

      // mirroring
      if (axis == X_AXIS) m_pVerts[i].x *= -1.0f;
      if (axis == Y_AXIS) m_pVerts[i].y *= -1.0f;
      if (axis == Z_AXIS) m_pVerts[i].z *= -1.0f;

      m_pVerts[i].x += vcPos.x;
```

```
            m_pVerts[i].y += vcPos.y;
            m_pVerts[i].z += vcPos.z;
            }

    CalcBoundingBox();
    if (m_bPartOfMesh) m_pDad->CalcBoundingBox();
    } // Mirror
```

Mirroring is done by just inverting the coordinate on the mirror axis, which equals multiplying this coordinate by –1. However, this works only if the object is centered in the origin. Therefore, you have to translate it back to the origin first; after inverting the coordinate, you then translate it back.

Texture Coordinates for Polygons

Besides the functions `CPolygon::GetTexOff` and `CPolygon::GetTexRep`, which are implemented in the class declaration already, you need three more functions to work with the texture coordinates. Basically, you do not set texture coordinates for single vertices, but for a whole polygon instead. Besides the base coordinates, there are also the values for a texture offset if you want to translate the texture on the polygon and for the texture repeat. This editor will only use planar texture mapping, which means that the textures are projected onto a plane. Because we are using only plane polygons, this suffices. Other kinds of texture mapping include spherical texture mapping and cylindrical texture mapping.

The projection of a texture map onto a plane is really easy. You just have to ignore the coordinates of the axis to which the plane is orthogonal. For the two remaining coordinates, you just calculate where a certain vertex is located with respect to the bounding box of the geometry you want to map the texture onto. If a vertex is exactly in the middle of the bounding box, for example, it gets the texture coordinates 0.5f on both axes. Here is the function for the planar mapping. Note that the texture repeat is initially set to 1, and the offset is set to 0:

```
void CPolygon::CalcTextureCoords(ZFXAXIS axis, const ZFXAabb *pAabb)
    {
    VERTEX *pVert=NULL;
    ZFXAabb aabb;

    if (pAabb) aabb = *pAabb;
    else aabb = m_Aabb;

    m_fTexOff[0] = m_fTexOff[1] = 0.0f;
    m_fTexRep[0] = m_fTexRep[1] = 1.0f;

    ZFXVector vcSize = aabb.vcMax - aabb.vcMin;
```

```
      for (UINT i=0; i<m_NumVerts; i++) {
         pVert = &m_pVerts[i];

         // planar texture mapping
         if (axis == X_AXIS) {
            pVert->tu = (pVert->z - aabb.vcMin.z)/vcSize.z;
            pVert->tv = (pVert->y - aabb.vcMax.y)/vcSize.y;
            }
         else if (axis == Y_AXIS) {
            pVert->tu = (pVert->x - aabb.vcMin.x)/vcSize.x;
            pVert->tv = (pVert->z - aabb.vcMax.z)/vcSize.z;
            }
         else if (axis == Z_AXIS) {
            pVert->tu = (pVert->x - aabb.vcMin.x)/vcSize.x;
            pVert->tv = (pVert->y - aabb.vcMax.y)/vcSize.y;
            }
         } // for
      } // CalcTextureCoords
```

For this function, you have to provide a bounding box as a parameter, too. You might ask yourself why. After all, a polygon should know its own bounding box quite well, right? Indeed, but who says that you want to map the texture limited to the polygon's bounding box only? If multiple polygons are selected, or if you want to map a texture on a whole mesh, for instance, you will, of course, provide another bounding box that includes all the geometry. The other option is to map the texture on each single polygon and try to adjust the texture repeat and offset in a way that the texture is mapped onto the whole geometry without visible artifacts.

If the texture coordinates are then generated by planar mapping, however, you are not done. There is still the texture offset and repeat, which must be integrated if the level designer wants the texture to be repeated or translated on the polygon. Here are the formulas to integrate those values into the base texture coordinates stemming from the planar mapping:

```
u = u_base * u_repeat + u_offset;
v = v_base * v_repeat + v_offset;
```

The base texture coordinates from the planar mapping are multiplied by the factor used for the texture repeat, and then the value for the offset is added. The problem is just that you cannot extract the values for the texture repeat and offset after they are integrated into the final texture coordinates. Because the editor enables you to edit the texture coordinates via a dialog box, however, you need to know the current offset and repeat in order to add more or less repeat and offset via slider controls. Therefore, the values for the texture repeat and offset are stored in separate variables.

If the level designer wants to texture a polygon, he calls the relevant dialog box by clicking the appropriate button. The dialog box will show the texture offset and repeat, which can then be adjusted. The following function integrates the new values for texture offset and repeat into the polygons vertices:

```
void CPolygon::TransTextureCoords(float ftU, float ftV, float frU, float frV)
   {
   if (frU == 0.0f) frU = 0.00001f;
   if (frV == 0.0f) frV = 0.00001f;

   for (UINT i=0; i<m_NumVerts; i++) {
      // undo old values
      if (m_fTexOff[0] != 0.0f) m_pVerts[i].tu -= m_fTexOff[0];
      if (m_fTexOff[1] != 0.0f) m_pVerts[i].tv -= m_fTexOff[1];

      if ((m_fTexRep[0] != 1.0f) && (m_fTexRep[0] != 0.0f) )
         {
         m_pVerts[i].tu /= m_fTexRep[0];
         }
      if ((m_fTexRep[1] != 1.0f) && (m_fTexRep[1] != 0.0f) )
         {
         m_pVerts[i].tv /= m_fTexRep[1];
         }

      m_pVerts[i].tu = m_pVerts[i].tu*frU + ftU;
      m_pVerts[i].tv = m_pVerts[i].tv*frV + ftV;
      }

   m_fTexOff[0] = ftU;
   m_fTexOff[1] = ftV;
   m_fTexRep[0] = frU;
   m_fTexRep[1] = frV;
   } // TransTextureCoors
```

At first, you have to separate the original texture coordinates from the offset and the repeat. To do this, use the formula shown above, but in an inverted manner. Then you use the original formula with the new values for the offset and the repeat. You only have to take care if the texture repeat is 0. In such a case, the texture would look like trash, but that is not the problem. The problem is that this would lead to a division by 0, which of course is not a good idea if you want to keep the application running.

Class Design of the Tool 695

The final function that deals with the texture coordinates is one that enables you to query the values for the offset and the texture repeat from the polygon. This is needed in the editor to display those values. Furthermore, if the user wants to change the texture coordinates, you need those values to extract the offset and repeat because those values cannot be calculated from the final texture coordinates after they have been integrated into them:

```
void CPolygon::GetTextureTrans(float *pftU, float *pftV,
                               float *pfrU, float *pfrV)
   {
   if (pftU) *pftU = m_fTexOff[0];
   if (pftV) *pftV = m_fTexOff[1];
   if (pfrU) *pfrU = m_fTexRep[0];
   if (pfrV) *pfrV = m_fTexRep[1];
   } // GetTextureTrans
```

Miscellaneous Functions for Polygons

The first supporting miscellaneous function the polygon class needs is the one that calculates the bounding box of the polygon, which is used for culling and, more importantly, for picking and selecting the polygon in the editor. For this purpose, a simple AABB will do. Calculating such a box is no big deal. You just loop through all vertices and store the maximum and minimum values separately for each axis:

```
void CPolygon::CalcBoundingBox(void)
   {
   ZFXVector vcMax, vcMin;

   // random starting value
   vcMax.x = vcMin.x = m_pVerts[0].x;
   vcMax.y = vcMin.y = m_pVerts[0].y;
   vcMax.z = vcMin.z = m_pVerts[0].z;

   for (UINT i=0; i<m_NumVerts; i++) {
      if ( m_pVerts[i].x > vcMax.x )
         vcMax.x = m_pVerts[i].x;
      else if ( m_pVerts[i].x < vcMin.x )
         vcMin.x = m_pVerts[i].x;
      if ( m_pVerts[i].y > vcMax.y )
         vcMax.y = m_pVerts[i].y;
      else if ( m_pVerts[i].y < vcMin.y )
         vcMin.y = m_pVerts[i].y;
      if ( m_pVerts[i].z > vcMax.z )
         vcMax.z = m_pVerts[i].z;
      else if ( m_pVerts[i].z < vcMin.z )
```

```
        vcMin.z = m_pVerts[i].z;
   } // for

m_Aabb.vcMax    = vcMax;
m_Aabb.vcMin    = vcMin;
m_Aabb.vcCenter = (vcMax + vcMin) / 2.0f;
} // CalcBoundingBox
```

The next function we need to have is one that calculates the normal vector for the polygon. The editor does only support normals on the base of polygons, so the normals of the vertices are just the normal of the polygon. And this normal will be created automatically so that it is sitting orthogonal on the polygon. For sharp-edged indoor settings, this is the most common usage, but you can and should implement a normal transformation for each vertex:

```
void CPolygon::CalcNormals(void)
   {
   ZFXVector vc0, vc1, vc2, vcN;

   vc0.x = m_pVerts[m_pIndis[0]].x;
   vc0.y = m_pVerts[m_pIndis[0]].y;
   vc0.z = m_pVerts[m_pIndis[0]].z;

   vc1.x = m_pVerts[m_pIndis[1]].x;
   vc1.y = m_pVerts[m_pIndis[1]].y;
   vc1.z = m_pVerts[m_pIndis[1]].z;

   vc2.x = m_pVerts[m_pIndis[2]].x;
   vc2.y = m_pVerts[m_pIndis[2]].y;
   vc2.z = m_pVerts[m_pIndis[2]].z;

   vcN.Cross( (vc1-vc0), (vc2-vc0) );
   vcN.Normalize();

   for (UINT i=0; i<m_NumVerts; i++) {
      m_pVerts[i].vcN[0] = vcN.x;
      m_pVerts[i].vcN[1] = vcN.y;
      m_pVerts[i].vcN[2] = vcN.z;
      }
   } // CalcNormals
```

While inserting a polygon into a level, you'll sometimes find that you have built the polygon with the wrong vertex orientation. Because the editor is using only single-sided polygons, the backface of a polygon will always be invisible. If the polygon was created with the wrong winding of the vertices, or if you copy a wall that should be located on the other side of the corridor, however, you must make the other side of the polygon visible.

You can do this by changing the ordering of the vertices to be in the inverse order. Just loop through the list of indices and copy those indices in the inverse order to a new index array. This new array is then used by the polygon, and now its front face and back face are swapped:

```
void CPolygon::InsideOut(void)
   {
   WORD *pNewIndis = new WORD[m_NumIndis];

   for (UINT i=0; i<m_NumIndis; i++)
      pNewIndis[i] = m_pIndis[m_NumIndis-1-i];

   SetIndices(pNewIndis, m_NumIndis);

   SAFE_DELETE_A(pNewIndis);
   } // InsideOut
```

Now it's time to reveal the big secret behind polymesh objects: A polymesh consists of CPolygon instances only, so you can reuse all the functionality. In some places, however, a polygon must access its parent (for instance, if you translate some vertices or the whole polygon). The bounding box of the mesh the polygon belongs to must then be updated accordingly. The following function enables you to set the mesh object to which a polygon belongs:

```
void CPolygon::SetAsPartOfMesh(CPolymesh *p)
   {
   if (p) {
      m_pDad = p;
      m_bPartOfMesh = true;
      }
   else {
      m_pDad = NULL;
      m_bPartOfMesh = false;
      }
   } // SetAsPartOfMesh
```

The final operation you can do on a polygon is to convert the polygon into a portal. In this editor, you cannot just build a portal by using something like a create-portal function. Instead, you must build a polygon first, then select this polygon, and then click a button in the editor that will build a portal from this polygon. Although you don't know the class for the portals yet, you can see from the following function what is going on. Note that this function only allows polygons with exactly four vertices to become portals. The only reason to restrict this number is to prevent the view frustum of this polygon from getting too many planes:

```
bool CPolygon::CreatePortal(CPortal *pPortal)
   {
   if (m_NumVerts != 4) return false;

   pPortal->SetGeometry(m_pVerts, m_pIndis, m_Aabb);

   return true;
   } // CreatePortal
```

And now we have finished off the class `CPolygon`. Or did it finish off us? Well, just don't care anymore. Now that this class is complete and we can now edit polygons and vertices from polygons we can move on to the parent layer of a polygon. A herd of polygons forms of course a polymesh.

Complex Models: CPolymesh

Do you like to be on your own all the time? Probably not, and neither do polygons. Therefore, we will support their sense of teamwork and provide them with a class they can jump into and come together in little (or big) groups. Such a group of polygons is called a *polymesh*. This can be all kinds of geometry, open or closed, and it is also possible in this editor that a single polygon can be a group of its own. That would not make much sense, but in the heat of level editing it might very well happen that a polygon has to stay alone as a mesh for a while.

A polymesh is nothing more than a management unit to group polygons. This proves very helpful if you have built complex objects such as a desk with a lot of stuff on it. If you want to move this desk around in a room to see where it fits best, you can just group all polygons from the desk and the stuff on it together into one group. This enables you to select the whole thing with a single click.

> **Tip**
>
> Besides being a management unit for polygons, polymeshes also serve another purpose in the game code of the next chapter. The game we are implementing there will have shadows for the animated characters as well as for selected objects from the level geometry. And guess what. Each mesh is such a selected object. Therefore, each mesh in the level will cast a shadow in the game.

Class Declaration

Did I mention that the `CPolygon` class is by far the most complex class used for the editor in this chapter? No need to panic, but that is absolutely true. Don't be shocked when you see the class declaration for the CPolymesh class. This class looks very comprehensive and very big. However, your first glance might be misleading. Many tasks that must be done by the mesh object class can be delegated to the according function of the polygon class, so the implementations of the functions are not very complex.

Here is the new class for mesh objects:

```
class CPolymesh : public CLevelObject
   {
   public:
      CPolymesh(void);
      virtual ~CPolymesh(void);

      void       CopyOf(CLevelObject*);
      void       Render(ZFXVertexCacheManager*, bool);
      void       Translate(const ZFXVector&);
      void       InsideOut(void);
      void       SetSkinID(UINT);
      void       CountNonRedundantSkins(UINT*,UINT*);
      CPolygon*  PickPoly(const ZFXRay&, float, float*);
      bool       Picked(const ZFXRay&, float*);
      bool       Intersects(const ZFXAabb&, ZFXAXIS);
      void       GetIntersectingPolys(const ZFXAabb&, CSelectionBuffer*,
                                      ZFXAXIS);
      void       GetIntersectingVerts(const ZFXAabb&, CSelectionBuffer*,
                                      ZFXAXIS);
      void       CreateFromPolygons(CPolygon*, UCHAR);
      HRESULT    RemovePolygon(const LPPOLYGON);
      HRESULT    AddPolygon(const CPolygon &);

      void       Save(FILE*);
      bool       Load(FILE*);
      void       SavePurePolys(FILE*);

      void       SelectAllPolys(CSelectionBuffer*);
      void       SelectInvert(CSelectionBuffer*);

      void       HideNoPolys(void);
      void       HideInvertPolys(void);
      void       HideSelectedPolys(void);
      void       HideUnselectedPolys(void);

      LPPOLYGON  GetPolygon(UINT i){return m_ppPoly[i];}
      void       CalcBoundingBox(void);
```

Chapter 14 ■ Computer-Aided Design (CAD) Tools

```
      void       CalcNormals(void);
      void       CalcTextureCoords(ZFXAXIS, ZFXAabb*);

      void       TransTextureCoords(float ftU,
                      float ftV, float frU, float frV);
      bool       GetTextureTrans(float *pftU, float *pftV, float *pfrU,
                           float *pfrV);
   private:
      LPPOLYGON *m_ppPoly;
      bool       m_bSupprBoxCalc;

      void       Init(void);
      void       Release(void);
   }; // class
typedef class CPolymesh *LPPOLYMESH;
```

From now on, I don't show the constructors and the destructors of the classes that are derived from the level object base class. They all look like the one used in the CPolygon class and just call the functions Init() and Release(). This scheme has the advantage that you can reset an instance without having to destroy the object itself.

During the initialization of an instance, there is just nothing going on. You set the type of the level object and initialize all attributes to some default values. The meanings of the member attributes are discussed in the following sections dealing with the implementation of the member functions. Most of the names are self-explanatory, though:

```
void CPolymesh::Init(void)
   {
   m_NumPolys      = 0;
   m_NumVerts      = 0;
   m_NumIndis      = 0;
   m_ppPoly        = NULL;
   m_bSelected     = false;
   m_bHidden       = false;
   m_bSupprBoxCalc = false;
   m_Type          = LOB_MESH;
   memset(&m_Aabb, 0, sizeof(ZFXAabb));
   } // Init
```

Releasing an instance from this class is no big deal. You just have to make sure that all the allocated memory is freed and that all created objects are deleted. After all, you would not want to have those nasty memory leaks, would you?

```
void CPolymesh::Release(void)
   {
```

```
    if (m_ppPoly) {

      for (UINT i=0; i<m_NumPolys; i++)
          SAFE_DELETE(m_ppPoly[i]);

      SAFE_FREE(m_ppPoly);
      }
    } // Release
```

Creating an Instance

To build a new instance of the mesh class, you only need to have a list of polygons that should make up the initial mesh. Of course, you can add polygons later on or remove some of them. Again, I'm not stating absolutes. You can, in fact, create an instance from this class without the data it should contain, but there would be no reason to do so.

Here is the function that lets you fuel data into the mesh object:

```
void CPolymesh::CreateFromPolygons(const CPolygon *pPolys, UCHAR n)
    {
    Release();
    Init();

    m_bSupprBoxCalc = true;

    for (UINT i=0; i<n; i++) AddPolygon(pPolys[i]);

    CalcBoundingBox();
    m_bSupprBoxCalc = false;
    } // CreateFromPolygons
```

As you can see, this function first ensures that the mesh does not contain anything at all. If it does, the existing data is just thrown away. The bounding box recalculation is suppressed because we are potentially adding a lot of polygons now to the mesh, which would require recalculating the box for each polygon. Then the CPolymesh::AddPolygon function is used to add all polygons from the given list. Finally, the bounding box is calculated in a separate call.

However, the function CPolymesh::AddPolygon can be used for more than just adding a bunch of polygons initially. It is, of course, also used to add a single polygon to an existing mesh. And, after all, adding a new polygon to a mesh is done in the blink of an eye. You only need to check that enough memory is available to take another instance of the polygon class, and then you can just add the polygon:

```
HRESULT CPolymesh::AddPolygon(const CPolygon &Poly)
    {
```

```
// allocate memory if needed
m_ppPoly = (LPPOLYGON*) CheckMem( (LPVOID*)m_ppPoly,
            m_NumPolys, sizeof(LPPOLYGON) );

// create new instance and copy data
m_ppPoly[m_NumPolys] = new CPolygon();
m_ppPoly[m_NumPolys]->CopyOf( (LPLEVELOBJECT)&Poly );
m_ppPoly[m_NumPolys]->SetAsPartOfMesh(this);

// adjust counters
m_NumVerts += m_ppPoly[m_NumPolys]->GetNumVerts();
m_NumIndis += m_ppPoly[m_NumPolys]->GetNumIndis();
m_NumPolys++;

if (m_bSuppressBoxCalc) return S_OK;

CalcBoundingBox();
return S_OK;
} // AddPolygon
```

It is also important to adjust the counters for the vertices and the indices of the mesh accordingly. Those are only used for statistics later on. If you provide statistics, however, they should be right. Calculating the bounding box could be made faster here. This function loops through all polygons and recalculates the box completely from scratch. It would be faster to loop through the vertices of the new polygon only and adjust the old box if necessary. If you can add polygons to the mesh, you should also be able to remove them from the mesh object. After all, the editor is all about editing objects, so it is most likely that the user wants to add polygons to meshes and remove them all the time without destroying the whole mesh for that purpose. The following function enables you to remove a specific polygon that you know by its address (as supplied by the selection buffer, for instance):

```
HRESULT CPolymesh::RemovePolygon(const LPPOLYGON pPoly)
   {
   UINT i=0;

   // search the pointer that should be deleted
   for (i=0; i<m_NumPolys; i++)
      if (m_ppPoly[i] == pPoly) break;

   if (i >= m_NumPolys) return ZFX_FAIL;

   // adjust counters
```

```
   m_NumVerts -= m_ppPoly[i]->GetNumVerts();
   m_NumIndis -= m_ppPoly[i]->GetNumIndis();

   // delete the object
   SAFE_DELETE(m_ppPoly[i]);
   if (i != (m_NumPolys-1))
      m_ppPoly[i] = m_ppPoly[m_NumPolys-1];

   m_NumPolys--;

   CalcBoundingBox();
   return ZFX_OK;
   } // RemovePolygon
```

This function takes the address of a polygon that should be deleted from the mesh. You search for this address in the list of polygons the mesh owns, and then pick the appropriate polygon from the list. This is done by addresses because the selection buffer works only with addresses referencing selected objects. If the polygon is found, it is then removed from the list and deleted. If it is the last object in the list of the mesh, the counter is just set accordingly by decreasing it. If it is not the last object in the list, you can just copy the pointer address of the last object in the list to this position to fill the hole in the list.

Loading and Saving

Loading and saving an instance of the mesh class is again using the same scheme as the polygon class. At first you pump the important attributes into the file or load them from the file accordingly. Then the main data part needs to be handled and, in this case, the data part is a bunch of polygons. The nice thing is now that they can take of themselves, you just have to loop through the list of polygons of the mesh and call their own functions to load and save them, respectively:

```
void CPolymesh::Save(FILE *pFile)
   {
   if (!pFile) return;

   fwrite(&m_NumPolys, sizeof(UINT), 1, pFile);
   fwrite(&m_Aabb, sizeof(ZFXAabb), 1, pFile);
   fflush(pFile);

   // sort polygons by texture
   qsort(m_ppPoly, m_NumPolys, sizeof(LPPOLYGON),
         SortBySkin);

   for (UINT i=0; i<m_NumPolys; i++)
```

```
      m_ppPoly[i]->Save(pFile);
   } // Save
/*------------------------*/


bool CPolymesh::Load(FILE *pFile) {
   if (!pFile) return false;

   fread(&m_NumPolys, sizeof(UINT), 1, pFile);
   fread(&m_Aabb, sizeof(ZFXAabb), 1, pFile);

   if (m_NumPolys == 0) return false;

   m_ppPoly = (LPPOLYGON*)InitMem( (LPVOID*)m_ppPoly,
                       m_NumPolys,sizeof(LPPOLYGON));

   for (UINT i=0; i<m_NumPolys; i++) {
      m_ppPoly[i] = new CPolygon();

      if ( !m_ppPoly[i]->Load(pFile) ) {
         // critical failure
         delete m_ppPoly[i];
         m_NumPolys = i;
         return false;
         }

      m_ppPoly[i]->SetAsPartOfMesh(this);
      }
   return true;
   } // Load
```

Saving the data is the easier thing, of course. You only have to store two attributes of the mesh; the class for polygons does the rest. It is worth mentioning that the polygons are sorted by the skin they use, which will make things easier for us when we are loading the data for a video game application (because we can take it for granted that the data is sorted to some degree).

We still need another function for saving data from a mesh, a function that stores only pure, single polygons without the information about the mesh object. The reason for this is simple. As stated previously, the editor should be able to save and load prefabs. However, the prefab format we use here knows nothing about meshes or any other kind of level object except for polygons. So if you have one or more meshes selected and want to save a prefab from the selection, only the polygons are stored, not the mesh to which they belong. Here is the function for this purpose:

```
void CPolymesh::SavePurePolys(FILE *pFile)
   {
   UINT n=0, SkinID=0;
   char buffer[2048];

   if (!pFile) return;
   for (UINT i=0; i<m_NumPolys; i++) {
      // name of the base texture
      SkinID = m_ppPoly[i]->GetSkinID();

      SendMessage(CApplication::m_G.hGUI[CSK_LIST],
                  CB_GETLBTEXT, SkinID,
                  (LPARAM)(LPCSTR)buffer);

      // save string length and string to the file
      n = strlen(buffer);
      fwrite(&n, sizeof(UINT), 1, pFile);
      fwrite(buffer, n, 1, pFile);

      m_ppPoly[i]->Save(pFile);
      }
   } // Save
```

As you can see, the polygons are not just saved to the file. There is also a request to a combo box to get a string from there, and then this string is also saved along with its length to the file. There is also a class CApplication mentioned. Okay, let's examine them one by one. The editor is a WinAPI application, even if we are working only on the geometry classes for now. The application is, as no surprise, mainly implemented in the class CApplication. One static attribute of this class is m_G, where every important thing that must be accessible from outside is stored (such as the handles of the control elements). This is how you get access to the combo box mentioned. This combo box contains a list of all textures that are used as skin objects in the current level, where the place in the list equals the ID of the skin. Therefore, the filename of the texture used by the polygon is saved to the file here.

Unfortunately, you cannot store just the ID of the skin. If you did, a prefab could be used in only the very same level. If you want to use it in a more general manner, however, such as for all levels where it should still show the same textures, you have to save the texture filename along with the geometry.

Copying an Instance

Copying an instance of the mesh class is just as boring as loading and saving a mesh object. No mesh class attribute needs copying, so we must only copy the polygons that form the mesh one by one. This is done by clearing the mesh object first and then looping through the list of polygons of the given mesh and adding them to the current mesh:

```
void CPolymesh::CopyOf(CLevelObject *pLob)
   {
   if ( !pLob->IsOfType(m_Type) ) return;

   LPPOLYMESH pMesh = (LPPOLYMESH)pLob;

   Reset();

   m_bSupprBoxCalc = true;

   for (UINT i=0; i<pMesh->m_NumPolys; i++)
      AddPolygon( *pMesh->m_ppPoly[i] );

   CalcBoundingBox();
   m_bSupprBoxCalc = false;
   } // CopyOf
```

Collision Detection

Again, this level object offers the functionality to be selected by the level designer. This is done just as in the class for the polygon level objects. You just provide a bounding box constructed from the selection rectangle the level designer has opened in its orthogonal views. Then you can use this bounding box to see whether the mesh is inside this selection area, which is true if at least one of its polygons is partially inside:

```
bool CPolymesh::Intersects(const ZFXAabb &aabb, ZFXAXIS axis)
   {
   if ( IsHidden() ) return false;

   // intersection with bounding box?
   if (!m_Aabb.Intersects(aabb)) return false;

   // intersection with polygon in the mesh
   for (UINT i=0; i<m_NumPolys; i++) {
      if (m_ppPoly[i]->IsHidden()) continue;
      if (m_ppPoly[i]->Intersects(aabb, axis))
         return true;
```

```
      }
   return false;
   } // Intersects
```

In some situations, a level designer may want to select single polygons from a mesh, not the whole mesh itself. The strategy stays the same. You open a selection rectangle by clicking in the orthogonal view. Then you extend this rectangle to a bounding box, where the missing coordinate in 3D space is running from +infinity to –infinity. If a mesh is intersecting this bounding box, you test its nonhidden polygons with their according function to evaluate whether they are contained inside the selection rectangle. If this is true, you just add the address of the concerned polygon to the selection buffer provided as a function parameter.

You can go one step further, however. It is not only possible to select polygons from a mesh object, but also to select single vertices from a mesh (which is, of course, a vertex that is part of a polygon belonging to the mesh). The function is more or less the same, but it will then call the appropriate function of the polygon class to select the vertices:

```
void CPolymesh::GetIntersectingPolys(const ZFXAabb &aabb, CSelectionBuffer *pSB,
                                     ZFXAXIS axis)
   {
   if ( IsHidden() ) return;

   // intersection with bounding box?
   if (!m_Aabb.Intersects(aabb)) return;

   // intersection with polygon in the mesh?
   for (UINT i=0; i<m_NumPolys; i++) {
      if (m_ppPoly[i]->IsHidden()) continue;
      if (m_ppPoly[i]->Intersects(aabb, axis))
         pSB->AddLob( m_ppPoly[i] );
      }
   } // GetIntersectingPolys
/*----------------------------*/


void CPolymesh::GetIntersectingVerts(const ZFXAabb
                        &aabb, CSelectionBuffer *pSB,
                        ZFXAXIS axis) {
   if ( IsHidden() ) return;

   // collect vertices
   for (UINT i=0; i<m_NumPolys; i++) {
      m_ppPoly[i]->GetIntersectingVerts(aabb, pSB,
```

```
                                               axis);
        }
    } // GetIntersectingVerts
```

And that is all you need to do to the selection in the orthogonal views. Of course, you would also want to select whole meshes or single polygons from a mesh in the perspective view by clicking them. This mouse click is then calculated into a ray in 3D world space, and so you have to do a collision detection of the level objects with this ray. It is rather easy to evaluate whether a mesh object was hit by checking its bounding box for an intersection first. Under this scenario, you still have to loop through the polygons of the mesh and check whether the ray has really hit one of the polygons or just the empty space between them. Finally, the distance to the point of intersection is returned as a reference parameter.

The same algorithm is used if the level designer wants to select single polygons only. Then you have to loop through all polygons of the mesh and compare the distance to the point of intersection, if any. It might very well be true that a ray hit more than one polygon from a single mesh. In such a case, you have to return the one that is the closest with regard to the origin of the viewer. Here are the two functions that enable you to do this:

```
bool CPolymesh::Picked(const ZFXRay &Ray, float *pfD)
    {
    if ( IsHidden() ) return false;

    if ( !m_Aabb.Intersects(Ray, NULL) ) return false;

    else if ( PickPoly(Ray,9999.9f,pfD) != NULL )
        return true;

    return false;
    } // Picked
/*----------------------------*/


CPolygon* CPolymesh::PickPoly(const ZFXRay &Ray, float fMin, float *pfD)
    {
    CPolygon *pPoly = NULL;

    if ( IsHidden() ) return NULL;

    for (UINT i=0; i<m_NumPolys; i++) {

        if ( m_ppPoly[i]->IsHidden() ) continue;
```

```
        // delegate to Picked()
        if ( m_ppPoly[i]->Picked(Ray, pfD) ) {

            // select the closet one
            if (*pfD < fMin) {
                fMin = *pfD;
                pPoly = m_ppPoly[i];
                }
            }
        }
    }
    return pPoly;
    } // PickPoly
```

Rendering an Instance

Rendering an instance of the mesh class is just a joke, honestly. The mesh is nothing more than just a container of polygon instances. And the polygon class has its own render function. Therefore, you just have to loop through all polygons in the mesh and kindly ask each to render itself. Note that hidden polygons are again not rendered if the parameter indicates that this flag should be taken into consideration. As mentioned previously, hidden level objects are rendered in the perspective view if the relevant check box in the editor is checked:

```
void CPolymesh::Render(ZFXVertexCacheManager *pVCMan, bool bHide)
    {
    if ( IsHidden() ) return;

    for (UINT i=0; i<m_NumPolys; i++) {
        // don't render hidden polygons
        if ( bHide && m_ppPoly[i]->IsHidden() ) continue;
        m_ppPoly[i]->Render(pVCMan, bHide);
        }
    } // Render
```

Texture Coordinates for the Mesh

As far as the texture coordinates are concerned, there is nothing new to report. Still there is only support for planar texture mapping. If this should be done for a selected mesh, the call is delegated to the polygon class. The same holds true for the transformation of the texture coordinates, which means the offset and the repeat of those coordinates. This issue is a bit tricky due to some reasons explained in a moment. First take a look at Figure 14.5. This figure shows the dialog box that enables you to adjust the texture repeat and offset for selected level objects.

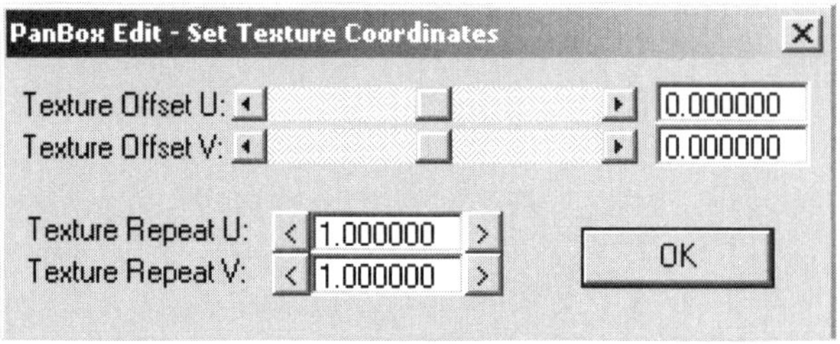

710   Chapter 14 ■ Computer-Aided Design (CAD) Tools

Figure 14.5 The dialog box to edit texture repeat and offset.

You can see from the figure that the offset of the texture on both axes will be controlled by using sliders or by putting the values directly into the input boxes. The repeat for the texture map can also be set directly into the according input boxes or it can be set using the relevant buttons to increase or decrease the value.

The problem now is that all values will apply for all selected polygons. If you have selected a mesh object and call this dialog box, you cannot display the current values for the texture repeat and offset with only one exception (only in the rare case that all polygons in the mesh have exactly the same values for the texture repeat and offset). If only one polygon uses different settings, this dialog box cannot reflect this, and the values are set to 0 and 1, respectively.

You might ask why someone would call this dialog box for more than one polygon if they don't have the same values. On the one hand, this might happen by chance, perhaps because the user forgot to select only a single polygon. On the other hand, and a more real case, is that the user has multiple polygons with different texture repeat values but wants to translate the textures on all selected polygons. This is not supported in this editor, but it is possible if you separate the offset from the adjustment of the texture repeat. You could also think about a separate box that will not let you adjust the final settings of the texture coordinates, but that will let you define additional number of repeats and offsets that should be added to the existing ones.

Anyway, enough talk for now. Here is the function to calculate the planar texture mapping coordinates:

```
void CPolymesh::CalcTextureCoords(ZFXAXIS axis, const ZFXAabb *pAabb)
   {
   if (!pAabb) pAabb = &m_Aabb;

   for (UINT i=0; i<m_NumPolys; i++) {
      m_ppPoly[i]->CalcTextureCoords(axis, pAabb);
      } // for
   } // CalcTextureCoords
```

```
/*-------------------------*/


void CPolymesh::TransTextureCoords(float ftU, float ftV,
                                   float frU, float frV)
   {
   // Brute Force protection against 0 repeat
   if ( (frU < 0.0001f) && (frU > -0.0001f))
      frU = 0.0001f;
   if ( (frV < 0.0001f) && (frV > -0.0001f))
      frV = 0.0001f;

   for (UINT i=0; i<m_NumPolys; i++)
      m_ppPoly[i]->TransTextureCoords(ftU,ftV,frU,frV);
   } // TransTextureCoors
/*-------------------------*/


bool CPolymesh::GetTextureTrans(float *pftU, float *pftV, float *pfrU,
                                float *pfrV)
   {
   float ftU=0.0f, ftV=0.0f, frU=0.0f, frV=0.0f;

   for (UINT i=0; i<m_NumPolys; i++) {
      m_ppPoly[i]->GetTextureTrans(&ftU, &ftV,
                                   &frU, &frV);
      if (i>0) {
         if ( (*pftU != ftU) || (*pftV != ftV) ||
              (*pfrU != frU) || (*pfrV != frV) )
            return false;
         }
      *pftU = ftU;   *pftV = ftV;
      *pfrU = frU;   *pfrV = frV;
      }
   return true;
   } // GetTextureTrans
```

Selection and Hiding Games

We are now back to hiding and selection operations. By now, you know two possible ways in the editor to select level objects. One way is to open a selection rectangle in the orthogonal views; the other is to click an object in the perspective view. However, you have two more options you don't know yet. On the one hand, you can just select all nonhidden objects of a certain type in the editor (for example, all meshes in the level). On the other hand, you can just invert an existing selection (making all selected objects deselected and all deselected objects selected).

Those selection processes are normally controlled by the application's management layer, which controls all the lists of polygons, meshes, and other level objects. However, the class `CPolymesh` is something of a big exception when compared to other level objects. The big difference stems from the fact that this level object is just a container for other objects, namely for the polygons. This results in the unwanted fact that the list of polygons sitting inside a mesh is not known to the management layer that is controlling all level objects (well, all level objects except for the polygons sitting inside meshes). Therefore, the class for the mesh objects needs to implement a bit more functionality, as you can see in the following functions:

```
void CPolymesh::SelectAllPolys(CSelectionBuffer *pSB)
   {
   for (UINT i=0; i<m_NumPolys; i++)
      {
      if ( !m_ppPoly[i]->IsHidden() )
         pSB->AddLob(m_ppPoly[i]);
      }
   } // SelectAllPolys
/*------------------------------*/


void CPolymesh::SelectInvert(CSelectionBuffer *pSB)
   {
   for (UINT i=0; i<m_NumPolys; i++)
      {
      if ( m_ppPoly[i]->IsHidden() ) continue;

      // select unselected
      if ( !m_ppPoly[i]->IsSelected() )
         pSB->AddLob(m_ppPoly[i]);
      // deselect selected
      else m_ppPoly[i]->DeSelect();
      }
   } // SelectInvert
```

In these functions, the selection buffer is also used. Normally, it is fed from a superior layer in the application. In this instance, however, handing over the selection buffer as a visitor to these functions is much easier. It's easier because if you want to select more than one object at a time, such as multiple vertices from a polygon or multiple polygons from a mesh, you need to return a list of selected objects rather than only one single object or its address. To prevent this, I decided to let the selection buffer come down to the class to collect the stuff for itself.

> **Note**
> The superior layer or the managing layer in this application refers to the `CSector` class, which is the single most important management unit in this implementation. The same is true for the video game that loads those levels, as you will see in the next chapter.

You have different ways you can hide level objects with the editing tool's interface. If an object is hidden, no operation can be performed on the object, except for an unhide operation. No hidden object is rendered in the orthogonal views, but they can be rendered in the perspective views if the level designer sets the relevant check box. The problem is that the level objects that are dumped into a mesh object (the polygons) are not recognized as level objects by the superior layer of management, which can only see the free polygons that are not grouped in a mesh (or the meshes, for that matter). So the class for the meshes has to supply the following functions to allow the management layer to control those polygons as well:

- Hide the selected polygons of the mesh
- Hide the unselected polygons of the mesh
- Invert the hidden flag of all polygons of the mesh
- Unhide all hidden polygons of the mesh

Note that this is not dealing with the state of the mesh itself. Even if all polygons contained inside the mesh are hidden, the instance of the `CPolymesh` class itself is not hidden because it has its own flag. Well, it won't get rendered anyway because the only visible parts of a mesh are its polygons. Although this is just a little catch, it'll be necessary to take care of it. After all, you cannot select a mesh that is not hidden but whose polygons are all hidden. On the other hand, you can use the mesh's flag to hide all of its polygons without the need to toggle the flag on each polygon. The following functions are mostly meant to deal with the single polygons from the mesh:

```
void CPolymesh::HideNoPolys(void)
   {
   for (UINT i=0; i<m_NumPolys; i++)
      m_ppPoly[i]->UnHide();
   } // HideNoPolys
/*----------------------------*/
```

```
void CPolymesh::HideSelectedPolys(void)
```

```
    {
    for (UINT i=0; i<m_NumPolys; i++)
        if ( m_ppPoly[i]->IsSelected() )
            m_ppPoly[i]->Hide();
    } // HideSelectedPolys
/*--------------------------*/


void CPolymesh::HideUnselectedPolys(void)
    {
    if ( IsSelected() ) return;

    for (UINT i=0; i<m_NumPolys; i++)
        if ( !m_ppPoly[i]->IsSelected() )
            m_ppPoly[i]->Hide();
    } // HideUnselectedPolys
/*--------------------------*/


void CPolymesh::HideInvertPolys(void)
    {
    for (UINT i=0; i<m_NumPolys; i++)
        if ( m_ppPoly[i]->IsHidden() )
            m_ppPoly[i]->UnHide();
        else
            m_ppPoly[i]->Hide();
    } // HideInvertPolys
```

Selecting and hiding level objects in this implementation is plain simple. The state of being hidden or selected or not is controlled by toggling the flags, which are declared as attributes in the base class along with their accessor functions. The value of the flag is then taken into consideration during the render operations. That isn't magic, but just a suitable interface to access the objects.

Miscellaneous Functions for Meshes

As well as for the polygon class, there are also some miscellaneous functions in the mesh class. Three of those helper functions only delegate the call to each polygon object in the mesh because the polygon class implements the functionality. The following functions are just a big loop over the polygon list of the mesh each:

- CPolymesh::InsideOut
- CPolymesh::SetSkinID
- CPolymesh::CalcNormals

The next helper function calculates the bounding box for the mesh, which is done almost the same way as for the polygon class. Instead of looping through vertex lists, we only need to loop through the corner pointer of the bounding boxes of the polygons contained in the mesh. Actually, you are then spanning a bounding box for the mesh by including all bounding boxes of the polygons:

```
void CPolymesh::CalcBoundingBox(void)
   {
   ZFXVector vcMax, vcMin, vcTemp;
   ZFXAabb   Aabb;

   Aabb = m_ppPoly[0]->GetAabb();
   vcMax = vcMin = Aabb.vcCenter;

   for (UINT i=0; i<m_NumPolys; i++)
      {
      Aabb = m_ppPoly[i]->GetAabb();

      vcTemp = Aabb.vcMax;
      if      ( vcTemp.x > vcMax.x ) vcMax.x = vcTemp.x;
      else if ( vcTemp.x < vcMin.x ) vcMin.x = vcTemp.x;
      if      ( vcTemp.y > vcMax.y ) vcMax.y = vcTemp.y;
      else if ( vcTemp.y < vcMin.y ) vcMin.y = vcTemp.y;
      if      ( vcTemp.z > vcMax.z ) vcMax.z = vcTemp.z;
      else if ( vcTemp.z < vcMin.z ) vcMin.z = vcTemp.z;

      vcTemp = Aabb.vcMin;
      if      ( vcTemp.x > vcMax.x ) vcMax.x = vcTemp.x;
      else if ( vcTemp.x < vcMin.x ) vcMin.x = vcTemp.x;
      if      ( vcTemp.y > vcMax.y ) vcMax.y = vcTemp.y;
      else if ( vcTemp.y < vcMin.y ) vcMin.y = vcTemp.y;
      if      ( vcTemp.z > vcMax.z ) vcMax.z = vcTemp.z;
      else if ( vcTemp.z < vcMin.z ) vcMin.z = vcTemp.z;
      }
   m_Aabb.vcCenter = (vcMax + vcMin) / 2.0f;
   m_Aabb.vcMax    = vcMax;
   m_Aabb.vcMin    = vcMin;
   } // CalcBoundingBox
```

One thing remains to be explained. In the class declaration, you have already seen this function declaration:

```
LPPOLYGON CPolymesh::GetPolygon(UINT i) { return m_ppPoly[i]; }
```

With the helping hand of this function, you can access a specific polygon that is part of the mesh. The question is how you get the index of the polygon you want to retrieve in the first place and why you might need a certain polygon from the mesh at all. Actually, this function is used only in a single place in the editor: where a mesh gets fragmented into free polygons. You would then destroy the mesh class. Before you do this, you just loop through the polygon list of the mesh, get each polygon from the mesh with the function shown above, and make a copy of the polygon, which is then placed as a free polygon inside the active sector.

Into a New World: CPortal

In Chapter 13, you learned a lot about portal engines, including how they work and their utility. Portals enable you to create connections between sectors and to build some kind of graph data structure that represents the whole level. In the simplest scenario, a single room in an indoor level is a single sector, and the doors leading from this room to neighboring rooms or corridors are each a portal. (You also learned about special effects you can create with portals, such as Star Gates, mirrors, and labyrinths.) Of course, a portal cannot lead to another neighboring sector. A portal can only lead to another portal, which in turn belongs to a certain sector. Note, however, that the portals in our editor do not fulfill any kind of task such as scene management, culling, or anything like that. The editor enables you only to *place* portals (if you think you need them and want to have them in the game loading the level data). Portal use is not a must, it is only recommended here.

Class Declaration

Remember that if you use a portal with a lot of edges, you sustain a performance penalty. If you want to do real portal clipping, this would result in an *n*-sided frustum, which leads to overhead in frustum culling even for bounding box objects due to the number of planes in the frustum. That is why a portal in this editor must not have more than or fewer than four vertices. There is also no direct way to create a portal. Instead, you must build a polygon and shape it to fit the place where the portal should reside. Then you call the function CPolygon::CreatePortal, which copies the geometry of the polygon and builds a portal object with that geometry. The editor should then remove the polygon from the world by deleting it.

Here is the declaration for the portal class:

```
class CPortal : public CLevelObject {
   public:
      CPortal(void);
      virtual ~CPortal(void);

      void      CopyOf(CLevelObject*);
```

```
    void      SetGeometry(const VERTEX*, const WORD*,
                          const ZFXAabb&);
    void      Render(ZFXVertexCacheManager*,bool);
    bool      Picked(const ZFXRay&, float*);
    bool      Intersects(const ZFXAabb&, ZFXAXIS);

    UINT      GetID(void)           {return m_ID;     }
    UINT      GetItsTargetID(void){return m_BID;   }
    CSector*  GetItsSector(void)    {return m_pDad;   }
    CPortal*  GetItsTarget(void)    {return m_pBrother;}
    void      SetID(UINT ID)          { m_ID = ID; }
    void      SetItsSector(CSector *pS) { m_pDad=pS; }
    void      SetItsTarget(CPortal *pP);
    void      DeconnectFrom(UINT id)
                              { if (m_BID==id) m_BID=0; }
    void      Save(FILE*);
    bool      Load(FILE*);

  private:
    CSector*  m_pDad;             // own sector
    CPortal*  m_pBrother;         // destination portal
    UINT      m_ID;               // own id
    UINT      m_BID;              // brother id
    VERTEX    *m_pVerts;          // vertices
    WORD      *m_pIndis;          // indices
    WORD      *m_pLineIndis;      // line indices
    bool      m_bVisible;         // destination sector visible?

    void      Init(void);
    void      Release(void);
  }; // class
typedef class CPortal *LPPORTAL;
```

Notice that the term *destination portal* is not used here; instead, the term *brother* is used (just to make it sound more friendly). Other than that, there is not much to see in this class. The portal knows its brother, if it has one. It knows to which sector its brother belongs, and it has some geometry so that it can be rendered in the editor.

Note

Keep in mind that portals are visible only in the editor. In the final game, they don't show up at all because they are used only to determine neighboring sectors of the one the player is currently in.

Creating an Instance

The initialization function and the one to release an instance of the portal class are just basic stuff like most of the level class startup and shutdown functions:

```
void CPortal::Init(void)
   {
   m_NumVerts    = 0;
   m_NumIndis    = 0;
   m_NumPolys    = 1;
   m_ID          = 0;
   m_BID         = 0;
   m_bSelected   = false;
   m_bHidden     = false;
   m_bVisible    = true;
   m_pVerts      = NULL;
   m_pIndis      = NULL;
   m_pLineIndis  = NULL;
   m_pDad        = NULL;
   m_pBrother    = NULL;
   m_Type        = LOB_PORTAL;
   memset(&m_Aabb, 0, sizeof(ZFXAabb));
   } // Init
/*----------------------------------*/


void CPortal::Release(void)
   {
   SAFE_DELETE_A(m_pVerts);
   SAFE_DELETE_A(m_pIndis);
   SAFE_DELETE_A(m_pLineIndis);
   } // Release
```

The only way to fill data into the portal class is by setting its geometry. Normally, you copy the data from a polygon into a new portal object, because the editor does not allow for another way to create a portal (other than converting a polygon into one). After this conversion has taken place, the portal cannot be moved or rotated or edited in another way. After all, doing so would not make sense and would require the editor to redo all the connections going to and from this portal. The only action you can do with a portal is to select and delete it. Therefore, first adjust the final shape and orientation of the polygon you want to convert into a portal, and then convert it using this function:

```
void CPortal::SetGeometry(const VERTEX *pVerts, const WORD *pIndis,
                          const ZFXAabb &aabb)
```

```
{
Reset();

m_NumVerts = 4;
m_NumIndis = 6;

m_pVerts = new VERTEX[m_NumVerts];
m_pIndis = new WORD[m_NumIndis];
m_pLineIndis = new WORD[m_NumVerts*2];

if (!m_pVerts || !m_pIndis || !m_pLineIndis) return;

memcpy(m_pVerts, pVerts, sizeof(VERTEX)*4);
memcpy(m_pIndis, pIndis, sizeof(WORD)*6);

for (UINT i=0; i<m_NumVerts; i++) {
   m_pLineIndis[(i*2)] = i;
   m_pLineIndis[(i*2)+1] = i+1;
   if (i==m_NumVerts-1) m_pLineIndis[(i*2)+1] = 0;
   }
memcpy(&m_Aabb, &aabb, sizeof(ZFXAabb));
} // SetGeometry
```

Loading and Saving

Loading and saving is just the same for all level objects. First you write out the counters and other attributes of this class or read it from a file. Then you loop through the dynamically allocated lists containing the main data of the instance:

```
void CPortal::Save(FILE *pFile) {
   fwrite(&m_ID,       sizeof(UINT),     1, pFile);
   fwrite(&m_BID,      sizeof(UINT),     1, pFile);
   fwrite(&m_NumVerts, sizeof(UINT),     1, pFile);
   fwrite(&m_NumIndis, sizeof(UINT),     1, pFile);
   fwrite(&m_bVisible, sizeof(bool),     1, pFile);
   fwrite(&m_Aabb,     sizeof(ZFXAabb),  1, pFile);

   fwrite(m_pVerts, sizeof(VERTEX), m_NumVerts, pFile);
   fwrite(m_pIndis, sizeof(WORD), m_NumIndis,   pFile);
   fwrite(m_pLineIndis,sizeof(WORD),m_NumVerts*2,pFile);
   } // Save
/*----------------------------------*/
```

```
bool CPortal::Load(FILE *pFile)
   {
   fread(&m_ID,       sizeof(UINT),    1, pFile);
   fread(&m_BID,      sizeof(UINT),    1, pFile);
   fread(&m_NumVerts, sizeof(UINT),    1, pFile);
   fread(&m_NumIndis, sizeof(UINT),    1, pFile);
   fread(&m_bVisible, sizeof(bool),    1, pFile);
   fread(&m_Aabb,     sizeof(ZFXAabb), 1, pFile);

   if (m_NumVerts == 0) return false;

   m_pVerts    = new VERTEX[m_NumVerts];
   m_pIndis    = new WORD[m_NumIndis];
   m_pLineIndis = new WORD[m_NumVerts*2];
   if ( !m_pVerts || !m_pIndis || !m_pLineIndis)
      return false;

   fread(m_pVerts, sizeof(VERTEX), m_NumVerts, pFile);
   fread(m_pIndis, sizeof(WORD),   m_NumIndis, pFile);
   fread(m_pLineIndis,sizeof(WORD),m_NumVerts*2,pFile);
   return true;
   } // Load
```

Copying an Instance

As always, copying an instance of a level object class is no big deal. Just copy the important attribute of the given object, which should be duplicated, and you are already done with this task:

```
void CPortal::CopyOf(CLevelObject *pLob)
   {
   if ( !pLob->IsOfType(m_Type) ) return;
   LPPORTAL pPort = (LPPORTAL)pLob;
   Reset();

   SetGeometry(pPort->m_pVerts, pPort->m_pIndis, pPort->m_Aabb);

   m_pDad     = pPort->m_pDad;
   m_pBrother = pPort->m_pBrother;
   m_ID       = pPort->m_ID;
   m_BID      = pPort->m_BID;
   m_bVisible = pPort->m_bVisible;
   } // CopyOf
```

Collision Detection and Rendering of an Instance

It's unnecessary to list the functions for selecting and picking a portal in the orthogonal views and the perspective view here. The code would just be redundant. As you already know, a portal is just a polygon, so the functions used for this purpose are similar implementations to the ones you can find in the `CPolygon` class.

The same is true for rendering a portal, which is done the same way as rendering a polygon. As seen from this perspective, it might have been a good idea to derive the portal class not directly from the level object base class but from the polygon class instead. (If you want to re-implement a similar tool or change this one, keep this idea in mind.)

Miscellaneous Functions for Portals

We must take care of one thing before we are done with the portals: establish a connection between two portals, which are then pointing to each other. The following function enables this. Note, however, that you have to prevent one thing from happening: a portal trying to connect to itself. Such a portal would result in an infinite loop in the application that uses this level, so we won't allow for that:

```
void CPortal::SetItsTarget(CPortal *pP)
    {
    // prevent infinite loops
    if (pP->GetID() == m_ID) return;

    if (pP) {
       m_pBrother = pP;
       m_BID = m_pBrother->GetID();
       }
    else {
       m_pBrother = NULL;
       m_BID = 0;
       }
    } // SetItsTarget
```

You may want to cut the connection between a portal and its brother if you want to connect the portal to another portal or if you want to make this portal a mirror or something like that. In this case, the function will also accept a `NULL` pointer value.

Let There Be Light: CLight

To create the lighting in our levels, we set and edit light sources in the level editor. For the sake of simplicity, only one type of light source is built in to the editor, the pixel-shader omni light (discussed earlier in this book). Essentially, the class `CLight` itself has nothing to do with how we make the lighting calculations. The only thing that this class will hold is the position and the radius of the light source as well as the color of the light. Therefore, this class is very easy to implement. The tricky thing is how you then implement the lighting itself later on.

One issue does require attention. We are just using omni lights here, which emit their light evenly in each direction. In reality, however, most light sources are some kind of spot light. This discrepancy doesn't create a fatal problem, however, because we can just fake a spot light by placing an omni light in a way that the lighting looks like a spot light. Figure 14.6 shows how to do this. The geometry that shows a light is located at the ceiling. But this is only a bunch of polygons, nothing else. However, the light source, which will not show up in the game later on, is placed just below the floor. The result of this is that the radius of influence of the omni light will include only the floor polygon, not the walls or the ceiling. Therefore, it looks like the spot of a spot light even though it is an omni light.

The problem with this approach is shadow casting. If you were to calculate the shadows from the given position of the light source, they would be optically wrong. For a person standing right below the light in the corridor, the shadow should go down on the floor. Because the light source is located below this person, however, the shadow would be cast up onto the ceiling. Weird. To overcome this problem, I separated the source of light from the source of shadow. In the class we use for a light, you can set a flag to indicate whether the object is a shadow source or a light source. A light source should be taken to calculate the lighting, and a shadow source should be used to cast the shadows. For the scene displayed in Figure 14.6, you would then place another object of this function call right below the ceiling and would set this as a shadow source. This will solve the problem.

Class Declaration

Now that calculating the light is clear to you, take a look at the class declaration for the level object of the light type. As with portals, the light source itself will not show up in an application that is using the level data. In the level editor, however, you should mark the position of a light source so that the level designer can see its location. In Figure 14.6, a rhombus shape for the geometrical object is used. Note that the editor also has a class CGeometry, which has a set of static functions to create simple geometrical objects, such as a rhombus or a cube, as a list of polygon objects or as a mesh object.

The class for the light sources has an attribute of the mesh class type that is used for all functions, such as rendering, collision detection, and so on. Here is the complete class declaration:

```
class CLight : public CLevelObject
   {
   public:
      CLight(void);
      virtual ~CLight(void);
```

Class Design of the Tool 723

Figure 14.6 Fake a spot light with a point light. The geometry for the light is located below the ceiling, whereas the actual light source is just above the floor.

```
void     CopyOf(CLevelObject*);

void     Render(ZFXVertexCacheManager*,bool);
void     Translate(const ZFXVector&);

bool     Picked(const ZFXRay &Ray, float *pfD)
            { return m_Mesh.Picked(Ray, pfD); }

bool     Intersects(const ZFXAabb &b, ZFXAXIS a)
            { return m_Mesh.Intersects(b, a); }

ZFXVector GetPosition(void) { return m_vcPos; }
void     SetPosition(const ZFXVector&);
```

```
    void     SetColor(const ZFXCOLOR &clr)
                {memcpy(&m_Clr,&clr,sizeof(ZFXCOLOR));}

    void     SetColor(float fR, float fG, float fB)
                { m_Clr.fR = fR; m_Clr.fB = fB;
                  m_Clr.fG = fG; m_Clr.fA = 1.0f; }

    ZFXCOLOR GetColor(void)       { return m_Clr; }
    void     SetRadius(float fR)  { m_fR = fR; }
    float    GetRadius(void)      { return m_fR; }
    void     SetFlickering(bool b) {m_bFlicker = b;}
    bool     IsFlickering(void)   {return m_bFlicker;}
    void     SetShadowCasting(bool b);
    bool     IsShadowCasting(void){return m_bShadow;}
    void     Save(FILE*);
    bool     Load(FILE*);

  private:
    CPolymesh m_Mesh;
    ZFXVector m_vcPos;
    ZFXCOLOR  m_Clr;
    float     m_fR;
    bool      m_bFlicker;
    bool      m_bShadow;

    void      Init(void);
    void      Release(void);

  }; // class
typedef class CLight *LPLIGHT;
```

Because this class does not use any kind of dynamically allocated memory and doesn't even create any object for a pointer, the Release() function can stay empty. In the initialization function, you can see that a static function of the class CGeometry is used here to create a geometrical object for the light. In its second parameter, you could also have supplied a list of polygon objects to be filled with the geometry instead of a mesh; because this class only deals with a mesh object, however, we can just create the geometry as a mesh object and copy it:

```
void CLight::Init(void)
   {
   CGeometry geo;
```

```
m_NumVerts   = 0;
m_NumIndis   = 0;
m_NumPolys   = 1;
m_vcPos      = ZFXVector(0,0,0);
m_bSelected  = false;
m_bHidden    = false;
m_bFlicker   = false;
m_bShadow    = false;
m_Type       = LOB_LIGHT;
memset(&m_Aabb, 0, sizeof(ZFXAabb));

geo.CreateLight(&m_Mesh, NULL, ZFXVector(0,0,0), 0.2f, 0.2f, 0.2f);
m_Mesh.SetSkinID(1);
} // Init
```

In this class, you will also find the attribute m_bFlicker, which is set to true or false to indicate whether this light should be flickering. Even the good old *Doom 1* had those flickering lights, which can create a lot of atmosphere. In the editor, this is only a flag, and you can leave it up to the application using our level data to interpret this flag and react accordingly.

Copying, Saving, and Loading an Instance

Copying, saving, and loading of an instance of this CLight class are the very same as in all the other level object classes. You just deal with the main attributes you need to restore all the information about the light object. Then you call the relevant function of the mesh object to let it take care of itself:

```
void CLight::CopyOf(CLevelObject *pLob)
   {
   if ( !pLob->IsOfType(m_Type) ) return;
   LPLIGHT pLight = (LPLIGHT)pLob;
   Reset();
   m_Aabb     = pLob->GetAabb();
   m_vcPos    = pLight->m_vcPos;
   m_Clr      = pLight->m_Clr;
   m_fR       = pLight->m_fR;
   m_bFlicker = pLight->m_bFlicker;
   m_bShadow  = pLight->m_bShadow;
   m_Mesh.CopyOf( &pLight->m_Mesh );
   } // CopyOf
/*----------------------------*/

void CLight::Save(FILE *pFile)
```

```
    {
    fwrite(&m_vcPos,    sizeof(ZFXVector), 1, pFile);
    fwrite(&m_Aabb,     sizeof(ZFXAabb),   1, pFile);
    fwrite(&m_Clr,      sizeof(ZFXCOLOR),  1, pFile);
    fwrite(&m_fR,       sizeof(float),     1, pFile);
    fwrite(&m_bFlicker, sizeof(bool),      1, pFile);
    fwrite(&m_bShadow,  sizeof(bool),      1, pFile);
    m_Mesh.Save(pFile);
    } // Save
/*------------------------*/

bool CLight::Load(FILE *pFile)
    {
    fread(&m_vcPos,    sizeof(ZFXVector), 1, pFile);
    fread(&m_Aabb,     sizeof(ZFXAabb),   1, pFile);
    fread(&m_Clr,      sizeof(ZFXCOLOR),  1, pFile);
    fread(&m_fR,       sizeof(float),     1, pFile);
    fread(&m_bFlicker, sizeof(bool),      1, pFile);
    fread(&m_bShadow,  sizeof(bool),      1, pFile);
    return m_Mesh.Load(pFile);
    } // Load
```

Collision Detection and Rendering

The collision detection and the rendering of a light source object are fairly easy. Because we are using a mesh object for a light source, we can utilize this mesh object for the purpose of collision detection and rendering. Therefore, the relevant functions just delegate the workload to the `CPolymesh` class.

Interactive Objects: CEntity

An entity in our game's context is just a geometrical model, such as a mesh object, but it is not static; it can be ordered to do certain animations or movements. Furthermore, the player who is close to the object and presses a certain key on his keyboard can activate such an animation or movement. You can build arbitrarily complex objects as entities (simple switches the player has to activate, moving platforms such as elevators, and subway train wagons driving through the level, for instance).

Such complex entities are beyond the scope of this book. Instead, you learn here how to implement one type of animated, activatable entity: a sliding door. As you will see, you can also use the editor to adjust the attributes for the door, such as sliding distance and the sliding axis. In the game in Chapter 15, the player can then activate those doors to open them, and the doors will close automatically after a certain pause.

With such a sample at hand, it won't be difficult for you to conceive of other types of entities that are a bit more complex (using a whole path for the movement, for example, with certain waypoints).

Class Declaration

Before implementing the class for the entity derived from the level object base class, you have to define some more things. An instance of this class will by just a plain entity without specific capability or utility. Although it would make sense to derive one class from this class for each type of entity you want to have in your level, for the sake of simplicity I chose another approach here by introducing a structure for a specific entity type, which is then used as an attribute in the class to hold specific attributes for a certain entity type:

```
typedef enum ZFXENTITY_TYPE
    {
    ENT_UNKNOWN,
    ENT_DOOR
    } ZFXENTITY;

typedef struct ENTITYDOOR_TYPE
    {
    float    fDist;
    float    fPause;
    ZFXAXIS  Axis;
    UINT     Portal[2];
    } ENTITYDOOR;
```

Now it's time to consider the class declaration for the entity objects. Such an entity does indeed have some geometry that needs to be displayed in the level. Instead of re-implementing a lot of functionality we already have available, however, we just take an attribute of the type CPolymesh and add it to this class to deal with all the geometrical issues. In this class, there is also a void pointer, which will store the describing structure of the entity with additional attributes. In this case of a door, it will always be the structure ENTITYDOOR:

```
class CEntity : public CLevelObject
    {
    public:
       CEntity(void);
       virtual ~CEntity(void);

       void     CopyOf(CLevelObject*);
       void     Render(ZFXVertexCacheManager*,bool);
       void     Translate(const ZFXVector&);
       bool     Picked(const ZFXRay&, float*);
```

```
    bool        Intersects(const ZFXAabb&, ZFXAXIS);
    void        Save(FILE*);
    bool        Load(FILE*);

    ZFXENTITY   GetSubType(void) { return m_SubType; }
    void        SetSubType(ZFXENTITY);
    void        SetGeometry(const CPolymesh *pMesh);
    void        SetData(const ENTITYDOOR&);
    void        SetData(const ENTITYPLAYER&);
    void*       GetData(void) { return m_pData; }

    void        RemovePortalConnections(UINT);
    bool        ConnectTo( CPortal* );

  private:
    ZFXENTITY   m_SubType;    // door, ...
    CPolymesh   m_Mesh;       // polymesh
    void        *m_pData;     // info structure
    UINT        m_nSize;      // size of pData

    void        Init(void);
    void        Release(void);
  }; // class
typedef class CEntity *LPENTITY;
```

Creating an Instance

Why should we make this more complex than necessary? Remember that we created a portal by just using the polygon class and converting an instance of the polygon class into a portal. Therefore, our editor already has the functionality to create a polygon.

For the entities, we'll follow a similar approach (albeit more elegant). In this case, we won't use just a single polygon to build an entity. Instead, we'll define a mesh object out of a set of polygons first. Then we can select this mesh and click a button in the level editor to create an entity instance out of this mesh object.

Thus the level designer can just build a set of polygons that forms a door, for example. Then he selects those polygons and groups them together into a mesh object and builds an entity object from this mesh.

Common Functionalities

This level object, like all the other types, has common functionalities such as picking, selecting, and so on. It's unnecessary to list them here because this class uses the functions of the CPolymesh class for these. That's one helpful thing about object orientation: You don't have to re-implement similar functions if you can just use other objects that are already at your disposal.

Miscellaneous Functions for the Entities

Although this version of the editor allows for only one type of entity, I still did not hard-code this type into the class. Instead, there is a function to set the subtype of the entity object. Currently, there is only one type to select, as you can see in Figure 14.7. However, you can add any type you want to have here. As of now, there are only sliding doors.

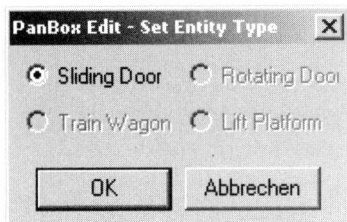

Figure 14.7 Dialog box for the entity type selection.

Here is the function used internally by the dialog box shown in Figure 14.7 to set the relevant type of the entity for an instance of the entity class:

```
void CEntity::SetSubType(ZFXENTITY SubType)
   {
   if (SubType == m_SubType) return;

   m_SubType = SubType;

   SAFE_FREE(m_pData);

   switch (m_SubType) {
      case ENT_DOOR:
         m_nSize = sizeof(ENTITYDOOR);
         m_pData = malloc(m_nSize);
         if (!m_pData) break;
         memset(m_pData, 0, m_nSize);
         break;
      default: break;
      } // switch
   } // SetSubType
```

As for the entities, you can use a second dialog box in the editor to set the attributes of an entity. To call this dialog box, you select one entity and click the relevant button in the GUI. Figure 14.8 shows this dialog box. In this dialog box, you can set the distance in units that the door should move when it is activated. Another field enables you to set the time that the door will pause in its open state before closing. You can also select the axis on which the door should move. To change the direction of the move, you just add a negative sign to the distance.

Although it would be more convenient if you could define an arbitrary axis for the movement, this would involve setting a vector in the editor and rotating this vector. Such complexity is beyond the scope of this book (and this version of the editor), but feel free to add this feature.

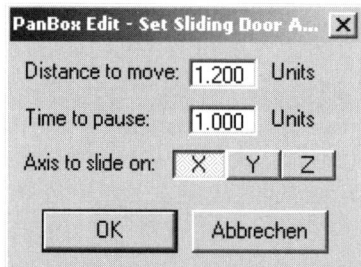

Figure 14.8 Dialog box to set the attributes of a door entity.

Connecting Entities with Portals

Now it's time for another helpful functionality to make its way into our editor. As mentioned in Chapter 13, you can activate and deactivate a portal. Just remember how the guys from the SG-1 team had to twist and whirl the Star Gate to bring it online and open it.

Think about the concept behind deactivating a portal that is just an invisible connection in a doorframe, for example. Suppose you have a room leading to another room through a door, and in this doorframe there is a portal sitting that takes care of rendering the neighboring room if the player can see the doorframe. If you have doorframes as well as doors, however, it is a waste of performance just to render the neighboring sectors if the portal is inside the view frustum—especially if you have doors that are closing automatically; after a few seconds, you have a situation where all doors in a level are closed most of the time. Hence even if the portal is in the view frustum, the neighboring room will not bring a single pixel onto the screen because the door hides the portal. You could do a hidden surface removal and ignore the portals that are occluded, but there is an easier way. If you have a door entity in your level, you can just connect this entity to the portal. The only thing you need to do is to save the ID of the two portals that are intersecting a door entity. Those portals are then deactivated and will not render their neighboring sectors until they are activated—and they will be activated whenever the door is activated.

The following two functions enable you to set the portal connection for the entity:

```
void CEntity::RemovePortalConnections(UINT id)
   {
   if (m_SubType != ENT_DOOR) return;

   ENTITYDOOR *pData=NULL;

   pData = (ENTITYDOOR*)m_pData;
   if (pData->Portal[0] == id) pData->Portal[0]=0;
   if (pData->Portal[1] == id) pData->Portal[1]=0;
   } // RemovePortalConnections
/*--------------------------*/


bool CEntity::ConnectTo(CPortal *pPortal)
   {
   if (m_SubType != ENT_DOOR) return false;

   ENTITYDOOR *pData=NULL;

   pData = (ENTITYDOOR*)m_pData;
   if (pData->Portal[0] != 0) {
      if (pData->Portal[1] == 0) {
         pData->Portal[1] = pPortal->GetID();
         return true;
         }
      else return false;
      }
   else {
      pData->Portal[0] = pPortal->GetID();
      return true;
      }
   } // RemovePortalConnections
```

This automated functionality to connect the portals to the other level objects is controlled and called by the management layer of the level, which is the CSector class. Therefore, each time a new portal is inserted into a level, the sector class has to loop through all of its level objects and determine where connections have to be made.

Go Fish: CSpawn

One more mini-LOB needs to be examined, which is done here in just a few lines of text and code. At this point, the level files still can't define points in the level where characters, such as players and bots, can initially be placed. Such points are normally called spawn points because the characters are spawned in these locations. Just the class declaration for those spawn points is shown here because it needs only two attributes and not very many functions. The first attribute is the location of the spawn point; the second is a mesh object.

This mesh object is used to render the spawn point in the editor. It is just to set a marker in the level so that the level designer can see where the spawn points are located. We are using the same mesh object here that we used for the visualization of the light sources, but we will render it in another color to differentiate the two of them.

Here is the class declaration:

```
class CSpawnPoint : public CLevelObject
   {
   public:
      CSpawnPoint(void);
      virtual ~CSpawnPoint(void);

      void      CopyOf(CLevelObject*);
      void      Render(ZFXVertexCacheManager*,bool);
      void      Translate(const ZFXVector&);

      bool      Picked(const ZFXRay &Ray, float *pfD)
                   { return m_Mesh.Picked(Ray, pfD); }
      bool      Intersects(const ZFXAabb &b, ZFXAXIS a)
                   { return m_Mesh.Intersects(b, a); }

      ZFXVector GetPosition(void) { return m_vcPos; }
      void      SetPosition(const ZFXVector&);
      void      Save(FILE*);
      bool      Load(FILE*);

   private:
      CPolymesh m_Mesh;
      ZFXVector m_vcPos;

      void      Init(void);
      void      Release(void);
   }; // class
typedef class CSpawnPoint *LPSPAWNPOINT;
```

Initially, a spawn point has the position (0,0,0) in 3D space, which is the origin of the world coordinate system. The function `CSpawnPoint::Translate` enables you to move this position, or you can query and set its value with the two accessor functions. All other functions of this class just delegate the call to the `CPolymesh` class.

Local Management: CSector

You read earlier that the `CPolygon` class is the most complex one in this chapter. Perhaps that was a bit of an overstatement. The class for the sector we are about to implement now is every bit as (and perhaps more) complex. Don't worry, though; it is not complicated (even though it requires many lines of source code). In this class, all the small pieces of the level editor puzzle come together. Think about all the classes implemented so far: a polygon, a polymesh, a portal, a light source, and an entity. All of those objects are derived from the level object base class, but as of now they are just standalone classes, more or less without any management involved.

Although you might think that the level class itself would manage all those objects in a level, that is not the case. We are dealing with a portal engine here, and you can think of the portal engine nowadays as connecting several small levels together. At least this is the way you should treat portal engines. Those small sublevels are called sectors in our case, and that is why the sector class is doing all this management of level objects. The level itself will know only about its sectors, nothing else.

Upon completion of this section, when you have the sector class up and working, most of your work will have been completed, and you will have the editor more or less ready. Honest.

Class Declaration and Basic Functions

Because of the size of this declaration, your understanding of it will be enhanced if we review it piece by piece. The easiest part in this class is the stuff for the statistics. The level editor should be able to determine the number of polygons, meshes, portals, and so on inside a level. For this reason, this class has a number of counters, set accordingly each time an object is added or deleted from the sector. The following functions return those counters to display the statistic:

```
UINT CSector::GetNumVertsM(void);    // vertices in meshes
UINT CSector::GetNumIndisM(void);    // indices in meshes
UINT CSector::GetNumMeshs(void);
UINT CSector::GetNumPorts(void);
UINT CSector::GetNumLights(void);
UINT CSector::GetNumEntities(void);
UINT CSector::GetNumPolysTotal(void);
```

This class also has the level object functions `CSector::Picked` and `CSector::Intersects`; these serve no real purpose in a sector, because you cannot pick or select a sector. You can actually select a sector, because there can be only one sector active for editing its level objects, but you do so via a combo box in the level editor's GUI. To be able to instantiate objects from the sector class, we don't really want to implement those functions to just return any value; after all, the sector class is also derived from the level object base class.

This section next shows the attributes from the class declaration for a sector object, so you can just look at them without being distracted by all those member functions and the class declaration syntax. As mentioned previously, portals must have unique IDs, the only level object in this editor with this requirement (and so this attribute must remain constant here; otherwise the entities would not be able to connect themselves to a portal, and the portals would not be able to reference each other). Just saving a pointer won't do the trick. After you save the level and reload it, the pointer is useless. In this case, the sectors also get a unique ID. Such sector IDs are necessary only if a level designer wants to be able to identify and select a specific sector from the list of sectors he wants to edit. Normally, only a single sector is active for editing in the level editor. The inactive sector can be rendered as well; if you want to edit another sector, however, you have to select it as active. To avoid using numeric IDs such as 0, 1, 2, . . ., which would tell the level designer nothing, each sector has a unique name string supplied by the level designer upon its creation. Besides the name, each sector also has an attribute for the ambient light. This can differ from sector to sector. The other attributes of the sector class are six lists for different level object types and counters for those lists. Note that there is an additional counter for the polygons that are part of a mesh.

Here is the list of attributes from the class declaration:

```
private:
   char         m_chName[256]; // name of the sector
   ZFXCOLOR     m_Ambient;     // ambient light

   LPPOLYGON    *m_ppPoly;     // polygons
   LPPOLYMESH   *m_ppMesh;     // meshes
   LPPORTAL     *m_ppPortal;   // portals
   LPLIGHT      *m_ppLight;    // lights
   LPENTITY     *m_ppEntity;   // entities
   LPSPAWNPOINT *m_ppSpawn;    // spawn points

   UINT         m_NumMeshs;      // number of meshes
   UINT         m_NumPsInMeshs;  // number of polygons in meshes
   UINT         m_NumPorts;      // number of portals
   UINT         m_NumLights;     // number of light
   UINT         m_NumEntys;      // number of entities
```

```
    UINT        m_NumSpawns;    // number of spawns

    // temporary pointer
    LPLEVELOBJECT *m_ppLob;
    UINT          *m_pC;
```

The secret of the temporary pointer will be revealed later on. Here I just want to mention that this pointer is used only to point to one of the six lists of level objects and the associated counter for this list. You can set the pointers to a certain type of level object by using the following functions:

```
bool CSector::SetPointers(SELECTMODE sm)
   {
   if (sm==SM_POLYGON) {
      m_pC = &m_NumPolys;
      m_ppLob = (LPLEVELOBJECT*)m_ppPoly;
      }
   else if (sm==SM_MESH) {
      m_pC = &m_NumMeshs;
      m_ppLob = (LPLEVELOBJECT*)m_ppMesh;
      }
   else if (sm==SM_PORTAL) {
      m_pC = &m_NumPorts;
      m_ppLob = (LPLEVELOBJECT*)m_ppPortal;
      }
   else if (sm==SM_LIGHT) {
      m_pC = &m_NumLights;
      m_ppLob = (LPLEVELOBJECT*)m_ppLight;
      }
   else if (sm==SM_ENTITY) {
      m_pC = &m_NumEntys;
      m_ppLob = (LPLEVELOBJECT*)m_ppEntity;
      }
   else if (sm==SM_SPAWN) {
      m_pC = &m_NumSpawns;
      m_ppLob = (LPLEVELOBJECT*)m_ppSpawn;
      }
   else return false;
   return true;
   } // SetPointers
/*------------------------------*/

bool CSector::SetPointers(UINT t)
```

```
    {
    if ( (t <= 0) || (t >= 6)) return false;
    else if (t == 1) {
        m_pC = &m_NumPolys;
        m_ppLob = (LPLEVELOBJECT*)m_ppPoly;
        }
    else if (t == 2) {
        m_pC = &m_NumPorts;
        m_ppLob = (LPLEVELOBJECT*)m_ppPortal;
        }
    else if (t == 3) {
        m_pC = &m_NumLights;
        m_ppLob = (LPLEVELOBJECT*)m_ppLight;
        }
    else if (t == 4) {
        m_pC = &m_NumEntys;
        m_ppLob = (LPLEVELOBJECT*)m_ppEntity;
        }
    else if (t == 5) {
        m_pC = &m_NumSpawns;
        m_ppLob = (LPLEVELOBJECT*)m_ppSpawn;
        }
    return true;
    } // SetPointers
```

One of the functions uses the type SELECTMODE as a parameter. Except for SM_NONE and SM_VERTEX, all possible values display in the switch. This enumerated type enables you to set the editor into a specific editing mode. Before you can start selecting and editing anything at all, you must switch the user interface to the relevant mode associated with the kinds of objects you want to select. A big advantage to this is that you don't have to worry about light sources or portals when you are in polygon select mode and open up a selection rectangle in one of the three orthogonal views. Any object other than polygons will just be ignored in the selection process, and, therefore, whether or not something is inside the selection rectangle does not matter.

The second version of the function takes a numeric ID as input to bend the pointers to a specific type of list. Here it does not matter which ID is used for which list as long as all IDs are used for a different list. You will see the reason for this function later on when it is used for the first time.

There are also three functions to deal with the name of a sector. Two function are used to set and to get the name of a sector, respectively. The third function enables you to check whether a given string is equal to the name of the sector. This is used to maintain the uniqueness of the sector names by comparing the name of a new sector to the names of the existing sectors:

```
void CSector::SetName(const char *chName)
   {
   int nL = strlen(chName)+1;
   if (nL>256) memcpy(m_chName, chName, 256);
   else memcpy(m_chName, chName, nL);
   } // SetName
/*------------------------*/

void CSector::GetName(char *chName)
   {
   memcpy(chName, m_chName, strlen(m_chName)+1);
   } // GetName
/*------------------------*/

bool CSector::NameEqual(const char *chName)
   {
   if (strnicmp(chName, m_chName, 65535)==0)
      return true;
   return false;
   } // NameEqual
```

By now, you have already seen a significant part of the class declaration and a part of the implementation. However, there is a bit more in this class. The following listing shows the class declaration, but without the members previously discussed:

```
class CSector : public CLevelObject
   {
   public:
      CSector(const char *chName);
      ~CSector(void);

      void Render(ZFXVertexCacheManager*, DWORD, bool bHide);
      void RenderLit(ZFXRenderDevice*,bool bHide);
      void Render(ZFXVertexCacheManager *pVCM, bool b)
              { Render(pVCM, LOB_ALL, b); }

      ZFXCOLOR GetAmbient(void) { return m_Ambient; }
      void     SetAmbient(float fR, float fG, float fB)
              { m_Ambient.fR = fR; m_Ambient.fG = fG; m_Ambient.fB = fB; }

      void SelectAll(SELECTMODE, CSelectionBuffer*);
```

```cpp
        void SelectInvert(SELECTMODE, CSelectionBuffer*);
        void SelectIntersecting(SELECTMODE, CSelectionBuffer*, const ZFXAabb&,
                                ZFXAXIS);

        void RecalcVertexNormals(void);

        void HideNone(void);
        void HideSelected(SELECTMODE);
        void HideUnselected(void);
        void HideInvert(void);

        void Pick(SELECTMODE, const ZFXRay&,
                  CSelectionBuffer*);

        LPLEVELOBJECT AddObject(const CLevelObject&);
        void RemoveObject(LPLEVELOBJECT);

        void RemovePortalConnections(UINT id);
        void NewPortalInTown( CPortal* );
        void NewDoorInTown( CEntity* );

        void Save(FILE *pFile);
        bool Load(FILE *pFile);
        void LoadPrefab(const char*, ZFXRenderDevice*, CSelectionBuffer*);
    private:
        void Init(void);
        void Release(void);
        void CalcBoundingBox(void);
    }; // class
typedef class CSector *LPSECTOR;
```

Now that you understand this class better, the declaration probably looks less ominous. Although it is still a big and comprehensive class, you can create a lot of functionality with just a few lines of code by looping through the lists of LOBs and calling their own functions to perform specific tasks.

Creating an Instance

Creating an instance of the sector class is not very difficult. After all, most of the attributes are set only later on for this object. In the graphical user interface, you can create a new sector by clicking the relevant button. In the resulting dialog box, you then must uniquely name this sector in the current level. Because the name is the unique ID of the

Class Design of the Tool

sector in the level, the dialog box won't go away until you cancel the operation or enter a valid name (one that is not already used for another sector in the level):

Then the constructor is called:

```
CSector::CSector(const char *chName)
    {
    Init();
    m_ID = 0;
    SetName(chName);
    } // constructor
/*----------------------*/

CSector::~CSector(void)
    {
    Release();
    } // destructor
/*----------------------*/

void CSector::Init(void)
    {
    m_NumVerts      = 0;
    m_NumIndis      = 0;
    m_NumPorts      = 0;
    m_NumPolys      = 0;
    m_NumMeshs      = 0;
    m_NumPsInMeshs  = 0;
    m_NumLights     = 0;
    m_NumEntys      = 0;
    m_NumSpawns     = 0;
    m_bHidden       = false;
    m_bSelected     = false;
    m_pC            = NULL;
    m_ppLob         = NULL;
    m_ppPoly        = NULL;
    m_ppMesh        = NULL;
    m_ppPortal      = NULL;
    m_ppLight       = NULL;
    m_ppEntity      = NULL;
    m_ppSpawn       = NULL;
    m_Type          = LOB_SECTOR;
    m_Ambient.fR    = 1.0f;
    m_Ambient.fG    = 1.0f;
```

```
   m_Ambient.fB   = 1.0f;
   m_Ambient.fA   = 1.0f;
   } // Init
/*------------------------*/

void CSector::Release(void)
   {
   UINT i=0;

   for (i=0; i<m_NumPolys; i++)
      SAFE_DELETE(m_ppPoly[i]);
   for (i=0; i<m_NumMeshs; i++)
      SAFE_DELETE(m_ppMesh[i]);
   for (i=0; i<m_NumPorts; i++)
      SAFE_DELETE(m_ppPortal[i]);
   for (i=0; i<m_NumLights; i++)
      SAFE_DELETE(m_ppLight[i]);
   for (i=0; i<m_NumEntys; i++)
      SAFE_DELETE(m_ppEntity[i]);
   for (i=0; i<m_NumSpawns; i++)
      SAFE_DELETE(m_ppSpawn[i]);

   SAFE_FREE(m_ppPoly);
   SAFE_FREE(m_ppMesh);
   SAFE_FREE(m_ppPortal);
   SAFE_FREE(m_ppLight);
   SAFE_FREE(m_ppEntity);
   SAFE_FREE(m_ppSpawn);
   } // Release
```

Upon releasing an instance of a sector, you have to free only the memory that was allocated. Note that you have to separate between freeing and deleting the memory, depending on the method you used to allocate the memory in the first place.

Loading and Saving

Loading and saving a level are basically just like in all the level object classes discussed so far. The only difference is that the functions are a bit longer, because we are not only dealing with one or two arrays of data here that must be loaded or saved. Instead, there are lists of all kinds of level objects in a sector that must be loaded or saved, respectively.

The saving of a sector requires you only to loop through the lists of level objects contained in this sector and request each entry of each list to save itself to the file. To save you time down the road, however, a bit more work was invested here. In fact, this function takes the

Class Design of the Tool 741

list of polygons and then sorts them by the texture they are using. Then you count the number of different skins used by the polygons; the skins not already used by the polygons are put on the mesh objects. Thus you determine the number of all the different skins used in a given sector and you just save it to the file. This value is not needed for the editor, but the game that is using our levels will find this very helpful.

The remainder of the saving routine is fairly trivial:

```
void CSector::Save(FILE *pFile)
   {
   UINT i=0, NumSkins=0;
   int  NewSkin=-1;
   int  n=0;

   UINT aSkins[400];

   if (m_NumPolys > 0) {
      // sort polygons by texture
      qsort(m_ppPoly, m_NumPolys, sizeof(LPPOLYGON), SortBySkin);

      // number of different skins in the sector
      UINT OldSkin = m_ppPoly[0]->GetSkinID();
      aSkins[NumSkins++] = OldSkin;

      for (i=1; i<m_NumPolys; i++)
         {
         NewSkin = m_ppPoly[i]->GetSkinID();
         if (NewSkin != OldSkin) {
            aSkins[NumSkins++] = NewSkin;
            }
         OldSkin = NewSkin;
         }
      }

   // number of different skins in mesh
   for (UINT m=0; m<m_NumMeshs; m++) {
      m_ppMesh[m]->CountNonRedundantSkins(aSkins, &NumSkins );
      }

   n = strlen(m_chName);
   fwrite(&n, sizeof(int), 1, pFile);
   fwrite(m_chName, n, 1, pFile);
```

```
   fwrite(&NumSkins,     sizeof(UINT),    1, pFile);
   fwrite(&m_NumVerts,   sizeof(UINT),    1, pFile);
   fwrite(&m_NumIndis,   sizeof(UINT),    1, pFile);
   fwrite(&m_NumPolys,   sizeof(UINT),    1, pFile);
   fwrite(&m_NumPsInMeshs, sizeof(UINT),  1, pFile);
   fwrite(&m_NumMeshs,   sizeof(UINT),    1, pFile);
   fwrite(&m_NumPorts,   sizeof(UINT),    1, pFile);
   fwrite(&m_NumLights,  sizeof(UINT),    1, pFile);
   fwrite(&m_NumEntys,   sizeof(UINT),    1, pFile);
   fwrite(&m_NumSpawns,  sizeof(UINT),    1, pFile);
   fwrite(&m_Aabb,       sizeof(ZFXAabb), 1, pFile);
   fwrite(&m_Ambient,    sizeof(ZFXCOLOR),1, pFile);
   fflush(pFile);

   for (i=0; i<m_NumMeshs;  i++)  m_ppMesh[i]->Save(pFile);
   for (i=0; i<m_NumPolys;  i++)  m_ppPoly[i]->Save(pFile);
   for (i=0; i<m_NumPorts;  i++)  m_ppPortal[i]->Save(pFile);
   for (i=0; i<m_NumLights; i++)  m_ppLight[i]->Save(pFile);
   for (i=0; i<m_NumEntys;  i++)  m_ppEntity[i]->Save(pFile);
   for (i=0; i<m_NumSpawns; i++)  m_ppSpawn[i]->Save(pFile);
   } // Save
```

Notice that you don't know the function `CPolymesh::CountNonRedundantSkins` yet. We have to add this to the polymesh class now because we need it here. You will find this very simple implementation on the CD-ROM. The function gets an array of skin IDs along with the number of entries in the array. Then it loops through all the polygons of the mesh object and counts how many skins are not inside the array yet but are used by the mesh. The counter is then adjusted accordingly.

Loading a sector is just as easy as it gets. You just have to load the attributes and the lists of elements from the file. Again, each object takes care of itself; the different types of level objects load themselves from the file. This function needs to supply only enough memory to store the objects:

```
bool CSector::Load(FILE *pFile)
   {
   UINT i=0, NumSkins=0;
   int  n=0;

   fread(&n, sizeof(int), 1, pFile);
   fread(m_chName, n, 1, pFile);
   m_chName[n] = '\0';

   fread(&NumSkins,     sizeof(UINT),    1, pFile);
```

```
fread(&m_NumVerts,    sizeof(UINT),    1, pFile);
fread(&m_NumIndis,    sizeof(UINT),    1, pFile);
fread(&m_NumPolys,    sizeof(UINT),    1, pFile);
fread(&m_NumPsInMeshs, sizeof(UINT),   1, pFile);
fread(&m_NumMeshs,    sizeof(UINT),    1, pFile);
fread(&m_NumPorts,    sizeof(UINT),    1, pFile);
fread(&m_NumLights,   sizeof(UINT),    1, pFile);
fread(&m_NumEntys,    sizeof(UINT),    1, pFile);
fread(&m_NumSpawns,   sizeof(UINT),    1, pFile);
fread(&m_Aabb,        sizeof(ZFXAabb), 1, pFile);
fread(&m_Ambient,     sizeof(ZFXCOLOR),1, pFile);

m_ppMesh   = (LPPOLYMESH*)InitMem( (LPVOID*) m_ppMesh, m_NumMeshs,
                sizeof(LPPOLYMESH));
m_ppPoly   = (LPPOLYGON*)   InitMem( (LPVOID*)m_ppPoly, m_NumPolys,
                sizeof(LPPOLYGON));
m_ppPortal = (LPPORTAL*)    InitMem( (LPVOID*)m_ppPortal, m_NumPorts,
                sizeof(LPPORTAL));
m_ppLight  = (LPLIGHT*)     InitMem( (LPVOID*)m_ppLight, m_NumLights,
                sizeof(LPLIGHT));
m_ppEntity = (LPENTITY*)    InitMem( (LPVOID*)m_ppEntity, m_NumEntys,
                sizeof(LPENTITY));
m_ppSpawn  = (LPSPAWNPOINT*)InitMem( (LPVOID*)m_ppSpawn, m_NumSpawns,
                sizeof(LPSPAWNPOINT));

for (i=0; i<m_NumMeshs; i++) {
   m_ppMesh[i] = new CPolymesh();
   m_ppMesh[i]->Load(pFile);
   }
for (i=0; i<m_NumPolys; i++) {
   m_ppPoly[i] = new CPolygon();
   m_ppPoly[i]->Load(pFile);
   }
for (i=0; i<m_NumPorts; i++) {
   m_ppPortal[i] = new CPortal();
   m_ppPortal[i]->Load(pFile);
   }
for (i=0; i<m_NumLights; i++) {
   m_ppLight[i] = new CLight();
   m_ppLight[i]->Load(pFile);
   }
for (i=0; i<m_NumEntys; i++) {
```

```
      m_ppEntity[i] = new CEntity();
      m_ppEntity[i]->Load(pFile);
      }
   for (i=0; i<m_NumSpawns; i++) {
      m_ppSpawn[i] = new CSpawnPoint();
      m_ppSpawn[i]->Load(pFile);
      }
   return true;
   } // Load
```

Loading a Prefab

Now that you know how you can load a sector of the level, it's time to learn how to load a prefab. By observing this class closely, you may have noticed already that the sector class can only load prefabs, not save them (because a sector can accept only level objects). Therefore, if we want to load a prefab, we just let the sector do this; then the loaded prefab will belong to a sector. If you want to save a prefab, select a number of polygons from the level and save the selected objects. You do this in the selection buffer, where you can access easily all necessary information about the selected object.

Here is the function to load a prefab:

```
void CSector::LoadPrefab(const char *ch, ZFXRenderDevice *pDevice,
                         CSelectionBuffer *pSB)
   {
   LPPOLYGON     pPoly = new CPolygon();
   LPLEVELOBJECT pLob = NULL;
   UINT NumPolys=0, n=0;
   int  nIndex=-1;
   char buffer[2048];

   FILE *pFile = fopen(ch, "rb");
   if (!pFile) return;

   pPoly->Reset();

   // how many new polygons?
   fread(&NumPolys, sizeof(UINT), 1, pFile);

   if (NumPolys == 0) return;

   for (UINT i=0; i<NumPolys; i++)
      {
      pPoly->Reset();
```

```
    // name of diffuse texture
    fread(&n, sizeof(UINT), 1, pFile);
    fread(buffer, n, 1, pFile);
    buffer[n] = '\0';

    // texture already loaded?
    nIndex = cbhContainsString(CApplication::m_G.hGUI[CSK_LIST], buffer);

    pPoly->Load(pFile);

    // load texture if needed
    if (nIndex == -1) {
        nIndex = CApplication::m_G.Level.CreateSkinID(pDevice, buffer, 1.0f);
        cbhAddItem(CApplication::m_G.hGUI[CSK_LIST], buffer, NULL, true);
        }

    pPoly->SetSkinID(nIndex);
    pLob = AddObject( *pPoly );
    pSB->AddLob( pLob );
    }

    delete pPoly;
    fclose(pFile);
    } // LoadPrefab
```

Because prefabs are just comprised of polygons, they are saved only as a list of polygons, even if those polygons belonged to a certain mesh at the time of saving the prefab. If you want to load such a prefab now, you just have to determine the number of polygons stored in the file and read them out of the file in a big loop. Luckily, the polygons can take care of themselves, so you just call the loading function of the polygon class. Each loaded polygon is then added to the sector list of level objects. In addition, the address of the new polygon is added to the selection buffer in order to have the whole geometry of the prefab selected after it is loaded. This makes translating the prefab right after loading it very easy.

Two functions use the prefix cbh in this function. The prefix is short for combo-box helper and is used for functions that allow easy access to elements in the list of a combo box. In this case, we are requesting information about the textures already loaded into the current level and stored in a WinAPI combo-box control with the handle CSK_LIST. If the texture a specific polygon from the prefab is using is already loaded, you get the ID from the combo box. Otherwise, you have to load this texture into the level first and store the new ID for the polygon. Then the prefab is loaded.

Collision Detection and Selection of LOBs

Now you will see why a base class for all level objects is a great help. In the various functions to pick and select or deselect objects of a certain type, you only need to bend the temporary pointers to the according list of the object type under consideration at the moment. When the temporary pointers are bent to the list and its counter, you can then just loop through the list and call the associated picking or selection function from the level object over the base class interface.

This is pretty easy to do, but there are some catches here and there. Those catches arise when a certain type of object is not directly accessible over a list of the sector. Such is the case of polygons that are not in the polygon list of a sector because they are part of a mesh. In this scenario, you also need to go through the list of meshes when seeking a polygon. The same holds true for vertices. Vertices can be part of a polygon only. However, in turn, this polygon could be part of a mesh.

With those special cases in mind, it is not difficult to come up with the relevant functions. Let's start with picking a level object by clicking it in the perspective view of the editor. This picking request is then delegated to the active sector using this function:

```
void CSector::Pick(SELECTMODE sm, const ZFXRay &Ray, CSelectionBuffer *pSB)
   {
   LPLEVELOBJECT  pPicked=NULL, pPoly = NULL;

   float fMin=65535.0f, fD=0.0f;

   // polygon is a special case

   if (!SetPointers(sm)) return;

   // loop through all LOBs
   for (UINT i=0; i<(*m_pC); i++)
      {
      // ignore hidden ones
      if (m_ppLob[i]->IsHidden()) continue;

      // try a pick
      if (m_ppLob[i]->Picked(Ray, &fD))
         {
         if (fD < fMin) {
            fMin = fD;
            pPicked = m_ppLob[i];
            }
         }
```

```
        }

    // if we need to pick polygons dont forget the ones in the meshes
    if (sm==SM_POLYGON)
        {
        for (i=0; i<m_NumMeshs; i++)
            {
            if (m_ppMesh[i]->IsHidden()) continue;

            if (pPoly=m_ppMesh[i]->PickPoly(Ray,fMin,&fD))
                {
                fMin = fD;
                pPicked = pPoly;
                pPoly = NULL;
                }
            }
        } // if [POLYGON]

    if (pPicked) pSB->AddLob(pPicked);
    } // Pick
```

As you can see, the picked polygon that the level designer has selected is placed directly into the selection buffer that is provided as a parameter to this function. Note that the editor enables you to place additional objects into the selection buffers if you are pressing the CTRL key while picking. Otherwise, the picking operation clears the selection buffer first.

The level designer can also simultaneously select all level objects of a certain type in the sector by just clicking a single button in the GUI. If you want to clean up a sector view by hiding all light objects, for instance, you just switch the selection mode to the light source type and click the button that selects all objects simultaneously. The following two functions are self-explanatory:

```
void CSector::SelectAll(SELECTMODE sm, CSelectionBuffer *pSB)
    {
    // special case polygon
    if (sm==SM_POLYGON)
        {
        // first polygons from meshes
        for (UINT m=0; m<m_NumMeshs; m++)
            {
            if (m_ppMesh[m]->IsHidden()) continue;
            m_ppMesh[m]->SelectAllPolys( pSB );
            }
        }
```

```
    if (!SetPointers(sm)) return;

    for (UINT i=0; i<(*m_pC); i++) {
       if (m_ppLob[i]->IsHidden()) continue;
       pSB->AddLob( m_ppLob[i] );
       }
    } // SelectAll
/*----------------------------*/

void CSector::SelectInvert(SELECTMODE sm, CSelectionBuffer *pSB)
    {
    UINT i=0;

    // special case polygons in meshes
    if (sm == SM_POLYGON)
       {
       for (i=0; i<m_NumMeshs; i++)
          {
          if ( m_ppMesh[i]->IsHidden() ) continue;
          else m_ppMesh[i]->SelectInvert(pSB);
          }
       }
    // ignore vertices here
    else if (sm == SM_VERTEX) { return; }

    if (!SetPointers(sm)) return;

    for (i=0; i<(*m_pC); i++)
       {
       if (m_ppLob[i]->IsHidden()) continue;

       if ( !m_ppLob[i]->IsSelected() )
          pSB->AddLob( m_ppLob[i] );
       else m_ppLob[i]->DeSelect();
       }
    } // SelectInvert
```

In the final scenario, the level designer opens a selection rectangle in one of the three orthogonal views by click-dragging. In this case, a bounding box is built from this two-dimensional rectangle, and the missing coordinate is set from −infinity to +infinity depending on the axis along which the viewer is looking in the orthogonal view.

Class Design of the Tool

The intersection query function is very easy to accomplish (as shown earlier). Besides the special case of the polygons that are also part of a mesh, vertices may produce another catch: They can be part of a polygon or part of a polygon that is in turn part of a mesh. Here is the function:

```
void CSector::SelectIntersecting(SELECTMODE sm, CSelectionBuffer *pSB,
                                 const ZFXAabb &aabb, ZFXAXIS axis)
   {
   UINT i=0;

   // 1. special case: vertices in polygons and meshes
   if (sm == SM_VERTEX)
      {
      for (i=0; i<m_NumMeshs; i++)
         {
         if ( m_ppMesh[i]->IsHidden() ) continue;
         else m_ppMesh[i]->GetIntersectingVerts(aabb,pSB,axis);
         }
      for (i=0; i<m_NumPolys; i++)
         {
         if ( m_ppPoly[i]->IsHidden() ) continue;
         else m_ppPoly[i]->GetIntersectingVerts(aabb, pSB, axis);
         }
      }

   // 2. special case: polygons in meshes
   else if (sm == SM_POLYGON)
      {
      for (i=0; i<m_NumMeshs; i++)
         {
         if ( m_ppMesh[i]->IsHidden() ) continue;
         else m_ppMesh[i]->GetIntersectingPolys(aabb,pSB,axis);
         }
      }

   if (!SetPointers(sm)) return;

   for (i=0; i<(*m_pC); i++)
      {
      if (m_ppLob[i]->IsHidden()) continue;
      if ( m_ppLob[i]->Intersects(aabb, axis) )
            pSB->AddLob( m_ppLob[i] );
```

```
        }
    } // SelectIntersecting
```

As you can see, the base class is doing a great job here. There is no need to differentiate among the different types of level objects. After the correct pointers are bent, you only need to loop through the list and call the appropriate function of the base class.

Hide Objects in the Sector

You have already seen how you can hide and unhide level objects as far as the derived classes are concerned. You have not yet seen how those functions to hide or unhide anything are called. Of course, this is done using the active sector object. The editor offers four buttons to do four different kinds of hiding operations:

- Hide nothing (unhide hidden objects)
- Hide selected objects
- Hide unselected objects
- Invert the hide state on all objects

The following four quickie functions will do the jobs listed here. Each of the functions has to take a special case into consideration, and this special case is connected to the polygons sitting inside the meshes. By now, you know how to handle this. You do need to know, however, that we are using the function `CSector::SetPointers` with the `UINT` parameter in three of the functions to bend the temporary pointers accordingly (because you only need to look at the select mode if you want to work on selected geometry). In the other cases, you have to loop through all lists; therefore, you let the function described earlier hand you the pointers to each list in a loop.

Here are the four functions for switching the hiding state:

```
void CSector::HideNone(void)
    {
    for (UINT t=0; t<6; t++) {
        // special case polygons in meshes
        if (t == 0) {
            for (UINT cm=0; cm<m_NumMeshs; cm++)
                {
                m_ppMesh[cm]->UnHide();
                m_ppMesh[cm]->HideNoPolys();
                }
            continue;
            }

        if ( !SetPointers(t) ) continue;
```

```cpp
        for (UINT i=0; i<(*m_pC); i++)
            m_ppLob[i]->UnHide();
        }
    } // HideNone
/*-------------------------*/

void CSector::HideSelected(SELECTMODE sm)
    {
    UINT i=0;

    // special case polygons in meshes
    if (sm == SM_POLYGON)
        {
        for (i=0; i<m_NumMeshs; i++)
            m_ppMesh[i]->HideSelectedPolys();
        }
    else if (sm == SM_VERTEX) { return; }

    if (!SetPointers(sm)) return;

    for (i=0; i<(*m_pC); i++)
        {
        if ( m_ppLob[i]->IsSelected() ) m_ppLob[i]->Hide();
        }
    } // HideSelected
/*-------------------------*/

void CSector::HideUnselected(void)
    {
    for (UINT t=0; t<6; t++)
        {
        // special case meshs
        if (t == 0)
            {
            for (UINT m=0; m<m_NumMeshs; m++)
                m_ppMesh[m]->HideUnselectedPolys();
            continue;
            }

        if ( !SetPointers(t) ) continue;
```

```
        for (UINT i=0; i<(*m_pC); i++) {
            if ( ! m_ppLob[i]->IsSelected() )
                m_ppLob[i]->Hide();
            }
        }
    } // HideUnselected
/*---------------------------*/

void CSector::HideInvert(void)
    {
    for (UINT t=0; t<6; t++) {
        // special case meshes
        if (t == 0) {
            for (UINT cm=0; cm<m_NumMeshs; cm++)
                {
                if ( m_ppMesh[cm]->IsHidden() )
                    {
                    m_ppMesh[cm]->UnHide();
                    m_ppMesh[cm]->HideNoPolys();
                    }
                else m_ppMesh[cm]->HideInvertPolys();
                }
            continue;
            }

        if ( !SetPointers(t) ) continue;

        for (UINT i=0; i<(*m_pC); i++)
            {
            if (m_ppLob[i]->IsHidden()) m_ppLob[i]->UnHide();
            else m_ppLob[i]->Hide();
            }
        }
    } // HideInvert
```

Adding and Removing Objects

Removing an object from the sector because it should be deleted is fairly simple. The selection buffer will hand over the address of a level object base class pointer. Then you just have to look at the type of the object that should be deleted, loop through the associated list of this level object type, and delete the entry for the object if the same address appears in the list.

Don't start to yawn just yet, however; there are a number of special cases. If you delete real geometry, such as polygons or meshes, you must adjust the counters accordingly. If you delete polygons, you also need to look inside the meshes, however, because this polygon could very well be part of a mesh. You also need to delete the mesh if you delete the last polygon of a mesh. Otherwise, there would be some ghost geometry left in the level (which means you could select and edit a mesh that is not visible because it has no polygons at all).

Well, here you go:

```
void CSector::RemoveObject(LPLEVELOBJECT pLob)
   {
   LPPOLYMESH pMesh=NULL;

   LPLEVELOBJECT *ppLob = NULL;
   UINT *pC=NULL;

   // search a polygon in meshes as well
   switch ( pLob->GetType() )
      {
      case LOB_POLYGON:
          m_NumVerts -= pLob->GetNumVerts();
          m_NumIndis -= pLob->GetNumIndis();

          if ( ((LPPOLYGON)pLob)->IsPartOfMesh() )
             {
             pMesh = ((LPPOLYGON)pLob)->GetParent();
             pMesh->RemovePolygon((LPPOLYGON)pLob);

             // delete empty meshes
             if ( !pMesh->GetNumPolys() )
                RemoveObject(pMesh);
             m_NumPsInMeshs--;
             return;
             }

          pC = &m_NumPolys;
          ppLob = (LPLEVELOBJECT*)m_ppPoly;
          break;

      case LOB_MESH:
          m_NumVerts -= pLob->GetNumVerts();
          m_NumIndis -= pLob->GetNumIndis();
```

```
            m_NumPsInMeshs -= pLob->GetNumPolys();

        pC = &m_NumMeshs;
        ppLob = (LPLEVELOBJECT*)m_ppMesh;
        break;
    case LOB_PORTAL:
        pC = &m_NumPorts;
        ppLob = (LPLEVELOBJECT*)m_ppPortal;
        break;
    case LOB_LIGHT:
        pC = &m_NumLights;
        ppLob = (LPLEVELOBJECT*)m_ppLight;
        break;
    case LOB_ENTITY:
        pC = &m_NumEntys;
        ppLob = (LPLEVELOBJECT*)m_ppEntity;
        break;
    case LOB_SPAWNPOINT:
        pC = &m_NumSpawns;
        ppLob = (LPLEVELOBJECT*)m_ppSpawn;
        break;
    default: return;
    } // switch

    for (UINT i=0; i<(*pC); i++)
        if (ppLob[i] == pLob) break;

    if (i>=(*pC)) return;

    SAFE_DELETE(ppLob[i]);

    if (i != ((*pC)-1)) ppLob[i] = ppLob[(*pC)-1];
    (*pC)--;
    return;
    } // RemoveObject
```

That was not too bad, right? And the good news is that adding an object to a sector is done more or less the same way. You only need to take care of the available memory in this case and enlarge the memory area of a certain list if there is not enough room to store one more element using the functions of the base class.

Note that the function to add an object to the sector will return the pointer of the newly added object. This is a different pointer from the parameter you provided because the sector copies the object into another place in memory. The returned address can then be stored in the selection buffer, for example:

```
LPLEVELOBJECT CSector::AddObject(const CLevelObject &Lob)
   {
   LPLEVELOBJECT pLob = (LPLEVELOBJECT)&Lob;

   switch ( pLob->GetType() ) {
      case LOB_POLYGON:
         m_ppPoly = (LPPOLYGON*) CheckMem( (LPVOID*)m_ppPoly, m_NumPolys,
                                           sizeof(LPPOLYGON) );

         m_ppPoly[m_NumPolys] = new CPolygon();
         m_ppPoly[m_NumPolys]->CopyOf( pLob );

         m_NumVerts += pLob->GetNumVerts();
         m_NumIndis += pLob->GetNumIndis();
         m_NumPolys++;
         return m_ppPoly[m_NumPolys-1];

      case LOB_MESH:
         m_ppMesh = (LPPOLYMESH*) CheckMem( (LPVOID*)
                              m_ppMesh, m_NumMeshs,
                              sizeof(LPPOLYMESH) );

         m_ppMesh[m_NumMeshs] = new CPolymesh();
         m_ppMesh[m_NumMeshs]->CopyOf( pLob );

         m_NumPsInMeshs += pLob->GetNumPolys();
         m_NumVerts += pLob->GetNumVerts();
         m_NumIndis += pLob->GetNumIndis();
         m_NumMeshs++;
         return m_ppMesh[m_NumMeshs-1];

      case LOB_ENTITY:
         m_ppEntity = (LPENTITY*) CheckMem( (LPVOID*)
                            m_ppEntity, m_NumEntys,
                            sizeof(LPENTITY) );

         m_ppEntity[m_NumEntys] = new CEntity();
         m_ppEntity[m_NumEntys]->CopyOf( pLob );
         m_NumEntys++;
         return m_ppEntity[m_NumEntys-1];
```

```
    case LOB_PORTAL:
        m_ppPortal = (LPPORTAL*) CheckMem( (LPVOID*)
                            m_ppPortal, m_NumPorts,
                            sizeof(LPPORTAL) );

        m_ppPortal[m_NumPorts] = new CPortal();
        m_ppPortal[m_NumPorts]->CopyOf( pLob );
        m_ppPortal[m_NumPorts]->SetItsSector(this);
        m_NumPorts++;
        return m_ppPortal[m_NumPorts-1];

    case LOB_LIGHT:
        m_ppLight = (LPLIGHT*) CheckMem( (LPVOID*)
                            m_ppLight, m_NumLights,
                            sizeof(LPLIGHT) );

        m_ppLight[m_NumLights] = new CLight();
        m_ppLight[m_NumLights]->CopyOf( pLob );
        m_NumLights++;
        return m_ppLight[m_NumLights-1];

    case LOB_SPAWNPOINT:
        m_ppSpawn = (LPSPAWNPOINT*) CheckMem( (LPVOID*)
                            m_ppSpawn, m_NumSpawns,
                            sizeof(LPSPAWNPOINT) );

        m_ppSpawn[m_NumSpawns] = new CSpawnPoint();
        m_ppSpawn[m_NumSpawns]->CopyOf( pLob );
        m_NumSpawns++;
        return m_ppSpawn[m_NumSpawns-1];

    default: return NULL;
    } // switch
} // AddObject
```

Rendering an Instance

The rendering of a sector is actually pretty easy. As you know, each level object has its own function to render itself, which is inherited from the base class but implemented in the derived classes. So you only have to loop through all lists of all level objects and call the render function of each object.

To provide a bit more flexibility, however, the render function takes a flag as an input parameter, which can be a combination of the available LOB types to indicate which types of LOBs should be rendered. The idea is that the editor will render polygons with a different line color than for meshes, for instance, so you have to make separate render calls:

```
void CSector::Render(ZFXVertexCacheManager *pVCM, DWORD Type, bool bHide)
   {
   UINT i=0;
   static ZFXCOLOR clrL = { 1.0f, 1.0f, 0.0f, 1.0f };
   static ZFXCOLOR clrS = { 1.0f, 0.0f, 1.0f, 1.0f };
   static ZFXRENDERSTATE sm = RS_SHADE_LINES;

   if ((Type & LOB_MESH) || (Type & LOB_ALL)) {
      for (i=0; i<m_NumMeshs; i++) {
         if ( !m_ppMesh[i]->IsSelected() )
            m_ppMesh[i]->Render( pVCM, bHide );
         }
      } // type

   if ((Type & LOB_POLYGON) || (Type & LOB_ALL)) {
      for (i=0; i<m_NumPolys; i++) {
         if ( !m_ppPoly[i]->IsSelected() )
            m_ppPoly[i]->Render( pVCM, bHide );
         }
      } // type

   if ((Type & LOB_ENTITY) || (Type & LOB_ALL)) {
      for (i=0; i<m_NumEntys; i++) {
         if ( !m_ppEntity[i]->IsSelected() )
            m_ppEntity[i]->Render( pVCM, bHide );
         }
      } // type

   if ((Type & LOB_SPAWNPOINT) || (Type & LOB_ALL)) {
      for (i=0; i<m_NumSpawns; i++) {
         if ( !m_ppSpawn[i]->IsSelected() )
            m_ppSpawn[i]->Render( pVCM, bHide );
         }
      } // type

   if ((Type & LOB_LIGHT) || (Type & LOB_ALL)) {
      for (i=0; i<m_NumLights; i++) {
         if ( !m_ppLight[i]->IsSelected() )
```

```
            m_ppLight[i]->Render( pVCM, bHide );
         }
      } // type

   if ((Type & LOB_PORTAL) || (Type & LOB_ALL)) {
      for (i=0; i<m_NumPorts; i++) {
         if ( !m_ppPortal[i]->IsSelected() )
            m_ppPortal[i]->Render( pVCM, bHide );
      }
   } // type
} // Render
```

Now it gets more interesting because the level editor also enables you to render a simplified per-pixel lighting using the omni-light vertex and pixel shaders discussed earlier in this book. However, the representation of the lit scene is really slow in the editor, and even the polygons facing away from the light source are lit if they are inside the radius of the light source. Therefore, you should switch on the lighting in the editor only to check how it looks after you place new light sources in the level.

In the video game in the next chapter, the level is rendered pretty fast, even with a lot of light sources active at the same time. Here is the function to render the lit pass in this editor:

```
void CSector::RenderLit(ZFXRenderDevice *pDevice, bool bHide)
   {
   ZFXMatrix matA;
   UINT i=0;

   ZFXVertexCacheManager *pVCM =
                        pDevice->GetVertexManager();

   // loop for all lights in the sector
   for (UINT l=0; l<m_NumLights; l++) {

      if (m_ppLight[l]->IsHidden()) continue;

      matA = g_CalcTransAttenNoRot(m_ppLight[l]->GetPosition(),
                              m_ppLight[l]->GetRadius());

      pDevice->SetShaderConstant(SHT_VERTEX, DAT_FLOAT,
                        20, 4, (void*)&matA);

      pDevice->SetShaderConstant(SHT_PIXEL, DAT_FLOAT,
              0, 1, (void*)&m_ppLight[l]->GetColor());
```

```
        for (i=0; i<m_NumMeshs; i++)
           {
           if ( !m_ppMesh[i]->IsSelected() )
              m_ppMesh[i]->Render( pVCM, bHide );
           }
        for (i=0; i<m_NumPolys; i++)
           {
           if ( !m_ppPoly[i]->IsSelected() )
              m_ppPoly[i]->Render( pVCM, bHide );
           }
     pVCM->ForcedFlushAll();
     }
  } // RenderLit
```

Note that the editor normally calls the function `CSector::Render` to render a sector with 100 % white ambient light. This is the mode in which you should edit levels at first. If the level designer wants to see the level correctly lit, however, it calls the function `CSector::RenderLit`, which uses a lighting render pass for each light source in the scene. The ambient pass is also rendered using the specific value of the sectors. See Chapter 7, "3D Pipelines and Shades," to review how the omni lighting with a pixel shader works.

Connecting Portals and Entities

The last issue that must be considered in the sector class is some kind of automation that will connect portals that abut each other or to connect entities to portals that are intersected by them. At first you need a function that informs a sector that a new portal was inserted into the level by the level designer. It is imperative that the sector is not only informed about the portals that are inserted in its own portal list, but also about portals belonging to other sectors. It is most likely that portals of other sectors will have connections to portals in a given sector to connect the two of them. The function `CSector::NewPortalInTown` loops through the list of all portals in the sector and checks whether any of these portals abut the new portal. If this is the case, the two of them become brothers. Then the function loops through all entities in this sector to determine whether a portal intersects a door. If this is the case, the portal is connected to the door entity.

It is also possible that the level designer will first place a portal and then place a door. In this case, the portal would not be connected to the door unless we call the appropriate function `CSector::NewDoorInTown` to inform each sector in the level about the new door. Note that in the case of the editor, the portal does not care at all whether it is intersecting a door. Only the door entity will store the portal. In the next chapter, however, the portal will care about that because the door is the only thing that can activate the portal.

Chapter 14 ■ Computer-Aided Design (CAD) Tools

It is also possible that the level designer is not satisfied with his work and that he wants to delete a portal. Of course, all connections that reference to this portal must be removed as well. The function CSector::RemovePortalConnections cleans up things before a portal is removed from the level:

```
void CSector::NewPortalInTown(CPortal *pPortal)
   {
   ZFXAabb aabb1 = pPortal->GetAabb();
   ZFXAabb aabb2;

   for (UINT e=0; e<m_NumEntys; e++) {
      aabb2 = m_ppEntity[e]->GetAabb();
      if ( aabb1.Intersects(aabb2) )
         m_ppEntity[e]->ConnectTo( pPortal );
      }

   for (UINT p=0; p<m_NumPorts; p++) {
      aabb2 = m_ppPortal[p]->GetAabb();
      if ( aabb1.Intersects(aabb2) )
         m_ppPortal[p]->SetItsTarget( pPortal );
      }

   } // NewPortalInTown
/*----------------------------*/

void CSector::NewDoorInTown(CEntity *pDoor)
   {
   ZFXAabb aabb1 = pDoor->GetAabb();
   ZFXAabb aabb2;

   for (UINT p=0; p<m_NumPorts; p++) {
      aabb2 = m_ppPortal[p]->GetAabb();
      if ( aabb1.Intersects(aabb2) )
         pDoor->ConnectTo( m_ppPortal[p] );
      }
   } // NewDoorInTown
/*----------------------------*/

void CSector::RemovePortalConnections(UINT id)
   {
   for (UINT e=0; e<m_NumEntys; e++)
      m_ppEntity[e]->RemovePortalConnections( id );
```

```
   for (UINT p=0; p<m_NumPorts; p++)
      m_ppPortal[p]->DeconnectFrom( id );
   } // RemovePortalConnections
```

And now it is truly done. The whole manager class `CSector`, which is taking care of all the level objects, is ready for action. Although it's taken quite a while, and more than a few pages in this chapter, to develop this class, it is now in place and ready to perform all the low-level work that the level class might require. The following section examines the level class, but most of its functions just boil down to a delegation of a call to the sector class.

All Together Now: CLevel

If you put together everything that can be contained in a level, you end up with a class for a level. However, the sector class is the real workhorse here; the level class is just a container that holds a number of sector objects and lets them do all the work.

Class Declaration

Most of the functions in this class are just delegated to the active sector object. Not many functions here have to be implemented in a different way.

This class is easy to understand, so a full listing of the code is not required here. Remember that only one sector is active at any given time. The level designer selects the active sector from the combo box in the GUI of the editor, and the sector is then set as the active one based on its name (which is stored in the combo box). Most of the functions of the level class are only working with the active sector object by calling its functions.

Here is the declaration of the class:

```
class CLevel {
   public:
      CLevel(void);
      ~CLevel(void);
      void     ClearAll(ZFXSkinManager*);
      void     SetName(const char *ch);
      void     GetName(char *ch);
      bool     HasName(void);
      bool     SaveLevel(const char*,ZFXRenderDevice*);
      bool     LoadLevel(const char*, HWND, HWND, ZFXRenderDevice*);
      void     SaveSkin(ZFXSkinManager*, FILE*, UINT);
      void     LoadSkin(HWND, ZFXSkinManager*, FILE*);
      void     RemovePortalConnections(UINT id);
      void     NewPortalInTown( CPortal* );
      void     NewDoorInTown( CEntity* );
      void     RecalcVertexNormals(void);
```

```
    UINT       CreatePortalID(void) {m_PID++;return m_PID;}
    UINT       CreateSkinID(ZFXRenderDevice*, const char*,float);
    void       RenderActive(ZFXRenderDevice*, DWORD, bool);
    void       RenderActiveLit(ZFXRenderDevice*,bool);
    void       RenderInActive(ZFXRenderDevice*, DWORD,bool);
    HRESULT    AddSector(const char *ch);
    HRESULT    RemoveSector(const char *ch);
    bool       SectorExists(const char *ch);
    bool       SelectSector(const char *ch);
    CSector*   GetSelectedSector(void) { return m_ppSector[m_nActive]; }
    UINT       GetNumSectors(void) { return m_NumSectors; }
    void       GetNumLobs(UINT *pVerts, UINT *pIndis, UINT *pPolys,
                          UINT *pMesh, UINT *pPorts, UINT *pLights,
                          UINT *pEntys);
  private:
    char       m_chName[MAX_PATH];   // level name
    LPSECTOR   *m_ppSector;          // sectors
    UINT       m_NumSectors;         // number of sectors
    UINT       m_nActive;            // active sector
    UINT       m_PID;                // portal IDs
    void       Init(void);
    void       Release(void);
  }; // class
typedef class CLevel *LPLEVEL;
```

Loading and Saving a Level

Loading and saving data from or into a binary file are nothing spectacular, as you should know by now. The function to save a level takes the name of the file as an input parameter as well as a render device object. This object is needed to extract the texture filenames from the skin manager.

You also already know the file format for a level file of our editor. At first you have to write out the important attributes of the level object into the file. This is the number of sectors, portals, and stuff like that. Then you loop through the list of sectors in this level and request the sectors to store themselves to the file one by one. After that, the list of skins is saved as well so that the editor can rebuild the list in the same order to maintain the ID of the skins. And that's it.

Loading a level is more or less the same, but instead of writing the attributes you just read them, and then construct the according number of sectors and request each sector object to load itself from the file. Finally, the list of skins is rebuilt so that the textures are available. Here are the two functions:

Class Design of the Tool

```cpp
bool CLevel::SaveLevel(const char *ch, ZFXRenderDevice *pDevice)
   {
   FILE *pFile=NULL;
   UINT i=0, NumSkins=0;

   if ( !(pFile = fopen(ch, "wb")) )
      return false;

   RecalcVertexNormals();

   NumSkins = pDevice->GetSkinManager()->GetNumSkins();

   fwrite(&m_NumSectors, sizeof(UINT), 1, pFile);
   fwrite(&m_PID,        sizeof(UINT), 1, pFile);
   fwrite(&NumSkins,     sizeof(UINT), 1, pFile);

   for (i=0; i<m_NumSectors; i++) {
      m_ppSector[i]->Save(pFile);
      fflush(pFile);
      }

   for (i=0; i<NumSkins; i++)
      SaveSkin(pDevice->GetSkinManager(), pFile, i);

   fclose(pFile);
   SetName(ch);
   return true;
   } // SaveLevel
/*----------------------------------*/

bool CLevel::LoadLevel(const char *ch, HWND hcbSector, HWND hcbSkins,
                       ZFXRenderDevice *pDevice)
   {
   FILE *pFile=NULL;
   char  buffer[1024];
   int   n=0;
   UINT  NumSkins=0, i=0;

   if ( !(pFile = fopen(ch, "rb")) ) return false;

   ClearAll( pDevice->GetSkinManager() );
   cbhResetContent(hcbSector);
```

```
    cbhResetContent(hcbSkins);

    fread(&m_NumSectors, sizeof(UINT), 1, pFile);
    fread(&m_PID,        sizeof(UINT), 1, pFile);
    fread(&NumSkins,     sizeof(UINT), 1, pFile);

    n = ((int)(((float)m_NumSectors)/50)+1)*50;
    m_ppSector = (LPSECTOR*)malloc(sizeof(LPSECTOR)*n);

    for (i=0; i<m_NumSectors; i++) {
       m_ppSector[i] = new CSector("Empty");
       m_ppSector[i]->Load(pFile);

       m_ppSector[i]->GetName(buffer);
       cbhAddItem(hcbSector, buffer, NULL, true);
       SelectSector(buffer);
       }

    for (i=0; i<NumSkins; i++)
       LoadSkin(hcbSkins, pDevice->GetSkinManager(), pFile);

    fclose(pFile);
    SetName(ch);
    return true;
    } // LoadLevel
```

Your Call: CSelectionBuffer

When designing the editing tool for this book, I had to ask myself how the level designer should be able to select objects from the level, and how this selection process should be implemented. Of course, the level designer has to be able to select all kinds of geometry and other objects such as spawn points. This is a must because the editing action, such as translation or rotation, should always affect only certain parts of the level. I considered a flag for the selection, similar to the hidden flag of the objects. Then I got lost in algorithms walking to the level and each sector twisting and toggling around flags. When I spoke to Oliver about this, he simply said, "You are using a selection buffer for this, aren't you?" At that moment, I thought of a forest and a lot of trees. I said: "Of course. At least, now I am."

So much for the story about how the selection buffer made its way into this tool. Thanks Oliver! The idea is just too simple for one to come up with on his own. A selection buffer is nothing more than a class whose instances can take references to arbitrary level objects of the base class type. Thus a selection buffer is something like a small sector for itself containing level objects, but with a slight difference. If you add a level object to a sector, the sector copies this object and stores it. If you add an object to the selection buffer, it only stores the address to reference the object, so the object itself has to be saved somewhere else. This *somewhere* is most likely a sector, of course.

Therefore, if the level designer selects polygon X in his level, which is part of sector Y, the selection buffer will receive the address of object X and store this address in its internal list. Notice that the class `CPolygon`, for instance, has several functions to translate or rotate the object or edit it in another way. However, neither the sector nor any other of the upper-level classes offer access to these functions to edit the low-level objects so far. Obviously, you can only edit selected objects, and, finally, the place where you can call the editing functions is the selection buffer, which will then delegate the calls to the low-level objects themselves using their addresses it has stored.

Class Declaration

In the following class declaration, you will recognize a lot of familiar functions. That is not surprising because functions such as `Translate()`, `Rotate()`, `Mirror()`, `TransTextureCoords()`, and others can be used by the editor only to edit selected geometry. Therefore, the selection buffer only delegates the function calls to the LOBs that are contained inside the buffer because they are selected. The functions aren't listed here because they are just a big loop over the selected objects.

Keep in mind that vertices are not a separate class, and not LOBs for that matter, but only a plain structure. However, you can still select, translate, and edit vertices in the editor. To do so, you need a little helper, the structure `VERTEX_SB`, which stores exactly two things: the address of the vertex in memory so that you can access its data, and the address of the polygon to which the vertex belongs. You need to know the polygon as well; because if you move the vertex, the bounding box of the polygon must be adjusted to include the new vertex position.

Now take a look at the declarations of the structure and the whole class for the selection buffer:

```
typedef struct VERTEX_SB_TYPE {
    VERTEX    *pV;     // address of a vertex
    LPPOLYGON pPoly;   // address of polygon
    } VERTEX_SB;

class CSelectionBuffer {
   public:
      CSelectionBuffer(void);
      ~CSelectionBuffer(void);

      void Reset(void);
```

```cpp
        void DestroyWithoutNotify(void);
        void DeleteSelectedObjects(CLevel*);
        void CopySelectedObjects(LPSECTOR);

        bool IsInside(const ZFXVector&, ZFXAXIS);

        UINT GetNumVerts(void)    { return m_NumVerts; }
        UINT GetNumLobs(void)     { return m_NumLobs;  }
        UINT GetNumObjects(void) { return m_NumLobs+m_NumVerts; }

        ZFXVector GetCenter(void){return m_Aabb.vcCenter;}

        LPPOLYGON     IsPolyQuad(void);
        LPLEVELOBJECT GetHeadPointer(void);

        void Render(ZFXRenderDevice*, float, bool, const ZFXVector*,
                    const ZFXCOLOR*);
        void Translate(const ZFXVector&);

        void AddLob(const LPLEVELOBJECT);
        void AddVertex(VERTEX*,const LPPOLYGON);
        void AddBoundingBox(const ZFXAabb&);

        void MergePolysToMesh(LPSECTOR,HWND);
        void MergeMeshs(LPSECTOR);
        void FragmentMeshs(LPSECTOR);
        void InsideOut(void);
        void Rotate(ZFXAXIS,float);
        void Mirror(ZFXAXIS);
        void Snap(void);
        void SaveAsPrefab(const char*);

        void SetSkinTo(UINT nID);
        void TextureRemap(ZFXAXIS);
        void TransTextureCoords(float ftU, float ftV, float frU, float frV);
        bool GetTextureTrans(float *pftU, float *pftV, float *pfrU, float *pfrV);
    private:
        LPLEVELOBJECT *m_ppLob;    // selected LOBs
        VERTEX_SB   *m_pVerts;     // selected vertices
        UINT         m_NumLobs;    // number of LOBs
        UINT         m_NumVerts;   // number of vertices
```

```
    ZFXAabb     m_Aabb;         // AABB
    float       m_fD;           // AABB delta

    void Init(void);
    void Release(void);
    void RenderBoundingBox(ZFXRenderDevice*);
    void RenderVertices(ZFXRenderDevice*, float);
  }; // class
typedef class CSelectionBuffer *LPSELECTIONBUFFER;
```

Is this a function to render a selection buffer in this class? Yes, of course. As you have seen earlier, the selected objects are not rendered using the render function of the sector itself. The selection buffer can be asked to render itself, just like any other object in the editor. The sense behind such a separate render call is that you can then render the selected geometry more easily with a different set of render states (such as a different color).

Also note that the selection buffer knows only objects of the type CLevelObject (or at least it just stores its contents in a single list of this type). This is in contrast to the CSector class, for example. However, nearly all the functionalities that the selection buffer needs to access for the selected objects are stored in the base class from which all different kinds of LOBs are inheriting.

During the construction or the destruction of an object, you must take care of one thing. If you want to destroy a selection buffer or reinitialize it, you must not leave the selected objects flagged as selected. To get the objects into a normal state, you have to deselect the objects first. Otherwise, they would be edited along with all other selected geometry in the worst case, even if they appear not to be selected:

```
CSelectionBuffer::CSelectionBuffer(void)   {Init();  }
CSelectionBuffer::~CSelectionBuffer(void)  {Release();}

void CSelectionBuffer::Init(void)
  {
  m_NumVerts    = 0;
  m_NumLobs     = 0;
  m_pVerts      = NULL;
  m_ppLob       = NULL;
  m_fD          = 0.05f;
  memset(&m_Aabb, 0, sizeof(ZFXAabb));
  } // Init
/*------------------------------------*/

void CSelectionBuffer::Release(void)
  {
```

```
      for (UINT i=0; i<m_NumLobs; i++)
         if (m_ppLob[i]) m_ppLob[i]->DeSelect();
   SAFE_FREE(m_ppLob);
   SAFE_FREE(m_pVerts);
   } // Release
/*-------------------------*/

void CSelectionBuffer::Reset(void)
   {
   Release();
   Init();
   m_Aabb.vcCenter = ZFXVector(0,0,0);
   m_Aabb.vcMax    = ZFXVector(0,0,0);
   m_Aabb.vcMin    = ZFXVector(0,0,0);
   } // Init
```

Adding Objects to the Buffer

By now it should be obvious how to use the editing tool. The level designer clicks an object in the active level to select it or he draws a selection rectangle by click-dragging over one of the three orthogonal views. The class `CSector` then hands over the address of any picked object or of any objects contained in the selection rectangle. In the case of the selection rectangle, the sector object gets a reference to the selection buffer so that it can insert each concerned object directly into the buffer to avoid returning a list of LOBs that are selected.

The following two functions enable you to add addresses of selected objects to the selection buffer. One function is needed to add LOBs to the selection buffer, and the second one will add addresses of vertices to the buffer. As you know, there is no level object for vertices in this tool, and hence the need for a separate function.

Finally, you must not forget to adjust the bounding box of the selection buffer to include the newly added object. In the class declaration, there is also a delta value for the bounding box, which is used to make the bounding box slightly bigger than the geometry inside. This way you can render the bounding box of the selected geometry later on without overdrawing some of the selected geometry.

Here are the two functions to add objects to the selection buffer:

```
void CSelectionBuffer::AddLob(const LPLEVELOBJECT pLob)
   {
   if ( pLob->IsSelected() ) return;

   if ( (m_NumLobs%50) == 0 )
      m_ppLob = (LPLEVELOBJECT*) realloc( m_ppLob, sizeof(LPLEVELOBJECT)
                                       * (m_NumLobs+50) );
```

```
      m_ppLob[m_NumLobs] = pLob;
      m_NumLobs++;

      // flag LOB as selected
      pLob->Select();

      // recalculate aabb
      AddBoundingBox( m_ppLob[m_NumLobs-1]->GetAabb() );
      } // AddLob
/*----------------------------*/


void CSelectionBuffer::AddVertex(VERTEX *pVertex, const LPPOLYGON pPoly)
   {
   ZFXAabb aabb;

   for (UINT i=0; i<m_NumVerts; i++) {
      if (m_pVerts[i].pV == pVertex) return;
      }

   if ( (m_NumVerts%50) == 0 )
      m_pVerts = (VERTEX_SB*) realloc(m_pVerts, sizeof(VERTEX_SB) *
                                      (m_NumVerts+50));
   m_pVerts[m_NumVerts].pV    = pVertex;
   m_pVerts[m_NumVerts].pPoly = pPoly;
   m_NumVerts++;

   aabb.vcMax    = ZFXVector(pVertex->x, pVertex->y, pVertex->z);
   aabb.vcMin    = ZFXVector(pVertex->x, pVertex->y, pVertex->z);
   aabb.vcCenter = ZFXVector(pVertex->x, pVertex->y, pVertex->z);
   aabb.vcMax += 0.05f;
   aabb.vcMin -= 0.05f;
   AddBoundingBox(aabb);
   } // AddVertex
```

Deleting and Copying Objects

Whatever you select in the level can then be edited. Of course, you should also be able to delete objects you have selected or copy them. In this section, you first learn how to delete objects permanently from a level. For this purpose, a selection buffer object needs the currently loaded CLevel object from the editor to get the active sector being edited at the moment. Then the selection buffer loops through its list of addresses of level objects and requests the sector to delete the object stored at this address. When this is done, you can reset the counter and the allocated memory of the selection buffer, which is then empty and ready for more action.

Caution

Note that there is no undo function in this editor. Therefore, after you have deleted something, there is no way to restore it from this level file. The only way to undo the operation is to load an old version of the level (if you have saved one, of course). So make it a habit to save a level regularly to different files.

Here is the implementation of the delete function:

```
void CSelectionBuffer::DeleteSelectedObjects(LPLEVEL pLevel)
    {
    UINT id=0;
    CSector *pSector = pLevel->GetSelectedSector();

    for (UINT i=0; i<m_NumLobs; i++) {

        // special case portal
        if (m_ppLob[i]->GetType() == LOB_PORTAL)
           {
           id = ( (LPPORTAL)m_ppLob[i] )->GetID();
           pLevel->RemovePortalConnections( id );
           }
        pSector->RemoveObject(m_ppLob[i]);
        }
    m_NumVerts = 0;
    m_NumLobs = 0;
    Reset();
    } // DeleteSelectedObjects
```

Besides the true deletion process of the selected objects, there is yet another way to delete objects. For this, we need a function that deletes the content of the selection buffer without deleting the objects that are selected and without notifying the selected objects that they are no longer selected. Such a function is needed, for example, when the level designer clicks the button to invert the selection. Then you clear the selection buffer without notifying the selected objects. After that you loop through the whole active sector and just invert the flags indicating the selection status of the objects and add the unselected ones to the selection buffer.

The normal `CSelectionBuffer::Reset` function would have reset the flags of the objects as well, so you would not have known afterward which ones had been deselected before and should now be selected:

```
void CSelectionBuffer::DestroyWithoutNotify(void)
   {
   SAFE_FREE(m_ppLob);
   SAFE_FREE(m_pVerts);
   Init();
   } // DestroyWithoutNotify
```

Just in time comes along another quite helpful function. After testing the editor a bit, I quickly implemented this function, which saves you from a lot of redundant work. After you have selected objects in the editor, you can now copy them with the following function. Using the function `CopyOf()`, which is implemented for all LOBs, the copying operation is not complicated at all. You just need to work a bit with the selection buffer to make this work. Suppose, for instance, that you have a number of objects selected and you want to copy them. You just loop through the objects in the selection buffer and build a copy of each object from the list. Before you copy an object, however, you have to deselect it. Then you can insert the copy into the active sector and mark the object as selected rather than the original one. With the address from the insertion operation, you overwrite the address of the original object you just copied.

After the copying operation, the originally selected objects are no longer selected. Instead, you have a copy of the selected object. Here is the function:

```
void CSelectionBuffer::CopySelectedObjects(LPSECTOR pSector)
   {
   DWORD    Type=LOB_NONE;
   CPolygon  Poly;
   CPolymesh Mesh;
   CLight   Light;
   ZFXVector vcT(0.2f,0.2f,0.2f);

   // deselect the object!!!
   for (UINT i=0; i<m_NumLobs; i++) {
      m_ppLob[i]->DeSelect();

      switch ( m_ppLob[i]->GetType() ) {
         case LOB_POLYGON:
            Poly.CopyOf( (LPPOLYGON)m_ppLob[i] );
            Poly.Translate(vcT);
            m_ppLob[i] = (LPPOLYGON)pSector->AddObject(Poly);
            break;
```

```
            case LOB_MESH:
                Mesh.CopyOf( (LPPOLYMESH)m_ppLob[i] );
                Mesh.Translate(vcT);
                m_ppLob[i] = (LPPOLYMESH)pSector->AddObject(Mesh);
                break;
            case LOB_LIGHT:
                Light.CopyOf( (LPLIGHT)m_ppLob[i] );
                Light.Translate(vcT);
                m_ppLob[i] = (LPLIGHT)pSector->AddObject(Light);
                break;
            default: break;
            } // switch
        m_ppLob[i]->Select();
        } // for
    m_Aabb.vcCenter += vcT;
    m_Aabb.vcMax    += vcT;
    m_Aabb.vcMin    += vcT;
    } // CopySelectedObjects
```

As you can see, the copies of the objects are translated by a certain vector. The only reason why we are doing this is because it makes it much easier to recognize visually the copy of the selected objects. If you didn't do this, the inserted copy of the object would sit right at the same position (which would look like the function did not work, because there seems to be no new geometry inserted). In the worst case, the level designer clicks the button several times, inserting multiple copies he can't even see.

Note that the function also allows for certain objects to be copied only. These include polygons, meshes, and light sources. In particular, it is not possible to copy entities and portals. That is because there are certain connections between those objects that should not be duplicated. At first, this may seem to be a strong restriction. If you build a complex, detailed object that is an entity, such as a door, you are not allowed to copy it? Well, the simple answer is this: You have to differentiate between the concept of the entity and the geometry that represents the entity. You can still copy the geometry of the entity by selecting the entity, hiding all nonselected objects, switching to the polygon selection mode, selecting everything that is not hidden, and then copying the object.

It is also recommended to save such complex objects as prefabs before you convert their geometry into an entity.

Polys to Meshes, Meshes to Polys

You have already read quite a lot about working with meshes and that meshs are built from single polygons that are just grouped together. However, you still don't know how to do this in the editor, even though you have all the low-level functions to add polygons and meshes to the active sector. Currently, no function enables you to group polygons into a mesh. However, this job can be done fairly easily. The level designer just needs to select a number of polygons he built using the GUI by setting the points for the polygon with clicks. A button on the GUI enables the level designer to issue the command that all currently selected polygons should be grouped into a mesh object.

That is why the selection buffer offers the according function to merge free polygons into a mesh. Therefore, you only need to create a new mesh object and loop through all selected polygons in the selection buffer. Those polygons are then copied into the mesh object, and the original polygons are deleted from the active sector. When this is done, the new mesh containing the copies of the original polygons is added to the active sector. Quite simple, isn't it?

```
void CSelectionBuffer::MergePolysToMesh(LPSECTOR pSector, HWND hWnd)
   {
   LPPOLYGON pPoly=NULL;
   CPolymesh Mesh;
   bool      bAsked=false;
   bool      bUseEm=false;

   if (m_NumLobs==0) return;

   for (UINT i=0; i<m_NumLobs; i++) {

      if ( m_ppLob[i]->GetType() != LOB_POLYGON )
         continue;
      else pPoly = (LPPOLYGON) m_ppLob[i];

      if ( pPoly->IsPartOfMesh() ) {
         if (bAsked && !bUseEm) continue;
         if (!bAsked) {
            if ( MessageBox(hWnd,
                  "At least one selected polygon is part of a mesh. Merge
                   them also?", "Warning", MB_YESNO | MB_ICONQUESTION)
                  == IDYES)
               bUseEm=true;
            bAsked=true;
            }
         }
      Mesh.AddPolygon( *pPoly );
      pSector->RemoveObject(pPoly);
      }
   pSector->AddObject(Mesh);
```

```
m_NumLobs = 0;
Reset();
} // MergePolysToMesh
```

As always, you must be aware of exceptions and special cases. The world would be boring without them, right? It can now happen that the level designer selects some polygons willingly or by chance which are already part of another mesh. If this function `CSelectionBuffer::MergePolysToMesh` finds at least one polygon that is already part of a mesh, it shows a WinAPI message box that asks the level designer whether the selected polygons should be ungrouped from the meshes they already belong to, to be part of the new mesh. If the level designer clicks Yes, the polygons are put into the selection buffer from which the new mesh will be built afterward. If he clicks No, the polygons belonging to a mesh already are ignored. The single decision applies to all concerned polygons.

The opposite case is when you want to select one or more meshes and want to destroy the grouping information without deleting the geometry. You can do this by copying the polygons from the selected meshes into the active sector as new free polygons. Then you just delete all selected meshes from the sector. The source code to do this is straightforward. There are no exceptions; you just need to confirm that a loop runs through the selected meshes and extracts their polygons in an inner loop that is running for all polygons of a mesh:

```
void CSelectionBuffer::FragmentMeshs(LPSECTOR pSector)
   {
   LPPOLYMESH pMesh=NULL;
   LPPOLYGON  pPoly=NULL;
   UINT n=0;

   for (UINT i=0; i<m_NumLobs; i++)
      {
      if ( m_ppLob[i]->GetType() != LOB_MESH ) continue;
      else pMesh = (LPPOLYMESH) m_ppLob[i];

      n = pMesh->GetNumPolys();

      for (UINT j=0; j<pMesh->GetNumPolys(); j++)
         {
         pPoly = pMesh->GetPolygon(j);
         pSector->AddObject( *pPoly );
         }
      pSector->RemoveObject(pMesh);
      }
   m_NumLobs = 0;
```

```
    Reset();
    } // FragmentMeshs
```

Saving Prefabs

Loading a prefab was already done directly in the class `CSector`, because this is the place where the loaded geometry is then placed. The editor enables you to save polygons only as prefabs, so you cannot include portals, spawn points, omni lights, and other level objects in the prefab file. Of course, you can save polygons that are part of a mesh. But again, the mesh information is not stored in the prefab; therefore, when you load a prefab, all polygons coming from it are interpreted as single, free polygons.

Our prefab format is now a very basic 3D model file format just like any other format. It is not as comprehensive as the x file format or the 3ds file format, but it serves the same purpose with regard to saving vertex and polygon data of a 3D model. After all, the prefab loading and saving function is nothing more than just importing and exporting a specific 3D file format. (This is just another hint that you should write your own exporters and importers for this editor to support other popular formats.)

Right after some geometry is selected into the selection buffer, the editor activates its controls, which enable the user to save a prefab. If the user selects such a control from the toolbar, for example, the editor hands the filename the user selected for the new prefab to the selection buffer. The selection buffer then opens the given file and saves all polygon data it contains into the open file. During the saving operation, the selection buffer loops through its list of LOBs to which it references. The buffer first counts the number of selected polygons (and polygons from meshes); this information is written to the file first. Then the buffer loops again through its list and saves all polygons (and polygons from meshes) into the open file one by one.

You read about the function `CPolymesh::SavePurePolys` earlier in this chapter. It will now be used to save polygons that are part of a mesh. However, it is most important here that you store the name of the texture with each polygon to the file. Keep in mind that you can access the name of the texture from the combo box of the user interface, where its skin ID equals the skin's position in the combo box's list.

Here is the function to save the polygons from the selection buffer as a prefab:

```
void CSelectionBuffer::SaveAsPrefab(const char *ch)
    {
    UINT nNumPolys=0;
    UINT i=0, n=0, SkinID=0;
    char buffer[2048];

    FILE *pPrefab = fopen(ch, "wb");
```

```
   for (i=0; i<m_NumLobs; i++)
      {
      if (m_ppLob[i]->GetType() == LOB_POLYGON)
         nNumPolys++;
      else if (m_ppLob[i]->GetType() == LOB_MESH)
         nNumPolys += m_ppLob[i]->GetNumPolys();
      }

   fwrite(&nNumPolys, sizeof(UINT), 1, pPrefab);

   for (i=0; i<m_NumLobs; i++)
      {
      if (m_ppLob[i]->GetType() == LOB_MESH) {
         ((LPPOLYMESH)m_ppLob[i])->SavePurePolys(pPrefab);
         }

      else if (m_ppLob[i]->GetType() == LOB_POLYGON)
         {
         SkinID = ((LPPOLYGON)m_ppLob[i])->GetSkinID();
         SendMessage(CApplication::m_G.hGUI[CSK_LIST], CB_GETLBTEXT, SkinID,
                     (LPARAM)(LPCSTR)buffer);
         n = strlen(buffer);
         fwrite(&n, sizeof(UINT), 1, pPrefab);
         fwrite(buffer, n, 1, pPrefab);

         ((LPPOLYGON)m_ppLob[i])->Save(pPrefab);
         }
      }
   fclose(pPrefab);
   } // SaveAsPrefab
```

You might be thinking that this prefab format is a rather plain and simple format in comparison to other 3D model file formats on the market. I agree. Normally, you save the list of vertices, then a list of indices making up the faces of the model, and so on. This model format is not meant to compete with commercial formats; it is just meant to be loaded as simply as possible in the editor. This editor is not oriented on building comprehensive vertex lists for a big vertex buffer to get good performance. It is oriented toward the base of polygons, and therefore the information is stored polygon by polygon in the file. If you want to support more model file formats, you would loop through the selected polygons, extract all their vertices, then all the indices, and so on to build lists of the attributes of the polygon. That is a bit more work to do, but it is no problem to write an exporter that writes the selected geometry as an x file model to your hard drive.

The source code for our full blown level-editing tool is now complete (after just a few dozen pages containing all the explanations and code to build it). There is still a bit of code missing to connect the classes shown so far with a GUI. However, this boils down to plain WinAPI code used to create buttons, text fields, and the like. You don't have to face that task alone, however; the following section focuses exclusively on the GUI.

Selected Aspects of the GUI

The complete *PanBox-Edit* project contains more classes than the ones covered here (including the one about to be introduced: CApplication). However, those other classes are neither very complex nor complicated (in code length or implementation). Because you will readily understand these classes from the accompanying CD-ROM, it's unnecessary to cover them in detail here. The project contains the following classes and objects besides the ones mentioned so far:

- The class CFile to encapsulate the WinAPI Open Filename dialog box
- The class CToolbar to encapsulate the WinAPI toolbar
- A combo box with helper functions to encapsulate the WinAPI combo box
- Dialog box callback functions for specific editor tasks

As you can see, most of this stuff is just very basic WinAPI programming. Now, however, it is time to screw up object-oriented C++ programming for the sake of simplicity. After all, sometimes you just want to have global variables that you can ignore using a straight class-oriented design. In some situations, however, a design implementation will drive you crazy because you need to implement a lot of overhead to get things running the way you want them. For instance, it is not easy with classes to use callback functions in the Windows messaging and event system.

In the following quick example, one global variable is used for the project, which is a structure that contains some fields. Note that this is an implicit class, so you could also have made the attributes static in order to cloak the global usage of this stuff. And you already know the name of the variable; it is CApplication::m_G, which is indeed a static attribute of the class CApplication. The attribute is an instance of the following structure:

```
typedef struct GLOBALS_TYPE {
    HINSTANCE        hInst;
    HWND             hWnd;
    HWND             hWnd3D[4];
    HWND             hGUI[100];
    HWND             hTexDlg;
    bool             bChanged;
    bool             bNeedRedraw[4];
    FILE             *pLog;
```

```
    CFile           FileDlg;
    CLevel          Level;
    CSelectionBuffer SelBuf;
    char            Dir[MAX_PATH];
} GLOBALS;
```

The structure GLOBALS shown here contains absolutely everything that must be accessible from different classes at different places in the application. For example, the callback functions of a control element need to have access to the level to extract data about certain objects the control should change or display. Table 14.1 lists the meaning of each of the fields in this structure.

Table 14.1 Fields of the Structure GLOBALS

Field	Meaning
HInst	Instance handle of the application
HWnd	Window handle of the application's main window
hWnd3D[4]	Handle of the four child windows used for rendering
hGUI[100]	Handles of the WinAPI control elements
hTexDlg	Handle of the nonmodal Texture Coordinates dialog box
bChanged	Level was changed and needs to be saved
bNeedRedraw[4]	Redraw of child windows necessary
pLog	Log file for error messages
FileDlg	Encapsulating the WinAPI Open Filename dialog box
Level	Currently loaded level
SelBuf	Selection buffer of the editor
Dir[MAX_PATH]	Path of the application itself

Class Declaration

This section covers the class CApplication, which provides the interface between the low-level classes containing the geometry, the objects, and so on and the level designer who wants to use those low-level classes. Interestingly, this class is not very big with regard to the number of functions it needs. Keep in mind that this class is mostly about reacting to input events and messages coming from controls such as buttons and menus. Those events and messages will then result in an action that concerns one of the low-level classes (and is implemented in those classes, of course).

The following listing shows the declaration of the class. Because you are familiar with programming the WinAPI, you can see from the source code on the CD-ROM what the functions of this class are doing in detail (and so they aren't discussed in detail in this chapter).

From the name of the functions, you can already guess what they are used for. Following this partial listing of the class declaration, this section discusses the most interesting parts of this class:

```cpp
class CApplication {
   public:
      CApplication(void) { }
      virtual ~CApplication(void) { }

      HRESULT Init(HWND, HINSTANCE);
      void    Update(void);
      void    RenderTick(void);
      void    Release(void);

      void    Done(void)     { m_bDone = true;     }
      bool    IsDone(void)   { return m_bDone;     }
      void    Active(bool b) { m_bActive = b;      }
      bool    IsActive(void) { return m_bActive;   }

      void    InvalidateView(int);
      void    InvalidateAllViews(void);

      bool    MsgProcMenu(WORD);
      bool    MsgProcGUI(WORD);
      bool    MsgProcToolbar(WORD wCmd) { return m_Toolbar.MsgProc(wCmd); }

      LPZFXRENDERDEVICE GetRenderDevice(void) { return m_pRDevice; }

      void    OnViewPerspective(void);
      void    OnViewOrthogonal(UCHAR);
      bool    OnClose(void);
      void    OnDeleteKey(void);
      void    OnMouseMove(WPARAM, LPARAM);
      void    OnMouseClick(bool, WPARAM, LPARAM);
      void    OnSelBufChange(void);

      ZFXSkinManager* GetSkinMan(void)
              { return m_pRDevice->GetSkinManager(); }

      CToolbar* GetToolbar(void) { return &m_Toolbar; }
      bool      CheckForcedSave(void);
      bool      MouseInside(HWND, POINT*);
```

```cpp
            static GLOBALS m_G;

private:
    DWORD              m_OldTime;       // frame counter
    DWORD              m_NewTime;       // frame counter
    float              m_dt;            // elapsed time
    LPZFXRENDERER      m_pRenderer;
    LPZFXRENDERDEVICE  m_pRDevice;
    CToolbar           m_Toolbar;
    HMENU              m_hm;
    POINT              m_ptCursorNew;
    POINT              m_ptCursorOld;
    int                m_CurView;       // viewport
    UINT               m_nFontID;       // font
    bool               m_bDone;
    bool               m_bActive;
    UINT               m_nZFXFont;

    // user settings for the editor
    bool               m_bDrawLight;    // rendering light
    bool               m_b3DHide;       // hide in 3d view also
    bool               m_bDrawGrid[2];
    bool               m_bDrawPoints[2];
    bool               m_bDrawWired[2];
    bool               m_bDrawInact[2];
    bool               m_bDrawInactW;
    bool               m_bSnap;
    UCHAR              m_bIsSelecting;
    UCHAR              m_bIsMovingSelection;
    UCHAR              m_bIsCreating;
    RECT               m_rcOrthoSel;
    ZFXVector          m_vcSel[2];
    ZFXAXIS            m_Axis[3];
    ZFXVector          m_vcEndMove;
    ZFXVector          m_vcStartMove;
    SELECTMODE         m_SelectMode;
    TOOL               m_CurrentTool;

    // view transformation stuff
    ZFXMatrix          m_World[4];
    ZFXVector          m_vcFix;
    float              m_fRotX;
```

```
    float           m_fRotY;
    float           m_fDistOrtho;
    float           m_fScale[3];
    float           m_fPosX[4];
    float           m_fPosY[4];
    float           m_fPosZ[4];

    VERTEX          m_vVerts[256];
    UCHAR           m_NumVerts;

    // Shader-IDs
    UINT            m_BaseVSH;
    UINT            m_OmniVSH;
    UINT            m_BasePSH;
    UINT            m_OmniPSH;

    // private functions
    HRESULT         InitRenderer(void);
    HRESULT         InitShaders(void);
    void            CreateGUI(void);
    void            UpdateCursor(void);
    void            SetSelectMode(SELECTMODE);
    bool            ChangeCheckState(UINT MenuID);
    void            OrthoSelection(bool,POINT);
    void            CheckTbState(UINT,UINT, SELECTMODE);
    void            RenderOrthoGrid(UCHAR n);
    void            RenderPerspGrid(void);
    void            RenderPolyUnderConstr(UINT);
    void            RenderSelectionRect(void);
    void            RenderInActive(bool);
    void            RenderGeometry(bool,float);
    void            RenderPortals(bool);
    void            RenderLights(bool);
    void            RenderEntities(bool);
    void            RenderSpawns(bool);
    bool            InvalidateSelectionRect(bool);
    void            OnPolyCreationEvent(bool bEnd, const ZFXVector*);
}; // class
```

Important Attributes

This class contains many attributes, not all of which are self-explanatory. Most of them are easy to understand, however, because they just control and adjust the behavior of the editor under certain circumstances or just save some important values such as the cursor position (over which child window the cursor currently hovers), and so on. Table 14.2 lists the most interesting and important attributes of this class; the other attributes should be self-explanatory (at least from the source code on the companion CD-ROM).

Table 14.2 Important Attributes of the Class CApplication

Data Type	Attribute	Meaning
UCHAR	m_bIsSelecting	By default, 255. If the value is set to 0, 1, or 2, it says that the user is drawing a selection rectangle in one of the orthogonal views, where the value identifies the concerned child window.
UCHAR	m_bIsMovingSelection	Like the one above, but indicating that the user is moving an existing selection rectangle.
UCHAR	m_bIsCreating	Values like above, but indicating that the user is currently creating a polygon in the ortho views.
RECT	m_rcOrthoSel	Contains the dimension and position of the selection rectangle if one is active. Else -1 for all entries.
ZFXVector	m_vcStartMove	Starting point for translating operation.
ZFXVector	m_vcEndMove	Endpoint for translating operation.
VERTEX	m_vVerts[256]	Vertex list for new polygon under construction.
UCHAR	m_NumVers	Number of entries in vertex list.
POINT	m_ptCursorOld	Mouse position in the last frame.
POINT	m_ptCursorNew	Mouse position in the current frame.
int	m_CurView	Identifies the child view the cursor is currently in. 0 to 3 starting clockwise in the upper-left view.
TOOL	m_CurrentTool	Currently active tool. As of now, there are only TL_SELECT, enabling you to select with the mouse and TL_POLYGON, enabling you to create a new polygon with the mouse.

Update Function

The editor performance is a critical element because we have to render the level not only four times, but also in a heavily nonoptimized and nonideal ordering and sorting. Performance drag may be noticed as longer execution times for rendering, delays while moving the cursor, and late reactions to mouse clicks and the like. Most of the problem is connected to the fact that you have to render all the data dynamically and cannot sort it into static buffers sitting in the VRAM.

You can fight bad performance, of course. Unlike in an interactive virtual environment such as a video game using such a level, in this editor you don't have to draw the level as often as possible. In fact, you only have to render everything anew when something in the level has changed. Remember the attribute in the class that is set accordingly to indicate a change that requires rendering. Even if no such event occurs, we will still redraw the level, but not each frame. We just count the number of frames being rendered and, at a certain number of frames, make a render call. I used 120 frames in this sample, but you can adjust the number and play around a bit with some values.

This "minor surgery" operation does the trick! All of a sudden, the editor is again very fast (even for huge levels with a lot of geometry) without noticeable delay:

```
void CApplication::Update(void)
   {
   static float fCount = 0.0f;

   UpdateCursor();

   if (fCount > 120.0f)
      {
      m_OldTime = timeGetTime();
      RenderTick();
      fCount = 0.0f;
      m_NewTime = timeGetTime();
      m_dt =  ((float)(m_NewTime-m_OldTime))/1000.0f;
      }
   else fCount += 1.0f;
   } // Update
```

The function CApplication::RenderTick will do nothing more than just call the functions that are taking care of rendering the objects in the level. There are separate render functions for geometrical data, portals, light sources, and so on in this class. Those functions are very simple indeed, because there is not much to do except for setting some line colors and calling the rendering functions of the LOB classes. The line color is used to render the objects in the wireframe mode with different colors (such as blue for mesh objects and bright gray for polygons).

Creating a Polygon

You can create a polygon without letting go of the mouse. First, the level designer using our tool has to click a button to indicate that he wants to start creating a polygon. This click sets the attribute m_CurrentTool to the value TL_POLYGON so that the application knows what is going on. If then the event of a mouse click occurs in any of the orthogonal views of the editor and the current tool is set to the polygon creation value, the function `CApplication::OnPolyCreationEvent` is called. If a right-click event occurs, the first parameter of the function is set to `true`, which indicates that the creation process is over now; otherwise, the value is `false`. The second parameter of the function is always the position where the mouse click occurred, which is calculated into 3D space with the missing coordinate set to 0.

If the level designer now left-clicks while the cursor is inside one of the three orthogonal views, a new vertex is created and added to a temporary list of vertices for the polygon under construction. If he right-clicks, the creation process is finished and a new polygon object is created from the temporary list of vertices. Then the texture coordinates are calculated according to the planar mapping of the concerned axis, and the polygon is then added to the active sector:

```
void CApplication::OnPolyCreationEvent(bool bEnd, const ZFXVector *pvc)
   {
   LPPOLYGON pPoly=NULL;
   CPolygon  NewPoly;
   CSector   *pSector=NULL;

   // note the child window in which the process started
   if (m_NumVerts == 0) m_bIsCreating = m_CurView;

   // end of creation
   if (bEnd) {
      // at least three edges?
      if (m_NumVerts>2) {
         // build new polygon
         NewPoly.Reset();
         NewPoly.SetVertices(m_vVerts, m_NumVerts);
         NewPoly.Triangulate();
         NewPoly.CalcTextureCoords(m_Axis[m_CurView],NULL);
         pSector = m_G.Level.GetSelectedSector();
         pPoly = (LPPOLYGON)pSector->AddObject(NewPoly);

         m_G.SelBuf.Reset();
         m_G.SelBuf.AddLob(pPoly);
         m_G.bChanged = true;
         OnSelBufChange();
         m_bIsCreating = 255;
         }

      // simulate button click to switch to polygon selection mode
```

```
         SendMessage(m_G.hGUI[CSM_POLYGON],BM_CLICK,0,0);
         SendMessage(m_G.hGUI[CT_SEL],BM_CLICK,0,0);
         m_CurrentTool = TL_SELECT;
         m_NumVerts = 0;
         }
   // creation process
   else if (!bEnd)
      {
      // too many vertices
      if (m_NumVerts > 255) return;

      // coordinates of the mouse click
      m_vVerts[m_NumVerts].x  = pvc->x;
      m_vVerts[m_NumVerts].y  = pvc->y;
      m_vVerts[m_NumVerts].z  = pvc->z;
      m_vVerts[m_NumVerts].tu = 0.0f;
      m_vVerts[m_NumVerts].tv = 0.0f;
      m_NumVerts++;
      }
   } // OnPolyCreationEvent
```

With that function done, you can now really start creating arbitrary geometry and place it inside the level. You do not need more than a function to create plane polygons, and with the function above you have that functionality now. However, you also have the class `CGeometry` in the project space, which can create certain geometrical objects as well as a list of polygons as meshes by static member functions. Even though this class only provides two simple shapes as of now, you can always add more and more additional objects to this class. After all, it is much easier to insert a complex shape into the level by just clicking a button on the toolbar. Creating such shapes by building them polygon by polygon is rather hard and boring. Therefore, the foundation of the editor is now provided and you can build it up from this point however you want.

One Look Back, Two Steps Forward

You've made it through the planning, the design, and the implementation of a fully functional low-polygon editor, and all in one chapter. Before completing this chapter, you may not have believed how easy implementing such an editing tool could be. Granted, our editor is somewhat different from famous tools that use a CSG approach, but still you can build levels and even 3D models. In fact, the game we are going to implement in the next chapter uses the level data generated with this tool.

Remember the enormous potential hidden inside this tool. You probably already have a lot of ideas in your head about how you can improve the editor and add more features.

Before you move on to the next chapter, however, I strongly recommend that you take a look at the `CApplication` class of the editor and check out how it works. (The times when level designers used to draw their levels on a piece of paper and then hack the coordinates into a plain-text file are long gone.)

In a real commercial project, a lot of time is dedicated to implementing the tools needed to build files for the game project. Nowadays, even the big commercial products such as Maya and XSI offer plug-in tools to support game-content creation and try to make custom level-editing tools obsolete.

Now that you are able to create 3D indoor content by just using a GUI, it is about time to let the light flow into our virtual universe and bring some interactivity to the level files by loading them into a game. In this interactive world, the player will be allowed to move through the world and experience the "feeling" of virtual reality. Just turn to the next chapter and get started.

CHAPTER 15

Deathmatch Shooter

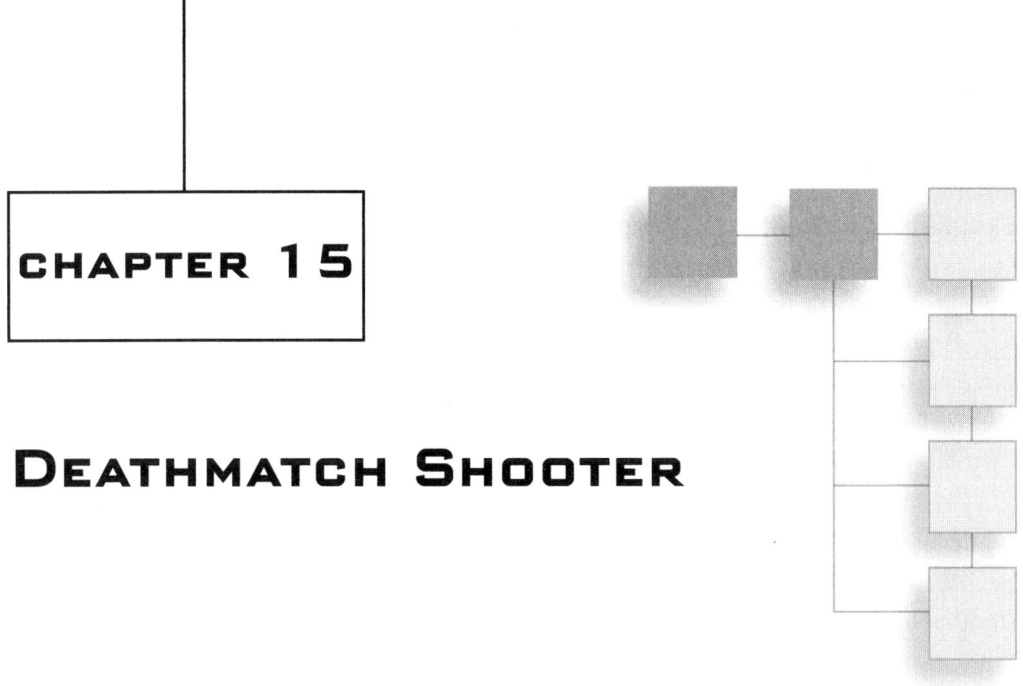

A lot of sense lies in childish playing.

Friedrich Schiller

For several hundreds of pages now, we have worked our way through writing a game engine. What use is the engine, however, if we don't have a chassis around the engine to be powered by it? You have seen a lot of small demo applications throughout the course of this book, but as of yet no comprehensive project that shows off with the engine. Now although this is a book about game engines, it just wouldn't be complete without a demo that can be played to a certain degree.

This chapter covers the following topics:

- A simple game design
- Building shadow volumes to render shadows
- Efficiently organizing level data for rendering
- Pixel lighting for an indoor level
- Connecting the portals
- Scene management with a portal engine

Deathmatch Shooter: *Pandora's Legacy*

This chapter finishes up with a simple network deathmatch shooter called *Pandora's Legacy*. The purpose of this game is not to implement a comprehensive game with a lot of features; instead, it is quite rudimentary. However, it does feature network support for multiple clients participating in the game and it can load the level data from the editor implemented in Chapter 14, "Computer-Aided Design (CAD) Tools."

Simple Game Design

There's not much to say about this game design, except this: it is quite simple. The only thing we are going to do in this game is to load the level data from our own editing tool *PanBox-Edit* as an interactive indoor environment and get the portal system working. Then the network interface of the ZFXEngine will allow multiple players to connect to the game and wander around in the level.

Even this simple design requires some good lines of code, especially if you want to store the data in an efficient way that is good for fast rendering. What's been described thus far would not be much of a game, however, so we will also enable the players to freeze each other by firing ice bullets. Frozen players have to wait some time while they warm up before they can continue walking around in the level freezing other guys.

Old Classes Redone

This implementation structure is similar to the layout of the level editor from Chapter 14. Of course, we also need classes for a level object, for a sector object, and so on. Because we are storing the data differently, however, those classes have to be different. Table 15.1 identifies the classes from Chapter 14 that have a counterpart in this chapter.

Still, the general layout of the management will be the same here as it was in the editor. That means the top-layer object is the level class, which stores a number of sectors, whereas the sector class keeps all the information about other objects in the level. Before we start to implement the code to handle all this stuff, this chapter provides an overview of the layout and design to enhance your understanding. Another interesting feature in all

Table 15.1 Counterpart Classes in This Chapter

Level Editor Class	Game Code Class
CLevel	CGameLevel
CSector	CGameSector
CPortal	CGamePortal
CLight	CGameLight
CPolygon	n/a
CPolymesh	n/a
CSpwawnPoint	n/a
CEntity	n/a

contemporary 3D games, and one that is used in this chapter (and introduced in the following section), is the real-time generation of shadows.

In the Shadows of Ourselves

In the virtual world of computer graphics, programmers must do all the work that is done in the real world by Mother Nature. Even if you have the world's most ingenious lighting calculation that brightens up pixels in real time using pixel shaders, you will soon realize that shadows are not cast automatically. Note that this discussion does not refer to global illumination methods such as radiosity, ray tracing, and photon mapping, which would cast shadows to a certain degree, but which are too slow for real time. Therefore, the bottom line is this: If you want to have a certain effect, you must implement it. Unfortunately, you can't just turn on a D3DRS_SHADOWGENERATION render state (at least not yet).

In the real world, darkness is all around; after all, it's just the absence of light. Mother Nature has to do little then to create shadows, which are just patches of darkness created when something blocks Mother Nature's attempt to illuminate (by blasting photons) a certain surface or area. And here you have the first hint as to how to implement shadows in computer graphics. You need to consider each object that is blocking the effect of a light source, or which *should be* blocking, for that matter. You can deal with potential "occluders" in different ways, such as shadow mapping, but this chapter focuses on just the shadow volume approach.

The Theory of Shadow Volumes

The theory behind shadow volumes is actually quite simple, as illustrated in Figure 15.1. This figure shows a triangle and a light source. Suppose now that you want to find out where the triangle should cast its shadow with respect to the light source. To do this, you have to draw the direction of the incoming light shining on the triangle. Then you take this direction vector and extrude each vertex of the triangle along this vector. By doing this, you extrude the whole triangle to a volume, and this volume is called the object's *shadow volume*, of course. Note that a front cap and a back cap are also needed; these ensure that the volume is closed on the front side and on the back side with regard to the light source. Note as well that the vector used here for extrusion is the same for all vertices, which is true only for directional light. Actually, you would have to draw a vector from the light source to each vertex to do the extrusion correctly.

Basically, that's all the theory you need to understand how shadow volumes work in general. Of course, the idea behind this approach is that each object that is sitting inside the shadow volume of an occluder is in shadow. This is similar to the viewing volume, where each object is visible that is inside the viewing volume. In this case, however, you are doing some kind of occlusion culling from the light source's point of view.

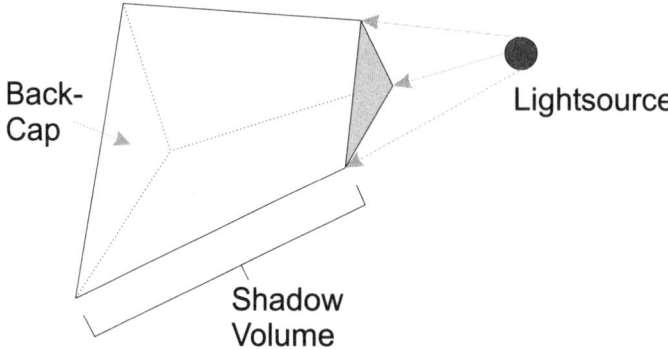

Figure 15.1 Extruding a shadow volume from a simple triangle with respect to a point light source. The triangle itself forms the front cap, and the extruded triangle is the back cap.

So far so good, but how should you now implement this? After all, you cannot assume that each object in the virtual world lies either totally inside a shadow volume or totally outside of all shadow volumes. Instead, you must calculate this on a per-pixel basis, and this is where the stencil buffers come into the game.

The following two subsections describe in detail two variants of the stencil shadow volume method. First, though, take a look at the basic layout of the algorithm to render with shadow volumes, which is the same for both variants:

- Render the scene without shadows into the depth buffer
- Recalculate the shadow volumes, if necessary
- Render the shadow volumes into the stencil buffer
- Render the scene into the frame buffer

You must render the shadow volumes into the stencil buffer only, not for visual output. This is done so that you can mask the areas of the color buffer that should receive shadow. (The two major variants of shadow volume rendering differ specifically on how to accomplish this, as discussed momentarily.) At this point, you have masked all the pixels that are in the shadow, and the stencil buffer will block those pixels from being rendered at all. If you then render your scene into the color buffer, all pixels now set in a region that is in shadow cannot break through to the color buffer. Hence the color buffer keeps its original clear color in this place, which should be jet black for the shadows. Note, however, that you must fill the depth buffer before the shadow volume rendering algorithm can run, because it needs the depth information.

Note

At the website Gamdev.net, you will find an excellent article called "The Theory of Stencil Shadow Volumes," by Hun Yen Kwoon. The following illustrations in this chapter are inspired by the ones you can find in this article. Check it out: http://www.gamedev.net/columns/hardcore/shadow volume.

Depth-Pass Variant

The first variant of the stencil shadow volume method is called the *depth-pass variant* or *z-pass variant*. You will soon understand the origin of this name. First, however, take a look at Figure 15.2, which shows a simplified 3D scene from bird's eye view. As you can see, there is a shadow volume, but the front cap and the back cap are not shown. Note that this volume will extrude into infinity.

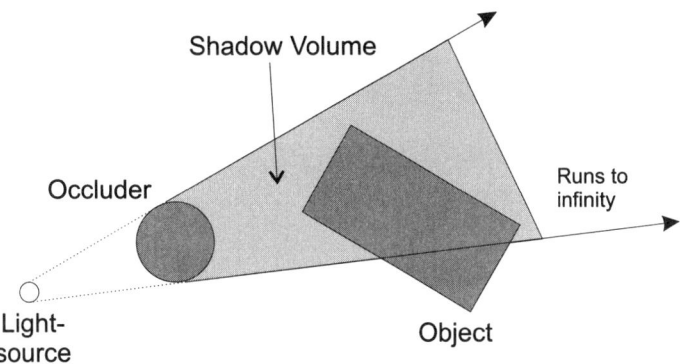

Figure 15.2 Bird's eye view of a 3D scene with a light source and one occlude (gray circle) and the occluder's shadow volume. Note the other geometrical object, which does not cast its own shadow here.

After you have constructed the shadow volume (you will see this in the source code later on), you must render it into the depth buffer. Keep in mind that the depth buffer is already filled with the 3D scene, which was rendered normally. While rendering the shadow volume into the stencil buffer, follow these steps:

1. Render all front faces of the volume. If the depth test is successfully passed, increase the according pixel in the stencil buffer.
2. Render all back faces of the volume. If the depth test is successfully passed, decrease the according pixel in the stencil buffer.

Therefore, at first you render the shadow volume with normal back-face culling. Then you render the volume again, but you toggle the back-face culling to render the opposite site of the triangles. As you can now see, this variant is called depth-pass because you just take an action in the stencil buffer if the depth test for a pixel of the volume is successfully passed. Now you have a mask in the stencil buffer that is doing the whole shadow trick for you. Take a look at Figure 15.3.

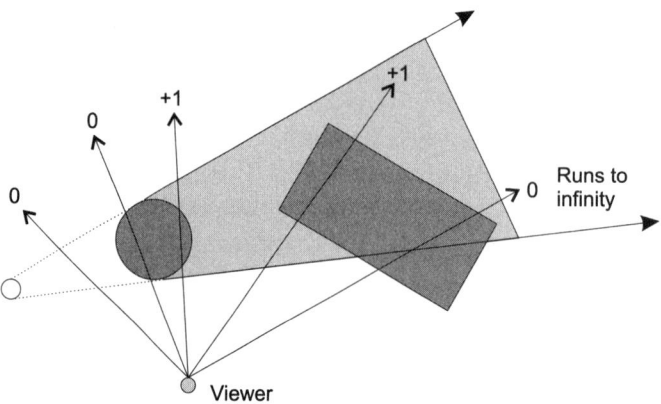

Figure 15.3 Depth-pass variant. If the viewing ray from the viewer intersects a front face of a shadow volume, the stencil value is incremented; if it is intersecting a back face, it is decremented.

Figure 15.3 shows how it works. This illustration shows five pixels. You can represent each of the pixels by a ray cast from the viewer into the direction of the pixel that is about to be rendered—or not, if it is in shadow. The first and the second ray starting from the left are not intersecting any shadow volumes, hence the stencil buffer's value will remain at 0. The third ray is more interesting. First the front face of the shadow volume is rendered, which works with the depth buffer, and hence the stencil value is set to 1. Then the back faces of this shadow volume are rendered, and this pixel fails at the depth buffer because the sphere (which generated the volume in the first place) is already closer to the viewer and blocks the depth buffer. So the value in the stencil buffer cannot be decremented to 0. Now this pixel is effectively masked in the stencil buffer and cannot be written to. Therefore, the part of the sphere that is in the shadow volume cannot be rendered later on and will stay dark (as it should, because it is inside the shadow). For the fourth ray, the exact same scenario plays out. The last ray is already blocked while rendering the front faces, which means that the stencil value is not even incremented so the pixel can be rendered later on.

Pretty smart, isn't it? That's the whole stencil shadow volume trick in this variant. After all, the stencil buffer does nothing other than just count the front faces and the back faces a ray from the viewer to a certain pixel intersects. If there is the same number of intersections for both types of faces, everything is okay. If the numbers are uneven, however, the ray has crossed one more front face of a shadow volume, but the ray has not left the same shadow volume through its back face after doing so. In this case, the pixel where the ray ends is inside the shadow volume, and thus inside the shadow.

This method is so robust that objects can even self-shadow. That is, a part of a mesh can cast a shadow on another part of itself. This even works when shadow volumes are located behind each other, and even when they are overlapping each other, as you can see in Figure 15.4.

In the Shadows of Ourselves   793

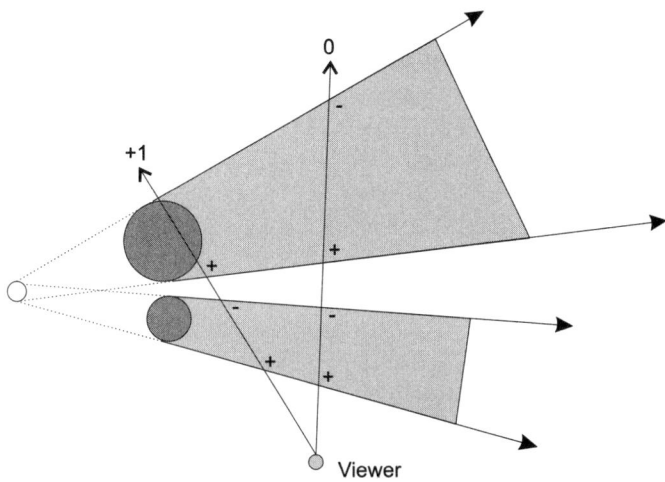

Figure 15.4 The depth-pass variant is even working if shadow volumes are located behind each other or if they are overlapping each other.

Very simple indeed. So is it too good to be true? Unfortunately, yes. The devil is in the details of this approach, and one minor nasty detail screws up the whole show, as you can see in Figure 15.5.

You can see here that the position of the view is the problem. If this position is located inside a shadow volume, the values in the stencil buffer are wrong (or at least they will have no meaning for the shadow calculation). Apparently, there is an easy solution to this. As soon as the viewer is inside the shadow volume, you clear the stencil buffer with the default value 1 rather than 0. However, that isn't a very robust solution. Using this solu-

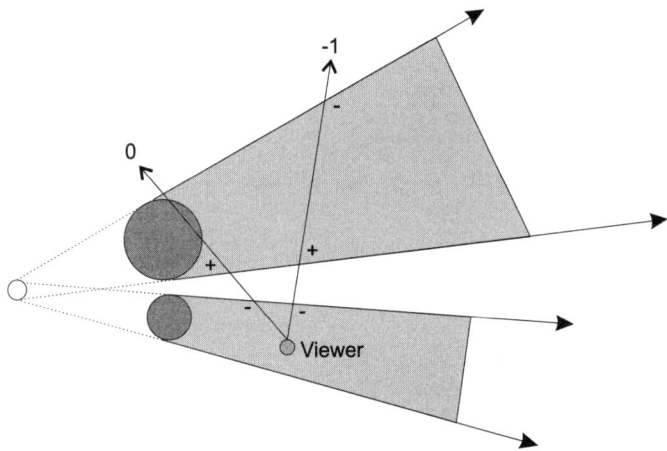

Figure 15.5 If the viewer is located inside the shadow volume, the depth-pass variant won't work.

tion, you will face problems with the near clipping plane. For instance, the viewer is standing right outside the shadow volume, but the rendering clips parts of the shadow volume because of the near plane. Therefore, the missing front faces of the shadow volume require an algorithm as if the player is actually already inside the shadow volume. In actuality, the problem is not the position of the viewer, but whether the near clipping plane is already inside the shadow volume.

Depth-Fail Variant

The second variant of the shadow volume method is called the *depth-fail variant* (or *z-fail variant*, as well as *Carmack's reverse*—Carmack being the one who brought us the binary space partitioning (BSP) tree for video game rendering in the first place). Due to the problems with the depth-pass variant described previously, John Carmack was looking for another approach to bypass the problems with this otherwise pretty smart way to create shadows. The variant he finally came up with is this:

1. Render all back faces of the volume. If the depth test fails, increase the according pixel in the stencil buffer.
2. Render all front faces of the volume. If the depth test fails, decrease the according pixel in the stencil buffer.

Under this variant, the stencil buffer sees action only if the depth test for a pixel under consideration fails (hence this variant's name). If you do the shadow volume dance with the pixels using the depth-fail variant, even a viewer standing right inside the shadow volume cannot cause any trouble, as you can see in Figure 15.6.

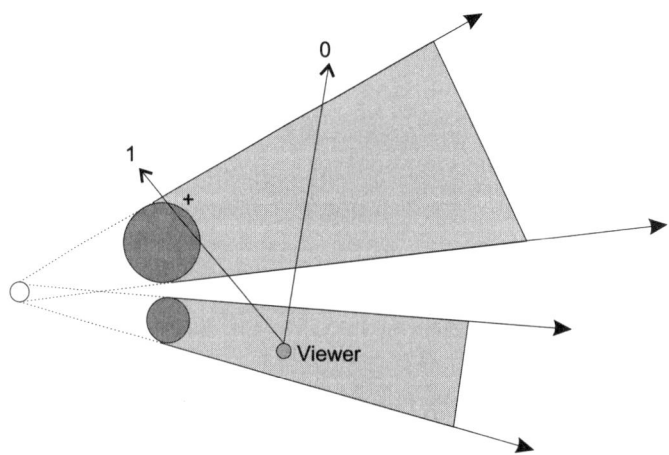

Figure 15.6 The depth-fail variant is still working even with the viewer standing inside the volume. The stencil value is incremented if rendering a back face fails because of the depth buffer and decremented if rendering a front face fails because of the depth buffer.

Be aware, however, that nothing comes free. The first drawback you have to deal with when using this variant is that the shadow volume needs to be capped, because this variant works only for closed shadow volumes (in contrast to the depth-pass variant, which does not care whether volumes are open or closed). This variant relies on the fact that the stencil value stays set when the rendering of a back face of the volume fails. If the viewer is standing in front of the volume or inside the volume and is looking into the direction of the open end where the back cap is missing, however, the algorithm won't work properly, even if pixels are in shadow. However, this is only a minor problem because caps can easily be calculated.

Note
> You can calculate the front cap in several ways. Mark Kilgard describes a complex method that enables you to project the polygons from the occluder that are facing away from the light source onto the near plane, which are then forming the front cap. However, you can do so more easily by just using the polygons of the occluder that are facing the light source. The back cap is then built from the same triangles, but with an inverted front-face orientation.

Now that the problem with the near clipping plane is solved, you encounter another pressing problem: the far clipping plane. Actually, that is basically the same problem as the open volume in this variant. Just think of the far plane cutting off a bit from the closed volume, which looks quite open afterwards. To overcome this problem, you can choose from two robust solutions. The first solution is to extrude the volume—not until infinity, but only for a small distance, guaranteeing that the far plane won't clip away parts of the volume. The more robust solution is to use what is called an infinite projection matrix. This matrix projects the geometry in a way that the far plane is assumed to lie in infinity. Therefore, it could not cut off the shadow volume, which ends somewhere before infinity "starts."

Okay, that is all you need to know about the gray theory behind shadows. Now it's time to implement a class that enables you to build and render those shadow volumes. Of course, this example uses the depth-fail variant.

Implementing Shadow Volumes

This section covers the creation of a shadow volume class that will build a shadow volume for arbitrary geometry that is independent of a specific vertex format. Building such a volume is not complicated at all, and there is even a nice sample in the DirectX Software Developer's Kit (SDK); that sample uses the depth-pass variant of the algorithm, however. You could still use that sample as a starting point, though, because in constructing the shadow volume you need to add only the front cap and the back cap to the volume. Most of the differences between the two variants concern only rendering.

Class Declaration

Before learning how to declare the class for a shadow volume, take a look at the following structure used to describe a triangle by pointing to three vertices and containing a normal vector for the triangle. This structure will prove quite handy for creating the shadow volume:

```
typedef struct TRIANGLE_TYPE
   {
   VERTEX *pV0;
   VERTEX *pV1;
   VERTEX *pV2;
   ZFXVector vcN;
   } TRIANGLE;
```

That this vertex format is used in the triangle structure shown here does not mean that the following shadow volume class is bound to a specific vertex format. We need to use this class for the vertex format of the characters and the level geometry, for example, which are different from the shadow volume class. Therefore, the vertex format does not really matter for the following class. Instead, a BYTE pointer is used on the input vertex list along with the size of one element in this list. However, it is assumed that the position data is the first information in the vertex structure.

Here is the class that enables us to build a shadow volume:

```
class CShadowVolume
   {
   public:
      CShadowVolume(void);
      virtual ~CShadowVolume(void);

      HRESULT Init(const void*, UINT, const WORD*, UINT,
                   UINT, ZFXAabb, ZFXRenderDevice*);

      HRESULT UpdateGeometry(const void*, const WORD*, ZFXAabb);

      HRESULT Render( CGameLight*, ZFXMatrix* );

   private:
      ZFXRenderDevice *m_pDevice;
      ZFXAabb          m_Aabb;

      // original mesh
      TRIANGLE        *m_pTris;
      BYTE            *m_pVerts;
```

```
    WORD            *m_pIndis;
    WORD            *m_pEdges;
    bool            *m_pIsCap;
    UINT            m_NumV;
    UINT            m_NumI;
    UINT            m_NumT;
    UINT            m_NumE;
    UINT            m_nSize;

    // used during initialization only
    PVERTEX         *m_pVolume;
    UINT            m_NumVV;

    void    BuildShadowVolume(ZFXVector);
    void    AddEdge(WORD v0, WORD v1);
    inline PVERTEX Extrude(const VERTEX*,
                           const ZFXVector&);
}; // class
typedef class CShadowVolume *LPSHADOWVOLUME;
```

The two functions `CShadowVolume::Init` and `CShadowVolume::UpdateGeometry` are doing more or less the very same things. They are used to build the geometry for the shadow volume, but the first function needs to get a bit more input data, which is then stored and can be reused in the second function later on. This is assuming that the model's triangulation and the vertex format have not changed since, and that only the positions of the vertices have moved.

The following subsections describe the other members of this class.

Initializing an Instance

Besides trivial tasks such as copying the vertex and the index data, you must complete another task during the initialization of an instance of the shadow volume class: create a list of TRIANGLE objects representing a copy of the geometry. This structure contains three pointers to vertices in the vertex list as well as a normal vector:

```
HRESULT CShadowVolume::Init(const void *pVerts, UINT NumV, const WORD *pIndis,
                            UINT NumI, UINT nSize, ZFXAabb aabb,
                            ZFXRenderDevice *pDevice)
   {
   m_pDevice = pDevice;
   m_Aabb    = aabb;
   m_nSize   = nSize;
```

```
   m_pVerts = new BYTE[NumV*nSize];
   m_pIndis = new WORD[NumI];
   m_pTris  = new TRIANGLE[NumI/3];
   m_pIsCap = new bool[NumI/3];
   m_NumV   = NumV;
   m_NumI   = NumI;
   m_NumT   = NumI/3;

   m_pEdges = new WORD[m_NumT*6];

   // worst case is one rectangle for each edge: 3*4
   m_pVolume = new PVERTEX[m_NumT*12];

   // copy data of original mesh
   memcpy(m_pVerts, pVerts, m_nSize*NumV);
   memcpy(m_pIndis, pIndis, sizeof(WORD) * NumI);

   int nFact = m_nSize/sizeof(BYTE);

   // build triangle data
   for (UINT i=0; i<m_NumT; i++)
     {
     m_pTris[i].pV0 = (VERTEX*)&m_pVerts[ m_pIndis[i*3+0] * nFact ];
     m_pTris[i].pV1 = (VERTEX*)&m_pVerts[ m_pIndis[i*3+1] * nFact ];
     m_pTris[i].pV2 = (VERTEX*)&m_pVerts[ m_pIndis[i*3+2] * nFact ];

     ZFXVector vc0( m_pTris[i].pV0->x, m_pTris[i].pV0->y, m_pTris[i].pV0->z);

     ZFXVector vc1( m_pTris[i].pV1->x, m_pTris[i].pV1->y, m_pTris[i].pV1->z);

     ZFXVector vc2( m_pTris[i].pV2->x, m_pTris[i].pV2->y, m_pTris[i].pV2->z);

     // calculate normal vector
     m_pTris[i].vcN.Cross( (vc2 - vc1), (vc1 - vc0));
     m_pTris[i].vcN.Normalize();
     }
   return ZFX_OK;
   } // Init
```

Here you can see the new structure, PVERTEX, which is also defined in the ZFXEngine like the other vertex types. Its only attribute is the position. If you want to render the shadow volume, you only have to render the volume into the stencil buffer. So there is no need for texture coordinates, normal vectors, and things such as that, which only affect the visual output.

Another remarkable thing is the attribute `m_pVolume`, which gets a lot more memory allocated than there is geometry in the model. This is because the shadow volume will need another amount of geometry because it adds addition geometry to the original one. Even if it is not using all the geometry of the original model, it is better to calculate for the worst-case scenario (regardless of whether this actually happens).

Build the Shadow Volume

This section shows you how to build a closed shadow volume for a geometric object. Before starting with that, however, it's necessary to separate the helper functions to keep the code more readable. The first little inline helper is doing nothing other than just moving a given VERTEX object along a given vector and returning it as the PVERTEX object. This function will prove helpful to extrude given vertices along the direction the light is running:

```
inline PVERTEX CShadowVolume::Extrude(const VERTEX *pv, const ZFXVector &vc)
   {
   PVERTEX v;
   v.x = pv->x - vc.x;
   v.y = pv->y - vc.y;
   v.z = pv->z - vc.z;
   return v;
   } // extrude
```

The second helper function is needed to build a list of edges from the geometry. During the shadow volume creation process, a number of edges will potentially be a part of the silhouette (outline) of the geometry as seen from the light source. Such an edge consists of two indices to the vertex list of the geometry. The following function takes two indices for an edge and tries to add them to the list. However, we need only to store edges here that are truly a part of the silhouette. You can evaluate this by looping through the whole list before you add the new pair of indices. If an edge is really part of the silhouette, it will be added only once to this list. If it is not part of the silhouette, it will occur two times from two different triangles sharing the same edge. Therefore, if an edge is redundant in the list, remove both entries:

```
void CShadowVolume::AddEdge(WORD v0, WORD v1)
   {
   // remove inner edges which are in the list twice
   for( UINT i=0; i < m_NumE; i++ )
      {
      if( (m_pEdges[2*i+0]==v0 && m_pEdges[2*i+1]==v1) ||
```

```
            (m_pEdges[2*i+0]==v1 && m_pEdges[2*i+1]==v0))
            {
            if( m_NumE > 1 ) {
               m_pEdges[2*i+0] = m_pEdges[2*(m_NumE-1)+0];
               m_pEdges[2*i+1] = m_pEdges[2*(m_NumE-1)+1];
               }
            m_NumE--;
            return;
            }
      }
   m_pEdges[2*m_NumE+0] = v0;
   m_pEdges[2*m_NumE+1] = v1;
   m_NumE++;
   } // AddEdge
```

Finally, we are ready to build the geometry for the shadow volume object. Remember, however, that you may need to recalculate the shadow volume each time the shadow casting object or the light source moves. Creating the shadow volume is done in two passes over the original geometry. In the first pass, we loop through all TRIANGLE objects from the original geometry and check their orientation with respect to the light source. If the angle between the normal of the face and the vector running from the object to the light source is less than 90 degrees (dot product >= 0), then this triangle is facing the light source, whereas its edges are potentially a part of the object's silhouette. Hence they are added to a list of edges. In addition, those triangles form the front cap of the shadow volume and will be added to its vertex list. For the back faces, we just use the same faces, but the vertices are extruded in the shadow-casting direction and their vertex order is changed to toggle their orientation.

After the first pass, you have already built the front cap and the back cap for the shadow volume. Now the only things missing are the rectangles connecting both caps. Of course, you do have the list with edges that form the silhouette of the front cap and the whole object. To close the front cap and the back , you need only to extrude the edges from the list into rectangles. Then the volume is closed.

Here is the function building the shadow volume:

```
void CShadowVolume::BuildShadowVolume(ZFXVector vcLight)
   {
   ZFXVector vc;
   PVERTEX v1, v2, v3, v4;

   vc = vcLight * 5.0f;

   // reset counters
```

```cpp
m_NumVV = 0;
m_NumE  = 0;

// 1st Pass: which tris are front which are back cap
for (UINT i=0; i<m_NumT; i++) {

   WORD wFace0 = m_pIndis[3*i+0];
   WORD wFace1 = m_pIndis[3*i+1];
   WORD wFace2 = m_pIndis[3*i+2];

   if ( (m_pTris[i].vcN * vcLight) >= 0.0f ) {

      AddEdge(wFace0, wFace1);
      AddEdge(wFace1, wFace2);
      AddEdge(wFace2, wFace0);

      memcpy(&v1, m_pTris[i].pV0, sizeof(PVERTEX));
      memcpy(&v2, m_pTris[i].pV2, sizeof(PVERTEX));
      memcpy(&v3, m_pTris[i].pV1, sizeof(PVERTEX));

      // frontfacing Tris build Front-Cap
      m_pVolume[m_NumVV++] = v1;
      m_pVolume[m_NumVV++] = v2;
      m_pVolume[m_NumVV++] = v3;

      // Back-Cap is extruded
      m_pVolume[m_NumVV++]=Extrude(m_pTris[i].pV0,vc);
      m_pVolume[m_NumVV++]=Extrude(m_pTris[i].pV1,vc);
      m_pVolume[m_NumVV++]=Extrude(m_pTris[i].pV2,vc);

      m_pIsCap[i] = true;
      }
   else m_pIsCap[i] = false;
   } // for

int nFact = m_nSize/sizeof(BYTE);

// 2. PASS: extract all edges to rectangles
for (UINT j=0; j<m_NumE; j++)
   {
   v3 = Extrude( (VERTEX*)&m_pVerts[ m_pEdges[2*j+0] * nFact ], vc);
   v4 = Extrude( (VERTEX*)&m_pVerts[ m_pEdges[2*j+1] * nFact ], vc);
```

```
            memcpy(&v1, (VERTEX*)&m_pVerts[m_pEdges[2*j+0]*nFact], sizeof(PVERTEX));
            memcpy(&v2, (VERTEX*)&m_pVerts[m_pEdges[2*j+1]*nFact], sizeof(PVERTEX));

            // add rectangle to vertex list
            m_pVolume[m_NumVV++] = v1;
            m_pVolume[m_NumVV++] = v2;
            m_pVolume[m_NumVV++] = v3;

            m_pVolume[m_NumVV++] = v2;
            m_pVolume[m_NumVV++] = v4;
            m_pVolume[m_NumVV++] = v3;
            }
      } // BuildShadowVolume
```

Rendering the Shadow Volume

The rendering process of the shadow volume geometry itself is implemented straightforwardly here. In particular, this code is not checking whether the light source or the shadow-casting object has moved compared to the preceding frame. If a shadow volume is rendered, you have to supply it with a light source that is emitting the light that causes the shadow in world coordinates as well as the world transformation matrix of the object the shadow volume belongs to. If the matrix is not provided, the function assumes the object to be in world coordinates.

If both the light source and the object are in world coordinates, you can just calculate the vector from the object to the light source. Otherwise, you need to transform the position of the light source into the local space of the object. Because the center of the object is the origin in the local space, the position of the light source equals the vector from the object to the light source in the local system.

With this vector from the object to the light source, you can calculate the distance between the two first. If this distance is greater than the radius of the light source, you can exit the function because no shadow can be cast. If this condition is checked and a shadow must be cast, however, you calculate the shadow volume with the function previously shown. Then the back faces of the shadow volume are rendered, and in a second pass the front faces are rendered. Here is what the according function looks like:

```
HRESULT CShadowVolume::Render( CGameLight *pLight, ZFXMatrix *pMat )
   {
   HRESULT    hr=ZFX_OK;
   ZFXVector  vcLookAtLight;

   ZFXVector  vcLightPos = pLight->GetPosition();
```

```
// transform light to model if needed
if (pMat) {
   ZFXMatrix mat; mat.InverseOf( *pMat );
   vcLightPos = mat * vcLightPos;
   vcLookAtLight = vcLightPos;
   }
else {
   vcLookAtLight = vcLightPos- m_Aabb.vcCenter;
   }

// light shining on the object at all?
float fDist_2 = vcLookAtLight.GetSqrLength();
float fRadi_2 = pLight->GetSqrRadius()*2;

if ( fDist_2 > fRadi_2 ) return ZFX_OK;

// build Shadow Volume
BuildShadowVolume(vcLookAtLight);

if ( pMat ) m_pDevice->SetWorldTransform( pMat );

// FIRST PASS: RENDER BACKFACES
m_pDevice->SetStencilBufferMode(RS_STENCIL_ZFAIL_INCR, 0);
m_pDevice->SetBackfaceCulling(RS_CULL_CW);

hr = m_pDevice->GetVertexManager()->RenderNaked(m_NumVV, m_pVolume, false);

// SECOND PASS: RENDER FRONTFACES
m_pDevice->SetStencilBufferMode(RS_STENCIL_ZFAIL_DECR, 0);
m_pDevice->SetBackfaceCulling(RS_CULL_CCW);

hr = m_pDevice->GetVertexManager()->RenderNaked(m_NumVV, m_pVolume, false);

if ( pMat ) m_pDevice->SetWorldTransform( NULL );
return hr;
} // Render
```

The ZFXRenderDevice interface offers two new things here that we have not seen as of yet. First there is the function of the vertex cache manager called ZFXVertexCacheManager::RenderNaked, which will render vertices that consist of only a position. That is the only vertex attribute you need for rendering the shadow volume geometry to the stencil buffer with PVERTEX elements. The second new thing in this interface are the settings `RS_STENCIL_ZFAIL_INCR` and `RS_STENCIL_ZFAIL_DECR` for the stencil buffer. Those are used to set the stencil buffer for incrementing or decrementing mode on a failure of the depth buffer test. Here is what this looks like in Direct3D:

```
pD3DDevice->SetRenderState(D3DRS_STENCILZFAIL, D3DSTENCILOP_DECR);
pD3DDevice->SetRenderState(D3DRS_STENCILZFAIL, D3DSTENCILOP_INCR);
```

This is all you need to do to activate the depth-fail version of the shadow volume rendering. The back faces are rendered first, and then the front faces. The values in the stencil buffer are set on a negative feedback from the depth buffer like they should be. Note that the stencil buffer is not activated in this function. Because we are most likely rendering lots of shadows one after the other, we can leave it switched on for all of these calls. Activating and deactivating is then done in the function calling this one shown above, and it is using the following function new to the `ZFXRenderDevice` interface:

```
void ZFXD3D::UseStencilShadowSettings(bool b)
   {
   ZFXMatrix matProj;

   m_pVertexMan->InvalidateStates();

   if (b) {
      m_pDevice->SetRenderState(D3DRS_ZWRITEENABLE, FALSE);
      m_pDevice->SetRenderState(D3DRS_STENCILENABLE, TRUE);
      m_pDevice->SetRenderState(D3DRS_SHADEMODE, D3DSHADE_FLAT);
      m_pDevice->SetRenderState(D3DRS_STENCILFUNC, D3DCMP_ALWAYS);
      m_pDevice->SetRenderState(D3DRS_STENCILPASS, D3DSTENCILOP_KEEP);
      m_pDevice->SetRenderState(D3DRS_STENCILFAIL, D3DSTENCILOP_KEEP);
      m_pDevice->SetRenderState(D3DRS_STENCILREF, 0x1);
      m_pDevice->SetRenderState(D3DRS_STENCILMASK, 0xffffffff);
      m_pDevice->SetRenderState(D3DRS_STENCILWRITEMASK, 0xffffffff);
      m_pDevice->SetRenderState(D3DRS_STENCILZFAIL, D3DSTENCILOP_INCR);
      UseColorBuffer(false);
      }
   else {
      m_pDevice->SetRenderState(D3DRS_SHADEMODE, D3DSHADE_GOURAUD);
      m_pDevice->SetRenderState(D3DRS_CULLMODE, D3DCULL_CCW);
      m_pDevice->SetRenderState(D3DRS_ZWRITEENABLE, TRUE);
      m_pDevice->SetRenderState(D3DRS_STENCILENABLE, FALSE);
      m_pDevice->SetRenderState(D3DRS_ALPHABLENDENABLE, FALSE);
      UseColorBuffer(true);
      SetMode(m_Mode, m_nStage);
      }
   } // UseStencilShadowSettings
```

These render states enable us to adjust the stencil buffer in a way that is correct for the shadow volume method we are using. If you are a bit rusty on how to set render states and how to adjust the stencil buffer, refer to the DirectX SDK documentation to see what each of the calls is meant for. Note how the color buffer is deactivated and activated in this function, because rendering the shadow volumes should take place in the stencil buffer only and not on the color buffer.

Now you have everything you need to do the shadow volume rendering and create the shadow in the color buffer. However, you have yet to see how this looks all together. Therefore, the following code snippet shows you how rendering the geometry and the shadows inside the level is done. Suppose, for instance, that the pointer pMesh is a valid instance of CModel; that m_pShadowVolume is the according attribute for the shadow volume geometry of this model; and that the object L is an instance of CgameLight, which is a class representing the position of a light source that creates shadows on the lit objects:

```
pDev->BeginRendering(true, true, true);

/* render now level geometry as usual */

/* now the Shadow Volume */
pDev->SetWorldTransform( pMesh->m_matWorld );
pDev->UseStencilShadowSettings(true);
pMesh->m_pShadowVolume->Render(L, pMesh->m_matWorld);
pDev->UseStencilShadowSettings(false);

/* and fade the screen */
pDev->SetStencilBufferMode(RS_STENCIL_ENABLE,0);
pDev->SetStencilBufferMode(RS_STENCIL_REF, 1);
pDev->SetStencilBufferMode(RS_STENCIL_FUNC_LESSEQUAL,0);
pDev->SetStencilBufferMode(RS_STENCIL_PASS_KEEP, 0);

pDev->FadeScreen(0.0f, 0.0f , 0.0f, 0.5f);
pDev->SetStencilBufferMode(RS_STENCIL_DISABLE, 0);

pDev->EndRendering();
```

The purpose of each call here should be clear by now. You first render the scene like you normally do. Then the stencil buffer is switched on and adjusted to render the shadow volumes as masks into the stencil buffer. Then the settings for the stencil buffer are switched so that rendering to the color buffer is allowed only in the places where shadow should be. Then we use the function to fade the screen to a dark color; this fade shades only the places on the color buffer where the shadow should be. Et voilá, there they are: your shadows.

This discussion now departs the dark world of shadows and proceeds to loading the level data from the level file in order to display it as an interactive gaming environment.

Loading a Level

It's about time to load the level from the file, and that means it's about time to put on the performance hat. To be honest, the data organization in the editor from Chapter 14 was ... well ... *nonexistent* seems to be the appropriate term here (at least with regard to rendering the data, as you can see from the poor rendering performance in the editor, which is hidden by rendering the scene only from time to time or when it becomes necessary because of editing changes). To display such a level in real time as an interactive environment, however, we must come up with another idea.

For you to understand what is going on while loading and organizing the data on the following pages, take a look at Figure 15.7. This figure shows the big picture of the *levelogram*. Each sector will have one single vertex buffer holding all its geometry. Therefore, for each skin used in a sector, the sector object has exactly one index buffer that contains the index lists of the geometry using a certain skin.

As you can see, there are no single objects such as polygons that are rendered dynamically. Unfortunately, this is the way the editing tool *PanBox-Edit* likes to handle the data (which made loading and saving the level data very easy in Chapter 14). For this chapter, however, it means that we have to invest some work into organizing the data. Therefore, the load-

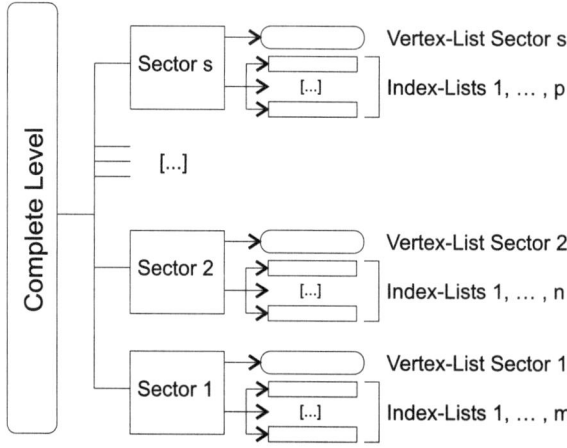

Figure 15.7 Organization of a level. The upper layer is comprised of the three sectors of a level. Each sector contains one static vertex buffer for all its vertices and one index buffer for each skin that is used.

ing functions you will see in a moment are a bit complex, but this is the secret to rendering the level data much faster than in the editor (even with dozens of per-pixel lights active on thousands of polygons in the view frustum). Hang in there; it'll be worth the effort.

Supporting Data Structures

For the loading process, we could just do the work like it was done in the editor in Chapter 14. For a video game application, however, it is imperative to have the data sorted in a way that is optimal for fast and efficient rendering. Hence we will invest a lot of work and code lines into rearranging the data, and we cannot do this with the data structures we have at hand.

We need two additional data structures used only for data loading. The first helper structure is called SECBUF, which means sector buffer. This will store three values: the skin ID, the number of triangles in a sector using this skin, and the ID of an index buffer from the ZFXEngine that contains the triangles using this skin. After an array of this structure has been filled with the data for each sector, it is then used for rendering.

The second structure is the one called POLYGON, which stores information about a polygon with vertices, as opposed to the plain position the ZFXPolygon class would save only. This structure is used as an array to extract all polygons from the file and then sort them by their skin before building a vertex buffer and the index buffers:

```
typedef struct SECBUF_TYPE
   {
   UINT SkinID;
   UINT NumTris;
   UINT IBID;
   } SECBUF;

typedef struct POLYGON_TYPE
   {
   VERTEX *pVerts;
   WORD    *pIndis;
   UINT    NumV;
   UINT    NumI;
   UINT    SkinID;
   } POLYGON;
```

Loading Routine in CGameLevel

Perhaps you're familiar with the principle of divide and conquer, a strategy just as applicable in computer science as in other aspects of life. Following this principle, you break down pieces of data that are too big to chew into smaller pieces and deal with them separately. Actually, that is what we are doing all the time. As no surprise, the loading function of the level class breaks down the work into loading the header data, the skins, and loading single sectors. The last task is then conquered by the sector class:

```
bool CGameLevel::Load(const char *pchName)
   {
   UINT       NumSkins   = 0;
   UINT       DummyUINT  = 0;

   FILE *pFile = fopen(pchName, "rb");

   if (!pFile) return false;

   fread(&m_NumSectors, sizeof(UINT), 1, pFile);
   fread(&DummyUINT,    sizeof(UINT), 1, pFile);
   fread(&NumSkins,     sizeof(UINT), 1, pFile);

   m_pSectors = new LPGAMESECTOR[m_NumSectors];

   // load all sectors from the file
   for (UINT s=0; s<m_NumSectors; s++) {
      m_pSectors[s] = new CGameSector(m_pDevice, s,
                                     this);
      m_pSectors[s]->Load(pFile);
      m_NumSpawns += m_pSectors[s]->GetNumSpawns();
      }

   // load all skins from the file
   for (UINT sn=0; sn<NumSkins; sn++) {
      LoadSkin( m_pDevice->GetSkinManager(), pFile );
      }

   fclose(pFile);

   BuildAllPortalRelationships();
   return true;
   } // Load
```

When compared to the loading function for a level object in the editing tool *PanBox-Edit*, nothing is new to you in this function. You can just draw the information piece by piece out of the open data file. Of course, the sector instances have their own loading function, and loading the skins is done just like in the editor in Chapter 14. Note, however, the call to `CGameLevel::BuildAllPortalRelationships`. The connections between portals and doors are discussed later in this chapter; for now, just understand that the loading function also takes care of building the connections for the portal engine system by this call.

Loading Routine in CGameSector

At first glance, loading the remaining data from each sector instance seems to be quite easy. And, indeed, the top-level loading function in the sector class does not show a single catch concerning rearranging the data. Thus the function looks quite straightforward and organized. The opposite is the case, however. As you can see, after reading the header data, this function calls the subfunctions only to do the groundwork; this is where the catches occur:

```
bool CGameSector::Load(FILE *pFile)
   {
   WORD       *pDummyWORD = NULL;
   UINT       NumPolys=0, NumPolysM=0, nSkin=0;
   UINT       NumV=0, NumI=0;
   int        nName      = 0;
   char       chName[2048];

   fread(&nName, sizeof(int), 1, pFile);
   fread(chName, nName, 1, pFile);
   chName[nName] = '\0';

   fread(&m_NumSkins,  sizeof(UINT),    1, pFile);
   fread(&m_NumVerts,  sizeof(UINT),    1, pFile);
   fread(&m_NumIndis,  sizeof(UINT),    1, pFile);
   fread(&NumPolys,    sizeof(UINT),    1, pFile);
   fread(&NumPolysM,   sizeof(UINT),    1, pFile);
   fread(&m_NumMeshs,  sizeof(UINT),    1, pFile);
   fread(&m_NumPorts,  sizeof(UINT),    1, pFile);
   fread(&m_NumLights, sizeof(UINT),    1, pFile);
   fread(&m_NumEntys,  sizeof(UINT),    1, pFile);
   fread(&m_NumSpawns, sizeof(UINT),    1, pFile);
   fread(&m_Aabb,      sizeof(ZFXAabb), 1, pFile);
   fread(&m_Ambient,   sizeof(ZFXCOLOR),1, pFile);

   // allocate memory for all lists
   m_pVerts  = new VERTEX[m_NumVerts];
   m_pIndis  = new WORD[m_NumIndis];
   m_pBuffer = new SECBUF[m_NumSkins];
```

```
        m_NumZFXPolys = NumPolysM + NumPolys;
        m_pZFXPolys = new ZFXPolygon[m_NumZFXPolys];

        if ( !LoadMeshs(pFile) ) return false;

        for (UINT p=0; p<NumPolys; p++) {
           if ( !LoadSinglePolygon(pFile) )
              return false;
           } // for

        if ( !LoadPortals(pFile) )   return false;
        if ( !LoadLights(pFile) )    return false;
        if ( !LoadEntities(pFile) )  return false;
        if ( !LoadSpawns(pFile) )    return false;
        if (FAILED( CreateOctree() )) return false;

        if ( FAILED( CompilePolygonList() ))
           return false;

        SAFE_DELETE_A(m_pZFXPolys);
        return true;
        } // Load
```

The only things here that should be new to you are compiling the polygon list at the end of the function and creating the octree. Otherwise, this function is similar to the loading function you saw for the editor in Chapter 14. You'll learn what compiling a polygon list is all about in a moment, but first take a look at the loading functions.

With the octree class on hand, creating the octree is not a complex task:

```
HRESULT CGameSector::CreateOctree(void)
   {
   if (!m_pZFXPolys) return ZFX_FAIL;
   if (m_Count < 1) return ZFX_OK;

   m_pOctree = new ZFXOctree();

   m_pOctree->BuildTree(m_pZFXPolys, m_Count);

   // we don't need those temporary lists any longer
   SAFE_DELETE_A(m_pZFXPolys);
   return ZFX_OK;
   } // CreateOctree
```

The octree for a sector is built from a list of ZFXPolygon objects that are stored in the member variable m_pZFXPolys in the sector class. During the loading process of the level, you must load all the polygons into this list (both the free ones as well as the ones stored in meshes). The following section describes loading the polygons.

Loading Polygons from Meshes

Now it gets hairy. Let's take a look at how we extract the mesh objects that are stored in the level file. The problem is that a mesh object is not treated as a separate mesh in the video game application (in contrast to the editor, which knows a mesh as a grouping tool for polygons). In this application here, however, it does not matter whether a polygon is a free polygon or whether it is part of a mesh. Well, as a general statement that is accurate, but it is not entirely true. For the rendering, all polygons from the mesh have to be inserted into the sector's list of free polygons. However, the meshes do have another meaning as well in the game code. Each mesh object is casting a shadow in the game. That means each object that is a mesh in the editor will have a shadow volume in the game later on. The free polygons do not have any shadows they cast themselves.

The following function loops through all meshes that are stored in the file and extracts each one of them as a bunch of POLYGON objects, which are stored in the according polygon list of the sector. This is done by a separate function: CGameSector::LoadSinglePolygon. Then we return to the first polygon of the mesh and start part one of the post-processing step. The polygonal data is then stored as a list of vertices and indices, which are small complete lists for a whole mesh as opposed to the per-polygon list in the original mesh structure from the file. As the second step, those lists are used to build a shadow volume object.

That is all you need to consider when loading a mesh:

```
bool CGameSector::LoadMeshs(FILE *pFile)
   {
   UINT NumPolys=0, StartPoly=0, VertexBase=0;
   UINT NumV=0, NumI=0;
   ZFXAabb Aabb;

   VERTEX *pV=NULL;
   WORD   *pI=NULL;

   if (m_NumMeshs < 1) return true;

   m_pMeshShadows = new CShadowVolume[m_NumMeshs];

   for (UINT m=0; m<m_NumMeshs; m++) {
      // mark the last polygon of this mesh because all of
```

812 Chapter 15 ■ Deathmatch Shooter

```
         // them are stored in the big list of the sector
         StartPoly = m_NumPolys;

         // 1. load mesh header
         fread(&NumPolys, sizeof(UINT), 1, pFile);
         fread(&Aabb, sizeof(ZFXAabb), 1, pFile);

         // 2. load polygons of the mesh
         for (UINT pm=0; pm<NumPolys; pm++)
            if ( !LoadSinglePolygon(pFile) )
               return false;

         // loop through all extracted polygons and build a temporary list
         // of the complete data of this mesh to build the shadow volume
         for (UINT i=0, NumV=0, NumI=0; i<NumPolys; i++)
            {
            POLYGON *pPoly = &m_pPolys[StartPoly];

            pV = (VERTEX*)realloc(pV, sizeof(VERTEX) * (NumV + pPoly[i].NumV));

            memcpy(&pV[NumV], pPoly[i].pVerts, sizeof(VERTEX) * pPoly[i].NumV);

            NumV += pPoly[i].NumV;

            pI = (WORD*)realloc(pI, sizeof(WORD) * (NumI + pPoly[i].NumI));

            for (UINT j=0; j<pPoly[i].NumI; j++)
               pI[NumI+j] = pPoly[i].pIndis[j]+VertexBase;

            NumI += pPoly[i].NumI;
            VertexBase += pPoly[i].NumV;
            }

         // 3. build shadow volume from temporary lists
         m_pMeshShadows[m].Init(pV, NumV, pI, NumI, sizeof(VERTEX), Aabb,
                                m_pDevice);
         NumV = NumI = 0;
         VertexBase = 0;
         SAFE_FREE(pV);
         SAFE_FREE(pI);
         } // meshs
```

```
    return true;
    } // LoadMeshs
```

In this function, you must recalculate the indices for each mesh. In the file, the indices are stored in such a way that each mesh's polygon starts with the index 0 to its own vertex list. Now, however, the vertices are stored in a big array, so the indices have to be adjusted. For building the shadow volume, the index list of the whole mesh must be a single list, just like the vertex list.

Loading Free Polygons

The single most important function here is the one to load a single polygon from the file. This function in this section is the one needed to load the free polygons from the file as well as the polygons, which are part of a mesh object. In the game code, all polygons are treated like free polygons, and there is no such thing as a mesh that is rendered separately.

Actually, loading a polygon is easy. First, you have to extract the header data from the file. Second, you allocate the memory for the POLYGON object into which the data is then read. When this data is in place, you have to generate a temporary list of vectors from the positions of the vertices and convert the indices to the UINT data type. Both lists are needed to build a list of ZFXPolygon objects, which is also created from the level geometry by this function:

```
bool CGameSector::LoadSinglePolygon(FILE *pFile)
    {
    bool        DummyBOOL = false;
    float       DummyFLOAT[2];
    ZFXAabb     DummyAABB;
    WORD        *pDummyWORD = NULL;

    // data containers
    ZFXVector    *pVC   = NULL;
    unsigned int *puI   = NULL;

    if (!pFile) return false;

    // allocate memory
    if ( (m_NumPolys%100) == 0)
       {
       m_pPolys = (POLYGON*)realloc(m_pPolys, sizeof(POLYGON)*(m_NumPolys+100));
       if (!m_pPolys) return false;
       }

    POLYGON *pPoly = &m_pPolys[m_NumPolys];
```

```
pPoly->pVerts = NULL;
pPoly->pIndis = NULL;

// load polygon header
fread(&pPoly->NumV,   sizeof(UINT), 1, pFile);
fread(&pPoly->NumI,   sizeof(UINT), 1, pFile);
fread(&pPoly->SkinID, sizeof(UINT), 1, pFile);
fread(&DummyAABB, sizeof(ZFXAabb), 1, pFile);
fread(&DummyBOOL, sizeof(bool),    1, pFile);
fread(DummyFLOAT, sizeof(float),   2, pFile);
fread(DummyFLOAT, sizeof(float),   2, pFile);

// allocate memory
pVC = new ZFXVector[pPoly->NumV];
puI = new unsigned int[pPoly->NumI];
pDummyWORD = new WORD[pPoly->NumV*2];

pPoly->pVerts = new VERTEX[pPoly->NumV];
pPoly->pIndis = new WORD[pPoly->NumI];

// load vertex and index data
fread(pPoly->pVerts, sizeof(VERTEX), pPoly->NumV, pFile);
fread(pPoly->pIndis, sizeof(WORD), pPoly->NumI, pFile);
fread(pDummyWORD, sizeof(WORD), pPoly->NumV*2, pFile);

// build vectors from vertices
for (UINT i=0; i<pPoly->NumV; i++) {
   pVC[i].Set(pPoly->pVerts[i].x, pPoly->pVerts[i].y, pPoly->pVerts[i].z);
   }

// extract indices to a list
for (UINT j=0; j<pPoly->NumI; j++)
   puI[j] = pPoly->pIndis[j];

// add polygon as ZFXPolygon to the complete list of the sector
m_pZFXPolys[m_Count++].Set(pVC, pPoly->NumV, puI, pPoly->NumI);
m_NumPolys++;

// clean up
SAFE_DELETE_A(pVC);
SAFE_DELETE_A(puI);
```

```
SAFE_DELETE_A(pDummyWORD);
return true;
} // LoadSinglePolygon
```

If this function were run once for each polygon in the level file, you would have all the polygon data of the whole sector stored in two ways: on one hand, as `ZFXPolygon` objects needed to build an octree or a BSP tree for collision detection; on the other hand, as a list of `POLYGON` structures. To do anything useful with this list, however, you have to compile it, which in this case means only preparing for rendering.

Compiling the Polygon List

After sending the loading routine across the whole level file, we now have all the polygon data in the big list `m_pPolys` as `POLYGON` objects. From this initial situation, we can now find a way to ensure an efficient rendering of those polygons. It is most important here that you can render lots of polygons in a single call. Depending on the graphics adapter (and perhaps the weather outside), something between 500 and 10,000 polygons should be a good number of polygons for rendering in a single call.

First you must sort the array of polygons by the skin ID they are using (because you can only render those polygons in a single call that are using the same skin). After you have the polygons ordered, you can run through their list and collect all vertices and store them in a single big vertex buffer for the sector. However, working with the indices is not that easy.

The indices are also saved in a big list of the sector. For a start, there is only one such list. But you should keep in mind each position in this list where a new skin ID is used by the indexed geometry, as well as the number of indices in the list using a certain skin. As soon as you find that a new skin is used for the following polygon, you create a static index buffer for the current skin and save the data into that buffer. When you have finished with the whole list, you will have one static index buffer for each skin that is used in this sector.

Now you can activate the vertex buffer of the sector and loop through the different skins. For each skin, you activate the according index buffer and render the geometry. This is the optimal way to sort the data for rendering on a sector layer.

You still must deal with one issue: the light sources. At this point, you can actually render the whole sector with ambient light and all of its textures and so on. You also know from the chapter about vertex and pixel shaders how to do the per-pixel lighting with omni lights. However, it would not be very fast to transform and render a whole sector again and again for each light source. Such a sector would have to be rather big to have a good performance in a single rendering pass. Luckily, however, each light normally shines on only a rather small part of the geometry. Therefore, you can easily save the indices of the triangles on which a certain light source shines directly into the light source object. Then each light source will render in an additional pass only the geometry it really shines on. This is called a *light cache*, and this light cache contains the concerned geometry.

> **Note**
>
> I want to say thanks again to Marco, who inspired me to use the light caches (which he thought I already knew about). In addition, he provided a lot of tips about how to make those omni lights render really fast.

While we are dealing with the indices of a polygon, we will take triplets of indices that form a triangle. Then we hand over this triangle to each of the light sources of the sector and ask the light source whether this triangle is inside its radius of influence, which basically means we're asking whether the triangle has to be included in the additional render pass needed for this light source. If so, this triangle is added to the cache of indices of the light source along with the skin that the triangle uses. Even an efficient light cache has to render the triangles sorted by the skins they are using.

Enough words. Take a look at the whole function:

```
HRESULT CGameSector::CompilePolygonList(void)
   {
   HRESULT     hr=ZFX_OK;
   POLYGON     *pPoly = NULL;
   ZFXVector   Tri[3];
   WORD        I[3];

   UINT     CountV=0, CountI=0, SkinIndis=0, Start=0, nSkin=0;

   if (m_NumPolys < 1) return ZFX_OK;

   // sort polygons by skin
   qsort(m_pPolys, m_NumPolys, sizeof(POLYGON), SortBySkin);

   for (UINT i=0; i<m_NumPolys; i++)
      {
      pPoly = &m_pPolys[i];

      // copy vertices into their own list
      memcpy(&m_pVerts[CountV], pPoly->pVerts, sizeof(VERTEX)*pPoly->NumV);

      // copy indices into their own list
      for (UINT j=0; j<pPoly->NumI; j+=3)
         {
```

```cpp
            I[0] = CountV + pPoly->pIndis[j];
            I[1] = CountV + pPoly->pIndis[j+1];
            I[2] = CountV + pPoly->pIndis[j+2];

            memcpy(&m_pIndis[CountI+j], I, sizeof(WORD)*3);

            Tri[0].Set(m_pVerts[I[0]].x, m_pVerts[I[0]].y, m_pVerts[I[0]].z);
            Tri[1].Set(m_pVerts[I[1]].x, m_pVerts[I[1]].y, m_pVerts[I[1]].z);
            Tri[2].Set(m_pVerts[I[2]].x, m_pVerts[I[2]].y, m_pVerts[I[2]].z);

            // loop through all lights
            for (UINT k=0; k<m_NumLights; k++)
               {
               if ( m_pLights[k].InfluencesTri(Tri) )
                  {
                  m_pLights[k].AddTriIndices(I[0],I[1],I[2],Tri,pPoly->SkinID);
                  }
               } // for
            }

         // reset counters
         CountV   += pPoly->NumV;
         CountI   += pPoly->NumI;
         SkinIndis += pPoly->NumI;

         // is skin changing for next polygon?
         if ( (i == (m_NumPolys-1)) || (pPoly->SkinID != m_pPolys[i+1].SkinID) )
            {
            hr = m_pDevice->GetVertexManager()->CreateIndexBuffer(SkinIndis,
                                                   &m_pIndis[Start],
                                                   &m_pBuffer[nSkin].IBID);
            if (FAILED(hr)) return hr;

            m_pBuffer[nSkin].SkinID  = pPoly->SkinID;
            m_pBuffer[nSkin].NumTris = (UINT)(((float)SkinIndis)/3);
            SkinIndis = 0;
            Start = CountI;
            nSkin++;
            }
         }

   // create a single static buffer
```

```
        hr = m_pDevice->GetVertexManager()->CreateStaticBuffer(VID_UU, 2, CountV,
                                                               0, m_pVerts,
                                                               NULL, &m_BufID);
    // close the caches for the lights
    for (UINT k=0; k<m_NumLights; k++)
        m_pLights[k].CloseCaches(m_pDevice);

    return hr;
    } // CompilePolygonList
```

The class for the light sources is not examined here; as you can see, all of its functions total just a couple of lines. The function CGameLight::CloseCaches will then tell an instance of the light class that no more data will be incoming. After the light source receives this call, it knows that it can then create static buffers for the indices it has collected in only a temporary list so far. As you learn during the render functions discussion later on, each light object has one index buffer on the sector's vertex buffer for each different skin it shines on.

Now we're at the point where the level is truly and totally loaded into the memory. You're now ready to rock. The functions for loading portals and spawn points are not shown here; instead, they will just be extracted from the data file without any problem and stored into the according lists.

Connecting Portals

Before we start connecting the portals in a level, it's important to recall a bit about portals. After all, the information about how portals work in general, and in particular for the editor and this game, is now spread throughout three chapters. Inside the level file, you will find portals with the following attributes:

- Four vertices are a rectangle for the portal.
- Each portal has a unique ID in the level.
- Each portal has the ID of its brother stored.
- Each door entity stores two portal IDs if they overlap each other.
- Portals are saved in a sector object.

So far, so good. This is all done inside the editor, so the data is already present. Now, however, look at the things we want to have from the portals in order for them to be of any use to us in doing the scene management here:

- Each portal should lead to one other portal.
- Each door needs pointers to portals if any are overlapping.
- If there are portals in a door entity, they should be deactivated if the door is closed.

This is a quite logical list of tasks, and they are relatively uncomplicated. Using the bounding box of a portal, you can check very easily whether the portal is overlapping with another portal or even a door entity. In this case, you just have to save the according connections by exchanging pointers between the concerned objects. If the player will then move through a portal, you just take the destination sector from the destination portal and then you know which sector the player is currently in. The following two functions automatically connect doors with portals and portals with other portals:

```
void CGameLevel::BuildAllPortalRelationships(void)
   {
   for (UINT s=0; s<m_NumSectors; s++) {
      m_pSectors[s]->BuildAllPortalRelationships();
      }
   } // BuildAllPortalRelationships


void CGameSector::BuildAllPortalRelationships(void)
   {
   // 1. connect doors with portal
   for (UINT e=0; e<m_NumEntys; e++)
      {
      // if door connect
      if ( m_ppEntities[e]->IsOfType(ENT_DOOR) )
         {
         ((CGameDoor**)m_ppEntities)[e]-> ConnectToPortals(m_pLevel);
         }
      }

   // 2. connect portals with each other
   for (UINT p=0; p<m_NumPorts; p++)
      {
      m_pLevel->FindBrother( &m_pPorts[p] );
      }
   } // BuildAllPortalRelationships
```

The door entities will know from the level editor whether they are overlapped or intersected by portals. If so, they already know the ID of the concerned portals. Therefore, the function CGameEntity::ConnectPortals does nothing more than just seek those portals in the level object to get a pointer to them. The level in turn then seeks the portal in its sectors. If it finds the portal, it returns the address. After all that searching, the door will then store the address to get access to the portal to be able to switch it on and off when it is opening and closing. Of course, a door entity needs to be connected to two portals or to none.

As you can understand, this is a trivial task, and so there's no need to show it here. It is more interesting to look at the function that establishes the connection between the portals themselves. A sector will, therefore, loop through its list of portals and will call the following function of the level with each of its portals to connect them to the rest of the virtual world:

```
bool CGameLevel::FindBrother(LPGAMEPORTAL pPortal)
   {
   if (pPortal->GetBrotherID() == 0) return true;

   for (UINT s=0; s<m_NumSectors; s++) {
      if (m_pSectors[s]->FindBrother(pPortal))
         return true;
      }
   return false;
   } // FindBrother
```

However, the level does not like to be pressed this way, so it hands the portals back to all of its sectors and lets them try to find the brother for this portal to satisfy the request of the original sector.

Caution

> If a portal still contains the value 0 for the ID of its brother after those connection requests, it means that there was no brother found for this portal. Normally this would be an error, but there are some exceptions. This is okay for special effect portals, and it is okay in a debug environment. If you load a level that is not yet finished, it might contain portals for which no counterpart exists yet.

And here is the according function of the sector class that loops through all portals of the sector and tries to find the brother for the given portal based on the ID of the portal. As you can see now, the ID has to be unique for the whole level, and not only for a sector:

```
bool CGameSector::FindBrother(LPGAMEPORTAL pPortal)
   {
   for (UINT i=0; i<m_NumPorts; i++)
      {
      if ( m_pPorts[i].GetID() == pPortal->GetBrotherID() )
         {
         m_pPorts[i].SetBrotherRelationship(pPortal);
         return true;
         }
      }
   return false;
   } // FindBrother
```

If the brother is found, the attribute pointers of the two are bound to each other so that they can find each other in memory pretty fast without searching. A check is also performed to confirm that the two portals are not the same one sitting at the same address. This should not happen, but then you never know . . . .

That's it! That's all you have to do to implement an automatic connection functionality for all the portals and doors inside a level.

Rendering a Level

After this little excursion into the world of the portals, we can now return to the roots of the action that is going on. While loading the level, we expended a lot of effort in organizing the data to be in a good ordering for performance during the render process, which is the focus of this section. As you will see, there is still a lot of work to do. You will also see here how the portal system works to cull sectors that the viewer has no visual contact with (that is, through any portals the viewer can see).

Rendering the Geometry

The very first render function the `CGameLevel` class needs to provide is, of course, a class that enables you to render the level's geometry. The function needs to get the ID of the sector the viewer is currently residing in as a parameter. Furthermore, you must provide the position of the viewer and two optional pointers in which the number of rendered triangles and the number of active lights will be saved.

> **Note**
>
> The ID of a sector is just the sector's index in the array of all sectors that is stored in the class `CGameLevel`. Based on the position of the camera, you could also calculate the sector in which the viewer is by using the octree or the BSP tree, but with overlapping bounding boxes of different sectors that is not so easy and would take some time. Therefore, it is easier to keep track of the sector that the player is in—starting from the ID of the sector where he spawned in the first place.

I hope you still remember the per-pixel lighting done with vertex and pixel shaders and how to simulate an omni light, because you'll use that knowledge here as well. However, there is a fallback, alternative option. Even though the shader versions I use here are really early ones, many graphics adapters still in use do not support shaders in hardware at all. This code path will not use any kind of lighting except for ambient light. Pretty ugly indeed, but the focus of this book is not indoor rendering, right? The following function of the `CGameLevel` class is the kickoff for the rendering process and selects the appropriate code path. Note that I don't print the plain, simple ambient render path here:

```
HRESULT CGameLevel::Render(UINT nSector, UINT *pNumT, UINT *pNumL,
                           const ZFXVector &vcPos)
```

```
{
ZFXPlane Frustum[6];
ZFXAabb   aabb;
HRESULT   hr=ZFX_OK;

m_pDevice->GetFrustrum(Frustum);
m_pDevice->SetWorldTransform(NULL);

if (nSector >= m_NumSectors)
   return ZFX_INVALIDPARAM;

   if ( !m_pDevice->CanDoShaders() )
      {
      m_pDevice->UseShaders(false);

      hr = m_pSectors[nSector]->RenderAmbient(Frustum, vcPos);
      }
   else {
      m_pDevice->UseShaders(true);
      m_pDevice->ActivateVShader(m_VSH, VID_UU);
      m_pDevice->ActivatePShader(m_PSH);

      m_pDevice->UseTextures(false);
      m_pDevice->UseColorBuffer(false);

      hr = m_pSectors[nSector]->RenderDepth(Frustum, vcPos);

      m_pDevice->UseTextures(true);
      m_pDevice->UseColorBuffer(true);
      m_pDevice->SetDepthBufferMode(RS_DEPTH_READONLY);

      hr = m_pSectors[nSector]->RenderLit(Frustum, vcPos, pNumT, pNumL);

      m_pDevice->SetDepthBufferMode(RS_DEPTH_READWRITE);
      m_pDevice->UseShaders(false);
      }
   return hr;
   } // Render
```

As you can see, this function will not just go directly to the sector and render it. Instead, it calls the ambient render path if the graphics adapter is missing shader support. On the other hand, many functions are being called. Interestingly, the textures and the color buffer are deactivated, and then the function `CGameSector::RenderDepth` is called. Then the textures are switched back on, as is the color buffer; the depth buffer is set to a read-only mode, and the function `CGameSector::RenderLit` is called. All this occurs for good cause: performance. As you know, we have to make a separate render pass of the geometry for each active light source. Normally each render pass draws its advantage from early z culling, but it will get even faster if you deactivate the depth buffer after the scene has been rendered completely a single time. In such a scenario, the additional render passes won't eat up fill rate of the depth buffer for the pixels they set onto the screen.

Although this might not result in a big gain in performance, it is still faster than rendering with the active depth buffer. In this case, filling the depth buffer is a render pass on its own. However, you could also combine it with an ambient pass, of course.

Rendering the Depth Pass

Now it's time to take a look at the depth pass. This is the first function that really renders anything from the sector. The rendering to the depth buffer only is just like an ambient render path, but with the slight difference that the color buffer is switched off. For each sector, rendering follows three steps:

1. Render the geometry of the sector.
2. Render the door entities of the sector.
3. Render the neighboring sectors.

In the first step, you render the geometry of the sector (that is, all polygons that were created in the level editor as free polygons or as polygons inside a mesh object). The rendering is done here using the index buffers, which were created on a per-skin basis. The second step involves rendering the door entities; these are treated a bit ... well ... separately. They are rendered dynamically, polygon by polygon. If you have a lot of door entities, this isn't such a great idea; you should choose a faster way to render. The issue is that each door has to use its own transformation matrix if it is animated. Finally, in the third step, the neighboring sectors are rendered if the portal leading to them is visible.

Any other sectors that exist in this virtual world do not matter for a given sector. A given section just knows the portals it owns. Therefore, you have to loop through all portals of a given sector, and for each portal you have to check the following three conditions:

1. Is the portal inside a closed door?
2. Is the portal outside of the view frustum?
3. Is the portal's front side looking away from the viewer more than 90 degrees?

As soon as one of these conditions returns true, you can skip this portal because the viewer cannot see it at all. Therefore, you don't have to render the sector that this portal leads to. You could add here a fourth condition that checks for the occlusion of the portal, which could be hidden behind other geometry of the level from the position of the viewer. If you find that a portal is potentially visible with the three conditions listed here, however, you request a pointer to the sector that the portal leads to and call the render function recursively for this neighboring sector.

Congratulations, mate. You have just implemented a fully functional portal engine scene-management approach:

```
HRESULT CGameSector::RenderDepth(ZFXPlane *pFrustum, const ZFXVector &vcPos)
   {
   static CGameSector *pSector=NULL;
   HRESULT hr=ZFX_OK;
   ZFXAabb aabb;

   // this sector had been drawn this frame in depth-pass mode
   if (m_bDepthRendered) return ZFX_OK;
   else m_bDepthRendered = true;

   if (m_NumZFXPolys == 0) return ZFX_OK;

   // 1. RENDER SECTOR GEOMETRY
   for (UINT i=0; i<this->m_NumSkins; i++) {

      hr = m_pDevice->GetVertexManager()->Render(m_BufID, m_pBuffer[i].IBID,
                                                 m_pBuffer[i].SkinID);
      if (FAILED(hr)) return ZFX_FAIL;
      }

   // 2. RENDER DOOR ENTITIES
   for (UINT k=0; k<m_NumEntys; k++) {
      if (!m_ppEntities[k]->IsOfType(ENT_DOOR)) continue;
      aabb = m_ppEntities[k]->GetAabb();

      if (aabb.Cull(pFrustum, 6) == ZFXCULLED ) continue;
      m_ppEntities[k]->Render( m_pDevice );
      }

   // 3. RENDER NEIGHBORING SECTORS
   for (UINT j=0; j<m_NumPorts; j++) {
      // portal inside a closed door
      if ( !m_pPorts[j].IsOpen() ) continue;

      // portal outside view frustum
      if ( m_pPorts[j].GetAabb().Cull(pFrustum, 6)
```

```
           == ZFXCULLED ) continue;

      // portal facing away from us
      if ( m_pPorts[j].IsBackfacingTo(vcPos) ) continue;

      pSector = m_pPorts[j].GetTargetSector();
      if (pSector) pSector->RenderDepth(pFrustum,vcPos);
      }
   return ZFX_OK;
   } // RenderDepth
```

The class `CGameSector` has some `bool` attributes, such as `m_bDepthRendered`. Of course, you have to avoid ending up caught in an infinite loop when the neighboring sector is returning through its own portal into the sector from which the render call just came. So each sector has this flag, which is set to `true` after a sector has been rendered in a given frame. At the start of each frame, the level object then sets all attributes of all its sectors to `false` to enable one rendering pass for each sector for the new frame.

Rendering the Ambient Pass

You render the ambient pass just like rendering the depth pass, except that now you use the shaders. In addition, you call the function `CGameSector::RenderLitPass` for each sector you visit while rendering. This function will do one additional pass for each light source in the sector to do the per-pixel lighting.

Rendering the door entities is outsourced into a separate function, because for this you need to render each door again with an ambient pass and additional light passes for each active omni light. You can find this function on the CD-ROM accompanying this book; it is very similar to the function that renders the additional light passes for the level geometry. Note that the rendering is done here based on the skin that is used by the geometry:

```
HRESULT CGameSector::RenderLit(ZFXPlane *pFrustum, const ZFXVector &vcPos,
                               UINT *pNumT, UINT *pNumL)
   {
   static CGameSector *pSector=NULL;

   static bool bTemp=true;
   static DWORD dwTick=0;

   HRESULT hr=ZFX_OK;

   if (m_bLitRendered) return ZFX_OK;
   else m_bLitRendered = true;
```

```cpp
   // set ambient light level
   m_pDevice->SetAmbientLight(m_Ambient.fR, m_Ambient.fG, m_Ambient.fB);

   // calculate flickering of lights by random
   if ( (dwTick==0) && ((rand()%8)==0))
      { bTemp=false; dwTick = GetTickCount(); }
   else if ((GetTickCount() - dwTick) > 100)
      { bTemp=true; dwTick = 0; }

   // 1. RENDER SECTOR GEOMETRY
   for (UINT i=0; i<this->m_NumSkins; i++) {

      m_pDevice->ActivatePShader(m_BasePSH);
      m_pDevice->ActivateVShader(m_BaseVSH, VID_UU);

      hr = m_pDevice->GetVertexManager()->Render(m_BufID, m_pBuffer[i].IBID,
                                                  m_pBuffer[i].SkinID);

      if (FAILED(hr)) return ZFX_FAIL;

      if (pNumT) (*pNumT) += m_pBuffer[i].NumTris;

      m_pDevice->ActivatePShader(m_OmniPSH);
      m_pDevice->ActivateVShader(m_OmniVSH, VID_UU);

      RenderLightPass(pFrustum, m_pBuffer[i].SkinID, bTemp);
      }

   // 2. RENDER DOOR ENTITIES
   RenderDoors(pFrustum, m_BaseVSH, m_BasePSH, m_OmniVSH, m_OmniPSH, bTemp);

   // 3. RENDER NEIGHBORING SECTORS
   for (UINT j=0; j<m_NumPorts; j++) {
      // portal inside a closed door
      if ( !m_pPorts[j].IsOpen() ) continue;

      // portal outside view frustum
      if ( m_pPorts[j].GetAabb().Cull(pFrustum, 6) == ZFXCULLED )
         continue;

      // portal facing away from us
      if ( m_pPorts[j].IsBackfacingTo(vcPos) ) continue;
```

```
        m_pPorts[j].ChopFrustum(pFrustum);

        pSector = m_pPorts[j].GetTargetSector();
        if (pSector)
            pSector->RenderLit(pFrustum,vcPos,pNumT,pNumL);
        }

    if (pNumL) (*pNumL) += m_NumLights;
    return ZFX_OK;
    } // RenderLit
```

Do you still remember all the attributes that you could adjust for each light source in the level editor? There was a flag to set the light to a flickering mode, and this flickering is calculated in this function here. A random variable decides whether all the flickering lights are switched on at this very moment. However, that means that all lights in the same sector that have their flickering flag active are on at the same time and off at the same time. Hence they flicker in a big group. This can be a nice effect to simulate all lights as being connected to the same broken power line. If you set the ambient light to jet-black and only use some flickering lights in a sector, it would look quite scary. However, it is not a good idea to let all lights in a sector flicker in the same rhythm to simulate flickering torches or open fires, for example. So add this to your to-do list. You would need another flag to indicate whether a light source should flicker in the sector's flickering rhythm or use its very own random flickering.

Rendering the Light Pass

And now we've come all the way down to the real-time lighting heart of *Pandora's Legacy*. The following function renders all additional render passes needed for the omni lights sitting inside a sector. Each light source has its own cache in the form of an index buffer that contains all the geometry from the sector onto which the light is shining. This function loops through all the omni lights and checks a number of things for each light source. First, this light source must not be a shadow caster, because those are only reference points for the shadow casting. Then, if the light is flickering, it must of course be switched on in this frame. And, finally, the light source has to own some geometry using the active skin, of course, and the cache of the light must be inside the view frustum. If all these conditions are okay, the attenuation matrix is calculated, and the additional pass for this light source under consideration is rendered:

```
void CGameSector::RenderLightPass(const ZFXPlane *pFrustum, UINT nSkin,
                                  bool bFlicker)
    {
    ZFXMatrix mat;
    UINT IBID=0;
```

```
if (!m_pDevice->CanDoShaders()) return;

m_pDevice->UseAdditiveBlending(true);

// RENDER ONE ADDITIVE PASS PER LIGHT
for (UINT i=0; i<m_NumLights; i++) {

   // only a shadow caster
   if (m_pLights[i].IsShadowCasting())
      continue;

   // light inactive due to flickering
   if (m_pLights[i].IsFlickering() && bFlicker)
      continue;

   // light shining on this skin?
   if ( !m_pLights[i].InfluencesSkin(nSkin, &IBID) )
      continue;

   // lit geometry inside the view frustum?
   if ( m_pLights[i].GetAabb().Cull(pFrustum, 6) == ZFXCULLED )
      continue;

   mat = CalcTransAttenNoRot(m_pLights[i].GetPosition(),
                             m_pLights[i].GetRadius());

   m_pDevice->SetShaderConstant(SHT_VERTEX, DAT_FLOAT, 20, 4, (void*)&mat);

   m_pDevice->SetShaderConstant(SHT_PIXEL, DAT_FLOAT, 0, 1,
                                (void*)&m_pLights[i].GetColor());

   m_pDevice->GetVertexManager()->Render(m_BufID, IBID, nSkin);
   } // for [lights]

m_pDevice->UseAdditiveBlending(false);
} // RenderLights
```

Rendering Shadows in the Level

Rendering the shadows in the class `CGameLevel` is now more or less identical to the small code sample provided at the beginning of this chapter. Therefore, there is nothing to say about it at all now. However, it is interesting that this function takes two pointers of the type `CGameCharacter` as a parameter. The characters wandering around in the level are stored in the class `CGame` and not in the level class, nor even in the sector class. So the list of players has to be provided to this function. The second list can be used for a list of bots, for example, but we don't have those here:

```
HRESULT CGameLevel::RenderShadows(UINT nSector, const ZFXVector &vcPos,
                                  CGameCharacter **pPlayers, UINT NumP,
                                  CGameCharacter **pBots, UINT NumB)
   {
   ZFXPlane Frustum[6];
   ZFXAabb  aabb;
   HRESULT  hr=ZFX_OK;

   m_pDevice->GetFrustrum(Frustum);
   m_pDevice->SetWorldTransform(NULL);

   if (nSector >= m_NumSectors)
      return ZFX_INVALIDPARAM;

   m_pDevice->UseStencilShadowSettings(true);

   hr = m_pSectors[nSector]->RenderShadows(Frustum, vcPos, pPlayers, NumP,
                                           pBots, NumB);

   m_pDevice->UseStencilShadowSettings(false);

   m_pDevice->SetStencilBufferMode(RS_STENCIL_ENABLE,0);
   m_pDevice->SetStencilBufferMode(RS_STENCIL_REF, 1);
   m_pDevice->SetStencilBufferMode(RS_STENCIL_FUNC_LESSEQUAL, 0);
   m_pDevice->SetStencilBufferMode(RS_STENCIL_PASS_KEEP,0);

   m_pDevice->FadeScreen(0.0f, 0.0f , 0.0f, 0.5f);

   m_pDevice->SetStencilBufferMode(RS_STENCIL_DISABLE,0);
   return hr;
   } // Render
```

Again, in this function the rendering is not done, but the work is dumped onto the poor sector class, which has to implement a function. This occurs because only the sector class knows where all the shadow casters are located. If one is found in the sector, the shadow volume of the mesh will be rendered. Of course, this function is also going recursively through the neighboring sectors to check the visibility of the characters and render all shadows in neighboring sectors:

```cpp
HRESULT CGameSector::RenderShadows(ZFXPlane *pFrustum, const ZFXVector &vcPos,
                                   CGameCharacter **pPlayers, UINT NumP,
                                   CGameCharacter **pBots, UINT NumB)
   {
   static CGameSector *pSector=NULL;
   HRESULT hr=ZFX_OK;

   if (m_bShadowsRendered) return ZFX_OK;
   else m_bShadowsRendered = true;

   // search shadow caster among the lights
   for (UINT l=0; l<m_NumLights; l++) {
      if ( !m_pLights[l].IsShadowCasting() ) continue;

      for (UINT m=0; m<m_NumMeshs; m++)
         m_pMeshShadows[m].Render(&m_pLights[l],NULL);

      for (UINT p=0; p<NumP; p++)
         pPlayers[p]->RenderShadow( &m_pLights[l] );

      for (UINT b=0; b<NumB; b++)
         pBots[b]->RenderShadow( &m_pLights[l] );
      }

   // render neighboring sectors
   for (UINT j=0; j<m_NumPorts; j++) {
      // portal inside closed door
      if ( !m_pPorts[j].IsOpen() ) continue;

      // portal outside the view frustum
      if ( m_pPorts[j].GetAabb().Cull(pFrustum, 6)
            == ZFXCULLED ) continue;

      // portal shows us its backface
      if ( m_pPorts[j].IsBackfacingTo(vcPos) ) continue;

      pSector = m_pPorts[j].GetTargetSector();
      if (pSector) pSector->RenderShadows(pFrustum, vcPos, pPlayers,
                                          NumP, pBots, NumB);
      }
   return ZFX_OK;
   } // RenderShadows
```

We have now loaded a level successfully and can render it efficiently. Before grabbing the code and playing around with it, however, read on throughout the rest of this chapter about some game class issues to get a big picture of what is going on in this game. But first take a look at a screenshot of this game, shown in Figure 15.8.

Figure 15.8 A screenshot of the sample game *Pandora's Legacy* with dynamic real-time lighting and shadows.

Integrating Characters

A video game would be very boring if there were no life forms around in the virtual world. Those life forms are normally called characters, and they should live in the virtual world as opponents, as neutral actors, or as teammates. This section shows you how to integrate those characters into the current game.

CGameCharacter, Base Class for Players and NPCs

In a video game, you need at least two different kinds of base characters. The first kind of character is an avatar, which represents a human player in the virtual world. The second kind of character is a bot or Non-Player Character (NPC). A bot is controlled by the computer by artificial intelligence (or by artificial stupidity, in some cases). Therefore, your game may have two classes like `CGamePlayer` and `CGameBot`. Because these classes share a lot of similar functionality, however, it makes sense to build a base class from which to derive these two classes. Here is just such a base class:

```
class CGameCharacter
   {
   public:
      CGameCharacter(void);
      virtual ~CGameCharacter(void);

      virtual void Update(CGameLevel*, bool, CGameCharacter**, UINT,
                          CGameCharacter**, UINT, float)=0;

      HRESULT      Render(void);
      HRESULT      RenderShadow(CGameLight*);

      virtual void ApplyDamage(UINT, UINT OwnerID);
      bool         TestCollision(const ZFXRay&, float, float*);
      HRESULT      FireBullet(void);
      HRESULT      TouchAndUse(void);

      // Network-Stuff
      UPDATEPKG    GetUpdate(void);
      void         SetUpdate(UPDATEPKG*);

      // Accessor-Methods
      void         SetID(UINT n)  { m_ID = n;      }
      UINT         GetID(void)    { return m_ID; }
      UINT         GetCS(void)    { return m_CS; }
      ZFXAabb      GetAabb(void);
      ZFXMatrix    GetWorldMatrix(void);
      ZFXVector    GetPos(void);
      ZFXVector    GetRight(void);
      ZFXVector    GetUp(void);
      ZFXVector    GetDir(void);
      UINT         GetEnergy(void){ return m_nEnergy; }
      UINT         GetAnimation(void);
      bool         IsFrozen(void){return(m_fFrozen>0.0f);}
      bool         IsBot(void)   {return m_bIsBot;}
      bool         IsIdle(void)  {return m_bIdle; }
      void         SetRotaSpeedY(float f);
```

```cpp
        void        SetRotaSpeedX(float f);
        void        SetSpeed(float f);
        void        SetSlideSpeed(float f);

    protected:
        LPZFXRENDERDEVICE   m_pRDevice;
        LPZFXNETWORKDEVICE  m_pNDevice;
        ZFXMCEgo            *m_pMCEgo;
        CZFXModel           *m_pModel;
        CShadowVolume       *m_pShadow;
        UINT                m_VSH;
        UINT                m_PSH;
        UINT                m_ID;
        UINT                m_CS;
        UINT                m_nEnergy;
        float               m_fFrozen;
        bool                m_bMoved;
        bool                m_bIsFalling;
        bool                m_bIdle;
        bool                m_bIsBot;

        void InitShadowVolume(void);
        void UpdateModel(float fElapsed);
        bool Intersects(CGameCharacter**, UINT);

        // Network-Messages
        HRESULT SendMsg_TouchAndUse(void);
        HRESULT SendMsg_FireBullet(void);
        HRESULT SendMsg_PlayerFrozen(UINT);
    }; // class
typedef class CGameCharacter *LPGAMECHARACTER;
```

The two attributes m_ID and m_CS are not very self-explanatory. The attribute m_CS is the variable identifying in which sector the character is currently ("cs" stands for current sector). This information is used to kick off the rendering process of the portal engine in this sector. For an artificial intelligence, this would also be needed to locate the bot in the level and calculate a path to its goal through the level. The attribute m_ID, on the other hand, is the ID of the character that was given to a client by the server, so it is actually the client ID. If the instance is not a human player, there will be no client. In this case, the server should come up with a unique ID for the bots.

Most of the member functions of this class are only references delegating the function call to the appropriate function of one of its member variables. The input control commands, for example, will be handed over to the movement controller, which will then calculate the new orientation and position for the object. Rendering the model for the character is done using the class `ZFXModel`, so there are only very few interesting tasks left to implement in this class. Still, however, most of the functions are not even very complex. You can figure them out on the companion CD-ROM. This section instead concentrates on the network stuff (which is more interesting, in my opinion).

Network Messages Concerning Characters

The network source code used in *Pandora's Legacy* is fairly simple for the sake of easy explanations here and because not many messages are going over the network. As you will see, a first-person shooter is not very complex with regard to the network issues. As far as the characters are concerned, they will build a simple package describing the important information about their state. This package is all the other clients need to know about a certain other client in order to display it correctly in the level. Note that the structure used for the update package is not really optimized with regard to its size in bytes:

```
typedef struct UPDATEPKG_TYPE
   {
   UINT      NID;
   ZFXVector vcPos;
   float     fRotY;
   char      nAnim;
   float     fASpd;
   } UPDATEPKG;
```

A character has to provide its unique network ID in the package as well as its current position, its rotation on the world up axis, the animation sequence it is using currently, and finally the speed at which the animation is run. Based on this update package that each client is sending to the server for his player character, all avatars in the game can be shown in more or less the same way on all clients. Sending and receiving this package is done in the class `Cgame`, which is utilizing the functions `CGameCharacter::GetUpdate` and `CGameCharacter::SetUpdate` for this purpose.

Because we are just talking about the `CGame` class and the network messages, I want to show you which messages are needed for this game. Sending an update package from a player and receiving update packages to update the list of client avatars on a local machine are just basic tasks that enable you to display the avatars for all clients correctly and their positions with the rotation, and so on. However, this would not make up a complete game. For a real game, you need more events that can occur besides receiving an update package. Our game is fairly simple, so there are only the following seven different messages that can happen in the network. Note that they start with the ID 4 because the IDs 0 to 3 are already used internally by the network component of the ZFXEngine:

```
const UINT MSG_UPDATE        = 4;
const UINT MSG_PLAYERLIST    = 5;
const UINT MSG_TOUCHANDUSE   = 6;
const UINT MSG_FIREBULLET    = 7;
const UINT MSG_PLAYERFROZEN  = 8;
const UINT MSG_BOTLIST       = 9;
const UINT MSG_BOTUPDATE     = 10;
```

Only three of those messages can be sent by the class CGamePlayer over the network. To do this, the class has three different member functions using the prefix SendMsg, and each one of them deals with a different message. One of these functions is shown here so that you can see what it looks like. The other two are then implemented similarly, with just a different message ID. Note that the attribute m_pNDevice of the class holds a pointer on the network device of the engine. The following function sends the message MSG_TOUCHANDUSE with the character ID:

```
HRESULT CGameCharacter::SendMsg_TouchAndUse(void)
   {
   ZFXPACKAGE msgPkg;

   ZFXVector vcPos = m_pMCEgo->GetPos();

   msgPkg.nLength  = sizeof(ZFXVector);
   msgPkg.nType    = MSG_TOUCHANDUSE;
   msgPkg.nSender  = m_ID;
   msgPkg.pData    = &vcPos;

   return m_pNDevice->SendToServer(&msgPkg);
   } // SendMsg_TouchAndUse
```

The message MSG_TOUCHANDUSE is meant for the purpose of activating objects in the level. If the player presses the RETURN key while playing the game, the character class sends this packet. On receiving this event, the CGame class has to react accordingly, which normally means checking nearby doors and other activate-able things. If there are things in the vicinity of the position where this event occurred and which are also included in the message, the objects should be told that they are activated now. In this simple video game, only the sliding doors are objects that can be activated by the play. This will also lead to activating the portal inside the door if there is one. From this, you can understand how **easy it is to program network games.**

CGame, a Class of Its Own

Up to this point, you have seen a lot of small details here and there that have to do with this and that. However, you control all those little details on a superior layer, and this superior layer is the class called CGame. This upper-management class initializes the necessary device objects from the engine, it contains an instance of the class CGameLevel, it updates the whole network, and so on. Unfortunately, although the whole class did not make it into this chapter, the most important parts of the class are covered here. The rest is just basic stuff you will find on the companion CD-ROM. You should now insert the CD-ROM in your drive and take a look at the class declaration before reading on.

Updating the Game

By now you should have an impression of what this class should do for us. Take a look at the CGame::Update function, which is called in every frame of the game. At first this function calls the update functions of the member variables, which have their own update functions. Then the network and the input are processed before the network is updated. This network update will not be done in each frame, but only at a certain time interval. This prevents the players from sending an update package each frame, for example, which would be hundreds of times a second. You don't need those updates that often. For simple player movements, it is even enough to update them once or twice every second.

Note

> The game *Pandora's Legacy* of this chapter is designed more or less as a game server, not as a dedicated server. That means that the server itself is also a player who is playing in the game with the clients. Only the server processes the movements of the bots if there are any. The clients have their own list of bots, but they won't let the bots move for themselves. Instead, they update the bots with the messages from the server. However, the clients themselves perform all other tasks. The server will distribute only the packages it receives from other clients, and it won't verify their movements. This is not the best architecture due to its potential for cheating, but it serves for the demonstration purpose of this chapter.

Here is the update function for the CGame class:

```
void CGame::Update(void)
    {
    float fET = m_pTimer->GetElapsed();

    m_pTimer->Update();
    m_pLevel->Update( fET );

    m_pBullets->Update( m_pLevel, (LPGAMECHARACTER*)m_pPlayers,
                       m_NumP, (LPGAMECHARACTER*)m_pBots,
```

```
                       m_NumB, fET );
m_fDT += fET;

ProcessNetwork();
ProcessInput();

// Network-Updates
if ( m_fDT >= 0.01f )
   {
   UpdateNetwork();
   m_fDT = 0.0f;
   }

// Player Updates
for (UINT i=0; i<m_NumP; i++)
   {
   m_pPlayers[i]->Update( m_pLevel, m_pPlayers[i] == m_pMe,
                       (LPGAMECHARACTER*)m_pPlayers,
                       m_NumP, (LPGAMECHARACTER*)m_pBots,
                       m_NumB, fET );
   }
} // Update
```

The Process...() functions are the most interesting ones. The function CGame::ProcessInput queries the player's input from the keyboard and the mouse and transforms that input into according commands for the movement controller. The avatar will then be moved, and the collision detection with the level geometry is calculated by using the octree class developed in Chapter 13, "Scene Management." This is simple stuff, so again I want to concentrate on the network functions here.

Networking Tasks

The most important network-processing task in each frame is checking the inbox of the client belonging to the application or the server if this instance of the application is the game server. As long as there are messages in the inbox, this function extracts them in a big loop and checks which message was received. For each message, the function recognizes it and then performs the appropriate steps to react to the message. A client would only need to react to certain messages, whereas the server has to do two things. First the server must react to the messages like a client because he is also a player in the game. Then, however, the server also must send the incoming message to all connected clients, because otherwise the clients would not see the messages other clients sent to the server.

Here is the function, which is just a big decision tree of different if and else cases:

```cpp
HRESULT CGame::ProcessNetwork(void)
   {
   HRESULT    hr=ZFX_OK;
   ZFXPACKAGE msgPkg = { 0, 0, 0, 0 };
   UINT       nNID=0;

   BYTE pBuffer[MAX_PKG_SIZE];
   memset(pBuffer, 0, MAX_PKG_SIZE);
   msgPkg.pData = pBuffer;

   // get all messages from the inbox
   while (m_pNDevice->IsPkgWaiting())
      {
      if (FAILED( m_pNDevice->GetNextPkg(&msgPkg) )) {
         hr = ZFX_FAIL;
         }
      else {
         // RECEIVING ID FORM SERVER
         if (msgPkg.nType == 0)
            {
            m_NID = *((UINT*)msgPkg.pData);
            AddPlayer(m_NID);
            m_pMe = m_pPlayers[m_NumP-1];
            }

         // A NEW CLIENT IS IN THE NETWORK
         else if (msgPkg.nType == 1)
            {
            nNID = *((UINT*)msgPkg.pData);
            if (m_NID!=nNID) AddPlayer(nNID);

            // SERVER INFORMS ABOUT THE OTHER CLIENT
            if (m_nmd==NMD_SERVER) {
               SendMsg_PlayerListTo(nNID);
               }
            }

         // A CLIENT IS GONE
         else if (msgPkg.nType == 2)
            {
            nNID = *((UINT*)msgPkg.pData);
            RemovePlayer(nNID);
```

```
      }

   // RECEIVING UPDATE PACKAGE FROM CLIENT
   else if (msgPkg.nType == MSG_UPDATE)
      {
      nNID = msgPkg.nSender;
      UpdatePlayer(nNID, (UPDATEPKG*)msgPkg.pData);

      if (m_nmd==NMD_SERVER) {
         m_pNDevice->SendToClients(&msgPkg);
         }
      }

   // RECEIVING PLAYERLIST FROM SERVER
   else if (msgPkg.nType == MSG_PLAYERLIST)
      {
      InitPlayerListOnClient( (CHARACTERLIST*)msgPkg.pData);
      }

   // TOUCHANDUSE-MESSAGE
   else if (msgPkg.nType == MSG_TOUCHANDUSE)
      {
      m_pLevel->TouchAndUse( *((ZFXVector*)msgPkg.pData) );
      if (m_nmd==NMD_SERVER) {
         m_pNDevice->SendToClients(&msgPkg);
         }
      }

   // FIREBULLET-MESSAGE FROM A PLAYER
   else if (msgPkg.nType == MSG_FIREBULLET)
      {
      m_pBullets->AddBullet( *((BULLET*)msgPkg.pData) );
      if (m_nmd==NMD_SERVER) {
         m_pNDevice->SendToClients(&msgPkg);
         }
      }

   // FROZEN-MESSAGE FROM A PLAYER
   else if (msgPkg.nType == MSG_PLAYERFROZEN)
      {
      UINT nBy = *((UINT*)msgPkg.pData);
      if (m_nmd==NMD_SERVER) {
```

```
                        m_pNDevice->SendToClients(&msgPkg);
                    }
                }
            } // if GetNextPkg() succeeded
        } // while [msg empfangen]
    return hr;
    } // ProcessNetwork
```

As an example, take a look at one of the functions that is called in reaction to a certain network message received by a player. A fairly complex network message is the one that contains the list of players. If a new player registers as a client to the network and comes into the game, this new client will automatically get a message from the server that contains a list of all connected clients. To render this list onscreen, the client then needs to process this message by creating an instance of the CGameCharacter class for each connected player in the game. This client must do this only one time. After that, the client receives only update packages from the other clients.

The following function sends the list of players from the master array of the server:

```
HRESULT CGame::SendMsg_PlayerListTo(UINT CID)
    {
    // only servers are allowed to do this
    if (m_nmd != NMD_SERVER) return ZFX_OK;

    ZFXPACKAGE     msgPkg;
    CHARACTERLIST  List;
    HRESULT        hr=ZFX_OK;

    List.Num = m_NumP;

    for (UINT i=0; i<m_NumP; i++)
        List.upkg[i] = m_pPlayers[i]->GetUpdate();

    msgPkg.nLength   = sizeof(CHARACTERLIST);
    msgPkg.nType     = MSG_PLAYERLIST;
    msgPkg.nSender   = m_NID;
    msgPkg.pData     = &List;

    return m_pNDevice->SendToClient(&msgPkg, CID);
    } // SendMsg_PlayerListTo
```

Of course, the client is the only one who is allowed to send this message. Clients will have only copies of this list, and they are not allowed to send data about other clients around in the network. A client should only send data concerning his own state and his own actions. The structure CHARACTERLIST is just an array of update packages for a character, with a maximum number of 256 allowed clients.

One Look Back, Two Steps Forward

That was certainly a full gallop through this chapter. Now we can slow down, glance back over our shoulder, and look at what we accomplished in this chapter. First you learned a lot about shadows—which algorithms are out there and how they are implemented. The second thing you learned is how you can manage and use a huge amount of data in a video game and display big levels pretty fast, even with per-pixel lighting effects. Of course, the simple system I've shown you here is very basic (and I'm already thinking about optimization possibilities). The management of the door entities is pretty rudimentary, for example. Although occlusion culling for the portals is another good idea, the simple game will do for the purposes of this book. The third thing you learned in this chapter is how to program a simple deathmatch network game.

I could have expanded this chapter to show you a lot more of the game code, but it wasn't really necessary. After all, rendering and collision detection inside the game boils down to just calling functions of other classes you have already seen. Furthermore, this book has focused mainly on game engine programming, and this chapter provides enough of a sample for you to actually use the engine developed over the course of this book.

As mentioned previously in this chapter, the game is already well prepared for integrating bots. The only thing you would need to come up with is a decent kind of artificial intelligence for the bots to let them navigate in an indoor environment safely. This is a good starting place for you to play around with this demo application a bit. Try to think of some more ideas about what to integrate into this game, and then see whether you can do it with the current version of the engine. If not, that's a good lesson, too: You now know what you have to change or to add in the engine.

After all, you will only realize what is good or bad about a design of an engine when you try to build a real project using the engine. Remember, there is no such thing as an ultimate engine.

Epilogue

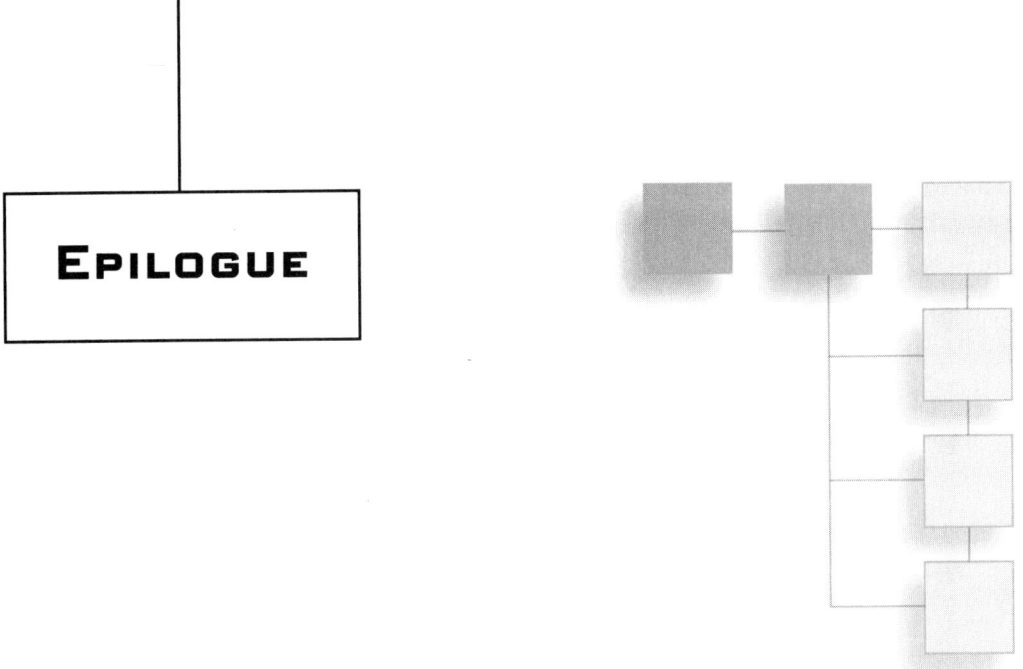

> *Rydell had a theory about virtual real estate. The smaller and cheaper the physical site of a given operation, the bigger and cheesier the website. According to this theory, Selwyn FX was probably operating out of rolled-up newspaper.*
>
> **William Gibson, All Tomorrow's Parties**

About 800 pages have flown by, and we are now at the end of a very long journey. If you feel like me, you are exhausted from the stress of reading and digesting this new knowledge about three-dimensional space. I hope you are eager to use this knowledge to create virtual worlds in your imagination and implement them on your computers so that you can crunch the virtual newspaper of William Gibson to the size of a molecule.

The preceding pages taught you how to do basic 3D programming, starting with the Direct3D fundamentals and moving on to a very simple 3D engine. Using this engine, you also learned how to program a rather complex tool for editing and creating 3D models and worlds. Both the tool and the engine were then utilized when you took that first step into video game programming by developing a small network deathmatch shooter.

In this book, you should have learned enough to start creating your own 3D worlds. The field of video game programming is a very creative one that lets you do everything you want to do. The hardware continually advances and provides more and more capabilities. It is up to you to explore how to use these capabilities to leverage your virtual world. You should not take this book or any other book out there as a step-by-step description on how to program certain things. A book is nothing more that a snapshot of a particular topic at a given point in time. Use this book as a mate that accompanies you on your journey and helps get you started.

That said, I would like to wish you success with your next 3D project, and even more important, I hope you have a lot of fun with it. That is what all this 3D stuff is about—fun!

INDEX

3D engine, 5–6
3DNow!, 101–102
3DNow! Professional, 108
3D Studio Max, 668

A

absolute matrix, joint parent, 426
abstract class interfaces
    creating, 42–43
    using, 50–52
accelerated graphics port (AGP), 8
accepting clients, 529–530
Active Project option, 49
aligning data, SSE, 103–104
alpha channels, 216, 227–233
alpha color keys, 229–233
    overall transparency, 231–233
alpha key function, 219
alpha testing, 228
ambient light, 194–195, 200, 201, 324
    vertex shading, 362–364, 368
ambient pass rendering, 825–827
AMD 3DNow!, 101–102
AMD Enhanced 3DNow!, 101
animated models
    calculating vertices, 428–430
    looping vertices, 435–438
    preparing, 430–435
    rendering, 439–440
        bones, 440–442
        normals, 442–444
    updating, 438–439
    using, 438
animations, reading, 414–415

application layer, 511
application programming interfaces (APIs)
    Berkeley Sockets, 514
    DirectPlay, 515
    independent interface classes, 34–35
    WinSock, 515, 539–553
ArchiCAD, 668
arithmetic logic unit (ALU), 340–343, 347
artificial intelligence (AI) math, 92
assembler languages, 92–94
assembler programming, 94–108
    AMD 3DNow!, 101–102, 108
    central processing unit (CPU), 96
    floating-point unit (FPU), 96–97
    multimedia extensions (MMX), 98–101
    processor architecture, 94–96
    single instruction multiple data (SIMD), 97–98
    streaming SIMD extensions (SSE), 102–107
    streaming SIMD extensions, second (SSE2), 107
asynchronous mode, 545, 546
attenuation, light, 365
audio interface
    implementation, 487
        initializing and releasing, 490–494
        loading and playing sounds, 494–499
        ZFXDA class, 487–490
    interface definition, 485–487
    overview, 484–485, 484–501
AutoCAD, 668
autonomy, game code, 32–33
axis-aligned bounding box (AABB)
    checking ray containment, 161–162
    class definition, 151
    clipping polygons, 167–168

Index

concepts, 138–142, 148–150
creation from OBB, 153–154
culling test, 154–157
extracting planes, 160–161
intersections with planes, 148–150
octrees, 638, 651–653
polygons, 166
scene management, 602
axis recalculations, 575–577, 581–583

B

back buffers
 defined, 82
 Direct3D, 76, 77
 viewport structure, 239
backface culling, 587
base class, 34
beginning scenes, 81
Berkeley Sockets, 514, 527
binary space partitioning (BSP), 9, 602–613
 algorithm, 605–607
 class declaration, 624–636
  collision detection, 633–636
  concepts, 624–625
  creating and releasing instances, 625–626
  recursive creation, 626–629
  securing best splitter, 629–631
  traversing tree, 631–633
 demo application, 653–663
 implementation, 622–624
 leafy, 613
 node-based, 612–613
 overview, 602–605
 potential visibility set, 621–622
 solid leaf, 613
 splitters, 610–612
 versus portal engines, 617–618
 video game history, 607–610
binding (naming socket), 527–528
bind position, 393
binormal vectors, 376–380, 381
bit string program, 93
bones, skinned meshes, 391–393
 setting up, 423–428
bot, 505
bounding boxes. *See also* axis-aligned bounding box (AABB); oriented bounding box (OBB)
 complex models, CAD, 702–703

culling with, 173–175
intersections between, 160
intersections with planes, 148–150
intersections with rays, 138–142
intersections with triangles, 157–160
octrees, 650–653
polygons, 695–696
polymesh, 715
recursive creation, 627–629
broadcasting data, SSE, 107
brother portal, 717, 820
brute force method, 588
budget development, 20–21
buffered data mode, 455
buffers
 back
  defined, 82
  Direct3D, 76, 77
  viewport structure, 239
 depth
  clearing, 81
  scene management, 604, 605
  vertex shading, 363
 dynamic
  performance, 298–300
  versus static buffers, 287–289, 290
  vertex cache object, 292, 297–298
 flushing, 311–312
 frame, 82
 front, 76, 82
 index, 287–290, 298–300, 316
 pixel, 81, 82
 selection, 764–777
  adding objects, 768–769
  class declaration, 765–768
  deleting and copying objects, 769–772
  overview, 764–765
  polygons, 772–774
  saving prefabs, 775–777
 sound, 495–497
 static
  creating, 303–304, 313–319
  versus dynamic, 287–289
  vertex cache object, 294
 stencil, 81
 vertex, 287–289, 298–300
bump mapping, 345, 370–385
 adding textures as, 219–221

heightmap conversion, 372–375
opening tangent space, 375–380
pixel shaders, 383–384
vertex shaders, 380–383
byte ordering, 528

C

C++ keyword operator, 117
cache manager. *See* vertex cache manager
cache object. *See* vertex cache object
caching, 286–287
callback procedure, 64–69, 73
camera, 242
    first-person, 570–571
    fixed, 572
    free cameras, 570
    modes, 570–572
    third-person, 570–571
camping effect, 506
cancel button, 69
capture the flag, 506
Carmack's reverse, 794–795
central processing unit (CPU), 8, 92
    capabilities increases, 94, 97
    identifying, 109–114
        CPUID instruction, 110
        feature list, 110–114
    instructions, 96
    limited category, 338–339, 340
    rendering hardware, 283–284
CGameLevel, 836–841
character integration, 831–835
chat application, 553–559
child nodes, octrees, 639–641
child windows, multiple
    dialog initialization, 76–79, 89
    virtual, 238
Chunk-Based Format (CBF), 389
    defining chunk, 394–396
    main function, 397–398
    overview, 394
    reading animations, 414–416
    reading chunk, 396–397
    reading faces, 403–404
    reading header, 398–399
    reading joints, 407–410
    reading key frame positions, 412–414
    reading key frame rotations, 411–412

    reading materials, 405–407
    reading mesh, 404–405
    reading vertices, 400–402
    set model scaling, 416–418
class declaration
    BSP trees, 624–636
    CLevel, 761–762
    entities, 727–728
    graphical user interface (GUI), 778–781
    lighting, 722–725
    octrees, 637–638
    polygons, 678–681
    polymesh, 698–701
    portals, 716–717
    sectors, 733–738
    selection buffer, 765–768
    shadow volume, 796–797
    spawn points, 732–733
class design, CAD tool. *See also* polygons; portals; sectors
    CLevelObject, 675–678
    level structure, 673–675
    overview, 672–673
clearing screens, 79–81
Clevel class, 761–764
ClevelObject class, 675–678
clients
    acceptance, 529–530
    sending data, 547–548
    socket object
        connecting, 549–550
        creating, 545–546
        disconnecting, 551–552
client/server networks, 509–510, 517
clipping pipeline, 336–338
clipping planes
    near and far, 239, 248–250
    setting, 248–250
clipping polygon lists, 643–644
clipping polygons, 167–173
clock speed, increasing, 97
collision detection, 92
    BSP trees, 633–636
    light source, 726
    octrees, 645–647
    planes, 145
    polygons, 685–688
    polymesh, 706–709

portals, 721
ray transformation matrix, 132–134
sectors, 746–750
color keys, 203
colors
comparing, 211–212
creating, 200–203
format conversion, 222–223
transparency effects, 228–233
combo box controls, creating dialogs, 63–64, 76
command and control centers (CCCs), 283–284
competitive advantage, 18–19
compilers
code optimization, 93–94
instruction set updating, 108–109
pixel shader, 277
vertex shader, 272–276
complex models, CAD tools. *See* polymesh
complex numbers, 177–178
Component Object Model (COM), 26, 491–494
computer-aided design (CAD) tools, 667–669. *See also specific subjects and functions*
computer graphics, transparency adjustments, 226–228
constructors
BSP trees, 625–626
dialog initialization, 70–71
DLL implementation, 62
interface, 473–475
joystick class, 468–470
keyboard class, 459
mouse class, 463–464
octrees, 638–639
polygons, 163–164, 680–681
skin manager, 209–211
vertex cache object, 292, 293–294
virtual, 52
continuous level of detail (CLOD), 589–590, 594–600
convex groups, 605–607
cooperative mission, 505–506
CPUID instruction, 110
cross products
plane intersections, 147–148
vector, 124–125
culling
backface, 587
bounding boxes, 154–157, 173–175

computer-aided design (CAD), 674
occlusion, 586
techniques, 152
test, 154–157
view frustum, 156, 587
BSP trees, 631–633
potential visibility set (PVS), 621
quadtrees, 592–593
cull member function, 152

D
D3DX, 28–29, 121
data, network
multimedia extensions, 99
receiving, 533–536
sending, 532–533
data-link layer, 512
data processing, 418–438
animating model, 428–430
animating vertices, 435–438
preparing animation, 430–435
preparing data, 419–423
setting up bones, 423–428
death match scenarios, 505
deathmatch shooter. *See Pandora's Legacy*
death-pass variant, 791–794
debug messages, 275
dedicated server, 510
depth buffers
clearing, 81
scene management, 604, 605
vertex shading, 363
depth-fail variant, 794–795
depth pass rendering, 823–825
design document, 15
designing
components, 15
implementing, 16–17
overview, 14
destructors
BSP trees, 625–626
dialog initialization, 70–71
interface, 473
keyboard class, 459
mouse class, 463–464
octrees, 638–639
polygons, 163–164, 680–681

Index

skin manager, 209–211
vertex cache object, 294
virtual, 52, 62
Deus Ex, 16
device-independent bitmap (DIB), 221–226
dialogs
    creating, 63–65
    message procedure, 66–69
    shutting down, 69–70
diffuse lighting model, 200–201, 383
Direct3D, 26–28
    combo dialog controls, 64
    dialog initialization, 73–76
    hardware lighting, 197–198
    rendering capabilities, 256
    render states, 282
    swap chains, 76–79
directional light, 195, 354–358
DirectInput functions, 450–480
direction vector, 244
direct light, 195–197, 200, 201
    directional, 195, 354–358
    point, 195–196
    spot, 196–197
DirectMusic, 487–501
DirectPlay, 515
DirectSound, 487–501
DirectX, 26–27
DirectX Software Development Kit (SDK), 60, 360
discrete level of detail (DLOD), 589–590
Doom, 7, 603, 604, 608, 609
dot product operation, 370
DownLoadable Sounds (DLS), 495
Duke Nukem 3D, 614
dynamic buffers
    performance, 298–300
    versus static buffers, 287–289, 290
    vertex cache object, 292, 297–298
dynamic link libraries (DLLs)
    advantages, 44–45
    demo application, 330–333
    exporting classes, 46
    functions, 36–37
    implementation, 58–89
        creating dialog, 63–65
        enumeration from DirectX, 60
        exported functions, 61–62
        initialization, 70–76
        message procedures, 66–69
        multiple child views, 77–79
        render functions, 79–89
        shutting down dialog, 69–70
        swap chains, 76–77
    loading, 45–46
    as render device, 48–50
dynamic render lists, 308–311

E

Early-Z-Culling, 363
emissive color, 356
emissive light, 202
Endians, 528
engines
    changing mode, 256–260
    components, 37–39
    defined, 5–6
    requirements
        code autonomy, 32–33
        naming engine, 31
        other, 33
    structure, 35–37
Enhanced 3DNow!, 101
entities, CAD tool, 726–731
    class declaration, 727–728
    common functionalities, 728–729
    connecting with portals, 730–731, 759–761
    creating instances, 728
    miscellaneous functions, 729–730
    overview, 726–727
enumeration, DirectX SDK, 60
Euler angles, 177, 182–183
executive summary, 18
exporting classes, 46
exporting functions
    in DLL implementation, 61–62
    sniffing for, 56–58
extended accumulator (EAX), 95
extended base (EBX), 95
extended base pointer (EBP), 95
extended counter (ECX), 95
extended data (EDX), 95, 110
extended destination index (EDI), 95, 105
extended features list, 110–111, 113
extended source index (ESI), 95, 105
extended stack pointer (ESP), 95
extern functions, 54

F

faces, reading, 403–404
fall, light, 365
far clipping plane, 239, 240, 248–250
feature list, processor, 110–114
field of view (fov), 240
file transfer application, 559–567
fill rate problem, 339
first in first out (FIFO), 516
first-person cameras, 570–571, 579–583
fixed cameras, 572
fixed-function pipeline, 268, 270, 336, 337
flame wars, 27
flexible pipeline, 268, 336, 337
flexible vertex format (FVF), 266–267, 270–271, 300, 341
floating-point registers, 98–99
    AMD 3DNow!, 101
    AMD 3DNow! Professional, 108
    Streaming SIMD Extensions (SSE), 102
floating-point unit (FPU)
    functions, 96–97
    multimedia extensions (MMX), 98–99
    vector descriptions, 98
float values
    AMD 3DNow!, 101
    Streaming SIMD Extensions (SSE), 102–103
font creation, 320–323
frag (kill), 505
fragment programs, 335
frame buffers, 82
free cameras, 570, 577–579
free polygons, 813–815
front buffers
    defined, 82
    Direct3D, 76
front cap, 795
full-screen mode, dialog initialization, 76, 89
fun-house effect, 618–619

G

game agent, 13
game engine, 5
games. *See* network games
geometry loader, 332–333
geometry rendering, 821–823
gimbal lock, 576

globally unique identifier (GUID), 453, 468
graphical user interface (GUI), 777–785
    class declaration, 778–781
    important attributes, 781–782
    overview, 777–778
    polygon creation, 783–785
    update function, 782–783
graphic files, loading, 221–226
graphics adapter, 92
graphics processing unit (GPU), 8–9
    limited category, 338–339, 340
    rendering hardware, 283–284
grayscale filter, 369, 374

H

hardware abstraction layer (HAL), 64, 69
hardware lights, 197–198, 202
headers
    audio interface, 485
    chunk, 395, 398–399
    foundations, 593–595
    heightmap, 370, 372–375
helper libraries, 28–29
hexadecimal numbers, 105–106
hidden surface removal (HSR), 586, 730
hiding games, polymesh, 711–714
hiding sector objects, 750–752
hierarchical occlusion map (HOM), 586
high-level language compilers, 93–94
Hovertank, 608

I

identifying central processing unit (CPU), 109–114
    CPUID instruction, 110
    processor feature list, 110–114
index buffers, 287–289, 290, 316
indoor games, 587
initialization
    audio interface, 490–494
    chat application, 553–554
    child nodes 639–641
    DLL implementation, 60, 70–76
    engine mode, 259–260
    file transfer, 559–561
    input devices, 453–454
    interface, 473–475

joystick class, 468–470
keyboard class, 459–460
mouse class, 463–464
network, 542–543
servers, 543–545
shadow volume, 797–799
socket, 526–527
inline assembler, 93
input class, 449–450
input devices, base class, 450–458
creation and destruction, 452
initialization, 453–454
input queries, 454–458
input interface, 477–480
instructions
multimedia extensions (MMX), 99–101
Streaming SIMD Extensions (SSE), 103
integrated development environment (IDE), 82, 108
interactive objects. *See* entities
interface, 472–477
interface definition
audio class, 485–487
input class, 449–450
network class, 537–539
skin manager, 204–207
vertex cache manager, 289–290
interfaces. *See also* audio interface
creating abstract classes, 42–43
defining, 43–45
definitions, 34–35
design, 448
functions, 36–37, 41–42
implementing, 472–477
input, 477–480
ZFXAudioDevice, 38
ZFXInputDevice, 37–38
Internet publishing, 26
intersections
between bounding boxes, 160
with bounding boxes, 138–142
with planes, 136–137
with triangles, 134–136, 157–160

J

Jesus position, 393
joints
animating vertices, 435–438

preparing animation, 430–435
reading, 407–410
setting up bones, 423–428
joystick class, 467–472

K

kd trees, 602
key frame animations
overview, 388–389
reading positions, 412–413
reading rotations, 411–412
keys
initializing and releasing, 459–460
querying input, 460–461
updating, 460
ZFXKeyboard, 458–459

L

lag, 508
latency, 508
lead programmer (technical director), 14, 15–16
leafy binary space partitioning trees, 613
least significant bit (LSB), 528
level-editing tools, 668–669
leveling games, 507
level objects (LOBs)
adding and removing, 752–756
hiding, 750–752
overview, 674–675
rendering, 756–759
selecting, 746–750
selection buffer, 768–772
level of detail (LOD), 588–590
light/lighting
ambient, 194–195
CAD tool, 721–726
class declaration, 722–725
collision detection, 721
copying, saving, loading instances, 725–726
miscellaneous functions, 721
overview, 721–722
direct, 195–197
directional, 195, 354–358
point, 195–196
spot, 196–197
emissive, 202
hardware, 197–198, 202

material's influence, 198–200
Pandora's Legacy, 815–818, 827–831
vertex shading, 194
line list, 325–327
lines, 131
Linux, 44
listening mode, sockets, 529
loading
    dynamic link libraries (DLLs), 45–46, 55–56
    game levels, 806–821
    graphic files, 221–226
    pixel shader, 277
    sound files, 494–501
    vertex shader, 272–276
local coordinates, 132–133
lock flags, 298–300
log files, skin manager, 208–209
logo images, callback procedure, 68
look-at matrix, 244
low-level optimization, 92

M

machine language, 93
main joints, 410
management, middle, 190–193
mapping, bump, 219–221
massive multiplayer online role-playing games, 507–508, 510
master socket object, 523
materials
    basic structures, 200–204
    comparing, 211–212
    influence on lighting, 198–200
    reading, 405–407
matrices, 126–130
matrix multiplication, vector, 125–126
member functions, 60
    axis-aligned bounding box (AABB), 151
    culling, 152
mesh, reading, 404–405
messages, 561–562
    chat application, 555–559
    dialog creation, 66–69
    socket objects, 548–549
Microsoft Developer Network (MSDN) Library, 68
Microsoft Visual Studio IDE, 108
Microsoft Visual Studio .NET, 109

Microsoft X file format, 190
mirror portal, 618
mnemonic codes, 93
mnemonics (mnemotechnology), 93
mode, engine, 256–260
model coordinates, 132–133
morphing between data sets, **271**
most significant bit (MSB), 528
mouse class, 462–467, 476
MOVAPS instruction, 103
move alignment, SSE, 103–104
movement controller, 572–584
    base class, 573, 573–577
        coupling to view matrix, 577
        implementing, 573–574
        recalculating axis, 575–577
        setting attributes, 574–575
    characteristics, 572
    demo application, 584
    deriving first-person camera, 579–583
        adjusting rotations, 580–581
        overview, 579–580
        recalculating axis, 581–583
        updating, 583
    deriving free camera, 577–579
        adjusting rotations, 578
        overview, 577–578
        updating camera, 579
moving data, SSE, 104–105
MOV instruction, 96, 100–101, 104–105, 602
MOVUPS instruction, 104
multimedia extensions (MMX), 98–101
    data types, 99
    instructions, 99–101
    registers, 99
multi-pass rendering, 203–204, 352–353
multitexturing, single-pass, 351–354
multitexturing unit, 337–338

N

name inventor, 32
naming
    engine, 31–32
    socket, 527–528
near clipping plane, 239, 240, 248–250
network architecture, 508–510
    client/server, 509–510

overview, 508
peer-to-peer, 509
network class interface definition, 537–539
network games, 504–508
    persistent worlds, 506–508
    session-based video, 504–506
networking tasks, *Pandora's Legacy*, **837–841**
network layer, 512
network library implementation, 515–553
    interface definition, 537–539
    overview, 516–517
    packing packages, 517–518
    server versus clients, 517
    socket objects, 523–537
        accepting clients, 529–530
        byte ordering, 528
        connecting to server, 530–531
        creation, 526–527
        disconnecting from server, 531–532
        listening mode, 529
        naming, 527–528
        overview, 523
        querying inbox, 536–537
        receiving data, 533–536
        sending data, 532–533
        ZFX class, 524–526
    waiting queues, 518–523
    WinSock encapsulation, 539–553
        connecting clients, 549–550
        creating client, 545–547
        creating server, 543–545
        disconnecting clients, 551–552
        initializing network, 542–543
        message procedure, 548–549
        receiving packages, 552–553
        sending data, 547–548
        ZFX class, 539–542
network technology, 511–515
    application protocol interfaces (APIs), 514–515
    Open System Interconnection (OSI) model, 511–513
    protocols, 513–514
node-based trees, 612–613
no-door games, 587–588
nonbuffered data mode, 455
non-player character (NPC), 832–834
normalization
    rays, 132
    vector, 122–123
normalized vectors, 143, 150, 151
normalizing cube map, 384
normal vectors
    planes, 143
    polygons, 164
    rendering, 442–444

O

object coordinates, 132–133
object culling, 152. See *also* culling; view frustum culling
object files, linking, 44
object linking and embedding (OLE), 491
object-orientation, 32–33
occlusion culling, 586
octrees, 161
    concepts, 600–602
    demo application, 653–663
    implementation, 636–653
        child node initialization, 639–641
        class declaration, 637–638
        clipping polygon list, 643–644
        collision detection, 645–647
        creating and releasing instances, 638–639
        overview, 636–637
        player's height, 647–650
        recursive creation, 641–643
        traversing tree, 650–653
    Pandora's Legacy, 810–811
odd-frame sorting, 287
OK button, 69, 70
Omni light matrix, 361–362
Omni lights, 359–368
OpenGL, 26–28
    rendering capabilities, 256
    render states, 282
Open System Interconnection (OSI), 511–513
optimization, code
    assembler languages, 93–94
    before starting process, 92
    low-level, 92
    rendering primitives, 287
oriented bounding box (OBB), 138, 140
    AABB creation, 153–154
    class definition, 151–152
    culling test, 154–157
    intersections with planes, 148, 150

orthogonal mode, 240, 259
orthogonal projection
    functions, 250–252
    uses, 237, 238, 240, 250–252
outdoor games, 587, 588

P

packages (packets), 517–518
Packed Double Word, 99, 100
packed floating-point values, SSE, 103
packets, 517–518
packing, 517–518
    receiving over networks, 552–553
    waiting queues, 518–523
PanBox-Edit
    capabilities, 671–672
    WinAPI framework, 672
Pandora's Legacy
    character integration, 831–835
    game design, 788
    loading a level, 806–821
        CGameLevel, 807–809
        CGameSector, 809–811
        connecting portals, 818–821
        free polygons, 813–815
        overview, 806–807
        polygon lists, 815–818
        polygons from meshes, 811–813
        supporting data structures, 807
    network messages, 834–835
    object classes, 788–789
    rendering a level, 821–831
        ambient pass, 825–827
        depth pass, 823–825
        geometry, 821–823
        light pass, 827–828
        shadows, 828–831
parallel data processing, 97–98
parallel projection, 250
peer-to-peer network, 509
performance, rendering primitives, 283–286
per-pixel light, 370
per-pixel Omni lights, 359–368
persistent data games, 507
persistent worlds, 506–508
perspective mode, 240, 259
perspective projection
    functions, 252–254
    uses, 237, 238, 240–241
physical layer, 513
pipeline, 3D, 336–338
pixel buffers. *See also* back buffers; front buffers
    clearing, 81
    defined, 82
pixel manipulation, 342–344
    rendering point lists, 324
    scene presentation, 329–330
    single-pass multitexturing, 353–354
    using prerequisites, 267–272
    using separately, 344
    world transformation issues, 265
pixel-pulp, 7
pixel shaders
    activating, 277
    applications, 338–339
    basics, 336
    bump mapping, 383–384
    directional lighting, 356
    loading and compiling, 277
    Omni lights, 364–366
    overusing, 338–339
    pipeline, 336–338
    transformations, 347–348
planes, 143–150
    axis-aligned bounding box (AABB), 160–161
    basic operations, 145–146
    clipping polygons, 168–173
    concepts, 143–145
    intersections between planes, 147–148
    intersections with bounding boxes, 148–150
    intersections with rays, 136–137
    intersections with triangles, 146–147
player base class, 832–834
player's height, 647–650
point light, 195–196, 359
point lists, 323–325
point sprites, 282
polygon lists, clipping to nodes, 643–644
polygons, 162–176, 678–698
    adding to selection buffer, 772–775
    basic operations, 163–164
    class declaration, 678–681
    class definition, 162–163
    clipping, 167–173
    collision detection, 685–688
    copying instances, 684–685

creating instances, 681–683, 783–785
culling with bounding boxes, 173–175
functionality, 678
intersections with rays, 175–176
loading and saving, 683–684
loading prefabs, 744–745
miscellaneous functions, 695–698
Pandora's Legacy, 811–818
rendering instances, 688–689
saving as prefabs, 775–777
setting up points, 164–167
texture coordinates, 692–695
transformations, 689–692

polymesh, 698
adding to selection buffer, 772–775
class declaration, 698–701
collision detection, 706–709
copying instances, 706
creating instances, 701–703
loading and saving, 703–706
miscellaneous functions, 714–716
overview, 698
rendering instances, 709
selection and hiding games, 711–714
texture coordinates, 709–711

polymesh objects, 697
"popping," 589
portals
class declaration, 716–717
collision detection, 721
connecting with entities, 730–731, 759–761
converting polygon into, 697–698
copying instances, 720
creating instances, 718–719
engines, 614–621
  automatic generation, 619–621
  concepts, 614–616
  special effects, 618–619
  versus binary space partitioning, 617–618
  zero overdraw, 616–617
loading and saving, 719–720
miscellaneous functions, 721
overview, 716
Pandora's Legacy, 818–821

position and orientation of camera, 242
potential visibility set (PVS), 9, 621–622
prefabs, 671
loading, 744–745

saving, selection buffer, 775–777
preparing data, 419–423
presentation layer, 511–512
processor architecture, 94–96
programming process, 13–14
projection. *See also* orthogonal projection; perspective projection
activating, 256–260
concepts, 237–240
summary, 264–265
projection matrix
combining, 254–256
orthogonal projection, 251–252
perspective projection, 253–254
view frustum definition, 246–248
proposal, game, 17–18
components, 17–18
  budget, 20–21
  competitive analysis, 18–19
  game treatment, 18
  other, 22–23
  schedule, 22
  team introduction, 19–20
protocols, network, 513–514
publishing, 23–26
pure virtual functions, 42–43

Q

quadtrees, 590–600
general, 590–593
heightmap foundations, 593–595
terrain rendering, 595–600
***Quake*, 604, 609, 621**
quaternions, 177–184
axis recalculation, 576, 581
background, 177
basic operations, 180–181
complex numbers, 178
concepts, 178–179
Euler angles, 182–183
multiplication, 181–182
need for, 179–180
rotation matrix, 183–184
querying data input, 454–458, 460–461, 476–477
querying inbox, 536–537
queues, network, 518–523

R

random access memory (RAM), 283–286
rays, 131–142
    axis-aligned bounding box (AABB), 161–162
    basic operations, 132–134
    bounding box intersections, 138–142
    defined, 131
    intersections with bounding boxes, 175–176
    overview, 131–132
    plane intersections, 136–137
    triangle intersections, 134–136
read access, 313
reading functions
    animations, 414–415
    faces, 403–404
    joints, 407–409
    key frame positions, 412–413
    key frame rotations, 411–412
    main joint, 410
    material, 405–407
    mesh, 404–405
receiving data, 533–536
receiving messages, chat application, 557–559
reciprocal square root, 123
recursion
    BSP trees, 626–629
    concepts, 624–625
    octrees, 641–643
recalculating constants, 190–191
reference rasterizer (REF), 64, 69
registers
    AMD 3DNow! Professional, 108
    central processing unit, 95–96
    floating-point unit, 97, 101
    multimedia extensions (MMX), 99, 100–101
    single instruction multiple data, 97–98
    Streaming SIMD Extensions (SSE), 102
    Streaming SIMD Extensions, Second (SSE2), 107
releasing
    audio interface, 493–494
    exported functions, 58
    interface, 473–475
    joystick class, 468–470
    keyboard class, 459–460
    mouse class, 463–464
    network clients, 542

render devices
    skin manager, 207–211
    ZFXD3D, 48–50
    ZFXRenderDevice, 37, 50–52
rendering
    animated model, 439–440
    beginning scenes, 81
    bones, 440–442
    clearing screens, 79–81
    coding, 83–89
    game levels, 821–831
    line lists, 325–327
    multi-pass, 203–204
    normals, 442–444
    point lists, 323–325
    polygon instances, 688–689
    polymesh instances, 709
    shadow volume, 802–806
    single-pass, 203
    terrain, 595–600
    testing implementation, 82–83
    text, 320–323
rendering primitives, 282–319
    buffer flushing, 311–312
    caching, 286–287
    dynamic list management, 308–311
    hardware and performance evaluation, 283–286
    static buffers, 313–319
    vertex and index buffers, 287–289, 298–300
    vertex cache manager, 289–290, 303–319
    vertex cache object, 290–303
render states, activating, 278–282
render target, Direct3D, 77–78
resource editor, 63
revenues, earning, 24–25
right vector, 245–246
role-playing games (RPGs), 507–508
root joint, 390, 392
rotation adjustments, cameras, 578, 580–581
rotation matrix, quaternions, 183–184

S

scalars, 177
scaling model, 416–418
scene management. *See also* binary space partitioning (BSP)
    concepts, 586–587
    patents, 602

techniques, 587–636
    binary space partitioning trees, 602–613
    octrees, 600–602
    overview, 587–590
    portal engines, 614–621
    potential visibility set (PVS), 621–622
    quadtrees, 590–600
scene presentation, 327–330
schedule, game proposal, 22
sectors, CAD tool, 733–761
    adding and removing objects, 752–756
    class declaration, 733–738
    collision detection, 746–750
    connecting portals, 759–761
    creating instances, 738–740
    hiding objects, 750–752
    loading and saving, 740–744
    loading prefabs, 744–745
    overview, 733
    rendering instances, 756–759
selection buffer, 764–777
    adding objects, 768–769
    class declaration, 765–768
    deleting and copying objects, 769–772
    overview, 764–765
    polygons, 772–774
    saving prefabs, 775–777
selection games, polymesh, 711–714
sending data
    to clients, 547–548
    file transfer, 561, 563–567
    over network, 532–533
    to server, 547
sending messages, chat application, 555–557
separation axis method, 157–160
servers
    connections, 530–531
    creating, 543–545
    disconnections, 531–532
    sending data to, 547
session-based video games, 504–506
session layer, 512
setting function, polygons, 164–167
shaders. *See also* pixel shaders; vertex shaders
    3D pipeline, 336–338
    applications, 338–339
    basic transformations, 344–351
    bump mapping, 370–385
    directional lighting, 354–358
    grayscale filter, 369
    overusing, 339–340
    per-pixel omni lights, 359–368
    single-pass multitexturing, 351–354
    switching, 340
    using prerequisites, 267–272
    uses, 335, 336
    world transformation issues, 265
shadow volumes, 340, 722
    building, 799–802
    class declaration, 796–797
    death-pass variant, 791–794
    depth-fail variant, 794–795
    implementing, 795
    initializing instances, 797–799
    rendering, 802–806, 828–831
    theory, 789–790
shared objects, 44
Short Packed Double Word **data type, 99**
Short Packed Word **data type, 99**
single instruction multiple data (SIMD), 29, 97–98
single-pass multitexturing, 351–354
single-pass rendering, 203
skeletal animation, 388–393
    key frame animations, 388–389
    processing data, 418
        animating model, 428–430
        animating vertices, 435–438
        preparing animation, 430–435
        preparing data, 419–423
        setting up bones, 423–428
    skinned meshes, 390–393
    using animated model, 438
        rendering bones, 440–442
        rendering model, 439–440
        rendering normals, 442–444
        updating model, 438–439
skin, 193
skin manager
    adding skins, 213–215, 237
    adding textures, 215–226
    comparing colors and materials, 211–212
    getting skins, 212–213
    heightmap conversion, 372–375
    interface definition, 204–207
    render device, 207–211

vertex cache object, 295
skinned meshes, 390–393
    bones in, 391–393
slabs method, 140–142
sniper scope, 240
socket objects, 523–537
    accepting clients, 529–530
    byte ordering, 528
    connecting to server, 530–531
    creating socket, 526–527
    disconnecting from server, 531–532
    listening mode, 529
    naming socket, 527–528
    overview, 523
    querying inbox, 536–537
    receiving data, 533–536
    sending data, 532–533
    ZFX class, 524–526
solid leaf binary space partitioning (BSP), 613
solutions (workspaces), 48
sound engine, 5–6
sounds
    listener and source for 3D, 499–501
    loading and playing, 494–501
spawn points, 732–733
special effects, portal engines, 618–619
specular color, 356
specular lighting model, 200–201
splitters, BSP, 606–607, 610–612, 627, 629–631
spot light, 196–197
square root, 123
static buffers
    creating, 303–304, 313–319
    versus dynamic buffers, 287–289
    vertex cache object, 294
static libraries, 36, 37
    in DLL loading, 45–46
    functions, 36, 37
    implementation, 52–58
        exported functions, 56–58
        loading DLLs, 55–56
    linking object files to, 44
    ZFX3D, 38–39
    ZFXGeneral, 39
    ZFXRenderer, 47–48
stencil buffers, 81
Streaming SIMD Extensions (SSE), 102–107
    alignment, 103–104
    broadcasting data, 107
    CPU identification, 109–114
    instructions, 103
    moving data, 104–105
    registers, 102
    shuffling data, 105–107
Streaming SIMD Extensions, Second (SSE2), 107
subdivision algorithms, 600–602
swap chains, 76–77
switching shaders, 340
synchronous mode, 545

T

tact rate, 97
tangent normal, 376–380
tangent space, opening, 375–380
tangent vectors, 345–346, 376–381
team games, 505–506
team introduction, 19–20
team killers, 505
technical director (lead programmer), 14, 15–16
terrain block, 595
terrain rendering, 595–600
text rendering, 320–323
texture manager, 192–193
textures
    adding, 215–226
        as normal maps, 219–221
        converting color formats, 222–223
        creating texture, 223–226
        loading graphic files, 221–222
        security checks, 216
        to skins, 216–219
    overview, 193–194
    polygons, 692–695
    polymesh coordinates, 709–711
transparency adjustments, 226–233
third-person cameras, 571
3D engine, 5–6
3DNow!, 101–102
3DNow! Professional, 108
3D Studio Max, 668
transformation matrices
    collision detection, 132–134, 177
    combined, 254–256
    conversion between 3D and 2D, 260–264
    polygons, 689–692

quaternions, 183–184
Transmission Control Protocol (TCP), 511, 514
transparency, 203, 206
    alpha channels, 229–233
    color formats, 228–229
    computer graphics, 226–228
transport layer, 512
traverse functions
    BSP trees, 625, 631–636
    octrees, 650–653
treatment, game, 18
triangles
    intersections with bounding boxes, 157–160
    intersections with planes, 146–147
    intersections with rays, 134–136
tweening, 271

U

updating
    animated model, 438–439
    first-person cameras, 583
    free cameras, 579
    graphical user interface, 782–783
    interface, 475
    joystick class, 471–472
    keyboard, 460
    mouse class, 464–467
    Pandora's Legacy, 836–837
up vector, 244
User Datagram Protocol (UDP), 511, 513–514
user pointer (UP), 288

V

vectors, 115–126
    basic operations, 117–120
    characteristics, 115–117
    complex operations, 120–122
    cross product, 124–125
    direction, 244
    matrix multiplication, 125–126
    normal, planes, 143
    normalizing, 122–123, 143
    right, 245–246
    up, 244
vertex buffers, 287–289, 290, 311–312
vertex cache manager, 303–319
    buffer flushing, 311–312
    concepts, 303–305
    creating and rendering, 305–307
    dynamic render lists, 308–311
    interface definition, 289–290
    static buffers, 313–319
vertex cache object
    adding data, 296–298
    concepts, 290–293
    creating and releasing, 293–294
    lock flags, 298–300
    rendering from, 300–303
    setting skin, 295
    world transformation, 265
vertex declaration, 270–272, 276–277
vertex manipulation, 340–342
vertex programs, 335
vertex shaders
    activating, 276–277
    applications, 338–339
    basics, 194, 242–243, 255, 336
    bump mapping, 380–383
    directional lighting, 355–356
    loading and compiling, 272–276
    Omni lights, 362–364
    overusing, 338–339
    pipeline, 336–338
    rendering point lists, 324
    scene presentation, 329–330
    single-pass multitexturing, 353
    transformations, 345–347
    use prerequisites, 267–272
    using separately, 344
    vertex manipulation, 340–342
    world transformation issues, 265
vertex structures, 266–267
vertices, 400–402
    animating, 435–438
    Chunk-Based Format (CBF), 400–402
view
    activating, 256–260
    concepts, 237–240
    conversion, 260–264
    multiple stages, 240–241
    summary, 264–265
view frustum, 240, 241
    concepts, 246–248
    portal engines, 616, 617

view frustum culling, 156, 587
    BSP trees, 631–633
    potential visibility set, 621
    quadtrees, 592–593
view matrix, 240
    combining, 254–256
    conversion, 260–264
    coupling, 577
    functions, 237–238
    orthogonal projection, 251–252
    setting up, 242–246
    view frustum, 246–248
viewports
    defining, 238, 240
    demo application, 330–332
virtual constructors, 52
virtual destructors, 52, 62
virtual member functions, 43, 60
virtual random access memory (VRAM), 283–286, 338–339
Visual Studio IDE, 108
Visual Studio .NET, 109
void pointer, 203, 272

W

WinAPI framework, 672
windowed mode
    demo application, 330–332
    dialog initialization, 76–79, 89
    viewports, 238
windows, transparency of, 226–227
Windows Sockets (WinSock), 515
WinSock API encapsulation, 539–553
    connecting clients, 549–551
    creating client, 545–547
    creating server, 543–545
    disconnecting clients, 551–552
    initializing network, 542–543
    message procedure, 548–549
    receiving packages, 552–553
    sending data, 547–548
    ZFX class, 539–542
wireframe mode, 282
Wolfenstein 3D, **608–609**
world transformation, 265–266
write access, 313

X

XMM registers, 125

Z

zero overdraw, 616–617
z-fail variant, 794–795
ZFXAudioDevice interface, 38
ZFXD3D, 48–50
ZFXDA class, 487–501
ZFXGeneral library, 39
ZFXInputDevice interface, 37–38
ZFXKeyboard class, 458–461
ZFXMouse class, 462–467
ZFXMovementController, 572–584
ZFXNetworkDevice interface, 38
ZFXRenderDevice, 37, 50–52
ZFXRenderer
    functions, 47–48
    implementing static libraries, 52–58
ZFXSocketObject class, 524–526
ZFXW class, 539–542
ZRXJoystick class, 467–472

Gamedev.net
The most comprehensive game development resource

- The latest news in game development
- The most active forums and chatrooms anywhere, with insights and tips from experienced game developers
- Links to thousands of additional game development resources
- Thorough book and product reviews
- Over 1000 game development articles!
  - Game design
  - Graphics
  - DirectX
  - OpenGL
  - AI
  - Art
  - Music
  - Physics
  - Source Code
  - Sound
  - Assembly
  - And More!

OpenGL is a registered trademark of Silicon Graphics, Inc.
Microsoft and DirectX are registered trademarks of Microsoft Corp. in the United States and/or other countries.

TAKE YOUR GAME TO THE XTREME!

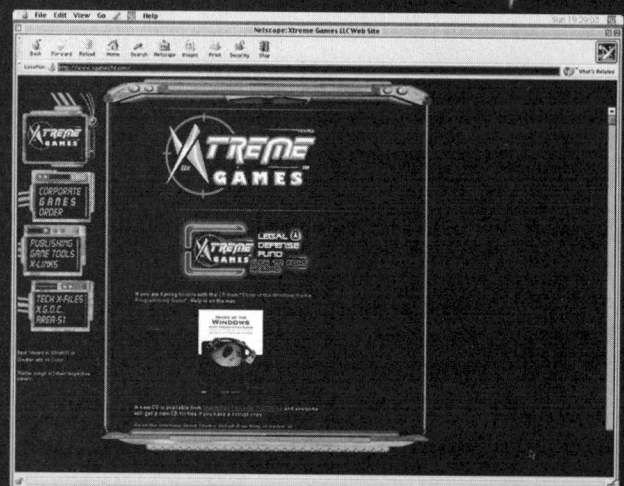
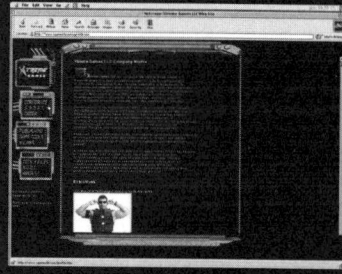
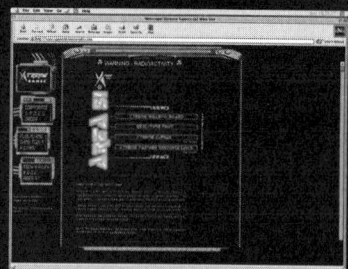
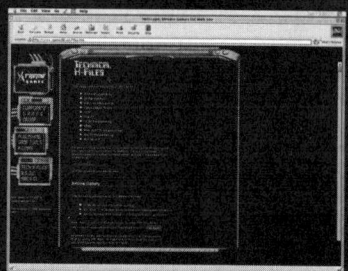

Xtreme Games LLC was founded to help small game developers around the world create and publish their games on the commercial market. Xtreme Games helps younger developers break into the field of game programming by insulating them from complex legal and business issues. Xtreme Games has hundreds of developers around the world. If you're interested in becoming one of them, then visit us at **www.xgames3d.com**.

www.xgames3d.com

THOMSON
COURSE TECHNOLOGY

Professional ■ Trade ■ Reference

GOT GAME?

Game Programming All in One,
2nd Edition
1-59200-383-4 ■ $49.99

Shaders for Game
Programmers and Artists
1-59200-092-4 ■ $39.99

Mathematics
for Game Developers
1-59200-038-X ■ $49.99

3D Game Programming
All in One
1-59200-136-X ■ $49.99

A division of Course Technology

PREMIER PRESS
GAME DEVELOPMENT

Call **1.800.354.9706** to order
Order online at **www.courseptr.com**

License Agreement/Notice of Limited Warranty

By opening the sealed disc container in this book, you agree to the following terms and conditions. If, upon reading the following license agreement and notice of limited warranty, you cannot agree to the terms and conditions set forth, return the unused book with unopened disc to the place where you purchased it for a refund.

License:

The enclosed software is copyrighted by the copyright holder(s) indicated on the software disc. You are licensed to copy the software onto a single computer for use by a single user and to a backup disc. You may not reproduce, make copies, or distribute copies or rent or lease the software in whole or in part, except with written permission of the copyright holder(s). You may transfer the enclosed disc only together with this license, and only if you destroy all other copies of the software and the transferee agrees to the terms of the license. You may not decompile, reverse assemble, or reverse engineer the software.

Notice of Limited Warranty:

The enclosed disc is warranted by Thomson Course Technology PTR to be free of physical defects in materials and workmanship for a period of sixty (60) days from end user's purchase of the book/disc combination. During the sixty-day term of the limited warranty, Thomson Course Technology PTR will provide a replacement disc upon the return of a defective disc.

Limited Liability:

THE SOLE REMEDY FOR BREACH OF THIS LIMITED WARRANTY SHALL CONSIST ENTIRELY OF REPLACEMENT OF THE DEFECTIVE DISC. IN NO EVENT SHALL THOMSON COURSE TECHNOLOGY PTR OR THE AUTHOR BE LIABLE FOR ANY OTHER DAMAGES, INCLUDING LOSS OR CORRUPTION OF DATA, CHANGES IN THE FUNCTIONAL CHARACTERISTICS OF THE HARDWARE OR OPERATING SYSTEM, DELETERIOUS INTERACTION WITH OTHER SOFTWARE, OR ANY OTHER SPECIAL, INCIDENTAL, OR CONSEQUENTIAL DAMAGES THAT MAY ARISE, EVEN IF THOMSON COURSE TECHNOLOGY PTR AND/OR THE AUTHOR HAS PREVIOUSLY BEEN NOTIFIED THAT THE POSSIBILITY OF SUCH DAMAGES EXISTS.

Disclaimer of Warranties:

THOMSON COURSE TECHNOLOGY PTR AND THE AUTHOR SPECIFICALLY DISCLAIM ANY AND ALL OTHER WARRANTIES, EITHER EXPRESS OR IMPLIED, INCLUDING WARRANTIES OF MERCHANTABILITY, SUITABILITY TO A PARTICULAR TASK OR PURPOSE, OR FREEDOM FROM ERRORS. SOME STATES DO NOT ALLOW FOR EXCLUSION OF IMPLIED WARRANTIES OR LIMITATION OF INCIDENTAL OR CONSEQUENTIAL DAMAGES, SO THESE LIMITATIONS MIGHT NOT APPLY TO YOU.

Other:

This Agreement is governed by the laws of the State of Massachusetts without regard to choice of law principles. The United Convention of Contracts for the International Sale of Goods is specifically disclaimed. This Agreement constitutes the entire agreement between you and Thomson Course Technology PTR regarding use of the software.